RUNNING YOUR BEST RACE
Programs for Improving Speed and Distance

Joe Henderson

wcb
Wm. C. Brown Publishers
Dubuque, Iowa

D1455742

Books by Joe Henderson

The Long Run Solution (1976)
Jog, Run, Race (1977)
Run Farther, Run Faster (1979)
The Running Revolution (1980)
Running, A to Z (1982)
Running for Fitness, for Sport,
and for Life (1984)
Running Your Best Race (1984)

Photography
Bob Coyle
34, 66, 72, 120
Dave Madison—
cover photo, 2, 8, 14, 22, 28, 38, 50, 56, 78, 90, 96, 102,
109, 114, 128, 134, 140, 146, 152, 158, 164, 170, 174, 180
Jim Schaffer
44, 48
Illustrations
All drawings by Don Person,
reprinted from *Running for Fitness, for Sport, and for Life*
(Wm. C. Brown Publishers, 1984)

Copyright © 1984 by Joe Henderson.
All rights reserved.

Paper
Library of Congress Catalog Card Number: 84–72143
ISBN 0–697–00458–9

Comb-Apple II Version
Library of Congress Catalog Card Number: 84–072145
ISBN 0–697–00459–7

Comb-IBM PC Version
Library of Congress Catalog Card Number: 84–072144
ISBN 0–697–00460–0

Printed in the United States of America

Dedication

For Fred Wilt, Arthur Newton, Ernst van Aaken, Arthur Lydiard and Bill Bowerman: the men whose writings taught me how to run my best races; the giants on whose shoulders I now stand as a writer.

Contents

Tables and Figures

Preface

*P*ublic speaking once topped my all-time list of painful acts. Facing crowds and letting my words reach them without editing used to terrify me. I dreaded the speech for days in advance, and after presenting it, needed weeks to work up the courage to speak again.

I list that trauma in the past tense, because I'm past being tense. I feel as relaxed on stage now as I do talking away the miles of a Sunday morning run or replaying a race over a meal with friends. The pain of speech-making vanished when I quit *speaking to* crowds of people and began *talking with* persons in those audiences.

After introductions, I now say, "That's enough about me. We're here tonight to talk about you and your interests. Any questions?"

This opening startles the audience into silence. These people came expecting to be lectured in normal running-clinic fashion for the next hour, and here the speaker is asking to be told what to say. No one speaks.

I ask who is in the crowd by calling for a show of hands to indicate running experience and interests. A second request for questions yields none.

"Come on," I plead. "You wouldn't be here if you didn't want to learn ways to run farther and faster, or to make your running healthier and happier. Who'll be first? Don't worry about asking something silly. The only foolish question is the one not asked."

As I look from face to face, eyes turn downward. No hand goes up.

"That's okay. I'll let you off the hook for a while by guessing your questions. Certain ones come up whenever runners meet. For instance, . . ."

That lead-in ploy seldom fails to tap a well of curiosity, and for the next hour or more, I respond to questions and comments from the floor. These runners seem to like the dialogue format as much as I do.

They teach me as much as I teach them. I learn from this two-way talk what runners really want to know, and how well the neat packages of advice in articles and books really work when the theories are put to a road test.

In the bad old days of speaking, my lectures parroted advice from my articles and earlier books. Now I've compiled a book along the lines of these public conversations. I introduce myself, and ask you to introduce yourself to me. Then I anticipate the questions that most concern you. Together, we arrive at solutions to your problems.

Introducing me: I have run for more than twenty-five years, raced more than 600 times at distances as short as 100 yards and as long as 100 miles. My personal mile record is 4:18, my 10-K 33:45, my marathon 2:49:48.

Those times came long ago and far away. All serious racing is behind me, and I run (and occasionally still race) without specific goals. I'm a Stage Three runner who runs for the fun of running.

Earlier, however, I evolved through the first two stages: exercising to establish basic fitness, and then training for higher speeds and longer distances. An already fit fourteen-year-old, I was a Stage One only a few weeks. Racing improvement, however, lasted a full 10 years, until I didn't need it any more to keep going. Stage Three, the recreational phase now in its sixteenth year, appears endless.

My story is not unique. My evolutionary course is similar to one that most runners follow.

Introducing you: I'm assuming a lot about you. You are a second-stage runner. You're long past jogging for fitness, but not yet ready to settle down to fun-running. Running in races "just to finish" no longer satisfies you, and you're not yet ready to treat races as social events. You want to learn how you can race faster and farther.

You don't place yourself among the competitive elite. You're concerned with improving your own times, not with beating other runners. You aren't interested in either the sprints or the ultradistances. You feel most at home in road races five kilometers to half-marathon, although you make rare forays down to the mile and up to the marathon.

You seek short-term gains in time and distance, but not at the expense of long-term health and enjoyment. You take your running seriously for the hour a day that you devote to it, but you don't let it become a second job.

I know who you are and where you want to go. I've been there.

Introducing the book: This is a do-it-yourself manual for racers. It is not a primer on establishing first-stage fitness; nor is it a philosophical roadmap for Stage Three runners. Two of my earlier books, *Running: The First Steps* and *Running: A to Z,* and dozens of volumes from other authors cover the territory on both sides of racing.

This isn't *my* book; it is *ours*. I provide a skeleton of advice, then leave to you the task of adding flesh and blood to those bare bones. I'm not your coach—only your advisor. I advise you on how to coach yourself, assess your abilities and ambitions, write your training schedules, and plan and execute your races.

The advice is mine; the work to implement it and then the better times ahead are yours. My past and your future come together on the pages that follow.

Joe Henderson
Eugene, Oregon
July 1984

Prologue

"Not in the clamour of the crowded streets nor in the shouts and plaudits of the throng, but within ourselves are victory and defeat."

Henry Wadsworth Longfellow

*T*wo somebodies with well-known names, one male and one female, lead their divisions at each big race. We watch them on television that day and read about them in the newspapers the next morning as if they were the only people running.

I don't begrudge these two runners their moments of glory. And since I'm in the news business myself, I know that the headlines and the choice video footage come from the front of the pack.

But as a runner who has been a small part of hundreds of big road races, and has never finished first, I also know how important the rest of the story is. It's the story you'll never read about in a newspaper or see as anything more than an oozing, multicolored mass when the TV cameras briefly shift their focus off the front-runners for a crowd shot from above.

This story really is thousands of individual stories, each one meaning much more to its author than any developments on the road up ahead. Runners have their own work to do, their own races to run, their own private victories to celebrate when their run is done.

While handing out awards at a race in Tacoma, Washington, I noted that most of the runners hadn't won any prizes they could place on a mantle or tack onto a bulletin board. Then I added, "You all are carrying home something of greater value."

I asked those who had run their first race to stand, then those who had run farther than ever before, finally those who had run their fastest at this distance. More than half of the crowd stood, and the people still seated applauded.

"Will those who think they failed or lost today please hold up your hands?" I said. No one did. This may only have shown reluctance to admit failure, but I doubt it.

"This," I said, "is what the running revolution is all about: everyone feeling like a winner and wanting to keep on winning. To participate is to win. To improve yourself is to win bigger, and the only way to lose is to stop."

This running revolution is not one of numbers. Sure, we've all heard that 20 or 25 or 30 million Americans run (depending upon which poll you believe, and how strictly you define running and runners), and more than a million of them race long distances on the roads.

The numbers boom is an effect of the running revolution, not a cause. Before the sport could enjoy its incredible growth spurt (which continues, by the way—much to the dismay of critics who've been predicting the decline and fall of running for years), we had to pass through a revolution of *attitudes*. Mainly, "losers" had to decide they could win.

I'm a reformed loser. When I began running in the 1950s, I believed what I know now to be the Three Great Lies of Sport: (1) There can be no gain without pain; (2) there can be but one winner; (3) there can be no running without success in racing.

To swallow the first lie is to believe that running must hurt all the time; that it is always serious, grinding work; that a strong mind must beat a reluctant body into shape; that this unpleasantness is tolerated only for the results it gives.

The second lie implies that second place means nothing; defeat is a step removed from death; only the person who finishes first is allowed to be happy, and then only for as long as he or she stays on top.

Lie three says that anyone whose painful work isn't paying off with first-place finishes or the reasonable prospect of achieving them should get out of the sport; be a spectator for the fastest and fittest people who survive this brutal natural-selection process.

When the sport still lived by these lies, as most other sports still do, not many people ran. If a group of high school or college runners had been asked 10 or 20 years ago, "When do you plan to quit?" most of them would have answered, "As soon as I graduate," or, "As soon as I stop improving." Many of them secretly hoped for a serious injury that would let them leave this dreary business sooner, yet with honor.

Ask today's runners the same question about when they intend to stop, and most of them will answer without hesitation, "Never!" They dread most an injury that might end their running.

This attitude shows how dramatically our ideas on racing and training have changed during the running revolution. The sport has evolved from painful to pleasurable, runners from being hero-worshippers to their own heroes, racing from a be-all to a by-product.

We have learned that this sport is too good to hurt all the time, too good to belong only to the people who race fastest, too good to leave behind when our own racing times stop improving.

We are free now to run with little pain, but who is to say we aren't gaining? We are free to finish far behind the leaders in races, but no one can call us anything but winners. We who run for fun want to run forever, and that is the greatest victory of all.

TRAINING

The Foundation

Simple as 1-2-3

The nicest compliment anyone can give me as a writer is to say that I made sense. Someone who reads or hears my words can't flatter me more than by saying, "You made everything so clear and simple." The reader doesn't need to say the delivery was eloquent or that he or she agreed with the messages—only that he or she understood. If a talk or article simplifies the complex, it is successful. If it complicates the simple, it is a failure.

Training for racing is really a very simple matter. Hundreds of books have been written about this subject, but they can be condensed to six essential words: *long enough, fast enough, easy enough.*

Essentially, training combines the elements of distance, speed and recovery into a schedule that matches one's running abilities and ambitions. These are the basic ingredients, the staples of a runner's diet, which will be combined later into palatable recipes.

The first two items are "tests"—a blanket term covering long runs, speedwork, and time trials. These are dress rehearsals for racing. By necessity, the tests are hard work. They prepare you for the even harder work of racing.

Long tests mimic the distance of the race, but at a slower pace. Fast tests prepare you for the race's full speed, but cover only part of its distance. You combine full distance with full speed only in the race itself, where it counts. Testing will be discussed more thoroughly in Part Two.

We examine the third ingredient—recovery—first, since it constitutes the bulk of any well-rounded training diet. For each race and race-like test, plan about ten times as much recovery running. Hard running tears you down, while easier running builds you back up. The tearing down occurs quickly; repairing takes much longer.

These recovery runs are neither very long nor very fast, and they should never be overly demanding. They are meant to restore energy and enthusiasm drained away by hard work.

We visit the extremes of distance and speed occasionally for challenge and excitement. But the spaces between races and tests are where we live.

Managing Stress

Athletic training is essentially an exercise in balancing stress loads. Apply the proper types of stresses in the proper amounts, and you become a fitter athlete. Understress, and you don't improve. Overstress, and your performance and perhaps even your health suffer.

Forbes Carlile translated Dr. Hans Selye's theories of stress management into athletic terms. Carlile, an Australian, gained attention in the 1960s and 70s as a coach of swimmers, including Olympic champion Shane Gould. But he entered the sports world as a long-distance runner, then graduated to studying the entire field of exercise physiology and athletic training.

Carlile developed ten guidelines applying to all types of athletic training and to all athletes. Physiologists and coaches now generally agree on a set of principles that read very much like Carlile's original list. Working within these physical laws should lead to the desired training effects.

1. **Principle of stress:**
    Stress, in manageable amounts, is the stimulus that provokes a training response. The stress must be regular and strong enough to stimulate adaptation. But it should not occur in such heavy and frequent doses that it overwhelms the adaptation system, causing a breakdown.

    Running itself is only one of many stresses acting on a runner. Others include faulty diet, psychic unrest, and environmental insults such as extreme heat and cold. Runners must consider the stress burden as a whole and then adapt their workloads to it.

2. **Principle of overload:**
    "Overload" is not the same as "overwork." Overloading is selective stressing: enough to stimulate the desired response without producing exhaustion.

Forbes Carlile said, "The training load must be severe, and must be applied frequently enough and with sufficient intensity to cause the body to adapt maximally to a particular activity." But he added, "It is at the same time true that sustained all-out efforts in training or in races should be made only sparingly."

This is what renowned coach Arthur Lydiard from New Zealand meant by his now-famous adage: "Train, don't strain." No results can come without training, yet straining too hard and too often is self-defeating. Lydiard asserted that training should be an everyday, year-round activity, but no more than ten percent of a runner's efforts should be race-like.

3. **Principle of specificity:**

Even though all training cannot be exactly like racing, it must be a close approximation. The system adapts to the specific exercise it is given. Walk, and you become fit for walking; bicycle, and you become a better biker; run, and you get into shape for running. There is little carry-over from one activity to another.

The training effect is even somewhat specific within running, with sprinting and distance running each requiring and producing different actions and reactions. How much speedwork helps a distance runner and how much endurance training helps a sprinter are still subjects of much controversy. But it is apparent that the bulk of one's training must fall within reasonable reach of racing distance, close to racing pace, or both, to be most effective.

4. **Principle of regularity:**

Almost any kind of running, in any amount, will yield some benefit if only it is taken regularly. Once a runner has the daily running habit, it's hard not to improve.

Physiologists say that runners need to train at least every other day—three or four days a week—to achieve and maintain basic fitness. Conditioning occurs quickly at first, with speed developing somewhat faster than endurance. But the reverse is also true. Conditioning vanishes quickly during layoffs, with speed diminishing somewhat more rapidly than endurance.

5. **Principle of progression:**

Obviously, progress is quickest and most apparent at the start of a racer's career, and it slows as one approaches maximum potential. The more the runner progresses, the harder it is to keep improving.

Progress, however, doesn't follow a smooth, upward course. There tends to be a "plateau" effect, with a series of sudden jumps separated by stagnant periods. The runner has to be prepared to work through these periods of no apparent improvement, waiting for the jumps. All else being equal, however, it is possible to hold the ground gained and move from strength to strength as condition and confidence increase over a period of many years.

6. **Principle of diminishing returns:**

The first mile is the most helpful one in terms of basic conditioning. Each succeeding mile yields less benefit. In other words, runners work more and more for less and less.

It doesn't take very much effort to reach ninety percent fitness—only a few miles a day. But you require progressively more training as you approach your ultimate potential until, at the highest levels, you're putting in a huge investment for very small additional gains.

7. **Principle of recovery:**

The interval-training system is more than simply mixing fast and slow running in a track workout. The principle of alternating effort with recovery applies to all training, regardless of the specific method used.

Forbes Carlile wrote: "Recuperation periods are essential, both during a single training session and throughout the year. Rest, with consequent physical and mental relaxation, must be carefully blended with doses of exercise. A rhythmical cycle of exercise and recuperation should be established."

Bill Bowerman, one of America's most successful coaches, pioneered what he called the "hard-easy" system. He staggered the intensity of workouts, scheduling a hard one only every two or three days. According to Bowerman, this allowed athletes to handle greater work loads with less strain, and stimulated faster improvement than a same-load-every-day plan.

All sound training programs leave room for rest and recovery. "There is a time for strenuous activity and a time for resting," Carlile cautions. "The rigidity of a too-definite program of training may easily drive the athlete to exhaustion."

8. **Principle of seasons:**

Sub-maximal training can be viewed as putting money in the bank; all-out racing as withdrawing those funds. No one can withdraw indefinitely. Eventually he or she must go back and restore the reserves. This explains the importance of racing sparingly during certain seasons and allowing race-free periods during the year.

Arthur Lydiard stated flatly, "You can't race well the year-round, because your condition will only take you so far. When you're racing hard, you can't train hard. If you compromise, you can hold your form for three or four months. But then you're going to have to go back and start to build up again."

If runners are lucky, Lydiard asserted, they may squeeze two peak periods of racing from a year, each lasting about three months and staggered with recovery breaks.

9. **Principle of pacing:**

Pace has two meanings. The first is obvious: the speed a runner travels during an individual run. The other is less apparent but just as important: the pace one maintains from week to week, month to month, year to year.

One principle rules both types of pacing: The harder and faster a person runs, the shorter he or she will be able to go. Fast pace lets you travel quickly; slow pace allows you to run longer. Set the training pace according to short-term (the distance of the run) and long-term (the projected length of the career) goals so as not to run down at the mid-point.

10. **Principle of individualizing:**

There can be no one plan suitable for everyone. Each program must be customized to accommodate the individual user's likes and needs, abilities and goals.

Forbes Carlile wisely said, "Always the most important consideration must be how the individual is responding to training, whether the athlete is carrying the physical load of training without strain or whether the body is slowly losing its capacity to adjust. Therefore training will always be an individual problem. No fixed training schedule should be followed rigidly. Blindly following any written schedule is unwise. For best results, training must be tailored to suit the individual."

In the Beginning

Fitness and Beyond

In the late 1960s, Dr. Kenneth Cooper presented us with the radical message that we should run more; we were suffering from inactivity. His aerobics books led millions of people onto the tracks and roads.

Looking back years later on the running boom which he helped inspire, Dr. Cooper observed that we runners might stay healthier and fitter if we ran less. In *The Aerobics Program for Total Health and Well-Being* (M. Evans and Company, 1982), he wrote, "Recent research has shown that unless a person is training for marathons or other competitive events, it's best to limit running to around twelve to fifteen miles per week. More than that will greatly increase the incidence of joint and bone injuries, and other ailments. On the other hand, less mileage will fail to achieve the desired improvement in the body."

Cooper and his staff at the Aerobics Center in Dallas were "overwhelmed" by the incidence of injuries in people running more than twenty-five miles a week. While a competitor may willingly take the risks associated with higher mileage, Cooper argued, the extra running first yields diminishing returns and eventually negative ones. For non-racers, he set minimums and maximums: no less than two miles, four times a week, and no more than three miles on five days.

Cooper's associate, John Duncan, remarked that people running five three-milers a week "have the same low risk of developing heart disease as someone running eighty miles per week." Cooper agreed: "If you run more than fifteen miles per week, you are running for something other than fitness."

Of course, most of you run for very good reasons other than fitness. Fitness, as Dr. George Sheehan has said, "is a stage you pass through on the way to becoming an athlete." You are probably past that stage.

Three miles may be the upper limit for absolute safety. But it may also be the lower limit for race training—as well as for attaching the runner firmly and permanently to the activity. Three miles or less, taken every other day as if it were a prescription item, will make you fit. Three miles and more, taken daily, will make you a complete runner.

If you want to shed a few pounds or prevent a heart attack in later life, observe the Cooper limit. But if you want to sample all that running has to offer, you need to run more. Three miles is about where running quits being simply an exercise and becomes a sport, quits being something you do to tone your body and becomes a vehicle for exploring the limits of your abilities.

As you begin your exploration, look realistically at what you are about to do and why. Be aware that racing has nothing to do with fitness as Kenneth Cooper defines it; the efforts involved are too great. When you train to race, you are no longer running to lose weight and keep your heart in shape (although those benefits still accrue). You're training primarily to immunize yourself against the stresses of the race so as not to be hurt too much by them.

The most obvious stress is distance, and your first task is getting used to staying on your feet for as long you plan to race. Most events last longer than thirty minutes, and many of them will require sixty minutes or more to finish. So you must form a daily habit of training at least a half hour and occasionally extend the length to an hour-plus. (If you aren't already at those time levels, Table 2.1 tells how to work toward them.) Only after you're running this far comfortably should you concern yourself with racing.

Graduating to Racing   What follows is a case history of one race, the huge and zany Bay to Breakers in San Francisco. Many cities host similar events; every city should have one. There is no better way to take the long step from running to fitness to training and racing for sport than by joining this type of crowd.

One of the great exercises in the Bay Area, practiced by runners who call themselves "serious," is derogating the Bay to Breakers race. They say they can't be bothered by this event because it is too crowded, too chaotic, too crazy for them. They miss the point.

The crowds and the zaniness of this event (the word *race* somehow doesn't fit) help it serve its most important purpose: introducing masses of runners to the organized sport. More people come into racing via this twelve-kilometer route across San Francisco than any other single way—because more have run here than in any other single race. Of the nearly 100,000 people who run here each year, about half have never raced before. This introduction will prompt hundreds of them to move on to other, smaller and better events.

Table 2.1 *Preliminary Steps*

Two prerequisites should be satisfied before attempting any race: daily runs of at least a half hour and a long run of an hour or more. If you now are running less than these amounts, enter this program one step up from current level. For instance, if you're averaging twenty minutes (total time divided by seven, even if not running every day), begin in fifth week. Run at a pace that allows you to finish these runs comfortably. Record your actual runs by day and your averages by week.

First Week (Average: 13 Minutes)

Day	Suggested Run	Actual Run
1	15 minutes	_____
2	15 minutes	_____
3	15 minutes	_____
4	15 minutes	_____
5	15 minutes	_____
6	20 minutes	_____
7	Off	_____
	Daily Average:	_____

Second Week (Average: 15 Minutes)

Day	Suggested Run	Actual Run
1	15 minutes	_____
2	15 minutes	_____
3	15 minutes	_____
4	15 minutes	_____
5	15 minutes	_____
6	30 minutes	_____
7	Off	_____
	Daily Average:	_____

Third Week (Average: 18 Minutes)

Day	Suggested Run	Actual Run
1	20 minutes	_____
2	20 minutes	_____
3	20 minutes	_____
4	20 minutes	_____
5	20 minutes	_____
6	30 minutes	_____
7	Off	_____
	Daily Average:	_____

Fourth Week (Average: 20 Minutes)

Day	Suggested Run	Actual Run
1	20 minutes	_____
2	20 minutes	_____
3	20 minutes	_____
4	20 minutes	_____
5	20 minutes	_____
6	40 minutes	_____
7	Off	_____
	Daily Average:	_____

Table 2.1—*Continued*

Fifth Week (Average: 23 Minutes)

Day	Suggested Run	Actual Run
1	25 minutes	_____
2	25 minutes	_____
3	25 minutes	_____
4	25 minutes	_____
5	25 minutes	_____
6	40 minutes	_____
7	Off	_____
	Daily Average:	_____

Sixth Week (Average: 25 Minutes)

Day	Suggested Run	Actual Run
1	25 minutes	_____
2	25 minutes	_____
3	25 minutes	_____
4	25 minutes	_____
5	25 minutes	_____
6	50 minutes	_____
7	Off	_____
	Daily Average:	_____

Seventh Week (Average: 28 Minutes)

Day	Suggested Run	Actual Run
1	30 minutes	_____
2	30 minutes	_____
3	30 minutes	_____
4	30 minutes	_____
5	30 minutes	_____
6	50 minutes	_____
7	Off	_____
	Daily Average:	_____

Eighth Week (Average: 30 Minutes)

Day	Suggested Run	Actual Run
1	30 minutes	_____
2	30 minutes	_____
3	30 minutes	_____
4	30 minutes	_____
5	30 minutes	_____
6	60 minutes	_____
7	Off	_____
	Daily Average	_____

No event anywhere is so welcoming of newcomers. While other races limit their number of entries, this one seeks ever-larger totals. While others work to rid themselves of "outlaws" who run without numbers, one-third of the San Francisco field doesn't enter and no one seems to mind. First-timers feel wanted here, and they are.

These novices don't feel intimidated, partly because this isn't truly a race except for the one percent of runners upfront. The other ninety-nine percent are packed together too tightly to generate the speed which is the essence of true racing. It's said that people are still leaving the starting line when the first runners are finishing seven and one-half miles away. That's crowded!

New racers, who imagine that the whole world is watching them and waiting to laugh when they fall, take comfort in this crowding. It gives them a place to hide and an excuse for running slowly. The crowd gives them little choice.

Hardly anyone takes racing seriously at Bay to Breakers. This is a mobile party, a celebration of running. The best way to celebrate, as the folks in San Francisco like to say, is to "go with the flow."

No matter how big the crowd is, however, each runner is responsible for keeping his or her flow going. That requires preparation. Twelve kilometers is a tough starting distance under ideal conditions, and those in San Francisco are far from ideal.

Besides putting in the recommended amounts of training time (regular runs of at least a half hour and long ones of an hour or more), the runner must anticipate the Hayes Street Hill. This dominant landmark of Bay to Breakers climbs 200 feet between two and one-half and three miles, then descends steadily for the remainder of the course.

Anyone who arrives at this event with only flatland training is in for a shock. The climb up the hill will hurt immediately and intensely, but the long run downhill will do more damage to the legs. The advice is obvious: train on hills, practicing a steep half-mile climb and a gradual four-mile descent before race day.

By training this way, a first-timer learns something important about all races: they begin long before he or she steps to the starting line.

Exercising of Opposites

Fully Fit

Like most runners with roots in the 1950s and 60s, I once thought extra exercises were a waste of time. The calisthenics of football and army basic training were used more to discipline the mind than train the body, and we runners already had plenty of self-discipline. Hurdlers and sprinters might need these contortions, but distance runners' time was better spent running.

I thought I had put extra exercises behind me when I stopped playing football at sixteen, only to have them return during a few unpleasant months in the Army at twenty-two. For almost ten years after that, I didn't do a pushup, situp, or toetouch. Why bother?

Meanwhile, injuries began to nag me—little ones at first, the kind that don't stop you but nibble away at the joy of moving freely. I ignored these little hurts, and they grew into big ones—the kind that cause you to miss a day here and there, then several days, then whole weeks. Eventually I ran myself into foot surgery and still hadn't figured out why.

George Sheehan told me why. Dr. Sheehan, the medical columnist and philosopher-in-residence at *Runner's World,* casually tosses off lines that are the envy of anyone who writes. His wisdom emerges in the form of short, simple statements which are easy to read and hard to forget. The Sheehan "proverb" on the subject of runners' exercises concerns strength and flexibility. He said: "When you run, three things happen—and two of them are bad." The good one is that you become a faster and more enduring runner; you adapt to the kind of exercise you give yourself. But if you don't take any exercise except running, the bad things happen and, in extreme cases, may stop you from running as they progress.

The first of these is tightness of the backside, all the way from the heels to the lower back. If you're a long-time, long-distance runner and aren't taking corrective exercises, you probably can't bend from the waist with your knees straight and touch your fingertips to the ground.

The second bad effect is loss of muscle strength in the upper body and development of strength imbalances in the legs. Runners' arms, shoulders, chest, and abdominal muscles are pretty much just along for the ride; if they're neglected, they shrink. The front-of-leg muscles from the hip on down get worked, but not as hard as the ones in back; this accounts for the imbalances.

At best, then, runners aren't as fit as they'd like to believe if they lack flexibility and balanced strength. At worst, they're wide open to all kinds of injuries.

I suffered the injuries, as hundreds of other runners have, when I specialized too much in running. (This is particularly true for those of us who do little speed training; faster running returns some of the strength and flexibility that long, slow distance takes away.) I know now that exercises are a good investment, giving hours of smooth running for a few minutes of supplemental work. I now invest in it every day and now tell other runners to do the same.

Try this: First, bend over and touch the ground (even if only with the fingertips). Then do ten honest pushups and bent-leg situps. If you can't pass these minimum tests of flexibility and strength, or if leg injuries are eroding the fun of your running, you need to do more than run.

Balancing Acts Let's begin our discussion about supplementary exercises by saying what they are not. They are not directly related to performance, and they are not the best way to warm up. You improve your racing times by training better, not by lifting weights like a shotputter. You warm up best for running by running slowly for the first mile or two, not by stretching like a yogi.

So why bother with supplemental exercises at all? In a word, *balance*. Running's effects on the upper body are nil, so if you don't want to end up with the stick-like arms and the stomach muscles of a plucked chicken, you might want to adopt the habit of regular strength-building. Among the simplest and most effective exercises are old-fashioned pushups and situps.

Stretching is meant to counteract the tightening effects of running, and is therefore best practiced immediately after finishing. The muscles respond best to stretching after they have been warmed.

The five stretching and strengthening exercises in the accompanying figures have been chosen with both benefits and practicalities in mind. They can be performed within a five-minute period that can be inserted into your cool-down activities; they require no apparatus or props; and none of them asks you to lie down on the cold, wet, or rough ground.

Five minutes a day will keep you as strong, loose, and balanced as a runner needs to be. You're not training for ballet or body-building.

Part one: Cradle a lower leg and pull it toward chest.

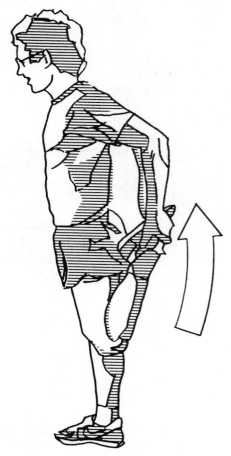

Part two: Grasp a foot behind back, and pull toward buttocks. Repeat parts one and two with other leg.

Figure 3.1 The Leg Puller

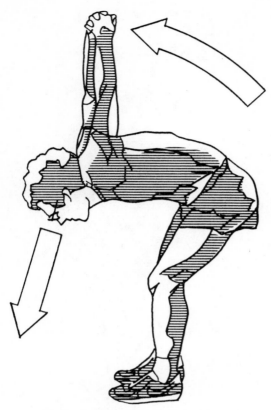

Part one: Clasp hands behind back, stand with feet together and knees slightly flexed. Bend forward while pulling arms upward. Stop at point of discomfort and hold.

Part two: Drop arms until palms touch ground in front of feet. The less flexible you are, the farther in front of the toes you will touch.

Figure 3.2 The Toe Touch

Part one: Stand with legs spread. Turn one foot outward, then bend in that direction.

Figure 3.3 The Triangle

Part two: Turn in the direction of bend, step forward, and reach as far ahead as possible. Repeat parts one and two on the other side.

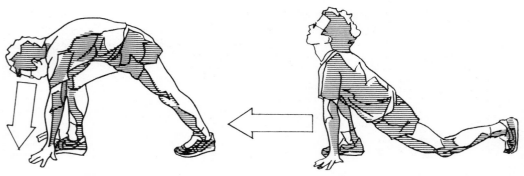

Part one: Crouch with one foot a few inches in front of other knee, hands on ground. Then straighten rear leg.

Figure 3.4 The Sprinter

Part two: Step forward with front foot for an extended version of part one. Repeat both exercises with opposite foot forward.

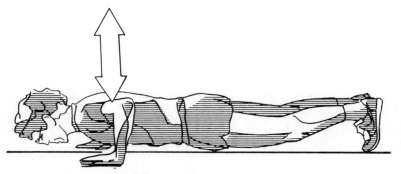

Standard pushup. From straight-armed starting position, touch nose, chest, and upper legs to floor, keeping back straight. Work up to 20 or more repetitions.

Figure 3.5 The Pushup

Training Table

Eat, Drink, and Be Wary

One hears contradictory dietary tales and ends up wondering what to believe. At one extreme, runners say they couldn't keep training and racing without their organic, unadulterated diets. At the other, Olympic marathoners report living on pizza and beer, and running on defizzed Coke. Diets of successful runners vary so widely—from vegetarian to vitamin J (for junk food)—that the normal conclusion you might draw is it doesn't really make any difference what you eat.

If diets are judged by the running results they give, "acceptable" eating habits obviously aren't limited to a few bland items. Runners can work well on a wide variety of fuels, and no one has yet determined a "best" diet for everyone, all the time. However, certain dietary adjustments do produce direct, measurable, and sometimes dramatic effects on running performance. Some involve adding items; others require taking things away.

The most important addition is liquids, particularly for long-distance runners. For events lasting more than an hour, drinks not only enhance performance but protect health itself. Marathon runners, for instance, need to drink immediately before and during races and long training runs. They can get by on plain water, but electrolyte mixtures put back more of what these runners lose.

Carbohydrate-loading—the popular practice of stoking up on bread, spaghetti, and similar foods prior to competition—adds extra fuel *before* the runner loses it. It is particularly beneficial in marathon running; researchers claim it can reduce a three-hour runner's time by as much as ten minutes. Carbo-loading is of little or no benefit in races lasting less than an hour, where performance is limited by factors other than fuel supply.

What runners *don't* eat is often more important than what they do consume. For example, the pre-race meal contributes little to the energy output of the event, and the potential for trouble is high when a runner puts food into a nervous stomach. Many runners prefer to go into their race hungry instead of risking the complications of eating too much, too late.

The big problem in nutrition is not *deficiency* but *overabundance.* Each pound above ideal weight (and "ideal" for runners is less than the figure shown on doctors' charts) is an extra burden to carry. It causes a drag on mechanical and oxygen-producing efficiency. The quickest way for most runners to improve is by losing a few pounds.

Weight is one of the most sensitive indicators of fitness, and all runners—whether overweight or not—should check theirs daily. Sudden gains, according to diet author Dr. Irwin Stillman, should be treated as if they were a serious illness. Sudden losses must be taken just as seriously. While a gradual reduction in weight is beneficial, a quick drop often signals trouble resulting from overwork, dehydration, or even true disease.

The runner's second-best training tool, after the digital wristwatch, is an accurate set of scales.

Last Suppers German doctor/coach/researcher Ernst van Aaken once remarked, "No one ever got fast by eating." Yet, as coach Arthur Lydiard pointed out, "The way runners eat before races, you'd think they were worried about dying of malnutrition after 50 meters."

The late Dr. Van Aaken thought runners shouldn't eat at all in the twelve to twenty-four hours before a race. They have all the stored fuel they need, he asserted, and putting more food into a tense system might cause indigestion, cramping, diarrhea, or other difficulties.

Van Aaken and Lydiard agreed that the best advice on eating immediately before competition is this: If in doubt, don't. This applies to the final hours before a race, when it is too late for the food to do much good but not too late for it to do harm.

The pre-race week is another matter. Evidence points to significant benefits from carbohydrate-loading during this period. This technique involves packing the body with high-energy fuel called *glycogen,* a product of foods rich in carbohydates.

The theory behind carbo-loading is that muscle glycogen supplies are limited. They are depleted in long races, causing us to slow down or stop. But these reserves can be built up by juggling carbohydrate intake, and we can go farther before a "collapse" occurs. The diet does not increase speed; it only delays slowing. It works best in races lasting longer than two hours, the point at which glycogen depletion would normally reach a critical stage.

The classic carbohydrate-loading routine involves three steps, summarized here:

1. A long "depletion" run seven days before the competition to drain the runner of glycogen.

2. The protein phase: three days of keeping the glycogen level low by eating high-protein, low-carbohydrate meals—meats, eggs, fish, etc.

3. The carbohydrate phase: three days of packing in the carbos for three days. (Don't interpret this as an invitation to overeat; maintain normal caloric levels.)

Paul Slovic, of the Oregon Research Institute, examined the results of "loading" in a marathon. He found that people on this diet typically improved by an average of eight minutes from their unloaded results.

The major complaint about the routine involves the high-protein phase. Runners say they feel exhausted and irritable then, and susceptible to illnesses and losses of confidence at the worst possible time. For them, a modified version of the carbo-loading routine gives some of the benefits while reducing the risks. They simply take the depletion run about four days before the race, then start loading immediately.

Whether or not you load with carbohydrates, you should examine the report of researchers from East Carolina University. This deals with what to eat—or more precisely, *not* eat—the day before a race. Dr. Ron Maughan, science columnist for *Running* magazine, reviewed the findings from the East Carolina study on rats:

> The authors of this report showed that treadmill-running endurance capacity can be increased if preceded by a 24-hour fast. The fast resulted in low values of blood glucose and also decreased the liver and muscle glycogen stores. In view of the well-recognized importance of these carbohydrate stores in determining the ability to perform prolonged exercise, the increase in endurance capacity seem somewhat paradoxical.
>
> However, in spite of the fact that resting glycogen levels were lower in the fasted animals, the glycogen content of skeletal muscle after the run to exhaustion was *higher* in the fasted than the fed rats. There was no difference in liver glycogen content at exhaustion between the fed and fasted groups.

A glycogen-sparing effect occurred, according to Maughan, and another energy-producing substance was recruited more heavily. He continued, "Clearly, the rate of glycogen utilization is much less in the fasted animals. However, they have a higher concentration of plasma free-fatty acids at rest and during exercise. These animals therefore conserve their limited glycogen stores by increasing the rate at which they oxidize fat"—a much more abundant fuel than glycogen.

Maughan cautioned that, while these results may not translate into human terms, they "may call for a re-examination of the use of the carbohydrate-loading diet by marathon runners"—particularly in the last day before racing.

I myself would stop short of recommending a full twenty-four-hour fast on the day before racing. However, I believe there is little to be gained from eating during those hours.

Drinks for the Road Bill Rodgers was on his way to winning the 1975 Boston Marathon, possibly headed for a world-best time. He was running at better than five minutes per mile, with a cool wind at his back.

Then Rodgers stopped, took a cup of water, stood in the middle of the road drinking it, and looked around to see if anyone was catching him. Two more times before the race ended Rodgers did the same thing. He explained afterward that he needed to drink and couldn't gulp the water while running.

This story says a lot about the value of drinking during long races. If a runner at world-record pace on a fifty-degree day needs to stop for water, then we all must need to.

Liquid replacement, or lack of it, has an effect on performance in distance races on any kind of day. When temperature and humidity are high, fluid loss can threaten health—even life itself.

Running doctors say that after you've sweated away about three percent (about five pints or five pounds for a person weighing 150 pounds) of body liquid, your temperature increases to the point where performance suffers. When sweat loss exceeds six percent of your weight, heat exhaustion or heat stroke are possible. The latter has killed more than a few runners.

What to drink? Water is the first priority, according to Dr. George Sheehan, *Runner's World* medical columnist. "The second priority is sodium chloride [salt], then potassium. These electrolytes, as they are called, are found in commercial 'ade' drinks."

Prepared drinks also contain sweeteners, on the theory that they provide quick energy. In fact, according to research by Dr. David Costill at Ball State University, heavily sugared drinks are slow to leave the stomach and may keep vital water and electrolytes from being absorbed as quickly as they are needed.

How often to drink? Dr. Costill recommends taking a pint ten minutes before the race, and a half-pint at ten- to fifteen-minute intervals during the run. If you wait to drink until you're thirsty and drink only as much as your thirst demands, he warns, you will become increasingly dry.

"Man generally relies on his thirst to control body-fluid balance," wrote Costill after conducting his initial tests on drinking while running. "Unfortunately, this mechanism is far from accurate. In laboratory tests that require about eight pounds of sweat loss, we found that thirst was temporarily satisfied by drinking as little as one pound of water."

Reduce that sweat debt. Drink up!

Dress for Success

Views on Shoes

An overrated rule is to provide the feet with the most protection that money can buy. The trend in shoemaking has been toward *more:* more padding, more support, more stability, more heel lift. However, you may be a runner who responds better to less. Two New Zealanders make a strong case for wearing the lightest shoes they can tolerate.

Jack Foster, fifty-two, has run hard for twenty years, completing a 2:11 marathon at age forty-one. Conventional wisdom insists that older bodies need more protection. Yet Foster prefers the least of all shoes.

"I was introduced to running over farmlands, where the underfoot conditions were soft and yielding, and one developed good strength and flexibility," he has said. "I ran in light tennis shoes, because there were no training flats in those days."

Jack believes those shoes forced him to learn proper running style: "We ran in those flimsy, light shoes and developed a 'feel' for the ground. We learned to land properly or got sore legs, since we couldn't rely on the shoes to absorb any shock. We got into a light-footed gait which moved us over hill and dale very effectively. I'm certain this [style] helped me stay injury free."

Even now, when shoe companies beg him to wear their latest high-tech training flats, Foster continues "to run daily in shoes most people consider too light even for racing."

It might be argued that he is one of the rare and lucky individuals born with perfect feet. Such is not the case with Anne Audain. If any runner has reason to give her feet maximum protection, it is Audain: an Olympic marathoner and former world record holder at 5000 meters. As a child, she could barely walk because of a deformity similar to clubfoot. Doctors corrected that when she reached her teens, and she started running as part of her therapy.

Those feet still aren't perfect, and Anne takes care of them in a most unusual way, as she once explained in a conversation with Bob Wischnia of *Runner's World*. Wischnia asked Audain how much her feet bothered her now.

"Sometimes they can be very painful and feel like they did before I had them operated on," she responded. "When it's cold, they have a tendency to throb a bit. However, they've never stopped me."

Does she wear special shoes?

"Heavens no! I race and train in the same pair of racing flats."

Racing shoes?!

"You have to understand that when I first started running, my doctors weren't too keen on the idea of it. One of them told me—and I think he may have been trying to discourage me—'If you're going to do this running, run in the nearest thing to bare feet.' Since that time, I've always raced and trained in the lightest shoes I can find."

While hesitating to recommend racing shoes for everyone, all the time, I do endorse several points made by the two New Zealanders. And I add a few thoughts of my own, as one who has always responded best to the least of all shoes.

- You're wise to wear the same type of shoes (if not the same pair) for all purposes, rather than switching models from training to racing. Raceday, the time of greatest stress, is not the time to risk a shoe change.
- You're built to run unshod, though modern surfaces no longer allow that luxury. Stay as close as possible to barefoot instead of removing yourself as far as possible from the earth.
- Light shoes enhance good running form. Heavy ones act as crutches which let the shoes instead of the feet and legs act as shock absorbers, thereby allowing the form to grow sloppy.
- If form improves in lighter shoes, but high mileage on hard surfaces still hurts you, maybe the fault lies in the running routine and not the shoes. Search the schedule for the trouble spot.
- The biggest drawback of racing shoes isn't the risk of injury but their cost. You usually pay more for less material and less durability.

Dressing Down Gone forever are the days of baggy, gray sweatsuits, cotton gym shorts and unmarked undershirts as standard running gear. Many contemporary races bear resemblance to sportswear fashion shows. Weatherproof jackets and pants (can't call them "sweats" any more), nylon mesh singlets (can't call them "jerseys"), and decorated T-shirts (can't call them "underwear") are all the rage. Runners who could once outfit themselves for racing for $25, counting the cost of shoes, might now spend ten times that much.

It's not necessary to spend that much. To be sure, some of the new items have made running more comfortable, but most of them are more fashionable than functional. You should concern yourself with function—with what effect your clothing has on performance.

Runners are most helped by what they *don't* wear. They more often overdress than underdress because they misread the temperature. They think the reading at the starting line will remain constant throughout the run or race. And it never does.

The human body works very effectively as a furnace, but rather poorly as an air conditioner. It creates heat better than it dissipates that warmth. As a result, the air temperature appears to rise by about twenty degrees during a run. A normally pleasant seventy-degree day soon feels like a steamy ninety. A near-freezing temperature rises to the pleasant fifties.

Dress with that "Twenty-Degree Rule" in mind. Feel a bit underdressed and chilly as you start, knowing that later you'll be cozy while runners around you are sweating in or stripping off their fashionable, expensive clothes.

Table 5.1 *What to Wear When*

Remember the "Twenty-Degree Rule": The temperture seems to rise by about that amount when you run. Dress with that warming trend in mind. Start with the basics of shoes, running shorts, and underwear; then, add layers according to the conditions.

Perceived Condition	Actual Temperature	Clothing to Wear
Hot	70s and up	Add only the skimpiest singlet (tank top) that modesty will allow; men may choose to go shirtless.
Warm	50s and 60s	Add a short-sleeved T-shirt to the basic uniform.
Cool	30s and 40s	Add long pants and a long-sleeved shirt or light jacket.
Cold	20s and down	Add a layer of protection for hands and ears, and perhaps another layer for legs and face in extreme cold.
Rain	Warm	Add a cap with a bill to keep vision clear; otherwise dress as on any warm day.
Rain	Cool	Add a cap plus a water-repelling jacket and pants; don't wear cotton "sweats" which soak up water.
Snow	Cold	Add extra socks to keep feet warm and dry; be sure the shoes provide adequate traction on slippery roads.

Reprinted from *Running for Fitness, for Sport, and for Life* (Wm. C. Brown Publishers, 1984)

CHAPTER SIX

How Far?

Time After Time

Ask me to name the single greatest advance in running during the recent Golden Age, and I'll talk about an attitude. I'll tell you that this sport boomed when dozens, then hundreds, then thousands of us decided running was too good to belong exclusively to young and fast males. We began to take running personally. The elite might travel longer and faster, but no one else could do our running for us—no one could break our PRs.

Ask me about the one great invention that supports this new attitude, and I'll point to my wrist. It holds a digital watch that has become as indispensable as shoes and shorts.

The watch is much more than a silicon chip wrapped in black plastic, and it's worth far more than its $21.95 price tag. This watch is a companion, a coach, even a conscience. It tells me what I have run, what I should run, and that I'm only as good as the run I take today.

Watchmaking technology is running wild. Manufacturers offer ingenious products that calculate distances and splits, count footsteps, and announce times. If you're easily bored while running, you can divert your attention with video games, radios, tape recorders, even tiny television sets built into watches.

But all I want to know is my time: the flickering black numbers between 0:00.00 and the day's stopping point. These readings are the most accurate measure of training effort, the most personal gauge of racing success, and the surest way to keep me living in the present.

My diary lists thirty- and forty-five- and sixty-minute runs, never four- or six- or eight-milers. Practicality led me to replace the mile with the minute standard. Running by time periods eases planning and record-keeping. For instance, I don't need to measure or follow courses, since an hour is an hour wherever it is run. And I never guess at distances, but simply look at the watch and note the elapsed time.

Running by the watch also encourages this ex-trackman to moderate his tendency to run too fast. My natural urge when running a set distance is to finish it as quickly as possible—*race* it, in other words. But because time can't be rushed, I settle into a comfortable pace during daily runs while training by the watch. That pace adjusts automatically to my day-to-day feelings, both good and bad.

Only in races do I dare allow distance and time to come together. There the whole purpose is to rush, and there the time is the truest measure of success. There the real victory ceremony occurs as the runner takes his or her first look at the result frozen on the face of the watch.

Times tell the truth. They say exactly what kind of runner I am, how I rank alongside runners everywhere, and—most importantly—how I compare with my old self. The current comparison shows almost a minute-per-mile slowdown from the PR years, and yet these are numbers I can accept.

Again, the digital stopwatch comes to the rescue. It gives visible proof that time doesn't stand still, and neither can I. No runner can hold onto precious moments for very long.

A man from Texas complained to me on the eve of his marathon, "I dread the next several weeks. I'll hurt for a few days, but that's not the half of it. The post-race blues will last much longer and will bother me much more than any stiffness ever could." He asked what he could do to ease the letdown he felt after every race. The longer the event, the bigger was the buildup and the harder the fall. Marathons were both the most exciting and most depressing events on his racing calendar.

"It's a matter of time," I said. "You look forward to the race for so long while you train that you're like a kid waiting for Christmas. Then it's all over in a few hours. Maybe those hours gave you what you wanted, maybe they didn't. Either way, they're gone just like that. The next morning, you wake up and see that you have little to show for your efforts except your pains and a line in your diary."

The runner nodded glumly, then asked, "But what can I do to ease myself through the blues?"

I tapped the black plastic watch on his wrist. "This is one of the greatest inventions in the history of running. It not only gives you the prize that counts most, an accurate record of your result, but it shows how fragile your prize is."

The man understood the first part of that answer but not the second, so I explained: "You put every number on that watch with your sweat. Wear the time proudly. Leave it on the face all day and night. Glance at it now and then, and smile as you celebrate your race.

"But pay special attention the next day when you zero that watch. This act tells you that the time has come to move on, to wipe away the old result and start putting new numbers on the dial."

Yesterday's races make sweet memories, but they don't take the place of today's and tomorrow's runs.

The 30-60 Formula Run far enough to feel you've accomplished something, but not so far that running seems like a second job. Most days, thirty minutes will satisfy the first requirement; sixty minutes is the dividing line between enough work and too much. Stop short of a half hour only when injured, ill, or taking a planned rest day. Exceed an hour only when you're preparing specifically for a race lasting that long, and go that far no more often than once a week.

This thirty-sixty formula is based on a rationale which we'll examine in a moment. But first, let's hear from the formula's detractors: the proponents of fitness who claim that even a half hour is too much to run daily, and the serious athletes who maintain that a steady diet of thirty- to sixty-minute runs is inadequate.

Graduates of the Kenneth Cooper School of Limited Mileage argue that even lower figures may be excessive, particularly if practiced without at least two rest days each week. Running this far every day is an invitation to injury, they warn.

Runners schooled on high-mileage training scoff at the one-hour limit. After I published the thirty-sixty formula in a magazine article, one athlete wrote: "The suggested training schedule is unrealistic. While I agree that recovery days are necessary, I don't believe that one hard day per week is sufficient training." He asserted that most "good to very good" runners exceed an hour at least every other day.

My recommendations fall between the extremes. Experience and observation tell me that most runners want, need, and can handle regular runs of a half hour or more, and that few of them can tolerate repeated runs of longer than an hour. To veteran runners, modestly paced thirty-minute runs become almost as easy as resting—and the more pleasant of the two alternatives. This running itself is a form of active recovery from hard work.

Extra-long and extra-fast training, and, of course, racing itself are the hard work. Precisely for that reason, a number of easy runs must separate the hard ones. We don't recover overnight, and we delay our healing by trying to put in too many miles at the wrong time.

Dr. Ron Maughan has addressed the question of what the recovery rates are from various amounts of running. Reviewing a Dutch study which used rats as subjects in assessing degrees of muscle damage, Dr. Maughan noted that "the exercise intensity was not severe and would correspond to a fairly moderate training session in [humans]." Results of the study indicated that thirty-minute runs on a treadmill caused no visible problem, while sixty-minute sessions produced significant signs of muscle damage. Healing began the third day after the trauma occurred and reversed itself completely a few days after that.

These experiments with laboratory rats lend scientific support to the arguments that hour-plus runs hurt and half hour runs don't, and that every day of hurting must be followed by many days of healing. It is important to note here that healing is not necessarily synonymous with resting. What it does mean is doing no further damage while recovery is taking place.

How Fast?

LSD Redefined

"Contrary to appearances," began my first book, which really was little more than a pamphlet, "I'm not attempting to establish myself as an apostle of LSD (long slow distance, in this case). I'm nothing more than a reporter, telling what happened to me and others who stumbled into this slow-motion running. This slim book contains a simple report of experiences from which you can draw your own conclusions, agree or disagree."

I neither invented nor named the LSD system: I merely wrote a booklet that describes it. Since the publication in 1969 of *LSD: The Humane Way to Train* (Tafnews Press, 1969) I have spent much time explaining to people who haven't read the original work what it does *not* say.

What LSD isn't:

- It isn't necessarily the best way to train. There are better ways to prepare for racing, but this is presented as an alternative for those who have tired of taking those harder, faster paths.
- It isn't mindlessly adding up mileage. Lengths of single runs and total distances should be the least you need, not the most you can tolerate.

- It isn't meant to be as slow as you can go. The ideal pace is neither too fast nor too slow, but fits into a comfort zone between the extremes.
- It isn't all long and slow. You learn to run faster by running fast, in small but regular doses of speedwork.
- It isn't surrender. You may even improve your racing performances, not so much by being better prepared as by staying healthier and hungrier.

LSD is running comfortably, both in terms of distance and pace. It is running at least a half-hour and no more than an hour, one to two minutes per mile slower than ten-kilometer race pace most of the time.

The system has served this long-time user well, but LSD is obsolete. Oh, I still believe enough in what I've done for the past twenty years to keep doing it. That's not the problem. The trouble lies with that name. Each of its three words urges extremism—something not intended for a system built on moderation.

The words *long, slow* and *distance* imply running as long as possible, as slowly as you can, adding up as much weekly distance as you're able. This can hurt as much as running too fast, as many runners have learned by taking LSD to extremes.

Runners who knew me in 1966, as my LSD phase was beginning, often asked, "Why are you running so much, and why are you going so slowly?" Runners who know me now say, "You run so little, and all of it is done at a fairly fast pace. Why did you change your LSD ideas?"

I haven't changed; the sport has. When I started doing what came to be known as LSD, runners still called anything beyond race length "overdistance." My thirty to sixty minutes a day seemed long. At a time when serious competitors still trained primarily on small, repeated parts of the racing distance and rarely ran them slower than race pace, even six minutes per mile seemed slow. My seven- to eight-minute pace appeared one step removed from walking.

I still run my thirty to sixty minutes daily; still run my miles at a comfortable seven to eight minutes apiece. I used to be so slow that no one would run with me, but now I pass nine runners for every one who passes me. Nine in ten of them run more than I do.

My running hasn't changed. I've stood still while the runners around me, their practices, and their perceptions, have passed through the distance/pace revolution.

Finding the Perfect Pace Take it from a racer who travels twenty times faster than the fastest runner does: Pacing is everything.

Johnny Rutherford drives the roads and tracks. In his kind of racing, pace doesn't just make the difference between good and bad performance. It determines, on one hand, if he goes home with a paycheck; on the other, if he goes home at all. The margin for pacing errors in cars traveling at 200 miles per hour is quite small.

Rutherford says that finding the right line between safety and speed is like holding a small bird in your hand. Hold it too loosely, and it flies away from you. Hold it too tightly, and you squeeze it to death.

He finds that delicate balance by driving at "red-line" pace. Hal Higdon, who writes about auto racing and the human variety, explains: "The red line is the mark on the tachometer of the racing automobile at which the engine, if constantly revved higher, will disintegrate. *Whoom!* Forty-thousand dollars worth of junk."

However, if the driver doesn't push that line, the race slips away from him. The same happens to a racing runner, of course. No one races well by pacing too easily. Yet everyone has a speed limit, beyond which lies disaster. Therefore, the first lesson in good racing is finding the line between fast enough and too fast, then holding it.

This is no secret. Racers who don't learn it quickly don't race well or for very long. And yet runners who tiptoe along the red line with the skill of Grand Prix drivers while racing may develop amnesia when it comes to carrying this lesson into training. The result? More races are lost in the spaces between events than in the competition itself. A runner lets good races fly away or squeezes them to death by ignoring the line between comfort and discomfort in the ninety percent of running time spent *not* racing.

Racing runners act like children spending a day at the beach. These youngsters may work for hours building elaborate castles of sand, then demolish their creations in a few seconds of gleeful kicking and stomping. They build to destroy.

Runners build for weeks or months in training, and then destroy much of that masterpiece they have created in a few minutes of racing—apparently taking great delight in this destruction. We, too, build so we can destroy.

In oversimplified terms, we use two gears: "running" and "racing." The first is rather easy to hold, and lets us run for *quantity*. The racing gear is hard to shift into and to tolerate once there; it allows us to achieve *quality,* but only temporarily.

To oversimplify again (ignoring the fact that some runners "race" their runs and others "run" their races), racing tears down. The problems runners who race have to solve are first, how to build more than they destroy, and second, how to rebuild adequately before destroying again.

We run for fitness. Running must be comparatively comfortable if it is to build and to last. We race for sport—not despite its destructiveness but *because* of it. Sport involves taking chances, seeing how far we can push before we break, gambling that we can bend without snapping.

Most of us want the best of two worlds. We want to run injury-free and enjoyably for the rest of our lives. We also want to race as well as possible. We can't have all of both at the same time, however, because the two goals conflict.

To run too easily is to risk racing slowly. To race too hard is to risk losing everything. Combining long-term, healthy running with immediate racing success requires careful juggling of quantity and quality—and a few compromises on both sides.

In the original LSD booklet, I offered the opinion that we build best by training at least a minute per mile slower than we race. I had no basis for that statement other than personal experience. On rare occasions when I checked everyday pace, it averaged that much more than long-distance racing rate.

Now I know that this guess was relatively accurate. Hal Higdon, surveying top road racers for *The Runner* magazine, found that the men were, as a group, 2:12 marathoners, while the women had run 2:35. These men averaged 6:07 mile pace in training; the women 6:48.

These times sound fast to those of us who have trouble *racing* at those speeds. But think of the times in relative terms: the men raced marathons near five-minute pace, and the women went below six.

There's that one-minute difference between training and racing pace for marathoners. The gap widens to about one and one-half minutes at ten kilometers and two full minutes for a single all-out mile. If these safety margins work for the best of us, they must also apply to the rest of us.

CHAPTER EIGHT

How Often?

Day by Day

If you run about ten kilometers a day, every day, a growing number of voices that ring with authority tell you that you're headed for trouble.

- *Item:* A now-infamous study from the University of Arizona implies that anyone who runs with an unusual degree of consistency and commitment displays unhealthy obsessive-compulsive tendencies.
- *Item:* Sports medicine author Dr. Gabe Mirkin comments that running is "the most dangerous exercise," and that "if you run every day, you're headed for disaster."
- *Item:* Evidence from the country's leading exercise physiology laboratory at Ball State University shows that people who continue training immediately after a race take about twice as long to recover as those who rest completely for several days.
- *Item:* Dr. Kenneth Cooper asserts that if you run more than three miles a day or more than five times a week, "you are running for something other than fitness."

Which is precisely the point. Most of you are past the stage of running purely for fitness. Three miles may be the upper limit for health maintenance, but it may also be the lower limit for race training and for attaching ourselves firmly to the sport.

The first thirty minutes of a run, says Dr. George Sheehan, is for your body; the extra time is for your mind. The first part is a warm-up for the good part. Three miles is the approximate point at which the exercise becomes a sport. And you take calculated risks in the name of sport.

Just so you won't think I'm advising taking foolhardy risks, let me say here that I accept without question Bill Bowerman's "hard-easy" concept. Alternating work with recovery is basic to any sensible running program. Each day of hard work must be followed by at least one and probably several easy days. Where I part company with the people who warn that we run too much, too often is over the definition of *easy*.

To George Sheehan, the word means "total rest." He once thought he had to train every day. To stay with that routine, he limited himself to about five miles a day. Any more than that, and he was tired and sore all the time.

Sheehan's racing performances leveled off, then began to slip. He is, above all, a racer; he wouldn't tolerate slowing down. So he tried taking a day off each week. He felt better, so he wondered, "Why not two days?" Feeling fresher yet, he dropped another training session to see what would happen—and then yet another.

What happened first on Sheehan's three-day-a-week program was that he could run more during each of his workouts. He both doubled the mileage and increased the pace on what became his Tuesday and Thursday ten-milers. The second effect was that his weekly races began to satisfy him again. At age sixty-five, Sheehan still regularly breaks forty minutes for ten kilometers. He has run as fast as 3:01 for the marathon on as little training as thirty miles a week.

This is hard-easy running at its extreme. The runs Sheehan does take last well over an hour each, are run at maximum pace, or both. Afterward, he forgets about running for the next forty-eight to seventy-two hours.

If you can stand waiting that long for your next run, you possess an unsual degree of patience. I'm not a patient man. I need my running more often than once every two or three days, so I compromise.

I can't race as fast or as far or as often as I once did without risking a breakdown, so I don't train for either miles or marathons anymore. And whenever I push to my present limits of speed or distance, I give myself at least an easy *week* to recover.

The compromise I make in the name of everyday running is that I *recover all the time* between race-like efforts. I rarely exceed ten kilometers of comfortably paced running. Ten-K a day keeps the doctor away.

One running course takes me past the local electric company's plant. Once a week, I check the sign at the gate reading "X Days Without an Injury." I keep this same kind of record myself. It has totaled as high as 1400 days.

This streak is not a bragging point. If maintaining it meant wading through injuries and illnesses, it would be foolish consistency. I am neither that tough nor that foolish.

What my streak means is that I've gone more than a year without *wanting or needing* a day off. I choose to think of this total not as a symptom of sickness, but as a sign of health: a sign that I've been doing lots of things right for a long time.

Our Hour Derek Clayton's stone wasn't aimed at me. He hadn't even heard my talk a few minutes before his, when I'd mentioned not missing a day's running in years. The former world marathon record-holder from Australia had been standing in the hallway, signing autographs and answering his fans' questions as I'd talked.

The same audience had heard both of us. These people heard me say I'd gone as long as four years without a day off. Then they heard Clayton say, "I know one bloke who won't even let himself have one day off. He runs right through everything—illness, injury, fatigue. That is bloody crazy. How can anyone have any fun in this game if he's so obsessed with it?"

Clayton did not intend personal criticism, but many of his listeners thought he did. As they stared in my direction, I wanted to crawl under my chair.

I had no chance to respond, but if I had replied my answer would have been one of agreement: "If I had to *force* myself to run through pain and exhaustion only for the sake of the streak, Derek would be right; I would be wrong. That would be an obsession, and those are never any fun.

"I enjoy my running. I like it enough to want to run day after day, and the way to continue day after day is to keep the distance and pace modest. I never let myself get so tired today that I can't run again tomorrow."

That means rarely running longer than an hour or within a minute per mile of current 10-K race pace. Few runners need to run or can tolerate running more than an hour or racing the clock regularly. The body and mind team up to shout, "Enough of this abuse!" Clayton had that problem.

One of the most ruggedly built men in high-level running, he still couldn't shoulder the training burden he heaped upon himself. Perhaps no one has ever trained more or faster than he did at his best. He went as high as 200 miles a week in training, most of those miles at or near five-minute pace.

And perhaps no top runner suffered more "down time." Clayton's medical history includes nine surgical operations. In spite of his record performances, he expressed some dissatisfaction with his career because it didn't net him an Olympic medal. His injuries occurred too often and at the wrong times.

When Clayton retired from marathoning after the 1972 Games, he made an incredible statement: "I can honestly say that I never enjoyed a minute of my running." He expressed relief at having put the suffering behind him.

It wasn't long, though, before Clayton began to miss his running. He didn't miss the racing, and he didn't miss the pain of his unrelenting hard training. The relief at being retired from those chores remained. But Derek missed something about the running itself.

He started again, this time averaging ten kilometers a day at a pace he could handle easily. For him, six-minute miles were easy compared to the five-minute pace at which he'd once raced and trained.

Clayton would start racing again, but never seriously, never again at his old distance and never with any special training. The man who once said he'd never enjoyed a minute of his running now calls his five- to six-milers at a comfortable pace a "highlight" of his day. That is exactly what the daily runs should be: a highlight, not a chore; a hobby, not a job; a time to be welcomed, not dreaded.

My own running became a dreaded chore twice. Early in my career, I ran too little and too fast. The ultimate price was an Achilles tendon damaged almost beyond repair and a damaged psyche that almost couldn't face another fast mile. Later, I ran too long and slowly, going two hours-plus every weekend and averaging more than an hour and a quarter each day. Its final result: heel surgery, which came as something of a relief when it took me off the high-mileage treadmill.

Only after settling into an hour-a-day routine did I feel I'd found my home. Only then did the running time become a highlight of my day. Once home, I didn't want to leave, even for a day.

I can't and don't fill those sixty minutes with running, but I can and do open up the full hour every day and run whatever I can within it. The best reason for taking that time has little to do with the physical results of the running. This is a quiet and creative hour when I call time out from the noise and confusion of the day, and spend an hour calming myself and collecting my thoughts. This would be a valuable and productive time even if one spent it sitting alone in a rocking chair in a quiet room.

Checks
and
Balances

Checkout Times

A reader chided me after he thought I'd advised in a magazine article to run an hour every day.

"You have excluded one crucial element," wrote James Menegazzi, a cardiac-rehabilitation specialist from Pennsylvania. "A day of rest. 'Rest' days have, oddly, come to take on the meaning of running for an hour at a comfortable pace. Whatever happened to the day off? One day off per week is not only refreshing; it makes good sense physiologically. If you have ever read Genesis, you know that even God took off one day a week."

I may never go so far as to *schedule* that day off for myself (although I suspect it might be a healthy practice). But I would surely neither preach nor practice running a full hour every day. Flexibility must be built into any program, or minor injuries will soon surface and evolve into major ones.

The best way to treat almost any ailment, from minimal ache to appreciable injury, is to do nothing. Nothing, that is, which produces any more pain. Never run with any pain or through any pain that interferes with the normal flow of the run.

"Run as you feel," the experts tell you. But how do you know how you feel? How can you be sure your head isn't lying to your body? One day, you might want to run for three hours when your physical limit is fifteen minutes. Another day, you may be able to go forever but don't feel like taking the first step.

I usually err on the long side, wanting to run more than I'm able. So I've adopted a set of checkout times that better match desires with abilities. My quarter-hour self-checks are outlined here.

- I start, unless it is painfully obvious that I'm going nowhere. Pre-run feelings, either good or bad, tell almost nothing about what to expect later on. The first fifteen minutes let me know realistically if I should bail out early.
- If no pains shout "Stop!" at that point, I go on to thirty minutes. Then I check out the main systems again, and call it a day if the run has become a struggle.
- With that test passed, I proceed to forty-five minutes. This is my usual stopping place, indicating a satisfactory run though not a great one.
- I continue to an hour only when all the gears are meshing perfectly. I know from many trials and errors that I can't or won't make a habit of going this far. That fact makes these rare days of overdistance extra-special.

When Running's a Pain A four-year streak, my longest period without a day off, ended on a crumbling bike path. I stepped the wrong way on a rough spot, and my left ankle went east while the rest of me kept going south. Diagnosis: Severe sprain. Treatment: A cast. Time off: Ten days.

I sulked for two days, which was the best therapy I could have practiced—both for early healing and to make myself thoroughly miserable. The complete rest made me so sick of inactivity that it built up my resolve to do something, *anything* active again.

Running was out of the question, but I have an active imagination. If I couldn't run, I could *pretend* I was running. I got up at my usual time, and went out for the usual time periods on my usual courses. The only unusual factor was the bicycle under me. I bicycled until I could walk without limping; then, I mixed walking and running until I was well enough healed that I didn't have to pretend to run any more. Anything felt better than nothing.

From negative experiences grow positive lessons. Those few weeks of pain yielded a plan for dealing with other bad breaks that inevitably disrupt running. Supporting it is a commitment to maintaining the thirty- to sixty-minutes-a-day exercise habit, even when a normal run cannot be done. The five stages of recovery, in sequential order, are presented here.

1. *Biking or swimming.* These activities are the alternatives for the most serious of injuries, those which don't even allow walking without limping. They take nearly all the pressure off most running wounds while still giving steady workouts.

2. *Walking.* Begin walking as soon as movement without a limp is possible, and continue as long as pain doesn't increase. These two limitations apply at all stages; the exercise should never aggravate the injury.

3. *Walking mixed with running.* Add brief periods of slow running to the walking—as little as one minute in five at first, then gradually decreasing the walks and adding to the runs.

4. *Running mixed with walking.* The balance tips in favor of the runs, but keep inserting intervals of walking—say, one minute in five—at this stage, when steady pressure can't yet be tolerated.

5. *Full-time running.* Approach it cautiously for a while, a little slower than normal, and with no tests or races until runs of thirty to sixty minutes have become a daily practice again.

By the Numbers After he won the 1968 Boston Marathon, Amby Burfoot coined a memorable phrase when he told about his persistent "fear of the precious minute," and how this compulsion to get on with another job sometimes kept him from doing all the running he could or should do. I admitted to him much later that I suffer from an opposite but equal complaint: a *fascination* with the precious minute that often drives me to run when I should be doing something else.

My whole running life is a numbers game, I told him. I give great meaning to what really are rather meaningless numbers. Most of them revolve around the watch.

- One minute or more faster than normal pace turns a "run" into a "race"; one minute or more slower than race pace defines a run as "LSD."
- Five minutes is the "time out" period—for breaks during long or fast interval work (race-like efforts which I call "tests"), for walking after a run, or for supplemental exercises.
- Ten minutes in every hundred—ten percent of the total—is a self-imposed limit on racing and race-like tests.
- Fifteen minutes—the warm-up period—determines how well or poorly the day's run will go. This also is my ideal length for intense speed sessions.
- Thirty minutes draws the line between fitness and sport; less than a half hour may make me fit, but more than a half hour makes me truly a runner.
- Forty-five minutes is my perfect run: long enough to be an honest effort but not so long that it does much damage.
- Sixty minutes is where running quits being recreation and starts resembling a second job. "Long" runs start here.

The flickering numbers on the face of a wristwatch run my running. Arbitrary figures tell me when to start and stop.

The only records I keep are the final daily readings on the Casio. Those numbers go into my diary as soon as I take my last step, and I don't erase the digital readout until I take the first step the next day.

I'm like a man lost in the snow who thinks he knows where a hidden path leads, but really can only see his footprints behind him. The trail of numbers gives me the illusion that I know where I'm going by looking at where I've been.

Keep it Simple Discus thrower John Powell's first rule of training: KISS. "Keep it simple, stupid." Any fool can complicate something simple, he says. But it takes wisdom to simplify something complicated.

I wouldn't call myself wise. But I am old in the ways that runners measure age: more than twenty-five years and 50,000 running miles old. One system that fails with age is memory, and complex formulas now confuse me.

So I keep my plans as simple. Nine days in ten (the non-race/non-test days) are distinguished only by what they do *not* contain.

- No hard/fast runs of race-like intensity.
- No short runs—"short" meaning less than thirty minutes.
- No long runs—counting anything above an hour as "long."
- No hard/easy pattern. I don't need to mix work with rest when none of it seems like work.
- No double sessions. Too much showering and changing of clothes.
- No peaking. If I'm running right and choosing the right races, I'm in shape to race reasonably well all the time.
- No tapering. If I'm not working too hard, I don't need to rest before races.
- No recovery runs. The pace of daily running adapts automatically for fatigue, and thirty to sixty minutes isn't long enough to hurt very much.
- No off-seasons. A runner who likes to run never wants to take a vacation from it.
- No days off. Almost all of the comments above apply here.

C H A P T E R   T E N

Your Training

Plan your overall running schedule by determining the following:

1. How Fast to Train

Indicate your most recent ten-kilometer race time or estimate your current potential at that distance.   _____

    Calculate your average pace per mile, dividing the time by the distance (see Table 10.1).   _____

That per-mile figure represents your current maximum pace for the approximate distance of your daily runs in this program.

    Indicate your current average pace per mile for a typical training run.   _____

    Copy your ten-kilometer racing pace from above.   _____

    Subtract your race pace from your training pace and list the result.   _____

Table 10.1 How Fast to Train

Use your most recent ten-kilometer race result, or an estimate of current potential, as a starting point. Calculate its pace, then add one to two minutes per mile. That is your ideal training-pace range for daily runs lasting thirty to sixty minutes. The reverse is also true. You should be able to race the 10-K one to two minutes per mile *faster* than you train at that distance.

Your 10-K Race Time	Your Pace per Mile	Your Fastest Training Pace	Your Slowest Training Pace
30:00	4:50	5:50	6:50
31:00	5:00	6:00	7:00
32:00	5:10	6:10	7:10
33:00	5:19	6:19	7:19
34:00	5:29	6:29	7:29
35:00	5:39	6:39	7:39
36:00	5:49	6:49	7:49
37:00	5:58	6:58	7:58
38:00	6:08	7:08	8:08
39:00	6:17	7:17	8:17
40:00	6:27	7:27	8:27
41:00	6:37	7:37	8:37
42:00	6:46	7:46	8:46
43:00	6:56	7:56	8:56
44:00	7:06	8:06	9:06
45:00	7:16	8:16	9:16
46:00	7:25	8:25	9:25

Table 10.1 —Continued

Your 10-K Race Time	Your Pace per Mile	Your Fastest Training Pace	Your Slowest Training Pace
47:00	7:35	8:35	9:35
48:00	7:44	8:44	9:44
49:00	7:54	8:54	9:54
50:00	8:04	9:04	10:04
51:00	8:14	9:14	10:14
52:00	8:23	9:23	10:23
53:00	8:33	9:33	10:33
54:00	8:43	9:43	10:43
55:00	8:52	9:52	10:52
56:00	9:02	10:02	11:02
57:00	9:11	10:11	11:11
58:00	9:21	10:21	11:21
59:00	9:31	10:31	11:31

If the difference is less than one minute, you are training too fast. If it is more than two minutes, your training pace is too slow. The ideal training-pace range is one to two minutes per mile slower than the racing rate.

Calculate your ideal proper training-pace range by adding one to two minutes per mile to your current ten-kilometer race pace (see Table 10.1).

Fastest training pace (add one minute). _____

Slowest training pace (add two minutes). _____

2. How Far to Train

Indicate the current average length of your training runs (in miles). _____

Indicate the current average pace per mile of your training runs. _____

Calculate the typical amount of time (in minutes) spent training, multiplying the mileage by the pace (see Table 10.2). _____

If the amount is less than thirty minutes, you need to run more. If it is more than sixty minutes, your training should run less. The ideal range for daily runs (not including long or fast races or tests) is a half hour to an hour.

Indicate your fastest recommended training pace (see Table 10.1). _____

Indicate your slowest recommended training pace (see Table 10.1). _____

Calculate the shortest and longest distances (in miles) that you should run in the minimum half-hour time period, dividing thirty by your pace (see Table 10.2).

Shortest (running two minutes per mile slower than ten-kilometer race pace). _____

Longest (running one minute per mile slower than ten-kilometer race pace). _____

Calculate the shortest and longest distances (in miles) that you should run in the maximum one-hour time period, dividing sixty by your pace (see Table 10.2).

Shortest (running two minutes per mile slower than ten-kilometer race pace). _____

Longest (running one minute per mile slower than ten-kilometer race pace). _____

Table 10.2 How Far to Train

Distances covered within a fixed time period vary widely according to pace. For instance, a runner averaging six-minute pace will travel five miles in a half hour, while someone running ten-minute miles will cover only five kilometers in that time. To convert your times to distances, estimate your average pace per mile for the appropriate running period.

Your Pace per Mile	Distance Run in 30 Minutes	Distance Run in 60 Minutes
6:00	5.0 miles	10.0 miles
6:15	4.8 miles	9.6 miles
6:30	4.6 miles	9.2 miles
6:45	4.4 miles	8.9 miles
7:00	4.3 miles	8.6 miles
7:15	4.1 miles	8.3 miles
7:30	4.0 miles	8.0 miles
7:45	3.9 miles	7.7 miles
8:00	3.8 miles	7.5 miles
8:15	3.6 miles	7.3 miles
8:30	3.5 miles	7.1 miles
8:45	3.4 miles	6.9 miles
9:00	3.3 miles	6.7 miles
9:15	3.2 miles	6.5 miles
9:30	3.1 miles	6.3 miles
9:45	3.1 miles	6.2 miles

3. How Often to Train

Indicate the number of days on which you typically run each week. _____

If the number is seven, make one of the days "optional" (to include a reduced amount of running, an optional activity, or rest). If the number is five or less, increase to six running days a week. Reserve one of those days for racing or testing. See Table 10.3 for a sample weekly program.

Table 10.3 How Often to Train

Make exercising a habit by planning to do something every day. That doesn't have to mean running seven days a week, and it certainly does not mean working hard each day. Mix training runs, races or tests, and optional days into the weekly recipe. *Training* is defined here as runs of thirty to sixty minutes (less than a half hour if injured or ill) at one to two minutes per mile slower that ten-kilometer racing pace. *Racing* is any all-out effort, and *testing* is running that mimics a race in either distance or pace. *Optional* days may include normal training runs, shortened runs, or alternative activities such as hiking, biking, swimming, and cross-country skiing. A typical weekly pattern might look like this:

Day	Running Plan
Monday	train 30 to 60 minutes
Tuesday	train 30 to 60 minutes
Wednesday	train 30 to 60 minutes
Thursday	train 30 to 60 minutes
Friday	train 30 to 60 minutes
Saturday	race or test
Sunday	optional

Write your own weekly plan based on training recommendations from Tables 10.1 and 10.2:

Day	Time	Length	Pace
1. _____	30-60 minutes	_____	_____
2. _____	30-60 minutes	_____	_____
3. _____	30-60 minutes	_____	_____
4. _____	30-60 minutes	_____	_____
5. _____	30-60 minutes	_____	_____
6. _____	race or test	_____	_____
7. _____	optional	_____	_____

TESTING

The Rehearsals

Three-Part Harmony

Be warned: A writer using my name authored a number of books in the 1970s that still rest on some bookshelves. That Joe Henderson is something of a stranger to me now. He occasionally offered advice I would no longer take, let alone give. His books froze ideas in time like photographs in a scrapbook. The cold type on those pages doesn't move, but I do. My theories and practices have evolved. Not that the old ideas were wrong; the new ones are improvements on them.

That earlier Henderson wrote about LSD running, but I rarely put in more than forty miles a week. He praised steady runs, but I'm not above stopping and walking. He scheduled a long run on weekends and avoided speedwork except in races; I plan a fast run most weeks and rarely run longer than an hour. He advised alternating hard days with easy days. I follow a hard day with an easy *week* and sometimes two.

The earlier Henderson published a marathon training plan that built to sixty-plus weekly miles. I tell people to follow Jeff Galloway's program which calls for as little as half that much mileage, and will use it myself if the marathon bug ever bites me again. Jeff's schedule for that race (see Chapter 19) may be the best anywhere, and its framework can support any kind of program. Our talks at his Tahoe Trails running camps certainly have led me to replot my own course.

Galloway ran in the Olympics of 1972, but he doesn't spend much time these days talking with fellow Olympians. Jeff is that rare sort of elite runner who knows how to advise the little people about the sport. He maintains that most of us run too much without going far or fast enough. The routines are . . . well, too *routine*.

Perhaps you know someone unhealthily preoccupied with mileage totals. He or she must reach a sixty-mile-a-week quota. He or she avoids taking easy days or speed days, since they would eat into that total. His or her main purpose in running seems to be adding up mileage totals in a diary. The old Joe Henderson would have pleaded guilty on those counts. But I know now that more harm than good results from running too much on the days meant to be easy, and then ending up too tired or bored to do justice to the runs meant to be hard.

I wholeheartedly endorse three Galloway principles:

1. To race well, we must get used to the stresses of racing distance and pace.

2. Most of us can't tolerate and don't even require more than one hard day—race, long run, or speed session—each week.

3. We probably need and can handle no more than an hour's running on all the other days.

Better racing comes from combining harmoniously the three elements of running: races, long and fast rehearsals for racing which I call "tests," and recovery/rebuilding training between hard efforts. For the purposes of this book, the elements combine in roughly this manner:

- Training—the majority of mileage, taken at a comfortable pace, seldom lasting less than a half hour or more than an hour, intended for R&R (recovery and rebuilding).
- Testing—a transition step between training and racing, farther and faster than training but easier than racing; at least one day and preferably as much as a week of R&R afterward.
- Racing—much farther and faster (and therefore harder) than normal; followed by at least one week of R&R or one day per racing mile, whichever is longer.

We talked of training in Part One and will move into racing in Part Three. Here, the subject is *testing*.

Simple or Simplistic? In one of my magazine articles, I included my thoughts about three-part harmony, recommending no more than one race or test a week, mixed with at least six recovery-rebuilding runs lasting less than an hour. One reader took issue with this advice.

"I find your view of training overly simplistic," wrote W. R. Elkman from California. "Apparently you feel that your running improves with less than one hour a day of training. I suspect you are among a minority of runners—or perhaps you simply aren't competitive."

True, my improvement stopped a long time ago, and my instincts as a competitor have withered. I'm running to keep running now, and three-part harmony is as much a survival technique as a training program.

Yet at my competitive best, I ran that simple way—without really knowing what I was doing. The more "sophisticated," demanding methods which I graduated to and gave five years of fair testing yielded no better results and far more injuries.

Elkman continued, "Most of the good to very good runners that I know improve on high mileage (eighty to 120 per week) and genuinely follow a pattern of hard-easy days." They push themselves several days a week, he explained, not just the one that I recommend.

Perhaps that's true of the best athletes. But most of us aren't "good to very good." We don't have the ability, the ambition, the time, or the resilience to pile up impressive amounts of work.

I've never tried to advise elite runners. They obviously take care of themselves quite well without my help. I'm not concerned with how much work these people can tolerate, but how little the others can get by with while still going where they want to go as runners. I've seen a little hard work go a long way for a lot of of people. I've also seen too many runners work too hard, too often, and wind up not being able to run at all.

I've been one of each type more than once. Rather than recount the worst of times, let's look at the stories behind the best of times.

My two best years were 1961 and 1968. As a high school senior in '61, I knew next to nothing about modern training techniques. Instinct alone led me to run around a four-mile section of land most days, occasionally adding a few miles to a session. The pace was rarely outside my comfort zone of seven to eight minutes per mile. To this, I simply added a weekly race or time trial when track season arrived.

My early race results were dreadful after I ran nothing fast all winter. I was lapped in my first indoor mile. But by season's end less than two months later, I'd improved my mile time by twenty-six seconds, won state championships in the mile and half-mile, and set a three-mile PR which would never be broken.

Five years of more complex and much harder training yielded only marginal improvement in the mile, my main event—and a growing amount of down-time for recovery from injuries. Only after I returned to my original, simple way of training did my health improve and times go down again. My running in 1968 involved little more than modestly paced thirty- to sixty-minute runs mixed with regular racing and simulated races at a wide variety of distances. Yet I came very close to the one-, two- and three-mile records I'd set as a fanatical kid, and ran all-time bests at almost every distance between six and twenty miles. Throughout that entire year, I lost not one day to injury or illness.

Much later, while reviewing the ups and downs of a long racing career with perfect hindsight, I discerned a clear pattern. If race-like effort (both true races and what came to be known as tests) totaled less than five percent of a month's running, I didn't race well; I felt sluggish. If the percentage went much beyond ten, I was too tired to race well and was courting injury. Racing five to ten percent of the time gave the best results and preserved the greatest level of health. Ten is my magic number: ten percent of total running taken as racing or testing, one minute or mile in every ten, a monthly average of one hard day in ten.

I list ten only as a starting point for your analysis. Your magic number eventually may be different, but that doesn't matter. The thing to remember here is the pattern of three-part harmony. Mixing training, testing, and racing in the right proportions may bring back harmony to a routine that has gone flat.

Hard and Fast Rules (Or How to Race and Test Often and Fairly Well without Really Suffering)

1. Treat racing and testing as prescription items. Taken in carefully measured doses and intervals, they give pleasant and predictable results. Underdose, and you get little benefit. Overdose, and you risk losing everything.

2. Count efforts as race-like whenever you time yourself for a measured distance and spend an unusual amount of effort on it. Races don't have to be official to take a race-like toll.

3. Don't mix training and racing, but do let training set your racing limits. Do no special speed or distance work on non-racing/non-testing days. Rarely race or test at more than two minutes per mile below the average pace or more than twice the average daily distance.

4. Don't race or test if you are ill, injured, or just don't feel in the mood for it. Leave the heroics to the heroes who race as if there were no tomorrow.

5. Make no firm promises as to pace or final time. Let them come as surprises. Goals preclude the element of surprise because you either reach them as expected, or fail and get frustrated.

6. Time the warmup according to the racing or testing distance. The shorter the race, the longer the preliminary run, and vice versa. In any case, total at least the daily minimum of thirty minutes.

7. Start cautiously and then accelerate, regardless of distance, attempting to run the two halves in equal time or the second slightly faster than the first. Give away a little time in the early going, knowing you'll probably get it back with interest later.

8. Leave the deepest reserves untouched. Rarely, if ever, go all the way to the bottom of the well. Stop before reaching the "survival-shuffle" stage.

9. Recover quickly and slowly. You should feel good enough to run almost normally the next day, but allow a week or more before racing or testing again.

10. Treat the race or the test as a bonus, not as the sole reason for running. Don't let the racing and testing taint the other ninety percent of runs.

Test
and
Rest

Pretending to Race

Test is a blanket term covering long runs, speedwork, and time trials. These are dress re-hearsals for racing. By necessity, the tests are hard work. They lead up to the even harder work of racing.

Long tests mimic the distance of the race but at a slower pace. Fast tests prepare you for the race's full speed but cover only part of its distance. You combine full distance at full speed only in the race itself.

The long test at least matches the time (not necessarily distance) of the longest race you plan to run, but is done a minute or so per mile slower than racing pace. For instance, as a 1:30 half-marathoner (about 7:00 pace) you would run one and one-half hours or more at eight minutes per mile or slower.

The fast test at least matches the pace of the shortest race you intend to enter, but lasts no more than half the racing distance. Say your lower limit is 10-K, which you race in about forty minutes (6:30 pace). You'd test at a 6:30 or slightly faster rate, for 5-K or less.

The idea, then, is to bring together the two factors—full distance at full speed—in the race, where it counts.

These tests are race-specific. They get a runner ready for a single race or set of distances. In later chapters, I put you on one-month cycles: usually a long test, a fast test, a race, then an easy weekend. If the race requires a special build-up of speed or distance—such as a mile or a marathon—the cycle may be longer.

If, like me, you simply enjoy the feeling of going longer or faster, try more general forms of testing which key off from your typical daily runs.

- *Double-time:* Up to twice your daily average time or distance, at normal training pace. If you usually run up to an hour's worth of eight-minute miles, test for as long as two hours at 8:00 pace.
- *Half-fast:* No more than half your daily average, at one to two minutes faster than normal training pace. If you usually run at least a half hour at 8:00 pace, drop to fifteen minutes at six to seven minutes per mile.

In both long and fast tests, consider exercising the interval option. Interval training allows you to run longer and faster than you otherwise could or would. Intervals can be particularly valuable when you're breaking into the higher ranges of distance and speed—say, more than double your normal training time or more than two minutes per mile faster than typical training pace.

- *Extra-long tests:* A five-minute break every half hour can as much as double your longest non-stop distance with little increase in effort. That is the Tom Osler Rule, and it works. Example: The intended testing time is two hours. Run twenty-five minutes, call a five-minute time out (most commonly for walking but sometimes for stopping and stretching). Repeat that cycle three more times to fill the allotted period.
- *Extra-fast tests:* Mixing fast portions with recovery walks, in classic interval fashion, allows you to run faster with no great increase in stress. Example: The test totals a mile on the track. Run a fast lap, then click off your watch while walking a lap. Repeat this process as you take a cumulative time for the mile, not counting recovery periods into the time or distance total.

Passing the Tests Like most of us who write about running, Marlene Cimons of the *Los Angeles Times* would trade a dozen by-lines for one personal-record time. She once called me, not to discuss an article she was writing for the magazine that employed us both, but to ask the question: "How do I improve my speed?"

Cimons had run her first marathon. Now she complained of feeling she could run forever, but that her times in the 10-K had stalled.

"How do I get off this plateau?" she pleaded.

I told her to go to the track for an introductory course in speed: "Run at or near your fastest mile pace. But to keep from tearing yourself apart, divide the mile into its four laps and walk a lap between. Just time the fast parts, and keep a record of what those mile times are." She called with weekly reports on her speed sessions—first telling me how tired and stiff they left her, later saying how she could run better times with apparently less effort.

After her next race, Marlene could hardly wait to let me know that she'd run almost "three minutes!" under her old 10-K best. She'd done it simply by testing herself with one mile a week for six weeks.

People who've done the least fast running improve the most when they add a small amount of it. The same effect applies to long-distance testing.

After running her fastest 10-K, Marlene Cimons set out to improve her stagnant marathon time. She turned to another experienced runner for advice. Jeff Galloway, a former U.S. Olympian, told her to make just one change in her program. Once every week or two, she should take a long run which gradually increased in distance to the full projected time (about three and one-half hours) of her marathon.

When Galloway sends marathoners into dramatic increases in their distances (often tripling their longest runs within a few months), he advises them to ease the stress the same way I'd told Cimons to make speedwork more tolerable. That is by employing one of the most discredited and least used secret weapons: walking breaks. In pre-marathon tests, the walks commonly amount to about five minutes every half hour.

Nothing changed for Cimons except the length of her long run and the way she took it. She ran quite moderately on weekdays, little more than would be recommended for fitness runners. Yet she improved her marathon time by nearly ten minutes.

She raced much faster than ever before at both the shortest and longest distances because she satisfied the two basic testing requirements: frequent runs at or below race pace, but at a shorter distance, to develop speed; and regular runs of race length, but at a slower pace, to develop staying power. Marlene Cimons' case also illustrates dramatically that the quickest way to race faster and farther may be to start walking.

Walk Talk *Walk*. It's a simple word for a noble act, but most runners don't think the word belongs in their vocabulary or the act in their program. They're wrong.

Most of us equate walking with quitting, but I think of it as a small miracle. Selective walks permit us to go longer and faster than we otherwise might—and with less effort and pain. This is the purpose of tests: to mimic the speeds or distances of races without absorbing their stress blows full force.

Tom Osler, a largely unsung genius in matters of running technique, wrote in his *Serious Runner's Handbook* (Anderson World Books, 1978) that any runner can immediately double his or her longest previous distance without doubling the effort. The trick: splitting up the run with five-minute walking breaks.

Dick Buerkle, two-time Olympian at 5000 meters and former world record-holder for the indoor mile, says the quickest way to build speed safely is to run a fast mile. This is the special type of mile that Marlene Cimons used: four individual laps on the track, each separated by a lap of walking (which again takes about five minutes).

After I repeated Osler's advice on walking in a magazine article on marathon training which recommended a twenty-five-minute run/five-minute walk formula, reader F. Gregg Bemis from New Mexico wrote with three questions. After expressing the usual runner's reluctance to walk, he asked three questions: Is there anything particularly sacred about the mix of twenty-five/five during the longest training runs? At what point, if ever, does one wean oneself from the walks? And, if one's last long run before a marathon included regular walks, does this mean he or she should walk during the marathon?

I prefaced my response to this reader's question by first advising him to think of walking as long-distance interval work. The intent of intervals is to cut up a big chunk of work into smaller and more manageable bites. In this case, they allow you to cover more total mileage at a faster pace than you could with straight running. I then went on to answer his specific questions.

The twenty-five/five formula isn't chiseled in stone. Experience has taught me that a five-minute break is long enough to provide some recovery, not so long that it has a stiffening effect. Your trials and errors may tell you otherwise. The frequency of these breaks depends upon how often you think you need them.

Wean yourself away from the walks only when you can run comfortably the full time of your next race and can recover from the test effort quickly. Most limited-mileage marathoners never reach this stage.

During long-distance testing, you rehearse the distance and pace of the race while still not shouldering their full workload. Save that experience for race day, when you start with every intention of running every step.

The plan for making a speed breakthrough without breaking down is similar. Dick Buerkle discussed it on his "Running People" show for CNN Radio. Run 440s, he advised runners who don't normally indulge in speedwork. Run just four of them and walk—don't run—a lap between.

"Some people think they should do more than four repeats," Buerkle remarked. "I like doing only four, because you can run close to top speed without worrying about saving yourself for, say, the ninth or tenth sprint. We're talking about quality here, not quantity." He recommended walking instead of jogging between intervals, because "if you have a walk to look forward to, your mind is free to concentrate on blasting the running part."

Whether the test is very long or very fast, the walk is the pause that refreshes.

Running Farther

Climbing "The Wall"

It isn't necessary for you to be a marathoner to learn from the marathoners. Their lessons here deal with how far you need to run and how best to run that far.

Several years ago, I wrote a schedule for first-time marathoners. *Runner's World* published it in 1977, and the program enjoyed several reincarnations in magazines and books. That plan held the conventional wisdom of marathon training in the late 1970s. It emphasized rather high mileage, while claiming it to be "the least a runner can do while avoiding The Wall." It gave more attention to raising the average length of runs than to extending the long one. It contained one hard run a week and two more of medium difficulty.

The long run peaked at two and one-half hours (less than twenty miles for most runners), the medium two at one and one-half hours each. The important feature of the program was thought to be that daily average, which reached well beyond an hour.

My marathon plan drew heavily upon the teachings of Ken Young. A man of limited talent, Young developed himself into a runner of American-record caliber. As befits one who now directs the National Running Data Center, he analyzed meticulously his own and other runners' statistics. One result was the "collapse-point theory."

"Collapse point," wrote Young in the mid-1970s, "is the maximum distance a runner can expect to go before the urge to slow down overwhelms him. More commonly, the collapse point is called 'The Wall' (which one runs into) or 'The Bear' (which jumps on one's back). It is characterized by a sudden decrease in performance, often occurring within a single mile. Pace may drop off by two to three minutes per mile or more." In other words, runners must train themselves to complete a distance without "collapsing" before they can hope to race it. As racing distances grow, just getting through them is increasingly difficult.

Much of the training for long-distance racing, according to Young, simply involved building the ability to go the distance. But without a strong foundation of endurance, speed-work would be irrelevant. Speed couldn't be used if you were unable to lift your feet in the last miles of the race.

The collapse-point theory held that endurance limits were drawn by the mileage habitually run in training. Required distances depended upon the length of the race. You could finish a 10-K on as little as two or three miles a day. Marathoners, on the other hand, required eight or ten a day for an extended period to get ready for their 26.2-mile race.

Young worked out a formula which predicted when a runner would reach his or her collapse point. In simple terms, the formula stated that a runner would stop or slow down dramatically at a point about three times his or her average daily distance for the past month or two. If an individual were averaging thirty-five miles a week during that time (five miles a day), his or her projected collapse point would be five times three, or fifteen miles. That runner could count on getting through a half-marathon rather comfortably. But to try a marathon would be an invitation to the trouble that lay at The Wall and beyond.

Young advised training at least a third of the racing distance daily, perhaps even little longer than the minimum, to give oneself a safety margin. A marathoner, for instance, might average nine miles a day. Tripling that amount would move the collapse point out beyond marathon distance, to twenty-seven miles. The farther above minimum mileage one went, the less he or she needed to worry about breaking down and the more he or she could dream about breaking personal records. That was the theory. How did it work in practice?

Quite well, according to Paul Slovic of the Oregon Research Institute, who studied runners at the Trail's End Marathon. By questionnaire, he asked their training mileages for two months before the race and compared those figures to their marathon times.

Those who ran the most generally raced the fastest. Slovic divided the subjects into four groups: (1) the sub-three-hour runners who averaged nine miles a day; (2) the 3:01 to 3:30 runners who ran six miles a day; (3) the 3:31 to 4:00 people who ran five miles daily; and (4) those who ran slower than four hours and who typically ran only four miles.

Using the Ken Young formula, only the first group was adequately trained for a marathon. The other groups would have had predicted collapse points of eighteen, fifteen and twelve miles, respectively. If Young's theory were valid, these undertrained runners should have slowed down dramatically after meeting their "Walls."

Slovic's data indicated that this was the case. Even Group One's pace dropped, by an average of fourteen percent, from twenty miles to the finish. This compared with a twenty-two-percent slowdown for Group Two, thirty-seven percent for Group Three and fifty-eight percent for Group Four.

To interpret these statistics another way, the sub-three-hour runners lost only about five and one-half minutes (relative to their twenty-mile pace) in that last stretch, while the four-hour-plus marathoners used up nearly thirty extra minutes on those last 6.2 miles. Their pace by then was a thirteen- to fourteen-minutes-per-mile shuffle.

Several years ago, I believed that the way for runners to collapse-proof themselves was to work from the bottom: push up the length of the day's runs until they averaged one-third of the racing distance. That principle formed the basis of my old marathon schedule.

The Galloway Way The old program wasn't a bad one. It certainly was better than having no plan at all, which was how most marathoners had previously groped their way toward their first race. Hundreds of people wrote to say they'd used the schedule, and ninety-eight percent of those who completed the program also completed their marathons.

This schedule worked most of the time: I have a file drawer full of unsolicited letters to prove it. But I have retired that plan in favor of a new, improved model that is both simpler and safer. It closely resembles Jeff Galloway's, since our lessons come from the same source: other marathoners putting themselves on the line for the first time.

Galloway and I advise runners from the safety of a speaker's platform or a printed page. Those men and women themselves must breathe life into the schedules, and they suffer when the numbers we give them are too high or too low. When those runners speak, I listen. In general, they had two complaints about my old program. First, it sometimes asked them to work too hard. The medium-long mid-week runs required for pushing the weekly mileage total above sixty seemed particularly draining and difficult to face. Second, it didn't ask them to work hard enough at other times. The long, weekend runs, which peaked at less than twenty miles, didn't seem to prepare these runners either physically or mentally for the surprises to come in the most difficult part of the race.

Some of them told me they were stopped short of the marathon starting line when the heavy weekly mileage total broke them down. Others said they hit "The Wall" in the marathon because they hadn't approached this distance in training.

Once the problems were noted, the solutions were obvious. Add distance to the long day; subtract it from the other days.

How far should the longest run be? Galloway's answer is simple: as long as the race. While Galloway accepts the collapse-point theory in principle, he uses a different method for establishing it. He says runners are likely to find their racing "Wall" at the point where their *longest testing run* ends. One who has trained no longer than two hours will have a very hard time racing beyond two hours, while one who has gone three hours will know the third hour of a marathon as familiar territory.

How often to run long? Galloway advises doing it once a week at most, and only every other week when distance totals are climbing rapidly toward marathon level. Take plenty of time to recover in between with no runs of more than an hour and most of them far less. Don't bother counting total mileage, since that raises the temptation to run too much on the days meant to be nice and easy, resulting in not being able to run enough on the days intended to be good and long. The run that counts is the long test.

Ken Young's collapse-point formula still has merit. It lives on here in a modified form, as a testing tool. The old Young rule now tells how long to test and how to test long. Results of those tests then determine racing limitations.

Normally, the long-distance testing should not exceed three times the daily training amount (calculated from at least the past month). Better yet, think of double the average as the safe limit. A forty-minute-a-day trainer, for instance, might go as far as two hours, but would run fewer risks by staying in the 1:20 range.

If you must go farther than this formula allows, consult Table 20.1. It explains how to cheat the collapse rule.

CHAPTER FOURTEEN

Running Faster

More from Less

Three letters arrived, independently and unsolicited, the same week that Brooks Johnson sounded off against LSD training in *The Runner* magazine. The coach of the 1984 U.S. Olympic women's team had written: "Long slow distance is fine—for those who want to run long and *slow*. But American competitive distance running has been held back for more than a decade by dependence on long slow distance at the expense of speed. Speed must be the centerpiece of any intelligent training program for the competitive runner—at any distance."

As if in response to an article they hadn't yet read, Elizabeth Stronge, Ted Fulton, and Richard Stiller told how they had combined adequate but unspectacular amounts of gentle running with small doses of speed to produce the best results of their long careers.

Elizabeth Stronge wrote from Alabama: "Previously in preparing for the 10-K season, I ran once a week with a male friend, and we went at a fairly fast clip. I found myself a little sore from those days and also a little hoarse from telling him to slow down.

"This season, I decided the speed necessary for a decent (whatever that means) 10-K was not worth those uncomfortable speedy runs. So I took the opposite road and slowed down my training runs to pure 'pleasure' pace. I also added some swimming. I found myself suddenly stronger.

"To my surprise, I ran a 35:22 10-K and felt wonderful. (I usually run a high thirty-six at my peak.) My legs were loose and eager, and somehow I gathered my speed from the strength I had built on the long, slow runs. I accelerated through the fourth, fifth and sixth miles rather than gradually running out of gas.

"I tell myself my training runs are just for building back up; I get enough tearing down in the races. Whenever I run with anybody, I just say, 'I'm going easy today,' as if I had run twenty quarters on the track the day before. Sometimes they take off without me, rarely do they believe me when I tell them how little speedwork I do. Who cares?"

Ted Fulton wrote from Florida: "I had been training and racing almost constantly since 1978. I had run twenty marathons and over 200 races of lesser distance. I went to Jeff Galloway's running camp seeking a method of improving from a level of performance at which I had been stagnant for the past year or two.

"While I respected Jeff's diagnosis of my overtraining and streak (twenty-six months without missing a day) having me in a burned-out state, I felt compelled to keep pushing until after the New York Marathon.

"Unfortunately—perhaps I should say *fortunately*—my Achilles tendon would not accept the wait until its promised post-New York rest. Most of that fall and early winter were spent seeking quick and miraculous cures, and alternating rests periods and easy running.

"When I was again able to run regularly, I decided to apply what I'd learned from Galloway and adopt a new program which would no longer have weekly mileage as its goal. I abandoned my normal eighty-five- to ninety-five-mile-weeks, two-workouts-per-day, two-long-runs-per-week routine in favor of a twenty-four- to twenty-five-mile run every other week, with races on alternate weekends. To my amazement, I approached both the long runs and the races with a refreshed and enthused feeling.

"Leading up to the Boston Marathon, I had set PRs for 8-K, 15-K, 10-K and 5-K. But I still had reservations about the fact that I'd averaged only fifty-five miles per week.

"Those doubts vanished early in the race. I ran three minutes faster than ever before, the last mile was the fastest, and I had never felt so good during or after a marathon."

Richard Stiller wrote from California: "I was and still am a believer in long, slow distance. I have never done well on extended interval training but have consistently produced good times (for me) on ninety to ninety-five percent LSD, with races for speedwork every second or third weekend.

"In the past few years, I have adopted a slight variation in my training that usually leads to a successful string of races. Three or four weeks before my first race, after running almost pure LSD (fifty to sixty miles a week at 7:00 to 7:30 pace), I insert a sub-maximal interval workout into my weekly schedule. It is usually eight 440s at 10-K goal pace with a 220 jog after each.

"I am quite capable of running those 440s down close to seventy seconds. But my goal is to prepare myself to race, not to blow myself down before I ever reach the starting line.

"I keep the effort controlled, and usually my first workout is eight times 440 in seventy-nine to eighty seconds per quarter [33:00 10-K pace]. Over a period of three weeks, that effort remains the same—but the times come down to the seventy-five- to seventy-six-second range [31:30 10-K]."

"Then I begin racing. At that point, I drop the intervals. They have served their purpose. I never, during the interval or racing period, do more than one hard session a week.

"At thirty-nine years old, I recently ran a 1:13:40 half-marathon and a 55:05 ten-mile. Both are PRs."

Nearly twenty years into my own LSD era, I'm still learning. What I've primarily learned in recent years is that this is less a training system than a recovery method. For this reason, I'm more inclined to call it "gentle running" than LSD: it gently replaces what the hard work takes away.

Stronge raced better by slowing down her training. That pace itself didn't make her faster in races; the recovery it gave her did. She went into her 10-Ks healthy and eager, with all the speed she needed.

Fulton and Stiller added small amounts of gentle speed to their gentle distance. Fulton sped up twice a week. "On one weekday," he wrote, "I would do form work (six to eight accelerations up a gradual incline of approximately 300 yards). On another day, I would do some relatively easy speedwork (total distance never exceeding four miles) on the track, again with emphasis on form rather than how fast the distance could be covered."

Stiller settled for a single fast day each week. That's all he is willing to do and all he thinks he needs. "Most runners never understood," he said, "that LSD was simply an alternative method of training for those who constantly overworked or injured themselves doing intervals—or simply disliked speedwork."

Speed Games John Salmonson of Honolulu found speed training distasteful. He wrote, "I run seventy-plus miles per week and do fairly well in long races (considering my six-foot-two, 175-pound size): 3:20 PR in the marathon. But I don't like speedwork, and subsequently my 10-K best is only 42:10. How can I get past this dislike/fear of short, hard races and get my time into the 39s?"

"If you don't like speed training," I replied, "don't do it. You obviously do like to race, so *race* yourself into anaerobic sharpness. Temporarily abandon all long racing and most long runs. In their place, race weekly at about half the 10-K distance.

"On weekends when there aren't races available, fake them. Run at or somewhat faster than your ideal 10-K pace, but for a much shorter distance in these tests. The beauty of this faster work is that you don't need to take it very often or for very long to see dramatic results. This is particularly true for those of us who normally shun faster running."

One of the all-time great racers, four-time Olympian George Young, advised sharpening for racing *by* racing; learn to handle the stresses of racing by experiencing the real thing. He called this the most specific, most exciting form of speedwork. The theory is sound, but in practice racing yourself into race shape is impractical and risky: impractical because you seldom find races of just the right distance at just the right time you need them, and risky because the leap from gently paced training to full-speed racing may be too long to make all at once.

Tests overcome both objections. You can schedule them anytime, at any distance, and you can insert them as transition steps between the relative ease of training and extreme effort of racing.

Or you can test for the reason I do: because running fast can be fun. In all my running life, I've never gone more than a few weeks between fast runs. I've never strayed far from racing and race-like testing. I never want to leave behind the sensation of lifted knees, extended strides, pumped arms, and labored breaths. This stopped being training long ago. It is my link to my running past. My first runs were all-out miles, and whenever I run a fast mile now I remember every one that came before. Times change; feelings don't.

My plan is to alternate fast tests one weekend with long ones the next. But I usually choose speed three weeks out of four. Long runs are just more of the same, while fast ones are a radical departure from the norm.

I've tested all sorts of recipes for these tests in recent years: a mile of four quarters with one-lap walks between; a mile with no walking; fifteen minutes of fast running mixed with jogging; fifteen minutes with no breaks. The mixture I now use is most appetizing.

My magic number on speed days is *ten*. The session totals ten laps on a quarter-mile or 400-meter track. I take a total time for the fast parts and later work out an average pace. That pace falls between one and two minutes per mile faster than normal; the faster it is, the more often I walk.

I may run the whole two and one-half miles without a pause, or break it into smaller pieces—miles, half-miles, quarters—with five-minute walks between bursts of speed. A lap of walking takes about five minutes (and, yes, that lap does count toward the total distance).

The decision on the exact mixture rests not on goals but on whims. I never plan what to run until I'm warming up, and sometimes wait to decide until the first fast laps. Half the fun of running fast is letting what happens happen, instead of trying to make the numbers fit a pre-determined plan.

Going
in
Style

On the Ball

"This is my thirtieth consecutive year of racing and training without so much as a two-week layoff," said Tom Osler in 1983. The ultramarathoner and author of the *Serious Runner's Handbook,* defines a "serious" problem as one that slows him even slightly.

"The most serious one I've had to endure has been a sore left heel which I injured after twisting my ankle in 1980," he explained. "This soreness has bothered me off and on ever since. It has never been so bad that it stopped me from running. But it has taken much of the fun from my runs and has caused me to lose interest in ultras."

The analytical Osler (he works as a college math professor) found relief by changing his running form—more specifically, his foot plant. "I switched to a ball-heel-toe foot placement. Like most long-distance runners, I had been a heel-toe lander, and it took me six weeks to grow accustomed to this new foot placement." That was time enough to cure his sore heel.

My experience was similar. Running slowly for the past several years had let me develop some form faults, and an injury had exaggerated them. A heel had bothered me almost constantly for a year when the thought finally struck me that I now ran like an arthritic old man: stiff-legged, flat-footed, short-strided. My feet felt like two clenched fists.

I ran this way to reduce pain, but in the process may have been adding to it. Running was jarring, jamming, and tightening the feet and lower legs. They were acting as ramrods instead of the shock-absorbers they are meant to be.

So I whispered new instructions to myself: "Lift the knees at pushoff, flex the ankles, spring from the big toes, land with the knees slightly bent, fall a little farther forward on the feet."

If a single word can define this style, it is *prance*. Not running like a drum major at a Saturday afternoon football game, but running as if I'm proud of myself. The prancing motion arises from three sources:

- *Foot*. Make full use of it. Land at midfoot, rock back gently onto the heel, then roll forward onto the toes—leaving the ground from the big one.
- *Ankle*. Flex it and snap it. Use it to get bounce from the ground. Think "flex" and "snap" as the ankle does its two jobs.
- *Knee*. Lift it. Pick up the knee and bend it.

This combination led Osler and me back to healthier running as we got up off our heels. We're beyond improving our PRs, but, for you, the more fluid way of moving might translate into faster times.

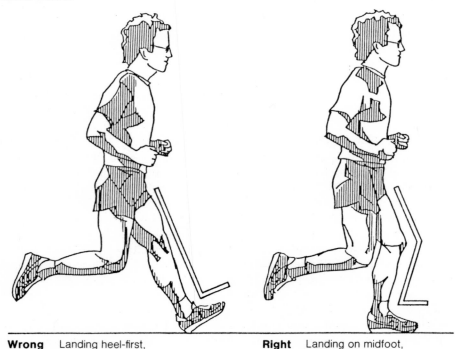

Wrong Landing heel-first,
Knee straightened,
ankle locked

Right Landing on midfoot,
Knee slightly flexed,
ankle unlocked

Figure 15.1 Running Footplant

Ups and Downs Shakespeare never ran a road or cross-country race, as far as we know, but runners everywhere will agree with his lament that hills "draw out the miles and make them wearisome."

Uphill running obviously slows us down, but without giving the usual recovery of slowing. You still may be working at six-minute-per-mile effort while moving at only eight- or nine-minute pace.

Downhill running is easier, but it isn't completely relaxing either. Gravity tugs you out of control. The feet, calves, knees, and thighs take almost twice the beating that they do on the flat.

Hill running has a set of rules all its own. The first word in running uphill is *preserve;* the most important word in running down is *protect.* "Preserving" means not wasting so much energy going uphill that you have no energy left for resuming normal pace when the course flattens. "Protecting" means not letting the downhills pound you so hard that you are not able to run normally when the hill bottoms out. In both cases, get over the hills without getting hurt by them.

Efficient climbing has less to do with technique than attitude. When you run up hills, neither fear them nor fight them; simply adjust to them. If you were riding a bicycle uphill, you would shift into a lower gear. The speed would drop, but you'd pedal with about the same effort. Do the same when you run: maintain a constant workload while ascending, even as the pace naturally declines.

Proper (read: *protective*) downhill running is more difficult than it might first appear, as illustrated by this exchange at a running clinic.

"I do okay on the uphills," one man said. "But the part that should be easy—coming back down—gives me the most trouble. What can I do?"

I offered the standard advice by quoting Kenny Moore, a consummate downhill specialist who once ran a sub-four-minute opening mile on a slope of a 10-K. Moore advised holding the body perpendicular to the surface and letting gravity do the work.

"I know all that," said the questioner. "But have you ever tried running that way down a steep hill? It pounds you to death. What I want to know is how to avoid that."

When I admitted ignorance, another speaker onstage at the clinic came to my rescue. Tom Miller was studying for an exercise-physiology doctorate at the University of Utah, giving particular emphasis to the ways runners move.

"Run like a question mark," said Miller. He explained the enigmatic advice as he assumed the wrong and right positions.

"The natural tendency when running downhill is to reach out with the front leg, lock the knee, and slam down heel-first. You lean backward, arch the back, and possibly throw back the head. That's all wrong. You're braking and taking more shock than you should."

Then Tom demonstrated the question-mark style. "Instead of 'running tall,' as you would on the flat, you 'run short,' as if you're sneaking up behind someone. Keep your feet under you and the footfall as quiet as possible. Bend the knees more than normal. Hold your rear down and slightly protruding. Look at the ground in front of you."

The time to learn about running hills is before the races, in hilly training and tests. Hill racing is strength work, and hill training/testing builds the necessary muscles for it.

According to Dr. Bob Fitts, former national-class road racer and now an exercise physiologist, "Hill training is the foundation upon which all of the other principles of successful hill racing must stand. There is a simple reason for this. When running up a hill, extra muscle fibers are used to perform the extra work. These fibers recruited for hill running are not generally used while running on level terrain." Simply put, untrained muscles fatigue quicker.

Fitts' conclusion: "Train on the hills, and almost any tactic will work. Without hill training, all tactics are doomed to failure."

My conclusion: Choose a test course as nearly identical to the racing course as you can make it.

Uphill. Keep effort constant by slowing pace somewhat. Lean into the hill, concentrating on pumping harder with the arms and "lifting" with the knees and ankles.

Figure 15.2 Uphill running

Downhill. Absorb the added shock by keeping center of gravity low and landing with exaggerated flex of knees. Look down to promote a forward lean.

Figure 15.3 Downhill running

Almost Like Race Day

Testing Everything

May all your race day surprises be pleasant ones!

The best surprise you can give yourself is to run farther or faster—or both—than you did before. Yet even that type of result shouldn't be too surprising. After all, haven't you trained and tested with that improvement in mind?

Testing means rehearsing in advance the stresses of the race so they won't occur as unpleasant shocks on race day. You test separately at the racing length and at race pace. Long tests (lasting the approximate length of your race but usually run at a slower pace) acquaint you with the feeling of covering the full distance. Fast tests (run at race pace but no more than half the distance) introduce you to the mechanics of moving at full speed. You bring the two factors together in the race itself.

The subject of testing doesn't end with distance and pace. These dress rehearsals serve many other purposes, all designed to immunize the runner against rude surprises. Very little that happens to you on race day should be happening for the first time.

Don't just simulate the race: mimic its whole day. Start the night before the event, by eating and sleeping as you would if you were about to compete, and continue pretending you were racing until you refuel and rest after the test. Pay special attention to five areas:

1. **What to eat and drink.**

    If what you normally do works, don't change it. If you normally eat several hours before running, eat the same items in the same amounts now; if you don't eat before a run, don't start now. If you drink a cup of coffee in the morning, drink that one cup. If you must experiment with items added to or deleted from the pre-event diet, make adjustments before race day. If something seems to help you test better, keep it in the race routine; if it bothers you now, cut it out then.

    When and what you drink during a long race protects your health and affects your performance. Practice drinking during long tests at intervals similar to those in races (generally every two to three miles). What to drink is the subject of some controversy. Some scientists claim that plain water works best, yet runners report good results from taking electrolyte mixtures such as ERG and sugared drinks such as defizzed cola. Again, the most important experiments are your own, and the time for experimenting is during long tests.

2. **What to wear.**

    The cardinal rule: *nothing new on raceday.* This applies most specifically to the single most critical item of equipment: the shoes. The temptation is to run in lighter footwear, thinking that every ounce of weight shed converts into minutes and seconds gained. This may be true in theory. In fact, you're giving up protection while adding greatly to impact stress. Any gains in time might be canceled out by muscle soreness at best, injuries at worst. When adding distance, speed, or both, stick with the shoes you know you can trust. Save the experimentation for everyday training runs. You might find (as noted in Chapter Five) that you can tolerate racing shoes all the time. On the other hand, realize that today's training shoes are lighter than the "racing" flats of a few years ago, so you never need to carry much of a load.

    The "nothing new" rule applies to clothing. Dress for the test exactly as you would for a race. Underdress rather than overdress, keeping in mind that temperatures automatically rise by twenty degrees when you start running. Being comfortable at the starting line means you'll soon feel too warm.

3. **When to test.**

    Most road races, for practical reasons of traffic and temperature, start in early to mid-morning. The hour may present problems if you normally aren't fully awake until noon, or if you don't generally run until sundown. You can't change the starting time, so a personal change is in order on this particular day. If the race starts at 8:00 A.M., test at eight o'clock. Much as this might hurt, get out of bed two hours earlier and perhaps take a shower *before* running to aid in the waking-up process.

You morning runners face a different set of problems on those rare occasions when races are scheduled in the afternoon or evening. You aren't accustomed to waiting all day to run; you aren't used to planning your daytime activities around a run; and, most of all, you aren't adapted to the warmer temperatures of afternoon. Delay your tests until the hour of the race in order to experience all of these conditions and to find ways of coping with them.

4. **Where to test.**

Familiarity breeds confidence. If you know what to expect from a race course, you're more confident that you can run it well. Test yourself on the course itself or on a reasonable facsimile thereof. Match the surface, terrain, and surroundings of race day as closely as possible. Test for road racing on the roads, for cross-country over the country, for track by running track. If the race has hills, practice running up and down slopes of the same steepness and number. Familiarity breeds competence.

5. **What to do before and after.**

A race doesn't start at the starting line, and it doesn't finish at the finishing chute. Neither should a test. The subjects of warming up and cooling down are important enough to fill the second half of this chapter.

Warming and Cooling The hardest, least pleasant effort doesn't come at the end of a run but at the start. Recall how you feel as you take your first steps each day. You're stiff, heavy, uncoordinated. You wonder if you've forgotten how to run and why you're bothering to re-learn the technique. Is this how you want to start a race or test?

Now recall how you feel after fifteen minutes have passed. Sweat is flowing as freely as your strides. The running has taken control of itself, and you're on automatic pilot. Your early doubts about how and why you run are gone. This is the way you want to feel at the starting line.

Spend fifteen minutes warming up. A quarter hour is long enough to loosen up both the legs and the head, but not so long that you squander the energy reserves you'll be needing soon. Keep this time period constant for races and tests of all distances and paces, but vary the routine somewhat as working conditions change.

For instance, when racing or testing at short distances (those lasting less than an hour and run quite fast), add two more elements after the fifteen-minute run: a set of stretching exercises, and striding 100 meters, three to five times, at the pace of the race or test.

Stretching and striding become options at longer distances (those taking longer than an hour to complete and more modest in pace). Take a separate fifteen-minute warm-up before any faster-than-normal effort of this length. However, if your objective is distance and not speed—if the test is gently paced or the race is an extra-long one, such as a marathon— simply warm up during its early miles as you would on a daily run.

Today's ambitious runners typically err on the side of too much warm-up. You see them pacing the streets a half hour to an hour before a 10-K race. This amount of pre-event warming serves no physical purpose: it is merely a reaction to anxiety. Think of how you feel after a normal day's thirty- to sixty-minute run. Do you want to *start* your hard work feeling this way?

Today's runners are just as likely to cool down too little. You see them crossing the finish line, stumbling to a grassy area nearby, and immediately starting the post-event celebration. This is no way to start recovering.

If the warm-up shifts gears between resting and hard work, the cool-down period is a necessary shift from racing to resting. Continued mild activity gradually slows down the racing metabolism, and also acts as a massage to gently work out the soreness and fatigue products generated by the earlier effort. The pattern and pace of recovery are set in the first few minutes after the race or test ends.

A report by J. E. Dimsdale, M.D. and colleagues, appearing in the *Journal of the American Medical Association* (February 3rd, 1984), offers a more sobering reason for cooling down properly. The authors studied ten healthy men, between the ages of twenty-two and thirty-five. They found that levels of two powerful hormones, norepinephrine and epinephrine, increased during exercise and continued to rise afterward. Dr. Dimsdale suggested that the continued rise in these hormones during the post-exercise period may be responsible for irregular heart beats and lack of adequate blood flow to the heart muscle.

"The worst possible strategy for exercise cessation," cautions Dimsdale, "would be to have the patient abruptly stop exercising and stand [still]. The best strategy would be for the work load to be diminished gradually."

The best strategy is to keep moving. Walk for at least fifteen minutes after the racing or testing ends. *Walk.* Some experts will advise you to run easily, but walking will give the same benefits with much less effort—and you've already worked hard enough.

Dr. Jack Rockett, a physician and veteran marathoner from Tennessee, values his post-race walking. "I've found that a walk at the end of a run keeps me from being so tight," explains Dr. Rockett. "Therefore, I need to do less stretching. Also, if I walk a mile or two the same day I run a marathon, I am less sore in the following days."

He has the backing of Tom Osler, who wrote in his *Serious Runner's Handbook:* "After a really hard effort, such as an all-out marathon race, the runner should try to keep his circulation going vigorously for some time. Brisk walking would be an excellent start on the road to recovery."

Osler recommends a brief walk immediately after finishing, then another stroll of up to an hour later that day. "The worst thing you can do," he says, "is stop immediately upon crossing the finish line and stand around talking to friends."

The talk can wait for fifteen minutes; the cool-down can't.

Ten-Kilometer Tests

The Perfect Ten

A case can be made for ten kilometers being the perfect racing distance. Certainly the 10-K is the most popular race: more than half of the events nationwide are the metric equivalent of 6.2 miles, and many of the others are eight kilometers (about five miles) or twelve kilometers (about seven and one-half miles) in distance. The discussion here centers on the "perfect ten," but extends across the range of 8-K to 12-K, because the training, testing, and racing requirements are nearly identical.

The fact that 10,000 meters is a traditional Olympic distance might explain the popularity of this race from the organizers' point of view. However, relatively few runners are aware of that fact, and almost certainly didn't know it when they first ran a 10-K. The primary appeal of the event arises from its close resemblance to everyday running. Training runs typically settle into the half hour to hour range, and almost every runner can finish a 10-K race within that same thirty- to sixty-minute range of times. Therefore, the distance is familiar, and neither too long nor too short.

Only the speed of the races is unique. The challenge of racing the 10-K lies in running that common distance faster than normal, but not so fast as to be reckless or dangerous. This is a true race (as opposed to marathons, which often come to resemble survival marches), and yet it is not a mad dash (such as happens in the mile).

The perfection of the 10-K takes other forms. Testing is simplified to a matter of improving speed, and no more than a weekly fast test is required to prepare for race speeds that aren't excessive. No long tests are needed because most runners go far enough in daily training to handle these distances.

If you enjoy racing, you want to race often. Ten-kilometer races allow this because recovery occurs quickly. Applying the standard formula of one easy day following each racing (see Chapter 29), you can safely run 10-K races as often as seven days apart. Marathon specialists, on the other hand, must limit themselves to about one race a month.

Ten kilometers is a great place for a racer to start, and an equally great stopping place for runners like myself who still like to race but don't care to work too hard at racing. I now enter these races almost exclusively; these are the distances I call "home."

I spent the first eight years of my running life training for and racing on the track. This netted me a 1:55 half mile, a 4:18 mile and a legacy of injuries. I spent the next seven years training for and racing in marathon-like events. This phase of my career allowed me to run unspectacular but satisfying sub-three-hour marathons and to survive runs as long as seventy miles. It also resulted in foot surgery from running too far, too often.

I'm proud of all the times and distances I ran in those fifteen years, and I don't regret any of the suffering that went into them. But those times are past now. I'm finished with that kind of working and wandering—at least as regular routines.

What I wrote many years ago in *Run Farther, Run Faster* (Anderson World Book, 1979) is even more true now: "I've been to the extremes of racing. Small, simple five- to ten-milers are the place I've decided to settle down. If I want to make rare trips out from here again, I'm familiar enough with the other neighborhoods to visit them briefly. But this is home." This home may not be as thrilling as the exotic places I visited at the extremes of pace and distance. But this is a place where I can relax, live comfortably and avoid much of the frenetic effort that very fast and very long travel involve.

I urge other runners to visit the places I have. If nothing else, this makes home look better when they return there to settle down.

The Need for Speed Adding distance is a matter of persistence: simply running more of what you already run daily. Increasing speed is a matter of style, of applying techniques not normally practiced day by day. Running fast is a learned skill, and you learn it by testing at that pace.

Dick Buerkle, a two-time Olympian, says a runner should practice the techniques of speed before worrying about the numbers on a watch. The digital watches on almost every running wrist are two-edged swords. On one hand, they give instant results. On the other, they sometimes tell us more about each run than we may want or need to know. The flickering numbers may blot out more important messages.

Buerkle writes in *Racing South* magazine: "I never use a watch during the first few weeks of speedwork. Instead, I think about knee lift, arm carriage, erect posture—all those things that make up the sweet stride. Time is not something you should be thinking about— at least not at first. Going without a watch was a significant factor in my running 3:54.9 for an indoor mile in 1978. Only in my last few workouts did I use a timepiece."

I apply this lesson during my nostalgic weekly visits to the track. I wear a watch only because I will want to know the results later, and no one else is there to time me. But I don't want to know how fast or slow the test is *until it ends*. I check no splits but concentrate instead, as Buerkle suggests, on the more important matters of running smoothly and strongly.

You might argue that speedwork in any form is distasteful and perhaps even unnecessary. I might have agreed with you once, before I found an unlikely hero in Doug Rennie. We've never met, and he may be surprised to hear his words repeated from this source— "Mr. LSD." I once overstated the case against speedwork because fifteen or twenty years ago training was out of balance in that direction. Now I speak favorably about speed because in recent years the balance has tipped too far toward slow distance.

Rennie argues persuasively for added speedwork. He has set all of his PRs—ranging from a 32:45 10-K to a 2:33:51 marathon—since turning forty, and attributes this improvement largely to his regular speed tests. Writing in *The Running Scene* magazine, he examined and rebutted common excuses for not training fast. To them, I add some of my own.

- *I don't need it.* "Ever run a 10-K race that felt like a fifty-yard dash lasting thirty-seven minutes?" A runner drawn into an unusually fast pace, a minute or more per mile faster than the training rate, feels that he or she is sprinting all the way. A sprint lasting more than a few seconds is no fun.
- *My races are my speedwork.* "If you race every weekend flat-out, and if every race is short and fast, then maybe you can get by with little or no formal speedwork. But how many can nod in affirmation to those ifs?" The races must be frequent and must mimic the pace of the shortest racing distance. Otherwise, speed tests must fill these needs.
- *I'll get injured.* "Running with your head and not just your legs greatly minimizes the risk of injury." Racing fast without a proper speed background maximizes the risk of injury. Testing at race pace eases the shock of an abrupt transition from gently paced training to hard racing.
- *Speedwork hurts.* "True, but so does racing. Speed sessions prepare both mind and body for the rigors endemic to flat-out racing." You most fear the unknown. Racing won't hurt as much if you know what to expect and have experienced it previously in tests.
- *Running on the track is boring.* "Who says you have to run on a track? The important thing is that you create [race-like] stress. How and where you do it doesn't really matter." The tests should match racing conditions, most notably the setting. You need to rehearse at racing speed on the track only if you plan to race there.

Table 17.1 Testing for a 10-K

While this is labeled a 10-K program, it applies to a range of short-distance races: those 8-K to 12-K in length and lasting between thirty minutes and an hour for most runners. Because you run that amount regularly in training, your concern in testing is not with distance but with speed. Temporarily eliminate all runs longer than an hour and spend the one big day each week learning to run faster.

This plan is designed to improve your speed during a month of testing and racing. The underlying assumptions are that you have not been racing regularly at distances 10-K and less, and that you have taken no recent speed tests. (If this doesn't describe you, the program in Table 20.3 may better fit your needs.)

The special ingredients here are: (1) testing at 10-K race pace but not more than half the racing distance; and (2) racing faster than 10-K pace at a shorter distance.

Week	Big Day	Other Days
1	5-K test at 10-K race pace	30 to 60 minutes
2	5-K or shorter race	30 to 60 minutes
3	5-K test at 10-K race pace	30 to 60 minutes
4	5-K or shorter race	30 to 60 minutes

Half-Marathon Tests

Making the "Half" Whole

My purpose here is to sell you on the hidden beauties of the half marathon, a perfectly lovely little event that is forced to hide behind an ugly name. I'm already sold on this race, for reasons that soon will become apparent.

I like everything about the half marathon except that name *half marathon*. No other road distance is known as a fraction of another. This is made to sound like a low-rent marathon, a discount item. It is treated as a second-rate event on a two-race program, added as an afterthought for those slackers who won't put out full marathoning effort.

Those who do run the "half" are also victims of its name. They think, "If I ran my half marathon in 1:30, I must now be ready for a three-hour race at the full distance."

No one expects Sebastian Coe to run two more laps at his world-record 800 pace for a 3:23 mile, yet we think a runner should be able to maintain half-marathon pace for another thirteen miles. If that were possible, American half marathon record-holder Paul Cummings would be a 2:03 marathoner instead of a 2:12 man (with, I quickly add, potential to break 2:10 if he concentrated on that event). Joan Benoit, who holds the U.S. women's mark in the half, would be running marathons in the 2:18 range instead of nearly five minutes slower.

The typical conversion formula between the two distances for runners of Cummings' and Benoit's ability is to double the half-marathon time and add at least five minutes to predict marathon capability. But here I am falling into the very trap I wanted to avoid. I, too, am cheapening the half by comparing it to its big brother.

The beauty of the half marathon is that it's a unique event, with its own special training and pacing requirements and its own rewards. Don't sell it short just because it isn't as popular as either the marathon or the 10-K. In my opinion, that very lack of popularity is one of this race's main attractions. Halves don't usually bring out the crowds of either the 10-Ks or the marathons. Very few of these events attract more than a thousand runners, and smallness may become an attraction after you've fought your way through a few mob scenes.

This distance—or more precisely, the range of distances well between fifteen and twenty-five kilometers, races requiring between one and two hours to complete—is the least-tapped source of personal records. These "middle distances" also offer unique experiences that frequently remain unexplored.

If I hadn't already applied the term "perfect race" to the 10-K in Chapter 17, I might have argued the perfection of the half marathon. Perhaps the word "attractive" is suitable. The attractiveness of the middle distances takes many forms, the most significant being that these races combine speed and distance better than the shorter and longer events. Ten-K testing almost exclusively emphasizes speed, while marathon tests lean heavily toward distance. The half marathon requires modest amounts of both elements.

The pace of this race is not so fast that it requires a great deal of special speedwork, as might the events of 10-K and less. Those short races themselves, taken regularly enough, can serve as your speedwork for the half.

By the same token, this distance is not so great that it demands extra-long training runs, as marathons do. Two hours is the most time you ever need to invest, and you can finish a half marathon on much less. This is a welcome change from spending all Saturday morning running and the rest of the weekend semi-comatose from the extreme effort of marathon testing.

Even if you train moderately (averaging thirty to forty-five minutes a day, for instance), no "Wall" is likely to loom between you and the half-marathon finish line. This is truly a *race* and not simply a survival exercise.

When you don't hit a "Wall," you spend much less time recovering. Dr. Jack Scaff, who conducts the popular Honolulu Marathon Clinic, tells the Hawaiian runners that crashing during the race is "an injury, and you need six weeks to recover just as you do for any other injury." By emerging from your half uninjured, you can repeat the distance as soon as two weeks later.

Combining Speed and Distance Another hidden beauty of the half marathon is that no one seems to train seriously and specifically for this event. Even people like Joan Benoit and Paul Cummings set their American records while pointing for something else: Benoit to break her national 10-K mark and Cummings for the New York City Marathon.

Runners of lesser ambition can be half marathoners without sacrificing their normal lives to the gods of speed or distance training. Preparation for a half fits so neatly into what they probably already run that they hardly need to break stride while getting ready for this type of race.

How much of the following describes you? Your typical daily run lasts at least thirty minutes but rarely more than an hour. Every week or two, you take a long run of one to two hours. You race often, mostly in the ten-kilometer range. These races are your only speed-work.

Now let's measure that routine against the accepted requirements of training. The two basic needs are frequent runs, taken somewhat faster than race pace but for a shorter distance, and regular runs of full distance but at a slower pace. (Full distance and full pace mix only during the race.)

If you fit the preceding profile, you typically don't train fast enough for the 10-K or long enough for the marathon. But this combination suits you well for the half. Your short races give the speed you need, your long runs provide the distance, and your everyday running allows full recovery between the harder sessions.

If I've just described you, don't change a thing. Don't make any attempt to "improve" your program or to peak for a certain half-marathon event. You're already trained perfectly for this race.

If, however, you're lacking in one of the basic ingredients, or if you want to adopt a new routine that allows more productive racing over a wider range of distances, consider adopting the following schedule of weekly races and tests. (Run the normal, comfortably paced thirty to sixty minutes on all other days.)

- *Week One:* long test, two hours maximum
- *Week Two:* fast test, one hour maximum
- *Week Three:* race, one to two hours
- *Week Three:* recovery weekend, nothing fast or long.

Inspiration for this program comes from Bill Bowerman. The legendary University of Oregon coach taught, as almost everyone now knows and practices, that good results can only come from mixing hard and easy days. Bowerman's years of experimentation taught him that no runner improved without working hard some of the time, but also that no one improved without taking breaks between bouts of extreme effort.

A lesser-known Bowerman principle involves training by cycles longer than a week. My variation on Bowerman's theme takes hard-easy to the extreme of no more than one day of racing or testing per week as part of a four-week cycle: short and fast first weekend, long and relatively slow the second weekend, race the third weekend, then repeating the cycle. This yields an average of about one hard day in ten, which appears to be a productive yet safe ratio not just for half marathoners but for racers at all distances.

Table 18.1 Testing for a Half Marathon

While this program applies specifically to the half marathon, it can be adapted to a range of middle-distance races: those 15-K to 30-K in length and lasting between one and two hours for most runners. These races will be both farther and faster than your normal training efforts, so you must prepare for both the added distance and speed.

The underlying assumptions of this plan are that you have not been racing regularly at these and shorter distances, and have taken no recent tests of race length or pace. (If this doesn't describe you, the program in Table 20.3 may better fit your needs.)

The special ingredients here are: (1) long tests at the projected time of your race but run at normal training pace; and (2) fast tests at race pace but not more than half the racing distance.

Week	Big Day	Other Days
1	test at full H-M race time	30 to 60 minutes
2	10-K test at H-M race pace	30 to 60 minutes
3	test at full H-M race time	30 to 60 minutes
4	10-K test at H-M race pace	30 to 60 minutes

Marathon Tests

What's in It for You?

On the face of it, running marathons makes no sense. What is a marathon, anyway? Twenty-six miles, 385 yards; forty-two kilometers, 195 meters. The people who devised this race didn't even have the good sense to make it an even distance, in either the mile or the metric system.

What purpose does running a marathon serve? I'm skeptical whenever anyone tells me, "It makes me feel so healthy." Maybe some of the early training makes a runner healthy, but much of the later, more serious training for marathons and the race itself should carry a "Caution: may be hazardous to your health" warning. A podiatrist—a marathoner himself—once told me, "I know without looking at the race schedule if there has been a marathon recently. Starting on Monday morning and continuing the next week or two, my office is filled with the casualties of the race."

We can't be going to these lengths because it makes us feel more alive and energetic, either. The hollow-eyed, glazed stare of a runner in the twenty-sixth-mile, post-collapse-point "survival shuffle" shows this can't be true, as do the finishers who hang limply on each other, too weak to stand alone.

It's unlikely that we run marathons because we like to view the scenery: we're running too hard and with too much concentration to know whether we're passing through a park or the city dump. Anyway, most marathon courses don't go anywhere except back to where they started.

Well, then, do we run marathons for the competition, the chance to be a winner, to earn prizes? Not in the usual meaning of these words. Not one marathoner in a hundred is rewarded for placing well, or runs for that reason, or knows or cares as much about the winner as he or she does about himself or herself.

Perhaps that's the point of marathoning. So many people are running the distance now because it means something to them personally. It's a major athletic goal they can reach with their own sweat—not second-hand from a stadium seat or through a TV screen. Whether the goal has any purpose is irrelevant as long as it has meaning.

Mark Twain once defined play as any activity which has meaning but no purpose. We forget sometimes that marathoning is just play—a sport, a game. We waste too much time trying to find purpose in it and to explain it in purposeful, practical terms.

Maybe it's time to admit that running 26.2 miles is as irrational and illogical as batting a fuzzy ball back and forth across a net, chasing a little white ball across a field, or committing assault and battery between two sets of goal posts. None of these games serves any great purpose, none has any great importance to the survival of humankind, but they all have great meaning to the people involved. That's all we should ask of our play.

Marathoning has whatever meaning we runners, by ourselves and as a group, decide to give it. And we've decided to give it more meaning than any other event in long-distance running—perhaps more than all the other races combined.

The marathon is meaningful because it gives a focus to the sport in general and to individual running careers in particular. This is the only distance above 10,000 meters with a history going back more than a century, with legends of its own, and with an Olympic tradition. It is an "ultimate" toward which an everyday runner can climb.

The first goal of a new marathoner is finishing. And to finish, he or she has to train longer than before. This training is a sneaky way of exposing him or her to other attractions of running that are not so obvious: the positively addicting sensations of runs beyond a half hour; the habit of maintaining a demanding schedule; the temporary stress and ultimate satisfaction of sub-marathon races; the support of a group of long training runs.

Once the ambition of finishing is satisfied, the new goal becomes time: improving one's own best time, running a time which all marathon runners understand and appreciate, achieving a time which has no intrinsic value but as much meaning as we place upon it. Times are important because everyone who runs can have one, and because the prospect of improving that time is a driving force which keeps many marathoners running.

First Marathon The first marathon is a graduation ceremony—a twenty-six-mile, 385-yard victory lap. The most demanding work, the build-up of distances which went on for months or even years, is behind you. If you have trained properly, you need not concern yourself too much with how the race will go; it is all but guaranteed to go well.

"The Wall" that marathoners talk about shouldn't give you any nightmares. Oh, it is a very real part of this event, but not an inevitable part. Your ability has little to do with whether you meet a "Wall" or not. Anyone, from the fastest to the slowest among us, can reach a collapse point, and anyone can avoid it. Those who hit "The Wall" have made mistakes, either in training or in pacing.

You will be well-trained long before marathon day if you follow a preparation plan similar to the one in Table 19.1. Like a student cramming for a final exam, you may think you need to pack in all the work you can in the last week or two. Don't! You draw your ability to finish the marathon from a reservoir of fitness filled gradually over several months. Extra-hard work in the final days does nothing but drain the pool at the worst possible time.

Go into the race well-rested. Allow two full weeks between the longest run and the big event. Run minimum distances during the last week, and perhaps rest completely the final day or two. Save your trained-in strength for when it counts.

There isn't much left to say about the marathon itself. The race almost runs itself. Just stay on course and keep alternating feet until you reach the end. You know by now how to choose a pace that will take you there, because you've rehearsed it dozens of times in practice.

Celebrate for the few hours of the race the good work done over the past few months. They are your reward.

Faster Marathon One of two thoughts occurs to marathoners after a race. If they ran as expected or better, they think, "If I did that well on that little training, think how much faster I'll go if I train harder!" And they up their mileage by fifty percent. If they ran poorly, they think, "I didn't train hard enough; I need more work." And they up their mileage by fifty percent.

We certainly must work hard in order to improve, but we can't tolerate ceaseless pounding. The harder the work on some days, the longer and easier the recovery period must be. The trick is to work hard *selectively*.

Run both more and less when training for a faster marathon—more on the big days and less on the little ones. Don't count miles; measure *efforts*. These come in two types: hard, to prepare you for the distance and speed of the marathon; and easy, to recover from that work.

The schedule in Table 19.2 contains two key features: a weekly test that mimics the stresses of the race, and a full week of recovery in between. Because your goal now is to run the marathon distance at a faster pace, you train for both distance and speed these two months.

Increase the long run until it matches the approximate *time* of your marathon, but run somewhat slower than your projected race pace. In other words, you aren't asked to attempt the full 26.2 miles before race day. A three-hour marathoner, for example, races at just below seven minutes per mile. He or she might train for three hours at *eight-minute* pace, covering about twenty-three miles in that time.

Table 19.1 *Testing for a First Marathon*

While this program applies specifically to the marathon, it can be adapted to a range of long-distance races: those longer than 30-K and lasting more than two hours for most runners. The goal for a first-timer at these distances is completing the race, which probably is more than three times as long as the typical training run. Temporarily eliminate all short- and middle-distance races as well as speed tests during this marathon preparation period, and spend one day each week learning to extend training pace over longer distances.

This plan is designed to increase your maximum distance over three months. The underlying assumption is that you have not regularly gone beyond two hours in races and tests. (If this doesn't describe you, the programs in Table 19.2 and Table 20.3 may better fit your needs.)

The special ingredients here are: (1) tests of two hours and more, taken with a five-minute walking break every half-hour; and (2) tests of about half that amount, taken without walks. Base the length of longer tests on your predicted race time.

Week	Big Day	Other Days
1	two hours with walk breaks	30 to 60 minutes
2	one hour without walks	30 to 60 minutes
3	2:00 to 2:15 with walks	30 to 60 minutes
4	1:00 to 1:15 without walks	30 to 60 minutes
5	2:15 to 2:30 with walks	30 to 60 minutes
6	1:15 to 1:30 without walks	30 to 60 minutes
7	2:30 to 3:00 with walks	30 to 60 minutes
8	1:15 to 1:45 without walks	30 to 60 minutes
9	2:45 to 3:30 with walks	30 to 60 minutes
10	1:30 to 2:00 without walks	30 to 60 minutes
11	3:00 to 4:00 with walks	30 to 60 minutes
12	one hour maximum	30 to 60 minutes
13	marathon race	about 30 minutes

Develop your speed on alternate weekends. Run at your projected race pace, but no more than half the marathon distance. For instance, a marathoner with a three-hour goal would test his or her speed with a half marathon in 1:30.

Do nothing long or hard on the recovery days. In fact, to compensate for the extra work involved in the tests, you may want to do even less on the weekdays than you did before entering this program.

Table 19.2 *Testing for a Faster Marathon*

While this program applies specifically to the marathon, it can be adapted to a range of long-distance races: those longer than 30-K and lasting more than two hours for most runners. You have achieved the goal of finishing a marathon-type event, and now you want to run that distance faster. The emphasis remains on long tests, but you now give more attention to speed.

This program is designed to increase your maximum distance over two months, while keeping in mind the importance of occasional faster runs. The underlying assumption is that you have not regularly gone beyond two hours in races or tests. (If this doesn't describe you, the program in Table 20.3 may better fit your needs.)

The special ingredients here are: (1) distance tests of two hours and more (maximum amount based upon your predicted race time), with five-minute walking breaks available as an optional feature; and (2) speed tests at race pace but not more than half the racing distance.

Week	Big Day	Other Days
1	2:00 to 2:30	30 to 60 minutes
2	10-K test	30 to 60 minutes
3	2:30 to 3:00	30 to 60 minutes
4	15-K test	30 to 60 minutes
5	2:45 to 3:30	30 to 60 minutes
6	half-marathon test	30 to 60 minutes
7	3:00 to 4:00	30 to 60 minutes
8	10-K test	30 to 60 minutes
9	marathon race	about 30 minutes

Your
Testing

Plan your pre-race testing schedule by determining the following information.

1. **Basic training**
   Indicate the average length of all your runs from the past month
(in minutes):   _____

If you have averaged less than thirty minutes, racing is not recommended. Delay entering any events or attempting any race-like testing until you have increased your daily average to a half hour or more.

If you have averaged more than thirty minutes, your training has prepared you for the testing recommended in this program. Maintain an average of at least thirty minutes per day. You are prepared for testing at about twice the length of your typical training run, unless a longer limit is indicated in part two below.

   Indicate the average pace per mile of your daily training from the
past month (not counting races or tests):   _____

You are prepared for testing at a pace up to two minutes per mile faster than you typically train, unless a faster limit is indicated in part three.

Table 20.1 *Distance Limits*

"Collapse point" is calculated according to the Ken Young formula: three times the average length of the daily run. Compute that average from at least the past month, dividing the total amount of running by the total number of days (even if you didn't run every day). Stop well short of "collapse," limiting the non-stop runs to twice the time of the average training run.

The test amounts can be extended significantly by inserting a five-minute walking break at least every half hour. Author and ultramarathoner Tom Osler maintains in his *Serious Runner's Handbook* that a runner can travel up to twice as far with the walks as without them. Adjust your figures upward by that amount when taking breaks.

Run at or near normal training pace (one to two minutes per mile slower than current 10-K racing ability). Count the walking breaks toward total time periods.

Daily Average	Safe Limit Non-Stop	"Collapse" Non-Stop	Safe Limit with Walks	"Collapse" with Walks
30 min.	1:00	1:30	2:00	3:00
35 min.	1:10	1:45	2:20	3:30
40 min.	1:20	2:00	2:40	4:00
45 min.	1:30	2:15	3:00	4:30
50 min.	1:40	2:30	3:20	5:00
55 min.	1:50	2:45	3:40	5:30
60 min.	2:00	3:00	4:00	6:00

2. **Distance limit**

Indicate the length of your longest run within the past month (in hours and minutes): _____

This amount represents the longest time you currently are prepared to race. To extend that limit, follow the distance-testing recommendations in Table 20.1.

3. **Speed limit**

Indicate the pace of your fastest run within the past month (in minutes and seconds per mile): _____

This figure represents the fastest pace at which you currently are prepared to race. To extend that limit, follow the speed-testing recommendations in Table 20.2.

Table 20.2 *Speed Limits*

These speed-testing recommendations are based upon length and pace of daily training runs. Do not exceed *one-half* of the distance that you average in training. Select the normal pace per mile at which you train, then determine how to test. Walking breaks are unnecessary at paces up to one minute per mile faster than training rate, are optional between one and two minutes faster, and are required at two-plus minutes.

Training Pace	Pace without Walk Breaks	Walk Breaks Optional	Walk Breaks Required
6:00	5:00-5:59	4:00-4:59	sub-4:00
6:15	5:15-6:14	4:15-5:15	sub-4:15
6:30	5:30-6:29	4:30-5:29	sub-4:30
6:45	5:45-6:44	4:45-5:44	sub-4:45
7:00	6:00-6:59	5:00-5:59	sub-5:00
7:15	6:15-7:14	5:15-6:14	sub-5:15
7:30	6:30-7:29	5:30-6:29	sub-5:30
7:45	6:45-7:44	5:45-6:44	sub-5:45
8:00	7:00-7:59	6:00-6:59	sub-6:00
8:15	7:15-8:14	6:15-7:14	sub-6:15
8:30	7:30-8:29	6:30-7:29	sub-6:30
8:45	7:45-8:44	6:45-7:44	sub-6:45
9:00	8:00-8:59	7:00-7:59	sub-7:00
9:15	8:15-9:14	7:15-8:14	sub-7:15
9:30	8:30-9:29	7:30-8:29	sub-7:30
9:45	8:45-9:44	7:45-8:44	sub-7:45

4. Race plans

Indicate in kilometers or miles the distance of the race you plan to run within the next month: _____

Indicate your projected time for the race: _____

Calculate the pace per mile that you intend to run for this distance (divide time by distance in miles):   _____

If your longest recent test (see part two) equals or exceeds the probable time of the race, and your fastest recent test (see part three) matches the projected pace of the race, you are adequately prepared for the upcoming event.

If you have matched or exceeded race pace, but are lacking in distance, attempt a long test before racing. Run the test at full race time but at a slower pace. If the test is not successful, reduce the length of your race until you are better prepared.

If you have met the distance requirement but are lacking in speed, attempt a speed test before racing. Run the test at full race pace for no more than half the racing distance. If the test is not successful, revise the pacing goal downward or race in a longer (and therefore slower) event.

If you have met neither the distance nor speed requirement, schedule both long and fast tests before racing. On the long test, run at your normal training pace for the probable race time. If the test is not successful, reduce the distance of the race. On the short test, run at race pace for no more than half the racing distance. If the test is not successful, revise the pacing goal downward.

5. Race-preparation schedule

Write your own monthly program for tests and races, based upon the answers in parts one to four above, and on the recommendations contained in Tables 20.1, 20.2 and 20.3. (Substitute a fast test for the long test in Week One if the race length is shorter than the average daily training run.)

Week	Type	Distance/time	Pace per mile
1	long test	_____	_____
1	fast test	_____	_____
2	fast test	_____	_____
3	race	_____	_____
4	recovery	no testing or racing this week	

Table 20.3 *Plan for the Month*

This program is best suited to runners who race regularly over a wide variety of distances. These people are well-grounded in both endurance and speed, and therefore can enter these events with a minimum of special preparation.

The plan is based upon one race a month. Two weekly tests, one long and one fast, precede the event. A weekend of recovery follows the race.

Week	Big Day	Other Days
1	long test, full race time*	30 to 60 minutes
2	fast test, half race length	30 to 60 minutes
3	race	30 to 60 minutes
4	no race or test	30 to 60 minutes

*If the race is to be shorter than the average training run, replace the distance test with another fast one.

RACING

CHAPTER TWENTY-ONE

The Competition

Pain in Perspective

"It's a horrible yet fascinating sight," wrote Sir Arthur Conan Doyle, "this strange struggle between a set purpose and an utterly exhausted frame. He was practically delirious, staggering along like a man in a dream."

In this short description of Doranto Pietri's arduous finish in the 1908 Olympic Marathon, the famous mystery writer and creator of Sherlock Holmes captured the essence of racing. A race puts the runner into the classic confrontation between a willing mind and a weak body. When you push to the limit, this conflict is unavoidable. There comes a point in all distance races when the "set purpose" and the "exhausted frame" do battle, as they did to the extreme in Pietri's case. The body has set limits; the mind determines how closely the runner will approach those limits.

European sports psychologist Miroslav Vanek declares, "Physical effort prevails in training, and psychic effort prevails in competition." Racing involves the hardest physical work you can do, but the emotional experiences of racing override the physical demands. These thoughts and feelings aren't experienced every day in training, and they set up conflicts that aren't a normal part of running. How you deal with these emotions determines the outcome of the race.

Before he or she races, a runner may be consumed by a mixture of anticipation and dread. The race itself involves paradoxical blends of control and recklessness, exhilaration and frustration, fear and courage. Afterward, you experience pain and pleasure, the proportion of each depending on whether or not the race met your expectations.

Racing might be described as organized, self-sought torture. It involves various types and degrees of pain, but the physical and psychic pain are constants before and during the race. The pleasure comes afterward.

"Jogging through the forest is pleasant," points out Kenny Moore, an Olympic marathoner-turned-writer, "as is relaxing by the fire with a glass of gentle Bordeaux and discussing one's travels. Racing is another matter. The front-runner's mind is filled with anguished fearfulness, a panic, which drives him into pain."

In describing Frank Shorter's performance in a Japanese marathon, Moore again refers to that pervasive pain experienced by those who race. "Shorter ran 140 miles per week all fall with consummate nonchalance. A thirty-mile day does not strain his prodigious physical resources. Yet in Fukuoka he [Shorter] said, 'The ordeal is between twenty miles and the finish. My only doubt is that my mind is ready to put my body through that.'

"Exploring the forest is easy," Moore contends. "Exploring the limits of human performance is excruciating."

Shorter agrees: "That's why you have to forget your last marathon before you run another. Your mind can't know what's coming."

Racing looks good from a distance. It's exciting to think ahead to it, pleasant to look back at it. But when you're involved in the immediate preliminaries and the race itself, the reality hits home. By the time you realize how unpleasant it can be, it is too late to turn back. Running away from the pain is not an acceptable alternative; that choice would keep hurting long after the immediate discomfort had vanished.

Ron Clarke, an Australian who held most of the world track records at distances 3000 meters and above during the 1960s, writes about his painful confrontations with himself in his autobiography *The Unforgiving Minute*. "In all my races, I feel some degree of pain. This is not remarkable, because any physical activity in which a person extends himself to the limit causes pain. Sometimes it is an agonizing pain which is scarcely tolerable, and when it comes an athlete has to cope with it as best he can—even if it means deluding himself. I remember in my first marathon the only way I could struggle over the last few miles was from lamp-post to lamp-post, promising myself that each lamp-post would be the last." Clarke concludes that "the pain in a race is caused by complete exhaustion. And the more intense it is, the greater the sense of achievement in overcoming it. Most people succumb to fatigue before they need to, because they have not conditioned their minds to cope with it."

Let me hasten to add, however, that the goal in racing is not to become a masochistic brute who embraces pain. Runners simply learn to live with their specialized discomforts, without developing a fondness for or an immunity to all pain.

Kenny Moore offers an example: "In the summer of 1967, I was included in a group of Oregon runners who were invited to participate in a United States Olympic Committee study of high altitude training and procedures. The price of our three-week vacation in the Rockies was to submit every Friday to a series of tests that measured lactic acid content in our blood.

It seemed strange to our doctors that, while we showed no reluctance to run ourselves into unconsciousness at the end of a hard workout (quite easy to do at 7500 feet), the mention of another session with the needles set us to whining like tormented alley cats."

Moore continues, "The explanation, of course, is that we were used to *our kind* of pain. Over the years, we had developed a familiarity with our bodies that let us know how much of the discomfort of extreme fatigue we could stand. Part of the runner's training consists of pushing back the limits of the mind, of proving to his doubting intellect that [racing] won't reduce him to another cinder on the track. But the needle pain was relatively new and exposed our 'innate toughness' for what it was: a learned specialty. . . . Good [runners] are reputed to possess either great resistance or little sensitivity to pain. Yet I doubt whether runners as a group are any more brave when it comes to sitting in dentist chairs or receiving tetanus boosters than the general populace."

Brian Mitchell, author of *Today's Athlete,* writes about runners and pain from a socio-logical-psychological perspective: "Perhaps one of the biggest mistakes which an observer can make about [racing] is to look upon it as a form of self-immolation. It is doubtful whether a wish for pain, or even for discomfort, characterizes the athlete. He does not look upon himself as a victim brought to the altar of the track to be sacrificed, and does not relish the pain that grows from the latter stages of a race. He distinguishes the pleasure in movement from the inevitable pain which has to be endured. The athlete will not like this pain; rather, he will accept it. . . . He knows if he is to achieve anything competitively, he must take himself through speeds and distances that will be uncomfortable. . . . If the athlete wished to cultivate pain, he would buy himself a bed of nails."

Useful Fears After setting a Boston Marathon record in 1970, Ron Hill commented, "I was worrying like hell all the way. But this is a good thing to develop, you know—this fear. It keeps you moving."

Hill had long since come to grips with fear, recognizing it as a component of competition that could be channeled to work on his behalf. It hadn't always been that way. He recalled how fear had worked against him in the 1964 Olympics.

"When I was in Tokyo," he said, "I was the second fastest man in the world at 10,000 meters and also the second fastest man in the world at the marathon. But the night before the 10,000 I was thinking, 'Tomorrow's the day.' There I was, lying in bed, turning the race over in my mind. And the first thing I thought about when I woke up was, 'Today's the day.' My stomach turned over. I didn't want to get out of bed, but finally I dragged myself out. During the warmup, my legs felt like lead, and I was just dragging them around the track during the race. There was no desire to get into the competition. In fact, the only desire was to get away from it; if somehow I could have gotten out of it, I wouldn't have run at all. I finished a disgusting eighteenth."

Hill immediately set about finding ways to cope with pre-race anxiety. He succeeded to the extent that he won at Boston, won at the Commonwealth Games and European Championships, and set world records. The fear remained, said Hill, but he learned to make it work *for* him instead of against him.

"The fear of running a long race can come from the fact that you know it's going to be physically painful. And unless you're a masochist, nobody likes pain; I certainly don't like it. If you dwell on the painful aspect, it can make you nervous. I've now developed some ways of turning off thoughts of the race, some ways I can step outside myself. I can even talk about the race in terms of what it's going to involve physically, and where the pain is going to come, and what it's going to be like, and how distressing it's going to be—without actually thinking that the guy who's speaking is going to be in that position so many hours hence."

Hill learned some important lessons about pre-race "nerves" that other runners might also find helpful. He realized that, within limits, his condition was normal and even beneficial, but that *fearing the fear* could push him outside the safe limits and hurt his performance. By knowing the signs and symptoms, and accepting them as natural, he was better able to control his anxiety.

Pre-race fear takes many forms: fear of pain, fear of competitors, fear of failure, fear of fear itself. And it goes by several names: "butterflies," "tension," "psyching." Whatever its form, a certain amount of uneasiness is a fact of the racer's life. It may feel unpleasant, but that isn't all bad. This is the mind's way of warming up the body for the big task ahead. Think of your fear as doing you a favor.

CHAPTER TWENTY-TWO

Emotional Experiences

Pre-Race Rituals

The mind becomes capricious as the race approaches. It distorts time and magnifies little, unimportant matters into big, crucial ones. The waiting is the worst. You can't wait to get started; at the same time, you don't know if you want to start—or if you will be able to. The last hours drag unmercifully, and a troubled mind fills them with a month's worth of worrying. Every move, every thought seems to pass under a microscope.

"I've got to get some sleep. How can I run if I can't keep my eyes open?"

"Should I eat this? It might upset my stomach."

"Oh no! My shorts are rubbing! What will this do to my legs after a couple of miles?"

"My left shoe has a flaw. Will my feet survive the race unblistered?"

"Nausea. Could it be the flu?"

"Uh-oh. A twinge in my calf."

"Is that wind I hear? Is the temperature climbing?"

"Look how fit and relaxed all those other people are."

Sportswriter Robert F. Jones went back to relive his glory as a swimmer after fifteen years away from the sport. Instead of glory, he rediscovered long-suppressed feelings of fear and dread that were equal parts of his races. He speaks for all racers when he says, "I looked at my watch when I felt *it* start; just twenty-three minutes after noon on the day of the relay; regular as clockwork, as they say, just like it was in the old days. At first it was only a flicker, a brief preoccupation, a butterfly emerging from its cocoon. I helped it along with some of the old rituals. A few curses, as obscene as I could make them, directed not only against my opponents and my coach, but against myself for letting me get into so grave a confrontation."

Jones notes that "the butterfly grew stronger with every obscenity. I fed it further with a mug of hot, strong tea, so thickly laced with honey you could feel it in your wrist when you stirred. I hadn't shaved or brushed my teeth that day, another of the old rituals. Makes you meaner and tougher, we used to believe. The butterfly began to flap its wings down at the base of my spinal cord, and pretty soon there were a dozen more tickling and flapping at the top of my gut."

Jones uses the right word: *ritual*. Jittery pre-racing runners concoct an odd mixture of science and superstition to both prepare themselves and calm themselves before races. The ritual probably works more to put their mind at ease than to benefit the race.

Tapering down on training and psyching up mentally can have some effect on the race's outcome (although training already has set its limits). Pre-race diet and warm-up can help. The idea is to get to the starting line fit, fresh, and ready to run. If the ritual contributes to these ends, it has served its purpose well. However, the principal intent of pre-race primping is to settle the mind. It is an attempt to grasp onto things familiar before plunging into the unknown.

Race plans serve somewhat the same purpose. The unknown can't be entirely charted or planned, of course, but it is comforting to have a general idea—based on past experiences—of what is going to happen and how you'll react. Once the race starts, the plan is used, modified, or discarded, according to what develops. Looking back later, you probably wouldn't have wanted to know exactly what would happen.

There is no easy way to avoid the worries that arise before races, any more than there is an easy way to get through the race. Deep down, runners probably wouldn't want an easy way out. Racing runners are funny people: they worry about hangnails, tummy aches, and any other minor problems that might prevent them from experiencing the real pains of the race.

Moment of Truth The race is not against other runners, but with oneself. Bruce Kidd won against almost everyone he faced while he was still a teenager, yet he wrote later: "Sport does not have to be so exclusively competitive that all but the most skilled must be discouraged from participating. Sport doesn't have to be unconditionally aggressive, either. Anyone who has been active well knows that man-versus-man is but one form of sports conflict. The athlete must compete against himself and the environment, and these common struggles outweigh the interpersonal struggle almost every time."

The struggle with self and environment becomes increasingly obvious as distances grow, and is most readily apparent in the marathon. Kenny Moore, who ran that distance in 2:11, described his approach to competition: "To be effective over the last six miles, one must harbor some sort of emotional as well as physical reserve. An intensive, highly competitive frame of mind over the early part of the run seems to evaporate after twenty miles, so I prefer to begin in a low-key, sort of yawning-sleepy state of semi-consciousness. I watch the scenery and the other runners with appreciation rather than with any sort of competitive response. I chat with anyone so inclined."

Only later, after the twenty-mile mark, does Moore "try to get enthusiastic about racing. A strong acceleration gives a lift, and I can usually hold a new rhythm to the finish. It's more fun to pass people late in the race when it means something. The last six miles is the stage where I try to honestly use everything I have left. That, of necessity, hurts."

But the key here is that the distance runner is hurting himself or herself, not inflicting pain on someone else. By this point in a long race, he or she may barely notice that anyone else is running. Each runner is fighting a private battle.

Early in his career, Frank Shorter often tied intentionally with Jack Bacheler for first place. This outraged some critics, who charged Shorter and Bacheler with working against the purpose of competition. To this, Frank replied: "Maybe in part our tying is sort of an attempt to thumb our noses at the attitude that it has to be like that—the whole idea that the goal is to trample everyone underfoot, to put on your spikes and run over them. It isn't all or nothing with me. I don't consider coming in second losing; it's just not winning. If you're satisfied with what you've done, you haven't lost."

Make no mistake: Shorter competes hard. One doesn't win Olympic gold medals and run 2:10 marathons without being a competitor. Frank, in common with most racers in his events, simply knows where his main competition lies.

Marty Liquori, once America's top miler, knew this too when he said, "Every race makes you a better man. It's not beating the other guy so much as triumphing over yourself."

After the Race Is Over The race is over, but talk of it lingers on. Post-race discussion seems to vary in direct proportion to the distance covered. The farther runners run, the more they're compelled to talk about it afterward.

Leonard Shecter once remarked in *Look* magazine that "people who live with pain, like boxers and long-distance runners, show very little aggression outside the sports arena."

George Sheehan expressed similar sentiments in *Runner's World:* "It is said that we live together and die alone. Runners live alone and die together. Only after a race does their reserve dissolve. In that common agony after the race, runners can reveal themselves to each other."

After long races, physical lows and emotional highs occur simultaneously. Runners who've gone through the agony alone now wallow in the ecstasy together. Perhaps the best explanation of this reaction comes from Kenny Moore: "Human beings are reluctant to accept meaningless suffering. Families of dead soldiers refuse to believe such sacrifice could be in vain. In that way, the pain in a marathon's closing stages can be so great as to *force* meaning upon the run. [Marathoners] submit to the ordeal not in spite of the pain but because of it."

Moore observes that, after the race, runners "hang stiffly to one another, too exhausted to untie their shoes, and they jabber uncontrollably. The pain has made everything suffered so extraordinarily important that it *has* to be expressed. The cramp that seized your leg coming off the hills at twenty miles must be described in loving, urgent detail, if only to the wall because nobody listens. Later, when you recover, you remember your babbling and the others', and in an embarrassed sort of recognition understand you shared something."

The "high" wears off—maybe in a few hours, maybe a day later. It often leaves a feeling much like a hangover in its wake. You realize you are very tired and very sore, and you may feel more than a little depressed. Strangely enough, the post-race blues may be their worst following your best performances. You wonder then, "Now what do I have to do to top this?"

Ron Clarke experienced these feelings time and again as he repeatedly broke world records. His book, *The Unforgiving Minute*, contains an eloquent description of those letdowns: "It has happened in Melbourne, in London, and in Oslo. In fact, almost every time that I've been fortunate enough to achieve a world record, a peculiar sense of disappointment has engulfed me soon afterward. The shouting and hand-shaking have ceased. The record has been confirmed and announced, and the crowd has drifted home. A man is able to think again, to give himself up entirely to his feelings. And invariably the exhilaration of achievement drains away, leaving the record-holder dejected and profoundly weary."

Clarke noted that "perhaps the experience of a record-holder is not unlike that of a young man who has just celebrated his twenty-first birthday. He has looked forward to the occasion for so long, but after the excitement of the party, the congratulations, and the gifts, he realizes that although he is now officially a man, he doesn't feel any different and that life will go on much the same."

There are new races to run, new standards to meet and to beat.

CHAPTER TWENTY-THREE

Forecasting Times

Five-Percent Formula

Before you plan how to run a faster race, think about how much faster you can run. "Set realistic goals," the running advisors tell us; the quickest way to discourage yourself is to choose a target you can never hit. But what is "realistic"? What do recent times at one distance tell you about your potential results at other distances?

For almost as long as I've been running, I've looked for ways to peer into the future. I've read graphs and formulas telling how to predict times ahead based on times past, from one distance to another. More often than not, the math involved in calculating rates of increase and decrease in pace bogged me down.

I was no better at explaining these systems. After I tried and failed at a running clinic, a man from the audience said, "It really isn't as complicated as you make it. All you need to do is add about twenty seconds per mile each time you double your racing distance."

"Your way sounds better than mine," I admitted. Later, I sat down with pen, paper, and calculator to test the man's theory. The difference in the men's world records—1500 to 3000 meters, 5000 to 10,000, 10-K to 20-K or half marathon, and half to full marathon—averaged sixteen seconds. For the top women, seventeen seconds typically separated the shorter and longer distances.

These are the world's fastest and most durable runners. I present myself as a case study for the average runner. My times typically slow by twenty-two seconds per mile as I double the length of the race. Someone who races more slowly may show a slightly larger gap, perhaps as much as thirty seconds per mile.

While I was trying to refine these calculations, an even simpler formula emerged: The typical slowdown factor at double the distance is a fixed percentage, regardless of your ability. Your time at one distance will always suggest your prospects at another, even when their lengths are many kilometers apart. It is a physiological fact that all runners slow down or speed up progressively and predictably as distances increase or decrease. It is my theory that one's pace typically slows by about five percent as the distance doubles and improves by that amount as the distance drops by half.

For instance, a half marathon is roughly twice the length of a 10-K. Say you run the shorter race at 6:30 mile pace. Add five percent to that, and you can count on running 6:50 miles during your half. A five-minute mile pace (thirty-one minutes) for 10-K predicts 5:15 pace (1:07) for a half marathon and a marathon at 5:30s (2:25). The five-percent formula yields probable times of 1:18 and 2:43 for a thirty-five-minute 10-K runner, 1:29 and 3:07 for one with forty-minute speed, and 1:40 and 3:30 based on forty-five-minute ability.

The formula has values even greater than predicting future results. It serves as an important guideline for pacing the upcoming race and for making changes in race preparation. You can't know in advance exactly how any race will end, but the five-percent formula can give you a better idea how it should *start*. Base your pace plans on the predicted time. (More on this subject in Chapter 24.)

Looking at the formula another way, you should expect about a five-minute improvement in marathon time, and two and one-half minutes in the half marathon for each one-minute drop in 10-K time. This assumes, of course, that you are equally proficient at the three most popular road distances. A runner with highly polished speed but limited endurance will slow by more than five percent as the distance doubles, while one who puts in mega-miles of low quality may run almost the same pace in every race.

Your speedup/slowdown factor probably won't be exactly five percent. Dramatic variations from this figure, however, may signal the need for changes in training. Whatever your slowdown factor is, it should remain fairly constant across the full racing spectrum. You can use this figure to test the effectiveness of your race preparation. If you see less than the expected difference between 10-K and marathon pace, for example, your speed needs attention. If you run a marathon slower than your 10-K time had predicted you should run the longer distance, give extra emphasis to your endurance.

More Formulas While I use the five-percent formula as a basis for time projections in Chapter 25 (races in the 10-K range), Chapter 26 (half-marathon range) and Chapter 27 (marathon range), two other systems of predicting bear mentioning here. The first, summarized in Table 23.1, came from Gerry Purdy of Colorado and his computer. Mike Tymn of Hawaii offered another formula after reading a magazine article of mine.

"Concerning your race predictions," wrote Tymn, "you might consider approaching them this way. Although the marathon is 4.22 times as long as ten kilometers, the average difference between the times of well-conditioned runners is 4.65. For example, a person capable of a 30:00 10-K should be able to run a 2:19:30 marathon [thirty minutes times 4.65 equals 139.5 minutes] if he has a good balance of strength and endurance. Conversely, a runner who can do a three-hour marathon should be able to turn in a 38:42 10-K [188 minutes divided by 4.65 equals 38.6 minutes]."

On the general subject of time predictions, runner-coach Larry Waldman of Pennsylvania issues this warning: "Runners should be advised not to allow formulas to place a limit on how fast they can run. Work and patience can enable the runner to reach goals thought to be unattainable."

Agreed. Formulas such as this can help the runner set realistic goals, and then plan training and pacing accordingly. They can provide road maps for the rather unfamiliar territory of the middle distances. These numbers, however, should not place artificial limits on performance or take the element of surprise out of racing results. Exploring the unknown and unknowable is a major reason to race—at any distance.

Table 23.1 *Equal Times*

Racing pace slows as distance increases; that much you already know. What you need to learn is the normal rate of slow-down. This helps you set a realistic race goal at an unfamiliar distance, plan a sensible pace, and know whether to feel glad or sad about the result.

Dr. Gerry Purdy, co-author of *Computerized Running Training Programs,* produced a set of equivalent times, from which the following table is adapted. To use this table, find your approximate time at any of the distances, then read across. The corresponding times (all rounded to the nearest minute) indicate your potential in these events, according to Dr. Purdy's calculations.

Note that these marks differ slightly from those in Tables 25.1, 26.1, and 27.1. Decide which formula works best for you.

10-K	15-K	20-K	H-M	25-K	30-K	Mar.
30 m.	46 m.	1:03	1:07	1:21	1:39	2:25
31 m.	48 m.	1:05	1:09	1:23	1:42	2:30
32 m.	49 m.	1:07	1:11	1:25	1:45	2:35
33 m.	50 m.	1:09	1:13	1:28	1:48	2:40
34 m.	52 m.	1:11	1:15	1:31	1:51	2:45
35 m.	53 m.	1:13	1:17	1:34	1:55	2:50
36 m.	55 m.	1:15	1:19	1:36	1:58	2:55
37 m.	57 m.	1:18	1:22	1:39	2:02	3:00

Table 23.1—Continued

10-K	15-K	20-K	H-M	25-K	30-K	Mar.
39 m.	59 m.	1:20	1:24	1:42	2:05	3:05
40 m.	1:00	1:22	1:27	1:45	2:08	3:10
41 m.	1:02	1:24	1:29	1:48	2:12	3:15
43 m.	1:05	1:27	1:32	1:51	2:16	3:20
44 m.	1:07	1:30	1:35	1:54	2:20	3:25
45 m.	1:09	1:33	1:38	1:58	2:24	3:30
47 m.	1:11	1:36	1:41	2:01	2:28	3:35
48 m.	1:13	1:38	1:44	2:04	2:31	3:40
49 m.	1:15	1:41	1:47	2:08	2:35	3:45
50 m.	1:18	1:44	1:50	2:12	2:39	3:50
52 m.	1:20	1:47	1:53	2:15	2:43	3:55
54 m.	1:22	1:50	1:56	2:18	2:47	4:00

CHAPTER TWENTY-FOUR

Pacing
and
Tactics

Your One Competitor

"Survival of the fittest" is the best way to describe most races. The typical pattern is seen most clearly in a mile race on the track. At the end of the first lap, all fifteen runners are bunched within a few yards. At the half-mile point, five of them have dropped off the pace and are slipping back. At three-quarters, five more have fallen away from the front runners. Three more slip behind on the backstretch. Coming off the final turn, two runners remain in contention. The strongest and fastest of the two wins the race.

A good race, you might say. It certainly was—for the leaders who could maintain the pace. But what about the other ten who tried to stay close to the leaders and couldn't? They started too fast, lost contact and momentum, and finished more slowly than if they'd let the front-runners get away at the start.

Dreams of glory and front running are fine—if you have the ability to carry through on them. In any race, however, only a few runners are capable of handling front-running pace. The majority will be hurt by this tactical blunder.

Arthur Lydiard, the renowned coach from New Zealand, advises that most runners "should firmly resist the temptation to go with the local champion for the first half-mile.

The ideal starting pace is the pace he knows he can maintain all the way. Only among top athletes who are fighting for championship honors should it be necessary to adopt this tactic. Between them, fast take-offs in an attempt to break up the field are expected and warranted. But others should be warned not to get tangled up in this sort of cut-throat running, as they are the ones whose throats will be cut first."

A key lesson of the running revolution has been that running is too good to be enjoyed only by the fittest and fastest runners. A lesson in racing from the sport's period of explosive growth has been that personal records are the most valuable prizes in any race. Not everyone can run fast, but anyone can break his or her own record. The way to break records is to ignore the runners out in front and to concentrate on pacing one's own race properly.

Split Decisions Every race is really two races. The parts are about equal size, but they differ dramatically in content.

The first half seems easy—often too easy. You know you should be saving something for later, but your body is pleading, "Faster!" You find it hard to hold back.

Then comes the second half, which is almost a different race. This is where you begin to hurt. Where did all that speed and energy go? Your body now cries, "Slower!" and you know you should be going faster. You find it hard to hold on.

Bad races are the result of a common human failing: running fast when we feel fresh, and slowing when we start to hurt. Good races, on the other hand, are largely the result of ignoring instincts of freshness and pain: holding back when we feel best, and saving energy to spend when we feel worst.

The difference between a good race and a bad race is how well or poorly we hold up in the last part. The first half merely sets the stage; the last half is where the main performance takes place. The strength of the final performance rests on the groundwork that was laid at the start.

The two-sided character of a race demands that the racer approach the event with a split personality. Ideally, you treat the stage-setting half with the coolness, care, and restraint of a technician. There's a definite job to do here, with certain narrow time limits; this is the businesslike part of racing.

In the second half, the race changes style, and the racer adopts a new role to match. Now you are an artist, an actor. You have to perform on the stage that has been set. You dispense with caution and inhibition, and race with creative abandon, with everything you have left. If the technician has done his or her job, the artist can perform well. If not, the mistakes of the first half come back to haunt you in the second.

Enough analogies; let's explore in some detail this concept of two-part racing. Arthur Lydiard has outlined a principle of pacing the mile race which applies to an even greater degree as the racing distance increases. "In my opinion," declares the coach from New Zealand, "the best way to get full benefit of ability in the mile is to go out with the attitude that it is a *half mile* race and, as far as you are concerned, the time to start putting on the pressure is when the first half mile is behind you."

Lydiard wasn't talking so much about a slow start as a *cautious* one. "The ideal starting pace," he maintained, "is the pace [the runner] knows he can maintain all the way." At first, it will seem too easy; later, the same pace will feel nearly impossible to maintain.

The coach, whose athletes have won three Olympic gold medals and held world records from 800 through 5000 meters, adds, "The three and six miles [5-K and 10-K] are far more exacting than the mile, and the athlete has to exercise more caution. It is far easier to go too fast, too soon in the six-mile than in the mile."

This advice is even more sound for races of marathon length. Here, the runner must exercise even more self-control. Early pacing mistakes that would mean a slower finish in a 10-K are likely to yield a non-finish in a marathon.

Lydiard has referred to even-pace running as "the best way to get the best out of yourself." For our purposes, "even pace" means that the times for the two halves of any race are very close to equal. The closer the two halves are to equality, the more efficient the pacing has been. If you start faster than you finish, you lose considerably more speed in the last half than you gained in the first. However, it is also possible to drop so far behind even pace in the early stages that the lost time can never be made up.

The "safety range" for pacing is about five seconds per mile on either side of even pace. For instance, a 12:00 two-miler would want to run between 5:55 and 6:05 for each of the miles.

These figures haven't been pulled from the sky. A review of world records indicates that most of the splits fall within one or two seconds per mile of even pace, and none of them varies by as much as five seconds. If this method applies to the fastest and finest-conditioned runners in the world, it should apply to those of average ability, too. Perhaps attention to pacing is even more critical to the runner with less basic speed, less training background, and far less to gain from bold tactical gambles.

Runners of all abilities can profit by timing at least the halfway split of races, and later analyzing pace. You find the five-seconds-per-mile tolerances by using this formula: subtract the fast half from the slow half, then divide the difference (in seconds) by the distance (in miles).

For example, if a forty-minute 10-K runner's times for the halves are 19:30 and 20:30, he or she slowed down by one minute—or about ten seconds per mile—en route. This slow-down factor is excessive. Next time, for the sake of more economical pacing and a faster overall time, the runner should start no faster than 19:45. (Table 24.1 summarizes the "safety margins" for all the standard racing distances. Chapter 25 gives more specific pacing recommendations for the 10-K, Chapter 26 covers the half marathon, and Chapter 27 advises marathoners on their splits.)

Table 24.1 *Perfect Pacing*

Steady pacing sets records. Start too quickly, and you lose at least two seconds late in the race for every one you thought you'd "put in the bank" in the early miles. Start too slowly, however, and you can't make up all the time you've squandered.

Pacing involves spreading scarce resources evenly over the entire distance. This is done by starting fast enough but not too fast. In practical terms, the two halves of the race should come within about five seconds per mile of equal time.

The "safety margins" below are based upon the five-seconds-per-mile factor. Divide both your racing distance and projected time by two, then add and subtract the appropriate amounts to determine what your fastest and slowest halves should be.

For instance, the distance is 10-K and the time forty minutes. The 5-Ks should be no faster than 19:29 and no slower than 20:31. If the splits fall outside this range, the race was run inefficiently.

Racing Distance	Halves	Safety Margin
8 kilometers	2.5 miles	plus/minus 25 sec.
10 kilometers	3.1 miles	plus/minus 31 sec.
12 kilometers	3.75 miles	plus/minus 38 sec.
15 kilometers	4.15 miles	plus/minus 47 sec.
20 kilometers	6.2 miles	plus/minus 1:02
half-marathon	6.55 miles	plus/minus 1:05
25 kilometers	7.25 miles	plus/minus 1:17
30 kilometers	9.3 miles	plus/minus 1:33
marathon	13.1 miles	plus/minus 2:35

CHAPTER TWENTY-FIVE

Ten-Kilometer Races

Smaller and Better

Bill Rataczak, listen closely to me. The race you direct is minor-league, with little to distinguish it from hundreds of other races like it, held any weekend of the year anywhere in the country. Don't take offense, Bill. I mean this not as a slur but as a high compliment.

Rataczak is an airline pilot. (In the 1970s, he flew the plane hijacked by that notorious air pirate, D. B. Cooper.) Annandale, Minnesota, is where Bill comes home to roost and where he conducts the annual Heart of the Lakes 10-K.

This race and others like it—races unknown outside of their immediate areas—form the base that supports the major-league events. These small races are the invisible bedrock of the sport, but I often forget that. Because of my job, I'm drawn to the bright lights and big crowds of the cities. The mega-races there are the most public face of running in the 1980s. But they aren't running as I first came to know it.

The Boston Marathon drew 200 runners when I started road racing. San Francisco held an annual event for a few dozen people, and it still hadn't been named Bay to Breakers. Peachtree and the New York Marathon were years away from their birth. The term "10-K" hadn't yet been coined.

I ran my first road races in California, in the company of fewer than a hundred fellow escapees from the track. The road sport attracted me because of its family-picnic atmosphere and the chance to make something besides left turns. I enjoyed running through the countryside with companions but away from crowds. I still do, but I'm too busy traveling the major-league circuit to do much racing at the roots of the sport.

The Annandale race isn't the New York Marathon, Bay to Breakers, or Peachtree; but then, it doesn't try to be anything but itself. You won't read any feature stories about it in national magazines, and Rataczak doesn't expect any to appear. His race features no celebrity runners. It pays no prize money.

He invited me to Minnesota not as a reporter but as a friend. I'd never been to Annandale before and knew only the Rataczaks when I arrived in this town, an hour from the Twin Cities. But I instantly felt at home there, because I'd run in dozens of towns and as many events just like this place and race. I felt I was coming home after too long on the road.

This was not a nostalgic return to the racing of yesteryear, and this is not an appeal to break up the big-city races. Running, 1980s style, offers the best of both worlds. We can visit the major leagues once or twice a year to sample the glitter and excitement that this sport didn't offer ten years ago. And then we can come back home to relax at the minor-league races that operate quietly, as they always have and, I hope, always will.

I came home to Annandale and saw there that the racing I remembered most fondly was not a dusty memory. It is alive and flourishing, just as I remembered it: no wait in line to start, country courses to run, good food and talk afterward. Bill Rataczak's event met my requirements for a perfect race in distance and size.

- Large enough so other runners are never out of sight, but small enough so we never bump into each other; large enough to take over the roads from the cars, but small enough so everyone can run right from the gun; large enough to form a post-race party, but small enough for you to find your friends in the crowd.
- Long enough to be a good workout, but short enough to avoid "The Wall"; long enough to race without the speedwork of a miler, but short enough to finish without the distance training of a marathoner; long enough to leave you pleasantly hung over from the effort the next day, but short enough to let you race again the next weekend.

A field of no fewer than a hundred people and no more than a thousand is my perfect size. Ten kilometers, give or take a few, is my perfect distance. Races of this size and distance make a much more comfortable home than either miles or marathons.

Mile races relate no more to what most of us run every day than a casual drive through the country does to a drag race. The mile is less than twenty percent of my usual distance and nearly fifty percent faster than my daily pace. To prepare correctly for a mile, I would have to do regular speedwork and accept its risks.

If I were a marathon specialist, I would have to give up short races in favor of long training runs on weekends for a couple of months before each twenty-six-miler. I would have to give up even more racing while recovering for at least a month after each marathon. If I ran four marathons a year, I would use up the whole twelve months just getting ready for and getting over them, with no time left for any other type of racing.

For someone who doesn't care to suffer daily or to delay gratification, the perfect run and the perfect race both last about ten kilometers.

Table 25.1 *Short-Distance Potential*

Performance at one distance accurately predicts potential at another. This table compares times for races in the 8-K to 12-K range. Find your most recent result in one of the two most popular racing distances, 10-K or half marathon, then read across to estimate your current ability in the other events. Eight-kilometer pace tends to be about two percent faster than 10-K pace, while the 12-K is run about one percent slower than the 10-K. All times here are rounded to the nearest minute.

If you have run. . . .		*You should expect to run about.* . . .	
10-K	**Half Marathon**	**8-K**	**12-K**
30:00	1:07:00	24:00	37:00
31:00	1:09:00	25:00	38:00
32:00	1:11:00	25:00	39:00
33:00	1:14:00	26:00	40:00
34:00	1:16:00	27:00	41:00
35:00	1:18:00	28:00	43:00
36:00	1:20:00	28:00	44:00
37:00	1:23:00	29:00	45:00
38:00	1:25:00	30:00	46:00
39:00	1:27:00	31:00	48:00
40:00	1:29:00	32:00	49:00
41:00	1:31:00	32:00	50:00
42:00	1:34:00	33:00	51:00
43:00	1:36:00	34:00	53:00
44:00	1:38:00	35:00	54:00

Table 25.1—Continued

If you have run. . . .		*You should expect to run about. . . . .*	
10-K	**Half Marathon**	**8-K**	**12-K**
45:00	1:40:00	36:00	55:00
46:00	1:43:00	36:00	56:00
47:00	1:45:00	37:00	57:00
48:00	1:47:00	38:00	59:00
49:00	1:49:00	39:00	60:00

Table 25.2 Ten-Kilometer Pacing

Talking about even-paced racing is easier than calculating it. The problem is that races combine two measurement systems. While most events are run at metric distances, such as 10-K, splits are often given at *mile* points and pace usually is computed in *per-mile* terms.

This table takes those practices into account. It lists the ideal paces per mile, and the desired splits at both three miles and 5-K (the approximate and exact halfway points). The ranges of times are based upon even pace, minus and plus five seconds per mile. Determine your probable final time, then plan to start no faster or slower than indicated here.

10-K	**Per-Mile**	**3 miles**	**5 kilometers**
30 minutes	4:45-4:55	14:16-14:46	14:44-15:16
31 minutes	4:55-5:05	14:45-15:15	15:14-15:46
32 minutes	5:05-5:15	15:14-15:44	15:44-16:16
33 minutes	5:14-5:24	15:43-16:13	16:14-16:46
34 minutes	5:24-5:34	16:12-16:43	16:44-17:16
35 minutes	5:34-5:44	16:41-17:11	17:14-17:46

Table 25.2—*Continued*

10-K	Per-Mile	3 miles	5 kilometers
36 minutes	5:43-5:53	17:10-17:40	17:44-18:16
37 minutes	5:53-6:03	17:39-18:09	18:14-18:46
38 minutes	6:03-6:13	18:08-18:38	18:44-19:16
39 minutes	6:12-6:22	18:38-19:07	19:14-19:46
40 minutes	6:22-6:32	19:06-19:36	19:44-20:16
41 minutes	6:32-6:42	19:35-20:05	20:14-20:46
42 minutes	6:41-6:51	20:04-20:34	20:44-21:16
43 minutes	6:51-7:01	20:33-21:03	21:14-21:46
44 minutes	7:01-7:11	21:02-21:32	21:44-22:16
45 minutes	7:10-7:20	21:31-22:01	22:14-22:46
46 minutes	7:20-7:30	22:00-22:30	22:44-23:16
47 minutes	7:30-7:40	22:29-22:59	23:14-23:46
48 minutes	7:40-7:50	22:59-23:29	23:44-24:16
49 minutes	7:49-7:59	23:38-23:58	24:14-24:46

Half-Marathon Races

For the Record

I readily admit to a special fondness for the half marathon, partly for the most crass of reasons. This distance has brought my only recent victories against a watch that seems to move faster as the years go by. All but one of my personal records is older than my first child, and Sarah is eleven as I write this. The lone exception to my slowing trend is the half marathon.

A few years ago, I set a personal record of sorts in my first race at this distance, which was rarely run until a few years ago. I bettered a time set a decade earlier en route to a marathon PR. Okay, so the "half" mark was a cheap one; I take whatever comes these days. More recently, I narrowly better that time.

Once in a while, even an over-the-hump racer can get lucky and sneak in a fast race. I can beat the clock and my old self without really trying. I may not push myself as hard in racing and training as I once did, but I compensate with a new economy of effort which comes from staying relaxed, healthy, fresh, and eager. None of these characteristics were present, however, in the hours preceding one half-marathon race.

A record attempt was the farthest thought from my mind on the trip to San Diego. My calves still ached dully from a fast mile three days earlier. I ate my last meal at McDonald's, gulping down a Big Mac and fries while driving to the airport.

The night flight was delayed in Los Angeles for two hours. I finally went to bed at 1:00 A.M. and slept fitfully. When my host knocked on the door at five o'clock, I told him, "Wake me when it's over." He stuck a cup of hot tea in my hand and guided me to his waiting car.

The temperature had already climbed to seventy degrees at race time. I didn't warm up; no need for that on a day like this and for the slow pace I planned to run.

The first mile seemed to take eight minutes, but my watch read just under seven. That turned out to be the slowest of the miles by nearly a minute. I never dared think "PR"; that would have frightened me away from it. I quit looking at my watch and listening for splits, fearing that would jinx me. I just let the right pace come, let old habits take over, and let time take care of itself. It came out a record by a single second.

Cheap as this PR was, I'm proud of it. I wouldn't have spent these paragraphs caressing its details if I weren't proud. It showed me I can still surprise myself with good times now and then, but I can't *want* them. The record was not the result of any special effort on my part, but of a standard routine naturally suited to half-marathon racing.

I've labeled the 10-K the "perfect" race distance. But as noted in Chapter 18, you may be better prepared to run half marathons. I think of myself not as unique among today's runners, but as fairly typical of them. Our regular daily runs cover about forty-five minutes, our races seldom dip below ten kilometers, our fast tests rarely are much faster than six-minute-mile pace, and our long tests don't often extend beyond one and one-half hours.

An honest appraisal of this schedule tells us that only the everyday training is adequate for all purposes. The short races and tests aren't fast or frequent enough for 10-Ks; the long tests aren't nearly long enough for a would-be marathoner. However, this routine suits a half marathoner. An occasional 10-K race gives experience at running about half the half-marathon distance at somewhat faster than its pace. The long runs of ninety minutes almost precisely match the half-marathon racing time.

Of course it isn't the best possible program for improving one's times at this distance. But it is the less inadequate for the "half" than for the two other popular racing events. A runner who doesn't care to run to the extremes of either speed or distance, but still wants his or her racing times to improve, might find happiness in the half marathon.

Table 26.1 *Middle-Distance Potential*

Performance at one distance accurately predicts potential at another. This table compares times for the commonly run 10-K and marathon with those in the 15-K to 25-K range. Find your most recent result at the popular short or long distance, then read across to estimate your current ability in the other events. The marks are based upon the expected five-percent slowdown or speedup in pace as distances are doubled or halved. All times here are rounded to the nearest minute.

| *If you have run.* . . . | | *You can expect to run about.* . . . | | | |
10-K	Marathon	15-K	20-K	H-M	25-K
30 min.	2:20	46 min.	1:03	1:07	1:21
31 min.	2:25	48 min.	1:05	1:09	1:23
32 min.	2:29	49 min.	1:07	1:11	1:26
33 min.	2:34	51 min.	1:09	1:14	1:29
34 min.	2:38	52 min.	1:11	1:16	1:31
35 min.	2:43	54 min.	1:14	1:18	1:34
36 min.	2:48	55 min.	1:16	1:20	1:37
37 min.	2:53	57 min.	1:18	1:23	1:40
38 min.	2:57	58 min.	1:20	1:25	1:42
39 min.	3:02	1:00	1:22	1:27	1:45
40 min.	3:07	1:01	1:24	1:29	1:47
41 min.	3:11	1:03	1:26	1:31	1:50
42 min.	3:16	1:05	1:28	1:34	1:53
43 min.	3:20	1:06	1:30	1:36	1:56
44 min.	3:25	1:08	1:32	1:38	1:58
45 min.	3:30	1:09	1:34	1:40	2:01

Table 26.1—*Continued*

If you have run. . . .		You can expect to run about. . . .			
10-K	**Marathon**	**15-K**	**20-K**	**H-M**	**25-K**
46 min.	3:34	1:11	1:37	1:43	2:04
47 min.	3:39	1:12	1:39	1:45	2:06
48 min.	3:43	1:14	1:41	1:47	2:09
49 min.	3:48	1:15	1:43	1:49	2:12

Table 26.2 *Half-Marathon Pacing*

Your halfway time is an important indicator of progress, but few half marathons post a timer at the 6.55-mile point. This table takes that oversight into account by listing the desired splits at the common checkpoints of five miles and 10-K. The ranges of times are based upon even pace, minus or plus five seconds per mile. Determine your probable final time, then plan to start no faster or slower than indicated here.

Half Marathon	Per-Mile	5 miles	10 Kilometers
1:10	5:16-5:26	26:19-27:09	32:37-33:39
1:12	5:25-5:35	27:04-27:54	33:34-34:36
1:14	5:34-5:44	27:50-28:40	34:30-35:32
1:16	5:43-5:53	28:10-29:00	35:27-36:29
1:18	5:52-6:02	29:21-30:11	36:24-37:26
1:20	6:01-6:11	30:07-30:57	37:21-38:23
1:22	6:11-6:21	30:53-31:43	38:18-39:20
1:24	6:20-6:30	31:39-32:29	39:14-40:16

Table 26.2—Continued

Half Marathon	Per-Mile	5 miles	10 Kilometers
1:26	6:29-6:39	32:24-33:14	40:11-41:13
1:28	6:38-6:48	33:10-34:00	41:08-42:10
1:30	6:47-6:57	33:56-34:46	42:05-43:07
1:32	6:57-7:07	34:42-35:32	43:02-44:04
1:34	7:06-7:16	35:28-36:18	43:58-45:00
1:36	7:15-7:25	36:13-37:03	44:55-45:57
1:38	7:24-7:34	36:59-37:49	45:52-46:54
1:40	7:33-7:43	37:45-38:35	46:49-47:51
1:42	7:42-7:52	38:31-39:21	47:46-48:48
1:44	7:51-8:01	39:17-40:07	48:42-49:44
1:46	8:00-8:10	40:02-40:52	49:39-50:41
1:48	8:10-8:20	40:48-41:38	50:36-51:38

CHAPTER TWENTY-SEVEN

Marathon Races

Race Against Time

Marathoning attracts both survivors and racers. The distinction between the two groups is important because it determines how they approach the event. Marathon survivors mainly want to complete the course, no matter how long it takes them. Marathon *racers* want to improve, and their times are the measure of that improvement.

Most runners first enter marathons as survivors, and only after the first marathon is behind them do they wonder, "How can I go faster?" When they ask that question, they have become racers. Later, they will ask, "How much faster can I go?" and finally, "Why can't I run any faster?"

This particular marathon happened to be in my home town of Eugene, Oregon, but it might have been anywhere. The emotions etched on the faces of the Nike-OTC marathoners were universal.

I enjoy watching a marathon in which I know many of the runners and can cheer them by name as they pass, sharing in a small way in their race well-run. And I hate seeing friends reduced to the post-"Wall" staggers in the late miles, when I'm unable to offer appropriate words of comfort.

I prefer to watch marathons a few miles from the finish, where my friends are wearing their most honest expressions—not the relaxed looks of the early miles or the relief of the final yards. Three faces come to mind from the Nike-OTC race.

One woman was near tears as she shuffled past and choked out the words, ". . . not my day." A man still moved well, but his shrug told me that he wasn't doing as well as he'd hoped. Another woman shouted, "I'm going to do it, really going to do it!" These reactions had nothing to do with place in the race. The last runner felt the happiest, the slightly disappointed one was fastest, and the devastated one finished between the other two.

All three runners measured themselves against their personal standards and not by the overall standards of marathoning. The watch gave each runner a chance to feel like a winner. But it also set a higher standard by which they could lose; simply finishing was no longer victory enough. All three had set out to improve their times, and only one did so.

This numbers game is both exciting and risky. Let's say you are new to this sport, and still have most of your improvement ahead of you. You ran your first marathon conservatively, trying only to survive it. Now you have a baseline PR that begs to be broken. This means you are no longer merely running the marathon: you now must *race* it.

Chasing a time adds excitement to your running. You'll probably break your marathon record several times, and each challenge will be replaced by a new and greater one. Each improvement will more satisfying than the last because of the extra effort involved. Be warned, however, that by trying to improve your time you are entering a race you ultimately must lose. The faster you go, the faster you *want* to go; the faster you think you *must* go. No one keeps going faster indefinitely.

In the early 1970s, John Loeschhorn ranked among the country's best cross-country and ten-kilometer runners. He ran his fastest marathon time in 1973, and decided he would let that PR stand forever. "Forever" ended as he approached age forty. Loeschhorn's goal in year leading up to that birthday was to run faster than ever before, and he narrowly missed that old mark six times in seven months.

"Maybe this is enough to expect from a man of my age and talent," he said after the sixth race. "But the greatest fault of racing is that it tends to make us unsatisfied with everything we have ever accomplished and impatient for better future results. Naturally, 'better' is defined as *faster*. This leaves many of us who race feeling forever unfulfilled."

He concluded on a happier note: "I'll be forty soon. Then I'll create a new set of PRs in Masters [ages forty and up] competition and start the foolish game all over again. You'd think that at my age I would be smarter, wouldn't you?"

Table 27.1 Long-Distance Potential

Performance at one distance accurately predicts potential at another. This table compares times for the commonly run 10-K and half marathon with those of the 30-K and marathon. Find your most recent result at one of those popular shorter distances, then read across to estimate your current ability in the longer events. The marks are based upon the expected five-percent slow-down in pace as distances are doubled. All times here are rounded to the nearest minute.

| *If you have run.* . . . | | *You should expect to run about.* . . . | |
10-K	Half-Marathon	30-K	Marathon
30 min.	1:07	1:37	2:20
31 min.	1:09	1:41	2:25
32 min.	1:11	1:44	2:29
33 min.	1:14	1:47	2:34
34 min.	1:16	1:50	2:38
35 min.	1:18	1:54	2:43
36 min.	1:20	1:57	2:48
37 min.	1:23	2:00	2:53
38 min.	1:25	2:03	2:57
39 min.	1:27	2:06	3:02
40 min.	1:29	2:10	3:07
41 min.	1:31	2:13	3:11
42 min.	1:34	2:16	3:16
43 min.	1:36	2:20	3:20
44 min.	1:38	2:23	3:25
45 min.	1:40	2:26	3:30

Table 27.1—*Continued*

| If you have run. . . . | | You should expect to run about. . . . | |
10-K	Half-Marathon	30-K	Marathon
46 min.	1:43	2:29	3:34
47 min.	1:45	2:32	3:39
48 min.	1:47	2:36	3:43
49 min.	1:49	2:39	3:48

Table 27.2 *Marathon Pacing*

In no other race is a controlled early pace more critical than in a marathon. "The Wall" awaits those runners who start too fast. (Starting too slowly is seldom a problem with marathoners.) This table lists the desired splits at the common checkpoints of ten miles and half marathon. The ranges of times are based upon even pace, minus or plus five seconds per mile. Determine your probable final time, then plan to start no faster or slower than indicated here.

Marathon	Per-Mile	10 miles	Half marathon
2:30	5:39-5:40	56:25-58:05	1:13:55-1:16:05
2:35	5:50-6:00	58:20-1:00:00	1:16:25-1:18:35
2:40	6:01-6:11	1:00:14-1:01:54	1:18:55-1:21:05
2:45	6:13-6:23	1:02:09-1:03:49	1:21:25-1:23:35
2:50	6:24-6:34	1:04:03-1:05:43	1:23:55-1:26:05
2:55	6:35-6:45	1:05:58-1:07:38	1:26:25-1:28:35
3:00	6:47-6:57	1:07:52-1:09:32	1:28:55-1:31:05

Table 27.2—Continued

Marathon	Per-Mile	10 miles	Half marathon
3:05	6:59-7:09	1:09:47-1:11:27	1:31:25-1:33:35
3:10	7:10-7:20	1:11:41-1:13:21	1:34:55-1:36:05
3:15	7:22-7:32	1:13:36-1:15:16	1:36:25-1:38:35
3:20	7:33-7:43	1:15:30-1:17:10	1:38:55-1:41:05
3:25	7:44-7:54	1:17:25-1:19:05	1:41:25-1:43:35
3:30	7:56-8:06	1:19:19-1:20:59	1:43:55-1:46:05
3:35	8:07-8:17	1:21:14-1:22:54	1:46:25-1:48:35
3:40	8:19-8:29	1:23:08-1:24:48	1:48:55-1:51:05
3:45	8:30-8:40	1:25:03-1:26:43	1:51:25-1:53:35
3:50	8:42-8:52	1:26:57-1:28:37	1:53:55-1:56:05
3:55	3:53-9:03	1:28:52-1:30:32	1:56:25-1:58:35

Your
Racing

Plan your racing pace and tactics by determining the following information.

1. **Race description**
    Indicate in miles or kilometers the distance of the race:

    Indicate your time goal:

    Calculate the pace per mile required to achieve this goal (divide time by distance in miles):

    Indicate the average length of your daily runs during the past month (in minutes):

    Calculate the difference in length between this race and the average training run (time longer or shorter):

    Indicate your longest race or test within the past month (in hours and minutes):

    Calculate the difference in length between this race and the longest recent race or test (time longer or shorter):

Indicate the average pace per mile of your daily runs during the past month: _____

Calculate the difference in pace per mile between this race and the average training run (time faster or slower): _____

Indicate your fastest race or test within the past month (pace per mile): _____

Calculate the difference in pace per mile between this race and the fastest recent race or test (time faster or slower): _____

You should have tested yourself at least once at the full time of the race (but at a slower pace), and at least once at the race's full pace (but at a shorter distance).

2. **Personal record**

Indicate the best time you have run at this racing distance: _____

Calculate the pace per mile of your record time (divide distance in miles by time): _____

Indicate your projected pace per mile in the current race (from part one above): _____

Calculate the difference between your projected pace for this race and your record pace (faster or slower): _____

The most important numbers in any race are those comparing your past and present abilities.

3. **Time projection**

Describe your most recent race performance.

Distance (in kilometers or miles): _____

Time: _____

Pace per mile (divide time by distance in miles): _____

If you are racing at the same distance after no major changes in training, and if the weather and course conditions are similar, the times in the last race and this one should be comparable.

If you are racing at a different distance, refer to tables in earlier chapters for comparable times. Table 25.1 lists short distances (8-K, 10-K and 12-K). Table 26.1 lists middle distances (15-K, 20-K, half-marathon and 25-K). Table 27.1 lists long distances (30-K and marathon).

Indicate your projected race time (based upon the appropriate table): _____

Calculate your projected race pace per mile (divide time by distance in miles): _____

Your actual race time probably will fall somewhere between your goal (in part one above) and the projection from the table. Select a realistic figure as a basis for outlining a pacing plan.

4. Pacing advice

Calculate the splits at key checkpoints if you run the recommended way, at an even pace (multiply pace per mile by the distance at the checkpoint in question):

Distance	Time
_____	_____
_____	_____
_____	_____
_____	_____
_____	_____

The most important checkpoint in any race lies at or near halfway. Calculate your ideal halfway time.

Halfway distance (divide length of race by two): _____

Half of total projected time (from part three above): _____

Average pace per mile to achieve the projected time (from part three above): _____

Fastest starting pace (subtract five seconds per mile from average pace): _____

Fastest halfway time (multiply maximum starting pace by half-way distance): _____

Slowest starting pace (add five seconds per mile to average pace): _____

Slowest halfway time (multiply minimum starting pace by half-way distance): _____

Tables in earlier chapters give recommended paces for the three most popular racing distances. Table 25.2 lists the 10-K, Table 26.2 lists the half-marathon, and Table 27.2 lists the marathon.

CHAPTER TWENTY-NINE

The Aftermath

Recovery Periods

There *is* life after racing, even though you may not think so in the days and weeks afterward. Once you've thought and talked the race to death, once the euphoria has worn off, the post-marathon blues are sure to follow.

We're not talking about post-race pains. You expect stiffness in the thighs and calves, and you wear your limp like a badge of courage. What you weren't prepared to deal with was the subtle destruction: the lingering deadness in your legs, yes, but an even more devastating deadness of spirit. You don't feel like running.

This effect is partly physiological, partly psychological. The goal that pulled you up the mountain for months is gone now, and nothing new has yet replaced it. Some loss of enthusiasm is inevitable. The psyche will heal along with the body, however, if you give them time. This takes more time than most runners imagine, and the worst mistake you can make now is to rush that natural timetable.

You'd be wrong to think that you were well again once the muscle soreness disappeared a few days after the marathon. You'd be begging for trouble by forcing yourself back into full training and racing before your energy debt has been repaid. Too many runners limp into doctors' offices a week or two after a hard race and complain, "I had no problems in the event itself, then this happened in yesterday's long run. What bad luck!"

Luck had nothing to do with it. Heaping abuse upon an already battered body yielded this predictable result. Distance racing is as destructive as it is exciting. Don't miss the excitement, but take extreme care in handling the destruction. Recover from the race as if it were an injury that takes time to heal.

Racing is like a vaccine. The right dose can make you faster than you've ever been before, but too much of it can hurt. Racing is the most common cause of injuries and poor performances. More precisely, *over-racing* is the cause: racing too often without enough recovery and rebuilding time in between.

Two innovative coaches on different sides of the world, Arthur Lydiard of New Zealand and Ernst van Aaken of Germany, hint at how often a person can race. Lydiard says hard speedwork should amount no more than ten percent of one's running. Van Aaken goes even lower; he limited racing and testing to five percent of total.

Using these formulas, a runner is limited to one racing mile in ten. And if you take frequent speed or distance tests, the amount of racing should be much less.

One method of insuring that races are spaced properly is to multiply the race distance or time by ten, then not race again until you've put in that much easy recovery running. This formula automatically lets you race more often at shorter, less taxing distances, and less frequently at longer, tougher ones.

Jack Foster, who has survived into his 50s as a top-level runner, offers an even simpler rule for clearing away the debris of the race. The New Zealander says he won't allow himself to run hard again until one day has passed for every mile of the race. (The race-spacing recommendations in Table 29.1 are based on Foster's formula.)

A Case of Over-racing After fifteen years of almost continuous racing and training, Lee Dorsey has learned much about running, and has lost most of his illusions about himself as a runner. He knows his long history in racing is unspectacular, that he has even less to brag about now, and that the future doesn't promise significantly better results than he has already achieved. But Dorsey also knows exactly where he has been, where he is, and where he is going. We should all be so lucky.

The Californian is a statistician by profession, and his running records reflect the same care that he applies to his job. Every workout, every race time and place, every split is committed to computer disks, awaiting the type of analysis that Dorsey eagerly gives these numbers.

Lee approaches his running as a rational scientist, with one significant exception. He has a blind spot when it comes to racing: he can't resist competition. He has raced more than 500 times, at distances as short as 100 yards and as long as 100 kilometers. For several years, he averaged a race a week, year-round. This racing mania caused Dorsey no end of trouble, and his legs still bear the scars of overindulgence.

"Pain burned one lesson into me right from the start," he recalls. "As a freshman in high school who had been running a slow mile each day for two weeks, I figured I was ready to win a mile race. My dreams came down hard. I started too fast and dropped out, exhausted, in the second lap."

Table 29.1 *Recovery Running*

A leading cause of chronic fatigue, injury, and illness among runners is incomplete recovery from race-like efforts. As a rule of thumb, allow at least one week or one day per racing mile, whichever is longer, to recover from all races and most tests. The recommendations in this table are based upon that rule. Run nothing unusually long or fast during the recovery period.

Race Length	Minimum Recovery
8 kilometers	one week
10 kilometers	one week
15 kilometers	two weeks
20 kilometers	two weeks
half-marathon	two weeks
25 kilometers	three weeks
30 kilometers	three weeks
marathon	four weeks

He learned in his first race how destructive an imprudent pace *during* a race can be. Only after running about 500 more races did he realize the value of pacing *between* races. Starting them too often can hurt even more than starting them too fast.

"What I'm talking about," says Dorsey, "is not recovering enough between races." He explains by pointing to a computer printout. "The last two years contrast sharply. The first year was my best ever. I set a personal record almost every time I ran. But then I went on an incredible year-long racing binge, often racing twice on a single weekend. I was injured or ill much of the time, and my racing results were disappointing."

Only after a knee injury stopped him completely did Dorsey review his old running literature. "I noticed Arthur Lydiard said that no more than ten percent of running should be at racing pace. Tom Osler called over-racing a form of 'self-abuse.' My recent medical history told me I was definitely abusing myself, so I sat down at the computer and figured my racing percentages to see if they correlated with my troubles."

One column of Lee's printout lists his total mileage. He averaged 200 miles a month during these four years, an amount that remained constant until the major injury.

The next column lists the number of racing miles. He did no speedwork outside of races, figuring he didn't need any when he raced so often. During the good year, he totaled seventeen racing miles a month; during the bad year, forty-two.

The third column lists percentages of racing. Dorsey raced about eight percent of his miles the first year, twenty-one percent the second year. "The unavoidable conclusion," he says, "is that I raced best when I raced least, or less than ten percent of my total mileage, anyway. When I went far above that limit, I first undermined my racing ability, then my health. I strive for quality in races now, not quantity."

Plan for All Seasons A runner can't sow and reap at the same time, which is another way of saying that the time for building up between races must far exceed the time spent tearing down during them. You now know this to be true from race to race, but the principle might also apply to seasons of the year. We may need to follow each season of heavy racing with an extended period of recovery and rebuilding.

Arthur Lydiard says a racer can hold peak form "for three or four months" before taking time off from racing. Tom Osler has reached the same conclusion independently. He writes, "One can rarely maintain a high performance level for more than three months."

Osler observes that he passes through cycles lasting about six months, each cycle including one high and one low period roughly corresponding to the seasons of the year. He finds he races best during the "highs" and prefers to run casually during the "lows."

"The six-month performance cycle is of importance to the runner for several reasons," writes Osler. "For one, it allows him to predict which times of the year he will perform best. Likewise, it allows him to determine when he should take a less serious attitude toward racing. Harder, shorter, faster runs can be tolerated during the peak phase and can produce dramatically improved racing performances. Easier, slower, longer training runs are best during the low phase."

Osler's advice grows more relevant as races spread throughout the year and there no longer is any off-season to the racing schedule. The pattern to adopt is alternating seasons of highs and lows (for instance, spring and autumn high, to take advantage of the best weather; summer and winter low, when conditions are least attractive for racing). The pattern to avoid is putting two or more serious racing seasons back to back.

Your Reviewing and Recovering

Review your race and plan for future racing by determining the following information.

1. **Time analysis**

   Indicate your race distance (in kilometers or miles): _____

   Indicate your race time: _____

   Calculate your race pace per mile (divide time by distance in miles): _____

   Indicate your previous best time (personal record) at this distance: _____

   Compare the result from this race with your previous best (amount faster or slower): _____

2. **Projection analysis**

   Indicate your projected time for this race (from Chapter 28): _____

   Calculate the amount by which you missed the projection (faster or slower): _____

A time faster than the projection indicates that you underestimated your potential; aim higher in your next race. It also suggests that your times at other distances (those upon which this prediction was based) are due for improvement.

A time slower than the projection generally means that you have trained inadequately, paced yourself improperly or both. Make the necessary corrections before and during your next race (see Chapters 20 and 28).

3. **Pace analysis**

Indicate your time for the first half of the race (estimate, if necessary, based on nearby splits):   _____

Distance of the first half (in miles):   _____

Calculate your pace per mile in the first half (divide time by distance in miles):   _____

Time for the second half (subtract time for first half from total time):   _____

Calculate your pace per mile in the second half (divide time by distance in miles):   _____

Difference in pace per mile between first half and second half (subtract lower from higher figure):   _____

The difference between first-half and second-half pace should not exceed ten seconds per mile (five seconds either side of even pace). If you ran within this range, you paced the race efficiently. If you slowed down by more than ten seconds per mile in the second half, you started too fast and lost more time later on. If you sped up more than ten seconds per mile, you lost more time early than you could make up at the end. Make the necessary correction in your next race (see Chapter 24).

4. **Place analysis**

Indicate your placings in this race (estimate if necessary).

Overall placing: _____

Total number of entrants: _____

Placing for your sex: _____

Number in this category: _____

Placing in your age-group: _____

Number in this category: _____

A percentage ranking gives a realistic picture of how you placed in comparison with other runners in races and divisions of varying sizes. Calculate those percentages as directed here.

Overall finish (divide your place by total number of starters): _____

Female or male finish (divide your place in this category by its number of starters): _____

Age-group finish (divide your place in this category by its number of starters): _____

5. **Recovery advice**
Indicate the distance of the race in miles: _____

Calculate your recommended number of recovery days (one day for each mile of the race): _____

Determine your minimum recovery period in weeks (divide number of days above by seven, then round up to next higher full week): _____

Avoid further races or tests until this number of weeks has passed, but continue normal training during this period. An additional recovery guideline: The amount of racing and testing during any month should not exceed ten percent of your total running time.

Epilogue

"*I*'m in my forties and still want to improve my racing performances," said the man in the pre-race seminar audience. "Am I too old to be thinking about that?"

"Calendar age means little," I told him. "What counts is running age, how long and how much you've run. After twenty-six years and 50,000 miles, I am quite old in the ways that really matter: the amount of running time and mileage I've put on my legs. You and I might have been born the same year, but you're still an infant if you've only recently begun to run. You probably can look forward to many years of improvement."

Dr. Joan Ullyot, author of *Women's Running* (Anderson World Books, 1976) wrote the Rule of Ten which appears to be quite sound as rules of thumb go: "You won't reach your full potential as an athlete until you have trained for about ten years." Runners adapt slowly and steadily to the stresses of racing, she says, and improvement usually continues for years on even modest amounts of consistent training. The beauty of this rule is that the ten-year clock doesn't begin ticking until the runner begins competing. A fifty-year-old runner is promised just as much improvement as a fifteen-year-old.

The rule was valid in my case. I started racing at fourteen, and the PRs didn't plateau out until my mid-twenties. I didn't suddenly fall apart then, like a car whose warranty had expired. I just found I was no longer interested in working harder and harder for smaller and smaller gains.

Jack Foster began competing much later and at a far higher level, but his timetable was similar. He ran a 2:11 marathon—still the fastest ever for a man his age—in his forty-second year. Then the New Zealander found that his devotion to hard training waned.

Foster, who now runs marathons ten minutes slower than he did at his best, speaks philosophically of the slowdown: "The dropoff in racing performances with age manifests itself only on timekeepers' stopwatches. The running action, the breathing, and the other experiences of racing all feel the same. Only the watch shows otherwise."

Times change; feelings don't. Everyone's times eventually slow, but the effort and excitement of racing can remain constant throughout your competitive lifetime if you don't pay too much attention to the watch.

If I don't look at the stopwatch, racing feels just like it did during my first trips around the track in 1958. The anticipation and dread beforehand, strength and strain during, and pride and relief afterward haven't changed—except now I'm visiting old friends instead of making new ones.

Dr. Peter Wood has run and raced longer than I have. He wrote about a feeling of continuity in his book, *Run for Health:* "Some of us can trace a direct line of descent, through running, to our youth. To run is to relive the exhilarating experience of running free that we first enjoyed as children."

"For some runners," Dr. Wood continued, "there is clearly a thin, continuous thread of running, linking many different phases of their lives." He tells of his thread, which extends back to wartime London.

"I first ran a mile at fifteen years of age, in 1944—four laps on a grass track in England. I still have precisely the same feelings of fatigue and excitement when I run a mile today. In fact, I can almost hear the flying bombs rumbling away in the distance as they did on that first day."

My thread doesn't reach back as far as Wood's in distance or time. But this year is far enough from 1958, and Oregon far enough from Iowa, to make me proud that I've kept unbroken the link between then and now, there and here. When I race, I remember all the good times that have come before: the ones on the watch, yes, but the even more important ones that can't be measured.

A generation has passed since I became a runner. I've gone from boyhood to young manhood to middle age. I've been a high school and college student, a reluctant soldier, a newspaper and magazine editor, a free-roaming writer. I've lived in five different states in three different regions of the country, and I've traveled just about everywhere. I've gone from living with my parents to having a family of my own. I've gone from attending track meets with my father to taking my own children to road races. I've gone from slow miler training easily, to fast miler training hard, to modestly fast marathoner training slowly, to slow marathoner and slow miler who doesn't think of running as "training."

Times and places change, youth fades, awards tarnish, old records gather dust. What stays constant and true through all the years and all the changes is the effort and enthusiasm that go into each new run and race.

Your Record-Keeping

You were told at the beginning that this was to be as much your book as mine. I write the guidelines; you bring them to life through your own efforts. The words here are mine, but the theories mean nothing until you put them into practice.

Your writing should have picked up where mine left off. You should be keeping records of your training, testing, and racing results. A daily log—which can be as simple as a notation on a calendar or as serious as a computer program—serves two important purposes: one personal and one practical.

On the first level, the log gives a feeling of substance and permanence to efforts that otherwise would remain as invisible and temporary as footprints on a hard road. You feel a growing sense of accomplishment as the records for past runs accumulate, knowing that you put every minute and mile onto those pages. Each number tells a story worth remembering.

The practical value of the log is that its numbers lend themselves to analysis. Rather than trusting hazy memories of what might have led to high and low periods in your running, you can find your answers by reviewing accumulated facts. As training, testing, and racing data pile up, the numbers form patterns which tell the story of how well or how poorly you respond to your running.

I've been a diary-keeper since 1959. My daily entries are now made mostly to satisfy creative urges, yet the diary has taught me most of my practical lessons. From the day-by-day notes grew patterns of responses to running, and from the patterns emerged the programs contained in this book.

From some 10,000 days of writing in a diary, I've learned which facts mean the most and how to review them. The essential information can fit onto one sheet of paper per month, divided into these columns:

- *Day of the month.* Keep a daily record, even if you don't run every day.
- *Amount of running.* Note the total time.
- *Amount of racing or testing.* Count only the part run significantly longer or faster than normal.
- *Notes.* Indicate extraordinary experiences, either good or bad: personal records, injuries, etc.

Most runners keep weekly records. This is too short a period to give an accurate reading of what you have accomplished. I prefer a monthly accounting (see the sample month in Table A). At month's end, add up the total running time for the month and divide by the total number of days (even if you have taken days off). This calculation yields the average daily length of your runs, which should fall in the thirty- to sixty-minute range.

Next, record the distances and times of the month's races and tests. Add up your amount of racing and testing for the month, and divide that figure into the total amount of running for the month. This gives the percentage of race-like effort, which should not exceed ten percent.

Finally, as you review the month's notes, look for connections between the numbers and your physical highs and lows. Then try to duplicate the conditions that led to the ups while eliminating the factors that produced the downs.

Table A *A Month's Records*

Month/Day	Run Time	Race/Test Distance	Race/Test Time	Race/Test Pace (mile)
4/1	30 minutes			
4/2	45 minutes			
4/3	45 minutes			
4/4	31 minutes			
4/5	36 minutes			

Month/Day	Run Time	Race/Test Distance	Race/Test Time	Race/Test Pace (mile)
4/6	40 minutes			
4/7	45 minutes	5-K	20:10	6:30
4/8	45 minutes			
4/9	47 minutes			
4/10	45 minutes			
4/11	30 minutes			
4/12	32 minutes			
4/13	45 minutes			
4/14	55 minutes	10-K	39:25	6:21
4/15	30 minutes			
4/16	32 minutes			
4/17	30 minutes			
4/18	15 minutes			
4/19	30 minutes			
4/20	17 minutes			
4/21	15 minutes			
4/22	30 minutes			
4/23	20 minutes			
4/24	30 minutes			

Month/Day	Run Time	Race/Test Distance	Race/Test Time	Race/Test Pace (mile)
4/25	15 minutes			
4/26	15 minutes			
4/27	21 minutes			
4/28	17 minutes			
4/29	20 minutes			
4/30	30 minutes			

- Days of running: 30 of 30
- Total running time: 930 minutes
- Average daily running time: 31 minutes
- Range of running times: 15 to 55 minutes
- Racing or testing days: 2 of 30
- Total racing/testing time: 59:35
- Range of racing/testing distances: 5 to 10 kilometers
- Range of racing paces: 6:21 to 6:30 per mile
- Percentage of racing/testing time: 6.4%
- Notes: Made the mistake of racing when a cold was developing, and it restricted running for the last half of the month.

Order the computerized edition of *Running Your Best Race*

Wm. C. Brown Publishers presents a new kind of sports book . . .

You can order a ready to run diskette for your Apple II series computer or IBM PC. The program diskette goes further than the book by allowing you to have an automated and personalized running program that plans, calculates, records, reviews, and updates your running program in no more time than it takes to select from the Menu of Programs and key in basic information about yourself.

The programs are advanced tools that go beyond the book to tailor Joe Henderson's advice to your needs in the areas of planning, pace, distance, running frequency, and training.

Apple II Series Version ISBN 0–697–00705–7

IBM PC Version ISBN 0–697–00727–8

Running Requirements: 48K and 1 disk drive

Quantity   Title/Order #   Price

Name _____

Address _____

City _____

State _____ Zip _____

Amount of order $ _____

Tax (CA, IA, LA residents add sales tax) $ _____

Please indicate method of payment.

☐ Check/money order enclosed (WCB pays shipping and handling)

Shipping & handling ($1.00 per selection) $ _____

☐ Charge my credit account   ☐ Visa   ☐ Mastercard   ☐ American Express

Total $ _____

Account No.   MC Bank #

Exp. Date _____ Signature _____
Required of all Charges

wcb
Wm. C. Brown Publishers
2460 Kerper Blvd. / P.O. Box 539 / Dubuque, Iowa 52001

马里奥·普佐作品01

教　父

马里奥·普佐 著

姚向辉 译

江苏文艺出版社
JIANGSU LITERATURE AND ART
PUBLISHING HOUSE

图书在版编目(CIP)数据

教父/(美)普佐(Puxo,M.)著;姚向辉译. —南京:江苏文艺出版社,2014.7

(读客全球顶级畅销小说文库)

书名原文:The go&father

ISBN 978 – 7 – 5399 – 6744 – 8

Ⅰ.①教…　Ⅱ.①普…②姚…　Ⅲ.①长篇小说—美国—现代

Ⅳ.①I712.45

中国版本图书馆 CIP 数据核字(2014)第 259928 号

书　　名　教父

著　　者　(美)马里奥·普佐

译　　者　姚向辉

出版发行　凤凰出版传媒股份有限公司

　　　　　江苏文艺出版社

社　　址　南京市中央路 165 号,邮编:210009

印　　刷　北京盛兰兄弟印刷装订有限公司

开　　本　710mm×1000mm　1/16

印　　张　18

字　　数　350 千

版　　次　2014 年 7 月第 1 版

印　　次　2014 年 7 月第 1 次印刷

标准书号　ISBN 978 – 7 – 5399 – 6744 – 8

定　　价　45.00 元

第一部

财富背后,总有犯罪。

——巴尔扎克

第一章

亚美利哥·邦纳塞拉坐在纽约第三刑事法庭里,等待正义得到伸张,等待报应落在那两个家伙头上,他们企图玷污他的女儿,残忍地伤害了她。

法官身材魁梧,他卷起黑袍的袖子,像是要动手惩罚站在法官席前的两个年轻人。他脸色冰冷,神情鄙夷。可是,眼前这一切却有什么地方不对劲,亚美利哥·邦纳塞拉感觉到了,此刻却还不理解。

"你们就像最堕落的变态。"法官厉声说。对,就是,亚美利哥·邦纳塞拉心想。畜生,畜生。两个年轻男人留着油亮的平头,脸蛋刮得干干净净,装出虔诚悔悟的神情,顺从地垂着脑袋。

法官继续道:"你们的表现活像丛林野兽,好在没有侵犯那可怜的姑娘,否则我一定关你们二十年大牢。"法官略一犹豫,一见难忘的粗眉底下,眼神朝脸色灰黄的亚美利哥·邦纳塞拉悄悄一闪,旋即望向面前的一叠鉴定报告。他皱起眉头,耸起肩膀,仿佛要压服油然而生的渴望。他重新开口。

"不过,考虑到你们年纪尚小,没有犯罪记录,家庭体面,而法律的出发点不是报复,因此我判处你们入感化院改造三年,缓期执行。"

要不是从事了四十年的殡葬行当,排山倒海而来的打击和仇恨肯定会爬上亚美利哥·邦纳塞拉的脸庞。漂亮的小女儿还在医院里,靠钢丝箍住断裂的下颌,两个小畜生居然要逍遥法外了?审判从头到尾就是一场闹剧。他望着快乐的父母围住爱子。

天哪,他们现在多么快乐,居然满脸微笑。

酸涩的黑色胆汁涌上喉咙,穿过紧咬的牙关满溢而出。邦纳塞拉取出胸袋里的白色亚麻手帕,按在嘴唇上。他站在那里,两个年轻人大踏步走下过道,狂妄而无所顾虑,笑嘻嘻的,甚至都没怎么看他。他望着他们走过,一言不发,用崭新的手帕压着嘴唇。

他们的父母走近了,两对男女和他年龄相仿,但衣着更有美国风范。他们瞥了他一眼,虽说面露惭色,眼里却流露出得意洋洋的藐视。

邦纳塞拉失去控制,探身对着过道大喊,嗓音嘶哑:"你们也会像我一样流泪!我要让你们流泪,就像你们的孩子让我流泪……"手帕举到了眼角。殿后的辩护律师把客户向前赶,父母紧紧围住两个年轻人,他们正沿着过道向回走,像是要去保护父母。大块头法警立刻堵住邦纳塞拉的那排座位。其实并没有这个必要。

亚美利哥·邦纳塞拉定居美国多年,相信法律和秩序,因而事业兴旺。此时此刻,尽管根得七窍生烟,买把枪杀了这两个人的念头仿佛要挣脱头骨,但邦纳塞拉还是扭头对仍在拼命理解情况的妻子解释说:"他们愚弄了我们。"他顿了顿,下定决心,不再害怕代价,"为了正义,我们必须去求唐·柯里昂。"

洛杉矶一个富丽堂皇的酒店套房里,约翰尼·方坦烂醉如泥,活脱脱一个寻常的吃醋丈夫。他四仰八叉躺在红色沙发上,抓起苏格兰威士忌酒瓶对着嘴喝,又把嘴唇泡进装着冰块和水的水晶玻璃桶冲掉酒味。凌晨四点,他喝得天旋地转,幻想等趾高气扬的老婆一回家就干掉她。但前提是她愿意回家才行。这会儿打电话给前妻问候孩子实在太晚,事业急转直下的人打电话给朋友似乎也不太妥当。有段时间他们凌晨四点接到电话会高兴得受宠若惊,但如今只可能觉得厌倦。想起当年走上坡路那会儿,约翰尼·方坦的烦心事还迷住过美国几位最耀眼的女星呢,他不禁自嘲地对自己笑了笑。

正在痛饮苏格兰威士忌,他总算听见妻子把钥匙插进了锁眼,但他只顾喝酒,直到她走进房间,在他面前站住。他眼中的老婆还是那么美丽,天使脸孔,深情的紫罗兰色眼眸,纤细柔弱但凹凸有致的身体。她的美在银幕上被放大无数倍,超脱世俗。全世界数以亿计的男人都爱上了玛格特·艾什顿的这张脸,肯掏钱在银幕上观赏这张脸。

"你他妈去哪儿了?"约翰尼·方坦问。

"出去鬼混。"她答道。

她低估了他的醉酒程度。他跳过鸡尾酒桌,抓住她的喉咙。但是,一凑近这张有魔力的脸,这双紫罗兰色的可爱眼睛,怒火凭空消散,他又变得无所适从。她犯了错误,看见他收起拳头,露出嘲讽的笑容。她喊道:"别打脸,约翰尼,还要拍戏呢。"

她哈哈大笑。他一拳打在她肚子上,她跌倒在地。他摔在她身上,她拼命喘息,他能闻到她芬芳的呼吸。拳头落在她的胳膊和光滑的棕褐色大腿肌肤上。他痛揍她,像是回到多年前纽约的地狱厨房,他还是个逞凶斗狠的少年,正在殴打流鼻涕的小孩。他能让对方吃苦头,但不会因为掉了牙齿或者打断鼻梁而破相。

可是,他揍得不够重。他下不了手。她对他咯咯傻笑。她摊开四肢躺在地上,织锦长衣拉到大腿根,一边咯咯笑一边奚落他。"来呀,捅进来呀。你倒是捅进来啊,约翰尼,你真正想要的是这个吧。"

约翰尼·方坦站起身。他憎恨地上的这个女人,但她的美貌仿佛魔力盾牌。玛格特翻个身,舞蹈演员似的一跃而起,面对他站住。她跳起孩子的嘲笑舞步,唱着说:"约翰尼永远不会伤害我,约翰尼永远不会伤害我。"随后板起美丽的脸蛋,近乎于哀伤地说,"可怜的傻瓜混蛋,打得我不痛不痒像个小孩。唉,约翰尼,永远是个傻乎乎意大利佬,那么浪漫,连做爱都像小孩,还以为打炮真像你唱的那些白痴小调。"她摇摇头,说,"可怜的约翰尼。再会了,约翰尼。"她走进卧室,他听见她转动钥匙锁门。

约翰尼坐在地上,脸埋在手里。屈辱得想吐的绝望淹没了他。但没过多久,帮他在好莱坞丛林活下来的草根韧性使他拿起电话,叫车送他去机场。有个人能救他。他要回纽约。回去找那个有权力、有智慧、让他信任的人。他的教父,柯里昂。

面包师纳佐里尼和他烤的意式长棍一样敦实,一样硬邦邦;他满身面粉,怒视老婆、正值婚龄的女儿凯瑟琳和帮工恩佐。恩佐换上了带绿字臂章的战俘制服,害怕这一幕会搞得他来不及回总督岛报到。他是成千上万的意大利战俘之一,每天假释出来为美国经济作贡献,他生活在持续的恐惧之中,唯恐假释被撤销。因此正在上演的这一幕小小喜剧,对他来说却严肃得无以复加。

纳佐里尼恶狠狠地问:"是不是你羞辱了我的家庭?战争已经结束,你知道美国要把你踢回遍地狗屎的西西里农村,所以给我女儿留了个小包裹做纪念?"

恩佐个头很矮,但筋骨强健,他伸手按住心口,虽然几乎泪流满面,但说起话来口齿伶俐:"主人,我向圣母发誓,我绝没有辜负你的善意。我全心全意敬爱你的女儿。我全心全意向她求婚。我知道我配不上她,他们要是送我回意大利,我就永远也没法回美国了,就永远没法娶凯瑟琳了。"

纳佐里尼的妻子菲洛蒙娜这时候开口了。"别犯浑,"她对矮胖的丈夫说,"你知道该怎么做。留下恩佐,让他去长岛和我们的远亲待在一起,避避风头。"

凯瑟琳在哭。她已经开始发福,不怎么漂亮,还长着淡淡的胡须。她永远也找不到第二个像恩佐这么英俊的男人肯娶她,肯带着尊重和爱意抚摸她的隐私部位了。"我愿意去意大利生活,"她朝父亲尖叫道,"要是你不让恩佐留下,我就离家出走。"

6 教 父

纳佐里尼凶巴巴地瞥了女儿一眼。他这个女儿啊,是个"烫手货"。他亲眼见过,恩佐从她背后挤过去,把刚出炉的热长棍放进柜台上的篮子里,女儿用圆滚滚的臀部磨蹭恩佐的下体。纳佐里尼下流地想:要是不采取恰当的措施,小流氓的热长棍就要钻进他女儿的烤炉了。恩佐必须留在美国,成为美国公民。能安排这种事情的,天底下只有一个人——教父唐·柯里昂。

上述所有人,还有其他许多人,都收到了华美精致的请柬,出席定于一九四五年八月最后一个星期六举行的康丝坦齐娅·柯里昂小姐的婚礼。新娘的父亲唐·维托·柯里昂尽管已经搬进长岛大宅,但从不忘记老朋友和旧邻居。招待宴会将在那幢大宅举办,欢庆仪式会持续一整天。毫无疑问,这次社交活动将分外盛大。和日本的战争刚刚结束,不必担心战场上的儿子。人们正需要一场婚礼来显示内心的欢乐。

就这样,在那个星期六早晨,唐·柯里昂的亲朋好友涌出纽约城,前来表达敬爱之意。他们送来的贺礼是塞满米黄色信封的现金,而不是支票。每个信封里都有一张卡片,标明送礼人的身份和他对教父奉献了多少敬意。每一分敬意教父都当之无愧。

人人向唐·维托·柯里昂求助,希望也从不落空。他不许空头支票,不找借口掩饰懦弱,说什么世上还有更强大的力量束缚他的双手。他不必是你的朋友,连你有没有能力报答也无关紧要。不可或缺的条件只有一个:你,你本人,要承认你对他的友谊。满足了这个条件,无论求助者多么贫穷多么卑微,唐·柯里昂都会把他的麻烦放在心上。为了解决求助者的灾难,他不会允许任何事情挡道。报答?友谊而已,以"唐"尊称他,时不时也用更有感情色彩的"教父"头衔。偶尔再送点朴素的小礼物——一加仑家酿的葡萄酒,一篮为他家圣诞餐桌特别烘制的胡椒烤饼——仅仅是为了表示尊敬,绝不图利。大家心照不宣,这只是善意的姿态,表达你欠他的人情,他有权随时请你做点什么小事抵债。

今天这个大喜之日,他女儿出嫁的日子,唐·维托·柯里昂站在长滩家的门口接待宾客,他认识每一个人,他信任每一个人。很多人多亏了唐才过上了舒适的生活,在这个亲密的场合可以当面称呼他"教父"。连庆典上负责招待的人也都是朋友。酒保是他的老伙计,礼物就是婚宴的全部酒水和他本人娴熟的技术。侍应生是唐·柯里昂几个儿子的朋友。花园餐台上的食物由唐的妻子和她的朋友烹制,花园足有一英亩大,张灯结彩,喜气洋洋,装饰出自新娘的密友之手。

唐·柯里昂招待每个人都同样热情,无论对方是穷是富,位高权重或者微不足道。他不怠慢任何一位。这就是他的性格。宾客纷纷称赞他身穿燕尾服多么风度翩翩,外人见了很容易以为唐就是幸运的新郎。

三个儿子里有两个陪他站在门口。老大的受洗教名是桑蒂诺,不过除父亲之外人人管他叫桑尼,年长的意大利人斜眼打量他,年轻的则一脸仰慕。就意大利父母在美国生下的第一代而言,桑尼·柯里昂个子算是很高了,差不多六英尺,加上剃成平头的浓密卷发,显得还要再高一点。他浓眉大眼,五官端正,长得像爱神丘比特,厚实的弓形嘴唇饱含肉欲,浅凹的下巴莫名地淫邪。他体格健壮如公牛,大家都知道上帝赋予他得天独厚的本钱,他的妻子把自己当成烈士,对婚床的恐惧不亚于当年异教徒害怕拷问台。有传闻说他年轻时常逛名声不好的院子,连最老练、无畏的老妓女,敬畏地检查过他偌大的家伙后,也要了双倍的价钱。

就在婚宴现场,几个大屁股大嘴巴的年轻妇人自信而节制地打量着桑尼·柯里昂。可是这次她们恐怕是在浪费时间了,因为桑尼·柯里昂已经准备对妹妹的伴娘露西·曼奇尼下手了,虽然他的老婆和三个孩子也在场。这姑娘也心领神会,身穿粉色礼服坐在花园餐桌前,油亮的黑发上戴着花冠。上周彩排的时候,她已经在和桑尼打情骂俏,那天上午更是在圣坛前捏了他的手。毕竟是姑娘家,只能做到这一步了。

桑尼没法成为他父亲那种了不起的男人,但露西并不在乎。桑尼·柯里昂有力量,有勇气。他很慷慨,心胸和硕大的本钱一样让人折服。然而,他欠缺父亲的谦逊,脾气暴躁而炽烈,导致他连连判断失误。尽管他是父亲事业的好帮手,不过很少有人相信他能接班。

二儿子弗雷德里科,大家叫他弗雷德或弗雷迪,是每个意大利人都会向圣贤祈求自己也能生一个的那种孩子。他孝顺忠诚,随时为父亲效劳,三十岁了还和父母同住。他个头不高,身材结实,并不英俊,但也有一颗家族遗传的爱神脑袋,浓密的卷发,圆润的脸庞,性感的弓形嘴唇。不过在弗雷德脸上,那双嘴唇并无肉欲,而是犹如花岗岩雕像。他性格阴郁,是父亲的左膀右臂,从不和父亲顶嘴,从不和女人勾三搭四,让父亲脸上无光。尽管有这么多优点,可他缺乏对领袖而言必不可少的人格魅力和兽性,也没有人指望他能继承家业。

三儿子迈克尔·柯里昂没有站在父亲和两个兄长的旁边,而是在花园找了个最僻静的角落,坐在一张酒桌前。但即便如此,他还是躲不过家族亲友的关注。

迈克尔·柯里昂是唐最小的儿子,也是唯一拒绝那位大人物摆布的孩子。他没有其他孩子的浓眉大眼爱神脸,连乌黑的头发都不打卷,而是满头直发。他纯净的橄榄棕肤色放在女孩身上肯定很美丽,他那种英俊颇为清秀。说实话,唐曾经担心过小儿子的男性气概。迈克尔·柯里昂长到十七岁,他的担忧才烟消云散。

此时此刻,他的小儿子坐在花园最偏僻的角落里,以显示他存心疏远父亲和家人。坐在他身边的美国女孩,人人都听说过,但直到今天才亲眼见到。恰当的礼数他当然不会忽略,他介绍她认识了在场各位,包括他的家人。家里人对她印象一般。她太瘦,

8 教　父

太白,脸孔对女人来说过于精明,举止对姑娘家来说过于随便。连名字听起来都那么怪异,她自称凯·亚当斯。就算她告诉大家她的家族两百年前定居美国,这个姓无人不知,他们恐怕也只会耸耸肩。

客人都注意到唐并不特别关注小儿子。迈克尔在战前曾是他的宠儿,似乎只等时机成熟,唐就会选择他继承家业。他继承了大人物父亲的沉稳魄力和智慧,天生的本能使得人们不得不尊敬他。二战爆发后,迈克尔·柯里昂志愿加入海军陆战队,违抗了父亲的明确命令。

唐·柯里昂不愿意也没兴趣让小儿子因为效忠一个与他无关的政权而送命。他已经贿赂好医生,私下里作了各种安排,花费大量金钱做足预防措施。可是,迈克尔已年满二十一岁,谁也扭转不了他的个人意愿。他参军,跨过太平洋作战,晋升上尉,赢得奖章。1944 年,《生活》杂志刊登了他的照片和赫赫战功。朋友把杂志拿给唐·柯里昂看(家人没这个胆子),唐轻蔑地嘟哝了几句,说:“他为陌生人创造了那些奇迹。”

1945 年,正在养伤的迈克尔·柯里昂提前退伍,他压根不知道是父亲安排了他的退役。他在家里住了几个星期,没和任何人商量,突然去了新罕布什尔州汉诺佛的达特茅斯学院,就此离开父亲的住所。这次回来一方面是参加妹妹的婚礼,另一方面是让家里人见见他的未婚妻,一个苍白无力的美国姑娘。

有几位宾客的人生格外多姿多彩,迈克尔·柯里昂在用他们的小趣闻逗凯·亚当斯开心。她觉得这些人异乎寻常,迈克尔因此觉得很好玩,她见了新鲜和陌生的事物总是目光炯炯,这和往常一样迷住了迈克尔。最终一小群人吸引住了她的视线,他们都聚集在家酿葡萄酒的木桶旁。那几个人分别是亚美利哥·邦纳塞拉、面包师纳佐里尼、安东尼·科波拉和卢卡·布拉齐。她用她一向敏锐的眼力指出这四个人显得不怎么开心。迈克尔微笑道:“对,他们是不开心。他们在等着私下见我父亲。求他办事。”很容易就看得出,四个人的眼神须臾不离唐的身影。

唐·柯里昂站在门口欢迎宾客,一辆黑色雪佛兰轿车开过来,在林荫路的另一侧停下。前排的两个男人从上衣口袋里掏出记事本,毫不掩饰地抄写附近车辆的牌号。桑尼扭头对父亲说:“那边的两个家伙,肯定是警察。”

唐·柯里昂耸耸肩。“马路又不是我家的,他们爱干什么就干什么。”

桑尼五官粗重的爱神脸气得通红。“下贱的狗杂种,什么都不尊重。”他走下门前台阶,穿过林荫道,来到黑色轿车停泊的地方。他愤怒地把脸凑近司机,司机没有畏缩,而是打开皮夹,亮出绿色证件。桑尼一言不发地后退,朝轿车后门啐了一口,扬长而去。他希望司机能跳出轿车追上来,但司机无动于衷。他回到台阶上,对父亲说:“联邦调查局的在抄车牌号码,没礼貌的混蛋。”

唐·柯里昂知道他们是谁。他最亲近的朋友早已得到提醒,别乘自己的轿车出席婚礼。尽管他并不赞同儿子傻愣愣地展示怒火,但儿子发发脾气也有好处,让不速之客们误以为他们的"意外"出现让人措手不及。唐·柯里昂本人并不生气。有个道理他早就弄清楚了,那就是你必须承受社会强加的侮辱,因为他明白,连最卑微的人,只要时刻擦亮眼睛,就迟早能抓住机会,报复最有权势的人。正是明白这个道理,唐才从不放弃他的谦逊风度,所有朋友都对此敬佩有加。

宅邸背后的花园里,四人乐队开始演奏。宾客都已到齐。唐把不速之客抛诸脑后,领着两个儿子走向婚宴现场。

几百名客人聚集在宽敞的花园里,有些在鲜花点缀的木台上跳舞,有些坐在摆满喷香食物和大罐家酿红酒的长桌边。新娘康妮·柯里昂光彩夺目,同新郎、伴娘、女傧相和迎宾员坐在一张特别垫高的餐桌周围。乡村风格的布置符合意大利传统,却不对新娘的胃口,但康妮选择这个丈夫已经触怒了父亲,因此只好用一场"黑皮"①式婚礼讨好他。

新郎卡洛·里齐是个混血儿,父亲是西西里人,母亲祖籍意大利北方,他遗传了母亲的金发蓝眼。卡洛的父母住在内华达州,他惹了点官司,不得不离开那里。他在纽约认识了桑尼·柯里昂,进而认识了桑尼的妹妹。唐·柯里昂当然派过几个信得过的朋友去内华达,他们汇报说卡洛和警方的纠葛是因为卡洛玩枪不慎,问题不严重,很容易就能抹掉记录,让他清白做人。他们还带回了有关内华达州合法赌博的情报,唐对此很感兴趣,最近一直在惦记这档子事。唐高明的手段之一,就是把利益的来源分布在不同的行当。

康妮·柯里昂不算漂亮,瘦巴巴的,有点神经质,以后肯定是个泼妇。但今天不同,白色婚纱和献出贞操的渴望改变了她,她容光焕发,几乎称得上美丽。木头桌面底下,她的手搁在新郎肌肉发达的大腿上,噘起爱神式的弓形嘴唇,隔着空气亲吻他。

她觉得卡洛·里齐英俊得无以复加。卡洛·里齐小时候曾顶着烈日在荒漠里劳作,非常辛苦的体力活儿,因此前臂和肩膀异常粗壮,燕尾服撑得鼓鼓囊囊的。他沐浴在新娘爱慕的视线中,为新娘斟满酒杯。他待她格外殷勤,仿佛两人是同台的演员,但眼睛不时扫向新娘挎在右肩上的特大号丝绒手包,装现金的信封填满了手包。到底有多少?一万?两万?卡洛·里齐微微一笑。这还只是开始。他总算和豪门结亲了,他们会照顾好他的。

客人里有个衣冠楚楚的年轻人,油光水滑的雪貂脑袋,也在打量那个丝绒手包。

---

① Guinea:对意大利裔美国人的蔑称。

保利·加图盘算着该怎么一把抢走那个胀鼓鼓的钱袋。想一想就让人开心。不过他知道这只是无聊无害的妄想，就像小孩做梦用气枪打倒坦克。他望着上司彼得·克莱门扎，中年胖子绕着几个姑娘在木头舞台上跳欢快的塔兰台拉民间舞。克莱门扎的个头高得吓人，块头也大得吓人，舞步娴熟而放肆，用硬邦邦的肚皮色迷迷地挨碰比他年轻得多也矮小得多的姑娘们的胸部，宾客不禁鼓掌喝彩。年纪较大的女人抓住他的胳膊，争抢下一轮的舞伴位置。年纪较小的男人恭敬地让出舞池，伴着曼陀林狂放的节奏拍巴掌。克莱门扎终于瘫坐在椅子上，保利·加图端来一杯冰镇的黑葡萄酒，掏出丝绸手帕帮他擦拭汗流不止的朱庇特额头。克莱门扎大口喝酒，鲸鱼似的喘气。他没有对保利道谢，而是直截了当地说："别杵在这儿当舞蹈裁判，去做你该做的事情。到附近多走两圈，看看有什么问题。"保利连忙钻进人群。

乐队暂停休息。一个叫尼诺·瓦伦蒂的年轻人捡起他们放下的曼陀林，抬起左脚踏着座椅，唱起粗俗的西西里情歌。尼诺·瓦伦蒂面容英俊，但因为常年饮酒而肿胀。他这会儿已经有点醉了，翻着白眼，舔着舌头，唱出淫秽的歌词。女人们开心尖叫，男人们跟着歌手喊出每个小节的最后一个词。

唐·柯里昂在这种事情上出了名地死板，尽管他的矮胖老婆兴高采烈地跟着大家起哄，他却一转身钻进屋子里。桑尼·柯里昂看在眼里，起身走向新娘的餐桌，在年轻的伴娘露西·曼奇尼身边坐下。他俩很安全。桑尼的妻子在厨房，忙着完成婚礼蛋糕的最后装饰。桑尼咬着女孩的耳朵说了几个字，女孩起身离开。桑尼等了几分钟，假装漫不经心地跟上去，他挤过人群，时不时停下和宾客聊几句。

所有人的眼睛都盯着他们。伴娘念了三年大学，已经完全成了美国人，是个名声在外的成熟女孩。婚礼彩排的时候，她从头到尾都在用挑逗和玩笑与桑尼·柯里昂调情，既然他是伴郎，和她在婚礼上扮演一对儿，她觉得这么做是受到允许的。她挽起粉色长袍，走进屋子，装出天真的笑脸，轻快地跑上楼梯，进了卫生间，在里面待了一小会儿。等她出来，看见桑尼·柯里昂在上面一层的楼梯平台向她招手。

唐·柯里昂的"办公室"是个略微垫高的拐角房间，此刻关着窗户，汤姆·黑根隔着玻璃俯视张灯结彩的花园婚宴。他背后的贴墙书架堆满法律书籍。黑根是唐的律师和顾问，是家族最重要的下属。他和唐在这个房间里解决了许多棘手问题，所以当他看见教父离开婚宴走进屋子，他就知道了，即便今天是大喜之日，有些小事还是非得处理不可，唐要来找他。紧接着，黑根看见桑尼·柯里昂和露西·曼奇尼咬耳朵，还有他尾随露西走进屋子的那一幕小小喜剧。黑根做个鬼脸，考虑要不要告诉唐，最后决定还是算了。他走到办公桌前，拿起手写的名单，列出的人都已得到私下面见唐·柯里昂的许可。唐走进房间，黑根把名单递给他。唐·柯里昂点点头，说："邦纳塞拉留到最后。"

黑根推开法式双开门,径直走进花园,走向聚在酒桶周围的央求者,指了指胖乎乎的面包师纳佐里尼。

唐·柯里昂用拥抱欢迎面包师。他们在意大利是小时候的玩伴,长大了也还是好朋友。每年复活节都有新鲜出炉的凝脂奶油麦芽派送到唐·柯里昂的家里,脆皮烤得金黄,又大又圆,堪比卡车轮胎。逢到圣诞节和家族成员的生日,纳佐里尼就用鲜美的奶油酥点表达敬意。这些年,不管生意好坏,纳佐里尼总是高高兴兴地向唐年轻时创立的面包业协会缴纳费用,除了战争期间希望能在黑市买到物价局的糖票之外,从没求过任何人情。现在这位忠诚的朋友有机会恳请援助了,唐·柯里昂很愿意答应他的请求。

他递给面包师一根"高贵"雪茄,一杯黄色"女巫"利口酒,按着面包师的肩膀,鼓励他说下去。这是唐有人情味的一面。他也有过苦涩的经历,知道人求人帮忙需要多少勇气。

面包师讲述女儿和恩佐的事情。一个意大利西西里的年轻人,被美国军队俘虏,以战俘身份来到美国,假释出来为美国的战事作贡献!诚实的恩佐和不谙世事的凯瑟琳萌发了纯洁而高尚的感情,但如今战争结束,可怜的小伙子要被遣返意大利,纳佐里尼的女儿肯定会心碎欲绝。只有教父柯里昂能帮助这对苦恼的男女。他是他们最后的希望。

唐陪着纳佐里尼踱来踱去,手按着面包师的肩膀,同情地点着头,鼓舞面包师的勇气。等他终于讲完,唐·柯里昂笑着对他说:"我亲爱的朋友,你可以不用担心了。"他开始仔细解释他的解决之道。首先向本选区的国会议员请愿。再由国会议员提出特别法案,允许恩佐入籍美国。法案肯定能在国会通过。这是恶棍狼狈为奸的特权。唐·柯里昂解释说办事需要钱,现行价格是两千块。他,唐·柯里昂本人,愿意保证事情顺利办成,费用由他代收。朋友你说怎么样?

面包师拼命点头。他早知道办这么大的事情肯定得花钱。完全可以理解。国会的特别法案可不便宜。纳佐里尼感激得热泪盈眶。唐·柯里昂陪他走到门口,保证派得力干将去找面包师,安排妥当所有细节,整理一应必须文书。面包师使劲拥抱他,随后消失在花园里。

黑根对唐笑着说:"纳佐里尼倒是做了一笔好投资。两千块一个女婿和一个面包房的终身帮工。"他顿了顿:"交给谁办?"

唐·柯里昂蹙眉思考道:"别找我们的人。交给隔壁选区的犹太佬。换个家庭住址。战争结束,估计会有很多类似的事。得在华盛顿再安排几个人,处理我们办不完的事情,免得价格上涨。"黑根在记事簿里做笔记,"别找鲁特科议员,试试费歇尔。"

黑根带进来第二个人,他的问题很简单。他叫安东尼·科波拉,父亲是唐·柯里昂年轻时在铁路货场的工作伙伴。科波拉想开比萨店,购置设施和特制烘箱需要五百块定金。出于某些无法深究的原因,对方不接受赊账。唐从衣袋里摸出一卷钞票。数量不够,他做个鬼脸,对汤姆·黑根说:"借我一百块,星期一我去了银行还你。"央求者再三声明,说四百块就够了,但唐·柯里昂拍拍他的肩膀,抱歉地说:"婚礼开销太大,搞得我有点缺现金。"他接过黑根递过来的钱,和他的那卷钞票一起塞给安东尼·科波拉。

黑根一言不发地望着这一幕,眼中满是仰慕。唐时常教导大家,必须用自己的风格表现慷慨。安东尼·科波拉这么一个人,唐这样的大人物居然找旁人借钱供他办事,你说他会多么受宠若惊。倒不是说科波拉不知道唐是百万富翁,而是有几个百万富翁会因为穷朋友而忍受哪怕一丁点儿不方便呢?

唐抬起头,像是在问下一个是谁。黑根答道:"卢卡·布拉齐,不在名单上,但他想见你。他明白他见不得人,可他想当面祝贺你。"

唐第一次露出不愉快的神色,他回答得拐弯抹角。"非得见他?"他问。

黑根耸耸肩。"你比我更熟悉他。不过你请他参加婚礼,他已经感恩戴德了。他没料到你会请他,估计他想表达一下谢意。"

唐·柯里昂点点头,打手势示意带卢卡·布拉齐来见他。

花园里,卢卡·布拉齐紫胀狂暴的脸色吓住了凯·亚当斯。她向迈克尔打听他。迈克尔之所以带凯参加婚礼,就是想让她慢慢了解他父亲的真面目,免得到时候大吃一惊。不过到目前,她似乎只把唐看作不怎么守规矩的生意人。迈克尔决定兜着圈子告诉她部分实情。他解释说卢卡·布拉齐是东部地区黑社会最可怕的角色之一,据说头号天赋就是能单枪匹马执行杀人任务,不需要帮凶协助,所以法律不可能发现他的罪行并给他定罪。迈克尔做个鬼脸,说:"我不知道这些说法有多少是真的,但我知道他算是我父亲的朋友。"

凯终于有点明白了,她半信半疑地问:"你不是想说这种人是你父亲的部下吧?"

他不想再顾及太多,直截了当答道:"差不多十五年前,有几个人想夺走我父亲的进口油生意。他们刺杀他,险些成功。卢卡·布拉齐杀上门去,风传他在两周内干掉了六个人,终结了著名的橄榄油战争。"他笑得仿佛在说笑话。

凯打个寒战:"你是说你父亲被黑帮放过冷枪?"

"十五年前,"迈克尔说,"从此就风平浪静了。"他害怕他说得太多了。

"你想吓唬我对不对?"凯说,"不想和我结婚就直说嘛。"她笑着用胳膊肘戳他的侧肋,"非常聪明。"

迈克尔报以微笑,说:"只是希望你考虑清楚而已。"

"他真的杀了六个人?"凯问。

"报纸这么说的,"迈克说,"反正没有证据。不过,有一桩他的事谁也不肯说。估计太恐怖了,连我父亲都避而不谈。汤姆·黑根知道,但不肯告诉我。有次我跟他开玩笑,说,'我得长到几岁才有资格听卢卡的那桩事?'汤姆答道,'一百岁吧。'"迈克尔抿了一口红酒,"事情肯定非同小可。卢卡也肯定不是平常人。"

地狱魔鬼见了卢卡·布拉齐也要害怕,他身材矮壮,骨架粗大,出现在哪儿,哪儿就警笛长鸣。他那张脸永远一副凶相。眼睛是棕色的,但毫无这种颜色的暖意,而是呈现出死气沉沉的黄褐色。嘴巴与其说残忍,不如说了无生机:薄嘴唇,橡皮质地,色如嫩牛肉。

布拉齐的残暴名声令人生畏,但对唐·柯里昂的忠诚也众所周知。有几根栋梁支撑起唐的权力大厦,他就是其中之一。他这种角色可不常见。

卢卡·布拉齐不怕警察,不怕社会,不怕上帝,不怕地狱,不怕也不爱身边的同伴。但是,他选择了心甘情愿地敬畏和爱戴唐·柯里昂。可怕的布拉齐来到唐面前,毕恭毕敬,手足无措。他结结巴巴地说了些锦上添花的贺词,一本正经地祝愿唐的第一个外孙是男孩。他奉上塞满现金的信封,是给新郎新娘的礼物。

这就是他的全部目的了。黑根注意到了唐·柯里昂的变化。唐接待布拉齐就像皇帝接见立下汗马功劳的臣子,并不特别亲昵,而是带着王者的尊严。唐·柯里昂的每个手势和每句话都表明他非常看重卢卡·布拉齐。对于布拉齐将礼物亲手交给他本人,他没有显露出丝毫惊讶。他理解其中的意义。

信封里的钱肯定比别人给的多。布拉齐考虑了好几个钟头才定下数目,和其他客人有可能送出的金额比了又比。他想当最慷慨的一个人,以表达他最尊敬唐,因此他非得把信封交到唐本人手里才行,这么做当然很笨拙,但唐没有理会,只是也用好听的词句表达谢意。黑根看着卢卡·布拉齐凶狠的脸变得满是自豪和喜悦。布拉齐亲吻唐的手背,走出黑根为他拉开的房门。黑根不多不少地对布拉齐露出友善的笑容,矮壮的男人彬彬有礼地扯了扯嫩牛肉颜色的橡皮嘴唇,以此还礼。

门徐徐关上,唐·柯里昂轻轻地长出一口气。全世界只有布拉齐能让他紧张。这家伙就像自然界的力量,实在不是能驯服的对象。对待他必须像处理炸药那样谨慎。唐耸耸肩。就算是炸药,也有办法引爆而不造成伤害。他探询地望着黑根,"只剩下邦纳塞拉了?"

黑根点点头。唐·柯里昂蹙眉思考,然后说:"带他进来之前,先叫桑蒂诺过来。

他该学着点儿。"

黑根来到花园里,心急火燎地寻找桑尼·柯里昂。他请邦纳塞拉耐心等待,走到迈克尔·柯里昂和女朋友身边,问:"见到桑尼了吗?"迈克尔摇摇头。该死,黑根心想,要是桑尼还在搞伴娘,那就麻烦了。桑尼的老婆和伴娘的家族要是发现了,那就是一场灾难。他急忙走向半小时前看见桑尼进去的那扇门。

见到黑根走进屋子,凯·亚当斯问迈克尔·柯里昂:"他是谁?你介绍说他是你哥哥,但他和你不是一个姓,而且怎么看都不是意大利人。"

"汤姆十二岁开始就和我们住在一起了,"迈克尔说,"父母双亡,他在街头流浪,眼睛严重感染。一天夜里,桑尼带他回家,他从此就住下了。他没别的地方可去,结婚以后才搬走。"

凯·亚当斯激动起来。"多么浪漫啊,"她说,"你父亲肯定是个热心肠,已经有好几个子女了,还二话不说就又收养了一个。"

迈克尔懒得说明意大利移民觉得四个孩子委实不多,只是答道:"没有收养汤姆,他只是和我们住在一起。"

"噢,"凯说,随后又好奇道,"为什么不收养他?"

迈克尔笑道:"因为我父亲说要汤姆改姓是不尊重他,不尊重汤姆的亲生父母。"

他们看见黑根赶着桑尼穿过法式双开门,走进唐的办公室,然后对亚美利哥·邦纳塞拉勾勾手指。"他们为什么要在今天这种日子拿公事打扰你父亲?"凯问。

迈克尔又笑道:"因为他们知道,按照传统,西西里人不能在女儿结婚的日子拒绝请求,也没有哪个西西里人会让这种机会平白溜走。"

露西·曼奇尼挽起粉色礼服,跑下楼梯。桑尼·柯里昂那张浓眉大眼的爱神脸,被酒气和色欲激得通红淫邪,吓得她魂不附体,但她挑逗他一个星期,本来就是为了这个。她在大学里有过两段恋情,不但没什么感觉,而且两次都没超过一个星期。和第二个情人拌嘴的时候,他抱怨说什么她"下面太大"。露西明白了,直到学期结束都拒绝再赴任何约会。

夏天,她帮最好的朋友康妮·柯里昂准备婚礼,听到人们传桑尼的闲话。一个星期天下午,在柯里昂家的厨房,桑尼的老婆珊德拉说得百无禁忌。珊德拉是个好脾气的粗鄙妇人,出生在意大利,小时候来到美国。她身体健壮,奶子硕大,结婚五年,已经生了三个孩子。珊德拉和其他妇人用婚床的恐怖故事挑逗康妮。"我的天,"珊德拉咯咯笑道,"第一眼瞅见桑尼那根铁棒,想到他要把那玩意儿捅进我身体里,我吓得直喊救命。过了第一年,我那里面软得就像通心粉煮了一个钟头。每次听说他睡了别的姑娘,我就去教堂点根蜡烛。"

她们哈哈大笑，只有露西觉得两腿之间阵阵发紧。

她跑上楼梯，奔向桑尼，难以抑制的欲望淌遍全身。来到拐角平台上，桑尼抓住她的手，拽着她沿着走廊钻进一间空卧室。门在背后关上，她两腿发软。她感觉到桑尼的嘴贴上她的嘴，他的嘴唇散发烟草烧焦的苦味，她张开了嘴。桑尼的手摸进了伴娘礼服，被分开的衣料发出沙沙声，露西感觉到一只热烘烘的手插进她两腿之间，分开丝绸内裤，爱抚她的阴户。她搂住他的脖子，吊在半空中，等他解开长裤。他用双手抱起她赤裸的臀部，举起她。她轻轻一跳，两腿裹住他的大腿根。他的舌头探进她的嘴里，她使劲吸吮。他拼命一顶，她的脑袋撞在门上。她感觉到某个炽热的东西穿过她的两腿之间。她的右手松开他的脖子，下去给他引路。她的手握住了一根硕大无朋的充血肉棒。肉棒在她手中搏动，像是什么小动物，她险些因为狂喜和感激哭出来，领着那东西钻进她湿漉漉、肿胀的身体。进入时的一刺，那种难以想象的愉悦让她不由得惊叫一声，几乎把双腿提起来绞住他的脖子，她的身体犹如箭囊，接纳他狂野的利箭，闪电般的穿刺；不知道多少次，她承受着折磨；她的骨盆越抬越高，终于平生第一次颤抖着达到了高潮，他的坚硬松弛，精液洪水般流下大腿。她缠住他身体的双腿慢慢松开，滑下来落回地面。两人彼此偎依，气喘吁吁。

两人本来可以再亲热一会儿，但轻轻的敲门声打断了他们。桑尼连忙扣上裤子，用身体堵住房门，免得外面的人进来。露西慌慌张张地抚平粉色长袍，眼睛闪闪发亮，但带给她无数欢愉的东西已经藏进了庄重的黑色礼服里。他们听见汤姆·黑根的低沉叫声："桑尼，在里面吗？"

桑尼松了一口气，朝露西使个眼色，"在，汤姆，什么事？"

黑根的声音仍旧很低："唐要你去他的办公室。就现在。"桑尼和露西听见他走远的脚步声。桑尼等了几秒钟，等露西使劲亲吻他的嘴唇，然后溜出房门，跟着黑根去了。

露西梳理头发，检查一遍衣服，拉起吊袜带。她的身体感觉受了擦伤，嘴唇软乎乎的一碰就疼。她走出房门，尽管觉得两腿之间黏糊糊湿漉漉的，但没有去卫生间清洗，而是径直下楼梯去了花园。她回到新娘那张餐桌，在康妮身旁坐下，康妮愠怒地叫道："露西，你去哪儿了？怎么像是喝醉了，现在不许再走开了。"

金发新郎给露西斟了一杯葡萄酒，心领神会地笑了笑。露西不在乎。她把深红色的葡萄酒端到灼热的嘴唇边，喝了一大口。她感觉到两腿之间又湿又黏，于是并拢双腿。她的身体在颤抖。她一边喝酒，一边隔着杯沿饥渴地寻觅桑尼·柯里昂。她没兴趣看其他任何人。她咬着康妮的耳朵，顽皮地说："再过几个小时，你就知道是怎么回事啦。"康妮咯咯直笑。露西端庄地把双手叠放在桌上，但掩不住脸上的喜气，就好像偷走了新娘的什么珍宝。

亚美利哥·邦纳塞拉跟着黑根走进拐角房间,见到唐·柯里昂坐在宽阔的写字台前。桑尼·柯里昂站在窗口,望着花园。今天下午,唐第一次显得这么冷酷,他没有拥抱客人,也不和客人握手。脸色灰黄的殡仪馆老板之所以能拿到请帖,仅仅因为他老婆和唐的妻子是好朋友。唐·柯里昂非常反感亚美利哥·邦纳塞拉。

邦纳塞拉的开场白拐弯抹角,颇为巧妙:"请您原谅我的女儿,您妻子的教女,她今天无法亲自登门,奉上敬意,因为她还没出院。"他瞥了桑尼·柯里昂和汤姆·黑根一眼,暗示他不想当着他们的面说下去,但唐的心肠可不软。

"我们都知道你女儿遭遇的不幸,"唐·柯里昂说,"要是我能帮得上什么忙,你尽管开口就是了。我妻子毕竟是她的教母。我可忘不了这份荣誉。"这是一份斥责,因为殡仪馆老板从不遵守习俗,用"教父"称呼唐。

邦纳塞拉脸色灰败,直截了当地说:"能和您单独聊聊吗?"

唐·柯里昂摇摇头。"这两位都是我愿意托付性命的人。他们是我的两条右臂。我不能打发他们走开,那太侮辱人了。"

殡仪馆老板闭上眼睛,隔了几秒钟,开始讲述事情经过。他的声音很沉静,这是他用来安慰死者家属的声音。"我按照美国习惯抚养女儿。我相信美国。美国帮我发家。我给女儿自由,但也教她不要让家族蒙羞。她找了个所谓的'男朋友',不是意大利人。她和他看电影,很晚回家,但她从没见过他的父母。我接受了这一切,没有反对,这都怪我。两个月前,他拉她去看电影,他还带了个伙伴,两人骗她喝威士忌,企图占她便宜。她奋起反抗,保住了贞操,却被他们像对待畜生似的殴打。我赶到医院,她顶着两个黑眼圈,鼻梁折断,下巴粉碎性骨折。医生得用钢丝箍起来才行。她痛得直哭:'爸爸,爸爸,他们为什么要那么做? 他们为什么要那么对我?'我也哭了。"邦纳塞拉说不下去了,他老泪纵横,但声音没有流露出情感。

唐·柯里昂不怎么情愿地做个同情的手势,邦纳塞拉说了下去,痛苦让他的声音有了人味儿。"我为什么哭? 我惹人疼爱的女儿,我的生命之光。一个漂亮的女孩。她以前信任别人,以后再也不会了。她再也不漂亮了。"邦纳塞拉浑身发抖,灰黄色的脸孔涨成了难看的深红色。

"我像正经美国人那样去报警。警察逮捕了那两个小伙子,送他们上法庭接受审判。证据确凿,他们认罪。法官判处他们监禁三年,却缓期执行,审判当天就释放了。我站在法庭上,活像个大傻瓜,那些杂种还对我笑。于是我对老婆说,'我们必须找唐·柯里昂伸张正义。'"

唐低了低头,对这个男人的痛苦表示尊重。可是,他开口说话的时候,言语却冷冰冰的,像是尊严受到了冒犯。"你为什么报警?为什么不一开始就来找我?"

邦纳塞拉几不可闻地喃喃答道:"你要我怎么做?就说你要什么吧。但请您实现我的恳求。"他的言辞近乎傲慢。

唐·柯里昂正色道:"你的恳求是什么?"

邦纳塞拉瞥了黑根和桑尼·柯里昂一眼,摇摇头。唐坐在黑根的办公桌前,没有起身,只是朝殡仪馆老板探出身子。邦纳塞拉犹豫片刻,随即弯下腰,把嘴唇凑得贴上了唐毛茸茸的耳朵。唐·柯里昂像告解室里的神父似的听着,眼望远方,冷漠而不动声色。这个姿势保持良久,最后邦纳塞拉结束耳语,挺直腰杆。唐抬起眼睛,严肃地打量着邦纳塞拉。邦纳塞拉脸孔通红,毫不畏惧地回视。

末了,唐开口道:"我做不到,你得意忘形了。"

邦纳塞拉提高嗓门,清清楚楚地说:"你要什么我都答应。"听见这话,黑根打个哆嗦,脑袋里一阵抽紧。桑尼·柯里昂抱起双臂,露出冷笑,从窗口转过身,第一次望向房间里的这幕戏。

唐·柯里昂从办公桌前起身。他仍旧不动声色,但声音仿佛冷酷的死神。"我们认识已经很多年了,你和我,"他对殡仪馆老板说,"但直到今天,你从没有征求过我的意见,或者寻求我的帮助。我妻子是你独生女儿的教母,但我记不得你上次请我去你家喝咖啡是什么时候了。你践踏我的友情,唯恐欠我的债。"

邦纳塞拉喃喃道:"我不想惹麻烦。"

唐抬起一只手。"算了,你别说了。你觉得美国是天堂。你生意兴隆,过得不错,以为这世界是个无忧无虑的地方,你可以随心所欲享受快乐。你不用真正的朋友武装自己,因为有警察保护你,还有法院,你和你的家人向他们求助不怕吃亏。你不需要唐·柯里昂。很好。我的感情受了伤害,但我不会把友谊硬塞给并不需要的人,尤其是那些看不起我的人。"唐顿了顿,对殡仪馆老板露出客气但嘲讽的笑容,"今天你却跑来找我,说什么'唐·柯里昂,请帮我伸张正义',求我却不尊重我。你没有拿出你的友谊。你在我女儿结婚的日子来找我,要我去杀人,还说什么——"唐轻蔑地模仿道,"'你要什么我都答应。'不,不,我并不生气,我只想知道,我做了什么,害得你待我这么缺乏礼数?"

苦闷而恐惧的邦纳塞拉叫道:"美国对我很好。我想当个好公民。我希望我的孩子能是美国人。"

唐一拍巴掌,表示坚决同意。"说得好。非常好。那你还有什么可抱怨的?法官已经作出判决。美国已经作了决定。带着鲜花和糖果去医院探望她吧,她见了会很欣慰的。还有什么不满足的吗?再说本来也不算什么大事嘛,小伙子还年轻,血气方刚,况且还有一个是高官的儿子。唉,我亲爱的,亚美利哥,你这人一直循规蹈矩。尽管你践踏我的友谊,我必须承认我完全相信亚美利哥·邦纳塞拉的诺言比别人的都靠得住。所以呢,你要答应我,你会打消那些疯狂的念头。这可不符合美国精神。要宽恕,要遗忘。生命本来就充满了不幸。"

唐克制着愤怒,不留情面、傲慢无情地冷嘲热讽,把可怜的殡仪馆老板变成了一团打战的果冻,但他还是鼓起勇气,再一次说:"我请你伸张正义。"

唐·柯里昂敷衍道:"法庭给了你正义。"

邦纳塞拉固执地摇摇头。"不,法庭把正义给了两个年轻人,而没有给我。"

唐点点头,认同这个是非分明的判断,他问:"你要什么正义?"

"以眼还眼。"邦纳塞拉说。

"你要得太多了,"唐说,"你女儿还活着。"

邦纳塞拉不情愿地说:"那就让他们受同样的苦。"唐等他继续说下去。邦纳塞拉鼓起最后一点勇气,说,"我要付给你多少?"这简直是绝望的悲鸣。

唐·柯里昂背过身去。这是明确的拒绝。邦纳塞拉一动不动。

最后,唐·柯里昂叹了口气,像个没法对犯错朋友长久生气的好心人,转身面对脸色苍白如尸体的殡仪馆老板。唐·柯里昂有雅量,唐·柯里昂有耐心。"你为什么害怕把第一忠诚献给我?"他说,"你告上法院,一等就是几个月。你花钱请律师,律师知道得很清楚,你最终只会自取其辱。你接受法官的判决,而法官就像街头最廉价的妓女一样出卖自己。早几年你手头紧,到银行去借钱,利息高得能杀人,你拿着帽子,乞丐似的站在一边等待,他们东闻西闻,把鼻子都伸到你屁眼里了,就为了确认你有能力还贷。"唐顿了顿,声音愈加严厉。

"但你要是来找我,我的钱包就是你的。你要是来找我伸张正义,侮辱你女儿的人渣今天只会哭得更加伤心。你这么老实的人要是不走运招惹了敌人,那他们也就是我的敌人……"唐抬起胳膊,指着邦纳塞拉,"那么,请相信我,他们只会害怕你。"

邦纳塞拉低下头,用被扼住的声音喃喃道:"做我的朋友吧。我全都接受。"

唐·柯里昂伸手按着他的肩膀。"很好,"他说,"你的正义将得到伸张。有一天——也许永远也不会有这一天——我会请你报答我,帮忙办点小事。在那天之前,就当这份正义是礼物吧,来自我的妻子,你女儿的教母。"

房门在感恩戴德的殡仪馆老板身后关上,唐·柯里昂转身对黑根说:"把事情交给克莱门扎,吩咐他派靠得住的人处理,不能是闻见血腥味就忘乎所以的手下。不管那个伺候尸体的笨脑瓜里做什么白日梦,我们毕竟不是杀人犯。"他注意到男子气概十足的大儿子在隔窗张望花园宴会。无可救药,唐·柯里昂心想,桑蒂诺如果一直这么抗拒教导,那就不可能领导家业,永远当不了唐。他必须尽快另觅人选,毕竟他只是凡人。

花园里传来惊天动地的欢呼声,吓了三个人一跳。桑尼·柯里昂凑近窗户,见到的情景让他快步走向房门,脸上露出愉快的笑容。"是约翰尼,他来参加婚礼了,我怎么说的来着?"黑根走向窗户,"确实是你的教子,"他对唐·柯里昂说,"要带他过来吗?"

"不用,"唐说,"让大家跟他开开心吧。叫他有空了再来见我。"他对黑根笑了笑,"看到了吗?真是个好教子。"

嫉妒让黑根感到一阵心痛。他干巴巴地说:"都两年没见了。多半又惹了麻烦,来找你帮忙。"

"有麻烦不找他的教父还能找谁呢?"唐·柯里昂问。

康妮·柯里昂头一个看见约翰尼·方坦走进花园,她忘了新娘的矜持,尖叫道:"约翰尼!"跑过去扑进他的怀抱。他紧紧拥抱康妮,亲吻她的嘴,其他人上来问候他的时候,他还是一直搂着康妮。他们都是他的老朋友,是他在西区一起长大的伙伴。康妮搂着他去见新郎。见到金发年轻人因为不再是今日焦点而面露不悦之色,约翰尼觉得有点好笑。他使出全部魅力,和新郎握手,端起一杯葡萄酒向他敬酒。

演奏台上响起一个熟悉的声音:"约翰尼,来给我们唱一首吧?"他抬起头,见到尼诺·瓦伦蒂的笑容。约翰尼·方坦跳上演奏台,抱住尼诺。他们当初形影不离,一起唱歌,一起约会姑娘,直到约翰尼开始出名、常去电台唱歌才分开。约翰尼去好莱坞拍电影之后,给尼诺打过几次电话,只是为了聊天,还答应安排他去俱乐部唱歌。不过他始终没有付诸行动。今天见到尼诺,见到他醉醺醺的促狭笑容,往日的情谊全回来了。

尼诺开始弹奏曼陀林。约翰尼·方坦搭上尼诺的肩膀。"这首歌献给新娘。"他说,踮着脚唱起一首下流的西西里情歌。他一边唱,尼诺一边用身体做猥琐动作。新娘自豪地涨红了脸,客人用欢呼表达赞赏。唱着唱着,众人都开始踮脚,吼叫每个小节末尾淘气的双关语。一曲唱罢,他们鼓掌鼓个不停,直到约翰尼清清嗓子,唱起第二首歌。

他们都为他感到骄傲。他是他们中的一员,现在是著名歌手、电影明星,和男人心中最性感的女神睡觉。尽管如此,他却长途跋涉三千英里参加婚礼,向教父表达足够的敬意。他仍旧喜爱尼诺·瓦伦蒂这些老朋友。很多人见过约翰尼和尼诺小时候的合唱,但谁曾料想约翰尼长大后能抓住五千万女性的心呢?

约翰尼·方坦俯身把新娘拽上演奏台,让康妮站在他和尼诺之间。两人弯下腰,面对面,尼诺猛地拨弦,奏出几个刺耳的和弦。这是他们的老花招,模仿情场争斗,拿声音当利刃,轮流吼叫一段迭句。约翰尼微妙地退让半步,允许尼诺盖过自己的声音,让尼诺抢过他怀里新娘,让尼诺轻快地接过最后一段凯旋的歌词,自己的声音渐渐小了下去。整个婚礼现场爆发出欢呼和掌声,歌曲结束,三个人彼此拥抱。宾客央求再来一首。

只有站在屋子拐角门口的唐·柯里昂感觉到有什么地方不对劲。他装出心情愉快的样子,尽量不触犯客人,快活地喊道:"我的教子跑了三千英里来向我们致敬,难道谁也不想让他润润嗓子?"马上有十几个斟满红酒的杯子伸向约翰尼·方坦。他从每个酒杯里各喝一口,接着跑过去拥抱他的教父,同时凑到老人的耳朵旁说了些什么。唐领着他走进屋子。

约翰尼走进房间,汤姆·黑根伸出手。约翰尼和他握手,说:"最近可好,汤姆?"但缺乏平时待人那种真诚和热情的魅力。他的冷淡让黑根有点受伤,但并没有放在心上。担任唐的心腹也有坏处,这就是其中之一。

约翰尼·方坦对唐说:"收到婚礼请帖,我心想,'我的教父不再生我的气了。'我离婚后给你打过五次电话,汤姆总说你出去了或者很忙,所以我知道你不高兴。"

唐·柯里昂拿起黄色的"女巫"酒瓶,斟满酒杯。"都是过去的事了。现在归现在。我还能为你做什么事情吗? 还是你名气太大,太有钱,已经不需要我的帮助了?"

约翰尼一饮而尽那杯黄澄澄的烈酒,伸出酒杯示意还要。他尽量用轻松自在的声音说:"我哪里算有钱啊,教父? 我在走下坡路。你说得对。我不该为了现在这个贱婆娘抛弃老婆和孩子。你生我的气,我不怪你。"

唐耸耸肩。"我只是担心你,你是我的教子,没别的。"

约翰尼在房间里踱来踱去。"我被那条母狗迷花了眼。好莱坞最了不起的明星。她貌若天仙。可你知道她拍完电影做什么吗? 要是化妆师是男人,把她的脸画得好看点,她就允许他操她。要是摄影师把她拍得格外上镜,她就领他去更衣室,跟他打一炮。随便什么人都行。她对她的肉体就像我对口袋里当小费的零钱。完全是魔鬼的婊子。"

唐·柯里昂突然打断道:"你的家人怎么样了?"

约翰尼叹了口气。"我照顾着呢。离婚后,我给金妮和孩子的比法庭的判决还要多。我每周见他们一次。我想念他们。有时候我觉得我要发疯了。"他又喝掉一杯酒,"现在的妻子成天嘲笑我。她不理解我为什么吃醋。她说我是死脑筋的黑皮,还取笑我的歌艺。我走前好好收拾了她一顿,但没打脸,因为她在拍电影。我揍得她抽筋,像小孩似的只打胳膊和腿,她笑个不停。"他点燃香烟,"就这样,教父,活得真没意思。"

唐·柯里昂答得很简单:"这些麻烦我可帮不了你。"他顿了顿,又问,"你的嗓子是怎么了?"

自信的魅力和自嘲的表情统统从约翰尼·方坦的脸上消失了。他几乎泣不成声地说:"教父啊,我没法再唱歌了,我的喉咙出了问题,医生也搞不清楚原因。"黑根和唐惊讶地看着他,约翰尼可从来都很硬气。方坦继续道:"我的两部电影挣了很多钱。我曾经是大明星,现在他们一脚把我踢开。电影公司老板对我恨之入骨,现在要打发我滚蛋了。"

唐·柯里昂站在教子面前,阴沉地问道:"他为什么讨厌你?"

"我以前唱过颂扬自由派组织的歌曲,你知道的,你很不喜欢我唱那些东西。唉,杰克·沃尔茨也不喜欢。他说我是共产党,不过没能把罪名栽给我。后来我勾搭了他的女人。完全是一夜情,她却反过来追我。我他妈能怎么办?再然后我的婊子老婆赶我出门,金妮和孩子不肯接受我,除非我愿意趴在地上哀求,而且我连歌都没法唱了。教父啊,我他妈该怎么办?"

唐·柯里昂脸色铁青,一丝同情也没有。他轻蔑地说:"首先,你得像个男人。"怒火忽然扭曲了他的脸庞。他吼道:"像个男人!"他探身过办公室,揪住约翰尼·方坦的头发,动作里充满了蛮狠的情谊,"老天在上,你在我身边待了那么久,怎么可能变成这个样子?好莱坞的软蛋?哭哭啼啼求人可怜?哭得像个娘儿们——'我该怎么办?哦,我该怎么办?'"

唐的模仿来得那么超乎寻常,那么出人意料,黑根和约翰尼先是大吃一惊,紧接着放声大笑。唐·柯里昂也有点沾沾自喜。他有几秒钟回想着他有多么爱这个教子。他自己的三个儿子被这样揶揄会如何反应?桑蒂诺会一连几个星期吊着脸,举止乖戾。弗雷迪会畏畏缩缩。迈克尔会冷笑一声,扬长而去,几个月不露面。可是,约翰尼,多么乖的小伙子啊,他已经露出笑容,正在打起精神,他明白教父的真正意图。

唐·柯里昂说了下去。"你抢了老板的女人,他比你有权势得多,然后居然还抱怨他不肯拉你一把。真是一派胡言。你抛弃了家庭,另娶一个婊子,让孩子没了父亲,现在因为他们不肯敞开怀抱迎接你而哭哭啼啼。那个婊子,你不肯打她的脸,就因为她在拍电影,她笑话你,你居然还吃惊。你活得像白痴,自然有白痴一样的下场。"

唐·柯里昂停下来,换上耐心的声音问:"这次愿意接受我的建议吗?"

约翰尼·方坦耸耸肩。"我不能和金妮复婚,我没法过她想要的日子。赌博、喝酒、和朋友一起鬼混,这些我都戒不掉。漂亮的女人追我,我拒绝不了她们。回到金妮面前,我总觉得自己在做贼。天哪,我可不想再受一遍那些折磨。"

唐·柯里昂难得露出恼怒的神色:"我没叫你复婚。你爱怎么过就怎么过。你愿意当孩子的父亲,这当然最好。男人要是不愿意好好当父亲就不是真正的男人。但另一方面,你不能强迫孩子的母亲接受你。谁说你不能每天去看孩子了?谁说你们不能住在一个屋檐下了?谁说你不能想怎么过日子就怎么过日子了?"

约翰尼·方坦笑道:"教父啊,不是所有女人都是老式的意大利妻子。金妮可不吃这套。"

唐开始挖苦他:"那是因为你活得就像个软蛋。你给的比法庭判的更多。你不打现在老婆的脸,因为她在拍电影。你让女人主宰你的世界,可她们无法胜任。虽说死后她们都会上天堂当圣人,我们只能在地狱受煎熬。另外,这些年我一直在看着你。"唐的声音变得真诚,"你始终是个好教子,给了我最大的尊敬。可是,你的老朋友呢?今年你跟这个人厮混,明年又是另外一个人。那个意大利小伙子怎么样了?他在电影里很有趣,可是运气不好,你见不到他了,因为你现在出名了。跟你一起上学的老伙计怎么样了?他可是你唱歌的搭档啊。对,尼诺。他很失望,拼命喝酒,但从不抱怨。他开卡车运砂土,干得很卖力,周末唱歌挣区区几个小钱。他从不说你的坏话。你就不能帮帮他?为什么?他唱得不错。"

约翰尼·方坦虽然厌倦,但还是耐心地解释道:"教父,他实在天赋不足。好是挺好,但并不出色。"

唐·柯里昂的眼皮几乎耷拉成了一条缝,他说:"你,我的教子,你啊,才是实在天赋不足。要不我给你找个和尼诺一起开卡车运砂土的工作?"约翰尼没有吭声,唐继续道:"友谊就是一切。比天赋更重要,比政府更重要。和家人差不多同样重要。千万别忘了这一点。你要是能用友谊筑起一道墙,就不需要求我帮忙了。来,说说看,你为什么没法唱歌了?你在花园里唱得不赖,都赶得上尼诺了。"

微妙的讽刺让黑根和约翰尼微微一笑。现在轮到约翰尼耐心解释了:"我的嗓子变得很脆弱。唱上一两首,然后有几个小时甚至几天没法唱歌。彩排和重拍我怎么都熬不下来。我的嗓子很脆弱,肯定得了什么毛病。"

"这么说,你有女人的麻烦,嗓子有毛病,现在又告诉我,你还和那位好莱坞的一把手不和,他拒绝让你工作。"唐开始谈正经事。

"他比你说的一把手还大,"约翰尼说,"他是电影公司的老板。他是总统的顾问,利用电影宣传战争。一个月前刚买了今年最热门的小说的电影改编权。一本畅销书,主角恰好就是我这种人,我都不需要表演,做我自己就行了。连唱歌都不需要。说不定能拿奥斯卡奖。大家都知道那个角色适合我,我会重新走红。这次是以演员的身份。可混蛋杰克·沃尔茨要赶我走,不肯把角色给我。我说我愿意白干,拿最低薪酬就行,但他还是说不行。他还放出风声说,我要是肯去电影公司的内部餐厅舔他的屁眼,说不定他还会稍微考虑一下。"

唐·柯里昂挥挥手,叫他别感情用事说废话。懂道理的人之间没什么生意纠纷是无法解决的。他拍拍教子的肩膀。"你泄气了。你觉得没有人关心你?你瘦多了,喝了不少酒吧?睡不着,吃安眠药?"他不满地摇摇头。

"我要你遵守我的命令,"唐说,"我要你在我家住一个月。好好吃饭,休息睡觉。我要你多陪陪我,我喜欢有你做伴,你说不定能从你教父身上学到点为人处世的道理,帮你在了不起的好莱坞混世界。但是,不许唱歌,不许喝酒,不许碰女人。一个月结束,你回好莱坞去,这个一把手、炮筒子,就会把你要的角色交给你。成交吗?"

约翰尼·方坦根本不相信唐有这么大的权力,但他的教父从没许过办不成的承诺。"这家伙和埃德加·胡佛有私交,"约翰尼说,"在他面前说话都不能太大声。"

"他是生意人,"唐不动声色地说,"我会给他一个他无法拒绝的条件。"

"太晚了,"约翰尼说,"合约都已经签好,一周内就要开始拍摄。怎么想都不可能啊。"

唐·柯里昂说:"去,参加宴会吧。朋友们在等你呢,一切都交给我了。"他把约翰尼·方坦赶出房间。

黑根在办公桌前坐下,开始记录。唐长叹一声,问:"还有事情吗?"

"索洛佐,没法继续拖延了,你本周必须见他。"黑根抬起笔,指着日历。

唐耸耸肩:"等婚礼结束,时间你来安排。"

这个答案告诉了黑根两件事。首先也是最重要的,维吉尔·索洛佐将得到否定的答案。其次,唐·柯里昂不肯在女儿的婚礼前回答索洛佐,是因为他知道拒绝会惹来麻烦。

黑根小心翼翼地问:"要我吩咐克莱门扎找几个人住在家里吗?"

唐不耐烦地说:"为什么?我不肯在婚礼前回答,是因为这么重要的日子容不得乌云,连远远的一丝乌云也不行。另外,我想事先知道他想谈什么。现在我们知道了。他的提议很见不得人。"

黑根问:"那么,你打算拒绝?"见到唐点头,黑根又说,"我觉得你回答之前,我们应该先讨论一下,全家一起讨论。"

唐笑着说:"你这么想?好吧,讨论一下也好。等你从加州回来好了。你明天飞过去,替约翰尼摆平这件事。见见那个电影业的大人物。告诉索洛佐,你从加州回来,我就见他。还有事情吗?"

黑根正色道:"医院打过电话。阿班丹多顾问快不行了,挺不过今天晚上。已经通知他家里人过去候着了。"

自从癌症把占科·阿班丹多禁锢在病床上之后，黑根代理行使顾问职务已有一年。他现在就等着唐·柯里昂永远承认他顾问的地位。可惜机会不大。这么高的位置按传统必须交给父母都是意大利人的男人。他暂时代理已经惹出了不少麻烦。另外，他今年三十五，按说岁数不够，也缺乏一名成功顾问必不可少的经验和狡猾。

唐并没有鼓励他。他问："我女儿什么时候和新郎离开？"

黑根看看手表。"几分钟后，他们切蛋糕，再过半个小时就走。"这提醒了他另外一件事，"你的新女婿，要给他在家族内部安排个重要职务吗？"

唐回答得那么斩钉截铁，让黑根吃了一惊。"没门。"唐用手掌猛拍桌面，"绝对没门。给他安排个挣钱过日子的活计，日子可以过得不错，但绝对不能让他了解家族生意。把这话告诉其他人，桑尼、弗雷迪、克莱门扎。"

唐顿了顿。"吩咐我的儿子，三个儿子，叫他们陪我去医院给可怜的占科送终。我要他们向他致以最后的敬意。叫弗雷德开大车，问约翰尼要不要一起去，就当给我个面子。"他见到黑根疑惑地望着他，"你今晚就去加州。你没时间见占科了。不过等我从医院回来，和你谈完你再走。明白了？"

"明白，"黑根说，"要弗雷德什么时候准备车子？"

"宾客离开以后，"唐·柯里昂说，"占科会等我的。"

"参议员打过电话，"黑根说，"道歉说他没法亲自登门贺喜，不过你也能理解。指的大概是马路对面抄车牌的两个调查局探员。不过他通过特别信使送了礼物。"

唐点点头。他不觉得有必要指出提醒参议员叫他别来的正是自己。"礼物像样吗？"

黑根做了个深感触动的表情，意大利式的表情放在德国—爱尔兰血统的脸孔上，显得非常别扭。"古董银器，很珍贵。年轻人卖了它至少能得一千块。参议员花了不少精力找这件恰到好处的礼物。对那种人来说，这比具体值多少钱重要得多。"

唐·柯里昂没有掩饰他的得意，参议员这种大人物也得如此尊重他。参议员和卢卡·布拉齐一样，也是唐的权力大厦的栋梁之一，也用礼物再次表达了忠心。

约翰尼·方坦一出现在花园里，凯·亚当斯就认出了他。她这次是真的吃惊了。"你没说你们家和约翰尼·方坦有交情，"她说，"现在我非得嫁给你了。"

"想会会他吗？"迈克尔问。

"现在就算了，"凯叹了口气，"我爱了他足足三年。只要他在大都会剧院开演唱会我就来纽约，尖叫得脑袋要爆炸。他实在无与伦比。"

"我们等会儿去找他。"迈克尔说。

约翰尼唱完歌，和唐·柯里昂一起钻进屋子，凯狡黠地说："你不是想说约翰尼·

方坦这样的大明星也要求你父亲帮忙吧?"

"他是我父亲的教子,"迈克尔说,"要不是我父亲,他今天也成不了大明星。"

凯·亚当斯笑得很开心:"听起来像是又一个了不起的故事。"

迈克尔摇摇头,说:"但我不能说。"

"你可以信任我。"她说。

他告诉了她,语气不像是在开玩笑,也没有任何自豪。他没有多加解释,只说八年前,他父亲比现在暴躁,事情和教子有关,所以唐就觉得牵涉到了个人荣誉。

前因后果说得很快。八年前,约翰尼·方坦和一个流行乐队合唱,大获成功。他成了电台节目里最吸引听众的明星。倒霉的是,乐队领班莱斯·哈雷,很有名气的演艺圈大人物,刚开始就和约翰尼签了长达五年的合作契约。这在演艺行业很常见。莱斯·哈雷凭合同转租约翰尼,大部分钞票进了他的腰包。

唐·柯里昂亲自参加磋商。他提出用两万块买断约翰尼·方坦签署的服务合约。哈雷提出他只分走约翰尼收入的五成。唐·柯里昂觉得很好玩,把两万块降到一万。乐队领班显然对他钟爱的演艺事业之外的世界一窍不通,彻底忽视了降价背后的真实意思。他一口回绝。

第二天,唐·柯里昂亲自去见乐队领班。他带了两个他最好的朋友,一个是顾问占科·阿班丹多,另一个是卢卡·布拉齐。见到没有旁人在场,唐·柯里昂硬是说服莱斯·哈雷签字放弃他持有的约翰尼·方坦的全部权利,代价是一张面额一万美元的保付支票。唐·柯里昂的说服手段是用手枪顶着乐队领班的脑门,拿出最严肃的态度让领班相信,一分钟内要么签字,要么脑浆洒满这份文件。莱斯·哈雷签了字。唐·柯里昂收起枪,把保付支票递给领班。

后来的事情大家都知道。约翰尼·方坦一路向上,成为全国最走红的歌手。他出演好莱坞音乐片,制片公司挣得盆满钵满。唱片赚的钞票以百万计算。随后,他和青梅竹马的妻子离婚,抛弃两个孩子,娶了电影界最灿烂的金发女星。他很快发现那女人是个"婊子"。他酗酒赌博,追逐其他女人。他的歌喉出了毛病。唱片销量下滑。电影公司不肯续约。现在只好回来找教父。

凯若有所思地说:"你确定你不羡慕你父亲吗?听你说的,他尽在为别人办好事了。他肯定是天生的热心肠。"她坏笑道,"当然啦,手段不完全遵纪守法。"

迈克尔叹了口气:"听起来确实是这么一回事,但请让我换个说法。知道极地探险家在通往北极的路上要沿途存放口粮,防止日后某天会需要食物吗?那就是我父亲的人情。他迟早会找上门,而他们最好按他说的做。"

临近黄昏,婚礼蛋糕终于推了出来,人们赞叹欣赏,分而食之。蛋糕是纳佐里尼特别烘焙的,巧妙地点缀着贝壳形状的成块奶油,美味可口,新娘贪婪地从蛋糕上挑了好几个吃掉,然后一阵风地离开,去和金发新郎去度蜜月了。唐彬彬有礼地催促宾客离开,同时注意到调查局探员的黑色轿车已经无影无踪。

最后,车道上只剩下了黑色的长车身凯迪拉克,弗雷迪坐在司机座位上。唐坐进前排,就他的年纪和庞大体型而言,动作颇为灵巧。桑尼、迈克尔和约翰尼·方坦坐进后排。唐·柯里昂对迈克尔说:"你的女朋友,她自己回市里没问题吧?"

迈克尔点点头:"汤姆说他会安排好的。"唐·柯里昂点点头,黑根的效率让他很满意。

燃油配给定量尚未取消,因此去曼哈顿的外环公园大道车流稀少。不到一个钟头,凯迪拉克就驶上了法兰西医院所在的街道。唐·柯里昂在路上问小儿子学业如何。迈克尔点头说不错。桑尼从后座问父亲:"约翰尼说你在帮他处理好莱坞的事情,要我过去帮忙吗?"

唐·柯里昂直截了当:"汤姆今晚过去。他不需要帮忙,事情很简单。"

桑尼·柯里昂笑道:"约翰尼觉得你搞不定,所以我想你会派我去。"

唐·柯里昂扭头道:"你为什么质疑我?"他问约翰尼·方坦:"你的教父曾经失信过吗? 我被人愚弄过吗?"

约翰尼紧张不安地道歉:"教父,幕后主使是个真正的炮筒子。油盐不进,连花钱都没用。他手眼通天,而且恨我。我实在想不出你还能怎么处理。"

唐用带着情谊的好笑语气说:"听我一句话:你能如愿以偿。"他用胳膊肘捅捅迈克尔。"我们可不能让我的教子失望,你说呢,迈克尔?"

迈克尔从来没有怀疑过父亲哪怕一秒钟,他摇摇头。

他们走向医院大门,唐·柯里昂拉住迈克尔的胳膊,让其他人先走。"等你念完大学,来找我谈谈,"唐说,"我有些计划,你会喜欢的。"

迈克尔没有说话。唐·柯里昂气咻咻地嘟囔道:"我知道你是什么人。我不会强迫你做你不赞成的事情。不过这次比较特殊。你现在尽管过你的日子,反正你已经成年了。但等你念完大学,请以儿子的身份来见我。"

占科·阿班丹多的家人是妻子和三个女儿,她们身穿黑衣,像一群胖乌鸦似的聚在医院的白色瓷砖走廊里,见到唐·柯里昂走出电梯,马上扑腾着离开瓷砖地面,被本能驱使着飞向他寻求保护。矮壮的母亲身穿黑衣显得挺庄重,肥胖的女儿则不太起眼。阿班丹多太太亲吻唐·柯里昂的面颊,啜泣着说:"噢,您是什么样的圣人啊,在女儿结婚的日子来这儿。"

唐·柯里昂一挥手扫开感谢之词。"我难道不该来向这么一位朋友表示敬意吗?

他担任我的右臂足有二十年啊。"他立刻醒悟过来,这位即将成为寡妇的女人,并不知道她的丈夫已经挺不过今夜了。占科·阿班丹多在医院住了将近一年,因为癌症渐渐死去,妻子已经觉得致命的疾病只是普通生活的一部分,今夜只是又一个难关罢了。她叽里咕噜讲个没完。"进去见见我可怜的丈夫吧,"她说,"他问起你来着。可怜的男人,他想去参加婚礼,表示敬意,但医生怎么都不许。他随后说你会在这个大喜之日来看他,但我怎么都不肯相信。唉,男人比女人更理解友谊。快进去吧,他见到你一定会很高兴。"

一名护士和一位医生走出占科·阿班丹多的私人病房。医生年纪很轻,表情严肃,天生发号施令的气度,也就是天生豪门巨富的风度。一个女儿怯生生地问:"肯尼迪医生,我们能进去看看他吗?"

肯尼迪医生恼怒地望着这一大群人。他们难道不明白房间里的病人正在承受痛苦的折磨,正在等死?要是大家能让他安安静静地辞世,对他反而比较幸运。"只能是直系亲属。"他用优雅而礼貌的语气说。他吃了一惊,因为妻子和三个女儿扭头望向一位身穿很不合身的燕尾服的矮胖男人,像是在等他决定。

矮胖的男人开口说话,声音里略微有一丝意大利口音。"亲爱的医生,"唐·柯里昂问,"他真的快死了吗?"

"对。"肯尼迪医生说。

"那你就没什么可做的了,"唐·柯里昂说,"把重任交给我们吧。我们会安慰他,帮他合眼。我们会埋葬他,在葬礼上流泪,之后照顾他的妻子和女儿。"听他把话说得这么直截了当,逼着她理解事态,阿班丹多太太哭了起来。

肯尼迪医生耸耸肩。你不可能向这些乡巴佬解释什么。另外一方面,他也注意到了对方言辞中自然而然的正当性。他的角色已经结束。他仍旧优雅而礼貌地说:"请等护士放你们进去,她还有些必要的事情要帮患者做。"他顺着走廊从他们身边走开,白大褂在身后翻飞。

护士重新走进病房,他们耐心等待。护士终于又出来,拉开门放他们进去。她悄声说:"疼痛和高烧害得他神志不清,尽量别惊动他。你们只能待几分钟,妻子可以留下。"约翰尼·方坦走过的时候,护士认出了他,猛地瞪大眼睛。他对护士浅浅一笑,护士用不加掩饰的挑逗眼神盯着他。他把护士归入以后可以考虑的类别,然后跟着其他人走进病房。

占科·阿班丹多和死神跑了一场马拉松,此刻终于被征服,他筋疲力尽地躺在抬高的床上。肉体消耗得只剩下一具骷髅,曾经生机勃勃的浓密黑发如今是脏兮兮的几缕细毛。唐·柯里昂兴高采烈地说:"占科,亲爱的朋友,我带几个儿子来向你致意了,还有啊,你看,连约翰尼都从好莱坞赶回来了。"

垂死的男人睁开烧红了的眼睛,感激地望着唐。他让几个年轻男人用血肉丰满的手握他瘦骨嶙峋的手。妻子和女儿在床边一字排开,亲吻他的面颊,轮流握他的另一只手。

唐握住老朋友的手,安慰道:"赶紧好起来,我们一起回意大利,去我们原来的村子,像父亲当年那样在酒馆门前玩地滚球。"

垂死的男人摇摇头。他示意年轻男人和家人从床边走开,抬起另一只瘦骨嶙峋的手,紧紧抓住唐。他想说话。唐垂下脑袋,坐进床边的椅子。占科·阿班丹多乱七八糟说着他们的童年。接着,他炭黑色的眼睛变得狡猾起来。他轻声说话,唐凑得更近。唐·柯里昂使劲摇头,眼泪滚滚而下,这一幕震惊了房间里的其他人。颤抖的声音越来越响,充满整个房间。饱受折磨的阿班丹多用超人的力量从枕头上抬起脑袋,眼神发直,抬起骷髅般的食指对着唐。"教父,教父啊,"他拼命高喊,"救救我,别让我死,我求你了。我的血肉要从骨头上烧掉了,我感觉虫子在吃我的脑浆。教父啊,医治我,你有力量,擦干我可怜妻子的眼泪。小时候我们在柯里昂村一起玩耍,现在怎能让我死去?我有罪,我害怕下地狱!"

唐默不作声。阿班丹多说:"今天是你女儿结婚的日子,你不能拒绝我啊。"

唐的声音沉静而郑重,穿透他亵渎神灵的胡言乱语。"老朋友啊,"他说,"我没有这种力量。要是有,我肯定比上帝更加仁慈,你要相信我。但是,我不畏惧死亡,不畏惧地狱。我将每晚每早为你的灵魂望弥撒。你的妻子和女儿也会为你祈祷。有这么多人求情,上帝怎么会惩罚你呢?"

骷髅般的脸露出奸诈得让人厌恶的表情,阿班丹多狡猾地说:"这么说,你都安排好了?"

唐冰冷的声音毫无安慰之意:"别亵渎神灵,你要认命。"

阿班丹多倒回枕头上,眼睛失去了狂野的希望之光。护士回到病房里,用严肃的职业态度驱赶大家出去。唐站起身,但阿班丹多伸出手。"教父,"他说,"留下陪我,帮我面对死神。他见到你在我身边,说不定会被吓跑,让我过得安稳。说不定你可以说点什么,拉拉关系,对吧?"垂死的男人使个眼色,像是在嘲讽唐,但并不特别认真。"再怎么说,你和死神都是亲兄弟嘛。"他像是害怕唐被触怒,连忙攥紧唐的手,"留下陪我,让我握着你的手。我们智取那个混蛋,就像我们智取其他人一样。教父啊,你不要出卖我。"

唐示意别人出去。众人离开。他用两只大手握住占科·阿班丹多枯瘦的手爪,温柔而笃定地安慰老朋友,一起等待死神。就仿佛唐真能从全人类最凶残的叛徒手上夺回占科·阿班丹多的生命。

康妮·柯里昂的大喜之日结束得很不错。新娘的手包里加起来一共收了两万块礼金,驱使卡洛·里齐以高超的技巧和旺盛的精力履行了新郎的职责。新娘十分愿意放弃贞操,却不愿意松开钱包。他不得不送她一个黑眼圈才得到后者。

露西·曼奇尼在家里等桑尼·柯里昂的电话,满心以为他会打来约她。最后,她打电话到他家,听见接电话的是个女人,连忙挂断。她不可能知道,几乎所有参加婚礼的人都注意到她和桑尼离席,过了要命的半小时才出现,已经有流言说桑蒂诺·柯里昂又找到一个玩弄对象,说他"办了"自己妹妹的伴娘。

亚美利哥·邦纳塞拉做了个可怕的噩梦。他梦见唐·柯里昂头顶军官帽,身穿工装裤,手戴厚手套,把一具浑身弹孔的尸体丢在殡仪馆门口,喊道:"记住,亚美利哥,一个字也别透露,尽快埋了尸体。"他在梦中呻吟得既响又久,最后被老婆摇醒。"唉,你怎么回事呀?"她抱怨道,"刚从婚礼上回来就做噩梦。"

保利·加图和克莱门扎送凯·亚当斯回她在纽约市的酒店。车很宽敞,装饰豪华,由加图驾驶。克莱门扎坐在后排,让出前排座位给凯。她觉得这两个人都充满了奇异的魅力,交谈用的是电影里的布鲁克林腔调,待她彬彬有礼得夸张。她和两个男人天南海北聊了一路,惊讶地发现他们提起迈克尔都带着深厚的情谊和尊敬,而迈克尔总让她以为他和他父亲的那个世界格格不入。克莱门扎用带着气音的低沉嗓门向她保证,"老头子"认为迈克尔是三个儿子里最优秀的,家业肯定会交给他继承。

"什么样的家业?"凯用最随便的语气问。

保利·加图转动方向盘,飞快地瞥她一眼。克莱门扎在她背后惊讶地说:"迈克没跟你说过?柯里昂先生是全美国最大的意大利橄榄油进口商。战争已经结束,这门生意保准能发大财。他很需要迈克这样的精明孩子。"

来到酒店,克莱门扎坚持送她到前台。她出言反对,克莱门扎却只是说:"老板说要保证送你到家。我非得做到才行。"

她拿到房间钥匙,克莱门扎陪她走到电梯口,一直送她进电梯。她朝克莱门扎挥手微笑,惊讶地见到他回礼的笑容是那么真诚,只可惜她没有见到他走回前台,问:"她登记的名字是什么?"

前台服务员冷冷地看着克莱门扎。克莱门扎将攥在手里的绿纸小球滚过台面,服务员一把抓起,马上答道:"迈克尔·柯里昂先生和夫人。"

回到车里,保利·加图说:"这小妞真不错。"

克莱门扎嘟囔道:"迈克已经和她睡过了。"除非,他心想,他们真的已经结婚了。"明天一大早来接我,"他对保利·加图说,"黑根有事情交给我们,得尽快解决。"

星期六深夜，汤姆·黑根吻别妻子，驱车赶往机场。他的首批登机特权（五角大楼一位参谋长的谢礼）帮助他不费吹灰之力就上了一架前往洛杉矶的飞机。

对汤姆·黑根来说，今天忙碌但充实。占科·阿班丹多凌晨三点咽气，唐·柯里昂从医院回来，通知黑根说他现在是家族的正式顾问了。黑根将变得非常有钱，权势就不消说了。

唐打破了长久以来的传统。顾问一直都是正统的西西里人，黑根由唐的家庭抚养长大也无法改变这个传统。问题的关键是血统。只有西西里出生的人才天生认同缄默规则——拒绝作证，保持沉默的规则，才能获得信任，坐上顾问这个重要位置。在下达命令的家族首领唐·柯里昂和执行命令的人之间还有三层组织，说是缓冲也行。这样的话，底下无论出什么事情都没法追查到上面。除非顾问叛变。星期天上午，唐·柯里昂对如何处理那两个殴打亚美利哥·邦纳塞拉女儿的年轻人，下达了明确的指示，但命令是关起门下达给汤姆·黑根的。当天晚些时候，黑根同样私下里向克莱门扎下达命令，当时也没有其他人在场。反过来，克莱门扎吩咐保利·加图执行任务。保利·加图召集人手，执行命令。保利·加图和他的人不知道任务的起因，也不知道最初是谁下达了命令。要把唐卷进去，链条上的每一环都必须背叛，尽管这种事尚无先例，但并非完全不可能。预防之道众所周知：让链条上的某个环节消失。

顾问，顾名思义，是唐的参谋，是唐的右手，是他的第二个大脑。他还是唐最亲密的伙伴和朋友。出门开重要会议，他给唐开车；谈判的时候，他为唐准备饮料、咖啡、三明治和新雪茄。他知道唐知道的所有（或者几乎所有）事情，了解权力的全部结构。全世界只有他能搞垮唐，但从来没有顾问背叛过唐，在美国站稳脚跟的任何一个西西里家族里都没有过，因为那么做没有前途。每个顾问都知道，只要保持忠诚就能发财，就能获得权势和尊敬。要是遭遇不幸，老婆和孩子会受到庇护，和他活着或自由时没有两样。但前提是他必须忠诚。

碰到某些情况，顾问必须以更加公开的方式代替唐露面，但又不能牵连首脑。黑根飞往加州要办的就是这种事情。他明白这次任务的成败将严重影响他的顾问生涯。约翰尼·方坦能不能拿到战争电影里他渴求的角色，就家族生意的标准而言只是小事一桩，黑根安排在下个星期五和维吉尔·索洛佐的会面更加重要。可是，黑根知道，对于唐来说，两件事同样重要，都关系到他这个顾问称不称职。

活塞引擎的飞机抖得厉害，汤姆·黑根本已紧绷的神经更加紧张，他向空姐要了一杯马丁尼安抚情绪。唐和约翰尼都和他大致说过那部电影的制片人杰克·沃尔茨是个什么角色。听约翰尼说完，黑根知道他不可能口头说服沃尔茨，同时也确信唐无论如何都要守住他对约翰尼的承诺。他的责任就是协商和联络。

黑根往后一躺，在脑子里过一遍手头的全部资料。杰克·沃尔茨是好莱坞最顶尖的三大制作人之一，拥有自己的电影公司，手头有几十个明星的合约。他是总统的战争情报咨询委员会电影业分会的成员，简而言之就是他协助拍摄战争宣传片。他去白宫赴宴，在好莱坞的家中招待埃德加·胡佛。不过，名头只是听起来很响亮而已。这些都是官方的联系，沃尔茨本人没有政治影响力，部分因为他是极端保守派，部分因为他妄自尊大，喜欢滥用权力，不曾想过这样做反而会让敌人如雨后春笋般冒出地面。

黑根叹了口气，实在找不到办法"解决"杰克·沃尔茨。他打开手提箱，想处理些什么文书，但他太累了。他又要了杯马丁尼，开始反思人生。他完全不后悔，只觉得自己幸运极了。原因暂且不论，事实证明十年前他选择了一条正确的道路。他事业成功，他很快乐——一个成年人的合理期望不过如此了，而且他活得很有意思。

汤姆·黑根今年三十五，高个子，平头，身材细瘦，长相普通。他是律师，尽管通过执业考试后从事过三年法律工作，但并不为柯里昂家族处理具体的法律事务。

十一岁的时候，他是十七岁的桑尼·柯里昂的玩伴。黑根的母亲瞎了眼睛，在他十一岁那年过世之后，一向酗酒的父亲更成了毫无指望的醉鬼。父亲是个勤勉的木匠，一辈子没做过亏心事，结果被喝酒毁了家庭，最终害他丧命。汤姆·黑根变成孤儿，流落街头，晚上睡在楼门口。妹妹被别人收养，但在 1920 年代，社会机构不会追查一个不知感恩、逃离他们庇护的十一岁男孩。黑根也有一只眼睛被感染，左邻右舍风传是他母亲传染或遗传的，和他接触也会被传染。众人都躲着他。十七岁的桑尼·柯里昂心肠很好，态度专横地要求收留他带回家的朋友。汤姆·黑根得到一盘热腾腾的意大利面，浇着油腻腻的番茄酱汁，那味道他到现在还忘不了，接着他睡在了家里的一张折叠铁床上。

唐·柯里昂什么话都没说，也没进行任何讨论，理所当然地允许这个孩子留在家里。他亲自带黑根见眼科医生，治疗他的眼部感染。他送黑根上大学和法学院。唐从未以父亲自居，而是像一名监护人。他从不表露感情，但奇怪的是，唐对黑根比对自家儿子更加客气，不强加父辈的意愿给他。大学毕业后去念法学院是他自己的决定，因为他曾听见唐·柯里昂说"律师拎着公文包，偷的钱比一百个人带着枪还要多"。另外一方面，桑尼和弗雷迪高中一毕业就坚持要加入家族生意，反而让他们的父亲恼怒不已。只有迈克尔去念了大学，但珍珠港事件后第二天就报名加入海军陆战队。

通过执业考试后，黑根结婚成家。新娘是个新泽西的意大利姑娘，大学毕业，这在当时还很罕见。婚礼自然还是在唐·柯里昂的家里举行，婚礼过后，唐答应支持黑根愿意建立的任何事业，给他介绍要打官司的客户，装修办公室，帮他置业。

而汤姆·黑根却垂下头，对唐说："我愿意为您做事。"

唐惊喜地问:"你知道我是什么人吗?"

黑根点点头。他并不真的知道唐到底有多少权势,当时还不知道。接下来的十年,他仍旧没有完全了解,直到占科·阿班丹多生病,他开始担任代理顾问。当时他只是使劲点头,盯着唐的双眼。"我愿意像你的儿子那样为你做事。"黑根说,言下之意是彻底忠诚,彻底接受唐的父辈权威。唐理解了黑根的意愿,在那时已经开始造就他的伟大传奇,也第一次对黑根流露出父亲的情谊。他搂住黑根,飞快地拥抱一下,从此待他就像亲生儿子,但他还是经常说,"汤姆,千万别忘了亲生父母。"就仿佛他不但要提醒黑根,也在提醒自己。

黑根绝对不可能忘记。他母亲近乎痴呆,邋里邋遢,严重贫血使得她对孩子毫无感情,连装也装不出来。黑根憎恶父亲。母亲死前的瞎眼吓坏了他,自己眼部感染就像一抹厄运的阴云。他确信自己会变瞎。父亲死后,汤姆·黑根十一岁的心智崩溃了,没人知道是怎么回事。他游荡街头,像动物等死,直到那个命运之日,桑尼发现他睡在楼门口,带他回家。接下来发生的完全是奇迹。可是,黑根做了很多年噩梦,梦见他是个成年瞎子,用白色拐杖咯咯嗒嗒探路,他瞎眼的孩子跟在背后,用白色小拐杖咯咯嗒嗒探路,他们在街上乞讨。有些早晨,他醒过来,唐·柯里昂的面容跳进刚刚恢复意识的大脑,他终于觉得安全了。

唐坚持要他除了履行对家族生意的职责外,先实践三年一般性法律事务。这段经历后来证明是无价之宝,同时打消了黑根为唐·柯里昂做事的残存疑虑。接下来,他进入一家唐能施加影响力的顶级刑事法律事务所,受训两年。大家公认他对法律的这个分支很有天赋。他做得不错,全身心效劳家族生意之后的六年里,唐·柯里昂硬是找不到一次斥责他的机会。

他开始担任代理顾问之后,其他有权势的西西里家族轻蔑地称柯里昂家族是"爱尔兰帮"。这让黑根觉得很好笑,同时也提醒他,他不可能接替唐,担任家族生意的领袖。但他很知足。那本来就不是他的目标,这种野心无论对他的恩人还是恩人的血亲都是极大的"不尊重"。

飞机在洛杉矶降落,天还没亮。黑根住进酒店,沐浴刮脸,望着城市渐渐破晓。他叫服务生把早餐和报纸送进房间,然后躺下休息,等待十点钟和杰克·沃尔茨碰面。预约出乎意料地顺利。

前一天,黑根打电话给一个叫比利·高夫的人,他在各种电影工会里拥有无上权威。黑根遵照唐·柯里昂的指示,请高夫帮忙安排明天黑根登门拜访沃尔茨,这同时是在暗示沃尔茨,要是会面的结果不能让黑根满意,电影公司就有可能爆发罢工。一小时后,黑根接到高夫的电话。会面约在上午十点。高夫说,沃尔茨明白有可能爆发罢工,但似乎并不在乎。他还说,"事情要是真的发展到那一步,我得先和唐本人谈谈才行。"

"要是真的发展到那一步,他一定会找你谈的。"黑根说,这样回答避免了作出任何承诺。高夫对唐如此百依百顺,黑根并不惊讶。从理论上说,家族的帝国仅限于纽约地区,但唐·柯里昂最初就是靠帮助工会领袖起家的,他们有很多人还欠他的人情债。

但约在十点钟可不是好兆头。说明他是见客名单上的第一位,说明对方不会请他共进午餐,说明沃尔茨没把他当回事。高夫并没有全力施压,说不定他已经上了沃尔茨的贿赂名单。唐远离聚光灯的做法对家族生意有时候也是不利条件,因为他的名字出了这个圈子就无人知晓。

事实证明他分析得很正确。沃尔茨让他在约定时间之外多等了半个钟头。黑根并不在乎。接待室非常奢华,相当舒适,对面的暗紫色沙发上坐着一个女孩,黑根这辈子都没见过这么漂亮的孩子。她顶多十一二岁,服饰昂贵而简洁,打扮得像个成年人。她长着一头美得超凡脱俗的金发,有深海蓝色的大眼睛和新鲜树莓颜色的红嘴唇。守在旁边的显然是她母亲,企图用冰冷的傲慢气势瞪得黑根屈服,反而让黑根很想一拳打在她脸上。天使般的孩子,恶龙般的母亲,黑根心想,同时毫不示弱地还以冷眼。

终于有个衣着优雅但身材矮胖的中年女人出来,领着黑根穿过一间又一间办公室,来到电影制片人的办公套间。办公室和办公室里的员工都很美丽,黑根不由赞叹。他微微一笑。这些精明孩子,以为在办公室打工就能涉足电影业,但其中绝大多数一辈子都是坐办公室的命,最终要么接受失败,要么返回家乡。

杰克·沃尔茨身量很高,体格粗壮,衣服剪裁得煞费苦心,差不多遮住了肥硕的肚皮。黑根知道他的来历。沃尔茨十岁就在西区搬运空啤酒桶和手推车,二十岁帮助父亲奴役制衣工人,三十岁离开纽约,搬到西海岸,投资五分戏院,开拓影业市场。四十八岁,他成了好莱坞最有权势的影业巨头,但仍旧口无遮拦,好色如命,像野狼一样追逐年轻女明星。五十岁,他改头换面,学习演讲,由英国男仆教他穿衣打扮,英国管家教他社交礼仪。第一任妻子过世,他娶了个不喜欢演电影的世界闻名的美丽女明星。今年他六十岁,搜集大师古画,是总统咨询委员会的成员,名义下有价值数百万美元的基金会,鼓励电影业的艺术创新。女儿嫁给一位英国勋爵,儿子娶了一名意大利公主。

根据全国电影专栏尽心尽力的报道,他最近的爱好是他名下的几个赛马训练场,仅过去一年就投入了上千万美元。他以六十万美元天价购入英国明星赛马"喀土穆",宣布这匹百战百胜的赛马即将荣休,担任种马,专门为沃尔茨的马厩繁育后代。

沃尔茨彬彬有礼地接待黑根,他那张脸晒成均匀而漂亮的古铜色,须发经过精心修剪,他随便歪了歪嘴,算是微笑打招呼。尽管花了那么多钱,尽管有技艺最高超的技师帮他收拾,但年龄毕竟还是摆在那儿;脸上的肌肉像是被勉强缝在一起的。不过,他的言行举止还是拥有勃然活力,这点和唐·柯里昂相同,也就是一个人对他所生活的世界拥有生杀大权的那种气度。

黑根开门见山,说他是约翰尼·方坦的一位朋友的传话人,说这位朋友很有权势,若是沃尔茨先生愿意帮个小忙,那么他保证会感激不尽,并愿意奉上一辈子的友谊。这个小忙呢,就是允许约翰尼·方坦主演贵公司下周开拍的那部战争电影。

那张勉强缝起来的脸不动声色,沃尔茨很有礼貌地说:"你那位朋友能帮我什么忙呢?"他的声音里有一丝掩不住的高傲。

黑根无视他的傲慢,解释道:"你会遇到一些劳工方面的麻烦。那位朋友百分之百能消除这个麻烦。你有个给公司挣了许多钱的头牌男星,癖好最近从大麻转到了海洛因。那位朋友能保证这个男星再也搞不到海洛因。今后要是再遇到这种小事情,打个电话就能解决你的问题。"

杰克·沃尔茨像听小孩吹牛似的听他说,最后存心换上东城口音,粗声粗气地说:"你在威胁我?"

黑根冷静答道:"绝对不是。我受朋友之托求你办事。我想说的重点是,这么做对你没有任何坏处。"

沃尔茨像是早有准备,忽然换上一脸怒容。嘴唇卷曲,染成黑色的浓眉皱成一条粗线,盖住闪闪发亮的眼睛。他俯身探过桌子对黑根说:"够了,油腔滑调的混蛋,我跟你和你的老板直说,我才不在乎他是谁。约翰尼·方坦绝对不可能主演那部电影。我不在乎有多少个黑皮黑手党大佬会从暗处钻出来。"他坐回去,"听我一句劝。埃德加·胡佛,知道这个名字吧——"沃尔茨哂笑道,"和我有私交。要是我告诉他有人逼我,你们死都不知道怎么死的。"

黑根耐心地听着。他高估了沃尔茨。这么愚蠢的人可能管理一家价值几百万美元的公司吗?这事值得思考一下,因为唐正在寻找新的投资机会。要是电影业的头目都这么低能,这个领域倒是挺适合。侮辱对他毫无影响。黑根的谈判技巧是唐亲自传授的。"永远不要动怒,"唐这么教导他,"决不要威胁,要讲道理。"用意大利语说"讲道理"听上去像"应对"。关键是忽视所有的侮辱和威胁,一边脸挨了打,就把另一边脸也凑上去。黑根曾经目睹唐在谈判桌边一坐就是八个小时,唾面自干,试图劝说一个臭名昭著、妄自尊大的暴徒别那么飞扬跋扈。八小时过后,唐·柯里昂扬起双手,打个绝望的手势,对谈判桌边的其他人说:"谁也没法和这家伙讲道理。"然后大踏步走出会议室。暴徒吓得脸色发白,连忙派手下请唐回会议室。各方达成谅解,但两个月后,那个暴徒在他最喜欢的理发店被乱枪打死。

于是,黑根重新开始,语气平常。"请看我的名片,"他说,"我是律师。难道我会自寻死路吗?我威胁你了吗?只要能让约翰尼·方坦主演那部电影,要求随便你提。我们为这个小忙提出了丰厚的回报。就我所知,这个忙对你只有好处。约翰尼说你承认他是完美的人选。正是因为这样我们才请你帮忙。如果你担心你的投资,我的客户愿意出资赞助这部电影。我们明白你说一不二。谁也不能强迫你,也不会强迫你。我们知道你和胡佛先生有私交,请允许我补充一句,我的老板因此很尊敬你。他非常尊敬这份关系。"

沃尔茨刚才一直拿着一杆大号红色羽毛笔胡写乱画,听见提到钱,忽然来了劲头,放下羽毛笔。他神气活现地说:"这部电影的预算是五百万。"

黑根轻轻吹声口哨,表示惊叹,然后漫不经心地说:"我老板的很多朋友都信任他的判断。"

沃尔茨第一次认真起来。他打量着黑根的名片。"我没听说过你,"他说,"我认识纽约大部分有头面的律师,你他妈到底是谁?"

"我在高级律师事务所执业,"黑根干巴巴地说,"只负责一个客户。"他站起身,"我就不耽搁你的时间了。"他伸出手,沃尔茨和他握手。黑根朝房门走了几步,然后又转身面对沃尔茨,"我明白你经常和一些自以为了不起的人打交道。但我恰恰相反。你不妨通过我们共同的朋友查证。要是愿意考虑,就打电话到我的酒店。"他顿了顿,"恕我无礼,有些事情,连胡佛先生都觉得无能为力,但我的客户做得到。"他见到电影制片人眯起双眼。沃尔茨终于明白了意思。"顺便说一句,我非常欣赏你的电影,"黑根用他最奉承的语气说,"希望你能再接再厉,我们的国家需要好电影。"

当天下午晚些时候,黑根接到制片人秘书的电话,说一小时内有车接他去沃尔茨先生在郊区的宅子吃晚饭。她说行程有三小时,但车上有酒吧和开胃点心。黑根知道沃尔茨是搭私人飞机去的,心想为什么不请他也飞过去。秘书又彬彬有礼地说:"沃尔茨先生建议你带上过夜行李,明天早晨送你去机场。"

"知道了。"黑根说。又是一个需要考虑的问题。沃尔茨怎么知道他打算明早飞回纽约?他想了几分钟。最合理的解释是沃尔茨请私家侦探调查他的行踪,尽可能搜集情报。这么说,沃尔茨肯定知道他代表的是唐,说明他对唐有几分了解,反过来说明他打算认真对待这整件事。说不定真有可能奏效,黑根心想,说不定沃尔茨比他今天上午的表现来得精明。

杰克·沃尔茨的家宅像是以假乱真的电影布景,有种植园风格的大屋,黑土马道围绕广阔的花园,有供马群起居的马厩和草场。树篱、花床和草坪经过仔细修剪,整齐得像是电影明星的指甲。

沃尔茨在有空调的玻璃门廊接待黑根。他身穿便装,蓝色丝绸衬衫敞开领口,芥末黄的便裤配软皮凉鞋。在鲜艳华服的衬托之下,那张缝起来的硬汉脸更加恐怖。他递给黑根一杯特大号马丁尼,自己也从托盘上拿起一杯。他比今天上午友善多了。他搂住黑根的肩膀说:"晚餐前还有一点时间,我们去看看我的马匹吧。"两人走向马厩,他说:"我摸了你的底细,汤姆,你怎么不说你的老板是柯里昂啊?我还以为你是约翰尼请来吓唬我的三流骗子呢。我可从来不吓唬人。倒不是说我喜欢树敌,我只是不吃这一套而已。我们现在先开心开心,吃过晚餐再谈生意。"

说来令人惊讶,沃尔茨居然很懂得款待宾客。他解释他的新方法和创新措施,希望能打造出全国最成功的马厩。马厩彻底防火,有最高等级的卫生设施,由私家侦探组成的特别保安队伍看守。最后,沃尔茨领着他走向一个隔间,外墙上镶着好大一块黄铜标牌。标牌上的名字是"喀土穆"。

黑根以外行人的眼睛都看得出隔间里的马有多美丽。喀土穆毛色漆黑,唯独宽阔的额头有一块钻石形状的白斑。棕色大眼闪着金苹果的光芒,绷紧肌肉上的黑色皮肤丝绸般柔滑。沃尔茨带着孩童般的自豪说:"全世界的头号赛马。我去年在英国用六十万买的。我打赌连俄国沙皇也没花过这么多钱买一匹马。但我不打算让它上场,我要让它当种马。我要建立起美国历史上最伟大的赛马马厩。"他梳理马的鬃毛,轻轻唤它的名字,"喀土穆,喀土穆。"他的声音里有爱意,马作出回应。沃尔茨对黑根说:"我是天生的骑手,知道吗?第一次上马背都五十岁了。"他哈哈笑道,"也许我的俄国祖母或外祖母被哥萨克骑兵强奸过,我继承了血脉。"他挠着喀土穆的肚皮,钦佩的语气不可能更真挚了,"看它的鸡巴,我真想也有那么一根。"

他们回到正厅吃晚饭。三名侍者在一名管家的指挥下伺候他们,桌布镶着金线,餐具全是银器,可惜黑根发现食物非常普通。沃尔茨显然独居已久,而且不懂得享受美食。等两人都点起粗大的哈瓦那雪茄,黑根才问沃尔茨:"约翰尼能不能拿到那个角色?"

"我没办法,"沃尔茨说,"就算我想,也没法把约翰尼塞进那部电影。演员的合同全都签好了,下周就要开拍。现在我哪儿还有回旋余地?"

黑根不耐烦道:"沃尔茨先生,和大人物打交道有个好处,就是知道这种借口一推就翻。实际上你想做什么就可以做什么。"他抽了一口雪茄,"不相信我的客户能信守承诺?"

沃尔茨干巴巴地说:"我相信我会遇到劳工纠纷。高夫打电话说过了,那个混蛋,听他说话的口气,绝对想不到我每年付他十万黑钱。我相信你能让我那个娘娘腔

'男'明星再也弄不到海洛因。但我不在乎,而且我能为电影提供资金。我恨方坦。告诉你的老板,我没法帮他这个忙,不过别的事情倒是可以考虑。随便什么事情。"

黑根心想,无耻混蛋,既然是这样,为什么让我大老远赶来?他还有别的事。黑根冷冷地说:"我认为你并不理解如今的局面。柯里昂先生是约翰尼·方坦的教父。这是非常亲密、非常神圣的宗教关系。"听见他提到宗教,沃尔茨谦恭地低了低头。黑根继续道,"意大利人有个玩笑话,说世界太残酷,所以一个人非得有两个父亲照看他,这就是教父的由来。约翰尼的父亲已经过世,因此柯里昂先生觉得他的责任更加重大。说到其他的要求,柯里昂先生可是很敏感的。第一个要求被回绝,他绝对不可能求你帮第二个忙。"

沃尔茨耸耸肩:"我很抱歉,可答案仍旧是不行。但既然你来都来了,说个价码吧,我得花多少钱摆平劳工纠纷这档事?现金,马上付。"

这解答了黑根的一个疑问。既然沃尔茨已经决定不把角色给约翰尼了,为什么还要花那么多时间和他周旋?这次会面根本不可能改变他的决定。沃尔茨有恃无恐,他不害怕唐·柯里昂的权势。当然,沃尔茨的政治关系分布全国,和联邦调查局局长也有交情,还有大量的个人财富和电影圈说一不二的权柄,他不觉得唐·柯里昂能构成任何威胁。要任何一个聪明人说,甚至要黑根说,沃尔茨的地位都确实似乎不可动摇。他愿意承受罢工有可能造成的损失,那么唐也就拿他无可奈何了。这种力量权衡没错,但是问题是:唐·柯里昂已经答应了教子,会帮他弄到那个角色,而就黑根所知,在这类事情上,唐·柯里昂决不食言。

黑根平静地说:"你存心歪曲我的意思。你想把我说成是勒索帮凶。柯里昂先生答应为你解决劳工纠纷,这是友情的表现,作为回报你要帮助他的客户。朋友之间交换影响力罢了,没别的意思。但是你并没有拿我当回事。我个人认为你犯了个错。"

沃尔茨像是早就在等这个机会撒泼发火。"我非常明白,"他说,"这是黑手党的风格,不是吗?嘴上说得好听,其实是在威胁。我跟你挑明了吧,约翰尼·方坦的确是完美的人选,那个角色会让他成为大明星,但他就是拿不到,绝对拿不到,因为我恨这个混蛋,我要把他赶出电影圈。听我告诉你原因,他毁了我最值钱的女明星。我培养了她五年,唱歌、跳舞、表演,什么都学了,我砸下去了几十万美元想要把她捧成明星。但你别以为我铁石心肠,眼里只有钱,坦白说,这个姑娘很漂亮,我这辈子从没玩过她那么漂亮的屁股,要知道我可是见识过各种各样的女人。她能像水泵一样榨干你。可是约翰尼出现了,用橄榄油似的嗓子和黑皮的魅力拐走了她。她抛弃了一切,害得我被人嘲笑。我这种地位的人,黑根先生,是不能忍受被耻笑的。我必须让约翰尼偿还我的损失。"

沃尔茨终于第一次让黑根吃了一惊。他觉得难以理解,一个这么富裕的成年人居然会让此等小事影响他对生意的判断,而且还是如此重要的生意。在黑根的世界里,柯里昂家族的世界里,女性的美丽肉体和性魅力对世俗事务毫无重要性可言。只要不涉及婚姻和家族的脸面,这就只是私人事务。黑根决定最后再试一次。

"你说得对极了,沃尔茨先生,"黑根说,"但你至于愤怒到这个地步吗?我觉得你并不理解这个小人情对我的客户有多重要。约翰尼小时候是在柯里昂先生怀里受洗的,他父亲过世后,柯里昂先生担负起了父亲的职责。有很多人称呼他'教父',表达尊敬和谢意,因为他曾经帮助过这些人。柯里昂先生从不让朋友失望。"

沃尔茨突然站起身。"我听够了。从来是我命令匪徒,匪徒哪儿有资格命令我?我要是拿起听筒,你今晚就得在牢里过夜。那位黑手党老大要是敢跟我动粗,他会发现我可不是什么乐队领头。没错,我也知道那个故事。听着,你们柯里昂先生死都不知道怎么死的。别逼我动用我在白宫的关系。"

白痴,愚蠢的杂种。他是怎么成为一把手的?黑根不由心想。总统的顾问,全世界最大的电影公司的老板。唐非得投资电影业不可。这家伙听话只听表面意思,没有理解其中的意义。

"谢谢你招待晚餐,让我度过这么愉快的夜晚,"黑根说,"能安排人送我去机场吗?我想我就不必过夜了。"他冷笑道,"柯里昂先生坚持要在第一时间听见坏消息。"

黑根在大屋那水银灯照射的柱廊上等车,见到两个女人登上等在车道上的加长林肯,正是他在沃尔茨办公室见过的十二岁漂亮金发女孩和女孩的母亲。可现在女孩那线条优雅的嘴唇成了乱七八糟的一团粉红色,海蓝色的双眼目光呆滞,沿着台阶走向打开的车门时,两条长腿像跛马似的蹒跚。母亲搀着女儿,扶她坐进车里,对着女儿的耳朵咬牙切齿地说着什么。母亲扭头鬼鬼祟祟地望向黑根,黑根见到她的眼神燃烧着秃鹫般的凯旋光彩,紧接着她也钻进了车里。

怪不得他没能坐飞机从洛杉矶过来,黑根心想。飞机上坐着母女俩和制片人。这样沃尔茨就有时间在晚餐前休息一下,搞那个小女孩。约翰尼想混的就是这样一个世界?祝他好运,也祝沃尔茨好运。

保利·加图不喜欢速战速决,特别是牵涉到暴力。他喜欢预先详细盘算。比方说今晚的任务,虽说只是揍两个小流氓,但要是有谁出错,就很容易酿成大祸。他一边小口啜饮啤酒,一边左顾右盼,看两个小流氓能不能勾搭上吧台的那两个小烂货。

保利·加图对这两个小流氓了若指掌。一个叫杰瑞·瓦格纳,一个叫凯文·穆南,今年都是二十岁,容貌出众,棕色头发,高个子,好身材。他们两周后要回城外的大学,父亲都有政治影响力,加上大学生的身份,所以躲过了征兵。他们因为侵犯亚美利哥·邦纳塞拉的女儿而被判缓刑。一对人渣,保利·加图心想。逃兵役,违反假释条例,午夜过后还在酒吧喝酒,追逐放荡女人。两个小流氓。保利·加图觉得他本人的缓役是另外一码事,因为医生向征兵委员会提供书面诊断书,证明这名二十六岁的未婚白种男性患者由于精神问题接受过弹震症治疗。加图经过"杀人明誓"的成人礼之后,克莱门扎帮他安排了这件事。

克莱门扎吩咐他这个任务必须在两个小伙子回学校前尽快完成。为什么非得在纽约下手? 加图不由心想。克莱门扎总是提点额外要求,不直接给命令。要是这两个小骚货跟着他们离开,那今晚可就又是白费了。

他听见一个姑娘笑着说:"你疯了吗,杰瑞? 我才不和你上车呢。我不想像某个可怜姑娘一样进医院。"她的声音饱含恶意的满足,倒是遂了加图的心愿。他喝完啤酒,走上黑洞洞的街道。好极了。时间过了午夜。还亮着灯的只有另外一家酒吧。其他店铺都已关门。克莱门扎关照过分局的巡逻车。在接到无线电调度之前,他们不会在附近出没,就算来也会来得很慢。

他靠在四门雪佛兰轿车上。后排虽说坐着两个大块头,但从外面几乎看不清楚。保利说:"他们一出来就动手。"

他还是觉得安排得过于仓促。克莱门扎搞来了两个小流氓的案底照片,还有他们每晚鬼混的酒吧地址。保利在家族内部找了两个打手,把小流氓指给他们。他的指示说得很清楚:不准打头顶和后脑,不能意外弄出人命。除此之外,爱怎么揍就怎么揍。他只提醒了一句:"要是两个小流氓没在医院里住满一个月,你们就回去开卡车。"

两个大块头钻出车门,他们以前是打拳的,但连小俱乐部都没熬出头,桑尼·柯里昂安排他们收高利贷,所以活得还算不赖。他们当然急于表达谢意。

杰瑞·瓦格纳和凯文·穆南走出酒吧,一头撞进陷阱。酒吧女郎的奚落刺痛了少年人的自尊心。保利·加图靠在挡泥板上,大声嘲笑道:"喂,情圣,被女人甩了吧。"

两人转过身,心情不坏。保利·加图一看就很适合拿来发泄屈辱。雪貂脸,矮个子,体格瘦削,而且还自作聪明。他们满怀渴望地扑上来,却立刻被两个男人从背后牢牢地抓住了胳膊。保利·加图趁机把带有十六分之一英寸铁刺的特制铜指套戴上右手。他每周在健身房训练三次,时间抓得很准,一拳镶在小流氓瓦格纳的鼻梁上。抱住瓦格纳的壮汉举起瓦格纳,保利挥动手臂,一记上勾拳不偏不倚正中下体。瓦格纳软瘫下去,大块头将他扔在地上。从头到尾还不到六秒钟。

两人的注意力转向凯文·穆南,他企图喊救命,从背后抱住他的男人伸出一条壮硕的手臂,轻而易举地勒住他,另一只手锁住穆南的喉咙,不让他发出任何声音。

保利·加图钻进车里,发动引擎。两个大块头把穆南揍成一坨果冻,动作不慌不忙得吓人,像是全世界的时间都归他们支配。他们不是慌乱地瞎打一通,而是一板一眼,用上躯体的全部力量,慢镜头似的慢慢收拾他。每一拳下去都带着皮开肉绽的声音。加图瞥了一眼穆南的脸——已经面目全非。两条壮汉撇开躺在人行道上的穆南,转身走向瓦格纳。瓦格纳正在尝试起身,张嘴就喊救命。有人从酒吧里出来,两个打手必须加快节奏了。他们把瓦格纳揍得跪倒在地。一个人抓住他的胳膊,用力一扭,接着一脚踢在他脊梁上。随着"咔嚓"一声,瓦格纳的惨叫声喊得整条街都推开了窗户。两个人下手飞快。一个双手像老虎钳似的夹住瓦格纳的脑袋,拽他起身。另一个挥舞偌大的拳头,猛砸固定的靶子。又有几个人跑出酒吧,但谁也没出头干预。保利·加图喊一声:"够了,快走。"两条大汉跳上车,保利一脚把油门踩到底。就算有人记下车型和牌照也无所谓。车是偷来的,牌照是加州的,纽约市有十万辆黑色雪佛兰轿车。

第二章

星期四早晨,汤姆·黑根走进他在市区的事务所。他打算先处理积欠的文书工作,好在周五和维吉尔·索洛佐会面前准备妥当资料。考虑到这次会面如此重要,他已经请求唐空出一个晚上讨论应对方法,他们知道索洛佐想和家族生做什么生意。黑根希望先处理完所有琐事,然后心无旁骛地参加这次初步的会面。

周二深夜,黑根从加州回来,通报他和沃尔茨的磋商结果,唐似乎并不惊讶。他让黑根仔细描述每个细节,听到小女孩和母亲的事情,他厌恶地皱起眉头,喃喃用令人发指①表达强烈的不满。他最后问了黑根一个问题:"这家伙真的有种吗?"

黑根琢磨着唐这个问题的真实用意。经过这些年,他早已明白唐的价值观和绝大多数人的大相径庭,因此他的话很可能还有其他意思。沃尔茨有性格吗?沃尔茨意志坚强吗?百分之百有。不过这并不是唐想知道的。这位电影制片人有不会被轻易吓住的勇气吗?他能承担电影延期导致的财务损失吗,能承受旗下大明星被曝出吸食海洛因吗?答案仍旧是肯定的。但是,这仍旧不是唐的意思。最后,他在脑海里正确地诠释出了唐的本意。杰克·沃尔茨有卵蛋甘冒失去一切的风险,以维护原则和荣誉吗?仅仅为了复仇?

黑根微微一笑。他很少和唐开玩笑,但这次实在忍不住:"你想问他是不是西西

---

① infanlità:原文意大利语,意为极度恶劣的行径。

里人。"唐愉快地点点头,认可这句奉承人的俏皮话,也表示黑根说得对。"不。"黑根答道。

这个话题到此为止。唐一直思考到第二天。星期三下午,他打电话叫黑根来家里,对他下达指令。黑根把这一天剩下的时间全用在了安排实施上,他对唐佩服得五体投地。毫无疑问,唐解决了问题,沃尔茨今天上午肯定会打电话来,说约翰尼·方坦将担任这部战争新片的男主角。

电话恰好响了,但打来的是亚美利哥·邦纳塞拉。殡仪馆老板感激得声音发颤。他请黑根转告唐,他的友谊至死不变。只需要唐一个电话,他亚美利哥·邦纳塞拉肯为敬爱的教父肝脑涂地。黑根保证一定转告。

《每日新闻》在版面正中间刊登了杰瑞·瓦格纳和凯文·穆南躺在马路上的照片。拍照的是行家里手,画面非常血腥,他们简直成了两堆肉块。报纸说他们还活着就是奇迹,但必须住院数月,还得接受整形手术。黑根要提醒克莱门扎:保利·加图值得关注。他做事似乎挺靠得住。

接下来的三个钟头,黑根高效地为唐的房地产公司、橄榄油进口生意和建筑公司合并收入报表。几家公司现在都不太景气,但战争已经结束,很快就能财源滚滚。他几乎忘了约翰尼·方坦,直到秘书说有加州的电话才想起来。拿起听筒,他颇为兴奋和期待,说:"我是黑根。"

线路那头的声音由于仇恨和激动而走了样。"你这个狗杂种,"沃尔茨扯着嗓子喊道,"我要你们一个个进监狱蹲一百年。我拿全部家产跟你们拼了。我要割了约翰尼·方坦的卵蛋,听见了吗,黑皮杂种?"

黑根友好地说:"我是德国和爱尔兰的血统。"对方沉默良久,"咔嗒"一声挂断电话。黑根露出微笑。沃尔茨一个字也没敢威胁唐·柯里昂本人。这就是唐的天才之处。

杰克·沃尔茨总是单独睡觉。他那张床容得下十个人,卧室足够拍摄电影里的舞厅场景,但自从第一任妻子十年前过世后,他始终单独睡觉。这并不意味着他不再享用女人。他是不年轻了,但他体力充沛,不过现在只有小女孩才能引起他的性欲,而晚上几个小时已经是身体和耐心的极限了。

星期四早晨,他不知为何醒得很早。黎明的光线使得宽敞的卧室影影绰绰,仿佛雾气弥漫的草场。床脚附近有个熟悉的轮廓,沃尔茨挣扎着用手肘撑起半个身子,想看得更清楚一些。那个轮廓属于马匹的头颅。沃尔茨还是看得有些模糊,伸手打开了床头柜上的台灯。

他被眼前的东西震惊得感到了生理上的不适。就仿佛胸口挨了大锤一击,心脏狂跳,阵阵反胃,呕吐物喷溅在厚实的熊皮地毯上。

名马喀土穆那丝绸般柔滑的黑色头颅,从躯体上割了下来,牢牢地粘在厚厚的一摊血迹中央。细长的白色筋腱露在外面,口鼻满是泡沫,曾经闪烁金光的苹果大眼因为死亡和失血,成了两颗斑驳的腐烂水果。纯粹原始的恐惧击倒了沃尔茨,出于恐惧,他大喊仆人,同样出于恐惧,他打电话给黑根,语无伦次地威胁。他的癫狂胡话吓坏了管家,管家打电话给沃尔茨的私人医生和电影公司的二把手。不过,沃尔茨在他们赶到前控制住了情绪。

他深感震惊。什么样的人能随便毁灭一头价值六十万美元的动物? 没有一句警告,不装腔作势,不按理出牌,不留任何余地。这种冷酷无情,这种对一切价值的全然蔑视,意味着这个人只认他自己的法律,甚至把自己视为上帝。这个人还有足够的权势和狡诈来支持他的意愿,马厩的安保力量在他眼中犹如儿戏。到了这个时候,沃尔茨已经得知有人给马下了强效麻醉剂,用斧头不慌不忙砍下硕大的三角形头颅。夜班警卫说没听到任何动静。要沃尔茨说,这不太可能。他们有可能是被逼着这么说的,也有可能被收买了,收买他们的人愿意要他们怎么说,他们就怎么说。

沃尔茨绝不愚蠢,只是极度自大,错误地以为他在自己的世界里比唐·柯里昂更有权力。他仅仅是需要看到与之相反的证据而已。他理解了对方的意思:尽管他很有钱,尽管他和美国总统有关系,尽管声称和联邦调查局局长有私交,一个躲在暗处的意大利橄榄油进口商就能要了他的命。真的可以杀了他! 就因为他不肯给约翰尼·方坦一个他想要的角色。谁有权这么做事? 要是大家都这么做事,世界会变成什么样子啊。太疯狂了。你有钱、有公司、有发号施令的权柄,却不能为所欲为。这种人必须碾碎,这种事决不允许。

沃尔茨请医生给他一剂药效温和的镇静剂,帮助他冷静头脑,理智思考。真正让他震惊的是这个叫柯里昂的家伙居然随随便便就下令毁灭了一匹价值六十万美元的世界名马。六十万美元啊! 只是个开始而已。沃尔茨打个寒战。他回想他已经建立起的好生活。他很有钱,勾勾手指、承诺一份合约就搞得到全世界最漂亮的女人。因为心血来潮就拿所有这些冒险? 那是发疯。他也许能揪出柯里昂,但杀一匹赛马能得到什么刑罚? 他狂笑起来,医生和仆人神情紧张地望着他。另一个想法涌上心头。有人如此公然地蔑视他的权力,他将沦为整个加州的笑柄。想到这里,他作了决定。除此之外,他还有个念头:也许他们不打算杀他,是因为手里还有更狡猾、更可怕的手段。

沃尔茨给了必要的指示,他的亲信班子行动起来。仆人和医生发誓保守秘密,否则就是电影公司和沃尔茨的死敌。透露给媒体的消息是赛马喀土穆在从英国来的路上不幸染病,终告不治。尸体被埋在大宅的一个秘密地点。

六小时后,那部电影的执行制片人打电话给约翰尼·方坦,通知他下周一报到。

那天晚上,黑根来到唐的家里,为明天和维吉尔·索洛佐的重要会面作准备。唐叫来了他的大儿子,桑尼·柯里昂那张浓眉大眼的爱神脸疲惫而憔悴,捧着一杯水小口啜饮。他肯定还在搞那个伴娘。黑根心想。又是一桩烦心事。

唐·柯里昂坐进扶手椅,吸着"高贵"牌雪茄。黑根在办公室存了一盒这种雪茄。他劝过唐改抽哈瓦那,但唐说哈瓦那伤喉咙。

"该知道的情况都搞清楚了吧?"唐问。

黑根打开他存放笔记的文件夹。这些笔记都不牵涉犯罪,只是些暗语一样的提示,以确保他没有遗漏任何重要的细节。"索洛佐找我们是为了求助,"黑根说,"他想请家族投资至少一百万美元,同时寻求法律方面的保护伞。答应这两个条件,我们就能分一杯羹,但具体数字没人知道。塔塔利亚家族为索洛佐作保,他们多半也有一份。生意是毒品。索洛佐在土耳其有关系,把土耳其种植的罂粟运往西西里没有任何问题。他在西西里有加工海洛因的地点,而且还能加工吗啡,如果有需要的话,这也是一种保险。不过他的加工厂似乎十分隐蔽安全。现在的障碍只剩下运进美国和分销。另外就是启动资金。一百万美元可没法从天上掉下来。"黑根见到唐·柯里昂皱起眉头。老头子不喜欢别人在谈论生意的时候乱加不必要的修饰。他连忙说了下去。

"大家管索洛佐叫'土佬'有两个原因。第一,他在土耳其待的时间很多,在土耳其有老婆和孩子。第二,据说他很容易拔刀子,至少年轻时是这样。不过只因为生意动刀,而且都有说得过去的理由。很有能力,不受别人的管教。他有案底,蹲过两次监狱,一次在意大利,一次在美国,政府知道他的毒贩身份。对我们是个优势。他被认为是黑帮大佬,而且有案底,意味着他不可能靠作证得到豁免。他在美国也有老婆和三个孩子,是个顾家的男人。只要知道家里人的生活费用有着落,他就愿意承担任何刑罚。"

唐抽着雪茄,说:"桑蒂诺,你怎么看?"

黑根知道桑尼会说什么。唐一直压制着他,他很气恼。他想大展身手。这是个完美的机会。

桑尼喝了一大口威士忌。"白粉是个金矿,"他说,"同时也很危险。最后得有人去蹲二十年大牢。要我说,别插手具体运营,只提供保护和资金,这么做应该不错。"

黑根赞赏地望着桑尼。他这手牌打得不错,着眼于显而易见的事实,提出了对他来说最有利的办法。

唐抽着雪茄说:"你呢,汤姆,你怎么想?"

黑根摆出百分之百诚实的样子。他已经得出结论,唐要拒绝索洛佐的提议。更糟糟的是,黑根确信唐想得不够透彻,眼光不够长远,类似的情况他只遇到过几次。

"直说吧,汤姆,"唐鼓励道,"西西里血统的顾问也不总是赞同老板。"三个人都笑了起来。

"我认为你该答应,"黑根说,"显而易见的原因你都清楚,但最重要的一条是毒品的盈利能力远远超过其他行当。就算我们不插手,也有其他人会,说不定就是塔塔利亚家族。借着毒品的利润,他们可以买通越来越多的警察和政客。他们的家族会变得比我们更强大,最后甚至动手抢走我们的产业。这就像国与国的关系。他们搞军备,我们也只能跟着搞。他们的经济力量越是强盛,对我们的威胁就越大。我们现在有赌场和工会,这两门生意暂时最挣钱。不过我认为毒品是未来的希望。我认为我们应该分一杯羹,否则就是在拿所有家业冒险。风险不在眼前,而是在十年以后。"

唐似乎很受触动。他抽着雪茄,喃喃道:"这确实是最重要的事情。"他叹了口气,站起身,"明天我几点见那个异教徒?"

黑根怀着希望说:"他上午十点到这儿。"唐也许会答应。

"你俩陪我见他。"唐说。他起身伸个懒腰,挽住儿子的胳膊,"桑蒂诺,好好睡一觉,你的脸色活像魔鬼他本人。照顾好自己,你不可能永远年轻。"

桑尼受到父亲关心的鼓舞,问了黑根不敢说出口的问题:"爸爸,你会怎么回答他?"

唐·柯里昂笑着说:"不了解怎么分账和其他的细节,我怎么知道?另外,我得考虑一下今晚得到的建议。我毕竟不是那种鲁莽行事的人。"就在他出门的时候,他语气随便地对黑根说:"你的笔记里有没有说土佬在战前靠妓院谋生?就像现在的塔塔利亚家族。记下这一条,免得忘了。"唐的声音里有最细微的一丝嘲笑,黑根涨红了脸。他故意没提这一点,一方面是无关紧要,另一方面是害怕这会先人为主地影响唐的判断。唐在男女之事上极其地古板。

维吉尔·"土佬"·索洛佐体格粗壮,中等块头,五官黝黑,说是真正的土耳其佬也混得过去。他鼻梁犹如弯刀,有一双冷酷的黑眼睛。他的神态也非常威严。

桑尼·柯里昂在门口迎接他,领他去办公室见黑根和唐。黑根觉得除了卢卡·布拉齐,这是他见过的最危险的人。

大家礼貌地握手寒暄。要是唐问我这家伙有没有卵蛋,黑根心想,我一定会说有。他从没在一个人身上见过如此可怕的力量,连唐也比不上。说实话,唐今天拿出了最糟糕的一面。和他打招呼的时候,唐显得有点过于单纯,过于像个农夫。

索洛佐开门见山。生意确实是贩毒。事情都安排妥当了。土耳其的罂粟田保证每年如数供货。他在法国有一家受到保护的工厂,把罂粟提炼成吗啡。他在西西里有个绝对安全的场地,把吗啡加工成海洛因。走私进入法国和意大利能有多保险就有多保险。运进美国会有百分之五左右的货损,因为大家都知道,联邦调查局实在无法收买。但是,利润大得惊人,风险近乎零。

"那为什么来找我呢?"唐很有礼貌地问,"我为何配得上你的慷慨?"

索洛佐的黑脸还是面无表情。"我需要两百万美元的现金,"他说,"另外一点同样重要,我需要一个伙伴,他得在重要位置有权势滔天的朋友。今后几年里,我的递送人员也许会有人被逮住,这是难免的。他们都是没有案底的人,这点我可以保证,因此法官从轻发落也合乎逻辑。我需要一个朋友,他能保证我的人就算进监狱,也只会蹲个一两年。这样他们就不会乱说话了。但要是被判个十年二十年的,那可就说不准了。天底下有很多软骨头。他们会乱说话,咬出更关键的角色。法律方面的保护伞必不可少。我听说,您,唐·柯里昂的口袋里装了很多法官,数量比得上擦鞋匠口袋里的零钱。"

唐·柯里昂没有费心去认可他的恭维。"我的家族能分多少?"他问。

索洛佐两眼一亮。"五成。"他顿了顿,用近乎于爱抚的声音说,"头一年,你的分红就有三四百万,往后只会越来越多。"

唐·柯里昂说:"塔塔利亚家族占多少呢?"

索洛佐第一次露出紧张的神色。"他们从我那份里拿分红,我在运作方面需要人手。"

"这么说,"唐·柯里昂说,"我只需要提供一点资金和法律保护就能拿五成,不必担心运作方面的问题,你想说的就是这些吧?"

索洛佐点点头。"假如你觉得两百万美元现金只是'一点资金',那么我要为你的成功喝彩了,唐·柯里昂。"

唐平静地说:"我之所以同意见你,是为了表示我对塔塔利亚家族的尊重,也因为我听说你做事认真,理当得到我的尊敬。我不得不拒绝你的提议,但请你听我的理由。你这门生意利润丰厚,但风险同样巨大。我要是参与你的运作,就会损害我的其他利益。没错,我在政坛上有许许多多朋友,但我的生意假如不是赌博而是毒品,他们对我恐怕就没那么友好了。他们认为赌博和烈酒一样,有伤风化但无害,但他们认为毒品很肮脏。不,你不用辩解。我说的是他们的看法,不是我的。一个人怎么谋生不关我的事。我想说的是,你的生意对我来说风险太大。我的家族成员过去这十年都过得很好,风平浪静。我不能因为贪婪而危害他们和他们的生计。"

索洛佐的失望仅有一个表现:眼神飞快地扫视整个房间,像是希望黑根或桑尼出言支持他。他说:"你担心你的两百万没有保障?"

唐冷冷一笑,答道:"不。"

索洛佐没有死心。"塔塔利亚家族愿意担保你的投资。"

这时候,桑尼·柯里昂犯了个判断和程序上的错误,一个不可饶恕的错误。他急切地问:"塔塔利亚能担保我们收回投资,但不需要任何佣金吗?"

黑根被他的插嘴吓傻了。他看着唐把凶恶而冷酷的视线转向大儿子,而桑尼因为莫名其妙受了斥责而手足无措。索洛佐的眼神又是一闪,但这次是出于满足。他发现唐的堡垒有一条裂缝。唐开口了,他驳回了桑尼的话。"年轻人嘛,免不了贪心,而且越来越没规矩,居然打断长辈说话,乱管闲事。唉,我对孩子总是很心软,宠坏了他们。你也看见了。索洛佐先生,我的拒绝是最终决定。请允许我恭祝您生意兴隆。你我在生意上没有冲突。很抱歉,我让你失望了。"

索洛佐低了低头,和唐握手,黑根送他到外面的车上。和黑根道别的时候,他脸上毫无表情。

回到房间里,唐·柯里昂问黑根:"你怎么看他?"

"西西里人。"黑根干巴巴地说。

唐若有所思地点点头,转向大儿子,心平气和地说:"桑蒂诺,绝对不要让家族外的人知道你在想什么。绝对不要让他们知道你手里有什么牌。我觉得你和那个小姑娘搞名堂把脑子搞坏了。别鬼混了,好好关心生意。现在从我面前滚开吧。"

对于唐的责骂,桑尼先是惊讶,然后是愤怒。黑根全看在眼里。他难道真以为唐不知道他四处猎艳?黑根心想,他真的不知道今天上午犯了多么危险的错误吗?要真是这样,桑蒂诺·柯里昂当上唐以后,黑根可不想当他的顾问。

唐·柯里昂等桑尼离开房间后,这才一屁股坐进皮革扶手椅,打个粗暴的手势示意倒酒。黑根给他斟了一杯茴香酒。唐抬起头看着他,说:"叫卢卡·布拉齐来见我。"

三个月后的一天,黑根正在市区的办公室忙着处理文件,希望能早点下班,去给老婆孩子挑选圣诞礼物。约翰尼·方坦兴高采烈地打来电话,打断了他的思路。电影已经拍完,毛片——天晓得那是什么鬼东西,黑根心想——好得没法说。他送了唐一件圣诞礼物,唐看了保准两眼发亮,他本打算亲自送来,但电影这边还有些小事,实在分身无术。他只能在西海岸过圣诞了。黑根试图掩饰他的不耐烦。他一向对约翰尼·方坦的魅力免疫,但胃口倒是被吊了起来。"什么礼物?"他问。约翰尼·方坦嘿嘿一笑,说:"不能说,保证是一等一的圣诞礼物。"黑根立刻失去了所有兴趣,决定有礼貌地挂断电话。

十分钟后,秘书说康妮·柯里昂在电话上,有话要跟他说。黑根叹了口气。康妮没出嫁之前是个好姑娘,结婚后成了讨厌鬼。她抱怨她的丈夫,经常回家探望母亲,一住就是两三天。事实证明卡洛·里齐是正牌窝囊废。家族安排他做点挣钱的小生意,却被他搞得一塌糊涂。他酗酒,嫖妓,赌博,动不动打老婆。康妮没和家里人说过,但告诉了黑根。不知道这次又要讲什么伤心事了。

然而,圣诞气氛似乎也让她高兴了起来。她只是想问黑根,她父亲还有桑尼、弗雷德和迈克会喜欢什么样的圣诞礼物。她已经想到了要送母亲什么。黑根给了些建议,她都觉得太俗气。最后,她总算放过了黑根。

电话铃再次响起,黑根把文件扔回待处理的档案篮。去他妈的,他要走了。不过,他可没有拒接电话的念头。秘书说打来的是迈克尔·柯里昂,他开开心心地拿起听筒。他一直很喜欢迈克。

"汤姆,"迈克尔·柯里昂说,"我明天带着凯开车进城。有些重要的事情想在圣诞节前告诉老头子。他明晚在家吗?"

"当然,"黑根说,"他过完圣诞才出城。需要我帮你安排什么吗?"

迈克的口风和他父亲一样紧。"不需要,"他说,"我们圣诞节见,大家都要去长滩,对吧?"

"对。"黑根说。迈克没有跟他聊天,而是直接挂断电话,黑根觉得很高兴。

他吩咐秘书打电话给他妻子,说他迟一点回家,不过还是在家吃饭。走出大楼,他脚步轻快地走向商业区的梅西百货。有人挡住他的去路。他惊讶地发现来者是索洛佐。

索洛佐抓住他的胳膊,轻声说:"别怕,我只想和你聊聊。"停在路边的轿车突然打开门。索洛佐催促道:"进去,我想和你聊聊。"

黑根抽出手臂。他并不害怕,只是有点恼怒。"我没这个工夫。"他说。这时有两个男人从他背后夹了过来,黑根突然觉得两腿发软。索洛佐温和地说:"上车。我要是想杀你,你已经是个死人了。请相信我。"

黑根钻进轿车,根本不相信他的话。

迈克尔·柯里昂对黑根撒了谎。他已经在纽约了,打电话的时候在离黑根不到十个街区的宾夕法尼亚酒店。他放下听筒,凯揿熄烟头,说:"迈克,你真是个撒谎精。"

迈克尔挨着她坐在床边。"都是为了你,亲爱的。要是告诉家里人我已经在城里了,那就非得立刻去见他们不可。那样今晚我们就没法出去吃饭、去戏院、一起睡觉了。我们还没结婚,在我父亲的家肯定没法睡在一起。"他搂住凯,轻轻亲吻她的嘴唇。她的嘴巴甜如蜜糖,他温柔地拉着她倒在床上。她闭上眼睛,等待他和她做爱,迈克尔感到无比幸福。他在太平洋打了好几年仗,在血腥的夺岛战斗之中,他做梦都想着凯·亚当斯这样的姑娘。她这么美丽的姑娘。苗条而柔软的身体，牛奶般的皮肤，燃烧着激情。她睁开眼睛，拽着他低头吻她。两人一直做爱到吃饭和去戏院的时候。

吃过饭，他们走过灯火通明的百货商店，店里挤满了为圣诞节购物的人，迈克尔对凯说："你要什么圣诞礼物？"

她贴紧迈克尔，说："只要你。你觉得你父亲会接受我吗？"

迈克尔柔声说："不成问题。你父母会接受我吗？"

凯耸耸肩："我不在乎。"

迈克尔说："我甚至想过走法律途径改名换姓，但要是出了事情也没什么用处。你确定愿意成为柯里昂家的一员吗？"他半开玩笑地说着。

"愿意。"她却没有笑。两人彼此贴紧。他们已经决定要在圣诞节这周结婚，到市政厅不声不响地举行世俗婚礼，只邀请两个朋友担任见证人。不过，迈克尔坚持要告诉父亲。他解释说，只要不秘密结婚，父亲就绝对不会反对。凯不太放心。她说她打算到婚礼后再通知她父母。"他们肯定会以为我怀孕了。"她说。迈克尔咧嘴一笑："我父母也是。"

他们谁都没有提起迈克尔将不得不斩断家族联系的问题。两人明白迈克尔已经在某种程度上这么做了，但内心对此都有点愧疚。他们决定念完大学，每周末见面，暑假住在一起。生活应该会很美好。

他们看的是音乐剧《竞技大赛》，主角是个吹牛皮的窃贼，故事有点感伤，看得两人互视微笑。他们走出剧院，外面天气很冷。凯偎依在他身边，说："我们结婚以后，你会先揍我，然后偷一颗星星当礼物吗？"

迈克尔笑道："我要当数学教授，"他说，"要不要先吃东西再回饭店？"

凯摇摇头。她意味深长地抬头看着他。和往常一样，她对做爱的渴望打动了迈克尔。他低头报以微笑，两人在冰冷的马路上拥吻。迈克尔很饿，决定叫客房服务送三明治。

走进饭店大堂，迈克尔让凯去报摊，说："你买报纸，我去拿钥匙。"前面有几个人在排队，尽管战争已经结束，但饭店还是缺少人手。迈克尔拿到房间钥匙，不耐烦地环顾四周找凯。她站在报摊前，低头盯着手里的一份报纸。他走了过去。凯抬头看他，两眼充满泪水。"噢，迈克，"她说，"噢，迈克。"他接过凯手里的报纸，第一眼见到的就是父亲躺在马路上的照片，脑袋浸在血泊之中。一个男人坐在马路牙子上，哭得像个孩子。那是他的二哥弗雷迪。迈克尔·柯里昂觉得身体在结冰。心里没有悲痛，也没有恐惧，只有冰冷的怒火。他对凯说："上楼回房间。"他不得不挽起凯的手臂，拉着她走进电梯，一路上谁也不说话。走进房间，迈克尔在床边坐下，打开报纸。头版头条：

维托·柯里昂遭到枪击。所谓的黑帮大佬严重受
伤。手术在警方重兵把守下进行。血腥的黑帮斗争令人
担忧。

迈克尔觉得两腿发软。他对凯说："他没死，那些杂种没能得逞。"他又读一遍报
道。父亲在今天下午五点遭到枪击。也就是说，他忙着和凯做爱、吃饭、欣赏音乐剧的
时候，父亲在死亡线上挣扎。迈克尔愧疚得难受。

凯说："我们这就去医院？"

迈克尔摇摇头："我先给家里打个电话。下手的人疯了，老头子没死，他们会孤注
一掷。天晓得下一步会搞什么名堂。"

长滩家宅的两部电话都占线，迈克尔打了二十分钟才拨通。听筒里传来桑尼的声
音："哪位？"

"桑尼，是我。"迈克尔说。

他听得出桑尼松了一口气。"天哪，小弟，我们都在担心你。你他妈在哪儿？我
派手下去你那小城打探情况了。"

"老头子怎么样？"迈克尔问，"伤得重吗？"

"很重，"桑尼说，"他们冲他开了五枪。不过他够硬气，"桑尼的声音充满自豪，
"医生说他熬得过来。听着，小弟，我很忙，没时间聊天，你在哪儿？"

"纽约，"迈克尔说，"汤姆没说我要进城？"

桑尼稍微压低了声音，"他们抓走了汤姆，所以我才担心你。他老婆在我这儿。
她还不知道，警察也一样。我不想告诉他们。策划这事的混蛋肯定是疯子。你给我马
上过来，别乱说话。明白吗？"

"好的，"迈克说，"知道是谁下的手吗？"

"当然，"桑尼说，"只要卢卡·布拉齐赶过来，他们就死定了。我们还是有优势。"

"我一小时内就到，"迈克尔说，"搭出租车。"他挂断电话。消息登报已经超过三
个钟头。电台肯定也播了这条新闻。卢卡不可能没有听到。迈克尔琢磨起了一个问
题：卢卡·布拉齐在哪儿？此时此刻，黑根也在问自己这个问题。长滩的桑尼·柯里
昂同样在担心这个问题。

当天下午四点三刻，唐·柯里昂看完橄榄油公司经理准备的报表。他拿起外衣，
用指节敲敲儿子弗雷迪的脑袋，让他别埋头看报纸了。"叫加图把车从停车场开过
来，"他说，"等几分钟我们就回家。"

弗雷迪嘟囔道："只能我自己去了。保利今天早上打电话请病假，说是又感
冒了。"

唐·柯里昂若有所思地想了几秒钟,"本月的第三次。看来你得找个更健康的伙计开车了。告诉汤姆。"

弗雷迪辩解道:"保利是个好小伙子。他要是说生病,那就肯定是生病了。没关系,我不怕开车。"他走出办公室。唐·柯里昂望着窗外,看见儿子穿过第九大道走向停车场。他打电话到黑根的办公室,但没人接。他打电话回长滩家里,还是没人接。他有点生气,又望向窗外。车已经停在了楼门口的路边。弗雷迪靠在挡泥板上,抱着胳膊看圣诞节的购物人潮。唐·柯里昂穿上外衣。经理帮他穿上大衣。唐·柯里昂嘟囔一声谢谢,出门走下两段楼梯。

来到街上,时值初冬,天光暗淡。弗雷迪漫不经心地靠在重型别克的挡泥板上。见到父亲走出大楼,弗雷迪跑上马路,到司机座那边钻进车里。唐·柯里昂正要从人行道这一侧上车,忽然停下,转身走向路口的露天水果摊。这是他最近的习惯,他喜欢反季的大水果,黄澄澄的桃子和橙子在绿色盒子里闪闪发亮。店主跑过来招呼他。唐·柯里昂没有动手去拿,只是用手指点。摊主只有一次违背了他的意愿,拿起他挑的一个水果,给他看底下有点烂。唐·柯里昂用左手接过纸袋,用一张五块钱付账。他接过找零,就在他转身走向等候的轿车时,两个男人突然绕过拐角出现。唐·柯里昂立刻意识到发生了什么。

两个男人穿黑大衣,黑帽子拉得很低,以防被目击证人记住长相。他们没料到唐·柯里昂竟有这么警觉。唐·柯里昂丢下水果,冲向停在路边的轿车,对他这种体型的人来说,他的速度快得惊人。他边跑边喊:"弗雷迪,弗雷迪!"就在这时,两个男人拔枪开始射击。

第一发子弹击中唐·柯里昂的后背。他感觉到子弹如榔头般的冲击力,但仍旧拖着身体跑向轿车。接下来的两颗子弹击中臀部,他摊手摊脚倒在马路上。两个枪手小心翼翼地避开滚动的水果,跟上来想解决他。此刻离唐呼唤儿子还不到五秒钟,弗雷德里科·柯里昂钻出车门,出现在车的另一边。枪手朝滚进了排水沟的唐匆匆忙忙又开两枪。一枪击中手臂多肉的部位,另一枪击中右侧小腿。伤都不重,但流血很多,在他身旁淌成了几小块血泊。这时候唐·柯里昂已经失去了知觉。

弗雷迪听见父亲的喊声,听见父亲喊他生下来的名字,紧接着听见两声响亮的枪响。他下车时已经慌了神,甚至忘了拔枪。两名刺客轻而易举就能撂倒他,但他们过于惊慌,一方面肯定知道二儿子有枪,另一方面耽搁的时间已经太久。他们拐过路口消失,留下弗雷迪一个人在路边陪着流血不止的父亲。大道上的购物客有几个躲进门洞或扑倒在地,剩下的三五成群聚在一起。

弗雷迪仍旧没有拔枪。他似乎吓傻了,盯着父亲脸朝下趴在柏油路上,身边发黑的血泊已经汇成湖泊。弗雷迪的肉体陷入休克。人们重新露头,有人见到他摇摇欲坠,扶着他到路边坐在马路牙子上。唐·柯里昂失去知觉的躯体周围聚起人群,直到第一辆警车拉着警笛分开一条路。紧跟着警车的是《每日新闻》的无线电报道车,车还没停稳,摄影师就跳下来,开始拍摄血泊中的唐·柯里昂。又过了几分钟,救护车赶到。摄影师把注意力转向弗雷迪·柯里昂,他哭得不加掩饰,这幅画面实在太滑稽了,因为他那张硬朗的爱神脸上,粗鼻梁和厚嘴唇沾满了鼻涕。警探在人群中散开,更多的警车陆续赶到。一名警探在弗雷迪身边跪下问话,但弗雷迪过于震惊,无法回答。警探伸手从弗雷迪的大衣里掏出钱包。他看了一眼证件,对搭档吹声口哨。几秒钟后,一群便衣警察把弗雷迪和人群隔开。第一个警探发现弗雷迪的肩套里有枪,掏出来拿走。他们抬起弗雷迪,把他塞进一辆没有标记的警车。见到这辆车开走,《每日新闻》的无线电报道车跟了上去。摄影师还在拍摄每一个人和每一件东西。

父亲遭到枪击后半小时,桑尼·柯里昂连续接到五个电话。第一个来自约翰·菲利普斯警探,他收柯里昂家的黑钱,坐在赶到枪击现场的第一辆便衣警车里。电话接通,他劈头就问桑尼:"听得出我是谁?"

"听得出。"桑尼答道。他刚才在打瞌睡,喊他来接电话的是他妻子。

菲利普斯也不废话,语速飞快:"有人在你父亲的办公楼外面刺杀他。十五分钟之前,他还活着,但伤得很重。救护车送他去了法兰西医院。警察把你弟弟弗雷迪带到切尔西分局去了。等他们释放他,你最好给他请个医生。我这就去医院,协助询问你家老头子,但前提是他能说话。有情况我随时通知你。"

隔着桌子,桑尼的妻子珊德拉发现丈夫涨红了脸,眼神发直。她悄声说:"出什么事了?"桑尼不耐烦地朝她一挥手,叫她安静,转身背对妻子,对着听筒说:"确定他还活着?"

"对,确定,"警探答道,"流了很多血,但我认为看起来可怕,实际上还好。"

"谢谢,"桑尼说,"明早八点整在家等着。有一千块送到。"

桑尼放下听筒,强迫自己坐着不动。他知道自己最大的弱点就是脾气火暴,此刻要是乱发脾气,结果可能是致命的。首先必须找到汤姆·黑根。他正要拿起听筒,电话又响了。来电者是家族许可的赌博簿记,负责唐的办公室所在的区域。簿记说唐遇到暗杀,在街上被乱枪打死。桑尼提了几个问题,得知簿记的线人未曾靠近尸体,桑尼认为他的消息并不确切。菲利普斯的内部线报更加准确。刚放下听筒,电话就第三次响起。打来的是《每日新闻》的记者,他刚说明身份,桑尼·柯里昂就挂断了电话。

他打到黑根家,问黑根的妻子:"汤姆还没到家吗?"她说:"没有。"还说离他应该到家的时间还有二十分钟,她在等他回家吃饭。"叫他打电话给我。"桑尼说。

他试着厘清思路,试着想象父亲遇到这种情况会怎么反应。他立刻想到肯定是索洛佐发动了袭击,但要是没有更强大的势力撑腰,索洛佐可没胆子清除唐这种地位的家族领袖。电话铃第四次响起,打断他的思绪。听筒里传来的声音非常柔和,彬彬有礼,问:"桑蒂诺·柯里昂吗?"

"对。"桑尼说。

"汤姆·黑根在我们手上,"对方说,"大约三小时后,我们将释放他,让他带来我们的提议。别匆忙下决定,先听听他怎么说。否则你只会惹来更多的麻烦。木已成舟,现在大家必须讲道理。别发你那出了名的脾气。"音调稍微有点嘲讽。桑尼拿不准,但听起来很像索洛佐。他装得意志消沉,有气无力地说:"我等着。"他听见对面咔嗒一声挂断,扭头看一眼沉重的镶金手表,把准确的来电时间写在台布上。

他坐在餐桌前,皱起眉头。妻子问:"桑尼,怎么了?"他冷静地说:"老头子被人放了冷枪。"见到妻子的震惊表情,他不耐烦地说:"别怕,他没死。不会发生其他事情了。"他没说黑根的事情。电话铃第五次响起。

打来的是克莱门扎。胖子呼哧呼哧的声音像是猪喘气,他问:"知道你父亲出事了?"

"知道,"桑尼答道,"不过他还活着。"电话沉默良久,接着响起克莱门扎饱含感情的声音,"感谢上帝,感谢上帝,"他又焦虑地说,"确定吗? 我听说他死在街上了。"

"他活着。"桑尼说。他仔细听着克莱门扎说话时的细微变化。情绪听起来很真诚,但演戏本来就是胖子的分内事。

"你必须接手,桑尼,"克莱门扎说,"要我做什么?"

"来我父亲家,"桑尼说,"带上保利·加图。"

"就这些?"克莱门扎问,"不用我派人去医院和你家?"

"不用,我只要你和保利·加图,"桑尼答道。电话又沉默良久,克莱门扎在掂量情况。桑尼不想搞得太僵,于是问:"保利他妈的到底在哪儿? 他到底在干什么?"

电话里不再有呼哧呼哧的声音了,克莱门扎显得有点戒备:"保利请病假,他感冒了,所以在家里。他今年冬天一直病快快的。"

桑尼立刻警觉起来:"这几个月他请了几次病假?"

"大概三四次吧,"克莱门扎答道,"我问了弗雷迪好几次要不要换人,但他说不用。没有理由,过去十年过得风平浪静,你知道的。"

"对,"桑尼说,"到我父亲家碰头吧。记得带上保利,过来的时候接上他。我不管他病得有多重。听明白了?"他没等克莱门扎回答,直接摔下电话。

妻子在默默垂泪。桑尼盯着她看了好一会儿,然后恶狠狠地说:"我们的人打电话,就说我在我父亲家,叫他们打他的特别专线。其他人打电话,一律回答你什么都不知道。要是汤姆的老婆打电话,就说他在忙生意上的事情,过一阵才能回家。"

他沉思片刻:"我们的人会过来看家。"他见到妻子面露惧色,不耐烦地说,"用不着害怕,我只是要他们过来守着而已。他们叫你做什么你就做什么。找我就打爸爸的特别专线,但除非有要紧事,否则别打过来。还有,别担心。"他走出家门。

夜幕已经落下,十二月的寒风抽打林荫道。桑尼不怕走进黑夜。这八幢房屋都属于唐·柯里昂。林荫道入口的左右两幢租给家族扈从以及家眷、明星情妇和住地下室房间的单身汉。另外六幢围成半圆形,汤姆·黑根和家人住一幢,唐本人住最小也最不起眼的一幢。另外三幢住着唐那些已经退休的老朋友,不收租金,但有个默契:只要唐提出要求,他们就必须搬走。这条林荫道看似和平安静,实际是一座坚不可摧的堡垒。

八幢房屋都有水银灯,周围照得通明,外人不可能潜入林荫道。桑尼穿过马路,到父亲的屋子门前,用他的钥匙开门。他喊道:"妈,你在哪儿?"母亲从厨房出来,她背后飘来煎辣椒的香味。没等她说话,桑尼就抓住她的胳膊,拉着她坐下。"我接到电话,"他说,"不过你别担心。爸爸受伤进医院了。你换身衣服,准备过去。我马上给你安排车子和司机。好吗?"

母亲盯着他看了几秒钟,然后用意大利语问:"中冷枪了?"

桑尼点点头。母亲垂首片刻,然后返回厨房。桑尼跟她进去,看着母亲关掉正在用平底锅煎辣椒的煤气炉,走出厨房,上楼去卧室。他用锅里的辣椒和桌上篮子里的面包凑合做了个三明治,滚烫的橄榄油从指缝间滴下来。他走进拐角的大房间,那是父亲的办公室,从上锁的柜橱抽屉里取出特别专线电话,这部电话登记在假名字和假地址之下。他首先打给卢卡·布拉齐。没人接电话。他接着打给布鲁克林的"安全阀"首领,此人名叫忒西奥,对唐的忠诚无可怀疑。桑尼把现状和计划告诉他。忒西奥的任务是召集五十个绝对忠诚的部下,派人守卫医院,派人到长滩办事。忒西奥问:"克莱门扎呢?也被他们抓走了?"桑尼答道:"我暂时不想用克莱门扎的人。"忒西奥马上明白过来,他顿了顿,然后说:"抱歉,桑尼,但换了你父亲也会这么说:别忙着下决定,我不相信克莱门扎会背叛我们。"

"谢谢,"桑尼说,"我也不这么认为,但此刻我必须谨慎。对吧?"

"对。"忒西奥说。

"还有一件事,"桑尼说,"我小弟迈克在新罕布什尔州汉诺威念大学。叫几个我们在波士顿的熟人过去接他,带他回纽约家里,等事情平息再说。我打电话通知他,让他等着。我只是想预防万一,免得出意外。"

"好的,"忒西奥说,"安排妥当了我马上去你父亲家,好吗?你认识我的人,对吧?"

"对。"桑尼说。他挂断电话,走到镶在墙里的小保险箱前开锁,取出一本蓝色皮革装订的索引簿子,翻到"账"字头部分,找到他要查的条目:雷·法瑞尔,五千块,圣诞夜。后面是个电话号码。桑尼拨打电话,说:"法瑞尔?"对方答道,"对。"桑尼说:"我是桑蒂诺·柯里昂。我想请你帮个忙,马上就要结果。请你帮我查两个电话号码,列出过去三个月内打进打出的所有通话。"他把保利·加图和克莱门扎两人家里的号码给对方,然后说:"非常重要,今晚十二点前给我,你会得到一份额外的圣诞礼物。"

整理思绪之前,他又打了一次卢卡·布拉齐的号码。还是没人接听。他有点担心,但马上抛诸脑后。卢卡一听到消息就会来这儿。桑尼坐进转椅。一小时之内,屋子里将满是家族人马,他要对他们发号施令。此刻他终于有时间思考,终于意识到情况有多么严重。十年来第一次有人挑战柯里昂家族和家族的权势。毫无疑问,幕后主使是索洛佐,但要是没有纽约五大家族中的至少一家撑腰,他绝对没有这个胆子。支持他的无疑是塔塔利亚家族。这意味着要么全面开战,要么按照索洛佐的条件立刻达成协议。桑尼露出狞笑。土佬固然老谋深算,可惜运气不好。老头子还活着,因此只能开战。有卢卡·布拉齐和柯里昂家族的资源,结果可想而知。然而,让人担心的问题又回来了:卢卡·布拉齐在哪儿?

第三章

算上司机,车里有四个人守着黑根。他们逼着他坐进后座,街上两个站在他背后的人这会儿坐在他两边。索洛佐坐在前排。黑根右边的男人探身过来,拉下黑根的帽子遮住眼睛,他什么都看不见了。"小拇指都不许动一下。"他说。

路程不远,顶多二十分钟,下车的时候天已经黑了,黑根认不出这个地点。他们领着他走进地下室,让他坐进一把直背餐椅。索洛佐隔着餐桌在对面坐下,黝黑的脸庞露出秃鹫般的凶相。

"我不希望你害怕,"他说,"我知道你不是家族的打手。我希望你帮助柯里昂家族,也希望你帮助我。"

黑根把香烟放进嘴里,他的手在颤抖。一个男人拿来一瓶黑麦威士忌放在桌上,用骨瓷咖啡杯给他斟了半杯。黑根怀着感激的心情一饮而尽。烈酒下肚,手不抖了,腿也不软了。

"你老板死了。"索洛佐说。他停下来,惊讶地看见黑根眼里涌出热泪。他继续道:"我们在他办公室外面的马路上伏击了他。我一得到消息就抓了你。你必须帮我和桑尼讲和。"

黑根没有搭腔,他惊讶于自己的悲痛。哀伤的感觉和怕死的恐惧在心头交织。索洛佐又说:"桑尼对我的生意很感兴趣,对吧? 你也知道这条路前途无量。毒品是未来。里面的钱太多了。用不了几年,大家都能发财。唐是个上了年纪的'胡子彼得'①,他的时代已经结束,只有他自己不知道。现在他死了,再怎么样也不可能让他起死回生。我打算提出新的建议,希望你说服桑尼接受。"

黑根说:"你一点机会都没有。桑尼会动用全部力量追杀你。"

索洛佐不耐烦地说:"这肯定是他的第一反应。你必须用道理说服他。塔塔利亚家族全力支持我。只要能阻止双方全面开战,纽约的其他几大家族什么都能接受。我们的战争会危及他们和他们的生意。要是桑尼接受提议,美国的其他家族都会认为事情和他们没关系,唐的老朋友也包括在内。"

黑根低头看着双手,没有吭声。索洛佐接着劝说:"唐在走下坡路。换了是以前,我绝对不可能碰他。另外几大家族不信任他,因为他任命你当顾问,而你连意大利人都不是,更别说西西里人了。要是全面开战,柯里昂家族会被碾碎,大家都是输家,包括我在内。比起金钱,我更需要柯里昂家族的政治影响力。所以请说服桑尼,说服各位首领,这样能少流很多血。"

黑根举起咖啡杯,示意倒酒。"我可以试试看,"他说,"但桑尼很顽固。再说,连桑尼也阻止不了卢卡。你得当心卢卡。要是我赞成你的提议,我也得当心卢卡。"

索洛佐平静地说:"卢卡让我操心好了。你只需要操心桑尼和唐的另外两个儿子。听着,你可以告诉他们,弗雷迪本来也会像他老头子那样吃子弹,但我严格命令手下,不准对他开枪。我不希望造成不必要的仇恨。记得告诉他们,弗雷迪还活着都是因为我。"

黑根的脑袋终于开始运转。他第一次真的相信索洛佐并不打算杀他或扣他当人质。恐惧解除,突如其来的解脱感流遍全身,他羞愧得脸色通红。索洛佐带着心照不宣的平静笑容看着他。黑根开始衡量情况。他要是不答应帮索洛佐说话就有可能送命。不过他随即醒悟过来,索洛佐期待他回去传话,原原本本地传话,因为这是一名负责的顾问的分内事。此刻仔细思考之下,他同时意识到索洛佐说得对。必须不惜一切代价阻止塔塔利亚家族和柯里昂家族之间无限制全面开战。柯里昂家族必须埋葬死

---

① 指二十世纪初来到美国的西西里黑手党成员.谨守故土规则。

者,忘记仇恨,达成交易。等时机成熟,再下手对付索洛佐。

抬头一看,他发现索洛佐很清楚他在想什么。土佬在笑。黑根突然一惊。卢卡·布拉齐出了什么事情,索洛佐为何不把他放在心上?卢卡和他达成了交易?他回忆起唐·柯里昂拒绝索洛佐的那天夜里,曾召唤卢卡到办公室闭门谈话。不过,现在不是为这种细节伤脑筋的时候。他必须返回长滩柯里昂家族的安全堡垒。"我尽量,"他对索洛佐说,"我觉得你说得对,甚至唐也会希望我们这么做。"

索洛佐肃然点头。"很好,"他说,"我不喜欢血流成河,我是一个商人,流血过于浪费金钱。"这时电话铃响了,坐在黑根背后的一个男人起身去接。他听了一会儿,最后简短地说:"好,我转告他。"他挂断电话,到索洛佐身边,凑到土佬耳旁悄声说话。黑根看着索洛佐脸色变得惨白,眼里闪烁怒火。他觉得又是一阵心慌。索洛佐看着他陷入沉思,黑根突然意识到他恐怕不会被释放了,意识到发生的某些事情多半判了他的死刑。索洛佐说:"老头子还活着。一身西西里老皮吃了五颗子弹,居然还活着。"他听天由命地耸耸肩,"运气不好,"他对黑根说,"我运气不好,你也运气不好。"

第四章

迈克尔·柯里昂赶到父亲的长滩家宅,发现一条铁链拦住了林荫道狭窄的入口。八幢屋子都亮起水银灯,林荫道照得通明,弯曲的水泥人行道前停着至少十辆轿车。

两个他不认识的男人靠在铁链上,其中一个用布鲁克林口音说:"你是谁?"

他报上姓名。另一个男人走出离他们最近的屋子,打量着他的脸。"唐的儿子,"他说,"我带他进去。"迈克跟着男人走向父亲家,守门的两个男人放他和向导进屋。

屋里满是他不认识的人,进了客厅才见到熟脸。迈克尔见到汤姆·黑根的妻子特蕾莎直挺挺地坐在沙发上抽着香烟,面前的咖啡桌上放着一杯威士忌。沙发的另一侧坐着壮硕的克莱门扎。这位首领面无表情,但汗流浃背,手里的雪茄被口水泡得发黑,闪着滑溜溜的光。

克莱门扎走过来,安慰地紧握住迈克尔的手,嘴里喃喃道:"你母亲在医院陪你父亲,他不会有事的。"保利·加图起身想和他握手。迈克尔好奇地看着他。他知道保利是父亲的保镖,但不知道保利今天请病假在家休息,不过他觉察到了这张细瘦黑脸上的紧张神情。他知道加图名声不错,前途光明,手脚麻利,知道怎么处理微妙的任务而不留下后遗症,今天却失职了。他注意到房间一角有几个陌生男人,不是克莱门扎的人。迈克尔把几点事实加在一起,马上醒悟过来。克莱门扎和加图有嫌疑。他以为保利也在场,于是问雪貂脸年轻人:"弗雷迪怎么样?他还好吧?"

"医生给他打了一针,"克莱门扎说,"他在睡觉。"

迈克尔走到黑根的妻子跟前,俯身亲吻她的面颊。他们一向处得很好。他耳语道:"别担心,汤姆不会有事的。你和桑尼谈过了吗?"

特蕾莎在他身上贴了一会儿,摇摇头。她是个优雅而美貌的女人,说是意大利人不如说是美国人,此刻非常害怕。迈克尔握住她的手,拉着她从沙发上起来,领着她走进父亲的拐角办公室。

桑尼摊在办公桌前的椅子里,左手拿黄色记事簿,右手拿铅笔。房间里另外只有一个人,是忒西奥首领,迈克尔认出了他,立刻意识到屋里那些生面孔肯定是他的人,他们正在组织新的保镖队伍。他手里也拿着记事簿和铅笔。

桑尼见到他们,从办公桌前出来,拥抱黑根的妻子。"别担心,特蕾莎,"他说,"汤姆没事。对方只是要他传话,说很快就放他。他不是动手的人,只是家族的律师。没理由伤害他。"

他松开特蕾莎,搂住迈克尔,亲吻他的面颊,迈克尔吃了一惊。迈克尔推开桑尼,咧嘴笑道:"当初被你揍习惯了,现在又得习惯这个?"他们小时候成天打架。

桑尼耸耸肩。"听着,小子,派人去那个乡下小城没接到你,我很担心。不是怕你被他们干掉,而是不想把坏消息带给妈妈。我跟她说爸爸出事就够受了。"

"她撑得住吗?"迈克尔问。

"还行,"桑尼说,"她经历过这种事。我也是。你那时候还小,到你懂事的时候,情况已经好得多了。"他顿了顿,又说,"她在医院陪老头子。他会挺过来的。"

"我们要不要也过去?"迈克尔问。

桑尼摇摇头,干巴巴地说:"事情了结之前,我不能离开这里。"电话铃响起。桑尼拿起听筒,仔细听着。趁他听电话,迈克尔踱到桌边,瞥了一眼桑尼在写字的黄色记事簿。上面是个名单,有七个人。前三个是索洛佐、菲利普·塔塔利亚和约翰·塔塔利亚。迈克尔突然明白过来,他闯进来的时候,桑尼和忒西奥正在制订暗杀名单。

桑尼挂断电话,对特蕾莎·黑根和迈克尔说:"你们到外面去等好吗?我有些事情还没和忒西奥安排妥当。"

黑根的妻子说:"是汤姆的电话吗?"她的语气几近狂暴,流着恐惧的眼泪。桑尼搂住她,领着她走向房门。"我发誓他不会有事,"他说,"在客厅等着。我有消息就出来通知你。"桑尼在她背后关上门。迈克尔已经坐进一把皮革扶手椅。桑尼瞪了他一眼,然后坐回办公桌前。

"你要是留在我这儿,迈克,"他说,"就会听到你不想听见的内容。"

迈克尔点燃香烟："我要帮忙。"

"不行，没门，"桑尼说，"老头子要是知道我让你掺和进来，会心疼死的。"

迈克尔起身吼道，"混蛋，他也是我父亲。我难道不该帮他吗？我可以帮忙。我不需要出去杀人，但我帮得上忙。别再当我是你的小弟了。我打过仗，挨过枪子，忘记了？我杀了不少日本人。你要干掉什么人，我知道了又怎么样？昏过去吗？"

桑尼咧嘴一笑："很快你就会希望我出手的。好吧，你留下，电话归你管。"他对忒西奥说："我刚才接到了内部消息。"他又对迈克尔说："肯定有人出卖了老头子。有可能是克莱门扎，有可能是保利·加图，这家伙今天请病假，倒是凑巧。我已经知道答案了，让我看看你有多聪明。迈克，你是大学生。是谁投靠了索洛佐？"

迈克尔重新坐下，躺进皮革扶手椅。他仔细琢磨着每一件事情。克莱门扎是柯里昂家族权力体系中的一名首领，能成为百万富翁全是拜唐·柯里昂所赐，两人的亲密友情已经持续了二十多年。克莱门扎占据着组织内部最有权势的位置之一。背叛他的唐，克莱门扎能得到什么？更多的金钱？他已经很有钱了，但人总是贪心不足的。更多的权势？报复臆想中的侮辱或轻视？因为黑根被任命为顾问？还是生意人的直觉，认为索洛佐终将获胜？不，克莱门扎不可能叛变，接着迈克尔悲哀地想到，他这么想只可能因为他不希望克莱门扎死。他从小到大收了胖子很多礼物，唐太忙的时候，克莱门扎有空就带他出去玩。他不可能相信克莱门扎犯了背叛罪。

可是，另外一方面，在柯里昂家族的所有人里，索洛佐最想收买的也正是克莱门扎。

迈克尔转而考虑保利·加图。保利还没有发财，但他受到器重，前途无量，不过他和别人一样，需要花时间奋斗才行。另外，他毕竟年轻，对权力有着更疯狂的念头。迈克尔记起念六年级的时候，他和保利是同班同学，因此也不希望保利是叛徒。

他摇摇头。"两个都不是。"他说。他这样说，仅仅因为桑尼说他已经有答案了。要是投票决定的话，他会投保利一票。

桑尼对他微笑道："别担心。克莱门扎没问题，是保利。"

迈克尔看得出忒西奥松了一口气。他们都是首领，他当然同情克莱门扎。既然叛徒是个小角色，形势也就没那么危急了。忒西奥小心翼翼地说："那么，明天我就可以让我的人回家了？"

桑尼说："后天。在此之前我不希望有别人知道这一点。听着，我要和我弟谈些家事，纯粹是私事。到外面客厅等我，好吗？我们等会儿继续列名单。你和克莱门扎一起解决这事。"

"好的。"忒西奥说，起身离开。

"你怎么确定是保利?"迈克尔问。

桑尼说:"电话公司有我们的线人,帮忙查到了保利家和克莱门扎家所有打进打出的电话。老头子办公楼的马路对面有个电话亭,保利本月请病假的三天里,都接到了从这个电话亭打来的电话。今天也是。对方想搞清楚保利是不是失势了,或者被谁顶替了位置。或者什么别的原因。无所谓。"桑尼耸耸肩,"感谢上帝,还好是保利。我们太需要克莱门扎了。"

迈克尔试探道:"那么,两边会全面开战吗?"

桑尼眼神坚定:"我就是这么打算的,现在只等汤姆回来。除非老头子有别的想法。"

迈克尔说:"那为什么不等老头子醒来跟你说?"

桑尼好玩地打量着他:"你的战斗勋章到底是怎么骗来的? 对方拿枪口指着我们,老弟,我们只能还击。我只害怕他们扣着汤姆不放。"

迈克尔听了很惊讶:"为什么不放?"

桑尼的声音又变得很有耐心:"他们抓汤姆是因为他们以为老头子死了,打算和我谈笔交易,汤姆是牵线人,带着他们的提议回来。现在,老头子还活着,他们知道我作不了决定,所以汤姆对他们毫无用处了,要杀要剐全凭索洛佐高兴。他们要是杀了他,就等于和我们摊牌,打算铲除我们。"

迈克尔平静地说:"索洛佐凭什么认为他能和你达成交易?"

桑尼红了脸,一时答不上来。过了一会儿,他说:"我们几个月前见过一面,索洛佐提议一起做毒品生意。老头子拒绝了他,但我没管住嘴,我表示愿意接受。这么做真是大错特错,要是说老头子对我有什么教导,那就是绝对不能做这种事情,让别人知道家族内部意见有分歧。于是索洛佐认为只要除掉老头子,我就会跟他合作搞毒品。老头子要是死了,家族的权力至少减半。要守住老头子积攒的家业,我非得拼死一搏才行。毒品是未来的大买卖,我们应该介入。就生意而言,我会跟他联手。当然了,他不可能让我太接近他,免得我一时心痒做掉他。但他同时也很清楚,要是我接受交易,其他几大家族就不会允许我几年后仅仅为了复仇而开战。另外,塔塔利亚家族给他撑腰。"

"如果他们真的干掉了老头子,你打算怎么办?"迈克尔问。

桑尼答得很简单:"索洛佐死定了。我不惜一切代价。不在乎我们是不是要同时和纽约五大家族开战。塔塔利亚家族会被抹掉,我不在乎同归于尽。"

迈克尔柔声说:"这可不是爸爸的做事风格。"

桑尼凶狠地打了个手势。"我知道我不是他那块料,但我向你保证——他也会向你保证的——论到真刀真枪,短兵相接,我不比任何人逊色。索洛佐知道这一点,克莱门扎和忒西奥也知道,我十九岁那年就杀了第一个人,那是家族最近一次开战,我是老头子的得力干将。所以我现在并不担心。我们家族处理这种事的人马都在。我只希望能尽快联系上卢卡。"

迈克尔好奇地问:"卢卡真有大家说的那么凶悍吗?他真那么厉害?"

桑尼点点头:"独一无二的人物。我打算派他对付塔塔利亚家的三个头目。我亲自收拾索洛佐。"

迈克尔不安地动了动。他看着自己的大哥,他记得桑尼虽说有时候粗暴凶恶,但本质上是个热心的好人。听他这么说话,感觉真是怪异,见到他像新登基的罗马皇帝,随手列出要处决的敌人名单,他觉得不寒而栗。他很高兴自己并没有参与其中,父亲还活着,他不必卷入江湖仇杀。他可以打打下手,接电话,跑腿,送信。桑尼和老头子能处理他们的事情,特别是还有卢卡这个后盾。

客厅忽然传来女人的叫声。天哪,迈克尔心想,像是汤姆的妻子。他冲过去打开门。客厅里的所有人都站了起来。汤姆·黑根在沙发前紧紧搂住特蕾莎,脸色有点尴尬。特蕾莎哭得上气不接下气,迈克尔意识到那声尖叫是她在狂喜中呼喊丈夫的名字。他望着汤姆·黑根挣脱出妻子的怀抱,让妻子坐回沙发上。他对迈克尔狰狞一笑:"很高兴见到你,迈克,真的很高兴。"他大踏步走进办公室,没有多看啜泣的妻子一眼。他和柯里昂家族生活了几十年,不可能什么都没学到,想到这里,奇特的自豪感觉涌上迈克尔心头。黑根有着老头子的风范,桑尼也是,令人惊讶的是,甚至他自己也是。

第五章

凌晨四点,桑尼、迈克尔、汤姆·黑根、克莱门扎和忒西奥,几个人都坐在拐角办公室里。汤姆·黑根说服特蕾莎回家了。保利·加图还在客厅等候,浑然不知忒西奥的手下已经得到指令,不准他离开,也不准他走出他们的视线。

汤姆·黑根复述索洛佐的提议。他说索洛佐得知唐还活着之后,显然想杀了黑根。黑根咧嘴一笑:"哪怕有一天我要向最高法院陈情,恐怕也比不上今晚我在该死的土佬面前的表现了。我说就算唐还活着,我也可以说服家族接受交易。我说我能随便摆布你,桑尼。我们从小就算好伙伴;另外,你别往心里去啊,我还让他觉得你要是能早点接老头子的班,并不会特别难过。上帝请宽恕我。"他对桑尼抱歉地笑了笑,桑尼打手势说他明白,这话说了也不算数。

迈克尔躺在扶手椅里,电话搁在右手边,打量着两个男人。黑根一进房间,桑尼就冲上去拥抱他。想到桑尼和汤姆·黑根这么亲近,各方各面都比他和他的亲生大哥更亲近,迈克尔不禁稍微有点嫉妒。

"我们说正经事吧,"桑尼说,"我们必须制订计划。看看我和忒西奥列出的名单。忒西奥,你把你那份给克莱门扎。"

"假如要制订计划,"迈克尔说,"弗雷迪应该也在场。"

桑尼恶狠狠地说:"弗雷迪眼下派不上用场。医生说他严重休克,必须彻底静养。真不明白。弗雷迪平时挺硬气的。估计见到老头子被放冷枪让他受了刺激,他一向以为唐就是上帝。迈克,他和你我不一样。"

黑根赞同道:"对,别让弗雷迪参与。什么都别让他参与,完全不参与。要我说,桑尼,风波过去之前,你应该留在家里,根本不要出门。你在家里很安全。别低估索洛佐的能力,他是个厉害的对手。医院安排了吗?"

桑尼点点头:"警察封锁了医院,我派我的手下不间断地探望爸爸。汤姆,你看看这份名单?"

黑根看得皱起了眉头:"老天在上,桑尼,你真的动了个人感情。唐会认为这纯粹是生意争端。索洛佐是关键人物。干掉索洛佐,事情就会恢复原样。没必要对塔塔利亚家族下手。"

桑尼望向两位首领。忒西奥耸耸肩。"棘手。"他说。克莱门扎根本不吭声。

桑尼对克莱门扎说:"有件事不需要讨论就能下结论。我不想再看见保利那张脸。把他列在名单的第一位。"胖子首领点了点头。

黑根说:"卢卡呢?索洛佐似乎并不担心卢卡。我很担心要是卢卡出卖了我们,那我们的麻烦就大了。我们必须首先搞清楚卢卡的下落。有谁联系上他了吗?"

"没有,"桑尼答道,"我整个晚上都在打电话找他。他也许在哪儿鬼混。"

"不,"黑根说,"他从不和情妇过夜,完事后总是回家。迈克,继续打他的电话,直到有人接为止。"迈克尔顺从地拿起听筒,拨出号码。他听到那边的振铃声,但久久无人接听,最后挂断了电话。"一刻钟打一次。"黑根说。

桑尼不耐烦地说:"好吧,汤姆,你是顾问,有什么好建议?你到底认为我们该怎么办?"

黑根拿起桌上的酒瓶给自己倒威士忌。"我们和索洛佐谈判,拖到你父亲恢复健康,能够控制局面为止。有必要的话,甚至可以和他达成交易。等你父亲从床上起来,他不费吹灰之力就能解决问题,其他家族都会听他的。"

桑尼怒道:"你认为我收拾不了索洛佐那家伙?"

汤姆·黑根直勾勾地看着他的眼睛:"桑尼,你当然能击败他,柯里昂家族有这个力量。你有克莱门扎和忒西奥帮你,假如爆发全面战争,他们可以召集上千人手。但要是那样,整个东海岸会血流成河,其他家族会怪罪柯里昂家族。我们会四面树敌。那是你父亲最忌讳的情况。"

迈克尔望着桑尼,以为他听了进去,但桑尼一开口却对黑根说:"要是老头子死了,顾问,你会建议我怎么做?"

黑根平静地说:"我知道你不会听我的,但我会建议你和索洛佐做毒品交易。没了你父亲的政治关系和个人影响力,柯里昂家族就会失去一半力量。没了你父亲,纽约其他几大家族会转而支持塔塔利亚家族和索洛佐,避免长期无益的斗争。要是你父亲死了,达成交易,然后等待时机。"

桑尼气得脸色发白:"你说得倒是轻巧,他们杀的又不是你父亲。"

黑根马上自豪地说:"对他来说,我和你还有迈克一样,都是他的好儿子,甚至更好。我给你的是职业意见。就个人而言,我想杀光那群杂种。"他声音里的情绪让桑尼后悔,桑尼说:"噢,天哪,汤姆,我不是那个意思。"但他确实是这个意思。血缘毕竟是血缘,其他什么都比不了。

桑尼沉思片刻,另外几个人在尴尬的寂静中等着他。最后,他叹了口气,静静地说:"好吧,我们按兵不动,等老头子回来作决定。汤姆,我要你也留在林荫道。别冒险。迈克,你要当心,虽说我觉得索洛佐不会把亲属拖进战争,因为那样所有人都会与他为敌。但你还是要当心。忒西奥,你的手下是后备力量,让他们在城里各处刺探情报。克莱门扎,处理掉狗东西保利·加图之后,把你的手下调进屋里和林荫道,替换忒西奥的人。忒西奥,你在医院的人就别动了。汤姆,明天一早就开始用电话和信使与索洛佐和塔塔利亚展开谈判。迈克,你明天带几个克莱门扎的人去卢卡家等他露面,要是他不露面,就搞清楚他到底去哪儿了。那个疯子说不定听到新闻,已经去找索洛佐算账了。我实在不相信他会背叛自己的唐,土佬给他多少钱都没用。"

黑根不情愿地说:"也许迈克不该这么直接地介入这种事。"

"也对,"桑尼说,"那就算了,迈克,我反正需要你在家等电话,这个任务比较重要。"

迈克尔没吭声。他觉得很惭愧,甚至羞耻,他注意到克莱门扎和忒西奥尽量不动声色,他很清楚他们在努力掩饰对他的轻蔑。他拿起电话,拨打卢卡·布拉齐的号码,把听筒压在耳朵上,听着铃声响了又响。

第六章

彼得·克莱门扎那晚睡得很不安稳,他早早起床,早餐是一杯渣酿白兰地、厚厚一片热那亚的萨拉米香肠和一节新鲜的意大利面包,和往常一样,面包还是直接送到他家门口。用过早餐,他端起大号素色瓷杯,喝着加了茴香酒的热咖啡。他身穿旧浴袍和红拖鞋在屋里走来走去,琢磨着今天要做的事情。昨晚桑尼·柯里昂说得很清楚,要尽快处理掉保利·加图。所谓尽快,就是今天。

克莱门扎有点犯难。倒不是因为加图是他手底下出来的叛徒。这件事和首领的判断力没关系。保利的背景毕竟挑不出毛病。他来自一个西西里家庭,和柯里昂家的孩子在同一个地区长大,甚至和其中一个孩子是同学。他顺理成章走到现在的地位。上头考验过他,没有发现缺点。杀了第一个人之后,他靠家族过上了好日子,东区的一个簿记生意有他的抽头,一个工会发他薪水。克莱门扎不是不知道保利·加图靠抢劫捞点钱,这么做当然违反家族的规定,但也能证明他的价值。打破这种规章制度说明他闲不住,就仿佛好赛马永远想挣脱缰绳。

再说保利从没因为抢劫而惹来麻烦。他的行动总是经过精心计划,实施时只造成最低限度的混乱,从不伤害别人:他只抢了曼哈顿时装中心的三千美元和布鲁克林贫民区一家瓷器厂的工人全部薪水。一个年轻人的口袋里有些闲钱终归是好事。事情并不出格。谁能料想保利·加图会叛变呢?

今天早晨让彼得·克莱门扎烦心的是个行政问题。处决加图这件事本身反而犹如家常便饭。问题在于他这个首领该提拔谁上位,在家族内取代加图?对于"纽扣人"①来说,这次晋升非常重要,不能轻易作决定。这个人必须悍勇、精明、足够安全,不能有麻烦就向警察开口,必须深受西西里的缄默规则的熏陶。另外,这个人有了新的位置,应该得到什么待遇呢?克莱门扎曾经好几次和唐谈过,应该给出事时顶在最前线的重要纽扣人提高奖金,但唐没有答应。要是保利的荷包更鼓,说不定就能抵抗奸诈土佬索洛佐的利诱了。

克莱门扎最后把候选名单缩小到了三个人。第一个是为哈莱姆的黑人非法彩票经营者做事的执法人,强壮而凶残,力大无穷,很有个人魅力,容易和别人打成一片,但必要时也能让他们害怕他。考虑了半小时,克莱门扎还是划掉了这个名字。这家伙和

---

① bucton man:纽扣人.犯罪组织内类似打手的低等级成员。

黑人走得太近,说明性格有缺陷。而且他现在的这个位置还没人能够取代。

克莱门扎几乎选了第二个人,这个小伙子很努力,为组织效力忠心耿耿,干得也不错。他为家族许可的曼哈顿地区高利贷头目服务,负责收回拖欠的账款。他刚人行的时候是一名簿记的代理员。他还没有准备好接受这么重要的提拔。

最后他选定的是洛可·兰坡。兰坡在家族的学徒生涯虽短但令人钦佩。战争期间,他在非洲负伤,四三年退伍。尽管受伤让他瘸得厉害,算是半个残废,但由于实在缺少年轻人,克莱门扎还是吸收了他。克莱门扎让他当时装中心黑市的联系人,同时联系控制物价局食品券的公务员。经过磨炼,兰坡成了整个行当里的麻烦解决专家。克莱门扎喜欢他出色的判断力。他知道有些事情蛮干毫无意义,只会受到重罚或者蹲上半年大牢,他明白要挣大钱就要舍小利。他眼力不错,明白凶恶恐吓不适合这一行,轻轻敲打就够了。他低调处理他负责的生意,完全合乎需要。

克莱门扎松了一口气,就像认真的办公室主任解决了棘手的人事问题。好了,洛可·兰坡将得到助手的位置。克莱门扎打算亲自处理这件事,帮助没有经验的新人杀人明誓,也了结他和保利·加图的个人恩怨。保利曾经是他的门生,他越过几个更有资格、更忠诚的人提拔了保利,他帮助保利杀了第一个人,处处提携他。保利背叛的不单是家族,还背叛了他的恩主彼得·克莱门扎。不知尊重的行为必须严惩。

其他的事情都安排好了。保利·加图接到命令,下午三点来接克莱门扎,开一辆自己的车,别开赃车。克莱门扎拿起电话,拨打洛可·兰坡的号码。他没有报上姓名,而只是说:"来我家,有事要你办。"他很高兴地发现尽管时间还早,兰坡既不惊讶也不睡意蒙咙,只是说:"行。"好小子。克莱门扎又说:"别着急,吃过早饭午饭再来,不过别超过下午两点。"

电话里又是言简意赅的一声"行",克莱门扎挂断电话。他早已通知手下去柯里昂家族的林荫道接替忒西奥首领的人,现在已经办妥了。他有几个得力部属,这种体力活不需要他操心。

他决定去洗他的凯迪拉克。他爱死了这辆车。开起来安静又稳当,内饰非常考究,天气好的时候,他偶尔会在车里坐上个把钟头,因为比坐在屋里舒服多了。另外,洗车总能帮助他思考。他记得父亲在意大利也喜欢洗刷驴子。

克莱门扎在有暖气的车库里忙活,他讨厌寒冷。他复查计划。对付保利非得加倍小心,这家伙就像耗子,能闻到危险。不过话也说回来,就算他很凶悍,这会儿肯定也吓得屁滚尿流,因为老头子还活着。他多半坐立不安,像是满屁股爬满蚂蚁的驴子。克莱门扎早就习惯了这种情况,在他的行当乃是家常便饭。首先,他要找个好借口,让洛可陪着他们。其次,他得想个说得过去的任务,需要他们三个人一起去办事。

当然了,严格来说,没必要这样。不需要任何麻烦也能做掉保利·加图。他已经被盯上了,不可能跑掉。可是,克莱门扎有个强烈的感觉,那就是遵守良好的工作习惯很重要,务必做到万无一失。论到生死问题,谁也说不准会发生什么。

彼得·克莱门扎一边洗浅蓝色的凯迪拉克,一边琢磨用什么样的表情说什么话。他要粗声大气,就像保利惹他发火似的。加图敏感多疑,这会打乱他的阵脚,至少能让他摸不着头脑。过度友善反而会让他警觉,但也不能大发雷霆,而要是心不在焉的恼火。兰坡为什么也在?这会使得保利非常惊慌,特别是兰坡还必须坐在后排。保利开车,后脑勺对着兰坡,他恐怕不会乖乖让自己置于险境。

克莱门扎使劲擦拭抛光凯迪拉克的金属表面。事情会很棘手,非常棘手。他考虑要不要再叫一个人来,但想想还是算了。这一点上他遵循了基本的逻辑判断。将来有可能会出现有人会因为利益而出卖他的情况,要是只有一名同伙,那就是正反双方各执一词。但要是还有第二名同伙作旁证,平衡就会被打破。不,办事必须严格按照程序。

克莱门扎最伤脑筋的是处决必须"公开"。言下之意:尸体要被发现。他更希望让尸体消失(通常的埋葬地点是附近的大海,或者家族朋友在新泽西拥有的沼泽地,或者其他更复杂的手段)。可是,这次必须公开,震慑潜在的叛徒,警告敌人:柯里昂家族绝对没有变得愚蠢或软弱。这么快就揪出了索洛佐的间谍,这会使得索洛佐警觉起来。柯里昂家族将挽回部分颜面。老头子吃冷枪让家族显得有点愚蠢。

克莱门扎叹了口气。凯迪拉克闪闪发亮,仿佛一枚硕大的蓝色钢蛋,可他离解决问题仍旧差了十万八千里。答案忽然冒了出来,既合情合理又切中要害,能解释洛可·兰坡、他本人和保利为何一起出现,能让这个任务足够隐秘和重要。

他要告诉保利,今天的任务是找一处公寓,以备家族决定"睡床垫"之用。

每当家族之间的战争变得残酷而激烈,双方会在秘密公寓设立指挥部,双方人手可以睡在摆满房间的一个个床垫上。这么做不是为了让妻儿远离危险,这样的斗争一般不会牵连家人,而是参加战斗的人很容易遭到报复。找个秘密地点住进去只是出于明智,因为你不想让敌手或想贸然插手的警察掌握你的一举一动。

因此,家族通常会派一位受到信任的首领去租一套秘密公寓,摆满床垫,作为据点,动手的时候方便进入城区。克莱门扎领命办这种事当然合情合理。他带上加图和兰坡安排各种细节(例如装饰公寓)同样合情合理。另外,事实证明保利·加图很贪婪,第一个念头肯定是这么重要的情报能从索洛佐手上换到多少钱,克莱门扎想着想着笑了。

洛可·兰坡来得很早,克莱门扎向他解释任务和各自的角色。惊讶和感激让兰坡喜形于色,他毕恭毕敬地感谢克莱门扎提拔他,允许他为家族效劳。克莱门扎相信他没看错人。他拍着兰坡的肩膀说:"过了今天,你的待遇会好得多。这个回头再谈。你明白家族现在还有更关键、更重要的事情要做。"兰坡打了个手势,意思是他不着急,知道少不了他的奖赏。

克莱门扎走进书房,打开保险柜,取出一把手枪交给兰坡。"用这把,"他说,"警察绝对查不到。和保利一起留在车里。等任务完成,我要你带着老婆孩子去佛罗里达度假。先用你的钱垫上,回头我补给你。放松放松,晒晒太阳。住家族在迈阿密海滩的酒店,要是有事我知道上哪儿找你。"

克莱门扎的妻子敲敲书房门,说保利·加图来了。他的车停在车道上。克莱门扎带着兰坡穿过车库。克莱门扎坐在前排加图旁边的座位,嘟囔一声算是打招呼,一脸不痛快的表情。他看看手表,像是预料到加图会迟到。

雪貂脸的纽扣人使劲打量他,寻找蛛丝马迹。兰坡坐进他背后的后排座位,他抖了一下,说:"洛可,坐到另一边去。你块头太大,会遮住后视镜。"兰坡乖乖地换到克莱门扎背后,仿佛这是全世界最自然不过的要求。

克莱门扎烦闷地对加图说:"该死的桑尼,他吓破胆了,已经开始考虑睡床垫。我们得在西区找个地方。保利,你和洛可准备东西,到时候其他人用得着。知道什么合适的地方吗?"

不出所料,加图的眼睛露出贪婪的光芒。保利吞下鱼饵,满脑子都是这条情报值多少钱,忘了考虑自己有没有危险。兰坡表现得很完美,他盯着窗外,一脸冷淡,懒洋洋的。克莱门扎不禁庆幸自己选对了人。

加图耸耸肩:"我得想想。"

克莱门扎嘟囔道:"边开车边想,我今天要去纽约。"

保利车技老练,下午进市区的车流稀少,因此初冬的夜幕刚开始降临,他们就赶到了城区。一路上他们没有闲聊。克莱门扎指挥保利驶向华盛顿高地。他看了几幢公寓楼,吩咐保利到阿瑟大道停车等候。他把洛可·兰坡也留在车上,走进维拉·马里奥餐厅,吃了一顿小牛肉和色拉的简餐,对几个熟人点头致意。一小时过后,他走了几个街区到停车的地方,坐进车里,加图和兰坡还在等候。"妈的,"克莱门扎说,"他们又要我们回长滩。有别的任务交给我们。桑尼说这事回头再说。洛可,你就住在市里,要么你就留下?"

洛可平静地说:"我把车停在你家了,我老婆明天一早就要用。"

"这倒是,"克莱门扎说,"那你只能跟我们回去了。"

回长滩仍旧一路无言。在进城区的最后一段路上,克莱门扎忽然说:"保利,停车，我要撒尿。"一起做事那么久，加图知道胖子首领憋不住尿。他经常提这种要求。加图开下公路，在通往沼泽的泥地上停车。克莱门扎下车，走了几步钻进灌木丛，真的撒了一泡尿。他回来打开车门，飞快地张望一眼公路上下。没有灯光，路上一片漆黑。"动手。"克莱门扎说。一秒钟后，车里轰然响起枪声。保利·加图像是蹿了起来，躯体撞在方向盘上，接着软软地倒在座位上。克莱门扎早就后退两步，免得溅上头骨碎片或血迹。

洛可·兰坡从后座手忙脚乱爬下车。枪还握在手里，他一抬手扔进沼泽。他和克莱门扎匆忙走向停在附近的一辆车，坐进车里，兰坡在座位底下摸索，找到留给他们的钥匙。他发动引擎，送克莱门扎回家。他没有走回头路，而是走琼斯海滩堤道穿过梅里克镇，取草原小溪公园大道，拐上州北公园大道，走长岛高速公路到白石大桥，经布朗克斯返回他在曼哈顿的家。

第七章

暗杀唐·柯里昂的前一天夜里，他最强大、最忠诚也是最令人恐惧的鹰从准备和敌人碰面。几个月前，卢卡·布拉齐就开始接触索洛佐。这是唐·柯里昂本人的命令。卢卡的办法是频繁光顾塔塔利亚家族控制的夜总会，勾搭他们最抢手的应召女郎。和应召女郎上床的时候，他抱怨说他在柯里昂家族受到压制，无人赏识他的价值。和应召女郎鬼混一周以后，夜总会老板布鲁诺·塔塔利亚开始接触他。布鲁诺是最小的儿子，表面上和家族的皮肉生意没有往来，但他那因长腿舞女而出名的夜总会却是城市应召女郎的进修学校。

第一次会面说的尽是场面话，塔塔利亚邀请他以执法人身份加入家族生意。这么你来我往了差不多一个月，卢卡像是个被年轻美女迷得神魂颠倒的男人，布鲁诺·塔塔利亚的角色是个生意人，试图挖对手的墙脚。在一次类似的会面中，卢卡假装有所动摇，说："但有一点你必须明白，我绝对不会背叛教父。唐·柯里昂是我非常尊敬的人。我理解他，因为在家族生意里，他必须把几个儿子摆在我前面。"

布鲁诺·塔塔利亚是新一代黑手党，几乎毫不掩饰对卢卡·布拉齐、唐·柯里昂甚至自己父亲这些胡子彼得的蔑视，但今天却有点过于虔敬，他说："我父亲不可能希望你做任何反对柯里昂家族的事情。何必呢？现在大家都相安无事，和以前不一样啦。只是说你要是想找份新工作，我可以给我父亲传个话。我们这一行永远用得上你这样的人。这不是简单的生意，只有手段强硬的人才能让事情顺利进行。你什么时候下了决心就告诉我。"

卢卡耸耸肩:"我现在过得也不坏。"于是这件事就算了。

他使塔塔利亚家族相信他想从油水很足的毒品生意中捞点好处。这样一来,要是土佬有什么盘算,他也许能听到风声,还能知道索洛佐是否打算招惹唐·柯里昂。等了两个月,风平浪静,卢卡报告唐,索洛佐大方地接受了失败。唐吩咐他接着试探,但旁敲侧击即可,别急于求成。

唐·柯里昂遇刺前的那天晚上,卢卡来到夜总会。布鲁诺·塔塔利亚很快在他的酒桌边坐了下来。

"我有个朋友想和你聊聊。"他说。

"带他过来好了,"卢卡说,"你的朋友我都欢迎。"

"不行,"布鲁诺说,"他想私下会会你。"

"他是谁?"卢卡问。

"就是个朋友,"布鲁诺·塔塔利亚说,"他有个提议想听听你的意见。夜里晚些时候行吗?"

"当然,"卢卡说,"时间地点?"

塔塔利亚悄声说:"夜总会凌晨四点打烊,服务员打扫卫生的时候,我们就在这儿碰头,怎么样?"

他们知道我的习惯,卢卡心想,他们肯定调查过我。他通常下午三四点起床吃早餐,然后和家族里的老伙伴赌博或者找姑娘消遣。有时候他看一场午夜场电影,然后找一家夜总会喝酒。天亮之前他从不上床。因此,提议凌晨四点碰面并不像听上去那么稀奇。

"行,好的,"他说,"我四点再来。"他走出夜总会,叫计程车去第十大道他租的房间。他和一家意大利远亲合住。这套公寓贴着铁轨,他的两个房间和其他房间隔开,中间是一扇特制的门。他喜欢这么住,因为既有家庭生活的感觉,也能避免在最缺乏防御的地方遭受突袭。

狡猾的土耳其狐狸要露出他毛茸茸的尾巴了,卢卡心想。事情要是发展得顺利,索洛佐今晚亲自露面,说不定可以就此一了百了;给唐送一份圣诞大礼。卢卡回到房间里,打开床底下的行李箱,取出沉重的防弹背心。他脱掉衣服,把防弹背心穿在羊毛内衣外面,套上衬衫和外衣。他考虑了几秒钟,要不要打电话到唐在长滩的住处,把最新进展告诉他,但他知道唐从不在电话上和任何人谈正事,再说这个任务是唐私下里布置的,不希望别人知道,黑根和他的大儿子也包括在内。

卢卡总是带枪,他有持枪许可证,这可能是有史以来最昂贵的一份许可证,总共花了万把块,但假如被警察搜身,他可以免于牢狱之灾。身为家族的最高行动指挥官,他配得上这东西。不过今夜不同,考虑到他也许能了结这个任务,他需要一把"安全"枪,一把不可能被追查的枪。不过,转念仔细一想,他决定今夜还是先听听对方的建议,然后向教父唐·柯里昂报告。

他动身返回夜总会,但没再喝酒,而是慢慢走到四十八街,拐进他最喜欢的意大利餐厅帕斯蒂小馆,吃了顿悠闲的夜宵。快到约定的时间了,他踱回夜总会门口。进去的时候,看门人已经走了。衣帽间的姑娘也走了。只有布鲁诺·塔塔利亚在等他,布鲁诺和他打招呼,领着他走向房间侧面空荡荡的酒吧。他前方是几张空荡荡的小酒桌,中央的抛光黄木舞池闪闪发亮,犹如一小粒钻石。阴影中是空无一人的演奏台,麦克风细长的金属支架悄然耸立。

卢卡在吧台前坐下,布鲁诺·塔塔利亚走进吧台。卢卡谢绝了布鲁诺递给他的酒杯,点燃香烟。要见他的有可能是别人,不是土佬。但就在这时,他看见索洛佐走出了房间另一头的暗处。

索洛佐和他握手,和他并排在吧台前落座。塔塔利亚把酒杯摆在土佬面前,索洛佐点头致谢。"知道我是谁吗?"索洛佐问。

卢卡点点头,露出一抹狞笑。老鼠被引出洞窟。他很乐于处理这个背叛西西里原则的家伙。

"知道我有什么提议吗?"索洛佐问。

卢卡摇摇头。

"有一桩大买卖,"索洛佐说,"真的大,顶层人员每人几百万的大生意。第一批货运到,我保证有你五万块。我说的是毒品。毒品是未来。"

卢卡说:"为什么找我?要我向唐传话?"

索洛佐做了个怪相:"我已经和唐谈过了。他不想参与。没关系,离了他我照样干。但我需要一个身手好的人,提供现场保护。我知道你和家族闹得不太愉快,也许愿意换个环境。"

卢卡耸耸肩:"那得看条件够不够好了。"

索洛佐一直在全神贯注地观察他,此刻似乎下了决定。"考虑几天我的提议,然后我们再聊聊看。"他说着伸出手,但卢卡假装没看见,忙着往嘴里塞香烟。吧台里的布鲁诺·塔塔利亚不知从哪儿摸出打火机,伸向卢卡的香烟。他忽然做了个怪动作,把打火机丢在吧台上,抓住卢卡的右手,死死按住。

卢卡的反应很快,身体滑下高脚凳,想挣脱布鲁诺的束缚。索洛佐扑上来抓住他的左腕。但卢卡比他们两人加起来都要强壮,他险些挣脱,但就在最后一刻,又一个男人走出他背后的暗处,用丝质细绳勒住他的脖子。细绳收紧,勒得卢卡无法呼吸。他脸色变紫,双臂渐渐没了力气。塔塔利亚和索洛佐很容易就能按住他的胳膊了,他们像孩子似的站在那儿,好奇地看着卢卡背后的男人继续收紧细绳。地板突然变得又湿又滑。卢卡的括约肌失去控制,屎尿倾泻而出。他失去了全部力量,两腿打弯,身体下坠。索洛佐和塔塔利亚松开他的手,只剩下勒杀者还支撑着他的身体,卢卡倒下,他跟着跪倒在地,收紧细绳,细绳深深陷进脖子上的肉里。卢卡的眼睛突出,像是受了极大的震惊,除了这种震惊,他和活人已经毫无相似之处。他死了。

"别让尸体被发现,"索洛佐说,"不能立刻被发现,这很重要。"他转身离去,消失在暗处。

第八章

唐·柯里昂吃冷枪后的第二天,整个家族忙得不可开交。迈克尔守在电话旁,一有消息就转达桑尼。汤姆·黑根忙着物色双方都能接受的调停人,安排和索洛佐的会谈。土佬突然变得谨慎,大概是知道了克莱门扎和忒西奥手下的家族纽扣人在全城搜寻他的踪迹。索洛佐寸步不离藏身之处,塔塔利亚家族的所有高层人物也一样。桑尼倒是早有预料,他知道敌人势必要采取这种最基本的预防措施。

克莱门扎忙着收拾保利·加图。忒西奥领命寻找卢卡·布拉齐的下落。卢卡从刺杀的前一天夜里开始就没回过家,这不是好兆头。但桑尼既不相信布拉齐会背叛家族,也不认为他有可能遭到突袭。

柯里昂妈妈留在市区,住进家族的朋友家里,好离医院近一些。女婿卡洛·里齐提出愿意帮忙,但家里说你管好唐·柯里昂安排的生意就行了,也就是曼哈顿意大利人聚居区的簿记业务。康妮和母亲住在市里,方便她探望医院里的父亲。

弗雷迪还在父母家自己的房间里,靠镇静剂维持情绪。桑尼和迈克尔去探望过他,见到他面色苍白,一脸病容,不禁大吃一惊。"老天。"走出弗雷迪的房间,桑尼对迈克尔说,"他看着比老头子受伤更重。"

迈克尔耸耸肩。他在战场上见过处于类似情况的士兵,但没想到这种事会落到弗雷迪身上。他记得小时候二哥是家里最强壮的,也是对父亲最恭顺的。可是,大家都知道唐已经放弃了二儿子,他不可能在家族生意里担当重要角色。他不够精明,也不够无情,性格过于孤僻,没有足够的魄力。

那天傍晚,迈克尔接到约翰尼·方坦从好莱坞打来的电话。桑尼拿起听筒:"算了,约翰尼,你回来看老头子也没啥用。他伤势太重,而且会让你招致非议,我知道老头子不会喜欢这样。等他好一点,我们把他接回家,你再来看他吧。好的,我会转达你的祝福。"桑尼挂断电话,扭头对迈克尔说:"爸爸听了肯定高兴,约翰尼想从加州飞回来看他。"

还是傍晚,克莱门扎的一名手下叫迈克尔去厨房接听那部公开的电话。打来的是凯。

"你父亲没事吧?"她问,声音有点紧张,不太自然。迈克尔知道她还不太相信发生的事情,不太相信他父亲真是报纸所称的"匪徒"。

"他会好起来的。"迈克尔说。

"我能陪你去医院看他吗?"凯问。

迈克尔笑了。她记得他说过的话:想和老意大利人相处得好,就必须经常做这种事情。"这次是特例,"他说,"要是记者知道了你的名字和背景,肯定立刻登上《每日新闻》的第三版。美国姑娘和黑手党老大的儿子有一腿。你父母恐怕不会喜欢吧?"

凯干巴巴地说:"我父母从来不看《每日新闻》。"她又尴尬地顿了顿,然后说,"你没事吧,迈克,你不会有危险吧?"

迈克尔又笑着说:"我是柯里昂家族出了名的胆小鬼。没有任何威胁。他们才懒得来收拾我呢。没事,凯,危机已经过去,不会再有麻烦了。本来就是个意外而已。见到你再跟你解释吧。"

"什么时候能再见?"她问。

迈克尔沉思道:"今天夜里如何? 先到你的酒店喝一杯吃顿饭,然后我去医院探望老头子。成天在这儿接电话,我倦透了。行吗? 但别告诉任何人。我可不想撞见报社记者拍我俩的照片。不是开玩笑,凯,那可就尴尬死了,特别是对你父母来说。"

"好的,"凯说,"我等你。要我帮你买圣诞礼物吗? 或者别的什么事情?"

"不用,"迈克尔说,"你准备一下就行。"

她有点兴奋地轻笑一声。"我会准备好的,"她说,"难道不是一向如此吗?"

"对,是的,"他说,"所以你是我最爱的姑娘。"

"我爱你。"她说,"你能说吗?"

迈克尔看着厨房里的四个小混混。"不行,"他说,"今晚,好吗?"

"好的。"她说。他挂断电话。

克莱门扎忙完当天的任务,终于回来,在厨房里忙着用大锅烹制番茄酱。迈克尔对他点点头,返回拐角办公室,发现黑根和桑尼等他等得很不耐烦。"克莱门扎在外面吗?"桑尼问。

迈克尔咧嘴一笑:"他在给手下煮面条,和军队似的。"

桑尼没好气地说:"叫他别浪费那个时间了,赶紧进来。我有更重要的任务交给他。叫忒西奥和他一起过来。"

几分钟后,几个人都集中在办公室。桑尼劈头就问克莱门扎:"处理掉了?"

克莱门扎点点头。"你再也不会看见他了。"

迈克尔像是被电打了一下,意识到他们说的是保利·加图,小保利已经毙命,被婚礼上高高兴兴跳舞的克莱门扎杀死了。

桑尼问黑根:"联系上索洛佐了?"

黑根摇摇头:"他的谈判热情似乎已经冷了,反正显得没那么急切了。也许只是格外小心而已,免得被我们的纽扣人盯上。再说我还没找到他信任的有地位的调解人。不过,他肯定明白现在必须谈判。老头子死里逃生,他已经错过了机会。"

桑尼说:"他很精明,是我们家族遇到的最精明的家伙。也许他猜到我们只是在拖延时间,等老头子情况好转,或者摸清他的底细。"

黑根耸耸肩:"对,他肯定猜到了,但他还是非得谈判不可。他别无选择。我明天一定安排妥当。不会有错。"

克莱门扎的一名手下敲敲门,走进办公室。他对克莱门扎说:"收音机里刚才说警察发现保利·加图死在他的车里。"

克莱门扎点点头,答道:"不用担心。"纽扣人惊讶地看着首领,随即露出了然的表情,转身返回厨房。

会议继续进行,像是没有受到任何打扰。桑尼问黑根:"唐的情况有变化吗?"

黑根摇摇头。"他没事了,但最近几天不能说话。他完全失去知觉,还没从手术中恢复回来。你母亲差不多守了他一天,康妮也是。医院里到处是警察,忒西奥的人也在附近,以防万一。几天后等他好转,我们去问他要我们怎么做。现在必须拖住索洛佐,免得他狗急跳墙。所以我才安排你和他商谈交易。"

桑尼冷哼道:"那也得他肯谈,我已经让克莱门扎和忒西奥去找他了,说不定我们能撞大运,一口气解决问题。"

"哪儿有这么好的运气,"黑根说,"索洛佐太精明了。"黑根顿了顿,"他知道一旦坐上谈判桌,就基本上只能任我们摆布了。所以他在拖延。我猜他正在寻求纽约另外几大家族的支持,这样就算老头子放出话来,我们也没法追杀他。"

桑尼皱起眉头:"他们为什么要支持他?"

黑根耐心地解释道:"为了避免大规模斗争,那样会伤害所有人,逼着报纸和政府采取行动。另外,索洛佐会让他们分一杯羹。你知道贩毒有多少油水可捞。柯里昂家族不需要,我们有赌博,那是和气生财的好生意。但另外几大家族在饿肚皮。索洛佐已经证明了他的能力,他们知道他能搞大贩毒买卖。他活着,他的钱就能流进他们的口袋,死了,他会带来麻烦。"

迈克尔从没见过桑尼此刻的脸色:厚实的爱神嘴唇和古铜色的皮肤变得灰白。"我他妈不在乎他们要什么。他们最好别插手这场战斗。"

克莱门扎和忒西奥不安地动了动,像是步兵首领害怕将军心血来潮,下令不惜一切代价攻克固若金汤的山头。黑根有点不耐烦了。"别这样,桑尼,你父亲不会喜欢你的想法。你知道他常说'那是白费劲'。没错,要是老头子下令追杀索洛佐,我们不会允许任何人挡道。但这并不是个人恩怨,而是生意。要是追杀土佬,其他家族插手,我们就展开谈判。要是其他家族发现我们决心干掉索洛佐,他们会放手的。唐会在其他领域让步,扯平得失。但千万别在这种事情上大开杀戒。这是生意。连暗杀你父亲也都是生意手段,不是个人恩怨。你现在应该明白这一点了。"

桑尼的眼神仍旧凶恶。"对,这些我都理解。但你也要明白一点,到我们想杀索洛佐的时候,谁也挡不住我们。"

桑尼问忒西奥:"卢卡有消息吗?"

忒西奥摇摇头。"完全没有,多半是被索洛佐抓走了。"

黑根静静地说:"索洛佐不担心卢卡,这让我觉得很有意思。他很精明,不可能不担心卢卡这样一个人。我相信不管用什么方法,他已经让卢卡置身事外了。"

桑尼嘟囔道:"天哪,希望卢卡别和我们作对。我怕的就是这种事。克莱门扎,忒西奥,你们怎么觉得?"

克莱门扎说得很慢:"任何人都有可能犯错,看看保利就知道。但卢卡不一样,他只认一条路。教父是他唯一信仰、畏惧的人。不仅如此,桑尼,他对你父亲的尊敬超过其他任何人,而教父赢得了所有人的尊敬。不,卢卡不可能背叛。要我说,索洛佐这种人,无论多么狡猾,也不可能成功突袭卢卡。卢卡怀疑所有人和所有事。他总是作最坏的打算。我估计他只是去什么地方休息几天。我们随时都会得到他的消息。"

桑尼转向忒西奥。布鲁克林首领耸耸肩。"任何人都有可能叛变。卢卡这人很敏感。也许唐不知怎的触犯了他。也有这个可能。但我认为是索洛佐成功突袭了他。这符合顾问刚才说的。我们得作最坏的打算。"

桑尼对大家说:"索洛佐应该很快就会听说保利·加图的下场,他会有什么反应?"

克莱门扎恶狠狠地说:"会让他好好思考一下。你会知道柯里昂家族不是傻瓜,会明白昨天算他非常走运。"

桑尼断然道:"那不是走运。索洛佐策划了好几周。他们肯定每天跟踪老头子去办公室,观察他的生活习惯,然后买通保利甚至卢卡。他们踩着时间点绑架汤姆。他们做到了所有想做的事情。他们不走运,运气不好,雇用的纽扣人不够出色,老头子动作又太快。他们要是杀了他,我就必须达成交易,索洛佐势必取胜,暂时取胜。我只能耐心等待,五年十年后才能报仇。你不能说他走运,彼得,那太低估他了。我们最近太过于低估别人。"

一个纽扣人从厨房端来一盆意大利面,然后送来盘子、叉子和红酒。他们边聊边吃,迈克尔看得很讶异。他没有吃,汤姆也没吃,但桑尼、克莱门扎和忒西奥狼吞虎咽,最后用面包皮把酱汁蘸得一干二净。场面甚至有点滑稽。他们继续讨论。

忒西奥不认为消灭保利·加图会让索洛佐不安,事实上土佬多半早就料到了,甚至还挺高兴。少了一张没用的嘴巴吃薪水。他并不会因此害怕;设身处地想一想,他们难道会害怕吗?

迈克尔不太有信心地说:"我知道我是外行,不过就你们对索洛佐的分析而言,加上他突然和汤姆切断联系,我猜他还藏着一张王牌。他很可能还会耍手段,重新占上风。要是能猜到他打算干什么,那我们就取得先机了。"

桑尼不情愿地说:"是啊,我也琢磨过这个,但能想到的只有卢卡。我已经放出风声,取消他享有的所有家族特权,一露面就带他来这儿。除此之外我只能想到一点,那就是索洛佐已经和纽约各大家族达成交易,明天我们就会得知他们要联合起来对付我们。那样的话,我们就必须答应土佬的条件了。汤姆,你说呢?"

黑根点点头:"我也是这么看的。没有你父亲领导,我们顶不住这种压力。只有他能反抗其他家族。他们需要他的政治关系,他能拿这些关系做交易,前提是他非常想这么做的话。"

克莱门扎开口说话,对一个刚刚被最得力的属下背叛的人来说,他有点过于自信:"索洛佐绝对不可能靠近这幢屋子,老板,你不必担心这个。"

桑尼若有所思地看了他几秒钟,然后对忒西奥说:"医院怎么样?你的人守得住吗?"

这次会议的第一次,忒西奥显得对自己完全有信心。"里里外外都有,"他说,"二十四小时看守。警察也戒备森严。警探在病房门口等着盘问老头子。真是笑话。唐还在打点滴,不吃不喝,所以不用担心食物,本来在这方面最应该提防的就是土耳其人,他们相信毒药。他们不可能接近唐,无论如何都不可能。"

桑尼躺进座椅。"也不可能对我下手,他们要和我谈生意,需要家族运转正常。"他朝迈克尔咧嘴一笑,"我猜会不会是你。也许索洛佐打算绑架你,拿你当人质威胁谈交易。"

迈克尔郁闷地想着,我和凯的约会没希望了,桑尼不可能允许我离开这里。但黑根急躁地说:"不,他要是需要谈判砝码,随时都可以抓迈克。但谁都知道迈克不参与家族生意,他是平民,要是索洛佐抓他,他会失去其他纽约家族的支持。连塔塔利亚家族都会帮我们追杀他。不,其实显而易见。明天我们要接待所有家族共同派出的一名使者,他会告诉我们必须和土佬联合做生意。他在等的就是这个。这就是他藏着的王牌。"

迈克尔松了一口气。"那就好,"他说,"我今晚得进城。"

"干什么?"桑尼厉声问。

迈克尔咧嘴一笑:"我打算去医院探望老头子,看看妈妈和康妮。另外还有些别的事情。"和唐一样,迈克尔从不吐露真实意图,他不想告诉桑尼说他要去见凯·亚当斯。没有理由要告诉他,只是习惯而已。

厨房里传来一阵嘈杂。克莱门扎出去看个究竟,回来的时候,他双手捧着卢卡·布拉齐的防弹背心,里面裹着一大条死鱼。

克莱门扎干巴巴地说:"土佬已经知道他的间谍保利·加图的下场了。"

忒西奥同样干巴巴地说:"我们知道卢卡·布拉齐的下落了。"

桑尼点燃雪茄,喝了一注威士忌。迈克尔摸不着头脑,问:"鱼是什么意思?"回答他的是顾问、爱尔兰人黑根。"鱼是说卢卡·布拉齐已经长眠海底。"他说,"这是西西里的传统。"

第九章

迈克尔·柯里昂那晚进城时心情低落。他觉得自己正逐渐陷入家族生意,这违背了他的意愿,他讨厌桑尼使唤他,哪怕只是接电话这种小事。参加家族会议让他感到不安,仿佛连谋杀这种秘密都可以托付给他似的。但现在去见凯,他觉得同样有愧于她。他跟她从没在家族问题上完全说过实话。他虽然也提起家人,但总穿插着笑话和奇闻轶事,比起现实生活中的他们,反而更像彩色电影里的冒险家。但现在,父亲当街挨了冷枪,大哥在策划杀人报复。事实清楚明白,只是这和他告诉凯的不一样。他说父亲遇刺是"意外",麻烦已经结束。妈的,看起来似乎刚开始。桑尼和汤姆没有认清索洛佐的本质,还低估了他,尽管桑尼足够精明,认识到危险。迈克尔试着思考土佬的底牌是什么。这个人显然胆大包天,心细如发,魄力非凡。你必须想到他会真的打你一个措手不及。可是,桑尼、汤姆、克莱门扎和忒西奥都自认为控制住了局势,而且他们都比迈克尔有经验。我是这场战争中的"平民",迈克尔挖苦地想着,要我参加这场战争,你们给我的勋章得比我在二战里拿到的勋章高级个一万倍才行。

想到这里,他又愧疚起来,因为他并不特别同情父亲。亲生父亲被打得满身枪眼,但说来奇怪,听汤姆说这只是生意而非个人恩怨,迈克尔却比任何人都理解这一点。父亲操纵了一辈子的权势,从周围的人身上勒索敬意,眼下付出了代价。

迈克尔只想退出,退出所有这些,去过他自己的生活。可是,在这次危机结束之前,他还不能切断和家族的关系。他必须以一介平民的能力帮忙。他突然意识到了,让他烦心的是分配给他的这个身份:有特权的非战斗人员,以良心为借口拒服兵役的人。怪不得"平民"二字总在脑海里蹦跶得这么烦人。

他来到酒店,凯在大堂等他(克莱门扎的两名手下开车送他进城,确定没有被跟踪后,在附近的一个路口让他下车)。

他们共进晚餐,喝了些酒。"你打算几点去探望父亲?"凯问。

迈克尔看看手表。"探视时间八点半结束。我打算等别人都走了再去。他们会让我上去的。他有私人病房和自己的护士,所以我可以陪他坐一会儿。他恐怕还没法说话,甚至不知道我在不在。但我必须去表达尊敬。"

凯悄声说:"我为你父亲觉得很难过,婚礼那天他看起来那么和气。我不相信报纸上说他的那些话。我认为大部分都是瞎编。"

迈克尔答得很委婉:"我也不这么认为。"他很惊讶地发现自己竟然对凯这么守口如瓶。他爱凯,信任凯,但父亲和家族的事情一句也不会告诉她。她是局外人。

"你怎么样?"凯问,"打算卷入报纸欢天喜地描述的这场黑帮战争吗?"

迈克尔咧嘴一笑,解开上衣纽扣,拉开左右两襟。"看,没有枪。"他说。凯笑出了声。

时间已晚,他们上楼来到她的房间。她为两人调酒,坐在他的大腿上喝酒。她的礼服底下是丝质内衣,他的手摸到她滚烫的大腿。两人倒在床上,穿着衣服做爱,嘴巴黏在一起。完事后,他们躺着一动不动,觉得身体的热气烧穿了衣服。凯喃喃道:"你们当兵的管这个叫吃快餐对吧?"

"对。"迈克尔说。

"倒也不坏。"尝到滋味的凯说。

他们打起瞌睡。迈克尔突然醒来,看看手表。"该死,"他说,"快十点了,我得赶紧去医院。"他到卫生间洗漱一番,梳理头发。凯跟着进来,从背后搂住他的腰。"我们什么时候结婚?"她问。

"随你定,"迈克尔说,"不过要等家里的事情平静下来,老头子情况好转。还有,我觉得你还是先跟父母解释一下比较好。"

"我该怎么说?"凯静静地问。

迈克尔梳着头发。"就说你遇到了一个意大利血统的男人,英勇帅气,达特茅斯学院的优等生,二战时得过杰出服役十字勋章和紫心勋章,诚恳,勤勉。但他父亲是黑手党首领,专杀坏人,有时候贿赂政府高官,因为职业原因被打得浑身枪眼。可是,这和那个诚恳又勤勉的儿子没关系。这么多全记住了?"

凯放开他的身体,靠在卫生间的门上。"真的吗?"她问。"他真的……"她顿了顿,"杀人?"

迈克尔停下梳头的手。"我不清楚,"他说,"没人清楚,但如果是真的,我也不会惊讶。"

他出门之前,她问:"什么时候能再见?"

迈克尔亲吻她。"你先回家,在乡下小城好好想一想。圣诞节假期过后,我回到学校,我们汉诺威再见。好吗?"

"好。"她说,目送他走出房门,看着他先挥手再走进电梯。她从没感觉这么贴近他,从没这么爱一个人,要是有谁说她要到三年之后才会再见到迈克尔,她恐怕不可能忍耐那种痛苦。

迈克尔在法兰西医院门口下了计程车,惊讶地发现街上完全空无一人。他走进医院,发现大厅空空荡荡,不禁更加惊讶。该死,克莱门扎和忒西奥在干什么? 就算他们没上过西点军校,也该有足够的常识去布置岗哨。大厅总得安排几个人吧。

连最后一拨探视者都已离开,现在差不多是晚间十点半。迈克尔既紧张又警觉。他没有在问询处耽搁,因为他知道父亲在四楼,也知道是哪一间病房。他搭自助电梯上去。太奇怪了,没有人拦他,直到四楼护士台才被叫住。他大踏步走过去,没有搭理她的问题,来到父亲的病房前。门外没有人。应该守在门口等待盘问老头子的两个警探在哪儿? 忒西奥和克莱门扎的手下在哪儿? 病房里有人吗? 门开着,迈克尔走进去。床上有个人影,借着照进窗口的月光,迈克尔看清了父亲的脸。父亲直到此刻仍旧面无表情,胸膛随着不均匀的呼吸微微起伏。床边的钢架上垂下软管,插进他的鼻孔。另外几条软管从腹部排出废物,滴进地上的玻璃罐。迈克尔站了几秒钟,确定父亲还活着,然后走出病房。

他对护士说:"我叫迈克尔·柯里昂,想陪我父亲坐一会儿。有两个警探应该守着他,他们去哪儿了?"

护士年轻貌美,对自己的权威很有信心。"噢,你父亲的访客实在太多,干扰到了医院的正常运行,"她说,"十分钟之前有几个警察过来,赶走了所有人。刚刚五分钟之前,我喊那两个警探接电话,他们总部有什么急事,把他们叫走了。不过你别担心,我经常进来查看情况,房间里有什么动静我都听得见,所以我们才敞着门。"

"谢谢。"迈克尔说,"我就陪他坐几分钟,好吗?"

她对迈克尔微笑:"只能几分钟,然后就得离开,你知道医院有规定。"

迈克尔回到父亲的病房里。他拿起话筒,请医院的接线员拨通长滩家里拐角办公室的号码。接电话的是桑尼。迈克尔悄声说:"桑尼,我在医院,我来得很晚。桑尼,这儿一个人都没有。没有忒西奥的人,门口没有警探。老头子完全没人保护。"他的声音在颤抖。

桑尼大吃一惊,过了很久才开口,声音低沉:"这就是你说的索洛佐的动作。"

迈克尔说:"我也这么觉得。可他是怎么让警察把所有人赶走的? 人都去了哪儿? 忒西奥的手下去哪儿了? 老天在上,索洛佐那王八蛋难道连纽约警局都买通了?"

"别着急,小子,"桑尼安慰道,"我们又走了好运,你这么晚才去医院。留在老头子的病房里。从里面锁上门。我打几个电话,十五分钟内就有人赶到。你别乱跑,也别惊慌。好吗,小子?"

"我不会惊慌。"迈克尔说。自从危机开始以来,他第一次感到胸中燃起了怒火,对父亲的敌人有了冰冷的恨意。

他挂断电话,按铃叫护士。他打算忽视桑尼的命令,按照自己的判断采取行动。护士进来,他说:"你千万别害怕,但我们必须马上移动我父亲,搬到另外一个病房,最好另外一层楼。你能拔掉所有管子吗? 好把床推出去。"

护士说:"开什么玩笑。这需要医生的批准。"

迈克尔说得飞快。"你肯定在报纸上读到过我父亲。你也看见了,今晚没人保护他。我刚刚听到风声,说有人要来医院杀他。请相信我,帮帮我。"碰到需要的时候,迈克尔很能说服别人。

护士说:"不需要拔掉管子,可以连支架一起推出去。"

"有空病房吗?"迈克尔轻声说。

"走廊到底有一间。"护士答道。

他们只用了几分钟,动作迅速而高效。迈克尔对护士说:"你和他留在这儿等帮手来。你要是待在外面的护士站,说不定会受伤。"

就在这时,病床上传来了父亲的声音,嘶哑但充满力量:"迈克尔,是你吗? 出什么事了,怎么了?"

迈克尔俯身到床边,握住父亲的手。"是我,迈克,"他说,"别害怕。听着,千万别发出声音,特别是假如有人喊你的名字。有人要来杀你,明白了吗? 但这儿有我,你别害怕。"

唐·柯里昂还没有完全明白前天自己遇到了什么事情,此刻被剧痛折磨,却还是对小儿子露出慈祥的笑容,他想说:"我为什么要害怕? 从我十二岁起就有陌生人想杀我。"但他实在没有足够的力气说出口。

第十章

医院规模不大,很私密,只有一个出入口。迈克尔隔窗扫视街面。底下是个弧形天井,有几级台阶通向街道,马路上一辆车也没有。不管谁要进医院,都必须经过这个出入口。他知道时间不多,于是跑出病房,蹿下四段楼梯,冲出底层出入口的宽幅双开门。他看到一边是救护车停车场,那里既没有救护车,也没有轿车。

迈克尔站在医院外的人行道上,点燃香烟,解开大衣,站在路灯底下,好让别人看见他的长相。一个年轻人沿着第九大道快步走近,胳膊底下夹着包东西,他上身穿着军服,一头浓密的黑发。他走到路灯底下,迈克尔觉得他有点面熟,但想不起来具体是谁。年轻人在他面前停下,伸出手,用浓重的意大利口音说:"唐·迈克尔,还记得我吗? 恩佐,面包师纳佐里尼的帮工,也是他的女婿。你父亲让政府允许我留在美国,救了我的命。"

迈克尔和他握手。他想起来了。

恩佐又说:"我来向你父亲表达敬意。这么晚了,我还能进医院吗?"

迈克尔笑着摇摇头:"不行了,但还是谢谢你。我会告诉唐,说你来过。"一辆轿车隆隆驶下街道,迈克尔立刻警觉起来。他对恩佐说:"快走吧。也许会有麻烦。你可不能被警察缠上。"

他见到意大利小伙子面露惧色,惹上警察的麻烦意味着遣返或被拒绝入籍,但年轻人站在那儿一动不动,用意大利语轻声说:"要是有麻烦,那我愿意留下帮忙。我欠教父的人情。"

迈克尔深受触动。他正要再次劝说年轻人快走,但转念一想,为什么不让他留下呢? 医院门口站着两个人,说不定能吓走索洛佐派来执行任务的人马。只站一个人就肯定不行了。他分了恩佐一根烟,帮他点燃。两人顶着十二月的寒冷夜风站在路灯下。圣诞节的绿色装饰切碎医院的黄色窗格,微光闪烁,照在他们身上。这根烟就快抽完,一辆低矮的黑色大轿车从三十街拐上第九大道,贴着路边向他们驶来。车速慢得几近停顿,迈克尔往车里张望,想看清对方的面容,身体不由自主地颤抖。车像是要停,但突然加速开走。有人认出了他。迈克尔又递给恩佐一根香烟,注意到面包师的手在颤抖,惊讶地发现自己的手却很稳定。

两人在街上抽了不到十分钟的烟,警笛突然划破夜空。一辆巡逻车吱吱嘎嘎拐上第九大道,在医院门前停下。另外两辆警车紧随其后。医院门前忽然挤满了制服警察和便衣警探。迈克尔松了一口气。桑尼好兄弟肯定打通了电话。他上前迎接他们。

两个身材魁梧的警察抓住他的胳膊,第三个搜他的身。戴金穗警帽的大块头警长走上台阶,手下恭恭敬敬让出一条路。他腰围惊人,帽子底下露出白发,但异常健壮,脸色赤红如牛肉。他走到迈克尔面前,粗声粗气道:"我以为你们这些黑皮流氓都给关起来了,你他妈是谁,在这儿干什么?"

迈克尔背后的一名警察说:"警长,他没有武器。"

迈克尔没有吭声。他在琢磨这个警长,冷静地打量他的面容和钢蓝色的眼睛。一名便衣警探说:"他是迈克尔·柯里昂,唐的儿子。"

迈克尔静静地说:"应该守卫我父亲的警探去哪儿了?是谁撤掉了岗哨?"

警长暴跳如雷:"他妈的小流氓,你以为你是谁,敢教我做事?是我撤掉的。我才不管意大利佬相互残杀,我不会动一根手指保护你的老头子。现在给我滚蛋。滚出这条马路,小地痞,不是探视时间就别在医院。"

迈克尔还在仔细打量他。警长的话并没有惹他生气。他的脑筋转得飞快。索洛佐会不会就在最开始那辆车里,见到他站在医院门口,索洛佐会不会打电话给这个警长,说:"柯里昂的人怎么还守在门口,我不是花钱让你把他们关起来了吗?"事情会不会如桑尼所说,都经过了精密策划?所有的事情都说得通了。他依然很冷静,对警长说:"你要是不在我父亲的病房附近安排警卫,我就不离开医院。"

警长都懒得搭理迈克尔,扭头对他旁边的警探说:"菲尔,把他抓起来。"

那名警探踌躇道:"这孩子没案底,警长。他是战争英雄,从不参与非法活动。报纸会闹翻天的。"

警长对那名警探怒目而视,气得满脸通红。他吼道:"去你妈的,我说把他抓起来。"

迈克尔仍旧头脑清楚,并没有动怒,存心挖苦道:"土佬给了你多少钱,要你出卖我父亲,警长?"

警长转向他,对两个身材魁梧的巡警说:"抓住他。"迈克尔感觉双臂被死死按住,见到警长偌大的拳头飞向自己的脸。他想闪避,但拳头重重地砸在颧骨上。一颗手雷在脑壳里爆炸。嘴里充满鲜血和碎骨,他意识到那是牙齿。他感觉半边脑袋充气似的肿了起来,两腿轻飘飘的,要不是两个警察拽着他,他已经倒在了地上。但他仍旧神志清醒,便衣警探上前拦住警长,免得他再动拳头,嘴里说:"老天,警长,你真的伤着他了。"

警长大声说:"我没碰他。他扑上来打我,自己摔倒了。你眼睛瞎了? 他拒捕。"

迈克尔在血色雾霭中见到又有几辆轿车贴着路边停下。好些人鱼贯而出。他认出里面有克莱门扎的律师,他在对那名警长说话,好言好语但饱含信心。"柯里昂家族雇用了私家侦探公司保卫柯里昂先生。我带来的这些人有持枪许可,警长,你要是逮捕他们,明早就要见法官,向他解释理由。"

律师看着迈克尔,问:"你要控告对你做出这种事的人吗?"

迈克尔说话有困难,上下颌合不拢,但他还是勉强嘟囔道:"我脚滑了,摔了一跤。"他见到警长得意洋洋地瞥了他一眼,他试着还以微笑。他不惜一切代价也要隐藏控制大脑那美妙森冷的寒意和严冬般充斥全身的恨意。他不想让任何人觉察到他此刻的感受。换了唐也是一样。他感觉自己被搀进医院,随即失去了知觉。

第二天上午醒来,他发现下颚戴上了铁箍,左边缺了四颗牙齿。黑根坐在床边。

"医生给我打了麻药?"迈克尔问。

"对,"黑根说,"他们要从牙龈里挖碎骨,认为会疼得难以忍耐。再说你反正也昏过去了。"

"我还受了别的伤吗?"迈克尔问。

"没了,"黑根说,"桑尼想送你回长滩家里,你撑得住吗?"

"当然,"迈克尔说,"唐没事吧?"

黑根脸色一亮:"我觉得问题已经解决了。我们雇了一家侦探公司,附近现在戒备森严。到车上我继续跟你说。"

开车的是克莱门扎,迈克尔和黑根坐在后排。迈克尔的脑袋抽痛不已。"昨晚到底发生了什么,你们算是搞清楚了吗?"

黑根平静地说:"桑尼有条内线,就是那位想保护你的菲利普斯警探。他给我们通了消息。那个警长叫麦克劳斯凯,从当巡警开始就收黑钱,胃口相当大。我们家族塞了他不少好处,但他非常贪婪,做事靠不住。索洛佐肯定塞了他好大一笔。昨晚探视时间一结束,麦克劳斯凯就抓了忒西奥在医院内外安排的所有人。有些人带着枪也无济于事。麦克劳斯凯紧接着撤走守在唐门口的警探,说需要他们帮忙,还声称另外派了几个警察顶上,他们却搞混了命令。放屁。他收了黑钱出卖唐。菲利普斯说他属于有一就有二的那种人。索洛佐那一大笔钱肯定只是预付金,答应得手后还有无数好处。"

"我受伤的事情见报了吗?"

"没有,"黑根说,"我们没有声张,谁也不希望这件事被捅出去。警察不希望,我们也不希望。"

"很好,"迈克尔说,"恩佐那孩子溜掉了吗?"

"溜掉了,"黑根说,"他比你机灵,警察一到就跑了。他说索洛佐的车经过时,他就站在你旁边。真的吗?"

"对,"迈克尔说,"小伙子挺不错。"

"会好好关照他的,"黑根说,"你感觉还好吧?"他关心地看着迈克尔,"样子不太妙。"

"我没事,"迈克尔说,"那个警长叫什么来着?"

"麦克劳斯凯,"黑根说,"倒是有个消息,说不定能让你心情好些,柯里昂家族总算扳回一分。布鲁诺·塔塔利亚,今天凌晨四点。"

迈克尔坐了起来。"怎么回事? 不是说我们应该按兵不动的吗?"

黑根耸耸肩:"医院出事之后,桑尼下了狠心。纽扣人洒遍纽约和新泽西。我们昨晚列了个名单。我还在劝说桑尼别冲动,迈克,也许你能跟他聊聊。不需要全面开战也能了结整个问题。"

"我会跟他聊聊的,"迈克尔说,"今天上午要碰头吗?"

"要,"黑根说,"索洛佐终于联系上了,想和我们坐下来谈谈。有个调解人在安排细节。说明我们赢了。索洛佐知道他输了,想保全他那条小命。"黑根顿了顿,"我们没有立刻还击,他也许以为我们软弱可欺。但塔塔利亚死了一个儿子以后,他知道我们动真格了。他敢对唐下黑手,算是豪赌一场。另外,卢卡的下落弄清楚了。伏击你父亲的前一天夜里,他们杀了卢卡。在布鲁诺的夜总会。简直不敢想象。"

迈克尔说:"肯定打了他一个措手不及。"

一辆黑色长车横过来堵住长滩家那条林荫道的人口。两个男人靠在引擎盖上。迈克尔注意到入口两边的两幢屋子开着楼上的窗户。天哪,桑尼是动真格的了。

克莱门扎在林荫道外停车,三个人走路进去。两名守卫是克莱门扎的手下,克莱门扎对他们皱皱眉头,算是打过招呼。守卫点头还礼。没有微笑,没有寒暄。克莱门扎领着黑根和迈克尔·柯里昂进屋。

他们还没按门铃,就有另外一名守卫打开门。他显然从窗口看见了他们。他们走进拐角办公室,发现桑尼和忒西奥在等他们。桑尼走到迈克尔面前,用双手捧着弟弟的脑袋,开玩笑道:"漂亮,真漂亮。"迈克尔拍开他的手,走到办公桌前倒了一杯苏格兰威士忌,希望烈酒能缓和下巴的剧痛。

　　五个人坐成一圈,气氛和前几次会议大不相同。桑尼显得更快活,迈克尔明白他的快活意味着什么。大哥心里不再犹豫不决。他下定决心,什么都没法动摇他。索洛佐昨晚的企图是最后一根稻草。休战已经没得谈了。

　　"你走了以后,调解人来过电话,"桑尼对黑根说,"土佬想会谈。"桑尼哈哈大笑,"他倒是有卵蛋,"他钦佩道,"经过昨晚的烂事,居然还敢约我们今天或明天谈一谈。难不成我们就老实待着,他上什么菜我们就吃什么? 算他有胆子。"

　　汤姆小心翼翼地问:"你怎么回答的?"

　　桑尼咧嘴一笑,"我说行啊,好呀,随便他定时间,我不着急。我有上百个纽扣人二十四小时巡街。要是索洛佐敢露一根屁股毛,他就死定了。他们要多少时间,我就给他们多少时间。"

　　黑根说:"有什么具体建议吗?"

　　"有,"桑尼说,"他要我们派迈克见他,听他的提议。调解人保证迈克的安全。索洛佐不要求我们保证他的安全,他知道他没这个资格,因此这次会面由他那边安排。他的人来接迈克,带迈克去会面地点。迈克听索洛佐怎么说,然后放他回来。但会面地点暂时保密。他们保证交易的条件好得我们没法拒绝。"

　　黑根问:"塔塔利亚家族呢? 布鲁诺死了,他们有什么打算?"

　　"那是交易的一部分。调解人说塔塔利亚家族答应听索洛佐的,会忘记布鲁诺·塔塔利亚。他们对我父亲下手,他就是代价。一命抵一命。"桑尼又笑道,"杂种真有胆子。"

　　黑根小心翼翼地说:"我们应该听听他们怎么说。"

　　桑尼使劲摇头,"不,不行,顾问,这次不行。"他带上一丝意大利口音,存心模仿父亲和大家开玩笑,"没什么可会谈的,没什么可讨论的,不再给索洛佐要心眼的机会。等调解人来问我们怎么回答,你替我回答他一句话:我要索洛佐,否则就全面战争。我们开始睡床垫,派所有纽扣人上街。大家鱼死网破。"

　　"另外几大家族不会答应全面开战的,"黑根说,"等于把所有人放在火上烤。"

　　桑尼耸耸肩。"他们有个很简单的解决办法啊,把索洛佐交给我。要么就和柯里昂家族开战。"桑尼顿了顿,接着粗鲁地说,"别再建议怎么息事宁人了,汤姆,我已经作了决定,你的任务是帮助我获胜。听懂了?"

　　黑根低下头,沉思片刻,然后说:"我和你在警局的联系人聊过。他说麦克劳斯凯警长肯定拿索洛佐的黑钱,而且胃口不小。不但如此,麦克劳斯凯还在贩毒生意里分一杯羹。麦克劳斯凯已经答应担任索洛佐的保镖。没有麦克劳斯凯陪着,土佬连鼻子都不敢探出狗洞。他和迈克会面的时候,麦克劳斯凯会坐在他旁边,穿便服,但带枪。你必须明白,桑尼,索洛佐有这种人护着,他就刀枪不入。从来没有谁枪杀一名纽约警长后还能安然脱身。报纸、整个警察局、教会等等都不会放过你,压力大得你难以想象。那会酿成灾难。各大家族将找你麻烦。柯里昂家族会被驱逐。连老头子的政治保护网都会明哲保身。你必须考虑到这些因素。"

桑尼耸耸肩。"麦克劳斯凯不可能一辈子陪着土佬,我们等得起。"

忒西奥和克莱门扎不安地抽着雪茄,不敢插嘴,汗流浃背。上头要是作了错误的决定,首先倒霉的就是他们。

迈克尔第一次开口,他问黑根:"能把老头子从医院搬回林荫道吗?"

黑根摇头道:"我一去就问过了。不可能。他的情况还很糟糕。他能活下来,但需要各种各样的护理,也许还需要再动手术。不可能。"

"那么你必须立刻做掉索洛佐,"迈克尔说,"我们不能等。这家伙太危险。他会想出什么新点子的。他明白,除掉老头子是最重要的。对,他知道现在情况不妙,所以愿意为了那条小命低头。但如果他知道自己左右是个死,那就会再次对唐下手。有那个警长帮他,天晓得这次会发生什么。我们不能冒险,必须立刻做掉索洛佐。"

桑尼若有所思地挠着下巴。"你说得对,小弟,"他说,"你这话算是一语中的。不能让索洛佐再对老头子下手了。"

黑根平静地说:"麦克劳斯凯警长呢?"

桑尼转向迈克尔,面露古怪的微笑:"对,小弟,那个难啃的警长呢?"

迈克尔说得很慢:"好吧,这很极端。但有些时候,最极端的手段也有正当的理由。考虑一下,假如我们必须杀死麦克劳斯凯,那么必须证明他和事情脱不开干系,所以他不是在履行职责的诚实警长,而是一名卷入黑帮勾当的腐败警官,招致杀身之祸完全是活该。我们有收我们钱的报社人员,把故事连同足够的证据交给他们,这样他们就能给我们撑腰了,减轻部分压力。听起来怎么样?"迈克尔用讨教的眼神打量众人。忒西奥和克莱门扎脸色阴沉,不肯说话。桑尼还是一脸古怪的笑容:"继续说,小弟,说得很好。童言无忌嘛,唐的口头禅。继续说,迈克,说下去。"

黑根也在微笑,侧过头去。迈克尔脸红了。"好,他们要我去和索洛佐会谈。只有我、索洛佐和麦克劳斯凯在场。把时间安排在两天以后,派我们的线人打听清楚会谈地点。坚持必须是公共场所,说我不愿意让他们带我去什么公寓或住宅。用餐高峰时间的餐馆或酒吧,诸如此类的,这样我觉得安全。他们也觉得安全。连索洛佐也猜不到我们敢枪杀警长。我和他们碰面的时候,他们会搜我的身,因此我身上不能带枪,你们要想个办法,在会谈期间让我拿到武器。然后我宰了他们两个人。"

四个脑袋转过来盯着他。克莱门扎和忒西奥大惊失色。黑根有点悲哀,但并不讶异。他想说什么,但想想还是算了。但桑尼,他那张浓眉大眼的爱神脸欢快地抽搐着,突然爆发出一阵大笑,是打心底里发出的笑声,绝非作假。他真的在捧腹大笑,用一根手指指着迈克,喘着粗气说,"你,高贵的大学生,从来不想掺和家族生意。现在想杀一个警长和土佬,就因为麦克劳斯凯打烂了你的脸。你当成了个人恩怨,只是生意而已,你却当真了。你想杀了这两个家伙,因为你脸上挨了拳头。真是放屁。这么多年,你尽在放屁。"

克莱门扎和忒西奥完全误会了桑尼,以为他在嘲笑弟弟提出这么一个建议是在虚张声势,也露出灿烂的笑容,有点同情迈克尔。只有黑根心生警惕,不动声色。

迈克尔环顾众人,瞪着笑得停不下来的桑尼。"你要宰了他们两个人?"桑尼说,"喂,小弟,他们可不会给你奖章,只会送你上电椅。明白吗?这可不是逞英雄啊,小弟,不是射击一里之外的敌人,而是在看得见他们眼白的地方开枪,就像当初在学校里挨的教训,明白吗?你得站在他们面前,轰掉他们的脑袋,脑浆会溅满你漂亮的常春藤校服。怎么,小弟,只因为一个白痴警察打了你的脸,你就想杀人?"他还在笑。

迈克尔站起身。"你最好别笑了。"他说。他突然变脸,克莱门扎和忒西奥的笑容立刻消失。迈克尔既不高也不健壮,但浑身上下散发着危险的气息。此时此刻,他仿佛唐·柯里昂的化身。他的眼睛变成了灰褐色,脸色青白,似乎随时会扑向他强壮的大哥。毫无疑问,他手里要是有枪,桑尼恐怕就危险了。桑尼停下笑声,迈克尔用杀人的语气冷冷地说:"狗娘养的,你以为我做不到?"

桑尼收起笑声。"我知道你做得到,"他说,"我笑的不是你说的话。我笑的是事情变成这样了。我一直说你是家里最硬气的,比唐本人都硬气。只有你敢和老头子作对。我记得你小时候什么样子,那脾气可真是够看的。妈的,你脾气上来了连我都敢揍,我比你大那么多。弗雷迪每个星期都得赏你一顿好揍。索洛佐居然以为你是家里的软蛋,因为你让麦克劳斯凯打你,但你没有还手,不肯参与家族争斗。麦克劳斯凯也是,他以为你是没胆子的小黑皮。"桑尼顿了顿,柔声说,"但你毕竟是一个柯里昂,狗娘养的,只有我知道这一点。从老头子挨枪子那天开始,我坐在这儿等了三天,等你脱掉常春藤战斗英雄的狗屁伪装,等你担任我的右手,一起杀了那些试图摧毁爸爸和家族的杂种。谁能想到你需要的只是在脸上挨一拳?"桑尼做个滑稽的挥拳手势,重复道,"真想不到。"

紧张气氛缓和下来。迈克摇摇头:"桑尼,我只是因为别无选择。我不能再给索洛佐机会对老头子下手。现在只有我能接近他。这我看出来了。另外,我觉得你找不到敢杀警长的人。也许你可以自己动手,桑尼,但你有老婆和孩子,在老头子恢复健康前,你要管理家族。这样就只剩下了我和弗雷迪。弗雷迪还没恢复,无法行动。那就只有我了。完全符合逻辑,和我下巴挨的那一拳毫无关系。"

桑尼过来拥抱他。"我他妈不在乎你的理由,只要你肯和我们并肩作战就行。我还要告诉你一件事:自始至终你都是正确的。汤姆,你说呢?"

黑根耸耸肩:"理由充足。我这么想是因为我不认为土佬是诚心谈交易。我认为他还在想办法对付唐。按照一个人的过去,就可以推断出他的未来。所以我得做掉索洛佐。必须做掉他,哪怕非得做掉那个警长也一样。但动手的人将承受极大的压力。难道非得是迈克吗?"

桑尼柔声说:"我可以去。"

黑根不耐烦地摇摇头:"就算有十个警长陪着,索洛佐也不敢让你靠近他一英里之内。再说现在家族由你代管。你不能冒险。"黑根顿了顿,对克莱门扎和忒西奥说:"你们有没有非常得力的顶尖纽扣人能接下这个任务?他这辈子都不需要担心钱了。"

克莱门扎首先说:"没有生面孔,索洛佐立刻会认出来的。我或者忒西奥去也一样。"

黑根说:"有没有够凶悍、身手好但还没建立起名声的新人?"

两个首领同时摇头。忒西奥用微笑抵消话里的刺:"这就像让小联盟的队员去打世界联赛。"

桑尼插嘴道:"只能是迈克。有成百上千条理由。最重要的是他们低估他,觉得他娘娘腔。但他有这个本事,我敢打包票,这一点很重要,因为我们只有这个机会做掉那个杂种土佬。所以现在必须盘算一下该怎么支援迈克。汤姆、克莱门扎、忒西奥,搞清楚索洛佐打算带他去哪儿会谈,花多少钱都无所谓。知道了以后,我们要想一想该怎么把武器送到迈克手里。克莱门扎,你从武器库里找一把真正'安全'的枪,最'冷'的一把——绝不可能被查到。枪管尽量短,破坏力足够大。不需要特别精确。开枪时他就对着他们的脑袋。迈克,用完之后,你把枪扔在地上。别被连人带枪抓个正着。克莱门扎,用那种特制胶带缠住枪管和扳机,这样不会留下指纹。记住,迈克,我们什么都摆得平,目击证人,任何事情,但要是连人带枪被逮住就没戏了。我们要准备好运输工具和掩护手段,让你消失一段时间,等风头过去再露面。你要离开很长时间,迈克,但你别去和你的女人告别,连电话也别打。等事情结束,你离开美国,我会帮你传话给她。以上都是命令。"桑尼对弟弟微笑,"现在和克莱门扎待在一起,熟悉他给你挑的枪。顺便练习一下。其他事情交给我们。所有事情。好吗,小弟?"

迈克尔·柯里昂又觉得那种美妙的寒意流遍全身。他对大哥说:"我的女朋友和私事不用你操心,我没那么蠢,你认为我会打电话告别吗?"

桑尼连忙说:"好吧,但你仍旧是新人,我只是帮你理理思路。别往心里去。"

迈克尔咧嘴笑着说:"你他妈什么意思,新人? 我和你一样,听从爸爸的教诲,否则你以为我为什么这么聪明?"两人哈哈大笑。

黑根为众人斟酒。他有点郁郁寡欢。政客希望诉诸战争,律师希望诉诸法规。"好吧,管他的,现在我们知道该怎么做了。"他说。

第十一章

马克·麦克劳斯凯警长坐在办公室里,摸着鼓鼓囊囊装满投注单的三个信封。他皱着眉头思考,希望能读懂投注单上的记号。这关系重大。前一天夜里,他的队伍突袭了柯里昂家族的一个簿记点,缴获的投注单就装在信封里。簿记现在必须赎回投注单,否则赌客就会自称获胜,掏空他的腰包。

但对于麦克劳斯凯警长来说,读懂投注单非常重要,他卖给簿记的时候可不想被蒙。要是赌注加起来有五万,他差不多能收到五千。但要是有些赌注特别大,投注单加起来有十万甚至二十万,那他的要价就要高得多了。麦克劳斯凯摆弄着信封,决定吊一吊簿记的胃口,让对方先出价,或许能从中猜到真正的价值。

麦克劳斯凯望向警局办公室墙上的挂钟。时间到了,他要去接滑头滑脑的土佬索洛佐,送那家伙去他和柯里昂家族约定会谈的地点。麦克劳斯凯走到壁柜前,开始换便装。换好衣服,他打电话给老婆说晚上有公事,不回家吃饭了。他从不跟老婆说实话。她以为靠警察那点薪水就能活得如此体面。麦克劳斯凯觉得很好笑,哼了一声。他母亲也曾这么以为,但他早就知道了实情。他父亲手把手教会了他。

他父亲曾经是个巡警,每周带着儿子走一遍辖区,向一个个店主介绍他六岁的儿子:"这是我家小子。"

店主会和他握手,甜言蜜语恭维他,打开收款机,五块十块地送给这个孩子。一天下来,马克·麦克劳斯凯的每个衣袋都会塞满纸钞,父亲的朋友这么喜欢他,每次见面都要送点礼物,他打心底里觉得骄傲。他父亲当然要把钱存进银行,为小马克念大学做准备,只给他留下顶多五毛零花。

等马克回到家里,他的警察叔伯问他长大了要干什么,他会幼稚地吃吃答道"警察",逗得他们哄堂大笑。后来,尽管父亲希望他先上大学,他还是高中一毕业就去考警校了。

他曾经是个好警察，是个英勇的警察。盘踞街角的凶狠小流氓见了他就逃跑，最后干脆只要他执勤就不露面。他曾经悍勇过人，公平处事，从不带着儿子去见店主，收现金当礼物，假装没看见违反垃圾规定和停车规定的行为；他直接收钱，之所以直接收，是因为他觉得这是他应得的。其他警察巡逻的时候，经常躲进电影院或在餐馆消磨时间，尤其是冬天的夜班，他却从不这么做。他总是认真巡查。他给他管理的店铺许多保护和服务。当班时遇到有酒鬼醉汉从鲍威利流窜过来，他驱赶他们的手段异常凶狠，那些家伙顶多只敢来一次。他辖区内的商人很欣赏他，用各种方法表达谢意。

另外一方面，他遵守体系规则。他辖区内的簿记知道他不会为了一己私利存心闹事，知道他满足于警局总数里的那一份。他的名字和很多人列在一起，但他从不敲诈勒索。他这人公平处事，只收干净的职务贿赂，他在警局的晋升之路不算出众，但很稳当。

他养活了一个大家庭，四个儿子没有一个当警察，而是都上了福特汉姆大学，马克从警佐升到副警长，最后当上警长，全家活得衣食无忧。也就在这段时间，麦克劳斯凯有了难以打交道的名声。他辖区内的簿记交的是全城最高的保护费，看来四个儿子念大学开销实在太大。

麦克劳斯凯觉得干净的职务贿赂并不出格。他的儿子凭什么要去念纽约市立学院或者不值钱的南方大学，难道就因为局里的薪水不够让警察过日子和照顾家人吗？他用他的生命保护所有人，档案证明他在巡逻时曾和盗匪殊死枪战，收拾过武装保镖和不懂事的皮条客。他把他们打得不敢露头。他好好治理他的这一角纽约，让普通人过得安心，当然有资格拿到比每周一百多得多的酬劳。薪水这么低，他倒是不愤慨，而是明白人终究只能靠自己。

布鲁诺·塔塔利亚是他的老朋友。布鲁诺和他的一个儿子是福特汉姆大学的同学，毕业后开了夜总会，麦克劳斯凯一家偶尔进城消遣，就去夜总会享受美酒佳肴和歌舞表演，请客的当然是夜总会。除夕之夜，他们会收到精致的请柬，以老板贵客的身份参加酒会，坐在最好的位置。布鲁诺一定会把他们介绍给来夜总会演出的名角，其中不乏著名歌手和好莱坞明星。当然了，他时不时请麦克劳斯凯帮些小忙，比方说抹掉某个雇员的犯罪记录，弄到歌舞表演的工作许可，通常是个有卖淫或骗赌案底的漂亮姑娘。麦克劳斯凯总是乐于助人。

麦克劳斯凯给自己立了条规矩，决不表现出他明白别人的企图。索洛佐找到他，提出要把老柯里昂无依无靠地丢在医院里，麦克劳斯凯没有问原因，只问给多少钱。索洛佐说一万，麦克劳斯凯就知道了原因。他没有犹豫。柯里昂是全国最大的黑手党头目之一，政治关系比当年的卡彭还要多。不管是谁想做掉他，都算是帮美国除了一害。麦克劳斯凯先收钱后办事，但紧接着又接到索洛佐的电话，说医院门口还有柯里昂的两个手下，他气得暴跳如雷。他已经把忒西奥的手下全抓了起来，还撤掉了守在病房门口的两名警探。身为一个有原则的人，他非得把一万块还给索洛佐不可，但他早就盘算好了这笔钱的用途，那是他孙子的教育经费。在愤怒的驱使下，他冲到医院，揍了迈克尔·柯里昂。

不过事情进展顺利。他在塔塔利亚夜总会和索洛佐碰头，谈定了一笔更好的交易。麦克劳斯凯还是没提问，因为他知道全部答案。他关心的只有价钱。他根本没想过自己有可能遇到危险，没想过有谁会一时间异想天开，杀死一名纽约市的警长。黑手党最凶悍的打手遇到最低阶的巡警想扇他耳光，也得乖乖站着任人摆布。杀警察没有任何好处，因为忽然间会有许多打手因为拒捕或企图逃离犯罪现场而被击毙，谁他妈敢做这种事情呢？

麦克劳斯凯叹了口气，准备离开分局。所谓祸不单行，他老婆在爱尔兰的姐姐和癌症斗争数年后终于逝世，这场病花了他不少钱。举办葬礼还要花更多。他自己在祖国的叔伯婶婶时不时需要拉一把，维持他们的土豆农庄，他寄钱去冲抵赤字。他并不吝啬。他和老婆回去探亲的时候，得到的待遇堪比国王皇后。战争已经结束，外快源源不断，不如今年夏天再去一趟好了。麦克劳斯凯把他要去哪儿告诉巡警秘书，免得局里有急事找不到他。他不觉得需要采取什么预防措施，退一万步说，他总是可以声称索洛佐是和他碰头的线人。出了分局，他走过几个街区，叫了辆计程车，前往他要和索洛佐会面的地方。

安排迈克尔逃离美国的是汤姆·黑根：假护照，海员证，将在西西里港口停泊的一艘意大利货轮上的铺位。他派出的几名密使当天下午出发，搭飞机赶往西西里，和那里的黑手党首脑商量，帮迈克尔找个藏身之地。

桑尼安排了一辆轿车和一个绝对靠得住的司机，等待迈克尔走出他将和索洛佐会面的那家餐厅。司机就是忒西奥本人，他自告奋勇给迈克尔开车。这辆车看起来破旧，但引擎很好。车将挂假牌照，本身也无法追查。特殊任务需要最安全的车，这辆车就是为此预留的。

迈克尔和克莱门扎待了一天，练习将会传递给他的小型手枪。这支点二二用的是软头子弹，打进人体只是针眼小洞，出去时则会撕开血淋淋的大窟窿。他发现这支枪在目标五步之内打得很准，之外就难说会飞到哪儿去了。扳机有点紧，克莱门扎用工具收拾一番之后就好用多了。他们决定不管枪声，免得无辜的旁观者搞错情况，出于愚蠢和勇气贸然出头。枪声会让旁观者远离迈克尔。

克莱门扎一边陪他练枪一边指导他。"开完枪就马上丢掉。垂下胳膊，让枪顺势滑出手。谁也不会注意到。大家都会以为你还有枪。他们只会盯着你的脸。快步离开，但别跑。别直接看任何人的眼睛，但也别扭头不看他们。记住，他们害怕你，请相信我，他们会害怕你。谁也不会出手干预。走出餐馆，忒西奥会在车里等你。进去，剩下的全交给他。别担心会出意外。你只会惊讶事情怎么这么顺利。来，戴上帽子，看看你的模样。"他把一顶灰色软呢帽扣在迈克尔的头上。从来不戴帽子的迈克尔做个鬼脸。克莱门扎安慰道："预防被指认。目击证人改变口供的也有了借口。别担心指纹。枪柄和扳机贴上了特制胶带。别碰枪身的其他部位，千万记住了。"

迈克尔说："桑尼已经知道索洛佐要带我去哪儿了吗？"

克莱门扎耸耸肩。"还没有。索洛佐非常小心。不过别担心他会伤害你。调解人在我们手上，你不安全回来，我们就不放他。要是你遇到什么意外，调解人会付出代价的。"

"他为什么要冒险？"迈克尔问。

"他收费很高，"克莱门扎说，"算是一小笔财富了。另外，他在各大家族都算重要角色。他知道索洛佐不敢让他出意外。对于索洛佐而言，你这条命不如调解人的值钱。就这么简单。你会安然无恙。事后天崩地裂都有我们撑着。"

"会有多糟糕？"迈克尔问。

"会非常糟糕，"克莱门扎说，"意味着柯里昂家族和塔塔利亚家族全面开战。其他大部分家族会站在塔塔利亚家族那一边。卫生部今年冬天要收拾许多尸体了。"他耸耸肩，"这种事每隔十来年就要发生一次，能释放彼此的仇怨。另外，要是放任他们在小事上随便摆布我们，那他们就会想要夺走我们的一切。必须一冒头就斩断。就像他们当初在慕尼黑就该阻止希特勒，他干了那种事，怎么能随便放过他，放过他就意味着后面的大麻烦都是自找苦吃。"

迈克尔听他父亲说过类似的话，但时间是三九年，战争尚未正式打响。唐说假如各大家族管理国务院，二次大战就不用打了，他想着，忍不住苦笑。

他们开车返回林荫道，走进唐的住所，桑尼已经把这里当成了指挥部。迈克尔琢磨着桑尼还能在林荫道这个安全地带忍耐多久。他迟早会冒险出门。他们发现桑尼在沙发上打瞌睡，咖啡桌上扔着午餐的残羹：牛排碎块、面包渣和半瓶威士忌。

父亲向来整洁的办公室如今成了乱七八糟的寄宿公寓。迈克尔摇醒大哥，说："你怎么活得像个流浪汉，就不能把房间收拾得干净点？"

桑尼打着哈欠说："你他妈是在检查兵营吗？我们还没打听到他们打算带你去哪儿，索洛佐和麦克劳斯凯这对杂种。要是不知道地方，他妈的该怎么把枪送到你手上？"

"要么我随身带着?"迈克尔说,"也许他们不会搜我的身,或者藏个好地方,就算搜也找不到。再说找到了又怎样?顶多让他们拿走,不会有什么损失。"

桑尼摇摇头,说:"不行。这次必须确保做掉索洛佐。记住,有机会就杀他。麦克劳斯凯动作慢,比较迟钝。你有足够时间杀他。克莱门扎有没有告诉你,千万记得扔掉枪?"

"一百万遍了。"迈克尔答道。

桑尼从沙发上起身,伸个懒腰。"下巴感觉怎么样?"

"难受。"迈克尔说,左半边脸疼得火烧火燎,但钢丝箍住的地方上了麻药,没有感觉。他拿起咖啡桌上的酒瓶,咕咚咕咚灌下几口威士忌,疼痛随之减轻。

桑尼说:"悠着点儿,迈克,现在可不能喝晕头。"

迈克尔说:"噢,天哪,桑尼,你就别装大哥了。我和比索洛佐更凶残的敌人打过仗,条件比现在艰苦得多。他有迫击炮吗,有空中掩护吗,有重炮吗?地雷?他只是个狡猾的混蛋,有个高级警察当打手。只要下决心杀他们,就不存在任何问题。下决心才是最困难的。他们死都不知道怎么死的。"

汤姆·黑根走进房间,点头和他们打招呼,走向以假名登记的电话。他打了几个电话,最后对桑尼摇摇头。"一点风声都没有,"他说,"索洛佐在尽量保守秘密。"

电话铃响了。桑尼接听,尽管没人说话,但他还是举起另一只手,像是叫大家都安静。他在记事簿上写了几笔,最后说:"好的,到时候见。"然后挂断电话。

桑尼笑道:"索洛佐真是个人物。他安排今晚八点,他和麦克劳斯凯警长在百老汇的杰克·邓普西酒吧门口接迈克,去其他地方谈事情,他要迈克和他用意大利语交谈,这样爱尔兰警察根本不知道他们在说什么。他居然还叫我别担心,他知道麦克劳斯凯只听得懂'索尔多'①这么一个意大利词。另外,迈克,他查过你的底细,知道你懂西西里方言。"

迈克尔干巴巴地说:"忘得差不多了,不过反正也聊不了几句。"

汤姆·黑根说:"调解人不来,我们就不让迈克去。这一点安排好了吗?"

克莱门扎点点头:"调解人在我家和我的三个手下打牌呢。他们要接到我的电话才会放他走。"

桑尼躺进皮革扶手椅。"妈的,我们怎么才能查清会面地点?汤姆,我们在塔塔利亚家族有内线,他们怎么一点消息都没有?"

黑根耸耸肩。"索洛佐实在太精明。他非常谨慎,甚至不用他们的人掩护。他觉

---

① 意大利货币单位。

得有那个警长就够了,秘密比刀枪更重要。他其实是对的。我们只能派人跟踪迈克,祈祷能有好结果。"

桑尼摇摇头:"不行,尾巴这东西,想甩总归是甩得掉的。他们首先要查的就是有没有人跟踪。"

这时已经是下午五点。桑尼满脸焦虑地说:"要么等车来的时候,直接让迈克朝车里射击,管他是谁。"

黑根耸耸肩。"要是索洛佐不在车里怎么办?我们岂不是白白浪费一把好牌?该死,必须查清索洛佐要带他去哪儿。"

克莱门扎插嘴道:"也许我们该想想他为啥弄得这么神神秘秘。"

迈克尔不耐烦地说:"因为要预防万一呗。能不让我们知道的事情为什么要让我们知道?再说了,他能闻到危险。就算有那个警长跟着他,他也还是疑神疑鬼。"

黑根打了个响指。"那个警探,叫菲利普斯的。桑尼,给他打电话。他也许能查到该去哪儿找那个警长。值得一试。麦克劳斯凯恐怕不在乎别人知不知道他的下落。"

桑尼拿起听筒,拨打号码,轻声说了几句,挂断电话。"等他回电。"桑尼说。

他们等了快三十分钟,电话铃响了。打来的是菲利普斯。桑尼在记事簿上写了几笔,挂断电话。他紧绷着脸。"我想我们搞清楚了,"他说,"麦克劳斯凯总要留话给同事,万一有急事该去哪儿找他。今晚八点到十点,他在布朗克斯的蓝月亮。有谁熟悉那地方吗?"

忒西奥很有把握地说:"我知道。非常合适我们。家庭式的小餐馆,隔间很宽敞,适合私下谈话。饭菜很好吃。顾客不多管闲事。太理想了。"他俯身在办公桌上把烟头摆成示意图,"这是大门。迈克,事成后你直接出来,左转,拐过路口。我看见你,点亮大灯,过来接上你。你要是遇到麻烦,喊一声,我马上进来接应。克莱门扎,你赶紧安排起来。派人过去放枪。那儿的卫生间是老式马桶,水箱和墙壁之间有缝隙。让你的人把枪用胶带粘在缝隙里。迈克尔,他们会在车里搜你的身,发现你没带武器,随后就不会担心你了。进了餐馆,等一段时间,找个借口上厕所。不,别起身,先征求对方的许可。装得好像憋得难受,要自然。他们不可能多想。等你从厕所出来,别浪费时间。别重新坐下,直接开枪。也别想当然。打脑袋,一人两枪,然后立刻出去,能走多快就走多快。"

桑尼听得非常仔细。"派个信得过的精明人去放枪,"他对克莱门扎说,"我可不希望我弟弟走出厕所的时候手里只有他的鸡巴。"

克莱门扎一字一顿道:"枪一定会在那儿。"

"好了。"桑尼说,"大家干活吧。"

忒西奥和克莱门扎走了,汤姆·黑根说:"桑尼,要我开车送迈克去纽约吗?"

"不用,"桑尼说,"你留在这儿。迈克得手后,我们会忙得不可开交,我需要你帮忙。报纸那头准备好了吗?"

黑根点点头:"一得手我就放消息给他们。"

桑尼起身,走到迈克尔面前站住。他抓住迈克尔的手。"好了,小弟,"他说,"都交给你了。我会跟妈妈解释你为什么不告而别。适当的时候,我会给你女朋友捎个信。好吗?"

"好的,"迈克说,"你觉得我这一去,什么时候能回来?"

"至少一年。"桑尼说。

汤姆·黑根插嘴道:"唐也许有办法,让你早点回家,但别抱太大希望。时间取决于许多因素:我们给记者准备的故事怎么样,警察局想花多大力气掩盖过去,其他家族的反应有多剧烈。这件事会闹得满城风雨,现在能确定的只有这一条。"

迈克尔和黑根握手。"你们尽力而为,"他说,"我可不想再离家苦熬三年了。"

黑根柔声说:"现在退出还不算晚,迈克,我们可以派别人去。我们可以重新思考其他方案。也许索洛佐并不是非得除掉不可。"

迈克尔哈哈一笑。"我们可以说服自己相信任何观点,"他说,"但第一次讨论出的方案就很正确。我这辈子一直过得无忧无虑,现在也该吃点苦头了。"

"你别被下巴左右了思路,"黑根说,"麦克劳斯凯很愚蠢,另外,这是生意,无关个人。"

他第二次见到迈克尔·柯里昂脸色一凝,表情和唐相似得可怕。"汤姆,你别是真的相信了这种玩笑话吧?生意的一点一滴,全都和个人有关。一个人一辈子每天吃什么拉什么,全都和个人有关。大家说这是生意,没问题,但他妈的还是和个人有关。知道这道理是谁教给我的吗?唐,我家的老头子。教父。就算他的朋友被雷劈了,老头子也会觉得这是个人恩怨。连我参加海军陆战队,他都觉得这是个人恩怨。所以他才这么了不起。了不起的唐。在他眼中,什么都是个人恩怨。简直像是上帝。哪怕一只麻雀尾巴上掉了根羽毛他都知道,连他妈怎么掉的也知道。对吧?明白道理了吗?一个人要是觉得意外是对个人的侮辱,那么意外就永远不会找上他。我入行晚,没错,但我赶上来了。对,我把下巴被打断看作个人恩怨;对,我把索洛佐想杀我父亲看作个人恩怨。"他笑着说,"告诉老头子,这些都是跟他学的,我很高兴有机会报答他为我做的那些事情。他是个好父亲。"他顿了顿,沉思着对黑根说,"知道吗?我不记得他打过我。或者打过桑尼,或者弗雷迪。当然还有康妮,他甚至没有大声吼过康妮。可是,汤姆,你跟我说实话,你估计唐杀过多少人?"

汤姆·黑根别过脸去:"有一点你倒不是跟他学的,就是像你现在这么说话。有些事情非做不可,做了也不值得再次提起,不需要给自己找正当的借口。这种事情正当不起来。反正做就是了,然后忘掉。"

迈克尔·柯里昂皱起眉头,静静地问:"身为家族的顾问,你是否同意索洛佐活着对唐和家族都很危险?"

"同意。"黑根说。

"好。"迈克尔说,"那么我就必须杀了他。"

迈克尔·柯里昂站在百老汇大街的杰克·邓普西餐馆门口等车接他。他看看手表,离八点还有五分钟。索洛佐将分秒不差。迈克尔却要确保不迟到,他已经等了一刻钟。

从长滩到市区的路上,他一直在试图忘记刚才对黑根说的那番话,因为要是相信了自己的那番话,他的人生就将走上不归路。可是,经过今晚,他还有可能回头吗?要是再这么胡思乱想,迈克尔郁闷地心想,今晚当心丧命。他必须把心思放在手头的事情上。索洛佐不是白痴,麦克劳斯凯很难啃。他感觉到下巴的剧痛,此刻他喜欢这疼痛,让他提高警惕。

这是个寒冷的冬夜,尽管夜场就快开演,百老汇却人烟稀少。一辆黑色大型轿车在路边停下,迈克尔打个寒战,司机探过身子,打开前门,说:"迈克,上车。"他不认识司机,司机是个年轻的小混混,光溜溜的黑发,衬衫敞着领口,但他还是坐了进去。后排坐着麦克劳斯凯警长和索洛佐。

索洛佐隔着座椅靠背伸出手,迈克和他握手。索洛佐握得很有力,手温暖而干燥,他说:"迈克,很高兴你能来。希望我们能谈妥所有事情。真是太糟糕了,情况完全出乎我的预想,完全不该变成这样。"

迈克尔·柯里昂平静地说:"希望今晚能谈定,我不希望父亲再受到打扰。"

"保证不会了,"索洛佐恳切地说,"我以我的孩子向你发誓,保证不会了。只是请你敞开心胸和我谈。希望你不像你哥哥桑尼那么容易头脑发热。跟他谈生意是不可能的。"

麦克劳斯凯警长哼了一声:"这孩子不错,他没问题的。"他俯身热情地拍拍迈克尔的肩膀。"迈克,那天晚上对不住了。干我这一行,年纪大了,容易发脾气。看来我应该早点退休才对。最受不了有人招惹我,可是又成天被人招惹。你知道那种滋味。"他喟然长叹,仔仔细细搜了迈克尔的身。

迈克尔注意到司机露出一丝微笑。车向西开,像是根本不在乎被跟踪。车拐上西区高速路,在车流里钻进钻出。要是有车跟踪,也得这么钻进钻出。接着,迈克尔惊恐地发现轿车拐下了通往乔治·华盛顿大桥的路口,他们要过桥去新泽西。桑尼的线人给错了情报。

轿车经过引桥,走上桥面,把灯火辉煌的纽约留在背后。迈克尔尽量不动声色。他们是要把他扔进沼泽,还是狡诈的索洛佐最后一分钟改变了会谈地点?但就在快开过大桥的时候,司机突然猛打方向盘。沉重的轿车碾过隔离带,飞上半空,弹回返回纽约的车道。麦克劳斯凯和索洛佐同时扭头张望,看有没有车辆做出同样的动作。司机确实在往纽约开,他们驶下大桥,朝着东布朗克斯而去,虽说没有车跟踪,但还是专走黑街后巷。将近九点,他们确定没有尾巴,索洛佐举着烟盒向麦克劳斯凯和迈克尔敬烟,两人都没有要,他自己点燃香烟,对司机说:"好技术,我会记着你的。"

十分钟后,轿车驶进一个意大利小聚居区,在一家餐馆门口停下。街上空荡荡的,时间已晚,餐馆里没几个人。迈克尔担心司机也会进餐馆,但司机留在了车上。调解人没提到另有司机,谁也没提过这一点。从原则上说,索洛佐带司机就算破坏了约定,不过迈克尔决定不就此发难,他知道他们会以为他不提是出于恐惧,害怕破坏会谈成功的机会。

他们围着餐馆里唯一的圆桌坐下,索洛佐不肯进小隔间。餐馆里另外只有两个人。迈克尔怀疑他们是索洛佐的暗桩。不过无所谓,等他们有机会出手,保准为时已晚。

麦克劳斯凯饶有兴致地问:"这里的意大利菜好吃吗?"

索洛佐再三保证:"试试小牛肉,全纽约最好的。"唯一的侍者送上红酒,拔掉软木塞,倒了满满三杯。令人惊讶的是,麦克劳斯凯竟然不喝酒。"不喝酒的爱尔兰人恐怕只有我一个,"他说,"见过太多好人因为烈酒惹上麻烦了。"

索洛佐对警长好言好语道:"我要用意大利语和迈克交谈,不是信不过你,而是我说英语表达不清我的意思,我想让迈克相信我没有恶意,今晚达成协议对所有人都有好处。绝对不是我不信任你,你千万别往心里去。"

麦克劳斯凯警长露出嘲讽的笑容。"好的,你们谈你们的,"他说,"正好我集中精神吃小牛肉和细面条。"

索洛用西西里方言对迈克尔说:"你必须理解,我和你父亲之间的事情纯粹是生意问题。我非常尊重唐·柯里昂,巴不得有机会能为他效劳。可是,你也必须明白,你父亲为人非常守旧。他挡住了发展的道路。我这门生意就是未来,是日后的潮流,每个人都能发大财。可是,你父亲因为某些不切实际的顾虑挡了财路。他这么做等于把意愿强加在我身上。对,对,我知道,他告诉我,'尽管去做,那是你的生意,'但我们都知道那是不现实的。我们迟早会妨碍对方。他的言下之意是不准我做这门生意。我有自尊，不允许别人把意愿强加在我身上，所以做了非做不可的事情。塔塔利亚成了我的合伙人。要是这场争端继续下去，柯里昂家族就会被迫对抗其他所有人。你父亲如果身体健康，也许还撑得下去。但教父的大儿子毕竟不是教父本人——绝没有不尊重的意思。爱尔兰顾问黑根更是比不上占科·阿班丹多——愿上帝让他的灵魂安息。因此我提出讲和，休战。我们暂时消除敌意，等你父亲恢复健康，能够参加谈判再说。我苦苦劝说，答应补偿，塔塔利亚同意不再为他家的儿子布鲁诺寻仇。双方讲和。而我呢，我得过日子，所以会在我这门生意里做点小买卖。我不求柯里昂家族合作，只求你们别干涉。以上就是我的提议。我想你有资格同意，敲定协议。”

迈克尔用西西里语说：“跟我说说你打算怎么开始做生意，特别是我们家族在其中的角色，还有我们能得到什么好处。”

“这么说，你想仔细听听整个方案了？”索洛佐问。

迈克尔肃容道：“首先最重要的，你必须保证再也不试图威胁我父亲的生命。”

索洛佐夸张地举起一只手。“我能怎么向你保证？现在被追杀的是我。我已经错过了机会。你太高估我啦，亲爱的朋友，我没那么能干。”

迈克尔终于确定了，这次会谈不过是为了争取几天时间，索洛佐肯定还要尝试刺杀唐。局势妙在土佬低估了他，以为他是个小毛孩。那种怪异而美妙的森冷感觉笼罩全身。他挤出难受的表情。索洛佐看在眼里，问：“怎么了？”

迈克尔有点尴尬地说：“酒下去就进膀胱了。我憋得慌。能让我去一下卫生间吗？”

索洛佐用黑眼睛使劲端详他的面容，他伸出手，粗鲁地探进迈克尔的裤裆，里里外外摸个遍，寻找武器。迈克尔露出被冒犯的表情。麦克劳斯凯不耐烦地说：“我搜过他了。我搜过成千上万个小流氓。他没带武器。”

索洛佐不喜欢这样，不知为何，但就是不喜欢。他望向对面桌边的男人，朝卫生间的方向挑了挑眉毛。男人微微点头，表示他检查过了，里面没人。索洛佐不情愿地说：“别耽搁太久。”这家伙的直觉真是敏锐，而且非常紧张。

迈克尔起身走进卫生间。小便池顶上有个铁丝篮子，里面搁着一条粉色肥皂。他走进隔间。他真的需要撒尿，括约肌都要夹不住了。他很快解决问题，伸手到搪瓷水箱背后，摸到用胶带固定的短管小手枪。他撕下手枪，想起克莱门扎说的不必担心会在胶带上留指纹。他把枪插进腰带，用上衣遮住，系好纽扣。他洗手，润湿头发，用手帕擦掉水龙头上的指纹，然后走出卫生间。

索洛佐正对卫生间的门坐着，黑眼睛闪着机警的光芒。迈克尔笑了笑。“现在尽管聊吧。"他说着松了一口气。

　　麦克劳斯凯警长正在吃刚端上来的小牛肉和细面条。对面墙边的男人原本全神贯注,浑身绷紧,现在也明显放松了。

　　迈克尔重新坐下。他记起克莱门扎说过别这么做,应该一出卫生间就开枪。他却没有这么做,原因或者出于本能的警觉,或者出于纯粹的怯懦。他的感觉告诉他,要是做什么突兀的动作,就会被立刻放翻。现在他觉得安全了,刚才肯定很害怕,因为他很高兴自己不需要用两条腿站着。他双腿发软,抖得厉害。

　　索洛佐凑近他,迈克尔用桌面遮住腹部,悄悄解开纽扣,聚精会神听索洛佐说话。他一个字也没听懂,对他而言完全是胡言乱语。脑袋里充满隆隆流动的热血,一个字也钻不进去。他的右手在桌子底下移向腰间的手枪,拔了出来。就在这时,侍者过来听他们点菜,索洛佐扭头对侍者说话。迈克尔用左手猛地掀起桌子,右手一抬,枪口几乎抵住了索洛佐的脑袋。这家伙的协调性可真好,险些跟着迈克尔的动作一步跳开,但迈克尔更年轻,反应更迅速,随手扣下扳机。子弹击中索洛佐的眼睛和耳朵之间,从另一头飞出去,一大团血雾和碎骨洒在呆若木鸡的侍者身上。迈克尔凭本能知道一颗子弹就够了。索洛佐在最后一瞬间扭过头,他见到索洛佐眼中的生命之光像蜡烛似的熄灭。

　　时间这才过去一秒钟,迈克尔转身把枪口对准麦克劳斯凯。警长盯着索洛佐,眼神漠然而惊讶,像是在说这件事和他没关系。他似乎没有意识到自己有危险。叉满小牛肉的叉子悬在半空中,双眼刚转回来盯着迈克尔。他脸上和眼睛里的神情饱含自信和愤慨,像是在等待迈克尔投降或逃跑,而迈克尔对他笑着扣动了扳机。这一枪没打准,不致命,而是打中了麦克劳斯凯粗如牛颈的脖子,麦克劳斯凯使劲呛咳,像是吞了一大口咽不下去的小牛肉。他的肺部被打穿了,使劲咳嗽,空气中弥漫起血雾。迈克尔冷静从容地瞄准,一枪打爆披满白发的脑袋。

　　空气中像是挂着粉红色的雾气。迈克尔转向坐在墙边的男人。男人刚才毫无反应,似乎是被吓瘫了,此刻他小心翼翼地把双手亮在台面上,转开视线。侍者踉踉跄跄退向厨房,满脸惊恐,难以置信地盯着迈克尔。索洛佐仍旧坐在椅子里,餐桌支撑着他的半边身子。麦克劳斯凯沉重的身体垮下去,从椅子上滑到了地上。迈克尔让枪滑出掌心,枪贴着身体落向地面,没有发出多少声音。他注意到墙边的男人和侍者都没注意到他扔枪的动作。他几步走到门口,打开门。索洛佐的轿车还停在路边,但司机不见踪影。迈克尔左转拐弯。车头灯亮起,一辆破旧的轿车在他身旁停下,车门打开。他钻进去,车呼啸开走。他看到忒西奥坐在司机座位上,轮廓分明的脸板得像块大理石。

"办了索洛佐?"忒西奥问。

有一瞬间迈克尔被忒西奥的话问住了。"办了"一般指男女之事,办了女人就是诱奸她。忒西奥用在这儿真是有趣。"两个都办了。"迈克尔说。

"确定?"忒西奥问。

"见到脑浆了。"迈克尔答道。

车里有一身迈克尔的替换衣服。二十分钟后,他登上驶往西西里的意大利货轮。两小时后,货轮起锚出海,迈克尔在船舱里望着纽约市犹如地狱烈火的灯光。他感到如释重负。他总算逃掉了。这种感觉很熟悉,他所在的分队在某个岛屿抢滩登陆时,他被抬下火线。战斗仍在继续,但他受了轻伤,被送上后方的医疗船。当时这种压倒一切的轻松感也油然而生。地狱血流成河,而他不必在场。

索洛佐和麦克劳斯凯警长遇刺身亡,第二天,纽约全城各个分局的所有警长和副警长同时发话:严禁赌博,严禁卖淫,严禁签订密约,直到杀死麦克劳斯凯警长的凶手落网。全城大搜捕,所有非法生意陷入瘫痪。

那天晚些时候,几大家族派出密使,问柯里昂家族是否打算交出凶手。他们得到的回答是此事与柯里昂家族无关。当晚,一颗炸弹在长滩的柯里昂家族林荫道爆炸,一辆轿车开到铁链前,扔下炸弹就呼啸而去。同样是当晚,柯里昂家族的两名纽扣人在格林尼治村的一家意大利餐馆吃饭时被杀。1946 年五大家族混战拉开帷幕。

第二部

第十二章

约翰尼·方坦朝男仆随便一挥手,说:"明早见,比利。"黑人管家鞠了一躬,走出面向太平洋的宽敞餐室兼客厅。这是朋友之间的鞠躬道别,而非仆役对主人,之所以要鞠躬,仅仅因为约翰尼·方坦在和客人共进晚餐。

约翰尼的客人是个姑娘,名叫莎朗·莫尔,家住纽约市格林尼治村,来纽约是因为有个老情人已经出人头地,她想在他制作的电影里捞个小角色。约翰尼拍摄沃尔茨那部电影的时候,她恰好来片场探班。约翰尼觉得她年轻鲜活,迷人聪慧,请她回家共进晚餐。他的晚餐邀请闻名遐迩,有着皇室宴请的魄力,她当然满口答应。

他名声在外,莎朗·莫尔显然在期待他的猛烈攻势,但约翰尼很讨厌好莱坞有肉就吃的做法。他从不随便和女孩睡觉,除非女孩身上有他特别喜欢的地方。当然也有例外,有时候他喝得酩酊大醉,醒来时发现身边睡着个他不记得怎么遇到甚至不知道有没有见过的姑娘。如今他已经三十五岁,离过一次婚,和第二任妻子逐渐疏远,睡过数不清的女孩,因此他实在没那么饥渴。可是,莎朗·莫尔身上有什么东西激起了他的怜爱,所以他才邀请她共进晚餐。

他一向吃得不多,但知道有野心的漂亮姑娘总要为了穿漂亮衣服饿肚子,约会时往往胃口大开,所以桌上有充足的食物。桌上的酒水同样充足,冰桶里有香槟,餐具柜上有苏格兰威士忌、黑麦威士忌、白兰地和利口酒。约翰尼不停斟酒,用事先准备的几盘好菜款待客人。吃完饭,他领着姑娘走进宽敞的客厅,隔着落地玻璃窗眺望太平洋。他把艾拉·菲茨杰拉德的唱片放进音响,和莎朗坐进沙发。他和莎朗闲聊,了解她小时候的情况,她当初是假小子还是小花痴,是模样平常还是相貌出众,是孤僻还是开朗。他总觉得这些小细节分外引人人胜,能撩起对他做爱而言必不可少的柔情。

两人偎依在沙发上,非常友好,非常舒适。他亲吻莎朗的嘴唇,这个吻冷静而友好,她这么吻他,所以他也如此回应。宽大的观景窗外,他看见暗蓝色的太平洋在月光下舒展。

"你怎么不放自己的唱片?"莎朗问他,语气里带着戏弄。约翰尼报以微笑。她的戏弄让他觉得很好玩。"我可没那么好莱坞。"他说。

"放一张给我听听。"她说,"现场唱一首? 就像在电影里。我会像银幕上的姑娘那样,热血沸腾,浑身瘫软。"

约翰尼放声大笑。换了早几年,他还会做这种事情,结果总像在舞台上,姑娘对着想象中的镜头,拼命假装性感,假装被他融化,眼泪水汪汪地充满欲望。现在他连做梦都不想给女孩唱歌。首先,他有几个月没唱歌了,信不过自己的声音。其次,外行不明白职业歌手唱歌那么好听,其实在很大程度上靠的是技术设备。他当然可以播放自己的唱片,但他听见自己饱含激情的年轻嗓音就害臊,那感觉正仿佛秃顶发胖的老头让别人看他风华正茂时的照片。

"我的嗓音已经不行了,"他说,"实话实说,我听见自己唱歌就恶心。"

两人慢慢喝酒。"听说你在这部电影里很出彩,"她说,"真的一分钱也不收?"

"只收了象征性的报酬。"约翰尼答道。

他起身斟满她的白兰地酒杯,递给她一根印着金色字母的香烟,用打火机给她点烟。她一边抽烟一边喝酒,他重新在她身旁坐下。他的酒杯比她的满得多,他需要白兰地热身、提神、充电。这和一般一夜情的情况相反,他需要灌醉的是自己,而不是女孩。因为女孩往往迫不及待,他却没那么起劲。最近两年,他的自尊心饱受摧残,他用这个简单的办法恢复自尊心:和年轻鲜活的女孩一夜风流,请她共进几次晚餐,送个昂贵的礼物,然后尽可能用最友好的办法甩掉她,以免她受到伤害。女孩事后总能说她们和了不起的约翰尼·方坦有过一段情。这不是真爱,但姑娘那么漂亮,那么真诚,你也挑不出什么毛病。他讨厌难搞的碎嘴女人,爬下他的床就跑去告诉朋友说她睡了伟大的约翰尼·方坦,最后还要加一句说她们睡过更好的。在他的职业生涯之中,最让他惊讶的是那些低声下气的丈夫,他们就差没当面告诉他,说他们愿意原谅老婆,因为大歌星兼影星约翰尼·方坦就算勾搭了最贞洁的烈妇也情有可原。这实在让他无话可说。

他喜欢艾拉·菲茨杰拉德的唱片,喜欢她干净的歌喉,清澈的抑扬顿挫。音乐是生活中他唯一真正理解的东西,他知道他比全世界任何人都更加理解。此刻躺在沙发上,白兰地温暖他的喉咙,他忽然想唱歌了,不是自己唱,而是跟着唱片哼哼,但当着陌生人他可不能这么做。他伸出空闲的手放在莎朗的大腿上,另一只手举起酒杯喝酒。他毫不掩饰,带着孩童寻找温暖的那种色欲,用她大腿上的那只手撩开裙摆,露出金色网眼丝袜上方的乳白色肌肤,尽管这么多年亲热过那么多女人,此情此景还是让约翰尼觉得有一股黏糊糊的暖流瞬间淌遍全身。奇迹仍旧在发生,要是有一天连性欲都像嗓子那样抛弃了他,他该怎么办呢?

他准备好了。他把酒杯放在嵌花的鸡尾酒台上,转身面对她。他的动作非常确定,非常有把握,但又非常温柔。他的爱抚并不鬼祟,也不淫靡。他亲吻她的嘴唇,双手摸上她的胸部,一只手落下去爱抚温暖的大腿,掌心感觉到的皮肤是那么光滑。她回吻他,温暖但并不炽烈,如今的他更喜欢这种亲吻。他讨厌女孩突然情欲勃发,就像她们的身体是引擎,一碰毛茸茸的开关就轰然转动。

他和平时一样,做了每次都能激起他性欲的事情。他用中指的指尖轻轻抚弄她两腿之间的部位,动作尽可能轻。有些女孩甚至觉察不到这是做爱的开始,有些女孩会略微分神,不确定这算不算是肌肤相亲,因为同时他总在深吻女孩的嘴。也有些女孩会一沉腰身,吸住甚至是包裹住他的手指。当然了,在他成名之前,还有些女孩会扇他耳光。这就是他的全部技巧,通常来说相当管用。

莎朗的反应却异乎寻常。爱抚和亲吻她全盘接受,紧接着却移开她的嘴唇,顺着沙发微微一扭,伸手拿起酒杯。这是冷静而肯定的拒绝。这种事也发生过,虽说很少,但确实发生过。约翰尼也拿起酒杯,点燃香烟。

她用非常甜蜜的声音轻轻说:"并不是我不喜欢你,约翰尼,你比我想象中还要好很多。也不是因为我不是那种女孩。只是我必须动情了才能和男人上床,明白我的意思吗?"

约翰尼·方坦对她微笑,他还是挺喜欢她:"而我没有让你动情?"

她有点尴尬:"呃,你要知道,你唱歌出名什么那会儿,我还很小。我恰巧错过了你,我和你隔了一代。实话实说,不是我假正经。假如你是影星的时候我已经长大了,现在想也不想就会脱掉内裤。"

此刻他不怎么喜欢她了。她很可爱,会说话,有头脑。尽管他的关系能帮她进入演艺事业,但她并没有贴上来跟他睡觉。她是个坦诚的好姑娘。可是,他还意识到了另外一点。这种事以前也发生过几次。女孩和他约会,但不管她有多喜欢他,却早就打定主意不和他上床,只因为这样可以告诉朋友和她自己,她主动放弃了和了不起的约翰尼·方坦睡觉的机会。随着年龄渐长,他现在能理解这种事了,他并不生气,只是不再那么喜欢她了,而原先他又是那么喜欢她。

既然不怎么喜欢她了,他也放松下来,喝着酒,眺望太平洋。她说:"希望你别生气,约翰尼:我想我大概比较保守,我想在好莱坞,女孩应该可以安然退场,就像男女亲吻道晚安那么简单。我来这儿还不久,不懂规矩。"

约翰尼对她微笑,拍拍她的面颊,手落下去拉起裙摆,遮住她光滑圆润的膝盖。"我没生气,"他说,"来个老式约会也不错。"他没有说心里话,其实他松了一口气,因为他不必证明自己是个美好的情人,他不必维持在屏幕上天神一样的形象,也不必听女孩试着作出夸张的反应,就好像他完美到能够和一个再普通不过的女人做出不同凡响的爱一样。

他们又喝了一杯,冷静地亲吻,然后她决定走了。约翰尼很有礼貌地问:"改天再找你吃晚饭?"

她说得坦白诚实。"我知道你不想浪费时间,最后落得失望,"她说,"谢谢这个美妙的晚上。有朝一日我会告诉我的孩子,我曾单独和约翰尼·方坦在他家共进晚餐。"

他对她微笑。"还要说你没有屈服。"他说。两人哈哈大笑。"他们恐怕不会相信。"她说。轮到约翰回应了,他虚情假意地说:"我可以写下来,你想要吗?"她摇摇头。他继续道:"要是有谁敢怀疑,你就打电话给我,我保证向他们澄清。我会说我撵着你满公寓跑,而你捍卫了自己的贞节。如何?"

他终于有点过于刻薄了,见到年轻的脸上露出伤痛,他不太舒服。她明白这话的意思是说他并没有太使劲,他剥夺了她获胜的美妙感觉。她会觉得其实是因为自己缺乏魅力,不够吸引人,因此才成了今夜的胜者。她这样的一个女孩,每次讲述如何拒绝了不起的约翰尼·方坦,最后都必须露出嘲讽的微笑,补充道:"当然啦,他并不是特别起劲。"现在他开始怜悯她了:"要是心情不好就打电话给我。好吗? 我也不是非得和我认识的每个女孩睡觉。"

"好的。"她说完就走了。

他有一个漫长的夜晚需要打发。他可以去杰克·沃尔茨所谓的"肉铺",愿意倒贴的小明星不计其数,但他想要个有人味儿的伴侣。他想像人类一样交谈。他想到第一任妻子维吉尼亚。拍片工作已经结束,他陪孩子的时间就多了。他想重新进入他们的生活。现在他也很担心维吉尼亚。她可没有应付好莱坞浪荡公子的本事,他们也许会去追她,只为了事后吹嘘他们搞过约翰尼·方坦的前妻。还好就他所知,还没有谁说过这种话。不过,是个人就能这么说他的第二任妻子,约翰尼冷笑着心想。他拿起听筒。

他立刻认出了她的声音,这不稀奇,因为第一次听见这个声音的时候他才十岁,念书时也是同班同学。"嗨,金妮,"他说,"今晚忙吗? 我能过来坐坐吗?"

"行啊，"她说，"不过孩子都睡了，我不想吵醒他们。"

"没问题，"他说，"我只想和你聊聊。"

她听起来有点犹豫，小心翼翼地控制自己，不流露出任何关心，她问："出什么大事了吗，什么严重的？"

"没事，"约翰尼说，"今天拍完那部电影了，我只是想见见你，和你聊聊天。要是你确定我不会吵醒孩子，就让我看一眼她们。"

"好吧，"她说，"你得到了你想要的角色，我很高兴。"

"谢谢，"他说，"半小时后见。"

约翰尼·方坦来到贝弗利山他过去的家，他在车里坐了几分钟，望着那幢屋子。他记起教父的叮嘱，说他可以创造出自己想要的生活。只要知道自己想要什么，多半就能心想事成。可是，他到底想要什么呢？

前妻在门口等他。她很漂亮，身材较小，浅黑肤色，是个意大利好姑娘，是从不和其他男人鬼混的邻家女孩——这点对他特别重要。你还想要她吗？他扪心自问，答案是否定的。首先，他不可能再和她做爱，他们的感情已经陈旧。其次还有另外几个原因，和性爱无关，虽然他们已经不再势如水火，但她绝对不可能原谅他。

她给她煮咖啡，请他在客厅吃自家做的点心。"沙发上躺会儿吧，"她说，"你看起来很疲惫。"他脱掉上衣和鞋子，解开领带，她坐进对面的靠椅，露出凝重的微笑。"好玩。"她说。

"什么好玩？"他问，喝一口咖啡，手一抖把咖啡洒在了衬衫上。

"了不起的约翰尼·方坦居然没有约会。"她说。

"了不起的约翰尼·方坦要是还能睡到姑娘就算走运了。"他说。

他这么直接可不寻常，金妮问："你到底是怎么了？"

约翰尼咧嘴苦笑："我和一个女孩在我家约会，她甩了我。可你知道吗？我却松了一口气。"

让他惊讶的是他见到怒气在金妮脸上一闪而过。"别为那些小婊子伤脑筋，"她说，"她肯定以为这样最能吸引你。"约翰尼很开心地意识到金妮真的很生气，因为居然有女孩拒绝约翰尼。

"哈，管他的，"他说，"我反正厌倦了这种事。一个人总得成长嘛。既然我再也没法唱歌，女人恐怕要对我没兴趣了。我可不是靠脸骗色的，你知道。"

她诚恳地说："你的真人从来比照片好看。"

约翰尼摇摇头。"我越来越胖，而且在脱发。该死，要是这部电影不能让我再出名，我干脆趁早学烤比萨去算了。要么想办法让你拍电影吧，你看起来很不错。"

她看起来有三十五岁了。保养得很好的三十五岁,但毕竟还是三十五岁。在好莱坞,三十五岁和一百岁没什么区别。年轻的漂亮女孩像旅鼠似的涌进洛杉矶,大部分人能混一年,有些两年。有些女孩美得能让男人心脏停跳,但只要一开口,对成功的贪婪欲望就遮蔽了可爱的眼神。普通女人在姿色上绝不可能和她们竞争。你尽可以扯什么魅力、智慧、优雅和仪态,但这些女孩的纯粹美丽彻底压倒了其他因素。要不是这种女孩有那么多,一个普通好看的女人或许还有机会。约翰尼·方坦搞得到所有这些女孩,至少是其中的绝大多数,因此金妮知道他这么说至少是为了哄她开心。他说话向来这么好听。他对女人总是彬彬有礼,哪怕名声最盛的时候也一样,恭维她们,给她们点烟,开门。平时受到如此礼遇的往往是他,所以和他约会的女孩愈加受到触动。他这么对待所有女人,哪怕是一夜情的对象,哪怕是连名字都不知道的姑娘。

她对他微笑,这是个友善的笑容。"你已经追到我了,约翰尼,还记得吗?十二年了,你犯不着跟我来这套。"

他叹了口气,在沙发上伸个懒腰。"不是开玩笑,金妮,你气色真的很好。但愿我也能这么好看。"

她没有答话,看得出他很沮丧。"觉得你那部电影怎么样?能帮助你吗?"她问。

约翰尼点点头。"挺好,能把我一路送回顶峰。我要是拿到奥斯卡,再好好谋划一番,就算不唱歌我也能重新出名。那样就可以给你和孩子更多的钱了。"

"我们的钱已经够多了。"金妮答道。

"我想多见见孩子,"约翰尼说,"我想稍微安生点儿了。我能每周五来吃晚饭吗?我发誓一次也不会落下,不管离家多远,不管我多忙。只要挤得出时间就陪孩子过周末,孩子放假也可以来和我住几天。"

金妮拿起烟灰缸放在他胸口。"我倒是没问题,"她说,"我不肯再结婚,就是因为想让你一直当她们的爸爸。"这句话她说得毫无感情色彩,但盯着天花板的约翰尼·方坦知道她这么说是为了修补裂痕,当初婚姻刚破裂,他的事业开始走下坡路那会儿,她说过一些很难听的话。

"说起来,猜猜谁给我打过电话?"她说。

约翰尼不肯陪她玩,他从不玩猜猜看的游戏。"谁?"他问。

金妮说:"你哪怕随便猜一次也好嘛。"约翰尼没有吭声。她说:"你的教父。"

约翰尼确实吃了一惊。"他从不和别人在电话上谈事情。他跟你说了什么?"

"他请我帮助你,"金妮说,"说你会和过去一样出名,你正在东山再起,但你需要别人信赖你。我问凭什么要我这么做,他说因为你是我的孩子的父亲。这位老先生真是热心,居然还有人说他的坏话。"

维吉尼亚讨厌电话,所以拆掉了家里的大多数分机,只留下卧室和厨房两部电话。他们听见厨房的电话响了。她过去接听,回到客厅时面露惊讶之色。"找你的,约翰尼,"她说,"是汤姆·黑根,说事情很重要。"

约翰尼走进厨房,拿起听筒。"是我,汤姆。"他说。

汤姆·黑根的声音很冷静:"约翰尼,电影已经完成拍摄,教父派我来找你,安排一下,帮你出头。他叫我搭早班飞机。我们在洛杉矶碰头如何?我当天晚上就得回纽约,所以你不必担心我连晚上也要纠缠你。"

"没问题,汤姆,"约翰尼说,"别担心什么晚上不晚上的。过一夜,放松放松。我办个酒会,介绍你认识几个电影圈的朋友。"他总是这么说,他不希望老邻居觉得受他嫌弃。

"多谢,"黑根说,"但我非得搭凌晨的航班回纽约不可。就这样,你来接十一点半从纽约起飞的航班。"

"没问题。"约翰尼说。

"你留在车里,"黑根说,"我下飞机的时候,你派个手下接我,领我去见你。"

"好。"约翰尼说。

他回到客厅,金妮好奇地看着他。"教父给我设计了什么计划,帮我出头,"约翰尼说,"他帮我弄到了电影里的那个角色,我不清楚他是怎么做到的。但我希望其他的事他就别插手了。"

他躺回沙发上,觉得疲惫不堪。金妮说:"你今晚别回家了,就睡客房吧。明天可以和孩子们吃早饭,免得半夜开车回家。想到你孤零零一个人待在家里我就难过。你不寂寞吗?"

"我很少回家。"约翰尼说。

她笑着说:"看来你改变的并不多。"她犹豫片刻,说:"我去收拾另一间卧室?"

约翰尼说:"不能睡你的卧室?"

她红了脸。"不行。"她说,对他微笑,他报以微笑。他们仍旧是朋友。

第二天,约翰尼醒来,百叶窗拉着,阳光照了进来,约翰尼看得出时间已经很晚。除非是下午,否则阳光不会有这个角度。他喊道:"嘿,金妮,还有早饭吃吗?"远远地传来她的叫声,"稍等片刻。"

真的只等了片刻。她肯定早就全都准备好了,热烘烘地放在炉子里,就等着装进餐盘,因为约翰尼刚点燃今天的第一支香烟,卧室门就被推开,他的两个女儿推着早餐小车进来了。

她们美得让他心碎。她们容光焕发,眼里闪着讶异和急于奔向他的渴望。她们的头发梳成老式长辫,身穿传统裙装,脚蹬漆皮鞋。她们站在早餐小车旁望着他揿熄香烟,等他召唤,张开双臂。她们随即奔向他。他把脸贴在两个芬芳鲜嫩的小脸蛋中间,用胡须茬刮得她们哇哇尖叫。金妮出现在卧室门口,把小车接着往前推,让他在床上吃早饭。她在床沿上坐下,帮他倒咖啡,给吐司抹黄油。两个女儿坐在沙发上望着他们。她们已经长大,不再是打枕头仗和能让人举起来摇晃的年龄了。她们已经知道要整理蓬乱的头发了。天哪,他心想,用不了多久她们就将成人,好莱坞的小流氓会追着她们跑。

他边吃边和女儿分享吐司和培根,还让她们喝了几小口咖啡。这是早几年留下来的习惯,那时候他和乐队唱歌,很少有机会和女儿一起吃饭,所以碰到他颠倒时间吃饭,比方说下午吃早饭,早晨吃晚餐,她们就喜欢抢他的食物吃。颠倒时间吃东西让她们很开心,早晨七点吃牛排和炸薯条,下午吃培根和煎蛋。

只有金妮和他的几个密友知道他有多宝贝这两个女儿。离婚和搬出家门的时候,和女儿分别最让他痛苦。他争取和为之奋斗的事情只有一件,那就是保留父亲地位。他拐弯抹角让金妮明白,她要是再婚,他会很不高兴,并非因为嫉妒,而是不愿失去父亲的地位。他对金钱作出安排,只要不再婚,她在财务方面就不需要发愁。另外一方面,她尽可以找情人,只要不让他们侵入家庭生活就行。不过,这方面他倒是完全信任金妮。她在情爱上出奇地害羞和守旧。好莱坞的小白脸闻到味道,蜂拥而至,想从她著名的丈夫那儿捞到钱财和好处,却每每空手而归。

他不担心她会因为昨晚他想和她睡觉而生出破镜重圆的念头。他们谁也不想恢复当初的婚姻关系。她明白他对美色的渴望,他对远比她美貌的女人有着难以遏制的冲动。众所周知,他和合演电影的女明星至少得睡一觉。女人抗拒不了他孩子气的魅力,正如他抗拒不了她们的美貌。

"你得赶快穿衣服了,"金妮说,"汤姆的航班很快就要降落。"她把女儿赶出卧室。

"好,"约翰尼说,"顺便说一句,金妮,知道我在离婚吗?我很快就又要自由了。"

她望着约翰尼穿衣服。唐·柯里昂女儿的婚礼之后,他们达成新的约定,他总在她家里放几身干净衣服。"还有两周就是圣诞节了,"她说,"要把你也计划在内吗?"

这还是他第一次考虑假日怎么过。他的嗓子出问题之前,假日是唱歌挣钱的好季节,但即便如此,圣诞节仍旧神圣不可侵犯。要是这次再错过,那就是一连两年了。去年他在西班牙追求第二任妻子,苦苦求她嫁给他。

"好,"他说,"圣诞夜和圣诞节。"他没提新年夜。新年夜也是他每隔一段时间就需要来一次的狂欢之夜,和朋友喝得烂醉,他可不希望老婆守在旁边。他对此并不愧疚。

她帮约翰尼穿上外衣,掸了掸灰尘。他向来讲究整洁。她看见他皱起眉头,因为换上的衬衫没有按照他的喜好清洗熨烫,袖扣是他很久没戴过的,对他最近的着装风格来说过于花哨。她轻轻一笑,说:"汤姆注意不到区别。"

家里的三个女人送他出门,到车道上车。两个女儿一边一个抓着他的手,妻子稍微落后两步。他显得那么高兴,她看得也很愉快。来到车前,他转过身,轮流把两个女儿举到半空中,一边放下一边亲吻。最后,他亲了亲妻子,坐进车里。他向来不喜欢啰唆的告别。

他的公关经理和助手已经安排好了。回到家里,一辆配有司机的包租车在等他。车里坐着公关经理和一名助理。约翰尼停好车,跳进包租车,赶往机场。他等在车里,公关经理去接飞机。汤姆上车,他们握手,车开回他家。

最后,只剩下他和汤姆坐在客厅里。两人之间有点冷淡。约翰尼一直没法原谅黑根,康妮婚礼之前,唐对约翰尼很生气,约翰尼想联系唐,拦在中间的正是黑根。黑根从不为他的行为找借口。他不能这么做。他的职责有一部分就是充当怨恨的避雷针,因为人们对唐过于敬畏,就算有气也不敢怨恨他本人。

"教父派我来在某些事情上帮你一把,"黑根说,"我想在圣诞节前解决问题。"

约翰尼·方坦耸耸肩。"电影已经拍完。导演待我很好。我的镜头很重要,不可能因为沃尔茨想打发我就被剪辑师扔掉。他不可能毁掉一部千万美元的大制作。所以现在全看观众觉得我在电影里有多出色了。"

黑根字斟句酌地说:"赢得奥斯卡奖对一个演员的职业生涯是真的非常重要,还只是普普通通的宣传噱头,不得也无所谓。"他顿了顿,又连忙说,"当然,荣誉除外,是人就喜欢荣誉。"

约翰尼·方坦对他咧咧嘴:"除了我那位教父,还有你。不,汤姆,那不是噱头。一尊奥斯卡奖能让一个演员红十年,他可以随便挑选角色,观众愿意进电影院看他。拿奥斯卡不是一切,但对于一名演员,却是这个行当最重要的东西。我指望这次能获奖。不是因为我这个演员有多了不起,而是我本来以歌手闻名,而这个角色万无一失。再说我演得也不错,不开玩笑。"

汤姆·黑根耸耸肩,说:"教父告诉我,按照现在的事态发展,你恐怕毫无获奖的机会。"

约翰尼·方坦怒道:"你在胡扯什么?电影都还没开始剪辑,更别说上映了。唐甚至都不是电影业的人。你他妈飞了三千英里,就是要说这种屁话?"他气得都快哭出来了。

黑根急忙解释道:"约翰尼,我对电影当然一窍不通。记住,我只是唐的信使。不过我们讨论过很多次你的事情。他担心你的未来。他觉得你还需要他的帮助,想一劳永逸解决你的问题。我这次来就是为了让事情能顺利进行。但约翰尼,你必须成长起来。你不能再把自己当成歌手和演员了。你要把自己当作能呼风唤雨的人,一个有权势的人。"

约翰尼·方坦笑着斟满酒杯。"要是我这次得不到奥斯卡,那我的权势恐怕也就和我女儿差不多了。我的嗓子完了,要是嗓子能恢复,我还可以试试。唉,该死。教父怎么知道我赢不了? 好吧,我相信他。他从不犯错。"

黑根点燃一支细雪茄。"我们听到风声,说杰克·沃尔茨不肯用电影公司的钱支持你候选。事实上,他甚至对投票者放话说他不希望你得奖。他还扣下了广告经费和有助于你获胜的所有开销。他尽可能安排人投另一个家伙的票。他用上了各种各样的贿赂:职位、金钱、女人……他这样做的同时还要设法让电影不受损失,至少尽可能少受损失。"

约翰尼·方坦耸耸肩。他倒了满满一杯威士忌,一饮而尽。"那我就死定了。"

黑根望着他,厌恶地皱起嘴唇。"喝酒对你的嗓子没好处。"他说。

"去你妈的。"约翰尼说。

黑根的脸突然拉下去,面无表情地说:"好吧,那我们只谈公事。"

约翰尼·方坦放下酒杯,走到黑根面前站住。"抱歉,汤姆,我没管住嘴巴,"他说,"天哪,真是对不起。我拿你撒气是因为我想宰了杰克·沃尔茨,但又不敢这么使唤教父他老人家,所以只好冲你嚷嚷。"他两眼含泪,把空酒杯砸向墙壁,但动作虚弱无力,厚实的酒杯没有破碎,而是顺着地板滚回了他面前,他低头看着酒杯,满心挫折和愤怒。他接着大笑起来,说,"我的天哪。"

他走到房间的另一头,在黑根对面坐下。"知道吗? 我的事业一直一帆风顺,然后我和金妮离了婚,所有事情都开始倒霉。我的嗓子坏了,唱片卖不出去,找不到拍电影的工作。然后我的教父对我生气,不肯接我的电话,我去纽约都不肯见我。挡路的一直是你,我责怪你,可我知道要是唐不下令,你也不会这么做。可谁能怨恨唐呢? 那就像怨恨上帝。因此我诅咒你。但你从来都是对的。为了向你表示歉意,我接受你的建议。嗓子一天不恢复,我就一天不喝酒。行吗?"

他的道歉发自肺腑。黑根忘记了恼怒。这个三十五岁的大男孩肯定有什么特殊之处,否则唐不可能那么宠爱他。他说:"算啦,约翰尼。"约翰尼的真诚让他感到尴尬,他怀疑约翰尼是害怕自己,害怕自己会挑拨他和唐的关系。当然了,谁都不可能以任何理由挑拨唐,唐的情感只受他自己左右。

"情况没那么糟糕,"他告诉约翰尼,"唐说他可以抵消沃尔茨对你做的所有坏事,说你几乎肯定能拿奖,但他觉得这并没有解决问题。他想知道你有没有脑子和卵蛋,自立门户当制片人,从头到尾自己制作电影。"

"他怎么能让我拿奖?"约翰尼怀疑道。

黑根答得不留情面:"你那么容易就相信沃尔茨能瞒天过海,却不相信你的教父也做得到?看来要让你对这桩事的另一面树立起信心,我非得和你说实话了。不过你可别到处乱说。教父的权势比杰克·沃尔茨大得多,尤其是在某些更加关键的领域。他打算怎么操纵奖项?他控制着——或者说控制了控制电影业所有工会的人,控制所有或者近乎所有投票者。当然,首先你必须足够优秀,能凭借自己的成就去竞争。另外,你的教父比杰克·沃尔茨有脑子。他不会跑到投票人面前,拿枪顶着他们的脑袋说'投票给约翰尼·方坦,否则就崩了你',遇到武力威胁不起作用或者会留下太多恶感的时候,他是不会这么做的,而是会让那些人心甘情愿地投你一票。可话也说回来,他要是不干涉,他们就不会把票投给你。现在你反正就相信我好了,他确实能让你得奖,而他要是不插手,你就没法得奖。"

"好吧,"约翰尼说,"我相信你。我有足够的卵蛋和头脑当制片人,但我没那么多钞票,也没有哪家银行肯资助我。拍摄一部电影需要几百万。"

黑根干巴巴地说:"你获奖以后就开始制订计划,制作三部由自己主演的电影。雇用这行最优秀的人——技术人员、明星,需要谁就雇谁。制订三到五部电影的计划。"

"你疯了,"约翰尼说,"那么多电影少说也要两千万美元。"

"等你需要钱了,"黑根说,"就联系我。我会告诉你联系加州的哪家银行,请他们提供资金帮助。别担心,他们多年来一直资助电影拍摄。你就按正常方式找他们借钱,理由必须正当,就像正规的生意往来。他们会批准。但你首先要见我,把数字和计划解释给我听。明白了?"

约翰尼沉默良久,最后静静地说:"还有什么条件?"

黑根笑了。"你是想知道,为了一笔两千万美元的贷款,你需要做些什么来报恩吗?当然会有的。"他等约翰尼开口,"可是,要是唐请你做事,你本来也不可能拒绝他吧?"

约翰尼说:"如果事关重大,那就必须是唐本人跟我说,明白我的意思吗?你和桑尼说了都没用。"

他敏锐的直觉让黑根吃惊,方坦终究还是有些头脑的。他凭直觉知道唐非常宠爱他,而且唐那么精明,不可能要他做什么危险的蠢事,而桑尼就说不准了。他对约翰尼说:"有一点你听了肯定安心。你的教父向我和桑尼下了死命令,不许我们以任何方式在任何事情上牵连你,防止因为我们犯错,损坏你的形象。你本人就更不可能这么做了。我向你保证,他会请你帮的那些忙,都是不等他开口你就会抢着做的事情。懂了?"

约翰尼微笑道:"懂了。"

黑根说:"还有,他对你很有信心。他认为你头脑很好,所以估计银行在这项投资上能挣钱,也就是说他能因此挣钱。所以,这确实是一桩商业交易,千万别忘记这一点。别拿了钱去乱花。就算他最喜欢你这个教子,但两千万美元也还是很大一笔钱。他冒了很大的风险才把钱交到你手上。"

"转告他,别担心,"约翰尼说,"连杰克·沃尔茨这种货色都能在电影界呼风唤雨,别人没理由不行。"

"教父也是这么想的,"黑根说,"能派车送我回机场吗?我的话说完了。签任何合约之前,先雇个好律师,这事情我不插手,但如果你不反对的话,我希望你签合同之前可以让我先过目一下。另外,你永远也不会遇到劳资纠纷,很能帮你降低一些成本,所以不管会计师在这类条目上填了多少,你抹掉那些数字就是了。"

约翰尼小心翼翼地问:"其他方面也要你点头吗?比方说剧本、选角之类的?"

黑根摇摇头。"不需要,"他说,"唐倒是有可能反对些什么,但他要是有意见就会直接跟你说。天晓得到底是什么。电影无论如何也打动不了他,因此他并不感兴趣。再说他不喜欢胡乱插手,这点我可以凭经验向你保证。"

"很好,"约翰尼说,"我开车送你去机场吧。替我谢谢教父。我很想打电话亲口感谢他,但他从来不接。说起来,这是怎么回事?"

黑根耸耸肩:"他难得对着听筒说话,他不希望自己的声音被录下来,哪怕说的是全然无关紧要的内容。他害怕别人会把字词拼凑起来,听上去像他在说别的什么事情。我猜就是这么一回事。他最担心的就是有朝一日会遭到政府陷害,所以不想被他们抓住把柄。"

他们坐进约翰尼的轿车,约翰尼开车赶往机场。黑根心想,约翰尼比他想象的要好,他看到了约翰尼的一些优点,亲自送他去机场就是一个证明。他对人的谦恭礼貌,这是唐一向重视的。还有道歉。约翰尼的道歉发自肺腑。他认识约翰尼很多年了,他知道约翰尼的道歉并非出自恐惧。约翰尼从小就胆大包天,所以才经常惹麻烦,跟公司老板和女人闹得不愉快。约翰尼是为数不多不害怕唐的人,在黑根认识人当中,只有方坦和迈克尔不害怕唐。因此他愿意接受真诚的道歉。接下来这几年,他和约翰尼将经常碰面。约翰尼必须通过这场考验,证明他到底有多精明。他必须为唐做一些事,这些事情唐既不会开口求他去做,也不会作为互相帮助的交换条件逼他去做。黑根琢磨着约翰尼·方坦到底够不够聪明,有没有意识到交易的这个部分。

约翰尼在机场放下黑根(黑根坚持不让约翰尼浪费时间陪他等飞机),驱车回到金妮家里。见到约翰尼,她很惊讶。他想待在她的家里,好有时间整理思绪,制订计划。他知道黑根的提议异常重要,他的人生轨迹随之改变。他曾经是大明星,但年纪轻轻三十五岁就被淘汰了。这一点上他不会自欺欺人。就算赢得最佳男主角奖项,那又能有多少意义呢?要是嗓子不恢复,就是零蛋。他只会是个二流人物,没有真正的权势,捞不到真正的油水。甚至那个拒绝了他的姑娘,聪明可爱,挺有时代气息,可他如果真是头面人物,她还会那么冷淡吗?现在有唐用钞票给他撑腰,他就有机会比肩好莱坞的任何大人物了。他也可以呼风唤雨。约翰尼不禁笑了。妈的,他甚至可以成为一个唐。

和金妮过上几周倒是不错,更久一点也可以考虑。他可以每天带着孩子出去玩,邀请几个朋友来坐坐。他要戒烟戒酒,好好保养。嗓子说不定还能恢复。要真能恢复,加上唐的金库,他将所向披靡。他可以在美国尽可能活得像个古代的国王或皇帝。情况将不取决于他的嗓子撑不撑得住,也不取决于公众对他这个演员能关注多久。帝国的根基将是金钱和最特殊、最令人垂涎的权力。

金妮给他整理好了客房。两人都明白,他不会睡在她的房间里,他们不会以夫妻身份同居。夫妻关系不可能恢复。尽管外界的闲话专栏和影迷把婚姻失败完全归咎于他,但有趣的是,对约翰尼和金妮而言,他们都知道更该负责的是金妮。

约翰尼·方坦成为最受欢迎的歌手和音乐电影明星之后,从没动过抛弃老婆孩子的念头。他骨子里是意大利人,很守旧。当然,他也时常偷腥——实在难以避免,因为干他这一行的,诱惑总是赤裸裸地摆在面前。尽管他看起来瘦弱,那话儿却和很多小骨架拉丁男人一样既长又硬。女人的讶异总是让他开心。他喜欢和端庄甜美、看似处女的姑娘约会,解开胸衣发现双乳饱满结实得出乎意料,沉甸甸的那么淫荡,与浮雕般的精致面容恰成对比。他喜欢在看似性感的姑娘身上寻找羞涩和胆怯,她们仿佛动作敏捷的篮球好手,用无数假动作装得像是睡过上百个男人,他和她们单独相处,你来我往几个钟头,插进去办完事才发现其实是处女。

好莱坞的家伙都嘲笑他对处女的偏好。他们当面说这是老掉牙的黑皮口味,处女要调教多久才肯给你口交啊,而且到头来往往还玩得没滋没味。但约翰尼知道关键在于你怎么操纵女孩。你要以正确的方式启发她,然后呢?还有比看着她平生第一次品味鸡巴还乐在其中更美妙的吗?啊哈,突破禁区实在美妙,教她们用双腿夹住你的腰实在美妙。她们的大腿各不相同,屁股各不相同,肤色各不相同,白色、棕色、褐色的色调各不相同。他在底特律睡过一个黑人姑娘,正经女孩,不是妓女,父亲是请他出场的一家夜总会的一位爵士歌手,她是他人生最美妙的经历之一。她温暖的嘴唇像是掺了胡椒的蜂蜜,深褐色的皮肤犹如凝脂,她是上帝创造的最甜美的女人,而且在遇到他之前还是处女。

其他人总喜欢谈论口交和各种花样,他其实并不那么喜欢口交。女孩尝试给他口交以后,他往往会对她们丧失兴趣,因为口交满足不了他。他和第二任妻子合不来就是因为她对 69 式的热衷超过一切,他非得动粗才能插入。她取笑他,说他太正经,进而说他做爱像小孩。也许这就是昨晚那姑娘拒绝他的原因。算了,去他妈的,她反正也不可能真有多棒。你看得出一个姑娘喜不喜欢做爱,真心喜欢的才做得最好。特别是初尝滋味的那些。他最讨厌那种十二岁就开始做爱,到二十岁已经厌倦的女人,只是按步照班扭动身体,虽说她们往往美艳动人,能用叫床蒙混过关。

金妮把咖啡和糕点端进他的卧室,放在会客区的长台上。他大致说了几句,说黑根在帮他聚拢信用贷款,准备制作电影,她听了非常兴奋。他将重新成为大人物。她其实并不知道唐·柯里昂究竟有多少权势,也不理解黑根从纽约来见他到底有多重要。他说黑根还会帮他处理法律事务。

喝完咖啡,他说他今晚就开始工作,打电话,为未来制订计划。"一半收益记在孩子的名下。"他告诉金妮。金妮露出感激的笑容,吻他道晚安,离开房间。

写字台上的玻璃盘里装满了有他姓名缩写图案的香烟,旁边的保湿盒里是铅笔粗细的古巴雪茄。约翰尼向后一躺,开始打电话。他的脑袋转得飞快。他打给新电影原著的畅销书作者。作家和他年龄相仿,成名之路也非常艰辛,如今是文学界的名人。他来好莱坞本希望能独当一面,却被当作狗屎对待。约翰尼有一天晚上在布朗德比餐馆亲眼见到作家受辱。有人安排作家和一个大胸的风骚小明星约会,吃完饭肯定还要睡一觉。可他们吃着吃着,一个獐头鼠目的喜剧演员朝小明星勾勾手指,小明星就撇下作家走了。这帮助作家对好莱坞的权势等级树立了正确观念。他的小说让他世界闻名也无济于事。小明星宁可勾搭最低级下贱、最獐头鼠目、最招摇撞骗的影坛大人物。

约翰尼打电话到作家在纽约的住所,感谢作家写活了他那个了不起的角色。马屁拍得作家忘乎所以。他假装随意地问起作家的新书进展如何,写的是什么内容。他点燃雪茄,听作家介绍书里特别有意思的章节,最后说:"天,写完了一定要让我先睹为快。寄给我一份样稿怎么样?说不定能帮你谈个好交易,比你和沃尔茨那个肯定强。"

作家的热切语气说明他猜对了。沃尔茨摆了他一道,用蝇头小利换走改编权。约翰尼提到长假过后他也许会去纽约,到时候请作家和他的几个朋友吃顿饭。"我认识几个漂亮姑娘。"约翰尼开玩笑道。作家哈哈大笑,说太好了。

接下来,约翰尼打给刚刚完成拍摄的那部电影的导演和摄影师,感谢他们在拍片时的大力帮助。他和他们推心置腹,说他知道沃尔茨跟他过不去,因此双倍感激他们的帮助,要是有机会能为他们效劳,打个电话知会一声就得。

最后,他打了最困难的一个电话,打给杰克·沃尔茨本人。他感谢沃尔茨愿意把角色给他,说他非常乐意能再为沃尔茨效劳。他这么做只是为了迷惑沃尔茨,因为他向来光明磊落,直来直往,几天后沃尔茨就将发现他耍的花招,对这通电话的虚情假意倍感吃惊,而这正是约翰尼·方坦希望他有的感觉。

打完电话,他坐在写字台前抽雪茄。边桌上有威士忌,但他已经对自己和黑根承诺过不再喝酒。他甚至连抽烟也不应该。或许很愚蠢,戒烟戒酒多半解决不了嗓子的问题。或许机会渺茫,但去他妈的,说不定有用呢,现在有了拼死一搏的机会,他希望所有概率都站在他这一边。

屋子已经静了下来,前妻在睡觉,他钟爱的女儿在睡觉,他可以回想生命中那段恐怖的时光,他怎么抛弃妻子和女儿。抛弃她们,投向一个臭婊子的怀抱,娶她当第二任老婆。可是,哪怕到了现在,想到她依然让他微笑,她在许多方面仍不失是个可爱的女人。再者说,拯救他一生的关键就是那天他下定决心,绝对不会去恨任何女人,更确切地说,那天他决定他不能恨第一任妻子、两个女儿、为数众多的女朋友、第二任妻子和之后的女朋友们,一直到莎朗·莫尔,她甩了他,好四处吹嘘她如何拒绝和了不起的约翰尼·方坦睡觉。

他曾经跟着乐队巡回卖艺,后来成为电台明星和舞台剧明星,最后终于打进电影圈。从头到尾都活得随心所欲,爱睡哪个女人就睡哪个女人,但从不让女人影响个人生活。接下来,很快成为他第二任妻子的玛格特·艾什顿迷住了他,他完全为她疯狂。他的职业生涯完蛋了,嗓子完蛋了,家庭生活也完蛋了。他走到了山穷水尽的那一天。

可情况是这样的,他为人向来慷慨公正。和第一任妻子离婚的时候,他把所有财产都给了她。他还确保他挣的每一块钱,不管来自唱片、电影还是夜总会表演,两个女儿都会分得一份。他名利双收的时候,对第一任妻子有求必应。他帮助过她的每一个兄弟姐妹和她的父母,甚至是她小时候学校里的朋友和她们的家属。他从来不是出了名就忘本的那种人。老婆的两个妹妹出嫁,他应邀在婚礼上唱歌,这其实是他最讨厌的事情。约翰尼没有拒绝过妻子,只要不完全违背他的人格,妻子的任何要求他都满足。

接下来他开始倒霉,找不到拍电影的工作,也没法继续唱歌,第二任妻子背叛他,他跑去与金妮和两个女儿过了几天。一天晚上,他的情绪低落到极点,他算是扑在她脚下,恳求她的怜悯。那天他听了自己新录的一首歌,声音难听得可怕,他指责是录音师存心破坏。但最终他不得不相信那就是他真实的声音。他砸碎母带,从此拒绝唱歌。他无地自容,除了和尼诺在康妮·柯里昂的婚礼上合唱一曲之外,连半个音符都没再唱过。

金妮了解到他的各种不幸遭遇,脸上的神情是他永远也忘不掉的。那神情只闪现了一秒钟,但足以让他永远也忘不了。那是无情的幸灾乐祸,让他不得不相信金妮这几年来对他怀着多么轻蔑的恨意。她很快恢复常态,对他表示出冷淡但彬彬有礼的同情。他假装接受。接下来的几天,他去见这些年来他最喜欢的三个姑娘,他和她们始终保持友谊,偶尔以伙伴的身份睡睡觉,他曾竭尽全力帮助她们,送出去的礼物和工作机会价值几十万。他瞥见同样的幸灾乐祸在她们脸上一闪而过。

就在那段时间里,他知道了他必须下定决心。一方面,他可以学习好莱坞的其他大人物,那些著名的制作人、编剧、导演和演员,他们带着性欲和仇恨捕猎美女。运用权势和金钱帮助别人的时候,他可以尽量吝惜,时刻警惕背叛,从心底里相信女人都会背叛和抛弃他,女人是他要击败的敌寇。但另一方面,他也可以拒绝仇恨女人,选择继续相信她们。

他知道自己承受不了不爱女人的代价,无论女人多么水性杨花,多么背信弃义,要是不能爱女人,他的一部分灵魂会随之死去。全世界他最爱的女人见到无常命运碾碎羞辱他,却暗自高兴,这没关系;她们以最可怖的方式——不是性爱——对他不忠,这也没关系。他别无选择。他必须接受她们。于是他和她们做爱,送她们礼物,隐藏她们的幸灾乐祸给他造成的创痛。他知道这是偿还女人给予他的极大的自由和热爱,因此他原谅她们。他并不后悔他那么对待金妮:坚持独占孩子的父亲地位,但决不考虑和她复婚,并且让她明白这一点。他从顶峰跌落,这是他抢救出来的唯一一件东西。对于他给女人造成的伤害,他早已变得铁石心肠。

他很累,准备上床睡觉,却怎么都摆脱不了记忆里的一件事:和尼诺·瓦伦蒂合唱。他忽然知道该怎么最大程度地取悦唐·柯里昂了。他拿起听筒,请接线生转纽约。他打给桑尼·柯里昂,问他要尼诺·瓦伦蒂的号码,接着打给尼诺。尼诺的声音和平时一样醉意盎然。

"喂,尼诺,愿不愿意过来帮我做事?"约翰尼说,"我需要一个信得过的兄弟。"

喜欢开玩笑的尼诺说:"天,我说不准啊,约翰尼,我有个开卡车的好工作,沿途可以和家庭主妇说说笑笑,每周净赚一百五。你的待遇怎么样?"

"起薪五百,外加安排你约会电影明星,怎么样?"约翰尼说,"说不定还可以让你在我的酒会上唱歌。"

"哦,好的,让我考虑一下,"尼诺说,"我先找律师、会计师和开卡车的帮工聊一聊。"

"喂,尼诺,别再开玩笑了,"约翰尼说,"我这儿需要你。你明天一早就给我飞过来,签一份每周五百的合同,为期一年。你要是勾搭我的姑娘,我就解雇你,但你能拿到至少一年的遣散费。如何?"

尼诺沉默良久,开口的时候声音很清醒:"喂,约翰尼,你开玩笑吧?"

约翰尼说,"我说真的,老兄。你跑一趟我经纪人在纽约的办公室,他们会给你机票和一些现金。明早我醒来就打电话给他们,所以你下午就在洛杉矶了。怎么样?我派人接你,带你回我家。"

尼诺又沉默良久才开口,声音犹犹豫豫,说:"好的,约翰尼。"听上去已经毫无醉意。

约翰尼挂断电话,起身准备睡觉。自从砸碎母带那天以来,他的感觉从没有这么好过。

第十三章

宽敞的录音室里,约翰尼·方坦抱着黄色记事簿估算开销。乐手鱼贯而入,都是他的朋友,他小时候和乐队唱歌那会儿就认识他们了。指挥正在发乐谱,口头指导乐手,他是流行乐伴奏领域最顶尖的人物,对事业低谷的约翰尼很是照顾。他叫艾迪·内尔斯,尽管日程表排得很满,但还是卖了约翰尼一个人情,来参加这次录音。

尼诺·瓦伦蒂坐在钢琴前,心情紧张,随手乱弹,不时拿起一大杯黑麦威士忌喝一口。约翰尼并不介意。他知道尼诺醉不醉唱得一样好,再说今天要录的歌曲也不需要尼诺有多少艺术家细胞。

艾迪·内尔斯特别编排了几首意大利和西西里的老歌,特地选了尼诺和约翰尼在康妮·柯里昂婚礼上的那首二重唱。约翰尼之所以想录这张唱片,主要是因为他知道唐喜欢这种歌曲,这将是给唐的一份完美的圣诞礼物。他凭直觉知道这张唱片的销量差不了,当然,恐怕到不了一百万。另外,他知道帮助尼诺正是唐所期待的报答方式。尼诺毕竟也是唐的教子。

约翰尼把写字板和记事簿放在身边的折叠椅上,起身站在钢琴旁。他说:"嘿,兄弟,"尼诺抬起头来,挤出笑容。他看起来病怏怏的。约翰尼俯身给他捏肩膀。"放松,老兄,"他说,"今天要是干得好,我保证给你安排好莱坞最出名的好屁股。"

尼诺喝了一大口威士忌:"谁? 莱丝?"

约翰尼笑道:"不,狄安娜·邓恩。保证是好货。"

尼诺食指大动,但还是忍不住装得好像希望落空:"就不能帮我安排莱丝吗?"

乐队开始演奏串烧曲的开场。约翰尼·方坦仔细听着。艾迪·内尔斯会先按照这次特别的编排演奏全部曲目,然后就是第一次录音了。约翰尼一边听,一边在脑子里记录,他该怎么处理每句唱词,该怎么切入下一首歌。他知道他的声音撑不了太久,但演唱大部分交给尼诺,约翰尼只需要跟着和声。当然,除了决斗二重唱。他得省着力气唱那首歌。

他把尼诺拽起来,两人站在麦克风前。尼诺唱砸了开场,接着又唱砸了第二次。他尴尬得满脸通红。约翰尼揶揄道:"喂,你这是存心拖延要加班费对吧?"

"没有曼陀林,我觉得很不自在,"尼诺说。

约翰尼琢磨了几秒钟,说:"喝点酒试试。"

这一招似乎管用了。尼诺一边唱,一边喝个不停,唱得很不错。约翰尼唱得很放松,没有用力,声音随着尼诺的主旋律上下翻飞。这么唱歌满足不了情感,但他暗自赞叹自己的技巧。玩了十年声音,他终究还是摸到了些门道。

唱到压轴的决斗二重唱,约翰尼放开嗓子,唱完之后,他的声带扯得生疼。乐手被最后这首歌带着走,对这些久经沙场的老将来说真是稀奇。他们敲打乐器,拿跺脚代表鼓掌。鼓手用一段连续轻擂向他们致敬。

加上停顿和商议,录音历经四个小时才结束。艾迪·内尔斯走过来对约翰尼轻声说:"听着很不赖嘛,小伙子。似乎又可以录唱片了,我有首新歌,完全适合你。"

约翰尼摇摇头:"算了,艾迪,别拿我开心了。再说,过几个钟头,我的嗓子会嘶哑得甚至没法说话。你觉得今天录的有多少需要补录?"

艾迪沉思着说:"尼诺明天得来一趟录音室。他唱错了几个地方。不过他比我预想中好得多。至于你的部分,我会请工程师修补我不喜欢的地方。可以吗?"

"可以,"约翰尼说,"什么时候听小样?"

"明天晚上,"艾迪·内尔斯说,"你家?"

"好,"约翰尼说,"感激不尽,艾迪。明天见。"他挽起尼诺的胳膊,走出录音室。他们没有去金妮家,而是去了他的住处。

时间已经临近傍晚。尼诺的酒意大半未消。约翰尼叫他去洗个淋浴,然后小睡一觉。他们晚上十一点要出席一个盛大酒会。

等尼诺醒来,约翰尼先向他介绍情况。"这次酒会是影星的孤独之心俱乐部,"他说,"今晚来的娘儿们都是你在电影里见过的妖娆贵妇,几百万男人情愿拿一条胳膊换一夜风流。她们今晚参加酒会只有一个目标，就是找个男人挨顿好操。知道为什么吗？因为她们太饥渴了，她们只是年纪稍微有点大。和所有贵妇一样，她们挑男人也讲究品位。"

"你的嗓子怎么了？"尼诺问。

约翰尼这会儿说话几近耳语。"每次稍微唱唱歌，嗓子就变成这样。接下来我会有一个月没法唱。不过嘶哑过几天就能好。"

尼诺体贴地说："很难受吧？"

约翰尼无所谓。"听着，尼诺，今晚你别喝太醉。你得给这些好莱坞的女人表演一下，我的朋友可不是吃素的。你必须给她们留下点印象。记住，这些贵妇里有些在电影圈很有权势，能帮你安排工作。搞完以后再卖卖魅力也没啥坏处。"

尼诺已经在给自己斟酒了。"我一向有魅力。"他说。他一口喝完，咧嘴笑道，"不开玩笑，真能让我亲近狄安娜·邓恩？"

"别心急火燎的，"约翰尼说，"其实和你想象的不一样。"

好莱坞明星的孤独之心俱乐部（这是被强制出席的新起之秀的叫法）每周五晚上聚会，地点是电影公司给罗伊·迈克艾尔罗伊安排的一处宫殿一样的住所，他是沃尔茨国际电影公司的媒体经纪人，更确切的头衔是公关顾问。实际上，尽管这是迈克艾尔罗伊举办的开门酒会，主意却来自杰克·沃尔茨那颗讲求实际的头脑。他有不少很挣钱的明星年龄渐长，没有特殊灯光和天才化妆师的帮助，时间的痕迹就昭然若揭。她们有各种各样的问题，灵魂和肉体都越来越迟钝，不再能够"坠入爱河"，不能想当然地认为自己是抢手货。另外一方面，她们也被金钱、名声和过去的美貌惯得过于颐指气使。沃尔茨召开酒会是方便她们挑选一夜情的情人，男人若是真有两下子，就能升格担任全职床伴，从此一路往上爬。这种活动有时候会堕落成争斗和纵欲，惹来警方找麻烦，因此沃尔茨决定干脆在公关顾问家召开酒会，公关顾问可以贿赂记者和警官，当场摆平问题。

对电影公司那些默默无闻、没演过主角但是精力旺盛的年轻男演员来说，参加周五晚上的酒会并不总是一桩美差。因为电影公司会安排在酒会上放映尚未发行的新片。事实上，这就开酒会的借口。大家会说，"我们去看看某人拍的新片怎么样。"于是酒会就有了正当的理由。

年轻的女明星被禁止参加周五晚上的酒会。更确切地说，是不鼓励参加。她们中的绝大多数人都心领神会。

新电影上映放在十二点开始，约翰尼和尼诺十一点赶到。罗伊·迈克艾尔罗伊乍一见是个格外讨人喜欢的男人，修饰整齐，衣冠楚楚。看见约翰尼·方坦，他欢喜得惊叫起来。"你他妈来这儿干什么?"他的惊讶是真心的。

约翰尼摇摇头:"来让乡下表弟开开眼界。这位是尼诺。"

迈克艾尔罗伊和尼诺握手,赞赏地打量着他。"她们会生吞活剥了他。"他对约翰尼说,领着两人来到后天井。

后天井其实是一连串大房间,玻璃门正对花园和池塘。这里聚集了百来号人,手里都拿着酒杯。天井的灯光经过精心布置,女人的面容和皮肤增色不少。这些都是尼诺小时候在昏暗银幕上见过的女人,在他的青春淫梦里扮演过角色。可是,现在见到活生生的真人,就像看见她们化了恐怖片的妆。什么也掩盖不了肉体和灵魂背后的疲惫,时间侵蚀了她们的神性。姿态和动作虽然和记忆中一样迷人,但她们就像蜡制水果,引不出他的半滴口水。尼诺连喝两杯,走到一张桌子旁,方便他接近酒瓶的巢穴。约翰尼跟着他,两人你一半我一杯喝酒,直到背后响起狄安娜·邓恩那有魔力的嗓音。

尼诺和其他几百万个男人一样,早把这个声音永远刻印在了脑海里。狄安娜·邓恩拿过两个奥斯卡,主演过好莱坞史上最赚钱的电影。银幕上的她有那种猫一般的女性魅力,没有哪个男人抵抗得了她的诱惑。可是,此刻她说的话却无论如何也上不了银幕。"混蛋约翰尼,你和我睡了一晚上,结果逼着我又开始看心理医生了。你怎么再也不找我了?"

约翰尼亲吻她送上来的面颊。"你害得我一个月起不了床,"他说,"认识一下我的表弟尼诺。强壮的意大利小伙。他说不定应付得了你。"

狄安娜·邓恩扭头冷冷打量尼诺:"他喜欢看试映?"

约翰尼笑道:"他以前没机会,不如你带他?"

单独和狄安娜·邓恩相处,尼诺不得不大喝特喝。他尽量表现得无动于衷,但这真的很难。狄安娜·邓恩鼻尖上翘,盎格鲁一撒克逊古典美女的脸型,轮廓分明。他实在太熟悉她了。他见过她孤零零地在卧室里心碎,为死去的飞行员丈夫痛哭,为失去父亲的孩子们流泪。他见过卑鄙小人克拉克·盖博先是占她便宜,接着撇下她去追求一个性感尤物,她发怒、受伤害、受屈辱,但仍旧保持光芒四射的尊严(狄安娜·邓恩从没在电影里扮演过性感尤物)。他见过她因为爱意得到回应而眉飞色舞,在她爱慕的男人怀里扭动;他还见过她凄美地死去至少六七次。他见过她,听过她,梦过她,但对独处时她说的第一句话还是毫无思想准备。

"约翰尼是这城市少数几个有卵蛋的男人之一,"她说,"剩下的都是同性恋和脓包,给他们阴囊里灌上一卡车西班牙苍蝇①,那玩意儿也硬不起来。"她抓住尼诺的手,

① spanish Fly:西班牙苍蝇,有催情作用,多用于动物。

领着他来到房间一角,远离人群和竞争。

她打听他的身世,仍旧散发着那种冷冷的魅力。他看穿了她。他明白她在扮演富家交际花的角色,友善对待马童或司机,但电影里的她要么会向他的情谊泼冷水(如果是斯宾塞·屈塞扮演他),要么会神魂颠倒得忘乎所以(如果是克拉克·盖博扮演他)。不过无所谓。他不由谈起他和约翰尼如何在纽约一起长大,他和约翰尼如何受邀在小俱乐部唱歌。他发现她出乎意料地同情和感兴趣。聊着聊着,她看似随意地问起:"知道约翰尼是怎么让杰克·沃尔茨那杂种把角色给他的吗?"尼诺愣了一下,摇摇头。她没有追问。

试映沃尔茨新片的时间到了。狄安娜·邓恩领着尼诺,温暖的手俘获了他的手,走进主宅深处的一个房间,这个房间没有窗户,有五十来张双人小沙发,沙发摆放得互不干扰,每一张都是个半隐蔽的小岛。

尼诺看见沙发旁有个小桌,小桌上是一碗冰块、几个酒杯、几瓶烈酒和一盘香烟。他递了一支香烟给狄安娜·邓恩,帮她点烟,然后给两人斟酒。他们没有交谈。几分钟后,灯光熄灭。

他猜到会有肆无忌惮的行为,他毕竟早就听说过好莱坞的荒淫传奇,但实在没料到狄安娜·邓恩会那么贪婪地径直扑向他的性器官,事先连半句客套和礼貌的话都没说。他喝着酒,望着银幕,但舌头尝不到味道,眼睛看不见电影。一方面,他体验到了从未有过的兴奋,部分是因为此刻在黑暗中伺候他的女人曾经是他春梦的主角。

但另一方面,他的男性尊严受到了侮辱。因此,举世闻名的狄安娜·邓恩得到满足,整理好他的衣物之后,他异常冷静地在黑暗中给她倒了杯酒,又点了支香烟,用他想象得到的最轻松的声音说:"这部电影似乎挺不错。"

他感觉到身边沙发上的她身体一僵。她难道在等他说什么恭维话?尼诺在黑暗中摸到最近的酒瓶,给自己倒了满满一杯。去他妈的。她当他是男妓。不知为何,此刻他对所有这些女人有了冰冷的怒意。他们又看了十五分钟电影。他侧过身子,两人不再接触。

最后,她用嘶哑的声音耳语道:"别装模作样,你也挺享受,你大得像头驴子。"

尼诺喝着酒,用天生不拘小节的口气答道:"平时就这德性,真该让你瞧瞧兴奋起来的样子。"

她轻轻一笑,从此没再开口。电影终于结束,灯光亮起。尼诺环顾四周。他看得出黑暗中有过一场狂欢,但奇怪的是他居然什么都没听见,不过有些贵妇满脸痛快,眼神闪亮,一看就是刚结束一场恶战。他们踱出放映室。狄安娜·邓恩立刻撇下他,去和一个年纪比他大些的男人攀谈,尼诺认出那男人是个著名演员,但现在见到他的真人,他才意识到那家伙是个基佬。他若有所思地喝着酒。

约翰尼·方坦来到他身边,说:"嗨,老伙计,玩得开心吗?"

尼诺咧咧嘴:"难说得很。反正不一样。不过等我回了老家,可以到处说狄安娜·邓恩上了我。"

约翰尼哈哈笑道:"要是她肯邀请你回家就不一样了。她没有吗?"

尼诺摇摇头:"我的注意力全放在电影上了。"这次约翰尼没有笑。

"认真点,兄弟,"他说,"这种女人能给你很多好处。再说你从来有洞就搞。妈的,有时候想起你上过的丑女人,我现在还要做噩梦。"

尼诺醉醺醺地挥舞酒杯,扯着嗓门说:"对,她们是丑,但她们是女人。"角落里的狄安娜·邓恩扭头看他们,尼诺抬抬酒杯和她打招呼。

约翰尼·方坦叹息道:"好吧,你就是个黑皮乡下人。"

"一辈子都是。"尼诺说,满脸醉酒后的迷人笑容。

约翰尼完全理解他。他知道尼诺没有装出来的那么醉。他知道尼诺之所以装醉,只因为想说说心里话,但要是清醒,这么说话对他的好莱坞新东家就太无礼了。他搂住尼诺的脖子,怀着感情说:"机灵鬼,你知道你有一份万无一失的全年合同,你爱说什么就说什么,我不能让你滚蛋。"

"你不能让我滚蛋?"尼诺用醉醺醺的狡黠语气说。

"不能。"约翰尼说。

"那就去你妈的吧。"尼诺说。

有几秒钟,约翰尼惊讶得要发火,但随即看清了尼诺脸上满不在乎的怪笑。过去这几年他活得越来越精明,从云端跌落凡尘也让他变得更加敏感,总之就在这时,他理解了尼诺,这个儿时的唱歌搭档为何总不成功,为何此刻要毁掉自己的成功机会:尼诺的反应与成功之路背道而驰,无论别人怎么帮他,他都觉得受了羞辱。

约翰尼拉着尼诺的胳膊,拽着他走出屋子。尼诺现在连站也站不稳了。约翰尼安慰他说:"好啦,小子,就算为我唱歌吧,我还想靠你发财呢。我不想操纵你的生活。你爱干什么就干什么。好吗,兄弟?你只需要为我唱歌,帮我挣钱,因为我现在没法唱歌了。听懂了吗?老伙计。"

尼诺站直身。"约翰尼,我愿意为你唱歌。"他说,他说得口齿不清,约翰尼听得半懂不懂,"我现在唱得比你好了。其实你知道吗?我唱得一直比你好。"

约翰尼站在那儿思考,原来如此。他知道他嗓子正常的时候,尼诺根本和他不是一个等级,小时候合唱那会儿就不是。他看见尼诺在等他回答,在加州的月光下醉醺醺地摇晃。"去你妈的。"他柔声说,两人同时大笑,又回到了他们年轻的时候。

听说唐·柯里昂遇刺,约翰尼·方坦不但担心他的教父,也害怕资助他制作电影的承诺就此落空。他想去纽约,到医院向教父表达敬意,但他们说那样会给他带来坏名声,唐·柯里昂最不希望发生的就是这种事。于是他只能等待。一周后,汤姆·黑根派来使者。资助仍旧算数,但一次只能拍一部电影。

在这段时间里,约翰尼放任尼诺去好莱坞和加州闯荡,尼诺和年轻的小明星厮混得很开心。约翰尼偶尔约他出去玩一个晚上,但从不强迫他。谈到唐遇刺,尼诺对约翰尼说:"知道吗?我曾经求唐在他的组织里给我找份工作,他却不肯。我受够了开卡车,想挣大钱。你知道他怎么说?他说每个男人只有一种命运,我的命运是当歌手。意思是说我吃不了江湖这碗饭。"

约翰尼琢磨起了这个问题。教父恐怕是全世界最聪明的人了。他一眼就看得出尼诺吃不了江湖这碗饭,只能惹上麻烦甚至丢掉小命。他会仅仅因为一句俏皮话就丢掉小命。可是,唐怎么知道他会成为歌手?因为,该死,他猜到我迟早会拉尼诺一把。他是怎么猜到的?因为他会提点我,而我会尽力表达谢意。他当然不会求我这么做。他只会让我知道,我要是这么做了,他会很高兴。约翰尼·方坦叹了口气。现在教父受了伤,麻烦缠身,他这边没人撑腰,沃尔茨又在暗地里使坏,他可以吻别奥斯卡奖杯了。只有唐能通过私人关系施加压力,而柯里昂家族有别的事情需要考虑。约翰尼主动提出帮忙,黑根斩钉截铁地说不用。

约翰尼忙着筹拍电影。之前那部电影的原著作者刚写完新书,应约翰尼的邀请来到西海岸,跳过经纪人和电影公司直接谈判。这本小说完全符合约翰尼的要求。他不需要唱歌,故事充满活力,有许多女人和性爱,约翰尼还立刻看到一个角色完全是为尼诺量身定制的。这个角色说话像尼诺,举动像尼诺,连长相也像。真是不可思议。尼诺只需要爬上银幕,扮演自己就行了。

约翰尼动作很快。他发现他对制片的了解超过自己的想象,但还是雇了个执行制片人,此人精通业务,但因为上了黑名单而找不到工作。约翰尼没有占他便宜,而是签了份公平的合同。"我指望你能帮我省更多的钱。"约翰尼直截了当地对他说。

因此当执行制片人来找他,说需要五万块打点工会代表,这时他吃了一惊。超时工作和用工方面有很多问题需要处理,五万块算是合情合理。约翰尼琢磨起了执行制片人是不是在骗他的钱,最后说:"让工会那家伙来见我。"

工会那家伙叫比利·高夫。约翰尼对他说:"我以为我的朋友已经摆平了工会。听说我不必担心这方面的事情。完全不必担心。"

高夫说:"谁说的?"

约翰尼说,"你他妈知道得一清二楚。我不会指名道姓,但只要他说过,我就相信。"

高夫说："世道变了。你的朋友有麻烦,他的话在西岸这么远的地方了已经不管用了。"

约翰尼耸耸肩。"我们过两天再见,如何?"

高夫笑了笑。"行啊,约翰尼,"他说,"但打电话给纽约也帮不了你。"

可是,打电话给纽约确实帮得了他。约翰尼打到黑根的办公室,黑根恶狠狠地说别付钱。"你要是给那杂种一毛钱,你的教父也会暴跳如雷的,"他对约翰尼说,"会让唐失去尊敬,现在他承担不了这个代价。"

"我能和唐谈谈吗?"约翰尼问,"你能和他谈谈吗? 我得让电影拍起来啊。"

"现在谁也没法和唐谈话,"黑根说,"他还太虚弱。我和桑尼谈谈,想办法解决问题。不过结论我可以先告诉你。一毛钱也别给那个混蛋。情况一有变化我就通知你。"

约翰尼挂断电话,心里不怎么痛快。劳资纠纷会大幅增加拍片成本,搅得鸡飞狗跳。他考虑了几秒钟,要不干脆悄悄塞给高夫五万块算了? 唐给他保证和黑根给他保证并发号施令毕竟是两码事。不过,他决定还是等几天看看。

等待帮他省下了五万块。第三天夜里,高夫在格伦代尔的家中遇刺身亡。再也没人说起劳资纠纷。杀人让约翰尼有点害怕。这是唐的触手第一次在他眼前发动致命攻击。

时间一周一周过去,约翰尼·方坦越来越忙,准备剧本、选角、研究制片细节,忙得忘了他的嗓子,忘了他不能唱歌。奥斯卡奖公布提名,他发现候选人里有他,组织者没有邀请他去向全国电视直播的颁奖仪式上演唱提名歌曲之一,他虽说不高兴,却只是耸耸肩就继续工作了。教父不再能够施加压力,因此他并不指望自己真能拿奖,不过获得提名也有点价值。

他和尼诺灌录的意大利名曲卖得比他近期的另几张唱片好得多,他知道这是尼诺的成功,和他关系不大。他已经听天由命,知道自己不再是职业歌手了。

他每周与金妮和孩子共进一次晚餐。无论忙得多么焦头烂额,他从不忘记这份责任。不过他不和金妮睡觉。另外一方面,他的第二任妻子耍花招搞了个墨西哥离婚①,因此他又是单身汉了。奇怪的是,他并不热衷于勾搭招之即来的小明星。说实话他也够势利的。那些年轻的明星,正当红的女演员,她们连搭理都懒得搭理他,所以他有点难受。但这对认真工作有好处。大部分晚上他都是单独回家,播放自己的旧唱

---

① 在墨西哥离婚比在美国的程序简单,开销也更少。

片,端杯酒,边听边哼唱几小节。他以前唱得很好,真他妈好。他从没意识到自己到底有多好。嗓音是否特别暂且不论(每个人都有可能得到一把好嗓子),他的唱功实在是好。他曾经是真正的艺术家,自己却不知道,不知道他有多热爱唱歌。他刚明白唱歌究竟是怎么一回事,却用酒精、烟草和女人毁了嗓子。

尼诺有时候过来喝杯酒,和他一起听唱片,约翰尼会嘲笑他说:"你个黑皮崽子,一辈子都没法这么唱歌。"尼诺会露出迷人得稀奇的笑容,摇摇头,用同情的语气说:"是啊,永远也做不到。"像是他知道约翰尼的心思似的。

新片开拍前一个星期,奥斯卡颁奖之夜即将来临。约翰尼邀请尼诺同行,尼诺拒绝了。约翰尼说:"伙计啊,我没求你帮过忙,对吧?今天算我求你,陪我一起去。要是我没得奖,只有你真心为我觉得可惜。"

尼诺有一瞬间似乎愣住了,回过神来,他说:"行啊,老伙计,我去就是了。"他犹豫了两秒钟,然后说:"你要是没得奖,那就忘记这回事好了。尽管喝个烂醉,有我照顾你。妈的,今晚我不喝酒都行。够朋友吧?"

"老兄,"约翰尼·方坦说,"确实是好朋友。"

奥斯卡颁奖之夜,尼诺信守承诺。他完全清醒地来到约翰尼家,两人出门前往举办仪式的剧院。尼诺心想约翰尼为什么不邀请他的女儿或者前妻参加颁奖晚会。特别是金妮。约翰尼难道认为金妮不会支持他?尼诺可真想喝酒,哪怕一杯也行,这个漫长的夜晚似乎会很难熬。

尼诺·瓦伦蒂觉得奥斯卡颁奖完全无聊透顶,直到最佳男演员揭晓为止。听见"约翰尼·方坦"这几个字,他不禁一跃而起,拼命鼓掌。约翰尼向他伸出手,尼诺紧紧握住。他知道他的老朋友需要和他信任的人亲密接触,尼诺一时间悲哀极了,因为约翰尼在这个辉煌的时刻,身边居然没有比他更好的伴侣。

接踵而至的彻底是一场噩梦。杰克·沃尔茨的电影横扫所有大奖,电影公司举办派对,报社记者和野心勃勃的男女投机分子蜂拥而至。尼诺信守承诺,保持清醒,尽量照顾约翰尼。但酒会上的女人不停把约翰尼·方坦拽进卧室去"聊天",约翰尼喝得越来越醉。

获得最佳女主角的女明星也遇到了同样命运,但她喜欢这一套,应付得也更好。尼诺不拿正眼看她,整个酒会上这么做的男人只有他。

最后,终于有人想到一个绝妙的点子:两位获奖者当众交媾,其他人充当观众。女演员被扒得精光,另外几个女人开始脱约翰尼·方坦的衣服。尼诺,场内唯一清醒的人,他抓起褪掉一半衣物的约翰尼扛在肩上,挣扎着冲出屋子上车。尼诺开车送约翰尼回家,心想:难道这就是成功?我宁可不要。

第三部

第十四章

十二岁的唐就已经是个男子汉了。他个子不高，肤色黝黑，身材瘦削，家住西西里一个独特的摩尔风貌村庄，村庄名叫柯里昂。他原名维托·安多里尼，陌生人杀死父亲，前来斩草除根，母亲把他送到美国，和朋友待在一起。来到新大陆，他改姓为柯里昂，以保持他和故乡的联系。他极少用行动表达感情，这是其中一次。

世纪之交的西西里，黑手党就是第二政府，比罗马的官方政府更有权势。维托·柯里昂的父亲和另一名村民有世仇，对方向黑手党告状。父亲拒绝屈服，在公开争吵中杀死了本地的黑手党首领。一周以后，人们发现他一命呜呼，尸体被"狼枪"①打得七零八落。葬礼后一个月，黑手党的枪手前来打听他的儿子维托。他们认为他差不多成年了，说不定等几年就会为父亲复仇。十二岁的维托在亲戚家东躲西藏，上船逃往美国。阿班丹多夫妇收留了他，他们的儿子占科日后会成为唐的顾问。

小维托在纽约地狱厨房第九大道的阿班丹多杂货店做事。十八岁那年，维托娶了个刚从西西里来的意大利姑娘，女孩年仅十六岁，擅长烹饪，是个好主妇。他们住进第十大道近三十五街的廉租公寓，离维托做事的杂货店只有几个路口，两年后，他们迎来了第一个孩子桑蒂诺，桑蒂诺仰慕父亲，所以朋友都叫他桑尼②。

附近住着个叫法努奇的男人。这个意大利汉子体格魁梧，模样凶狠，身穿昂贵的浅色套装，头戴米色软呢帽，据说是一名"黑手"，黑手党的一个分支，专用暴力手段向

---

① 狼枪：短筒霰弹猎枪。
② Sonny：英文中亦是对小男孩的昵称，相当于"小儿子"。

家庭和店主勒索钱财。不过,这附近的居民大多数可不是吃素的,所以法努奇的身体伤害威胁只对缺少男性后代保护的老夫妻奏效。也有些店主用一点小钱打发他,只是懒得麻烦而已。然而,法努奇同时也黑吃黑,对非法售卖意大利奖券和经营家庭赌场的人下手。阿班丹多杂货店给他上点小贡,虽说小占科极力反对,对父亲说他可以教训教训法努奇。占科的父亲禁止他这么做。维托·柯里昂看在眼里,觉得和他毫无关系。

一天,三个年轻人收拾了法努奇一顿,从左耳到右耳割开他的喉咙,深度不足以要命,但足够吓得他魂飞魄散,让他血流成河。维托看见法努奇从惩罚他的年轻人那里逃跑,环形伤口鲜血淋漓。有个细节他永远也忘不了:法努奇一边跑,一边把米色软呢帽垫在下巴底下接血。就仿佛他不愿玷污那身套装,或者不想留下一道可耻的猩红印记。

这次袭击到头来却成全了法努奇。三个年轻人不是杀人犯,只是几个凶悍的小伙子,想教训法努奇一顿,不让他继续黑吃黑。法努奇却证明他能杀人。几周后,对他动刀子的年轻人遭到枪杀,另外两个年轻人的家属用补偿金换取法努奇发誓不再报复。经过这件事,贡钱水涨船高,法努奇成了附近赌博事业的合伙人。至于维托·柯里昂,这些都和他没关系。他过眼就忘。

第一次世界大战期间,进口橄榄油货源匮乏,法努奇不但向阿班丹多杂货店供应橄榄油,还供应意大利萨拉米香肠、火腿和干酪,以此换得部分收益。他安排一个侄子进杂货店,维托·柯里昂愕然发现自己失业了。

这时,次子弗雷德里科也已出生,维托·柯里昂有四张嘴要喂。直到这一天,他还是个非常内敛文静的年轻人,想法都闷在心里。杂货店老板的儿子、年轻的占科·阿班丹多是他最亲密的朋友,维托因为占科父亲的行为而责怪了朋友,这个发展让两人都有些吃惊。事情是这样的:占科羞愧得满脸通红,向维托发誓说你不必担心食物。他,占科,会从杂货店偷食物,满足朋友之需。维托断然拒绝他的提议,因为这实在太可耻了,儿子怎么能偷父亲的东西?

年轻的维托对可怖的法努奇却生出了冰冷的怒意。他没有以任何方式表露愤怒,只是默默等待时机。他在铁路上打了几个月零工。没多久,战争结束,工作机会越来越少,他一个月只能挣到几天的工钱。另外,大部分工头是爱尔兰人或美国人,用最肮脏的语言辱骂工人,维托总是板着脸,假装听不懂,实际上尽管说话有口音,他的英语好得很。

一天晚上,维托正在和家人吃饭,忽然听见有人敲窗户,窗外是隔开两幢楼的通风井。维托拉开窗帘,惊讶地发现彼得·克莱门扎,一个住在附近的年轻人,从通风井另一头的窗户探出身子,把一个白布包裹伸向维托。

"嘿,兄弟,"克莱门扎说,"帮我收着,我会回来取的。快点。"维托不由自主地探出身子,隔着空荡荡的通风井接过包裹。克莱门扎脸色紧张而焦急。他似乎惹了什么麻烦,维托出自本能帮助了他。他在厨房解开包裹,里面却是五把上了油的枪。他将包裹收进卧室的壁橱,等待后续发展。他得知警察抓走了克莱门扎。他把包裹隔着通风井递给维托的时候,警察多半正在砸他的门。

维托没有对任何人提起,他惊恐的老婆害怕丈夫被送进监狱,哪怕闲聊都不敢开口。两天后,彼得·克莱门扎重新露面,随随便便地问维托:"我的货还在你那儿?"

维托点点头。他生性寡言少语。克莱门扎来到他的廉租公寓,接过一杯红酒,维托从卧室壁橱深处翻出那个包裹。

克莱门扎喝着红酒,一张和善的大脸警惕地盯着维托。"打开看过?"

维托面无表情,摇头答道:"和我没关系的事情我不感兴趣。"

两人喝了一晚上红酒,发现彼此性情相投。克莱门扎口若悬河,维托·柯里昂擅长聆听。他们成了点头之交。

几天后,克莱门扎问维托·柯里昂的妻子,她的客厅地板要不要铺块上等地毯。他领着维托去搬地毯。

克莱门扎领着维托来到一幢公寓楼,大理石露台,有两根大理石廊柱。他用钥匙开门,走进一套奢华的公寓。克莱门扎哼了一声,说:"到房间那头去,帮我把地毯卷起来。"

这是一块厚实的红色羊毛地毯。克莱门扎如此慷慨,维托·柯里昂为之震惊。两人卷起地毯,克莱门扎抬起一头,维托抬起另一头。两人抬着地毯,走向大门。

就在这时,公寓楼的门铃响了。克莱门扎丢下地毯,跑向窗口。他把窗帘拉开一条缝,瞅了一眼,马上从衣服里面拔出手枪。直到此刻,震惊的维托·柯里昂才醒悟过来,他们这是在某个陌生人家里偷地毯。

门铃又响了第二遍。维托走到克莱门扎身旁,看清外面的情况。门口站着一名制服警察。他们看着警察第三次按门铃,然后耸耸肩,走下大理石台阶,顺着马路走远了。

克莱门扎满意地咕哝一声,说:"来,我们走。"他抬起他那头地毯,维托抬起另一头。警察刚拐弯,他们就挪出沉重的橡木大门,抬着地毯走上马路。三十分钟后,他们按维托·柯里昂公寓客厅的尺寸剪裁地毯,剩下的足够装饰卧室。克莱门扎是个熟练工,从不合身的宽大上衣口袋里(那会儿他还不太胖,但已经喜欢穿松松垮垮的衣服了)掏出剪裁地毯所需的全部工具。

　　时间一天天过去,局势却不好转。柯里昂一家又不能吃漂亮的地毯。唉,找不到工作,老婆孩子只能挨饿。维托接受了朋友占科给他的几包食物,一边思考出路。最后还是克莱门扎和忒西奥找上了他,忒西奥是附近的另一个勇悍小子。克莱门扎和忒西奥觉得他不错,喜欢他的做派,也知道他走投无路。他们拉他入伙,这个帮派专门抢劫运输丝绸服装的卡车,卡车在三十一街的工厂装货,没有危险,司机是懂事的普通工人,见到枪口就像天使似的跳上人行道,劫匪开走卡车,到朋友的仓库卸货。有些商品卖给意大利批发商,有些则在意大利社区挨门挨户兜售,这些社区包括布朗克斯的亚瑟大道、曼哈顿的桑树街和切尔西区,住的都是等便宜货的意大利穷人,按照正价,那些人家的女儿一辈子也买不起这么精致的服装。克莱门扎和忒西奥请维托开为他们知道阿班丹多杂货店的送货卡车就是他当司机的。1919 年,技术熟练的汽车驾驶员还很稀奇。

　　维托·柯里昂知道不该这么做,却接受了他们的邀请。一番讨价还价之后,敲定他这次出马的份额至少是一千块。不过,这两位毛头同伴让他觉得太冒失,全盘计划不够周详,赃物分配过于随便。就他而言,整套手法都失之轻率。但他觉得这两个人不错,靠得住。彼得·克莱门扎已是虎背熊腰,赢得了他一定的信任,瘦削阴沉的忒西奥赢得的则是信心。

　　这个活儿本身倒是轻而易举。两名同伙亮出手枪,逼着丝绸卡车的司机下车,维托·柯里昂并不觉得有什么可怕。克莱门扎和忒西奥的冷静也给他留下了深刻印象。他们没有头脑发热,反而和司机有说有笑,说他只要乖乖的,他们就送他老婆几身衣裳。维托觉得自己兜售衣服有点傻气,于是把分得的赃物卖给销赃人,只拿到七百块。不过七百块在 1919 年已经是很大一笔钱了。

　　第二天,米色套装、白色软呢帽的法努奇在街上拦住维托·柯里昂。法努奇面相凶恶,毫不掩饰下巴底下从左耳到右耳的半环形白色伤疤。他有两道浓密的黑眉毛,五官粗鄙,笑起来却不知怎的挺和气。

　　他带着浓重的西西里口音说:“哎呀,年轻人,据说你们发财啦。你和你的两个朋友,不觉得对我有点太吝啬吗?这附近毕竟归我管,总得让我湿湿嘴嘛。”他说了句西西里黑手党的黑话,意思是要求分赃。

　　维托·柯里昂按照他的习惯没有回答。他当然明白暗示的意思,只是在等待对方明确提出要求。

　　法努奇对他笑笑,露出金牙,绞索般的伤疤贴着面颊伸展。他用手帕擦擦脸,解开上衣的纽扣,像是要凉快一下,其实是为了亮出插在宽松舒适长裤腰间的手枪。他叹了口气,说:“给我五百块,我就忘了这次侮辱。年轻人毕竟不知道我这样的人应该得到什么尊敬。"

维托·柯里昂对他笑笑，尽管他还是个手上没沾过血的年轻人，但笑容里的刺骨寒意仍旧让法努奇愣了几秒钟，这才说下去，"否则警察就会来找你，你的老婆和孩子会蒙羞，失去依靠。当然了，要是我的情报不准确，弄错了你的收益，嘴也可以少沾点水。但不能少于三百块。还有，别想蒙我。"

维托·柯里昂终于开口。他的语气通情达理，毫无怒气，谦恭有礼，年轻人对法努奇这种有地位的长者就该这么说话。他轻声说："我那份在我的两个朋友手里。我得跟他们说说。"

法努奇放心了。"记得转告你的两位朋友，我指望他们也能同样让我湿湿嘴。别害怕，尽管去说，"他宽慰道，"克莱门扎和我很熟，他明白事理。你跟着他好好混。他在这些事情上比较有经验。"

维托·柯里昂耸耸肩，挤出有点尴尬的神情。"当然啦，"他说，"你得理解，我是新入行的。谢谢你像教父一样和我说话。"

法努奇很受触动。"小伙子人不错嘛。"他说着拉起维托的手，攥在他毛乎乎的两只大手里，"你懂得尊重，"他说，"在年轻人身上是美德。下次要先和我谈谈，明白了？也许我还能帮你们策划一下呢。"

日后，维托·柯里昂逐渐明白，他之所以能和法努奇周旋得那么成功，那么知道进退，正是因为他脾气暴躁的父亲死在了西西里的黑手党手上。但此时此刻，他只感到一种森冷的怒意，这家伙居然要抢他冒着生命和自由的风险挣来的钱。他并不害怕，恰恰相反，他当时在想，法努奇真是个疯狂的傻瓜。以他眼中的克莱门扎而言，这条粗壮的西西里大汉宁可不要命，也不肯放弃劫来的一分钱。说到底，克莱门扎愿意仅仅为了偷一块地毯杀死警察，而瘦削的忒西奥有着蝰蛇的致命气质。

那天夜里，在通风井另一头克莱门扎的廉租公寓里，维托·柯里昂刚又领教了一课。克莱门扎破口大骂，忒西奥愁眉苦脸，但话锋一转，他们居然讨论起了法努奇拿到两百块会不会就此收手。忒西奥觉得有这个可能。

克莱门扎固执己见："不行，刀疤脸杂种肯定找过收衣服的批发商，打听到我们得了多少钱。三百块，少一毛钱法努奇都不会作罢。我们只能付钱。"

维托大吃一惊，但他很谨慎，没有流露出他的惊讶。"我们为什么非得付钱？他能把我们三个怎么样？我们比他强壮，我们还有枪，凭什么要把血汗钱交给他？"

克莱门扎耐心解释。"法努奇的朋友是真正的野兽。他在警察局也有关系。他想听我们的计划，无非是打算出卖我们，博得警察的欢心。这样警察就欠他一个人情了。这就是他的道道儿。另外，他有马兰扎拉本人点头的特许权，这片地区归他管。"

马兰扎拉是个经常见报的匪首,据说手下有个犯罪集团,专门从事敲诈勒索、赌博和武装抢劫。

克莱门扎给大家倒家酿的葡萄酒。他老婆把一盘萨拉米香肠、橄榄和一条意大利面包放在桌上,带着椅子下楼,去和女伴坐在门口聊天。她是个意大利姑娘,来美国好几年了,但还听不懂英语。

维托·柯里昂和两个朋友坐着喝酒。他从未像今天这样运用过智慧。他惊讶于自己的思路竟然如此明晰。他回想他对法努奇的所有了解。他回忆法努奇喉咙被割的那天,法努奇如何用软呢帽垫在下巴底下,接住滴落的鲜血。他想起动刀子的年轻人死于非命,另外两个被迫破财消灾。他突然想通了,法努奇肯定没什么像样的关系,不可能有。一个向警方通风报信的人,一个收钱就可以不寻仇的人,肯定没有过硬的后台。真正的黑手党头目不会放过另外那两个人。不,法努奇只是运气好,杀了动刀子的年轻人,知道另外两个人有所提防,他奈何不了他们,因此才情愿收钱买命。他能向店主和公寓楼里的赌场勒索保护费,完全是因为他身上的那股蛮劲。可是,维托·柯里昂知道至少有一个赌场从不向法努奇进贡,老板也没有遇到任何事情。

这样看来,法努奇是个独行侠。他雇用枪手执行特殊的任务,不过这都是纯粹的金钱关系。维托·柯里昂于是作了另外一个决定:他的人生要走一条什么道路。

这段经验催生了他的座右铭:一个人只能有一种命运。那天晚上,他大可以向法努奇进贡,回去当他的杂货店伙计,过几年自己也开个杂货店。可是,命运决定他必须成为唐,命运把法努奇带给他,他要走命中注定的道路。

喝完那瓶红酒,维托谨慎地对克莱门扎和忒西奥说:"你们要是愿意,不如一人给我两百块,我去交给法努奇?我保证他会接受我给他的这个数字。剩下的事情全交给我。我会把问题解决得包你们满意。"

克莱门扎顿时露出怀疑的眼神。维托冷冷地对他说:"只要我承认一个人是我的朋友,我就绝对不会骗他。你们明天自己去找法努奇,让他向你们要钱,但别立刻付给他,也无论如何别和他吵。就说要去取钱,会通过我转交给他。让他明白你们愿意按他的价码付钱。别讨价还价,这个交给我。他要是真像你说的那么危险,那就没必要激怒他。"

当晚谈到这里结束。第二天,克莱门扎找法努奇谈话,确定事情不是维托编出来的。接着,克莱门扎来到维托家,给了维托两百块。他盯着维托·柯里昂说:"法努奇说不能少于三百,你怎么让他接受这个数目?"

维托·柯里昂通情达理地说:"这就不是你需要关心的了。你记住我帮了你一次就好。"

随后来的是忒西奥。忒西奥比克莱门扎内敛和敏锐,更狡猾,但少些冲劲。他感觉到有蹊跷,什么地方不对劲。他有点担心,对维托·柯里昂说:"和那个黑手杂种打交道要当心,他奸诈得像个神父。给钱的时候需要我在场当证人吗?"

维托·柯里昂摇摇头,甚至没费心回答,只是对忒西奥说:"告诉法努奇,今天晚上九点到我家来收钱。我请他喝杯酒,聊一聊,说服他接受这个数目。"

忒西奥摇摇头:"你恐怕没那个好运气,法努奇从不让步。"

"我会和他讲道理。"维托·柯里昂说,这句话后来成了他的名言,致命攻击前的最后警告。后来他成为唐,每次请对手坐下来和他讲道理,对手就明白这是解决争端而不流血杀人的最后一次机会了。

吃过晚饭,维托·柯里昂吩咐老婆带着两个孩子——桑尼和弗雷德——到街上去,没有他的允许,就无论如何也不准他们回家。她必须守在公寓门口。他和法努奇有些私事要讨论,不能被打扰。他看见妻子脸上的惧意,很生气,平静地说:"你以为你嫁了个傻瓜吗?"妻子没有回答,不回答是因为她害怕,但此刻害怕的不是法努奇,而是自己的丈夫。他就在她的眼前发生变化,每个小时都有所不同,变成一个散发着危险气息的男人。他向来安静,沉默寡言,但总是很斯文,通情达理,就西西里年轻男子而言非同寻常。妻子见到的是他在褪去与世无争的保护色,准备迎接自己的命运。他起步很晚,已经二十六岁,但一登场就技惊四座。

维托·柯里昂决定杀死法努奇。杀了法努奇,他的银行户头上就会多七百块。三百块是他必须付给黑手恐怖分子的钱,还有忒西奥的两百和克莱门扎的两百。要是不杀法努奇,他就要让出这七百块现金。在他眼里,法努奇那条命值不了七百块。他不会用七百块换取法努奇的小命。就算法努奇需要七百块动手术救命,他也不会给他七百块让他找医生。他不欠法努奇的人情债,他们没有血缘关系,他对法努奇也没有感情。那么,凭什么要给法努奇七百块呢?

接下来的结论理所当然,既然法努奇想用武力夺走他的七百块,那么他为什么不杀了法努奇呢?地球没了这么一个角色也照样转。

当然,还有一些现实因素需要考虑。法努奇也许真有几个手握权柄的朋友,会来为他寻仇。法努奇本人就很危险,不那么容易杀,而且还有警察和电椅候着呢。可是,自从父亲遇害以后,维托·柯里昂本来就活在死刑判决之下。十二岁那年,他逃脱处刑人的追杀,远涉重洋来到陌生的土地,换了个陌生的名字。多年默默的观察告诉他,他远比芸芸众生更聪明、更勇敢,只是缺少机会运用智慧和运气罢了。

可是,在向命运迈出第一步之前,他还是犹豫了。他甚至把七百块单独叠成一卷,揣进长裤的口袋。不过,他把钱放进了左边裤兜。右边裤兜是克莱门扎为了抢劫丝绸卡车而交给他的手枪。

法努奇准九点登门拜访。维托·柯里昂端出一罐克莱门扎送他的家酿葡萄酒。

法努奇把白色软呢帽挨着酒罐放在桌上。他松开领带,一条宽边的花纹领带,明艳的图案掩盖住了番茄汁的污渍。这是个炎热的夏夜,煤气灯火苗微弱,公寓里悄静无声。维托·柯里昂却浑身冰冷。为了表示真诚,他先递上那卷钞票,仔细观察法努奇,法努奇一张一张点钱,接着拿出大号皮夹,把钱塞进去。法努奇喝着葡萄酒,说:"你还欠我两百。"他两道浓眉下的脸上毫无表情。

维托·柯里昂用冷静而通情达理的声音说:"我手头有点紧,我最近失业。请允许我拖欠几周吧。"

法努奇可以接受这个小小让步。钱已经到手大部分,剩下的等等也无妨。说服之下甚至还可能多等几天甚至就此作罢。他边喝酒边嘿嘿笑道:"哎呀,你这个年轻人倒是机灵。我以前怎么没有注意到你? 小伙子你太安静了,对自己没好处。我可以帮你安排些事情,能挣大钱。"

维托·柯里昂礼貌地点点头,表示很有兴趣,拿起紫色酒罐斟满法努奇的酒杯。法努奇想到他会说些什么,觉得还是不多坐为妙,于是起身握住维托的手。"晚安啦,年轻人,"他说,"别往心里去哟。要是有什么我能效劳的,打个招呼就行。你今晚为自己办了件好事。"

维托目送法努奇下楼,走出大门。马路上满是目击者,能证明法努奇安然离开柯里昂家。维托在窗口观察,见到法努奇拐弯上了第十一大道,知道法努奇这是要回家,多半打算先放下战利品,然后再出门。很可能还要放下手枪。维托·柯里昂走出公寓,沿着楼梯跑上屋顶。他跑过一整个街区的屋顶,爬下一幢空厂房的防火楼梯,来到那幢楼的后院。他踢开后门,走前门出去。马路对面就是法努奇居住的公寓楼。

这一片廉租公寓向西只延伸到第十大道。第十一大道多数是仓库和厂房,租用给依靠纽约中央铁路跑运输的公司,他们需要就近利用从第十一大道到哈德逊河之间星罗棋布的堆场。这片空旷地区里剩下的公寓楼已经寥寥无几,法努奇那幢是其中之一,大部分住户是单身列车员、货场工人和最廉价的妓女。他们不像老实的意大利人那样坐在街上聊天,而是在酒馆里挥霍薪水。因此,维托·柯里昂发现他很容易就溜过了空荡荡的第十一大道,钻进法努奇那幢公寓楼的门厅。他在这里拔出他从没用过的枪,等待法努奇回家。

他隔着门厅的玻璃门张望,知道法努奇会从第十大道过来。克莱门扎给他看过枪上的保险,他空膛扣过扳机。不过,小时候在西西里,他九岁就经常和父亲上山打猎,经常端起当地叫"狼枪"的沉重霰弹枪开火。正因为他那么小就熟悉狼枪,杀死他父亲的凶手才判了他死刑。

　　他等在黑洞洞的门厅里，看见法努奇的白色身影穿过马路，走向大门。维托后退一步，肩膀抵着通往楼梯的内门。他举枪准备开火，伸出的手离大门仅有两步之遥。门向内打开。法努奇，白色的法努奇，肩宽体阔的法努奇，臭烘烘的法努奇，填满了门口那一方亮光。维托·柯里昂扣动扳机。

　　枪火撼动了整幢楼，声音从敞开的大门传到街上。法努奇抓住两边门框，尽量站直，竭力去掏枪。挣扎的力量扯开纽扣，衣襟左右敞开。枪露了出来，衬衫前襟靠腹部位置犹如蛛网的一团红色也露了出来。维托·柯里昂瞄得非常仔细，像是在把钢针插进血管，对着红色蛛网的中心又开了一枪。

　　法努奇跪倒在地，撑开大门。他发出可怕的呻吟声，一个人肉体受到巨大折磨时的呻吟声，听起来几乎有点滑稽。这个呻吟声维托记得他听到了至少三次，他把枪口抵着法努奇汗津津油汪汪的面颊，一枪打进他的脑子。从头到尾不到五秒钟，法努奇瘫倒在地死去，尸体堵住敞开的大门。

　　维托小心翼翼地从尸体的上衣口袋里取出大号皮夹，揣进自己的衬衫。他跑过马路，穿过对面的空厂房，来到后院，爬防火楼梯到屋顶。他在屋顶俯瞰街道。法努奇的尸体仍旧躺在门口，但见不到其他人影。公寓楼上有两扇窗户被人打开，他能看见黑乎乎的脑袋探出窗口，但他看不清他们的面容，他们肯定也看不清他的面容。再说这种人也不会向警方通风报信。尸体估计要在门口躺到天亮，或者哪个警察巡逻时被绊倒。公寓楼里的住户不会存心出头，引来警察的怀疑和盘问。他们会锁好门，假装什么都没听见。

　　时间绰绰有余。他走过几个屋顶，进了自己那幢楼的屋顶小门，下楼回到住处。他打开门锁，进去，转身又锁上门。他翻看死者的皮夹。除了他交给法努奇的七百块，里面只有几张一块和一张五块。

　　皮夹翻盖里塞着一枚五块钱的老金币，多半是幸运符。就算法努奇是个有钱的匪徒，他也肯定没把家当带在身边。这证实了维托的部分猜测。

　　他知道他必须处理掉皮夹和手枪（当年他就知道必须把金币留在皮夹里）。他再次爬上屋顶，走过几段屋脊，把皮夹扔进一个通风井，然后倒空枪里的子弹，在屋脊上猛砸枪管。枪管怎么敲都不断。他调转枪身，把枪托砸向烟囱侧面。枪托裂成两半。再一下，枪身断成枪管和枪柄两部分。他把它们分别扔进两个通风井。枪管和枪柄从五层楼高处掉下去，却没有发出什么响动，而是陷进了底下堆积如山的稀烂垃圾。明天早晨，住户会从窗户扔出更多的垃圾，要是运气好，证据会消失得无影无踪。维托回到公寓里。

他有点发抖，但完全控制得住。他脱掉衣服，害怕溅上了污血，于是把它们塞进妻子洗衣服的铁皮桶里，用碱水和棕色洗衣皂浸泡，用水槽下的铁皮洗衣板搓洗，最后用碱水和洗衣皂洗刷铁皮桶和水槽。他在卧室一角找到刚洗好的一堆衣服，把这身衣服混进去。接着，他换上干净的衬衫和长裤，下楼在大门口找到老婆和孩子，与邻居谈天说地。

实际上，这些预防措施都是白费力气。天亮后警察发现尸体，根本没来查问维托·柯里昂。他惊讶地发现警察完全不知道法努奇被杀当晚来过他家。他本打算把法努奇活着离开他家当作不在场证明。事后他发现法努奇死了，警察只觉得高兴，并不急于追查凶手。警察理所当然地以为这是又一场黑帮处决，只盘问了有敲诈和暴力抢劫前科的无赖。维托从没惹过麻烦，所以也没有进入警方的视野。

虽然他瞒过了警察，但搭档就是另外一码事了。彼得·克莱门扎和忒西奥躲了他一个星期，接着又是两个星期，最后在一天傍晚登门拜访。他们明显带着敬意。维托·柯里昂不动声色地殷勤问候，用葡萄酒款待他们。

先开口的是克莱门扎，他轻声说："第九大道不再有人找店主收保护费了，也没有人收这附近玩牌和赌博的抽头了。"

维托·柯里昂盯着他们，没有吭声。忒西奥说："我们可以接管法努奇的地盘。他们会付钱的。"

维托·柯里昂耸耸肩："为什么要找我？我对这种事不感兴趣。"

克莱门扎哈哈大笑。这时候他还年轻，还没有长出硕大无朋的肥肚皮，但已经有了胖子的笑声。他对维托·柯里昂说："抢劫卡车那次我不是给了你一把枪吗？现在不需要了吧，能还给我吗？"

维托·柯里昂从侧袋里拿出一沓钞票，动作慢而用心，剥下五张十块。"拿着，我给你钱。抢完卡车我就扔掉了。"他笑呵呵地看着两人。

当时维托·柯里昂还不知道这个笑容的威力。之所以让人毛骨悚然，正是因为毫无威胁的意思，像是听到了只有自己才明白的什么私人玩笑。可是，他只在性命攸关的事情上露出这个笑容，玩笑也并不真的私密，他的双眼毫无笑意，外在性格平时又是那么通情达理和沉默寡言，因此突然摘下面具，露出真实的自我才那么吓人。

克莱门扎摇摇头。"我不要钱。"他说。维托收起钞票，静静等待。他们彼此心照不宣。克莱门扎和忒西奥知道他杀了法努奇，尽管他们没告诉过任何人，但几周之后，街坊邻居全知道了。百姓敬维托·柯里昂为"值得尊重的人"，但他并没有试图接手法努奇的生意和贡钱。

随即发生的事情顺理成章。一天晚上，维托的妻子把一位寡居的邻居带回家。这位女士是意大利人,品格无可指摘。她辛勤工作,抚养没有父亲的几个孩子。她十六岁的儿子依照意大利传统,工资袋连封口都不拆就交给母亲;十七岁的女儿是个裁缝,同样这么做。晚上,全家人把纽扣缝在硬纸板上,挣点奴工的计件工资。这位女士名叫科伦坡夫人。

维托·柯里昂的妻子说:"夫人想请你帮个忙。她遇上了麻烦。"

维托·柯里昂以为是要借钱,准备慷慨解囊,结果事情是这样的:科伦坡夫人有条狗,她最小的儿子宝贝得不得了。房东接到投诉,说狗半夜叫唤,因此请科伦坡夫人处理掉。夫人假装答应,房东后来发现夫人骗了他,于是命令她搬出去。她发誓说这次保证处理掉那条狗,而且说到也做到了。但房东实在气愤,不肯收回成命。她要么自己搬出去,要么就叫警察轰她出去。夫人把狗送给住在长岛的亲戚,她可怜的小儿子哭得可伤心了。但这也无济于事,他们眼看着就将无家可归。

维托·柯里昂和善地问她:"为什么请我帮忙?"

科伦坡夫人对他妻子点点头:"她叫我来请你帮忙。"

他吃了一惊。他妻子从没问过他为何要在杀死法努奇的那天晚上洗衣服,从没问过他这个没工作的人靠什么挣钱。即便此时此刻,她还是面无表情。维托对科伦坡夫人说:"我可以资助你点钱来帮你搬家,是这个意思吗?"

女人摇摇头,她泪流满面:"我的朋友全住在这儿,都是和我从小在意大利长大的姑娘们。我怎么能搬到别的地方,和陌生人生活?我想请你说服房东让我留下。"

维托点点头:"这个没问题,你不用搬家。我明天一早就找他聊聊。"

他的妻子对他露出笑容,他不明所以,但很高兴。科伦坡夫人有点不放心。"那个房东,你确定他会答应吗?"她问。

"罗贝托先生?"维托用惊讶的语气说,"当然会。他是个热心人。等我解释清楚你的情况,他保准会同情你的不幸遭遇。哪,别再担心这件事啦。你别着急。为了孩子,你要保重身体啊。"

房东罗贝托先生每天来这个居民区,查看他拥有的一排五幢廉租公寓楼。他是个包工头,把刚下船的意大利劳工卖给大公司,用得到的利润一幢接一幢买下这些公寓楼。他来自意大利北部,受过教育,看不起西西里和那不勒斯的文盲南方佬,他们像害虫一样挤满他的公寓楼,朝通风井里乱扔垃圾,任由蟑螂和耗子啃空墙壁,懒得抬起手保护他的资产。他不是坏人,是个好丈夫和好父亲,但每时每刻都在担心他的投资、他挣来的钱和有产人士不得不支出的开销,结果把自己的神经折磨得疲惫不堪,因此他的精神永远那么烦躁。维托·柯里昂在街上拦住他,想和他聊两句,罗贝托先生表现得有点唐突——当然不算粗鲁,因为尽管这个年轻人模样文静,但万一要是说错什么,这种南方佬随时都有可能一刀子捅了你。

"罗贝托先生，"维托·柯里昂说，"我妻子的一个朋友，一位可怜的寡妇，缺少男人的保护，告诉我说出于某些原因，你命令她搬出你的公寓楼。她绝望极了。她没有钱，朋友都住在这附近。我告诉她说我会找你聊聊，说你通情达理，只是有了误会而已。她已经送走了引起麻烦的小动物，为什么还是不让她留下呢？我们都是意大利人，算我求你赏个人情。"

罗贝托先生打量着面前的年轻人，见到的是个中等块头但身强力壮的男人，是个乡下人而不是匪徒，居然很可笑地胆敢自称意大利人。罗贝托耸耸肩。"我已经把那套公寓租给另一户人家了，租金也高了些，"他说，"总不能为了照顾你的朋友而让他们失望吧。"

维托·柯里昂理解地点点头。"每个月加了多少钱？"他问。

"五块。"罗贝托先生答道。这是撒谎。这套公寓面对铁路，四个房间都很阴暗，租给寡妇每个月收十二块钱，新房客的租金绝不可能高出这个数。

维托·柯里昂掏出一卷钞票，剥下三张十块。"这是六个月增加的总数，现在一次全给你。别告诉她，她是个有尊严的女人。过六个月再来见我。当然啦，你会让她留下那条狗。"

"见鬼去吧，"罗贝托先生说，"你算什么东西，对我发号施令？给我放尊重点儿，否则你的西西里屁股也要流落街头。"

维托·柯里昂惊讶地举起双手。"我只是在求你赏个人情呀。天晓得一个人什么时候会需要朋友，你说对不对？拿着，这钱你收下，就当是我在表达善意，主意您自己拿。我怎么敢反对你的决定。"他把钞票塞进罗贝托先生的手心，"就当帮我一个小忙，收下钱，稍微考虑考虑。明天早上，你要是非得把钱还给我，那就只能这样了。你想让那女人搬出你的房子，我怎么能阻止呢？那毕竟是你的产业啊。你不想让狗留下，这我完全理解。我本人也讨厌动物。"他拍拍罗贝托先生的肩膀，"就帮我这个小忙，好吗？我不会忘记你的。向你在这附近的朋友打听一下我，他们保证会说我这人从来知恩图报。"

实际上，罗贝托先生已经开始明白过来了。那天晚上，他打听了一下维托·柯里昂。他没有等到第二天早上，而是深更半夜就去敲柯里昂家的门，为这么晚还叨扰主人而道歉，接过柯里昂夫人送上的一杯葡萄酒。他向维托·柯里昂保证，整件事情都是天大的误会，科伦坡夫人当然可以继续住下去，当然可以留下那条狗。那帮下三烂房客就付那一丁点儿租金，凭什么抱怨一只可怜的小动物闹得太凶？最后，他把维托·柯里昂硬塞给他的三十块钱扔在桌上，用最真诚的语气说："你这么好心帮助一位可怜的寡妇,我倍感羞愧,也想表达身为一名基督徒的善心。她的房租就和原来一样吧。"

这出喜剧的几个角色都演得漂亮。维托斟酒,叫妻子端上点心,使劲握住罗贝托先生的手,称颂他的热心肠。罗贝托先生叹着气说结识维托·柯里昂这样的好邻居,真是恢复了他对人性的信心。末了,两人依依不合地分别。罗贝托先生死里逃生,骨头都吓软了,跳上电车,逃回他在布朗克斯的住处,径直上床。他有三天没在那几幢公寓楼露面。

维托·柯里昂已经成了这片地区"值得尊重的人",传言说他是西西里黑手党的成员。一天,一个在日租公寓主持扑克赌局的男人来找他,主动提出每周付他二十块,换取他的"友谊"。他只需要每周光临两次赌局,让赌客明白他们受到他的保护。

受到小流氓滋扰的店主请他调停。他照办了,事后得到相应的报酬。不久,他的收入就达到了每周一百块,这个数字在那个时候的那块区域算是一笔巨款。克莱门扎和忒西奥是他的伙伴和盟友,所以他必须分他们一杯羹,他们并没有开口,他是主动这么做的。最后,他决定和他的童年伙伴占科·阿班丹多一起开展橄榄油进口业务。生意归占科管,从意大利进口橄榄油,按照合理的价格买入,储存在他父亲的仓库里。占科在这方面很有经验。克莱门扎和忒西奥主管销售。他们拜访了曼哈顿、布鲁克林和布朗克斯的每一家杂货店,说服店主进"占科纯净"牌橄榄油(维托·柯里昂以他典型的谦虚态度,拒绝用他的名字为品牌命名)。大部分本金由维托提供,他理所当然成了公司的老大。要是遇到特殊情况,克莱门扎和忒西奥说得天花乱坠也说服不了某些店主,维托·柯里昂就亲自出马,运用他令人畏惧的说服力。

接下来的几年,维托·柯里昂过着小商人的满足生活,在一个生机勃勃的经济扩张时代,全心全意建立他的企业。他是个尽心尽责的父亲和丈夫,但忙得没有多少时间顾家。"占科纯净"橄榄油慢慢成为美国最畅销的意大利进口橄榄油,他的组织如雨后春笋般膨胀。和任何一位优秀的销售者一样,他逐渐认识到用价格战打击竞争对手的好处,说服店主少进其他品牌的橄榄油,从而阻塞他们的分销渠道。和任何一位优秀的销售者一样,他把目标瞄准垄断,左手强迫竞争对手放弃这片战场,右手将他们并入自己的公司。刚起步的时候,他在经济上缺少助力,而且不相信广告,仅仅凭借口耳相传,再加上他的橄榄油实际上并不比竞争者的好,因此他无法使用守法商人常用的压制手段,只得依赖他的人格魅力和"值得尊重的人"的威望。

年轻的时候,维托·柯里昂就有了"通情达理"的名声。他从不出言威胁,他的逻辑总是无可辩驳。他始终保证人人都能分得应有的利益,谁也不吃亏。他的手段当然也很简单。和许多天才商人一样,他意识到自由竞争浪费资源,而垄断最有效率。因此,顺理成章,他的奋斗目标就是高效的垄断。布鲁克林有几位橄榄油批发商,脾气暴躁,头脑固执,不讲道理,哪怕在维托·柯里昂以最大限度的耐心仔细说明情况之后,仍旧拒绝了解和认同他的远大理想。对于这些人,维托·柯里昂无可奈何,只能派忒西奥去布鲁克林,建立指挥部解决问题。几间仓库失火被烧,许多卡车的橄榄油倒在沿河的鹅卵石马路上,形成茶青色的湖泊。有个傲慢的米兰人头脑发热,对警察的信任超过圣人对基督的信仰,居然跑去向政府告意大利同伴的状,打破了已有千年历史的缄默规则。可是,还没等案情有所进展,这位批发商就失踪了,从此人间蒸发,留下深爱他的妻子和三个孩子,不过感谢上帝,孩子已经是成年人,接管他的生意,和占科纯净橄榄油公司达成协议。

有言道,伟大的人并非生而伟大,而是越活越伟大,维托·柯里昂就是明证。禁酒法得到通过,全国禁止销售酒类,维托·柯里昂走出最后一步,从有点冷酷无情的普通商人成为违法经济世界里一位了不起的唐。转变并不是在一天里发生的,也不是一年,但是到禁酒法末期和大萧条初期的时候,维托·柯里昂已经成了教父,唐,唐·柯里昂。

事情的开端非常不起眼。占科纯净橄榄油公司当时有六辆送货卡车组成车队。有一帮意大利私酒贩子从加拿大走私烈酒和威士忌到美国,通过克莱门扎找到维托·柯里昂。他们需要卡车和送货员在纽约市分销他们的商品。他们需要靠得住、嘴巴牢的送货员,而且要意志坚强,有点武力。他们愿意付钱给维托·柯里昂,雇用他的卡车和员工,价码高得吓人,维托·柯里昂当机立断,削减橄榄油生意,把卡车几乎全部拿去服务私酒走私者。尽管这帮人在提议时也没少笑里藏刀威胁他,但维托·柯里昂在当时就已经见过风浪,没有把威胁当作侮辱,也没有因此生气而拒绝有利可图的建议。他掂量了一下他们的威胁,发现没什么说服力,于是降低了对新伙伴的评价,因为他们太愚蠢,在毫无必要的情况下滥用威胁。这条情报很有用,遇到合适的机会会很有参考价值。

他再次大发横财。不过更重要的是,他获得了知识、关系和经验。他慢慢积累可靠的言行,就仿佛银行家积累债券。接下来几年,事实越来越清楚了:维托·柯里昂不只能力过人,而且独具天才。

他自愿担任在住处开地下小酒馆的意大利家庭的保护者,这些人以一毛五一杯的价钱把威士忌卖给单身劳工。科伦坡太太最小的儿子举行坚信礼,他成了孩子的教父,大方地拿出一枚二十美元金币当礼物。另外一方面,卡车总有被警察拦下的时候,占科·阿班丹多雇了个在警局和司法部有很多门路的好律师。柯里昂组织建立起贿赂体系,很快有了可观的"工资单",列出按月塞钱的官员。律师尽量缩小名单,为高昂的费用道歉,维托·柯里昂却安慰他说,"不,别这样,把大家都列上,哪怕暂时还帮不上忙。我相信友谊,我愿意先表达我的友情。"

岁月流逝,柯里昂帝国逐渐壮大,卡车越来越多,"工资单"越来越长,直接为忒西奥和克莱门扎效力的人数也在增加。整个机构越来越难以控制。最后,维托·柯里昂琢磨出一套组织体系。他给克莱门扎和忒西奥安上"首领"的头衔,为他们工作的人是部下。他给占科·阿班丹多安上"顾问"的头衔。他在他本人和实际行动之间建立起好几个缓冲层。每次下达指令,指令都下给占科或两名首领中的一个。向他们中的任何人下达指令的时候,旁边难得还有其他见证者。接下来,他分出忒西奥的一拨人,让他们专门负责布鲁克林。他要忒西奥和克莱门扎相互疏远,多年来一直表达得很清楚:除非绝对必要,否则他不希望这两个人互相协作,哪怕只是社交往来。他向比较精明的忒西奥解释过这一点,忒西奥立刻心领神会,尽管维托说这是预防法律风险的安全措施,但忒西奥明白维托不希望他的两名首领有机会密谋对付他,忒西奥也明白这并非出于恶意,只是策略上的预防。作为回报,维托放手忒西奥经营布鲁克林,但把克莱门扎的布朗克斯牢牢握在手心。克莱门扎更勇猛、更无畏,虽说表面上总是乐呵呵的,其实却更无情,因此需要严加管束。

大萧条继续增强维托·柯里昂的权势。事实上,正是在大萧条时期,众人开始称他唐·柯里昂。全城到处都是老实人祈求一份正经工作,却都徒劳无功。有尊严的人降低自己和家人的身份,向不拿正眼看人的官僚机构讨要官方救济。只有唐·柯里昂的手下昂首阔步上街,口袋里塞满银币和纸钞,不担心会丢掉工作。就连唐·柯里昂这个最谦逊的男人,也忍不住要感到自豪。他在照顾他的世界、他的子民。那些人依赖于他,为他累得满头大汗,冒着自由和生命的危险为他效劳,他没有让他们失望。雇员若是不走运被捕入狱,家人就会得到生活补贴,不是打发乞丐似的一点微薄资助,而是他入狱前的薪水。

这当然不完全是基督徒的善心。连最好的朋友也不会说唐·柯里昂是圣人下凡。这种慷慨的背后也有私心。进监狱的雇员明白,只要守口如瓶,他的老婆孩子就有人照看。只要不向警方通风报信,出狱时就会得到热烈欢迎,家里会有盛大宴会等着他,有上等食物,自家做的小方饺、葡萄酒和各色糕点,亲戚朋友济济一堂欢迎他重获自由。夜里某个时候,顾问占科·阿班丹多,甚至唐本人,会登门向这么忠诚的一名部下表示敬意,为他干一杯,留下一笔丰厚的现金当礼物,让他和家人快活享受一两个星期,再回去继续辛苦工作。唐·柯里昂的同情和体谅就有这么无微不至。

也就在这段时期,唐开始觉得他主宰的世界比总是妨碍他的政府所管理的国家要好得多,这种感觉与日俱增,因为他身边的贫民不断来寻求他的帮助——家庭救济、安排工作、保释犯人、小额贷款、在不通情理的房东和失业的房客之间周旋。

唐·维托·柯里昂向所有求助者伸出援手。不只如此,他怀着善意帮助他们,说些鼓励的话,安慰被接受施恩刺痛的自尊心。于是,自然而然地,当这些意大利人举棋不定,不知道该选谁代表他们进入州立法机构、市政厅和国会,就会向他们的朋友唐·柯里昂、他们的教父征求意见。他就这样成了一股政治力量,各方首脑都来找他出谋划策。他以政治家的远见卓识进一步巩固这种力量,帮助意大利穷苦人家的聪明孩童上大学,有些孩子日后成为律师、助理地检官甚至法官。他以伟大领袖般的高瞻远瞩规划帝国未来。

禁酒令的撤销严重打击了这个帝国,但他早已采取了预防措施。1933 年,他派遣特使去见一个人,这个人控制着曼哈顿的所有赌博活动,包括码头的掷骰子和与之相辅相成的高利贷(两者的关系犹如棒球比赛和热狗)、体育和赛马的外围赌博、玩扑克的非法赌场、哈莱姆的地下抽奖和彩票。这个人名叫萨瓦托雷·马伦扎诺,他是纽约地下世界有数的一把手、炮筒子、大人物之一。柯里昂的特使向马伦扎诺建议双方缔结平等互利的伙伴关系。维托·柯里昂有他的组织,在警方与政界关系良好,能为马伦扎诺的犯罪活动提供牢固的保护伞,还拥有向布鲁克林与布朗克斯扩张所需的新生力量。可惜马伦扎诺很短视,轻蔑地驳回了柯里昂的提议。著名匪首艾尔·卡彭是马伦扎诺的朋友,马伦扎诺拥有自己的组织、自己的队伍和雄厚的战争基金。他无法容忍这个暴发户,不像正牌黑手党,更像国会里的辩论家。马伦扎诺的拒绝触发了 1933 年大战,纽约地下世界的格局因此风云变幻。

乍一看,对抗双方力量悬殊。萨瓦托雷·马伦扎诺有个打手如云的强大组织。他和芝加哥的卡彭是好朋友,可以召唤那个地区的帮手。他和塔塔利亚家族的关系也不错,塔塔利亚家族控制全城的卖淫业和当时刚崭露头角的贩毒业。他和强大的商界领袖有政治联系,商人用他的打手施加恐怖统治,胁迫时装中心的犹太工会分子和建筑业的意大利零散财团。

面对这些,唐·柯里昂只能投入克莱门扎和忒西奥执掌的两个组织严密的小团伙。商界领袖支持马伦扎诺,这抵消了他在政坛和警方的关系。对他有利的是敌人不够了解他的组织。地下世界不知道他的部下的真正力量,甚至误以为布鲁克林的忒西奥是另一支独立力量。

尽管如此,双方还是力量悬殊,直到维托·柯里昂用巧计扯平了差距。

马伦扎诺捎信给卡彭,请卡彭派两个最优秀的枪手,来纽约干掉那个暴发户。柯里昂家族在芝加哥有朋友和情报人员,传回消息说两名枪手将搭火车抵达。维托·柯里昂派出卢卡·布拉齐解决他们,他的命令释放了这个怪物最残暴的本性。

布拉齐和三个手下在火车站截住芝加哥来的两名匪徒。布拉齐的一名手下事先搞到一辆计程车,自己充当司机。火车站的搬运工拎着行李,把卡彭的枪手带上那辆车。两人刚坐进去,布拉齐和另一名手下跟着钻进轿车,用枪逼着两个芝加哥小子躺在地上。计程车驶进码头区附近的一间仓库,布拉齐为他们布置好了场地。

卡彭的枪手被捆住手脚,嘴里塞上小浴巾,免得喊出声。

布拉齐从墙边拎起斧头,挨个收拾卡彭的枪手。他先剁掉一个人的双脚,然后齐膝断小腿,然后齐大腿根断大腿。布拉齐力大无穷,但也抡了许多下才达成目标,这时候受害者当然早已毙命,地上滑溜溜的全是碎肉和鲜血。布拉齐转向第二个受害者,发现已经不必白费力气了。卡彭的第二个枪手被吓得失魂落魄,天晓得怎么一口吞掉了浴巾,被活活憋死。警方尸检确定死因,在他胃里发现了那条浴巾。

几天后,芝加哥的卡彭家族收到维托·柯里昂的口信。大意如下:"你现在知道我怎么对待敌人了。一个那不勒斯人为何要介入两个西西里人的争端呢?假如你希望我把你看作朋友,那我就欠你一个人情,随时可以兑现。您这样的人肯定明白,要是你的朋友能够解决自己的问题,愿意帮你的忙,而不是随便使唤你,对你的好处无疑更多。你要是没兴趣考虑和我交朋友,那就算了。但我不得不告诉你,纽约的天气非常潮湿,不利于那不勒斯人的健康,所以我建议你这辈子都别来拜访。"

信件的傲慢语气是精心设计的。唐看不起卡彭家族,觉得他们就是一帮明目张胆、愚蠢的杀人狂。他的智慧告诉他,卡彭飞扬跋扈、喜欢炫耀非法财富,已经丧失了所有的政坛影响力。唐知道,甚至非常确定,没有政坛影响力,没有社会掩护,卡彭的世界,还有其他与此类似的世界,都很容易被消灭。他知道卡彭已经走上毁灭之路。他还知道卡彭的影响力尽管可怕,尽管无孔不入,但仅限于芝加哥。

这个战术相当成功,不完全归功于手段凶残,还因为唐的反应速度迅速敏捷。他要是这么睿智,那么下一步的行动就将充满危险。接受友谊和附带的报酬要好得多,也明智得多。卡彭回话说他们不会干涉。

这一局势力均衡。维托·柯里昂如此羞辱卡彭家族,赢得了美国地下世界的大量"尊敬"。六个月后,他击败了马伦扎诺。他扫荡马伦扎诺保护的骰子赌局,找到他在哈莱姆的头号私彩庄家,抢走他一整天的收入和记录。他从各个方面打击敌人,连时装中心都不放过,他派克莱门扎带人支援工会分子,对抗马伦扎诺雇用的打手和服装公司的老板。在各条战线上,他出色的智慧和组织都让他克敌制胜。柯里昂很擅长利用克莱门扎的残暴,帮助他扭转局势。最后,唐·柯里昂派出藏在暗处的忒西奥军团,前去收拾马伦扎诺本人。

这时,马伦扎诺派遣特使议和。维托·柯里昂拒绝接见,用各种各样的理由搪塞。

马伦扎诺的兵卒抛弃首领,不愿为了注定失败的事业丧命。簿记和高利贷转而向柯里昂的组织付保护费。战争将近结束。

1933 年的新年夜,武西奥打人马伦扎诺的防御圈。马伦扎诺的副手急于求和,答应将首脑引向屠场。他们说约了柯里昂在布鲁克林的一家饭馆会面,他们以保镖身份陪马伦扎诺出席。他们溜出饭馆,撇下马伦扎诺坐在格子布的餐桌前,愁眉苦脸地嚼着面包,武西奥领着四名部下进门,处决迅速而稳妥。马伦扎诺嘴里的面包还没咽下去,就被子弹打得浑身窟窿。战争彻底结束。

马伦扎诺帝国并入柯里昂麾下。唐·柯里昂建立起进贡的体系,所有簿记和私彩投注点的人员保留原职。他从时装区工会得到的额外收入在未来几年非常重要。解决完生意上的问题,唐·柯里昂却发现家里出了麻烦。

桑蒂诺·柯里昂,也就是桑尼,十六岁就长到了出奇的六英尺,肩宽体阔,一张脸浓眉大眼,性感但不柔弱。弗雷迪性格安静,迈克尔才学会走路,但桑蒂诺却总是麻烦缠身。他成天打架,学业糟糕。一天晚上,身为他的教父,克莱门扎不得不担负起进言的责任,来见唐·柯里昂,说他儿子卷入武装抢劫,这桩愚蠢的勾当有可能闹出大事。桑尼显然是主谋,另外两个小子是他的追随者。

维托·柯里昂极少发脾气,这是其中一次。汤姆·黑根在他家已经住了三年,他问克莱门扎这个孤儿有没有卷入。克莱门扎摇摇头。唐·柯里昂派车把桑蒂诺带到他在占科纯净橄榄油公司的办公室。

唐第一次遭遇挫折。他单独见儿子,大发雷霆,咒骂大块头桑尼时他用的是西西里方言,这种语言最适合用来表达怒气。末了,他问:"谁给你权力做这种事?你有什么理由要干这种事?"

桑尼站在那儿,气汹汹地拒绝回答。唐轻蔑地说:"而且还这么愚蠢。忙活一晚上能挣几个钱?一天五十块?二十块?拿小命冒险,就为了二十块?"

桑尼像是没听见最后这几句话,挑衅道:"我看见你杀了法努奇。"

唐说:"啊……"倒在椅子上,他等着。

桑尼说:"法努奇离开公寓楼,妈妈说我可以回屋了。我看见你爬上屋顶,于是跟踪你。你做的事情我看得一清二楚。我待在屋顶上,看见你丢掉皮夹和枪。"

唐叹息道:"唉,看来我没法教你怎么做人了。你难道不想好好上学,不想当个律师?律师拎着手提箱能偷的钱,一千个强盗戴着面具拿着枪也比不上。"

桑尼咧嘴一笑,顽皮地说:"我想加入家族生意。"他见到唐仍旧面无表情,没有被这个笑话逗乐。他又连忙补充道,"我可以学着卖橄榄油。"

唐还是没有回答。最后,他耸耸肩,"一个人只有一种命运。"他说。他没说目睹法努奇被杀已经决定了儿子的命运,只是转过身,轻声说:"明天上午九点过来。占科会教你的。"

占科·阿班丹多拥有顾问必不可少的敏锐洞察力,明白唐的真正意图,交给桑尼的任务主要是贴身保护父亲,在这个位置上,他同样能学习担任唐的微妙诀窍。这个安排也引出了唐本人的职业本能,经常长篇大论教导大儿子如何继承事业。

除了他时常重复的"一个人只有一种命运"理论,唐还喜欢责备桑尼动不动就发脾气的毛病。唐认为威胁是最愚蠢的自我暴露,不假思索就释放怒火是最危险的任性表现。没有谁听唐发出过赤裸裸的威胁,没有谁见过他陷入无法控制的狂怒。那是难以想象的事情。他就这么尽量向桑尼传授自己的准则。他说除了朋友低估你的优点,世上最大的天然优势就是敌人高估你的缺陷。

克莱门扎首领手把手教桑尼射击和使用绳索。桑尼对意大利绳子不感兴趣,他太美国化了。他更喜欢简单直接、保持距离的盎格鲁—撒克逊枪械,这让克莱门扎很伤心。不过桑尼很快就成了很受父亲欢迎的好搭档,为他开车,帮他处理各种小事。随后的两年里,他怎么看都是个普通人家的儿子,正在进入父亲的生意圈,不怎么聪明,也不怎么急切,满足于一份清闲的工作。

与此同时,他童年的玩伴、义兄汤姆·黑根却要上大学了。弗雷迪还在念高中,最小的迈克尔在读初中,小妹康妮才四岁,还在满地乱跑。全家人早就搬进布朗克斯的公寓住宅。唐·柯里昂在考虑去长岛买房子,但想把这件事和他正在盘算的另外几个计划结合起来。

维托·柯里昂很有远见。黑帮斗争让美国的所有大城市陷入混乱。几十起游击战同时打响,野心勃勃的暴徒尝试建立自己的小帝国,柯里昂这种角色尽量保卫疆界和生计的安全。唐·柯里昂看到报纸和政府部门在利用这些杀戮制定越来越严厉的法规,采取越来越残酷的警方手段。他预见到大众的义愤会挂起民主程序,给他和他的手下引来致命打击。他自己的帝国就内部而言很稳固。他决定给交战各方带去和平,从纽约开始到全国。

他知道这个任务很危险。他把第一年花在会见纽约各大帮派的首领上,奠定基础,试探口风,提议划分势力范围,由一个组织松散的联合委员会批准,各方共同遵守。可是帮派和利益冲突太多。大家不可能达成协议。和历史上所有伟大的统治者和立法者一样,唐·柯里昂看明白了,除非把王国的数量缩减到可控范围之内,否则就不可能缔造秩序与和平。

纽约有五六个强大的"家族"无法清除。但剩下的那些,例如控制社区的"黑手"恐怖分子、无组织的高利贷放债人、使用暴力手段的簿记(缺乏执法部门的保护,也就是说,还没有买通他们),都必须消失。于是,他对这些人发动了一场实质意义上的殖民战争,投入柯里昂组织的全部资源对付他们。

缔造纽约地区的和平花了他三年时间,得到了一些意料之外的奖赏,不过奖赏刚露面的时候,却披着厄运的外衣。一群被唐判了死刑的爱尔兰疯狗歹徒借着绿宝石岛①的冲劲,险些侥幸获胜。一名爱尔兰枪手凭借偶然的机会和自杀式的血勇,突破了唐的警戒圈,冲着唐的胸口放了一枪。刺客立刻被子弹打成了筛子,但损害已经造成。

不过,这却给了桑蒂诺·柯里昂一个机会。父亲暂时退出行动,桑尼以首领的头衔组织起一支队伍,那是他自己的小王国,他就像年轻时初出茅庐的拿破仑,显露出了城市战方面的天赋。他还表现出冷酷无情的作风,这是唐·柯里昂缺少的特质。

从 1935 年到 1937 年,桑尼·柯里昂在地下世界获得了有史以来最狡诈最无情的刽子手的名声。可是,单就恐怖而言,他在卢卡·布拉齐这位可怕人物面前也要黯然失色。

布拉齐追杀其他的爱尔兰枪手,单枪匹马将他们扫除干净。六个强大家族中有一个试图干涉,充当独立匪徒的保护人,刺杀家族领袖以杀一儆百的也是布拉齐。不久,唐养好了伤,与这个家族讲和。

1937 年,除了一些小摩擦小误会(当然,有时候结果也很致命),纽约市平静而和谐。

古代城邦统治者总要留个心眼,盯着在城墙外游荡的蛮人部落,唐·柯里昂也很关注他的王国之外的世界局势。他注意到希特勒的得势、西班牙的陷落,注意到德国在慕尼黑如何恐吓英国。他没有受到外部世界的蒙蔽,清楚看到全球大战即将打响,明白这场战争的意义。他的王国将比以前更加坚不可摧。不但如此,有远见的机灵人能靠战争大发横财。不过,想达到这个目标,无论外部世界如何炮火震天,他的版图之内必须维持和平。

唐·柯里昂带着他的信念走遍美国。他与洛杉矶、旧金山、克利夫兰、芝加哥、费城、迈阿密和波士顿的同胞商谈。他是地下世界的和平传道人,到了 1939 年,他比哪一任教皇都要成功,经他斡旋,全国地下世界最强大的各个组织之间缔结了切实可行的和平协议。这份协议就像美国宪法,充分尊重各个成员在各州各市的内部权威地位。协议只约定了各方的势力范围,以及各方应一致维护地下世界的和平。

就这样,1939 年二战打响,1941 年美国参战,唐·维托·柯里昂的世界却和平有

---

① 爱尔兰的别称。

序,与蓬勃美国的其他产业平起平坐,准备好了摘取金色果实。柯里昂家族插手向黑市供应物价局的食品票和汽油票,甚至旅行优先证。时装中心有些制衣企业没有政府合同,因而就得不到足够的原材料,家族帮他们搞到军方合同,接着再通过黑市搞到原材料。他甚至有能耐帮组织内符合征兵条件的所有年轻男子找到理由,不去海外打仗。他或者给年轻人安排军工企业的免役岗位,或者请医生帮忙,建议在体检前吃什么药。

唐对他的统治倍感骄傲。对于发誓效忠的臣民来说,他的王国非常安全,而信仰法律和秩序的普通人却大量死去。唯一美中不足的是儿子迈克尔·柯里昂拒绝了他的帮助,坚持志愿参军,报效祖国。让唐惊讶的是,组织另外还有几个年轻人也这么做了。其中一个年轻人对他的首领解释说,"这个国家待我一直不错。"首领向唐复述这段话的时候,唐气愤地对首领说,"我待他也很好啊。"这些人本来也许会倒霉,但既然他原谅了儿子迈克尔,就必须也原谅其他那些错误理解了他们对唐和自己的义务的年轻人。

二战结束时,唐·柯里昂知道他的王国必须再次改变行事策略,更好地适应外部世界的形势变化。他相信他能做到这一点,而且不损失任何利益。

这份信念有来自他亲身经历的理由。引领他走上光辉大道的是两桩个人遭遇。事业刚起步的时候,当时还年轻的纳佐里尼只是一个面包师的助手,正打算结婚,跑来求他帮忙。他未来的新娘是个意大利好姑娘,两人辛苦存钱,向一名别人引荐给他们的家具批发商付了三百块巨款。这位批发商让他们任意挑选家具,拿去装点他们的廉租公寓。一套精致而耐用的卧室家具,有两个衣橱和各色灯具。一套客厅家具,有松软厚实的沙发和扶手椅,蒙的是鲜艳的金线细纺面料。纳佐里尼和未婚妻在塞满家具的巨大仓库里花了一整天,快快活活地挑选物件。批发商接过他们的三百块血汗钱,揣进口袋,保证家具一周内送到他们已经租好的公寓里。

可是,就在第二周,家具公司宣告破产。塞满家具的大仓库被查封,物资转给债权人抵账。批发商溜得无影无踪,其他债权人只能对空发怒。纳佐里尼就是其中之一,律师说无计可施,除非法院裁决,满足所有债权人的诉求。整个过程大概需要三年,纳佐里尼要是能挽回一成损失就算走运了。

维托·柯里昂听完经过,又是好笑又是不敢相信。法律怎能允许这种强盗行径?批发商在长岛有宫殿般的豪宅,有一辆豪华轿车,还在供几个孩子念大学。他怎能收下可怜的面包师的三百块钱,但不把家具交给纳佐里尼?为了验证这番话,维托·柯里昂让占科·阿班丹多请占科纯净公司的律师去查一查。

结果证实了纳佐里尼的说法。批发商把个人财产都放在妻子名下。家具事业是个股份有限公司,他不承担个人责任。是啊,他收下纳佐里尼的钱那会儿已经打算申报破产了,确实显得不守信用,但这是业内的普遍做法。法律对此束手无策。

事情倒是很容易纠正。唐·柯里昂派顾问占科·阿班丹多找批发商谈话。不出所料,精明的商人立刻心领神会,安排让纳佐里尼拿到家具。对于年轻的维托·柯里昂来说,这堂课也算小开眼界。

第二桩遭遇的影响更加深远。1939 年,唐·柯里昂决定搬出纽约市。和其他父母一样,他也希望自家孩子能上更好的学校,交往更像样的伙伴。出于个人原因,他希望能找一个他的名声还不为人知的市郊,过点隐姓埋名的生活。他买下长滩的那条林荫道,当时那里只有四幢新落成的住宅,不过地皮足够再建几幢。桑尼已经和珊德拉正式订婚,很快就将结婚,一幢屋子将属于他。唐本人住一幢,另一幢给占科·阿班丹多和家人。最后一幢暂时空置。

人住林荫道后一周,三个工人开着卡车正大光明进来,声称是长滩镇的锅炉检查员。唐的一名年轻保镖放他们进来,领他们去看地下室的锅炉。唐、妻子和桑尼在花园休息,享受带着咸味的海风。

保镖喊唐回屋,唐觉得大为扫兴。三个工人都是虎背熊腰的大块头,围着锅炉站成一圈。他们拆开了锅炉,零件乱糟糟地扔在地下室的水泥地面上。领头的是个专横男人,用粗暴的语气对唐说:"你的炉子一塌糊涂。要我们修好重新装起来的话,劳务费和零件得花你一百五,否则就不让你通过本郡的检查。"他掏出一张红色纸标签,"贴上我们的签条,明白吗? 本郡的弟兄们就不会找你麻烦了。"

唐被逗乐了。这一周风平浪静,他过得很无聊;他丢下了生意,处理搬家的各种琐碎小事。他换上比平时更加浓重的口音,结结巴巴地说:"我要是不付你钱,我的锅炉会怎么着?"

领头的耸耸肩,朝地上七零八落的零件打个手势,"我们就这么扔着呗。"

唐温顺地说,"你等一等,我去拿钱。"他回到花园里,对桑尼说,"听着,有几个人在收拾锅炉,我不明白他们到底要什么。你下去处理一下。"这不只是个玩笑,他正在考虑让儿子担任二老板。这是高级管理人员必须通过的测验之一。

桑尼的解决方法并没有让父亲完全满意。过于直接,缺乏西西里人的微妙手腕。他是大棒,而非轻剑。桑尼听完首领的要求,立刻掏枪指着三个人,让保镖用棍子狠狠收拾了他们一顿。接着,他逼着他们装好锅炉,收拾地下室。他搜他们的身,发现他们实际上受雇于一家总部设在萨福克郡的住宅改造公司。他问清楚公司老板的名字,然后一路拳打脚踢把三个男人送回卡车上。"别让我再见到你们在长滩出现,"他说,"否则就割了你们卵蛋挂在耳朵上。"

这是桑蒂诺年轻时的典型作风,随着年岁渐长,他越来越残忍,把保护范围扩大到了所居住的整个社区。桑尼亲自拜访那个住宅改造公司的老板,叫他别再派人来长滩了。柯里昂家族和当地警方建立了日常业务联系之后,警方把这类投诉和职业罪犯的罪行通报给他们。不到一年,长滩成了全美同等规模城镇中犯罪率最低的地方。职业盗贼和劫匪得到警告:不得在本镇犯案。初犯尚可忍耐,再犯就消失得无影无踪。狮子大开口的住宅改造诈骗犯和巧舌如簧的登门骗子手得到礼貌的警告:长滩不欢迎你们。有些家伙过于自信,胆敢无视警告,被揍得离死只差一口气。对法律和权威缺乏尊重的当地小流氓得到了最有父爱的忠告:滚蛋。长滩成了模范小城。

唐觉得不可理喻的是这些销售欺诈居然合法。显然,在那个循规蹈矩没有活路的世界,他利用自己的天赋才能立足。于是,他就走上了那条路,进入了那个世界。

就这样,他幸福地住在长滩的林荫道上,巩固和扩展他的帝国,直到二战结束,土佬索洛佐破坏和平,将唐的王国卷入他的战争,把唐送上医院的病床。

第四部

第十五章

在这个新罕布什尔的村庄里,隔窗窥视的家庭主妇和门里消磨时间的店主不会漏掉任何异样的动静。因此,一辆纽约牌照的黑色轿车停在亚当斯家门口,所有居民没几分钟就都知道了。

凯·亚当斯虽说在念大学,骨子里还只是个小镇姑娘,所以也在卧室窗口偷看。见到那辆车沿着马路开过来的时候,她正在复习备考,刚打算下楼吃午饭;车在她家草坪前停下,她不知为何并不惊讶。两个男人钻出车门,都是身材魁梧的大块头,活像电影里的匪徒,她飞奔下楼,抢先开门。她确定他们是迈克尔或迈克尔的家里人派来的,不希望他们未经介绍就和父母说话。倒不是说迈克的朋友会让她觉得丢人,只是她的父母都是老派的新英格兰居民,甚至无法理解她怎么会认识这种人。

门铃响起,她恰好走到门口,她对母亲喊道:"我来。"她打开门,两个大块头站在门口。其中一个的手伸进胸袋,动作就像匪徒掏枪,凯吓得惊叫一声,但他掏出来的只是个小皮夹,男人翻开皮夹,露出证件。"我是纽约警察局的约翰·菲利普斯警探,"他说,朝另一个男人打个手势,他的同伴肤色黝黑,两道眉毛非常浓、非常黑。"这位是我的搭档,塞瑞昂尼警探。您是凯·亚当斯小姐吗?"

凯点点头。菲利普斯说:"我们能进去和你谈几分钟吗?和迈克尔·柯里昂有关。"

她站到旁边,让他们进门。就在这时,父亲出现在通向书房的侧走廊口。他问:"凯,什么事?"

他父亲头发灰白,身材瘦削,容貌出众,不但是本镇浸信会的牧师,而且是宗教界的著名学者。凯其实并不特别了解父亲,父亲对她来说是个谜,但她知道父亲爱她,尽管看起来父亲总觉得她这个人很无趣。虽说一向不太亲近,但凯还是很信任父亲。因此,她直截了当答道:"他们是纽约的警探,想问我几个问题,和我认识的一个小伙子有关。"

亚当斯先生似乎并不吃惊,他说:"不如来我的书房吧?"

菲利普斯警探客气地说:"亚当斯先生,我们希望能和您的女儿单独谈谈。"

亚当斯先生答得也很有礼貌:"那得看凯的意见了。亲爱的,你愿意和这两位先生单独谈,还是希望我陪着你,或者让你母亲陪着?"

凯摇摇头。"我单独和他们谈吧。"

亚当斯先生对菲利普斯说:"到我的书房谈吧。留下吃午饭吗?"两个男人摇摇头,凯领着他们走进书房。

他们不怎么舒服地坐在沙发的边缘上,她坐进父亲的皮椅。菲利普斯警探的开场白是:"亚当斯小姐,过去这三周你见过迈克尔·柯里昂或者听到过他的消息吗?"这个问题足以让她警觉起来。三周前,她打开波士顿的报纸,赫然发现头版头条是一名纽约警长和名叫维吉尔·索洛佐的毒贩同时被杀。报纸说这场血案属于柯里昂家族参与的帮派战争。

凯摇摇头。"没有,最后一次见到他的时候,他正要去医院探望父亲。差不多是一个月以前了。"

另外一名警探用粗哑的声音说:"那次我们知道得很清楚,后来没再见过他或者得到他的消息?"

"没有。"凯说。

菲利普斯警探用礼貌的语气说:"如果你确实和他有联系,我们希望你能告诉我们。我们必须和迈克尔·柯里昂谈一谈,事情极其重要。我得提醒你,如果你确实和他有联系,就有可能处于非常危险的境地。如果你以任何方式帮助他,就有可能惹上非常严重的麻烦。"

凯在椅子里坐得笔直。"我为什么不能帮助他?"她问,"我们就快结婚了,夫妻理当互相帮助。"

接话的是塞瑞昂尼警探。"如果你帮助他,那就有可能成为谋杀从犯。我们之所以要找你的男朋友,是因为他杀死了一名纽约的警长和警长正在接触的线人。我们知道开枪的就是迈克尔·柯里昂。"

凯哈哈大笑。她的笑声发自肺腑,充满怀疑,确实打动了两名警察。"迈克才不会做这种事情,"她说,"他和家族没有任何关系。参加他妹妹婚礼的时候,大家明显当他是外人，和待我差不多。他最近要是藏了起来，肯定是因为不想见人，免得自己的名字被卷进这场风波。迈克不是匪徒。我比你们或者任何人都了解他。他为人太好，不可能做出杀人这么可耻的事情。他是我认识的最守法的人，而且就我所知，他从不撒谎。"

菲利普斯警探温和地问："你认识他多久了？"

"一年多了。"凯说，两个男人的笑容让她吃了一惊。

"我认为有几件事情得让你知道，"菲利普斯警探说，"那天晚上他和你分开以后就去了医院。从医院出来，他和一位去医院办正经事的警长吵了起来。他主动攻击警官，但挨了一顿揍。具体说是下巴骨折，还掉了几颗牙齿。他的朋友带他回到柯里昂家族在长滩的住处。第二天夜里，和他争吵的那名警长遭到枪杀，迈克尔·柯里昂就此失踪，人间蒸发。我们有我们的联络人和线人。他们都说凶手是迈克尔·柯里昂，但我们没有证据可供呈交法庭。目击凶案的侍者见到他的照片说不认识，但面对面也许认得出。我们还问了索洛佐的司机，他不肯开口，但迈克尔·柯里昂要是在我们手上，他也许就愿意说话了。因此我们警察全在找他，联邦调查局在找他，所有人都在找他。可惜目前还没有结果，我们以为你也许能提供一点线索。"

凯冷冰冰地说："我一个字也不相信。"可是，她知道迈克被人打断了下巴这一点肯定是真的，这让她有点难过，但不认为这会驱使迈克动手杀人。

"要是迈克联系你，能通知我们一声吗？"菲利普斯问。

凯摇摇头。叫塞瑞昂尼的另一名警探粗鲁地说："我们知道你俩一直在睡觉。我们有旅馆的记录和目击证人。这种消息要是不小心见了报，你父母肯定会很不愉快。他们这么可敬，恐怕会看不起一个和匪徒睡觉的女儿。你要是不马上交代清楚，我就叫你老头子进来，把话跟他挑明白。"

凯讶异地瞪着他，然后起身过去打开书房的门。她看见父亲站在客厅窗口抽烟斗。她喊道："爸，能进来一下吗？"父亲转过身，对她微笑，走向书房。进了门，他搂住女儿的腰，面对两名警探，说："二位先生，如何？"

他们没有回答，凯冷冰冰地对塞瑞昂尼警探说："警官先生，你跟他挑明白好了。"

塞瑞昂尼涨红了脸："亚当斯先生，我说这些是为了你女儿好。她和一个小流氓有瓜葛，我们有理由相信此人谋杀了一名警官。我只是想说她要是不肯合作，就有可能惹上严重的麻烦，但她似乎不明白这件事到底有多严重。也许你能和她说说。"

"真是难以置信。"亚当斯先生礼貌地说。

塞瑞昂尼一挺下巴。"你女儿和迈克尔·柯里昂已经交往一年多了，他们在旅馆过夜，以夫妻身份登记。迈克尔·柯里昂受到通缉，要因为一起刺杀警官的案件接受盘问。你女儿拒绝提供有可能帮助我们的信息。这些都是事实。你爱说难以置信就说吧,但每一句我都有充足的证据。"

"我并不怀疑你的话,先生,"亚当斯先生不紧不慢地说,"我觉得难以置信的是我女儿会惹上严重的麻烦。难道你在暗示她是个——"他露出学者的怀疑神情,"匪徒的'姘头',是这么说的吧?"

凯惊讶地望向父亲。她知道父亲这是在以学究派头开玩笑,吃惊的是父亲居然并不把这件事看得很严重。

亚当斯先生确定地说:"不过请二位放心,那位年轻人要是敢在这儿露面,我保证马上报警。我女儿也同样。现在,不好意思,我们的午饭快凉了。"

他彬彬有礼地把警察送出家门,在他们背后慢吞吞地斩钉截铁地关上门。他挽起凯的胳膊,领着她走向屋后的厨房。"来吧,亲爱的,你母亲在等我们吃饭。"

他们走进厨房,凯在悄悄流泪,既因为刚从紧张中解脱出来,也因为父亲不问缘由的爱护。厨房里,母亲假装没看见她在哭,凯明白父亲肯定和母亲说了警察的事。她坐进老位子,母亲默不作声地上菜。三个人都在桌边坐下,父亲低头谢恩祷告。

亚当斯夫人身材矮胖,总是衣着整洁,发型一丝不乱。凯从没见过她蓬头垢面。母亲对她总是有点冷淡,保持一臂距离,连此刻也不例外。"凯,别那么夸张了。这些到头来肯定都是瞎忙活。那孩子毕竟是达特茅斯的学生,怎么可能卷入这么下贱的勾当?"

凯惊讶地抬起头。"你怎么知道迈克是达特茅斯的学生?"

母亲得意地说:"你们年轻人就喜欢神神秘秘的,以为自己很聪明。我们早就知道他了,但你不说,我们也不想提起。"

"可你们是怎么知道的?"凯问。她无法面对父亲,因为父亲知道她和迈克睡过觉了,因此没有看见他说话时脸上的笑容。"我们拆了你的信呗。"

凯又是气又是怒。这下她可以面对父亲了。他的行为比她的罪过更加不可饶恕。她无法相信他会做这种事。"父亲,不会吧,怎么可能?"

亚当斯先生对她笑着说:"我思考过哪种行为的罪过更大,是拆你的信,还是不管不顾我的独生女儿有可能遇到的危险。答案很简单,也符合道德。"

亚当斯夫人咽下一口炖鸡,在吃下一口之前说:"再怎么说,亲爱的,对于你这个年龄来说,你实在天真得可怕。我们不得不留神。再说你从不提起他。"

凯第一次庆幸迈克尔写信时从不情意绵绵,庆幸父母没见过她写的某些信件。"我之所以不提起他,是害怕他的出身会吓住你们。"

"确实吓住了,"亚当斯先生喜滋滋地说,"说起来,迈克尔真的没有联系过你?"

凯摇摇头。"我不相信他会犯任何罪。"

她见到父母隔着餐桌交换眼神,亚当斯先生柔声说:"他要是没有犯罪,又忽然消失,那么也许是遇到了别的什么事情。"

凯刚开始没听明白,紧接着,她从桌边起身,跑回自己的房间。

三天后的长滩,凯·亚当斯在柯里昂家族的林荫道路口下了计程车。她接到电话,满怀期待。汤姆·黑根在门口迎接,见到是他,凯很失望。凯知道他一句实话都不会说。

来到客厅,他给凯倒了杯酒。她看见有几个人走来走去,但桑尼不在其中。她直截了当地问汤姆·黑根:"知道迈克在哪儿吗?知道我该怎么联系他吗?"

黑根把话说得滴水不漏。"我们知道他没事,但不知道他这两天在哪儿。他听说警长被枪杀,害怕警察会诬告他,于是决定藏起来。他说他过几个月再联系我们。"

这个故事不但是假的,而且存心要让人一眼看穿——他只能透露这么多。"警长真的打断了他的下巴?"凯问。

"很抱歉,确实如此,"汤姆说,"但迈克并不是睚眦必报的那种人。我相信他和后来的事情毫无关系。"

凯打开手包,取出一封信。"要是他和你们联系,能把这封信交给他吗?"

黑根摇摇头。"我要是收下这封信,而你上法庭说我收下了这封信,就可以解读为我知道他的下落。你不如再等一等吧?我相信迈克会和你联系的。"

她喝完酒,起身离开。黑根陪她走向门厅,他刚打开门,就有一个女人从外面进来。这是个矮胖妇人,穿一身黑衣。凯认出她是迈克尔的母亲。她伸出手,说:"柯里昂夫人,近来可好?"

女人小小的黑眼睛盯着她看了几秒钟,皱巴巴的橄榄色面孔忽然露出笑容,笑容有点唐突,不知为何却显得真诚而友善。"哎呀,这不是米基的小女友吗?"柯里昂夫人说。她的意大利口音很重,凯几乎听不懂。"吃东西吗?"凯说不,意思是说不想吃东西,柯里昂夫人却怒气冲冲地转向汤姆·黑根,用意大利语骂了他几句,最后说:"连一杯咖啡都不请可怜的姑娘喝,真是耻辱。"她拉起凯的手,老妇人的手出奇地温暖和充满活力,领着凯走进厨房,"你喝杯咖啡,吃点东西,然后有人开车送你回家。你这样的好姑娘,我不要你坐火车。"她按着凯坐下,在厨房里忙前忙后,脱掉大衣和帽子挂在椅背上。没过几秒钟,桌上就摆上了面包、干酪和萨拉米香肠,炉子上热着咖啡。

凯腼腆地说:"我来问迈克的事情,我一直没有他的消息。黑根先生说谁也不知道他的下落,说他过一阵就会露面。"

黑根连忙插嘴:"妈,我们现在只能跟她说这些。"

柯里昂夫人用能瞪死人的轻蔑眼神看了看他。"如今轮到你教我怎么做了? 我丈夫都不敢教训我——愿上帝保佑他。"她在胸前画个十字。

"柯里昂先生还好吧?"凯问。

"好,"柯里昂夫人说,"还好。他年纪大了,糊涂了,会让这种事发生。"她不怎么恭敬地敲敲脑袋。她倒上咖啡,逼着凯吃了些面包和干酪。

喝完咖啡,柯里昂夫人用两只棕色的手捏住凯的双手,轻声说:"米基不会写信给你,你不会听到米基的消息。他要躲两三年。也许更久,也许久得多。你回去和家人团聚,找个好小伙子结婚吧。"

凯从手包里拿出那封信。"能帮我交给他吗?"

老妇人接过信,拍拍凯的面颊。"当然,当然,"她说。黑根正要反对,她用意大利语吼了他几句,然后领着凯走向大门。她在门口轻轻亲吻凯的面颊,说:"忘了米基吧,他不再是你的男人了。"

门口有辆车等她,前排坐着两个男人。他们开车送她回到纽约的酒店,一路上一声不吭,凯也同样。她在尽量让自己适应现实:她深爱的年轻人是个冷血凶手。消息的来源不容怀疑,因为正是他的母亲。

第十六章

卡洛·里齐对整个世界满腹牢骚。他入赘柯里昂家族,却被冷落一旁,只得到曼哈顿上东区一摊小小的簿记生意。他原先还指望能住进长滩林荫道的一幢屋子呢。他知道唐只要愿意,说句话就能让扈从家属搬走,他以为这是板上钉钉的事,这样他能进入所有生意的内部了。可是,唐却没有公正地待他。那个"伟大的唐",他轻蔑地想着。一个老胡子彼得,居然会像小流氓似的在马路上遭到枪手刺杀。他希望老东西一命呜呼。桑尼曾经和他是朋友,要是桑尼成为家族首领,他也许就有机会进入内部了。

他望着妻子倒咖啡。天哪,她成了什么邋遢样子。结婚才五个月,她已经开始发福,肚皮也像吹气球似的。意大利东边的婆娘,都是真正的黑皮贱种。

他伸手摸了摸康妮日益膨胀的臀部。她对他微笑,他嘲笑道:"肥肉比猪身上的还多。"见到她的刺痛表情,眼里淌泪,他却很高兴。她也许是了不起的唐的女儿,但终究是他的老婆,现在是他的私人财产,他愿意怎么待她就怎么待她。随便践踏柯里昂家族的一员让他觉得自己很有能耐。

他刚开始就收拾得她服服帖帖的。她企图留下那个装满礼金的拎包,他却赏她一个漂漂亮亮的黑眼圈,抢走了钞票。钱的下落也根本不告诉她。要是说了反而会招惹麻烦。他到今天还略略有那么一丝内疚。天哪,他在赛马和歌舞女郎身上挥霍了差不多一万五。

他感觉到康妮在背后看着他,于是张弛肌肉,伸手去拿桌子另一头的一盘甜面包。他刚把火腿和炒蛋一扫而空,但他是个大块头,早餐的饭量也大。他对自己展现给妻子的画面很满足,不是一般油腻腻的黑皮意大利丈夫,而是金发平头,手臂粗壮,长满金色汗毛,肩宽腰细。他知道从体格上说,那些给家族效命的所谓硬汉子根本比不上他。什么克莱门扎,什么忒西奥,什么洛可·兰坡,什么被人做掉的保利小子。天晓得那到底是怎么一回事。不知为何,他想到了桑尼。一对一连桑尼都不是他的对手,尽管桑尼比他块头稍微大点,身体稍微壮些。真正让他害怕的是桑尼的名声,虽说他只见过好脾气、乱开玩笑的桑尼。没错,桑尼是他的好哥们儿。等现在这个唐完蛋,事情也许会有新发展。

他慢吞吞地喝着咖啡。他讨厌这套公寓。他已经习惯了西区更宽敞的居住区,过一会儿他就得穿过全城去他的簿记点,经营午间的生意。今天是星期天,一周里生意最兴旺的一天,棒球已经开打,篮球快要结束,晚间的赛马即将开盘。他逐渐意识到康妮在背后忙来忙去,于是扭头看她。

她正在着装打扮,正是他最讨厌的地道纽约黑皮风格。丝绸印花长裙,扎腰带,俗丽的手镯和耳环,荷叶边衣袖。模样少说老了二十岁。"你他妈这是去哪儿?"他问。

她冷冰冰地答道:"去长滩看我父亲。他还没法起床,需要陪伴。"

卡洛好奇道:"管事的还是桑尼吗?"

康妮半冷不热地看看他。"怎么了?"

他气急败坏道:"下贱的黑皮婊子,敢再这么和我说话,我就把你肚皮里的小崽子揍出来。"她一脸惊慌,反而让他更加恼火。他跳起来,就手便是一记耳光,抽出一道红印子。他正正反反又是三记耳光,打得又快又准。他见到她的上嘴唇劈裂,流血肿起,于是见好就收。他不想留下伤疤。她跑进卧室,摔上门,他听见钥匙在锁眼里转动。他哈哈大笑,坐下继续喝咖啡。

他一根接一根抽烟,直到该换衣服才起身,敲敲门,说:"开门,别逼我出脚。"里面没有回应。"快点,我得换衣服。"他大声说。他听见她起床,走到门口,钥匙在锁眼里转动。他走进房间,她背对着他,走回床边躺下,别过脸对着墙。

他三下两下换好衣服,发现她只穿着衬裙。他希望她回家探望父亲,带回消息告诉他。"怎么?几个耳光就扇得你没精神了?"真是个淫贱的懒婆娘。

"我不想去。"她带着哭腔嘟囔道。他不耐烦地伸出手,把她翻过来面对自己。他看见了她为什么不想去,确实不去为妙。

他出手大概没掌握好轻重。她的左脸肿了起来,上嘴唇肿得奇形怪状,鼻子底下涨得发白。"好吧,"他说,"不过我很晚才回家。星期天比较忙。"

他离开公寓,发现车上有张罚单,而且是十五块的绿单子。他把罚单塞进手套箱,让它加入厚厚一摞伙伴的行列。他心情不错。扇那个被宠坏了的小婊子总是让他心情愉快,既然柯里昂家族不肯善待他,就这么拿她出出气倒也不错。

第一次打得她青一块紫一块的时候,他还有点担心。她马上跑回长滩,向父母告状,给他们看她的黑眼圈。他吓得出了一身冷汗。不过,等她回来,却非常温顺,成了个本分的意大利小妻子。接下来的几个星期,他尽量扮演好丈夫的角色,各方各面都好好待她,亲热体贴,每天从早到晚搞她。最后,她以为他不会再下那种狠手了,于是把回家的遭遇告诉了他。

她发现父母不以为然,不但不同情,很奇怪地还觉得好笑。她母亲稍微有点同情,请她父亲找卡洛·里齐谈谈。父亲却拒绝了。"她是我女儿不假,"他这么回答,"但现在她属于她的丈夫。他知道他的责任。在意大利连皇帝都不敢掺和夫妻间的家务事。回家吧,等你学会怎么当个好老婆,他就不会揍你了。"

康妮气愤地对父亲说:"你揍过你老婆吗?"她是父亲的心头肉,可以这么放肆地说话。父亲答道:"她可没有给过我揍她的理由。"母亲笑呵呵地点头。

她描述丈夫怎么抢走结婚的礼金,甚至不说一声钱都用在了哪儿。父亲耸耸肩,说:"要是我老婆也像你这么专横,我恐怕也会和他一样。"

她就这么回到家,有点困惑,有点害怕。她一直是父亲的心头肉,没法理解他现在为何如此冷淡。

然而,唐并不像他装出来的那么冷漠。他问了问,知道了卡洛·里齐把结婚礼金都花在了哪儿。他在卡洛·里齐的簿记点安排了几个手下,他们会向黑根事无巨细地报告里齐的一举一动。但唐没法插手。一个男人要是害怕他老婆的家族,怎么能好好履行丈夫的职责呢?这是个难解的僵局,他不敢贸然干涉。后来,康妮怀孕了,他觉得自己的决定很明智,更加认定他绝对不能插手。尽管康妮向母亲诉苦说她又揍了几次打,母亲终于开始担心,对唐提起这件事。康妮甚至暗示说她也许打算离婚。唐这辈子第一次向康妮发了火。他说:"他是你的孩子的父亲。一个孩子来到世上,怎么能没有父亲呢?"

得知这些,卡洛·里齐愈发有信心了。他百分之百安全,甚至对手下的两个"登记员"——萨利·雷格斯和寇奇——吹牛说只要看老婆不顺眼,他就揍得她满地乱爬。他看到他们面露敬佩之色,因为他有胆子这么粗暴对待了不起的唐·柯里昂的女儿。

可是,里齐之所以觉得安全,只是因为他不知道桑尼·柯里昂在得知妹妹挨揍以后,爆发出了能杀人的狂怒,唐本人下了最严厉、最强硬、连桑尼都不敢违抗的命令,这才约束住他,所以桑尼才对里齐避而不见,他不相信他能控制住自己的脾气。

就这样,在这个美丽的星期天早晨,自以为百分之百安全的卡洛·里齐驱车穿城,沿着九十六街驶向东区。他没注意到桑尼的轿车从对面驶来,驶向他的住处。

桑尼·柯里昂离开保卫森严的林荫道,在城里和露西·曼奇尼过夜。这会儿他在回家的路上,有四个保镖陪着他,前车两个,后车两个。他身边不需要帮手,他能应付从一个方向来的袭击。保镖自己开车,住在露西房间的左右两个房间里。只要不是每天去,偶尔见见露西应该无妨。不过既然已经在城里了,他打算接上康妮小妹回长滩看看。他知道卡洛应该在簿记点,小气的王八蛋不肯给康妮叫车,所以他想让小妹搭个顺风车。

他等前车的两个人走进公寓楼,然后下车跟着进去。他看见后车的两个人在他那辆车背后停下,下车盯着街道。他保持警惕。敌手知道他进城的概率顶多百万分之一,但小心终归没错。这是1930年代的战争给他的教训。

他从不搭电梯。电梯犹如死亡陷阱。他脚步飞快,爬了八层楼,来到康妮的公寓门口。他敲敲门。之前他眼看着卡洛的车经过,知道家里只有康妮一个。没人应门。他又敲敲门,听见妹妹问:"是谁?"声音惊恐而胆怯。

声音里的惊恐让他大吃一惊。小妹向来是家里最活泼、鲁莽、倔强的一个。她这是出了什么事? 他说:"是我,桑尼。"门闩拨开,门开了,康妮哭着扑进他的怀里。桑尼惊讶得没法动弹,他拉开康妮,见到一张肿胀的脸,顿时明白发生了什么事。

他转身跑下楼梯,去追她的丈夫。怒火熊熊燃烧,扭曲了他的面容。康妮看见他愤怒的样子,死死抱住他,不放他走,拖着他走进公寓。这会儿她是因为恐惧而哭。她了解大哥,害怕他的脾气,所以没有向他埋怨过卡洛。她好不容易才拖着桑尼回到公寓里。

"都怪我,"她说,"我先挑衅,想打他,所以他才打我。他的下手没那么重,是我撞上去的。"

桑尼控制住了那张爱神脸上的表情。"今天你不是要去看老头子吗?"

她没有回答,他又说:"我记得你要去的,所以过来接你,反正已经在城里了。"

她摇摇头。"我不想让他们看见我这个样子,下星期吧。"

"好。"桑尼说。他拿起厨房里的电话,拨了个号码,"我叫医生过来看你,包扎一下。你这个情况得多加小心。孩子还有几个月?"

"两个月,"康妮说,"桑尼,你别插手,求你了。"

桑尼哈哈一笑,说话时满脸凶相,"别担心,不会让你的孩子没出生就成孤儿的。"他轻轻亲吻小妹没受伤的那一侧面颊,然后离开公寓。

东121街的一家糖果店门前,马路上并排停了长长一溜轿车,那里就是卡洛·里齐的簿记点。店门口的人行道上,父亲在和小孩抛接球,星期天早晨,他们带着孩子出门兜风,下注的时候陪着孩子玩耍。见到卡洛·里齐来了,父亲们放下球,买冰激凌给孩子,免得他们吵闹。父亲们开始研究报纸上的首发投球手名单,苦苦琢磨今天的棒球赔率。

卡洛走进糖果店里面的大房间。他的两名登记员——精瘦的小个子萨利·雷格斯,壮实的大个子寇奇——已经在等待接单了。他们面前摆着一排横格大开本记事簿,用来记录赌注。木架上放着黑板,用粉笔写着十六个大联盟球队的名字,两个一对,表示今天谁打谁。每对球队旁边是个空心方框,准备填写赔率。

卡洛问寇奇:"店里的电话能窃听了吗?"

寇奇摇摇头。"还没搭上。"

卡洛走到墙边,拿起听筒,拨了个号码。萨拉·雷格斯和寇奇不动声色地看着他记录"赛线",也就是当日比赛的赔率。他们看着他挂断电话,走到黑板前,用粉笔抄写各场比赛的赔率。尽管卡洛不知道,但他们早就知道赛线,此刻正在核查他写的数字。卡洛接手的第一周就犯错,抄反了赔率,造出所有赌徒梦寐以求的所谓"中间盘",也就是在他这儿按这个赔率下注,再找另一个簿记,对同一支队伍按正确的赔率下注,赌徒就必胜无疑。只有卡洛的簿记生意会亏钱。这次犯错害得簿记点一周亏了六千块,证实了唐对女婿的判断。他下令说卡洛不管做什么都要再三核查。

柯里昂家族的高级成员一般从不过问运营中的这种细节,两头至少隔着五个缓冲层。可是,这个簿记点毕竟是考验女婿的测试场,所以始终处在汤姆·黑根的直接监管之下,每天都要向他报告情况。

赛线贴出,赌徒涌入糖果店的里屋,把赔率贴着比赛和投手名单抄在报纸上。有些男人拉着小孩的手,抬头看着黑板,一个家伙押的赌注很大,他低头看看领着的小女孩,开玩笑道:"宝贝儿,你觉得今天谁会赢?巨人还是海盗?"光怪陆离的队名迷住了小女孩,她说:"巨人比海盗厉害吗?"父亲哈哈大笑。

两名登记员前方排起队伍。登记员每填满一张单子就扯下来,包上收到的赌注,递给卡洛。卡洛从后门出去,爬上几级楼梯,走进糖果店老板居住的公寓。他打电话向中央交易所报告金额,撩开一段加宽的窗帘,把钱放进墙上的小保险箱。接下来,他烧掉登记单,用马桶冲掉灰烬,下楼返回糖果店。

由于蓝法①的规定,周日的比赛只能在下午两点以后开打,因此第一批下注的都是有家室的男人,投注后匆忙回家,带着妻小去海滩。随后陆续到来的是单身汉赌徒,还有星期天让家人困守城里闷热公寓的死硬派。单身汉赌徒都是豪客,下的赌注比较大,一般四点左右回来,接着赌连场开打的第二场比赛。正是因为他们,卡洛的星期天才需要从早干到晚和加班,也有已婚男子从海滩打来电话,尝试挽回损失。

一点半,赌客逐渐散去,卡洛和萨拉·雷格斯可以出来,坐在糖果店旁边的露台上透透气。他们看着小孩打棍球。一辆警车经过。他们就当没看见。这个簿记点在本辖区后台过硬,当地警察碰都不敢碰。要扫荡这里,非得警局最高层下令不可,即便真要扫荡,他们也会早早得到警告。

寇奇出来在两人旁边坐下。他们闲聊棒球和女人。卡洛笑着说:"我今天没忍住,又教训了一顿我老婆,让她知道谁说了算。"

寇奇看似随意地说:"她肚皮已经很大了,对吧?"

"所以我只扇了她几个耳光,"卡洛说,"没伤到她。"他想了几秒钟,又说,"她以为她能随便支使我,我可不吃这一套。"

还有几个赌客在附近吹牛扯淡聊棒球,其中两三个坐在卡洛和两名登记员上方的台阶上。忽然,街上打棍球的小孩四散奔逃,一辆轿车呼啸驶近这个街区,猛地停在糖果店门前。急刹车伴着一声尖啸,车还没停稳,一个男人就从驾驶座上蹿了出来,他的动作实在太快,所有人都来不及反应。来者正是桑尼·柯里昂。

他浓眉大眼的爱神脸和弓形的厚嘴唇拧成暴怒的凶相。才一眨眼,他就跳上露台,扼住卡洛·里齐的喉咙。他把卡洛和其他人分开,想把他拖上马路,但卡洛用两条肌肉发达的胳膊死死抱住露台的铁栏杆,再也不肯松手。他蜷成一团,耸起两肩,尽量护住脑袋和脸。桑尼扯碎了他的衬衫。

接下来的事情让人恶心。桑尼用拳头痛揍蜷缩的卡洛,用被怒火烧哑的嗓子辱骂他。卡洛虽说体型庞大,却毫不抵抗,不喊饶命也不叫冤枉。寇奇和萨利·雷格斯不敢插手。他们以为桑尼打算杀了妹夫,不想跟着卡洛倒霉。打棍球的孩子刚才还围过来,想骂那个害他们奔逃的司机,此刻却带着敬畏和兴趣看着这一幕。这都是些野小子,但见到如此愤怒的桑尼,他们谁也不敢作声。这时,另一辆车开到桑尼那辆车背后停下,两名保镖跳下车。见到眼前的场景,他们也不敢插手。他们警觉地守在旁边,准备保护首领,提防哪个旁观者蠢得会上去帮助卡洛。

___

① 禁止在星期日从事商业交易的法律。

卡洛的完全屈服,看着令人厌恶,但也许正是因为这样才救了他的小命。他用双手抱着铁栏杆,所以桑尼没法把他拖到街上,尽管他的力气也不小,但他就是不还击。他让拳头像雨点似的落在没有防护的后脑勺和脖子上,等待桑尼的怒火消退。最后,桑尼喘着粗气,低头看着他,说:"肮脏的狗杂种,再碰我妹妹一下,我就宰了你。"

这几句话缓和了紧张,因为要是桑尼想杀了他,就不可能发出这种威胁。他说得很无奈,是因为他不可能付诸行动。卡洛不肯看桑尼。他低着头,手和胳膊缠着铁栏杆。他一直那么抱着,直到轿车呼啸而去,听见寇奇用慈爱得出奇的声音说:"好啦,卡洛,进店里去吧。别在外面丢人了。"

直到这时,贴着露台石阶蜷成一团的卡洛才敢起身,松开他攥住铁栏杆的双手。他站起来,看见孩子盯着他的表情分外厌恶,好像目睹了一个人类同胞的堕落。他有点头晕,但主要是因为震惊,因为被纯粹的恐惧控制了身体;尽管桑尼的重拳犹如暴雨,但他伤得并不重。他任由寇奇拉着他的胳膊,领着他走进糖果店的里屋,用冰块帮他敷脸,虽说没有破皮流血,但整张脸青肿得很难看。恐惧逐渐退去,受到的羞辱让他犯恶心,他非得呕吐不可,寇奇扶着他的脑袋对准水槽,像搀醉汉似的扶着他,带他上楼走进公寓,帮他躺在一张床上。卡洛没有注意到萨利·雷格斯已经不见踪影。

萨利·雷格斯走到第三大道,打电话给洛可·兰坡,报告刚才发生的事。洛可冷静地听着,接着打电话给首领彼得·克莱门扎。克莱门扎呻吟道:"唉,我的天,该死的桑尼,他的臭脾气。"但说话前先谨慎地按下了插簧,免得洛可听见他的唠叨。

克莱门扎打电话到长滩家里,找到汤姆·黑根。黑根沉吟片刻,然后说:"尽快派你的部下开几辆车到通往长滩的路上,以防桑尼遇到塞车或出事故。他每次那么大发雷霆,自己都不知道自己会干出什么事。难说另一边的朋友会不会听说他在城里。说不准啊。"

克莱门扎怀疑地说:"等我派的人赶到路上,桑尼都已经到家了。塔塔利亚家族的人也一样。"

"我知道,"黑根耐心解释道,"但万一出了什么意外,桑尼说不定会被堵住。尽力而为吧,彼得。"

克莱门扎不情不愿地打电话给洛可·兰坡,吩咐他带几个人开车控制住回长滩的道路。他自己坐进他钟爱的凯迪拉克,带上三名驻扎在家里的护卫队成员,赶往大西洋海滩大桥,驶向纽约市区。

糖果店门口的闲汉里有一个小赌徒是塔塔利亚家族花钱雇的线人,他打电话通知了他的联络人。可是,塔塔利亚家族并没有因为战争而精简机构,联络人必须一层层向上传递消息,找到与塔塔利亚家族首脑有联系的首领。这时候,桑尼·柯里昂已经安全回到长滩的林荫道，走进父亲的住处，准备迎接父亲的怒火。

第十七章

　　1947 年柯里昂家族与五大家族的战争使各方都耗费巨大。警方为了麦克劳斯凯警长的案件，向各方施加压力，情况因此愈加复杂。调查警官对保护赌博和色情业的政治力量置之不理这种情况十分少见，政客遇到这种时候也无能为力，就仿佛参谋部面对一支烧杀劫掠的军队，而前线指挥官拒绝服从命令。

　　缺乏保护对敌手的伤害超过了对柯里昂家族的伤害。柯里昂集团的大部分收入来自赌博业，受到打击的主要是其中"街头彩票"和"摸奖"两个分支。经营这些赌局的代理员被警方纳入网络，通常先不重不轻收拾一顿，然后登记入册。警方甚至查到几家彩票金库的地址，上门扫荡，钱财损失惨重。那些庄家也都是一方炮筒子，纷纷向首领诉苦，首领带着他们的怨言上家族议事会讨论。可是，他们无能为力。庄家得到的答复是暂时歇业。哈莱姆的黑人散户得到允许，接管这个最挣钱的区域，他们的活动方式非常分散，警方发现很难给他们定罪。

　　麦克劳斯凯警长死后，有些报纸报道他和索洛佐有来往。他们公布证据，说麦克劳斯凯在死前不久接受大笔贿赂。报纸刊登的报道是黑根安排的，情报由他本人提供。警察局既不承认也不否认，但报道收到了效果。警方通过线人和被家族贿赂的警察得到消息：麦克劳斯凯是个堕落警察。倒不是因为他收钱和干净的职务贿赂——底层警察没有这方面的限制——而是他收了最肮脏的赃钱：杀人犯和贩毒的钱。对于警察的道德准则而言，这是不可原谅的罪过。

　　黑根知道警察对法律和秩序的信任天真得可笑。警察比他们服务的大众更相信这两样东西。说到底，法律和秩序犹如魔法，警察从中汲取权力——个人权力，他们对这种权力的珍惜，不亚于任何人对个人权力的珍惜。然而，警察对他们服务的大众又总怀着郁结于心的怨恨。大众既是警察要保护的对象，也是警察的猎物。作为被保护的对象，大众忘恩负义、态度恶劣、索求无度。作为猎物，大众狡猾而危险，一肚子坏水。一个人落到警察手里，警察维护的社会制度就会动用所有资源，营救警察捕获的猎物。操纵这些把戏的是政客。法官慈悲为怀，判处罪大恶极的流氓缓刑。州长和总统动不动大赦天下，觉得备受尊敬的律师还没有帮罪犯脱尽罪名。过了一段时间，警察学乖了。流氓奉上钞票，警察为什么不收下呢？警察更需要钱哪。警察的孩子凭什么不能上大学？老婆凭什么不能去更奢侈的商店购物？他凭什么不能冬天去佛罗里达度假晒太阳？警察毕竟每天都在冒生命危险，这可不是说着玩的。

但是，警察通常有规矩，不接受肮脏的贿赂。警察可以收钱让簿记做生意，可以收钱少开停车罚单和超速罚单，可以允许应召女郎和妓女挣点皮肉钱——当然，报酬不能少。这些恶习都是凡人的本性。然而，警察通常不会接受贿赂而放纵贩毒、武装抢劫、强奸、杀人和其他重大罪行。在警察眼里，这些行为损害的是他个人权威的核心，绝对不能纵容。

杀死一名警长相当于弑君。可是，等消息传出来，麦克劳斯凯被杀时身边是个臭名昭著的毒品贩子，涉嫌参与谋杀，警察的复仇欲望开始减退。另外，说到底，警察还有贷款要还，还有车款要付，还有孩子要长大成人。没了份子钱，警察就得节衣缩食，量人为出。没有执照的摊贩适合捞点午饭钱。停车罚单的酬劳也能积少成多。有些更不顾一切的警察甚至开始在管辖区的警厅搜刮搞同性恋、人身攻击、斗殴的嫌犯的财务。最后，高官发了善心。他们提高要价，允许各大家族恢复营业。各个辖区的中间人又开始登记贿赂名单，列出所属分局的所有警察和每个月的份额。社会秩序的假象得以恢复。

派私家侦探护卫唐·柯里昂的病房是黑根的主意。忒西奥组织里更加凶悍的手下从旁辅助。即便如此，桑尼还是不放心。二月中旬，唐可以活动了，桑尼安排救护车把唐送回林荫道的家里。屋子经过改造，唐的卧室成了一间设备齐全的病房，足以应付任何紧急情况。家里特别为此招募护士，检查背景后雇用，二十四小时值班。肯尼迪医生得到丰厚报酬，被说服担任这家私人医院的住院医师，时间至少到唐只需要护理为止。

林荫道本身加固得坚不可摧。纽扣人搬进另外两幢屋子，原先的房客送回意大利老家度假，费用由家族承担。

弗雷迪·柯里昂领命去了拉斯维加斯，一方面是休养，另一方面是打探情况，为家族打入日益兴隆的豪华旅馆兼赌场这一行作准备。拉斯维加斯属于仍旧中立的西海岸帝国，那个帝国的唐保证弗雷迪的安全。纽约的五大家族无意去拉斯维加斯追杀弗雷迪而继续树敌。他们在纽约的麻烦已经够多了。

肯尼迪医生严禁他们在唐面前讨论生意，但谁也不遵守这条禁令。唐坚持在病房里召开战时议事会。他回家的第一个晚上，桑尼、汤姆·黑根、彼得·克莱门扎和忒西奥就齐聚一堂。

唐·柯里昂还虚弱得没法说话，但他希望听一听情况，行使否决权。听到弗雷迪受命去拉斯维加斯了解赌场业务，他赞同地点了点头。听到柯里昂家族的纽扣人杀死了布鲁诺·塔塔利亚，他摇头叹息。但最让他揪心的是得知迈克尔刺杀了索洛佐和麦克劳斯凯警长,然后被迫流亡西西里。听到这个,他示意所有人出去;他们在存放法律书籍的拐角房间继续讨论。

桑尼·柯里昂躺在写字台前的大扶手椅里。"我想我们最好先让老头子轻松几个星期,等医生说他可以处理生意再说,"他顿了顿,"我想在他恢复之前让生意运转起来。警察已经开了绿灯。首先是哈莱姆的地下彩票。黑人兄弟在那儿弄得有声有色,现在我们要收回地盘了。他们总是瞎搞,不管做什么生意都这样。很多代理员不付钱给赢家。他们开着凯迪拉克上街,却告诉赌客说要么慢慢等,要么只拿一半奖金。我不喜欢他们开新车,不喜欢他们赖赢家的钱,所以我不希望这些单干户留在这个行当里,他们坏了我们的名声。汤姆,我们马上推进这个计划。告诉外界我们要整顿这个行当,其他事情都会恢复正轨。"

黑根说:"哈莱姆有些弟兄很难对付。他们已经尝到了挣大钱的甜头,怕是不愿意回去重新当代理员或者分销人。"

桑尼耸耸肩。"把名字报给克莱门扎。这是他的工作,端正一下他们的态度。"

克莱门扎对黑根说:"没问题。"

忒西奥提出了至关重要的问题:"我们一旦开始营业,五大家族就会跟着扫荡。他们会袭击我们在哈莱姆的彩票庄家和东区的簿记,甚至会让我们保护的时装中心员工吃苦头。这场战争会耗费许多金钱。"

"他们也许不会,"桑尼说,"五大家族知道我们会以牙还牙。我派了和平使者出去试水温,说不定为塔塔利亚家那小子赔偿一笔就行了。"

黑根说:"我们在这些谈判里会贴上冷屁股。五大家族最近这几个月损失了很多钱,把责任全怪在我们头上。怪得也有道理。我估计他们会希望我们答应参与贩毒,利用柯里昂家族的政治影响力。换句话说,就是索洛佐的交易,只是少了索洛佐。不过,他们会先用战斗行为伤害我们,然后再提出这个建议。他们认为这样能说服我们考虑贩毒的提议。"

桑尼毫不犹豫道:"贩毒没得谈。唐说不行,只要他不改主意,那就是不行。"

黑根很快回答:"那我们就会面临一个战术问题。我们的钱摆在明处——簿记和彩票,容易受到打击。可是,塔塔利亚控制的是妓女、应召女郎和码头工会。我们该怎么打击他们呢?另外几大家族也经营赌博,但大部分收入来自建筑业和高利贷,控制工会,招揽政府合同。他们凭敲诈勒索和其他手段从无辜百姓身上捞钱。他们的钱不是从街上来的。塔塔利亚夜总会太有名,我们没法碰,会惹大麻烦。唐不出面,双方的政治影响力旗鼓相当。我们面临的问题很严峻。"

"这是我的问题,汤姆,"桑尼说,"我来寻找答案。你继续谈判,跟进其他事情。

先把生意恢复起来,然后看情况再作定夺。克莱门扎和忒西奥有足够多的部下,真要动手,我们拼得过整个五大家族。我们要对抗到底。"

解决业内的黑人散户不成问题。警方收到线报,四处取缔,干得格外起劲。在那个时代,黑人还不可能贿赂高级警官或政治官员,以得到许可维持活动。主要原因是种族偏见和种族猜忌。不过,哈莱姆一向被认为是个小问题,平定局面本来就在预料之内。

五大家族却从出乎意料的方向发动突袭。服装工会两名有影响力的高级骨干被杀,两人都是柯里昂家族的成员。紧接着,柯里昂家族的高利贷放债人被禁止进入码头地区,柯里昂家族的簿记也是一样。码头工会纷纷倒向五大家族。五大家族威胁全市所有柯里昂的簿记变节。哈莱姆最大的街头彩票庄家,柯里昂家族的老朋友和盟友,遭到血腥谋杀。再也不存在其他出路。桑尼吩咐首领,开始睡床垫。

市区内收拾出两套公寓,摆满床垫供纽扣人歇息,搬进冰箱存放食物,储存大量枪支弹药。克莱门扎的部下驻扎一套,忒西奥另一套。家族旗下的所有簿记配备保镖小队。但是,哈莱姆的彩票庄家投靠了敌人,柯里昂家族暂时无能为力。家族耗费了大量金钱,进账寥寥无几。又是几个月过去,其他问题越来越明显。最重要的是柯里昂家族寡不敌众。

原因有几点。唐还太虚弱,无法参与决策,家族的许多政治力量保持中立。另外,过去的十年和平严重损害了两名首领的作战能力。克莱门扎是称职的行刑人和行政官,但不再拥有领兵作战的精力和青春活力了。年龄让忒西奥变得温和,不再冷酷无情。汤姆·黑根尽管能力过人,但就是不适合担任战时顾问。他最大的缺点是他不是西西里人。

桑尼·柯里昂意识到了家族战时阵容的缺陷,但无法采取措施补救。他不是唐,只有唐才可以撤换首领和顾问;而撤换他们这个动作本身就会让局势更加危险,有可能造成叛乱。起初,桑尼只想以守为攻,等待唐恢复健康,接过指挥权,但彩票庄家背叛和簿记受到恐怖威胁使得家族的地位岌岌可危。他决定发动反击。

他决定的反击手段是直取心脏。他制定了一套宏大的战术行动,打算同时刺杀五大家族的首脑,为此建立了针对这些人的严密监控体系。可是,一周过后,敌方首脑突然潜入地下,再也不公开露面。

五大家族和柯里昂帝国陷入僵持。

第十八章

亚美利哥·邦纳塞拉的住处和他在桑树街的殡仪馆只隔着几条马路,所以他通常回家吃晚饭。晚饭过后,他总是返回殡仪馆,尽职地陪着悼念者向躺在肃穆店堂里的死者致敬。

他向来讨厌别人取笑他的职业和给死人化妆的繁琐技术。他的朋友、家人和邻居当然不会开这种玩笑。一个人靠汗水挣面包钱,做什么职业都值得尊敬。

今天,他和妻子在装饰华丽的公寓里共进晚餐,餐具柜上摆着圣母玛利亚的镏金雕像,红玻璃筒里烛光闪烁。邦纳塞拉点燃骆驼牌香烟,喝一口美国威士忌缓神。妻子把热气腾腾的两碗汤放在桌上。家里只有他和妻子,他把女儿送到波士顿,在妻子的姐姐家暂住,在那里忘记那段可怕的遭遇和创伤,让她受伤的两个恶棍已经受到了唐·柯里昂的惩罚。

妻子一边喝汤一边问:"今晚还要回去工作吗?"

亚美利哥·邦纳塞拉点点头。妻子敬重他的工作,但并不理解技术在这个行当是最不重要的。她和其他人一样,以为他挣钱凭的是让死者在灵柩里宛如在世的手艺。当然,他在这方面的技术确实远近闻名,但更重要也更必要的是他从不缺席守灵式。痛失亲人的家属晚上待在所爱之人的灵柩旁,接受亲友的悼念,他们确实需要亚美利哥·邦纳塞拉的陪伴。

他对死者的陪护一丝不苟,面容总那么庄重,但又很坚强,懂得安慰人;他的声音总那么沉稳,但又压低嗓门,主导整个哀悼仪式。他能缓和有失体面的悲恸,能斥责不守规矩但父母无心约束的孩子。他吊唁时从不哭哭啼啼,但也决不敷衍。一家人只要让亚美利哥·邦纳塞拉送别过一个亲人,下次就还会再来找他。下葬前,他会陪伴死者度过在这个世界的最后一晚。

他通常吃过晚饭要打个瞌睡,然后洗脸剃须,拼命抹粉以掩住浓黑的须茬儿,当然还要刷牙。他怀着敬意换上干净的亚麻内衣、白得发亮的衬衫、黑色的领带、刚熨烫过的黑色正装、黑色袜子和哑光的黑色皮鞋。不过,整体效果并不阴沉,反而很安慰人。他总把头发染得乌黑,这是他这一代意大利男人里闻所未闻的轻浮举动,但这不是出于虚荣,而是因为他有一头漂亮的花白头发,颜色在他看来与他的职业很不相称。

喝完汤,妻子把一小块牛排和几叉渗着黄油的波菜放在他面前。他食量不大。吃完这些,他喝着一杯咖啡,又点燃一根骆驼牌香烟。他边喝咖啡边想可怜的女儿。她再也不是原先的那个人了。外在的美丽已经恢复,但眼神像是受惊的动物,他见到就受不了。因此,他们决定送她去波士顿生活一段时间。时间能治好创伤。痛苦和恐惧不是死亡,还有挽回的余地,这一点他知道得很清楚。他的职业让他乐观处世。

刚喝完咖啡,客厅的电话忽然响了。只要他在家,妻子就不接电话,他站起身,喝完最后一口咖啡,揿熄香烟。他走向电话,边走边扯掉领带,开始解衬衫的纽扣,准备小睡片刻。他拿起听筒,彬彬有礼而平静地说:"你好。"

另一头的声音粗哑而紧张。"我是汤姆·黑根,"声音说,"我应唐·柯里昂的要求给你打电话。"

亚美利哥·邦纳塞拉觉得咖啡在胃里翻腾泛酸,有点想吐。为了给女儿报仇而欠下唐的人情债已经是一年多以前了,有恩必报的念头日益淡薄。当初看到两个小恶棍那血淋淋的脸,他感激得愿意为唐赴汤蹈火,但时间对谢意的侵蚀比对美的侵蚀还要更快。此刻邦纳塞拉难受得像是大难临头,答话的声音随之颤抖:"好的,我明白。我听着呢。"

黑根声音里的冷酷让他惊讶。顾问尽管不是意大利人,但待人一向彬彬有礼,此刻却显得粗暴蛮横。"你欠唐一个人情,"黑根说,"他相信你会报答他,你会乐于见到这个机会。一小时后——不会更早,但可能更晚,他会去你的殡仪馆请你帮忙。你去那儿迎接他。你的员工不必在场,打发他们回家。如果你有任何异议,请现在就开口,我来转告唐·柯里昂。他还有其他朋友愿意帮他这个忙。"

亚美利哥·邦纳塞拉吓得险些叫起来:"我怎么会拒绝教父?你怎么会这样想?我当然愿意照他说的办。我没有忘记我的人情债。我这就去殡仪馆,马上就去。"

黑根的声音软了下来,但语气有些奇怪。"谢谢,"他说,"唐对你很放心。有疑问的是我。今晚你帮他这次,以后遇到麻烦尽管来找我,你得到的将是我的个人友谊。"

这话吓得亚美利哥·邦纳塞拉愈加魂不附体。他结结巴巴地说:"唐本人今晚要过来?"

"对。"黑根说。

"这么说,他的伤势已经完全恢复了,感谢上帝。"邦纳塞拉说。他的语气让这句话像是个问题。

电话那头犹豫片刻,黑根最后异常平静地说:"对。"咔嗒一声,电话断了。

邦纳塞拉汗流浃背,他冲进卧室,换衬衫,漱口;但他没有刮脸和换新领带。他系上白天那条领带,打电话到殡仪馆,吩咐助手今晚和死者家属留在前厅,他在后面的整容工作区有事情要忙。助手疑惑发问,邦纳塞拉粗暴地打断他,命令助手严格执行他的指示。

他穿好正装上衣,还在吃饭的妻子惊讶地抬头看他。"我有事情要忙。"他说。妻子见到他的表情,没敢多问。邦纳塞拉走出住处,走了几个街区来到殡仪馆。

这幢屋子孤零零地矗立在一大片建筑用地上,四周围着白色栅栏,背后有一条狭窄的车道连接马路,宽度仅够救护车和灵车通行。邦纳塞拉打开门锁,敞开大门,自己走到屋后,从宽幅门进屋,一路上看见几个吊唁者从前门走进殡仪馆,去告别亲友的遗体。

许多年前,邦纳塞拉从一位打算退休的殡仪馆老板手上买下这幢屋子,当时屋前有个门廊,吊唁者必须爬上十级台阶才能进入殡仪馆。这就造成了一个问题。年迈的和行动不便的吊唁者有心想见死者最后一面,却不太可能爬上这些台阶,于是前老板就让他们使用货运升降机,这是个金属小平台,搭在屋子旁边的地面上。升降机是用来运送灵柩和遗体的,能降到地下,再向上进入吊唁厅,于是行动不便的吊唁者愕然发现他们从灵柩旁边冒了出来,而其他吊唁者还得挪开各自的黑色座椅,让升降机通过翻板活门。行动不便或年迈的吊唁者告别遗体之后,升降机再次钻出打磨抛光的地板,带他们入地再出去。

亚美利哥·邦纳塞拉觉得这个办法既不体面又吝啬,于是他翻修了殡仪馆的前院,去掉门廊,换成小坡度的行走步道。当然了,灵柩和遗体还是由升降机搬运。

屋子的后半部是业务办公室、防腐处理室、灵柩储藏室和存放化学药品和可怕工具的上锁密室,用一道厚实的隔音门与吊唁厅和接待室隔开。邦纳塞拉走进办公室,在办公桌前坐下,点燃一支骆驼牌香烟——他难得在殡仪馆抽烟——开始等待唐·柯里昂。

他在极度绝望中等待。他心里有数,自己是要接受什么任务。过去这一年,柯里昂家族和纽约的五大黑手党家族爆发战争,报纸上充斥着流血事件。双方各有很多人被杀。这次肯定是柯里昂家族杀了某个重要角色,他们想隐藏尸体,让尸体消失得无影无踪,还有什么办法比通过有执照的殡仪馆正式下葬更好吗?亚美利哥·邦纳塞拉对要交给他的任务不抱幻想。他将成为谋杀从犯。事情若是败露,他得蹲几年大牢。女儿和妻子将会蒙羞,他的好名声,亚美利哥·邦纳塞拉广受尊敬的名声,将被拖进黑帮恶战的血腥泥沼。

他破罐子破摔,又抽了一根骆驼牌香烟,继续想到更可怕的后果。别的黑手党家族发现他帮助了柯里昂家族,会把他当作敌人,会杀死他。他开始诅咒他去找教父求他报仇的那一天,诅咒妻子和唐·柯里昂的妻子交上朋友的那一天,诅咒女儿和美国和他的事业成功。再一转念,乐观精神回来了。不会出事的。唐·柯里昂很精明,为了保守秘密,肯定前前后后都安排好了。他只需要鼓足勇气就行,因为天底下没有比惹唐不高兴更致命的事情了。

他听见轮胎碾过砾石路面。他久经训练的耳朵说有车开过狭窄的车道,停进了后院。他打开后门,请他们进屋。大块头胖子克莱门扎先进来,接着是两个模样凶恶的年轻人。他们一个字也没和邦纳塞拉说,搜查了一遍各个房间;克莱门扎转身出门,两个年轻人和殡仪馆老板留在屋里。

几分钟过后,邦纳塞拉辨认出沉重的救护车开上车道的声音。克莱门扎出现在门口,背后是两个男人抬着一副担架。亚美利哥·邦纳塞拉最害怕的噩梦成了现实。担架上是一具尸体,用灰色毯子裹着,发黄的双脚在担架一头露了出来。

克莱门扎示意抬担架的人进防腐处理室。这时候,一个男人从后院的暗处走进灯光明亮的办公室。来者是唐·柯里昂。

唐在受伤期间掉了不少体重,动作僵硬得奇怪。他用双手拿着帽子,硕大头颅上的毛发显得很稀疏。比起邦纳塞拉在婚礼上见到的唐,他老了很多,缩了几圈,但仍旧散发着权势感。他把帽子按在胸口,对邦纳塞拉说:"唉,老朋友,准备好帮我这个忙了吗?"

邦纳塞拉点点头。唐跟着担架走进防腐处理室,邦纳塞拉缀在后面。尸体放在一张有沟槽的台子上。唐拿着帽子轻轻打个手势,其他人退出房间。

邦纳塞拉轻声说:"您要我做什么?"

唐·柯里昂盯着台子。"既然你敬爱我,那么我要你施展所有本领,所有技术,"他说,"我不希望他的母亲见到他这个样子。"他走到台子前,掀开灰色毯子。亚美利哥·邦纳塞拉违背了他的全部意愿,违背了他多年的锻炼和经验,禁不住惊叫起来。防腐处理台上那张被子弹打烂的脸属于桑尼·柯里昂。左眼浸在血里,晶状体上有一道星状裂纹,鼻梁和左颧骨打得稀烂。

唐伸手扶住邦纳塞拉,以免跌倒,但只持续了一瞬间。"看哪,他们怎么残杀我的儿子。"他说。

第十九章

也许是因为局势僵持,桑尼·柯里昂才踏上消耗战的血路,最终以他自己的死亡作结。也许是他阴沉暴力的天性失去约束,才落得如此下场。总而言之,那年春夏,他向敌方的从属人员发动了毫无意义的扫荡战。塔塔利亚家族在哈莱姆的皮条客被乱枪打死,码头的雇用打手遭到屠杀。警告效忠五大家族的工会上层保持中立。柯里昂家族的簿记和放债人仍旧被禁止进入码头地区,桑尼派遣克莱门扎率领分部在湾岸地区肆意破坏。

这种屠戮毫无意义,因为无法影响战局。桑尼是个出色的战术大师,战果辉煌。可是,此刻需要的却是唐·柯里昂的战略天赋。战争陷入你死我活的游击战,双方断送了大量的利益和性命,结果却得不偿失。柯里昂家族终于被迫关闭了一些最挣钱的簿记登记点,其中就包括送给女婿卡洛·里齐讨生活的那一个。卡洛从此沉溺酒色,成天和歌舞女郎鬼混,弄得妻子康妮的日子很不好过。自从挨了桑尼一顿痛揍,他再也不敢打老婆,但也不肯和她睡觉。康妮趴在他脚边哀求,却被他轻蔑踢开,他觉得自己简直是个古罗马人,举手投足带着优雅的贵族气息。他嘲笑他说:"打电话给你大哥呀,说我不肯搞你,说不定他会揍得我硬起来。"

其实他怕桑尼怕得要死,虽说两人还能冷冰冰地礼貌相待。卡洛觉察到桑尼会杀了他,明白桑尼拥有动物本性,能杀死另一名人类;而他要想杀人,却必须聚集起全部勇气和全部意志力。卡洛从没想到过,这是因为他比桑尼·柯里昂更有人情味——如果"人情味"能用在他们头上的话;他嫉妒桑尼身上那种被镀上传奇色彩的、可怕的凶残。

汤姆·黑根,身为顾问,他不赞同桑尼的战术,却决定不向唐提出异议,只因为这种战术在某种程度上也取得了一定效果。随着消耗战的继续,五大家族似乎终于低头,反击越来越弱,终于完全停止。黑根刚开始并不相信敌人表现出的和解姿态,桑尼却喜气洋洋。"我要乘胜追击,"他对黑根说,"那些杂种会来求我们和谈的。"

桑尼有别的事情要担心。他老婆给他脸色看,因为风言风语已经传进她的耳朵,说露西·曼奇尼迷住了她的丈夫。尽管她喜欢公开拿桑尼的尺寸和技巧开玩笑,但桑尼这次疏远她的时间太久了,她怀念两人的床上时光。她唠叨得桑尼很不好受。

除此以外,身为猎杀目标的桑尼还处于巨大的精神压力之下。他一举一动都得分外小心,他知道敌人肯定记录下了他屡次探访露西·曼奇尼。不过话也说回来,这是他一辈子的弱点,因此也防范得非常严密。他在露西那儿很安全。尽管露西一丁点儿都没有察觉,但桑蒂诺的部下每天二十四小时监视着她,她的那层楼一旦有公寓搬空,桑尼的可靠部属就会去租下来。

唐在逐渐恢复,很快将重新掌权。到那时候,战局必定会倒向柯里昂家族这边。桑尼对此深信不疑。在这段时间里,他必须捍卫家族的帝国,赢得父亲的尊重;另外,由于王位并不一定非得传给长子,桑尼还得巩固他的继承权。

可是,敌人也在制订计划。他们分析局势,得出结论:避免彻底失败的唯一出路就是杀死桑尼·柯里昂。他们现在对局面理解得愈加透彻了,知道他们有可能与唐和谈,因为唐是出了名的讲求逻辑和通情达理。他们越来越憎恨嗜血的桑尼,他们认为这种行径很野蛮,而且缺乏生意人的好嗅觉。没有人想回到兵荒马乱的从前。

一天晚上,康妮·柯里昂接到一个匿名电话,说话的是个姑娘,说要找卡洛。"你是谁?"康妮问。

电话那头的姑娘咯咯笑着说:"我是卡洛的朋友。我只想告诉他,今晚我没法见他了。我得出城一趟。"

"臭婊子,"康妮·柯里昂说,她对听筒尖叫道,"下三烂的臭婊子!"电话咔哒一声挂了。

那天下午卡洛去赌马了,半夜三更才回到家,由于输了钱而一肚子怨气,因为随身带着酒瓶而喝得半醉。他刚进门,康妮就破口大骂。他置之不理,进屋冲澡。从卫生间出来,他光溜溜地对着康妮擦身子,梳妆打扮准备出门。

康妮叉着腰站在那儿,气得横眉冷对,脸色发白。"你哪儿都不准去,"她说,"你的女朋友打过电话,说她今晚来不了。你个狗杂种,居然有脸让你那些婊子打到这个号码上。我要宰了你这个混蛋!"她扑向卡洛,又是踢又是挠。

他用肌肉发达的前臂挡开她。"你疯了。"他冷冷地说。康妮看得出他在担心,像是知道最近在搞的疯姑娘真会玩这种把戏。"她在捉弄人,神经病。"卡洛说。

康妮躲过他的胳膊,一爪挠向他的面门,指甲勾到了他的面颊。他耐心好得出奇,只是推开了她。康妮注意到他很小心,因为她在怀孕,这激起她的勇气,给怒火添了一把柴。她很快就什么都不能做了,医生说分娩前的两个月不能有性生活,而她很想做爱,因为最后两个月就快开始了。另外,她想在卡洛身上留下个伤口的愿望也很真实。她跟着卡洛走进卧室。

她看得出卡洛有点害怕,顿时满心轻蔑和欢喜。"你给我留在家里,"她说,"不准出去。"

"好的,好的。"他说。他只套了条短裤,没穿衣服。他喜欢这么在家里走来走去,他对自己的倒三角体型和金黄的肤色很骄傲。康妮饥渴地盯着他。他勉强笑道:"至少得给我弄点吃的吧?"

他在请她履行妻子的职责——至少是其中一项职责——这让康妮消了气。她做饭很有一手,这是从母亲那儿学来的。她嫩煎小牛肉和青椒,趁平底锅还在火上煨着,又拌了色拉。卡洛往床上一躺,研究明天的赛马日程表。他手边有满满一水杯的威士忌,时不时拿起来喝一口。

康妮走进卧室,站在门口,像是未经邀请就不敢靠近床边。"饭菜好了。"她说。

"我还不饿。"他说,眼睛仍旧盯着赛马日程表。

"已经在桌上了。"康妮固执地说。

"填你的屁眼去吧。"卡洛说，一口喝完水杯里剩下的威士忌，拿起酒瓶斟满，一眼也没看康妮。

康妮走进厨房，拿起盛满食物的盘子，狠狠摔进水槽。炸裂声引得卡洛走出卧室，他看着油腻腻的小牛肉和青椒溅得厨房满墙都是，引起了他的洁癖。"娇生惯养的黑皮臭婆娘，"他恶狠狠地说，"给我打扫干净，否则我就踢死你。"

"他妈的没门。"康妮说。她举起爪子似的双手，准备挠他赤裸的胸膛。

卡洛回到卧室里，拿着对折的皮带出来。"打扫干净。"他说，威胁的口吻毋庸置疑。她站在那儿一动不动，他挥舞皮带，抽在她垫得高高的臀部上，有点刺痛，但并不真有多疼。康妮回到厨房里，拉开橱柜，从抽屉里拿出一柄长面包刀，握在手里准备迎战。

卡洛哈哈大笑。"柯里昂家的娘儿们也能杀人。"他说。他把皮带放在餐桌上，大步走向康妮。康妮突然挥刀猛刺，但怀孕的沉重躯体拖慢了动作，他闪过攻击，她怀着杀人的渴望瞄准卡洛的腹股沟。他轻而易举抢下面包刀，开始扇她耳光，下手中等偏重，免得打破皮肤。他一巴掌连一巴掌扇过去，她绕着餐桌后退，想逃离他的魔爪，他追着康妮走进卧室。她想咬卡洛的手，卡洛揪住她的头发，拎起她的脑袋，又是几个耳光上去，直到她哭得像个小孩，因为疼痛也因为屈辱。卡洛轻蔑地把康妮摔在床上，拿起床头柜上的威士忌喝了几口。他这会儿已经烂醉，蓝眼睛闪着狂野的光芒，康妮终于真的怕了起来。

卡洛骑在她身上，就着酒瓶狂饮，伸手揪住一大块因为怀孕而发胖的大腿，使劲一捏，她疼得直喊饶命。"比猪都肥。"他厌恶地说，走出卧室。

康妮又是害怕又是胆怯，躺在床上，不敢去看丈夫在隔壁干什么。过了好久才起身到门口，偷看客厅里的动静。卡洛又开了一瓶威士忌，四仰八叉躺在沙发上，没多久就喝得不省人事沉沉睡去，她轻手轻脚走进厨房，打电话给长滩家里。她想请母亲派人来接她，但希望接电话的千万别是桑尼，最好是汤姆·黑根或母亲。

晚上将近十点，唐·柯里昂家厨房的电话响了。唐的一名保镖接起电话，恭恭敬敬把听筒交给康妮的母亲。可是，柯里昂夫人听不太懂女儿在说什么，康妮急得歇斯底里，一边却要压低嗓门，免得被隔壁房间的丈夫听见。丈夫打肿了她的脸，嘴唇鼓胀害得她口齿不清。柯里昂夫人向保镖打个手势，示意去找桑尼，他正在客厅和黑根谈话。

桑尼走进厨房，从母亲手里接过听筒。"是我，康妮。"他说。

康妮吓坏了，一方面怕她的丈夫，另一方面也怕大哥的反应，因此愈加口齿不清。

她说得颠三倒四："桑尼，派车接我回家就行，我回来了再和你说，没事的，桑尼。你别来。叫汤姆来，求你了，桑尼。没事的。我只想回家。"

这时黑根刚好走进厨房。唐在楼上的卧室，服了镇静剂已经睡下，黑根想盯着点儿桑尼，以防万一。屋里的两个保镖也走进厨房。所有人都看着桑尼听电话。

毫无疑问，桑尼·柯里昂骨子里的暴虐从某一口神秘泉眼里冒了出来。大家看得一清二楚，血液涌向青筋暴起的脖子，仇恨蒙住双眼，五官绷紧，继而抽紧；脸色变得灰白，就像病人正在抵抗死神，奔流全身的肾上腺素让双手颤抖。不过，他却控制住了自己的声音，压低嗓门对妹妹说："你等着，你等着就好。"说完，他挂断电话。

他站了几秒钟，被怒火烧得有点不知所措，嘴里骂着"狗娘养的，他妈的狗娘养的"，跑出了屋子。

黑根认得桑尼的这种表情，桑尼已经丧失了全部理性。这时候的桑尼什么都干得出来。黑根还知道进城那段路会让桑尼冷静下来，恢复部分理智。可是，那部分理智会让桑尼变得更加危险，保护桑尼不受愤怒带来的后果所害。黑根听见汽车引擎轰然发动，对两名保镖说："去追他。"

他拿起听筒，打了几个电话，安排桑尼住在城里的几名部下去卡洛·里齐家，带走卡洛。另外几个人陪着康妮等桑尼。阻挠桑尼发泄怒火有点冒险，但他知道唐会支持他。他害怕桑尼会当着目击证人杀死卡洛。他倒是不害怕敌方会搞什么名堂。五大家族已经沉默了很久，显然正在谋求和解。

桑尼开着别克冲出林荫道，这时候他已经部分恢复了神志。他注意到两名保镖开车跟了上来，暗暗嘉许。他不觉得会遇到危险，五大家族已经停止反击，不再继续交火。他出门时在前厅抓上了外衣，手套箱的暗格里有枪，车登记在分舵的一名成员名下，因此他本人不会惹上官司。不过，他不觉得会需要武器。他甚至都不知道该怎么收拾卡洛·里齐。

这会儿他有机会琢磨了，桑尼知道他不能让孩子没出生就死了爹，尤其这个爹还是妹妹的丈夫。不能因为两口子吵架就杀人，除非事情超出两口子吵架的范围。卡洛是条恶棍，桑尼觉得他有责任，因为妹妹是通过他认识这个杂种的。

桑尼的暴虐天性还有另一面：他没法打女人，也从来没打过；他不能伤害孩子和软骨头。卡洛那天不肯还手，桑尼因此没杀人；彻底投降解除了他的暴力武装。小时候他的心肠也很软，长大后杀人如麻只是命运使然。

这次我要一劳永逸地解决问题，桑尼心想，他开着别克驶向堤道过河，从长滩开到琼斯海滩的公园大道。他每次去纽约都走这条路，因为道路比较通畅。

他决定先打发康妮和保镖回家，然后和妹夫认真谈谈。接下来会发生什么就天晓得了。要是龟孙子真的伤害了康妮，他就打残那个小杂种。晚风吹过堤道，带着咸味的新鲜空气平息了他的怒气。他把车窗摇到底。

他和平时一样开上琼斯海滩堤道，因为在这个时节的这个深夜钟点，这条路总是空空荡荡，他可以肆意加速，一口气开到另外一边的公园大道。连公园大道也不会有多少车辆。开快车发泄一下有助于缓解情绪，他知道过度紧张很危险。他把保镖的车甩了很远。

堤道光线昏暗，除他之外一辆车也没有。他远远看见前方的白色锥形屋顶：一个有人值守的收费亭。

旁边还有几个收费亭，但只在白天交通繁忙的时候才有人值守。桑尼一边刹车，一边在口袋里翻零钱。口袋里没有。他用一只手掏出皮夹，打开，摸出一张纸币。开进有照明的通道，他有点惊讶地发现前面那辆车堵住了去路，司机似乎在向收费员打听方向。桑尼按喇叭，那辆车闻声前进，让他的车开到收费口。

桑尼把一块钱的纸币递给收费员，等着找零。他急着想摇上窗户。大西洋的晚风吹得车里凉飕飕的。收费员笨手笨脚地拿零钱，拿着拿着居然还弄掉了。收费员弯腰去捡零钱，头部和身体消失在收费亭里。

就在这时，桑尼发现前面那辆车没有走，而是停在前面几英尺的地方，仍旧挡住他的去路。与此同时，他的侧面余光瞥见右边黑洞洞的收费亭里还有个人。他没有时间思考了，因为前面那辆车里钻出两个男人，正在向他走来。收费员仍旧不见踪影。离一切爆发还有最后千分之一秒，桑蒂诺·柯里昂瞬间就知道他死定了。此刻他的思绪异常清楚，沥空了所有暴虐情绪，就仿佛潜藏的恐惧终于成为现实，净化了他的头脑。

即使这样，求生本能驱动他粗壮的躯身，撞向别克的车门，撞开了门锁。桑尼壮硕的躯体刚冲出车门，黑灯的收费亭里的男人就开火了。前面那辆车里下来的两个男人也举起枪，黑灯的收费亭里的男人停止射击，桑尼扑倒在马路上，两条腿有一半还在车里。前面过来的两个人朝桑尼身上又开了几枪，冲着他的脸连踢几脚，进一步毁坏他的容貌，表明这次刺杀有浓重的个人恩怨气息。

几秒钟后，四个人——三名刺客和假收费员——坐进车里，飞速逃向琼斯海滩另一边的草原小溪公园大道。桑尼的车和收费口的尸体挡住了追击的通道，但几分钟后，等桑尼的保镖停车看见桑尼的尸体躺在地上，却无意追赶凶手。他们兜个大圈子，调头返回长滩。在堤道上遇到第一部公用电话，一名保镖就跳下车，打电话给汤姆·黑根。他说得干脆而直接："桑尼死了，他们在琼斯海滩收费站截住了他。"

黑根的声音非常平静。"明白，"他说，"去克莱门扎家，叫他立刻过来。他会告诉你们该怎么做的。"

黑根是在厨房里接电话的,柯里昂老太太忙着准备夜宵迎接女儿。他表情镇定,老妇人没有注意到任何异样。倒不是她想注意也注意不到,而是她和唐生活了一辈子,早就明白别去注意才更聪明;明白如果她有必要知道的坏事,那么马上就会有人来通知她;如果是坏事但她不知道也无所谓,那么她还是不要知道为妙。她早就习惯了不去分担男人的痛苦,因为他们难道分担过女人的痛苦吗?她不动声色,给自己煮咖啡,把食物摆在桌上。就她的经验而言,痛苦和恐惧不会减轻肉体的饥饿感;就她的经验而言,吃东西能减轻痛苦。要是有医生企图给她用镇静药,她会勃然大怒,咖啡和面包就是另外一码事了;不过,熏陶她长大的毕竟是另一种更加原始的文化。

就这样,她望着汤姆·黑根逃进拐角会议室;而黑根一进会议室就开始颤抖,抖得太厉害,他只得坐下,并拢双腿,脑袋缩在拱起的两肩之间,双掌牢牢合起,放在两膝之间,仿佛在向魔鬼祈祷。

此刻他知道了,他不配做家族的战时顾问。他受到愚弄,上了大当,五大家族用表面上的退缩骗过了他。他们不声不响,布阵伏击。他们仔细策划,耐心等待,不管怎么挑衅都不出手。他们的等待是为了发动一次致命攻击。他们做到了。老占科·阿班丹多不可能犯这种错误,事有蹊跷,他肯定会想方设法弄清楚,会三倍小心提防。除了这些,黑根还感到悲伤。桑尼是他真正的兄弟,他的救世主,从小就是他的英雄。桑尼从不虐待他欺负他,始终用爱待他。索洛佐放他回来那天,桑尼紧紧拥抱他,重逢的欢喜发自肺腑。尽管他长大后变得残忍暴虐嗜血,但对黑根来说,这些都无关紧要。

他之所以要走出厨房,是因为他知道他无论如何也没法开口,告诉柯里昂妈妈说她儿子死了。尽管他视唐为父亲,视桑尼为兄弟,但他从未把她视为母亲。黑根对她的感情与对弗雷迪、迈克尔和康妮的一样,是对亲近他但并不爱他的人的那种感情。可是,他还是无法开口。短短几个月,她失去了所有的儿子:弗雷迪流亡内华达,迈克尔为了保命藏在西西里,现在桑蒂诺又死了。三个儿子里她最爱哪一个?她从没表现出来过。

仅仅几分钟,黑根就重新控制住了自己。他拿起听筒,拨通康妮的号码。铃声响了很久才传来康妮耳语般的声音。

黑根轻柔地说:"康妮,是我,汤姆,叫醒你丈夫,我有话要和他说。"

康妮惊恐地低声说:"汤姆,桑尼过来了吗?"

"不,"黑根说,"桑尼不会过去。别担心。你叫醒卡洛,说我有非常重要的话要和他说。"

康妮带着哭腔说:"汤姆,他揍我,要是他知道我打给家里,我怕他会再伤害我。"

黑根安慰道:"他不会的。他会听我说话,我会点拨他。一切都会好的。告诉他事情很重要,非常重要,他必须来听电话。懂了?"

过了差不多五分钟,听筒里才传来卡洛的声音,威士忌和睡意让他说得含混不清。黑根厉声说话,让他警醒。

"听着,卡洛,"他说,"我下面要说的事很糟糕,你给我准备好了,等我说的时候,你要用非常随便的语气回答我,我刚才告诉康妮说很重要,所以你得跟她说个故事,就说家族决定让你俩搬进林荫道的一幢屋子,给你安排一份好工作;说唐终于决定给你机会,希望能让你们过得更舒服。听明白了?"

卡洛答话时满怀希望:"是的,明白了。"

黑根继续道:"几分钟后,我的两个人会来敲门,带你们走。告诉他们,我要他们先打电话给我。这一句就行了,别多嘴。我会命令他们让你和康妮留在家里。听明白了?"

"明白,明白,我听明白了。"卡洛连声说,声音很激动。黑根紧张的语气总算让他警觉起来,知道接下来的消息会非常重要。

黑根没多废话:"敌人今晚杀死了桑尼。别说话。康妮趁你睡觉打电话给他,他在去找你们的路上被杀了,但我不想让她知道这一点,哪怕她已经猜到了,我也不想让她确切知道。她会认为这都是她的错。听着,今晚我要你陪着她,什么也别说。我要你和她修补关系,当一个完美的好丈夫。我要你一直保持这样,至少等到孩子出生。明天早上,也许是你,也许是唐,也许是康妮的母亲会告诉康妮,她的大哥被杀了。到时候我要你陪着她。帮我这个忙,以后有机会我一定照顾你。听明白了?"

卡洛的声音有点颤抖:"明白,汤姆,明白了。听着,我和你向来处得不错。我很感激。你知道的,对吧?"

"对,"黑根说,"不会有人责怪是你打康妮导致了这个结果,别担心。我会处理好的。"他顿了顿,轻声鼓励道,"去吧,照顾好康妮。"他挂断电话。

他已经学会从不出言威胁,唐教了他这一点,但卡洛完全明白了他的意思:他离死只差半步。

黑根又打电话给忒西奥,叫他立刻来长滩林荫道。他没有说原因,忒西奥也没问。黑根叹了口气。现在轮到最困难的一部分了。

他必须唤醒服药昏睡的唐,必须告诉全世界他最敬爱的一个人:我辜负了您,我没能守住您的国土和您大儿子的性命。他必须告诉唐:除非受伤的您披挂上阵,否则我们就将失去一切。黑根不想自欺欺人。只有伟大的唐亲自出马,才能收拾目前的惨败局面,哪怕只是返回僵持状态也好。黑根没有费神询问医生的意见,眼下没有这个必要。就算医生说唐死都不能从病床上起来,他也必须向养父报告情况,然后遵从一切指示。唐会怎么应对,这方面毫无疑问。医生的看法在此刻无关紧要,一切事情都无关紧要。唐必须得到消息,然后要么接过指挥权,要么命令黑根向五大家族交出柯里昂帝国的权力。

话虽如此,但黑根还是万分惧怕接下来的这一个小时。他尽量做好精神准备,克制自己的内疚。过分自责只会增加唐的负担,过分悲恸只会加重唐的哀伤。指出他本人担任战时顾问的缺陷,只会让唐自认判断失误,竟然选了这么一个人坐上如此重要的位置。

黑根知道,他必须通报消息,提出他的分析,说明该怎么办才能扭转局势,然后保持沉默。接下来唐要他怎么回应,他就怎么回应。唐要他悔罪,他就悔罪;唐要他悲伤,他就袒露心底的哀恸。

听见几辆轿车驶进林荫道的隆隆声,黑根抬起头。两位首领到了。他打算先和他们简单说两句,然后上楼叫醒唐·柯里昂。他起身走到办公桌旁的酒柜前,拿出酒瓶和一个杯子。他呆站片刻,魂不附体,甚至没法举起酒瓶斟酒。他听见背后的房门轻轻打开,转过身,见到的赫然是自遇刺以来第一次打扮整齐的唐·柯里昂。

唐穿过房间,坐进他那张宽大的皮革扶手椅。他的步伐有点僵硬,衣服挂在身上有点松垮垮的,但在黑根眼中,他和以前没什么区别。好像唐单凭意志就可以摆脱身体的虚弱。他面容坚定,带着往日的全部力量和强韧。他直挺挺地坐在扶手椅里,对黑根说:"给我一点茴香酒。"

黑根换了一瓶酒,给两人各倒一杯甘草味的烈酒。这是乡下土酿,比店里卖的烈得多,是一个老朋友的礼物,他每年都要送唐一小卡车这种酒。

"我老婆睡前在哭,"唐·柯里昂说,"我朝窗外看,见到两个首领都来了,但这会儿是半夜,所以,我的顾问,我想你应该把大家都知道的事情也告诉你的唐。"

黑根静静地说:"我对妈妈什么也没说。我正想上楼叫醒你,把消息直接告诉你。本来再过一分钟我就要上楼去叫醒你的。"

唐·柯里昂不动声色道:"但你必须先喝点酒。"

"对。"黑根说。

"酒你已经喝完了,"唐说,"现在请告诉我吧。"声音里有一丝最细微的斥责,针对的是黑根的软弱。

"敌人在堤道上对桑尼开枪,"黑根说,"他死了。"

唐·柯里昂连眨眼睛。有那么半秒钟,他的意志之墙土崩瓦解,肉身力量的枯竭清清楚楚写在脸上。但他立刻恢复原样。

他合拢双手,放在面前的办公桌上,直勾勾地盯着黑根的眼睛。"告诉我,都发生了什么。"他说,他举起一只手,"不,等克莱门扎和忒西奥来了再说,免得你再从头说起。"

没过几秒钟,两位首领就在保镖的护送下走进房间。他们立刻看出唐已经知道了儿子的死讯,因为唐起身迎接他们。他们拥抱唐,老战友当然有这个资格。黑根先给他们各倒一杯茴香酒,两人喝完一杯,黑根开始讲述今晚的前因后果。

听到最后,唐·柯里昂只问了一个问题:"确定我儿子已经死了吗?"

克莱门扎答道:"对。保镖虽然是桑蒂诺的人,但都是我亲自挑选的。他们来我家以后,我仔细盘问了好几遍。他们在收费站的灯光下看清了他的尸体。按照他们见到的伤口,他不可能还活着。他们敢用生命担保。"

唐·柯里昂接受了最终宣判的结果,没有流露任何感情,只是沉默了几秒钟。他说:"没有我的明确命令,你们谁都不准插手,谁都不准发动报复行动,谁都不准追查凶手的下落。我个人不点头,就不准再对五大家族采取任何战争行动。在我儿子下葬之前,我们家族将中止一切生意活动,并中止保护我们的所有生意活动。过后我们再在这里碰头,讨论接下来该怎么办。今夜我们必须尽量为桑蒂诺准备丧事,要让他有一个基督徒的葬礼。我会请朋友找警方和其他人安排各种琐事。克莱门扎,你带上部下,时刻陪着我,担任保镖。忒西奥,你保护我的家人。汤姆,你打电话给亚美利哥·邦纳塞拉,就说我今晚需要他的服务。请他在殡仪馆等我。也许要等一两个,甚至三个小时。都明白我的意思了吗?"

三个男人点点头。唐·柯里昂说:"克莱门扎,安排几个人和几辆车等我。我过几分钟就准备好。汤姆,你做得不错。明天早晨,我要康丝坦齐娅来陪母亲。安排她和她丈夫住进林荫道。叫珊德拉的那些女伴去她家陪她。等我告诉我妻子,她也会过去。我妻子会把不幸的消息告诉她,让女人们安排教堂望弥撒,为他的灵魂祈祷。"

说完,唐从扶手椅上起身。另外三个人跟着他站起来,克莱门扎和忒西奥再次拥抱他。黑根为唐拉开门,唐停下盯着黑根看了几秒钟,然后伸手摸着黑根的面颊,轻轻拥抱他,用意大利语说:"你是个好儿子,你安慰了我。"言下之意是说,黑根在这个可怕的时刻表现得体。唐上楼走向卧室,去通知妻子。就是在这个时候,黑根打电话给亚美利哥·邦纳塞拉,请殡仪馆老板偿还他欠柯里昂家族的人情债。

第五部

第二十章

桑蒂诺·柯里昂的死震惊了地下世界。等唐·柯里昂从病床上起身主持家族事务的消息传回来,参加葬礼的探子报告说唐似乎已经康复,五大家族的首脑发狂般开始准备抵抗必将爆发的复仇血战。谁也不会犯错,误以为唐·柯里昂遭遇了不幸就会变得容易应付。他这个人一辈子只犯过几次错误,而且每次都从中吸取了教训。

只有黑根猜到了唐的真正意图,见到唐派遣使者向五大家族提出和谈,他并没有吃惊。唐不仅提出和谈,还建议纽约市的所有家族举行会议,并邀请全国各地的家族参加。纽约黑帮家族的势力在全国占有优势,因此他们的福祉影响着全美国的福祉。

刚开始还有疑惑。莫非唐·柯里昂布下了陷阱?他想让敌人放松警惕?他打算用全场大屠杀给儿子报仇?不过,唐·柯里昂很快就证明了他的诚意。他不仅邀请全国所有家族参加会议,而且也没有采取任何备战行动或谋求盟友。接着,他迈出决定性的最后一步,证实了他的意图,让大家确信会议能够安全地召开:他请布其奇奥家族出面作保。

布其奇奥家族是个独一无二的势力,在西西里曾经是黑手党里特别凶恶的一个分支,来到美国却成了和谈工具。这群人曾经靠残暴和决绝讨生活,但现在的谋生方式甚至称得上圣贤之道。布其奇奥家族有个强项:他们靠血缘关系紧密结合,哪怕在这个对家族的忠诚高于对妻子的地下世界中,他们对家族的忠诚也称得上严苛。

加上三代以内的堂表兄弟,布其奇奥家族一度有两百来号人,完全统治着西西里南部一小块地区的经济。整个家族的收入来自四五个面粉厂,面粉厂绝非共有,只保障家庭成员的就业、生计和最低限度的安全。加上内部通婚,足以让他们构建起统一阵线抵抗敌人。

他们控制着西西里的一角,其他人不准修建面粉厂与他们竞争,不准修建水坝,不准向竞争者提供水源或损害他们的水力买卖。一次,某个有权势的大地主企图修建一个仅供自家使用的小磨坊,但磨坊遭到焚毁,他告到宪兵队和上级机关,导致布其奇奥家族的三名成员被捕。甚至还没等到开庭,大地主的庄园宅邸就被付之一炬。起诉和指控悉数撤销。几个月后,意大利政府的一名高级官员抵达西西里,建议修建大型水坝,以解决危害该岛多年的水源短缺问题。工程师从罗马来勘测地形,愠怒的当地人——特别是布其奇奥家族的成员——盯着他们的一举一动。警察涌入这片地区,住进专门建造的营房。

修建水坝似乎是势在必行了,给养和设备已经在巴勒莫卸下货轮,不过这些物资最远也就只到了巴勒莫。布其奇奥家族联系上其他黑手党首领,商谈之后得到支持。重型设备遭到毁坏,轻型设备干脆被盗。意大利国会的黑手党议员在政治上向水坝的规划者发动了反击。争论持续了好几年,直到墨索里尼掌权。独裁者判定水坝务必修建。结果仍旧事与愿违。独裁者知道黑手党业已形成法外之法,将有可能威胁他的政权。他全权委托一名高级警官办理此事,高级警官解决问题的办法很简单,他把所有人扔进监狱或流放去苦役岛。短短几年,他单靠随意逮捕有黑手党嫌疑的任何人,就打破了黑手党的势力,同时也毁灭了许多无辜百姓的家庭。

布其奇奥家族过于轻率,居然以暴制暴对抗这种不被约束的权力。半数男人丧命于武装冲突,另外一半被流放去了苦役殖民小岛。最后只剩下了屈指可数的几个人,朋友安排他们通过秘密途径跳船经加拿大迁居美国。移民不到二十人,他们在哈得孙河谷离纽约市不远的一个小镇定居下来,从最底层开始奋斗,后来有了自己的垃圾搬运公司和几辆卡车。没有竞争,他们渐渐兴旺发达。之所以没有竞争,是因为竞争者都会发现卡车被烧毁或破坏。有个固执的家伙压价抢生意,被发现埋在他收来的垃圾底下,窒息而死。

这些男人娶了西西里的姑娘,孩子当然要降生,而垃圾生意虽然能马马虎虎过日子,但买不起美国能提供的更加精致的生活。于是,布其奇奥家族拓宽思路,开始担任交战的各个家族之间的调解人和人质。

布其奇奥家族的血脉里有着愚钝,说是不开化也行。总而言之,他们明白自己能力有限,在组织和控制更复杂的生意体系(例如卖淫、赌博、毒品和公众欺诈)方面,没法和其他黑手党家族竞争。他们是直来直去的角色,能向普通巡警送礼,却不懂怎么接触政治掮客。他们的资本只有两个:信誉和残忍。

布其奇奥家族的成员从不撒谎,决不背叛。这些行为过于复杂。另外,布其奇奥家族的成员从不忘记受到的伤害,不惜一切代价也要报复。阴差阳错之下,他们意外发现了这个日后将证明对他们而言最挣钱的行当。

交战之中的家族若是想和谈和安排会面,就会联系布其奇奥家族。布其奇奥家族的首领亲自斡旋最初几次谈判,安排必要的人质。举例来说,迈克尔前去会见索洛佐的时候,就有一名布其奇奥家族的成员留在柯里昂家里,以保证迈克尔的安全,费用由索洛佐承担。要是索洛佐杀了迈克尔,那么柯里昂家族就将杀死那名布其奇奥家族的男性人质。接下来,布其奇奥家族将为这名族人之死向索洛佐寻仇。布其奇奥家族实在太不开化,所以决不允许任何东西、任何形式的惩罚挡了他们的寻仇之路。若是遭到背叛,那么你无论如何也防备不了他们,因为他们不要命也要复仇。布其奇奥家族的人质相当于烫金的保证书。

因此,见到唐·柯里昂雇用布其奇奥家族担任调解人,安排他们为参加和平会谈的所有家族提供人质,他的诚意再也毋庸置疑。背叛的可能性不复存在,这次会谈将和婚礼一样安全。

人质到位之后,和谈在一家小型商业银行的董事会议室举行,这家银行的总裁欠唐·柯里昂的人情,而且有一部分股份虽然归在总裁名下,但实际上属于唐·柯里昂。总裁的记忆中有珍宝般的一刻:他提出用书面文件证明唐·柯里昂对这些股份的所有权,以排除背叛的全部可能性,柯里昂却大惊失色。"我愿意把我的所有财产托付给你,"他告诉总裁,"我愿意把我的生命和儿孙的福祉托付给你。我无法想象你会耍花招或者背叛我。我的整个世界,我对我看人眼光的信心会土崩瓦解。当然了,我有我自己的书面记录,那是为了万一我遭遇不测,我的继承人会知道你替他们保管了这些东西。但是,我知道哪怕我不在这世上守护我儿孙的利益了,你也会忠实地满足他们的要求。"

银行总裁虽然不是西西里人,但一样很重感情。他完全明白唐的意思。教父的请求就是总裁的命令。就这样,在这个星期六的上午,银行的行政套间,配有松软皮椅的会议室,百分之百的私密环境,全都准备好了供各大家族使用。

一支精心挑选的小部队换上警卫制服,替代了银行的保安队伍。星期六上午十点,人们开始进入会议室。除了纽约五大家族,来自全国各地的另外十个家族也派代表参加——芝加哥除外,芝加哥是地下世界的害群之马,大家已经放弃了驯服芝加哥的打算,觉得允许那群疯狗出席这么重要的会议毫无意义。

会议室里搭起了小酒吧和自助餐台。每名与会代表允许带一个助手出席。大部分唐带的是顾问,因此房间里的年轻人相对较少,汤姆·黑根是其中之一,而且只有他不是西西里血统。他身上聚集了众人好奇的目光,是个异类。

黑根知道进退。他不说话,也没有笑容。他伺候唐·柯里昂,恭敬程度不亚于宠臣伺候国王;他给唐端冷饮,点雪茄,把烟灰缸摆在唐的面前——恭敬,但不谄媚。

房间里这么多人,只有黑根认得暗色镶板墙壁上挂的那些肖像画里都是谁。这些浓墨重彩的油画,大部分描绘的是金融界传奇人物。一幅是财政部长汉密尔顿。黑根忍不住要想,汉密尔顿肯定会同意在银行机构举办这场和谈。没有比金钱更能平心静气,更有助于纯粹理性发挥作用了。

召集时间定在上午九点半到十点之间。唐·柯里昂既然是和谈的发起者,所以算是主人,因此第一个到场;他的优点很多,准时就是其中之一。第二个抵达的是卡洛·特拉蒙蒂,他把美国南部变成了私人领地。这位中年人英俊出众,是西西里罕见的高个子,皮肤晒得非常黑,衣服和发型异常精致。他看着不像意大利人,更像杂志封面懒洋洋地躺在游艇甲板上的富豪钓客。特拉蒙蒂家族靠赌博业吃饭,见到这位唐,你很难想象他凭借什么样的残忍才建立起他的帝国。

他很小就离开西西里,定居佛罗里达,在那里长大成人,受雇于控制赌博业的南部小镇政客辛迪加。那些人是一群狠角色,有更加凶狠的警官撑腰,做梦也没想到会被这么一个初来乍到的移民打败。他们对他的残忍毫无准备,也无法匹敌,因为在他们眼中,要争取的利益实在不值得流这么多血。特拉蒙蒂用更大的份额争取警方,消灭了原先操纵赌博业的极其缺乏想象力的红脖子流氓。特拉蒙蒂与古巴的巴蒂斯塔政权建立联系,把金钱注入哈瓦那的赌场和妓院,诱惑美国本土的赌客成群结队前往。特拉蒙蒂如今的资产许多倍于百万富翁,拥有迈阿密海滩最奢华的酒店。

同样晒得黝黑的顾问陪伴特拉蒙蒂走进会议室,特拉蒙蒂拥抱唐·柯里昂,以同情的神色表达他对教父丧子的哀悼。

其他的唐陆续来到。他们彼此相识,打过许多年的交道,有时候是因为社交,有时候是因为追逐利益。他们一向以职业性的礼节彼此相待,在年轻还没发胖的时候都帮过别人的小忙。第三位到场的唐是底特律的约瑟夫·扎卢奇。通过恰当的伪装和掩护,扎卢奇家族在底特律地区拥有一家赛马场和很大一部分赌博业。扎卢奇面如满月,模样和蔼,家住底特律最时髦的格罗斯角,住宅价值十万美元。他的一个儿子娶了美国一个老牌世家的女儿。扎卢奇和唐·柯里昂一样精明世故。在由黑帮家族控制的各个城市里,底特律的暴力犯罪率最低,过去三年统共只处了三起死刑。他厌恶贩毒。

扎卢奇带着顾问,两人上来拥抱唐·柯里昂。扎卢奇一口美国腔,声音洪亮,只带着最细微的一丝乡音。他衣着守旧,很有生意人派头,也有良好的商誉与之相配。他对唐·柯里昂说:"只有你的声音才能召唤我来这儿。"唐·柯里昂颔首表示感谢。他可以指望扎卢奇的支持。

随后赶到的两位唐来自西海岸，他们在各方各面都联系紧密，所以乘同一辆车到场。两人是弗兰克·法尔康和安东尼·莫雷纳里，四十刚出头，比与会的其他人都年轻。他们的衣着比其他人稍微随便一点，言谈举止有一丝好莱坞风度，热情得稍微有点过头。弗兰克·法尔康控制电影工会和各片厂的赌博活动，并通过复杂的管道向西部各州的妓院输送女孩。一个唐混娱乐界不太现实，但是法尔康却干出了一点门道。其他的唐因此不信任他。

安东尼·莫雷纳里控制旧金山的滨海地区，在体育赌博的帝国里数一数二。他有意大利渔民的血统，拥有旧金山最好的海鲜餐馆，据说他以低价供应上等的食物，他对此颇感骄傲。他有一张职业赌徒的扑克脸，传闻他插手美墨边境和远东航道的贩毒事业。两人的助手年轻健壮，一看就知道不是顾问而是保镖，只是不敢携带武器参加会议。大家都知道他们的保镖会空手道，其他的唐只觉得很好玩，但毫无警觉之意，不会比见到加州这两位唐带着教皇祝福过的护身符进门更加警觉。显然这里有几位笃信上帝的虔诚信徒。

接着赶到的是波士顿家族的代表。没有赢得同侪尊重的唐只有这一位。他名声在外，不善待部下，无情地瞒骗手下。这倒是可以原谅，毕竟一个人的贪婪尺度全靠自己把握。不能原谅的是他无法维持帝国的秩序。波士顿地区有太多的凶案，有太多争夺权力的小规模战争，没人撑腰的散户犯罪，过于明目张胆地藐视法律。如果说芝加哥的黑手党是野蛮人，那么波士顿这帮人就是没教养的蠢货、土鳖。波士顿的唐叫多米尼克·潘查，是个敦实的矮子，按照某位唐的说法，越看越像小偷。

克利夫兰辛迪加也许是美国纯赌博业内最有权势的帮派，出席的代表是一位容貌秀气的老人，他苍白瘦弱，头发雪白。他的外号是"犹太佬"，理由和长相无关，是因为他身边的助手全是犹太人，而不是西西里人。有传闻说要是他愿意，他甚至会任命一个犹太人做顾问。正如唐·柯里昂的家族因为吸收了黑根而有"爱尔兰帮"的绰号，唐·文森特·弗伦扎的家族也有"犹太家族"的雅称，只是相比之下更加实至名归。不过他执掌的组织效率奇高，尽管长相秀气，但他可不怕见血，他用铁拳统治帝国，辅以柔和的政治手腕。

纽约五大家族的代表最后到场，汤姆·黑根不无讶异地注意到，这五个人比外埠的乡巴佬显得更加仪表堂堂，威严出众。比方说，纽约的五位唐符合西西里的古老传统，一个个都是"大肚汉"，象征着力量和勇气，也代表着身材肥胖，他们在西西里仿佛是这两种意思结合的化身。纽约的五位唐矮胖粗壮，生着狮子般的硕大头颅，五官也比常人更大，肉乎乎的鼻子，厚实的嘴唇，赘肉下垂的面颊。他们的衣服和发型都不怎么考究,完全是实打实不虚荣的生意人派头。

首先是安东尼·斯特拉齐,他控制新泽西地区,还有曼哈顿西区码头的航运业。他在新泽西经营赌博业,和民主党的政治机器联系紧密。他有一支货运卡车队伍,帮他挣了大钱,主要因为他的卡车可以超载,不会被公路超重检查员拦住罚款。卡车压坏路面,他的路政公司和州政府签合同修路,再捞一笔油水。这种环环相扣的生意链让任何人心里都美滋滋的。斯特拉齐也很老派,拒绝经营卖淫业,但生意范围在码头区,所以很难不卷入贩毒。在和柯里昂家族敌对的五大家族中,他的势力最弱,但组织性最强。

控制纽约州北部地区的家族负责安排意大利移民从加拿大偷越国境,经营州北部的赌博业,对州政府下发赛马场的许可证有否决权,家族的首脑是欧蒂里奥·库尼奥。他长着乡间面包师的快活圆脸,特别能让人放松警惕,台面上的生意是一家大型牛奶公司。库尼奥喜欢小孩,口袋里总是装满糖果,希望能逗他的众多孙儿或同事的孩子开心。他戴一顶软呢圆帽,帽檐像女人的遮阳帽似的垂下来,把圆脸盘衬托得愈加宽大,模样非常可笑。他不但是少数几个从未被捕过的唐之一,甚至无人怀疑他的真正营生,他进入几个市民委员会任职,而且被商会投票选为"纽约州年度优秀商人"。

塔塔利亚家族最亲密的盟友是唐·埃米利奥·巴齐尼。他经营布鲁克林和皇后区的部分赌博活动,经营部分卖淫活动,从事敲诈勒索。斯坦顿岛完全受他控制。他经营布朗克斯和西切斯特的部分体育赌博。毒品买卖有他一份。他与克利夫兰和西海岸联系紧密,是少数几个精明得对内华达州开放的拉斯维加斯和里诺感兴趣的人之一。他对迈阿密海滩和古巴也感兴趣。他在纽约和全国的势力仅次于柯里昂家族,影响力甚至远至西西里。只要是非法的生意,就有他的一杯羹——据说在华尔街都有个立足点。从开战以来,他用金钱和影响力支持塔塔利亚家族。他的野心是取代唐·柯里昂,成为全国最有权势、最受尊敬的黑手党首领,并接管柯里昂帝国的部分版图。他和唐·柯里昂颇为相似,但更摩登、世故,更有商业头脑。谁都不会说他是胡子彼得,还在往上爬的年轻而鲁莽的新一代首领都很敬重他。他冷酷无情,完全不像唐·柯里昂的温和,此刻他大概是这群人里最受尊敬的一位了。

最后一个到场的是唐·菲利普·塔塔利亚,也就是塔塔利亚家族的首领,他们支持索洛佐,从而直接挑战柯里昂家族的权威,险些获胜。有意思的是其他人都有点瞧不起他。原因很简单,大家知道他任凭自己受索洛佐摆布,甚至是被土耳其佬的手巧妙地牵着鼻子走。他要承担这场动乱的责任,这次骚乱严重影响了纽约各大家族的日常业务。另外,他是个六十岁的花花公子和老色鬼,而且有充足的机会放纵自己。

这是因为塔塔利亚家族经营的就是女人。家族的生意是卖淫业,而且控制着全国各地的大部分夜总会,能把有天赋的人安插去美国的任何地方。菲利普·塔塔利亚利用暴力手段控制有前途的歌手和喜剧演员,强行进入唱片公司。不过,卖淫业是家族收入的主要来源。

大家都不喜欢他的性格。他爱抱怨,总是唠叨家族生意开销太大。洗衣店的账单,那么多毛巾,吃干净了利润(但洗衣公司其实也还是他的)。姑娘们懒惰,不安分,有的逃跑,有的自杀。皮条客两面三刀,一丁点儿忠诚都不懂。好帮手真是难找。西西里血统的小伙子对这种工作嗤之以鼻,认为贩运和虐待女人有违尊严;他们宁可唱着山歌割喉咙,用棕榈叶编个十字架挂在翻领上。菲利普·塔塔利亚说话总是大吼大叫,居高临下,毫无同情心。他最嘹亮的吼声留给政府,因为政府有权颁发或撤销夜总会和歌舞秀场的酒类许可证。他发誓他付给这些管公章的窃贼的钞票比华尔街造就了更多的百万富翁。

说来奇怪,尽管他对柯里昂家族发动的战争险些取胜,却没能给他赢来应有的尊敬。他们知道他的力量刚开始来自索洛佐,后来又来自巴齐尼家族。还有一点是占尽先机的突袭没能让他全面取胜,这是他受到蔑视的缘由。他要是更有效率,就可以避免所有这些麻烦了。唐·柯里昂的死亡将意味着战争结束。

唐·柯里昂和菲利普·塔塔利亚在敌对的战争中都失去了儿子,因此两人只是拘谨地点头打个招呼也完全合乎情理。唐·柯里昂是注意力的焦点,其他人都在打量他,观察伤情和挫败是否让他流露出软弱。大家困惑的问题是唐·柯里昂为何要在爱子死后启动和谈,这等于承认失败,几乎肯定将导致他的失势。他们很快就会知道答案了。

众人打招呼,斟酒寒暄,又过了半个小时,唐·柯里昂在锃亮的胡桃木会议桌前落座。黑根谦逊地在唐的左后方就座。这个信号使得其他的唐纷纷走向会议室。助手坐在唐的背后,顾问坐得比较近,方便在需要的时候提供建议。

唐·柯里昂首先发言,说话的神态像是没有发生过这一切——他受重伤,大儿子惨死,帝国摇摇欲坠,家庭分崩离析,弗雷迪逃往西部受莫雷纳里家族的庇护,迈克尔没有躲在西西里的荒郊野外。他自然地说起了西西里方言。

"我想感谢大家赏光肯来,"他说,"我认为这是帮了我个人的忙,我欠你们每个人一份人情债。有句话我说在前头,我今天来不是为了争吵什么或者说服谁,只是想说说道理,尽一个有理性的人的全部力量,希望大家今天分手时都还是朋友。这是我保证要做到的,你们有些熟悉我的人知道我从不轻易保证什么。好了,我们谈正经事吧。今天在座各位都是有信誉的人,不像律师那样需要彼此签字画押。"

他顿了顿。其他人都没有说话。有几个人在抽雪茄,有几个人在喝酒。他们都是有耐心的好听众。他们有个共同的特点,属于那种罕有的人物,拒绝接受有组织社会的制约,拒绝听从他人的命令。除非他们自己愿意,否则绝不会向任何势力和个人屈服。他们用欺诈和谋杀守护自由意志。只有死亡,或者最符合逻辑的说理能摧毁他们的意志力。

唐·柯里昂叹息道;"事情怎么会走到这一步?"他没有期待回答,"唉,算了,愚蠢的事情已经发生。太不幸了,完全没有必要。请允许我从我的角度说一说究竟发生了什么。"

他停下来,看有没有人反对他讲述他看到的前因后果。

"感谢上帝,我恢复了健康,也许能及时纠正这件事。我的儿子大概太鲁莽、太固执了,这点我不否认。总之就这么说吧,索洛佐找我谈生意,请我用金钱和影响力援助他。他说塔塔利亚家族已经表示了兴趣。这门生意是贩毒,我对此不感兴趣。我喜欢安静,这么有进取心的生意对我来说过于闹腾。我怀着对他和塔塔利亚家族的尊敬,向索洛佐解释我的看法。我以最高程度的礼貌表达了拒绝。我说他的生意和我的生意毫无关系,说我不反对他以他的方式谋生。他误会了意思,于是给所有人带来不幸。唉,这就是生活。在座各位谁没有自己的伤心事?接下来的发展实在不符合我的意图。"

唐·柯里昂停下来,向黑根打手势,示意要喝冷饮,黑根马上递给他。唐·柯里昂润了润喉咙。"我决定讲和,"他说,"塔塔利亚失去了一个儿子,我也失去了一个儿子。我们扯平了。要是人们放弃全部理性,死揪住怨恨不放,这个世界会变成什么样子?这就是西西里的苦难根源,男人忙着复仇,没时间供养家人。实在愚蠢。因此现在我想说,过去的事情就让它过去吧。在今天之前,我没有采取措施调查是谁背叛了我的儿子,又是谁杀死了他。只要讲和,从今往后我也不会这么做。我的一个儿子有家不能回,我必须得到保证,等我安排妥当,他可以安全回家的时候,不会受到干扰,不需要担心政府。这件事安排好,我们再来谈与大家利益攸关的其他事情,就让我们今天帮我们自己——我们所有人——一个有利可图的大忙吧。"柯里昂用双手打个富有感染力的谦逊手势,"这就是我的全部愿望。"

这番话说得很好。正是大家熟悉的那个唐·柯里昂。讲究理性,能屈能伸,好声好气。可是,大家都注意到他声称已经恢复健康,这说明你绝对不能因为柯里昂家族遭遇种种不幸而轻视他。大家还注意到在所有人答应他提出的和平条件之前,讨论其他的事情毫无意义。还注意到他要求恢复原状,除了他在过去一年间的惨重损失,再也不会放弃任何东西。

回答他的却不是塔塔利亚,而是埃米利奥·巴齐尼。他说得言简意赅,既不粗鲁也不侮辱人。

　　"你说的都没错，"巴齐尼说，"但我必须稍微补充一下。唐·柯里昂太谦虚了。其实，要是没有唐·柯里昂的帮助，索洛佐和塔塔利亚就不可能开展那门新生意。事实上，他的拒绝损害了他们的利益。当然，这不能怪他，可事实仍旧是事实：法官和政客肯买唐·柯里昂的人情债，哪怕是贩毒也一样，但事情牵涉到毒品，他们不可能被除他之外的任何人影响。要是索洛佐不能保证他的手下会得到网开一面的待遇，那他就不可能开展行动。我们都清楚这一点，否则我们就是一帮穷汉了。另外，官方最近加重了刑罚，一旦我们的人惹了毒品的麻烦，法官和检察官就会狮子大开口。面对二十年徒刑，连西西里人都会打破缄默规则法则，知道什么就说什么。不能允许这种事发生。这个系统完全掌握在唐·柯里昂手上。他拒绝让我们使用，实在不是朋友应有的举动。他从我们家人的嘴里夺走面包。时代变了，如今不比从前，大家可以各行其是。假如柯里昂操纵着纽约的所有法官，那么他就必须共享资源，或者允许其他人使用。当然，他可以为此收费，我们毕竟不是共产主义。可是，他必须允许我们从这口井里打水。问题就这么简单。"

　　巴齐尼说完，会场陷入寂静。分界线已经画出，情况不可能恢复原状。更重要的是，巴齐尼的言下之意是假如和谈失败，他将在塔塔利亚与柯里昂的战争中公开加入塔塔利亚一方。另外，他的一个论点很有说服力。他们的生活和财富依赖于互相帮忙，朋友求你办事而被拒绝，这就属于侵犯行为。朋友不会轻易求你帮忙，你也不能轻易拒绝。

　　唐·柯里昂最后开口作答。"各位朋友，"他说，"我的拒绝并没有敌意。大家都了解我。我几时拒绝过行个方便的请求？那么做实在违背我的天性。但这次我不得不拒绝。为什么？因为我认为毒品生意在未来几年内将摧毁我们。美国对贩毒的恶感过于强烈。毒品和威士忌、赌博甚至女人不同，大众需要那些东西，只有教会和政府的上层想禁止。但毒品不同，牵涉到的人都要倒霉。毒品有可能破坏其他生意。有人认为我在法官和执法部门有那么大的影响力，我不得不说我受宠若惊，我真希望这是真的。影响力我确实有一些，但如果牵涉到毒品，许多平时很尊重我的看法的人就有可能不再尊重我。他们害怕卷入这门生意，对此有强烈的厌恶感。肯在赌博和其他事情上帮助我们的警察，说到毒品也会拒绝帮忙。因此，求我在这方面帮忙办事，就等于请我危害自己。可是，假如在座各位都认为这么做就可以解决其他问题，那么我也愿意配合。"

　　唐·柯里昂说完，会议室里的气氛顿时放松下来，众人开始交头接耳。他作出了重大让步。他将为有组织的贩毒生意提供保护。实际上，他几乎完全同意了索洛佐最初的提案,只可惜当初的提案没有今天齐聚此处的全国首脑一致支持。大家心照不宣,他不会参与直接经营,也不会出钱投资。他将仅仅运用他在法律体系内的影响力保驾护航。可是,这个让步已经堪称惊世骇俗了。

洛杉矶的唐·弗兰克·法尔康开口作答。"不可能阻止我们的手下进入这门生意。他们反正会自己下水,招惹麻烦。这门生意的利润太丰厚,诱惑无法抵御。因此,我们不插手反而更加危险。如果在我们的控制之下,至少我们能掩盖得更好些、组织得更好些,保证少惹些麻烦。经营这门生意也没那么糟糕,因为反正要有人控制、要有人保护、要有人组织,我们不能允许乱七八糟的人跑来跑去,像一群无政府分子似的,爱怎么折腾就怎么折腾。"

底特律的唐,他对柯里昂比其他人更加友好,出于理性也出言反对老朋友的立场。"我不喜欢毒品,"他说,"这些年我一直在花钱让手下不插手这门生意。可是没有用,做不到。有人找到他们说,'我能搞到白粉,你筹个三四千块投资,我们靠分销就能挣五千。'谁能拒绝这么高的利润?然后他们一个个忙着搞副业,撇下我花钱请他们做的事情。毒品里的钱更多,而且一天天越来越大。谁也不可能阻止,因此我们必须控制住这门生意,做得像样点儿。我不允许学校附近出现毒品,不允许卖给儿童。那是伤天害理。在我的城市里,我尽量把毒品生意限制在黑人——有色人种——内部。他们是最好的顾客,最不容易惹麻烦,再说他们本来就是动物嘛。他们不尊重老婆,不尊重家人,甚至不尊重自己。让他们吸毒丢掉灵魂好了。但是,我们必须采取措施,不能让乱七八糟的家伙为所欲为,给所有人带来麻烦。"

底特律的唐激起了众人响亮的赞同声。他说中了要害。你甚至不可能花钱让别人不贩毒。另外,他关于儿童的那番议论,是他众所周知的慈悲和温厚在说话。可话也说回来,谁会卖毒品给儿童?儿童又怎么会有钱买?至于让有色人种去贩毒,那简直是天方夜谭。黑人没有分量和影响力,他们允许社会如此践踏他们就是最好的证明。底特律的唐提起他们,也足以说明他总是被不相干的事所动摇。

所有的唐轮流发言。大家都哀叹贩毒是坏事,会招惹麻烦,但又同意无法限制。理由很简单,这门生意的利润实在太丰厚,因此必然会有人冒着一切风险去染指。这就是人性啊。

最后大家达成共识:开放毒品买卖,唐·柯里昂必须为东部的毒品生意提供一定程度的法律保护。不言而喻,巴齐尼和塔塔利亚两个家族将负责大部分成规模的活动。搬开了这块大石头,会议转向牵涉到更广大的利益的其他问题,还有许多复杂问题等待解决。众人同意设拉斯维加斯和迈阿密为开放城市,所有家族都可进驻。大家都认为这两个城市前途无量。众人同意这两个城市不得展开暴力犯罪,形形色色的小型犯罪将被清除。众人同意在遇到重大事件时,处决虽有必要但有可能招来公众抗议,那么处决必须经过本委员会的批准。众人同意必须约束纽扣人及其他部下的暴力犯罪和彼此间因个人原因而起的复仇行为。众人同意各大家族在接到请求时应该互相帮助,例如提供处刑人,例如在贿赂法官这种特定行动中提供技术支持,这在某些场合关系到生死。这种高层人员非正式的谈话很花时间,中间休会一段时间,在餐台和酒吧吃午饭喝酒。

最后,唐·巴齐尼试图把会议引向结束。"那么,所有问题都讨论完了,"他说,"我们得到了和平,请允许我向唐·柯里昂表示敬意,和他打了这么多年交道,我们都知道他言出必行。若是再有什么分歧,我们可以重新开会,不必冲动犯傻。要我说,这条新路充满生机。我很高兴事情终于得到解决。"

只有菲利普·塔塔利亚还有点担心。若是战争重新爆发,杀死桑蒂诺·柯里昂已使他成为群体里最脆弱的一个人。他第一次长篇大论发言。

"我同意刚才的所有决定,我愿意忘记我自己的不幸。可是,我想听到柯里昂家族的严格保证。他会不会尝试个人复仇? 随着时间过去,他的位置也许会更加牢固,他会忘记我们发誓永葆友谊吗? 我怎么知道他过三四年不会觉得自己受到了亏待,违背意愿被迫答应今天的协议,因此可以随心所欲打破誓言? 我们是不是非得时刻互相警惕,还是可以真的心怀和平去过和平的日子? 我愿意给出保证,柯里昂能向所有人给出他的保证吗?"

就在这时,唐·柯里昂发表了将被长久纪念的演说,巩固了他在众人中最具远见的领袖地位,演说充满逻辑常理,发自肺腑,切中要害。他在演说中创造了一个短语,日后像丘吉尔的"铁幕"一样变得人尽皆知,但到十年后才进入公众视线。

他第一次起身对委员会说话。他个子不高,因为"病况"有点消瘦,六十岁的年龄终究显出了几分老态,但无疑已经恢复了过去的全部力量,仍旧拥有过去的所有智慧。

"我们如果失去理性,那算是什么样的人啊,"他说,"没有理性,我们和丛林野兽还有什么分别? 但是,我们毕竟有理性,能够彼此说理,能够和自己说理。重新挑起所有争端,诉诸暴力和混战,能够满足我的什么目标呢? 我的儿子死了,这是不幸,我必须承受,不能让我周围的世界随我一同受苦。因此,我今天说,我以名誉发誓,我不会寻求复仇,不会追查往事的前因后果。我将胸怀坦荡离开这里。

"有一点我想说的是,我们必须看顾自己的利益。我们这些人都拒绝当傻瓜,拒绝当傀儡,被高处的人扯着线蹦蹦跳跳。我们在这个国家运气不错。我们的大部分子女已经过上了更好的生活。你们有些人的儿子是教授、科学家、音乐家——真是走运。你们的孙子也许会成为新的首领。我们谁都不希望见到儿孙走上我们的老路,那样过日子太艰难了。他们可以和其他人一样,我们的勇气赢来了他们的地位和安稳。我已经有了孙子,希望他们的孩子有朝一日能成为——谁知道呢?——州长?总统?在美国一切皆有可能。可是,我们必须跟着时代向前走。刀枪刺杀的年月已经过去。我们要像商人一样狡猾,从商的钱更多,对我们的儿孙更好。

"至于我们的行为,我们不需要对那些炮筒子、那些首领负责,他们擅自决定我们该怎么处理我们的生命,他们宣战,希望我们用血肉保护他们的战果。我们凭什么为了保护他人的利益而伤害自己?而我们看顾我们自己的利益,他们凭什么插手?这是我们的事业①。"唐·柯里昂说,"这是我们自己的事业。我们管理自己的世界,因为这就是我们的世界,我们的事业。我们必须紧密团结,抵抗外来的干涉。否则他们就会给我们套上鼻环,就像他们已经给美国的另外几百万那不勒斯人和意大利人套上了鼻环一样。

"为了这个原因,我愿意为儿子报仇,这是为了大家的利益。我现在发誓,只要我还负责指挥家族的行动,若是没有正当理由和遇到最激烈的挑衅,就连一个指头也不会举起来反对在座各位。我愿意为了共同利益牺牲我的商业利益。我发誓保证,以名誉保证,你们都清楚我从没有违背过誓言和名誉。

"不过,我也有个自私的目的。因为受到索洛佐和那位警长的凶杀指控,我最小的儿子不得不逃跑。我必须安排他安全回国,洗清污名。这是我个人的事情,我会自己做些安排。也许我必须找到真凶,或者向政府证明他的无辜,也许证人和线人会撤回他们的谎言。可是,我还是要说,这是我个人的事情,我相信我能把我的儿子带回家。

"但是,有句话我得说在前头。我是个迷信的人,这个毛病多么可笑,但我不得不说,要是什么倒霉的变故落在我的小儿子头上,要是某个警察不小心开枪打死他,要是他在牢房里上吊自杀,要是什么新证人冒出来证明他有罪,那迷信就会让我觉得这是因为在座有人还对我心怀恶意。再进一步说,假如我的儿子被雷劈了,我都会怪罪在座的某些人。要是他乘的飞机坠海,乘的船只沉入滚滚波涛,他得上致命的热病,汽车被火车撞了,迷信同样会让我归咎于在座某些人的恶意。各位先生,这种恶意,这种厄运,我可永远不会原谅。但除此之外,我愿意拿我孙子辈的灵魂起誓,我绝对不会打破我们缔结的和平。说到底,我们毕竟比那些双手沾满无数人类鲜血的领袖要好,不是吗?"

说完这些,唐·柯里昂从他的位置顺着会议桌走向唐·塔塔利亚的座位。塔塔利

---

① Cosa nostra:原文为意大利语,意为"我们的事业",指代黑手党。

亚起身迎接他，两人拥抱，彼此亲吻面颊。房间里的其他唐鼓掌，见到谁都使劲握手，祝贺唐·柯里昂和唐·塔塔利亚新建立的友谊。这恐怕不是全世界最美好的友谊，他们不会互送圣诞礼物，但他们也不会彼此仇杀。在他们的世界里，这样的友谊就足够了，需要的也只是这样的友谊。

由于西部的莫雷纳里家族庇护了他的儿子弗雷迪，唐·柯里昂在散会后和旧金山的唐多聊了一阵，感谢他的善意。莫雷纳里的话足以让唐·柯里昂明白弗雷迪在那头如鱼得水，过得很高兴，很受女人的欢迎。他似乎很有经营酒店的天赋。唐·柯里昂赞叹摇头，就像平常父亲得知孩子拥有他做梦也没想到的天赋一样。有时候最大的不幸也能带来意料之外的报酬，难道不是这样吗？他们都同意确实如此。柯里昂向旧金山的唐明确表示，因为庇护弗雷迪帮了他一个大忙，所以他欠旧金山的唐一笔人情债。柯里昂郑重表示会施加影响力，无论未来几年的权力结构发生什么变化，都保证旧金山的人能用上至关重要的赛马电报线，这个保证非常重要，因为围绕这个设施而起的争斗是个一直在流血的老伤疤，而芝加哥那帮人死抓着不放又让事态更加复杂。不过，唐·柯里昂在那个法外之地也并非毫无影响力，他的承诺就是价值千金的礼物。

傍晚时分，唐·柯里昂、汤姆·黑根和保镖兼司机——凑巧就是洛可·兰坡——回到长滩的林荫道。走进屋子，唐对黑根说，"今天的司机，那个叫兰坡的，多注意他。我觉得这个小伙子值得好好培养。"这句评语让黑根有点吃惊。兰坡一整天半个字都没说过，甚至没有瞥一眼后座上的唐和黑根。他为唐开车门，他们走出银行时车已经停在门口，他的每件事情都做得恰如其分，但这正是一个训练有素的司机应该做的。显然唐的眼睛见到了他没看清的东西。

唐让黑根先离开，吃过晚饭再来，抓紧时间休息一下，因为他们要彻夜讨论。他还吩咐黑根叫上克莱门扎和忒西奥。夜里十点，别早到。黑根要向克莱门扎和忒西奥通报下午会议的情况。

十点，唐在配备法律书籍和特别电话的拐角办公室等待他们三人。桌上的托盘盛着冰块、苏打水和几瓶威士忌。唐开始发布命令。

"今天下午我们缔结了和约，"他说，"我用誓言和名誉作了保证，这对你们几个人应该足够了。可是，那些朋友恐怕没那么值得信赖，所以我们还不能放松警惕。可别被下三烂打个措手不及。"唐转向黑根，"已经放布其奇奥家族的人质回去了吧？"

黑根点点头："我一到家就打电话通知了克莱门扎。"

唐·柯里昂转向大块头克莱门扎。首领点点头："我放他们走了。教父啊，我有个问题，西西里人真能像布其奥家表现出来的那么愚钝吗？"

唐·柯里昂微微一笑："他们够精明了，能过上好日子。有什么必要比这更精明呢? 搞得天下大乱的可不是布其奇奥家族这种人。不过你说得对,他们缺少西西里人的头脑。"

战争已经结束,众人的情绪都很放松。唐·柯里昂亲自调酒端给大家。唐品着他的那杯酒,点燃雪茄。

"我不要你们采取行动搞清楚桑尼的死因,过去的事情就忘了吧。我要你们与其他家族全面合作,哪怕他们稍微贪婪一点,我们没有拿到应得的份额也让着点。在找到办法接迈克尔回家之前,无论遇到什么挑衅,我都不允许破坏和平。这是你们考虑问题的首要前提。千万记住,他要回来就必须彻底安全地回来。我说的不是塔塔利亚和巴齐尼,我担心的是警察。没错,我们可以除掉不利于他的关键证据,侍者不会作证,另外一个人不管他是旁观者还是枪手也不会。我们最不需要担心的就是关键证据,因为我们知根知底。我们要担心的是警察会不会因为线人让他们相信就是迈克尔·柯里昂杀死了警长,从而炮制假证据。明白吗? 我们必须要求五大家族尽其所能纠正警方的观念。他们与警方合作的线人必须捏造出新说法。我认为听完今天下午我的演说,他们会明白这么做也符合他们的利益。不过这还不够。我们要想出更特别的办法,让迈克尔永远不需要担心这件事。否则他回美国也没有任何意义。我们都好好想一想,这是目前最重要的。

"唉,老天应该允许每个人一辈子犯一次傻。我已经犯过了。我要买下林荫道附近的所有土地和房屋。一英里之内,我不希望有人推开窗户能看见我的花园。我要在林荫道附近筑起围墙,我要二十四小时全面保护林荫道。我要在围墙上开一道大门。简而言之,我现在希望活在要塞里。就这么说吧,从今往后,我再也不去市区办事了。我将半隐退。我忽然很想摆弄摆弄花园,葡萄收成好就酿酿酒。我想住在这幢屋子里。只有度假或者有急事需要见什么人的时候才出去,出门的时候也必须采取所有预防措施。你们别误会,这不是准备打仗,只是小心谨慎而已,我这人向来很谨慎,生活中最不合我心思的就是粗心大意。女人和孩子能够承担粗心大意的后果,男人却不行。做这些事情的时候要慢慢来,免得心急火燎地惊扰了我们的朋友。表面上要做得自然而然。

"现在我打算把生意逐渐转交给你们三个人。我要解散桑蒂诺的手下,把那些人安排进你们的组织。这会让我们的朋友安心,表明我的和平立场。汤姆,我要你调遣一组人去拉斯维加斯,向我全面汇报当地的情况。汇报弗雷迪的情况,那边究竟在发生什么,听说我都要认不出我的儿子了。听说他天天下厨,和小姑娘寻欢作乐,超过了成年人应有的范围。唉,他小时候过于严肃,一直不是从事家族生意的那块料。不过我们先搞清楚那边究竟能做些什么再说。"

黑根静静地说:"要派你的女婿去吗? 说起来卡洛还是内华达人,他应该熟门熟路。"

唐·柯里昂摇摇头。"不行,孩子都不在身边,我老婆很孤独。我要康丝坦齐娅和丈夫搬进林荫道的一幢屋子。我要给卡洛一份有职权的工作,也许我以前对他太严厉了,再说,"唐做个鬼脸,"我的儿子不够数。把他从赌博业撤出来,安插进工会,让他做些文书工作,尽量多说话。他这人很健谈。"唐的声音里有最细微的一丝轻蔑。

黑根点点头:"好的,克莱门扎和我过一遍人选,调遣队伍去拉斯维加斯。要我把弗雷迪叫回家住几天吗?"

唐摇摇头,他冷酷地说:"回来干什么? 我老婆还能给大家做饭呢。就让他待在那儿吧。"三个人不安地动了动。他们没有意识到弗雷迪居然激起了父亲这么强烈的反感,怀疑里面有些他们还不了解的原因。

唐·柯里昂叹息道:"今年我打算在花园里种些青椒和番茄,吃不完就当礼物送给你们。我年纪大了,想享受一点和平,一点安静和清净。好吧,就这些。还想再喝一杯吗?"

这句话就是解散的意思。三个人站起身,黑根送克莱门扎和忒西奥上车,约定开会商量细节,实现唐刚才表达的愿望。接着,他回到房间里,他知道唐·柯里昂还在等他。

唐已经脱掉上衣和领带,躺在沙发上,严厉的面容松弛下来,露出疲惫的皱纹。他挥手示意黑根坐进扶手椅,说:"好了,顾问,你不赞成我今天的那些决定吗?"

黑根考虑清楚,最后答道:"倒是没什么不赞成的,但我觉得那些决定既不符合也没有真实表现你的性格。你说你不想查清桑蒂诺是怎么死的,也不打算复仇。我不信。你发誓维护和平,因此你将捍卫和平,但我无法相信你会拱手把敌人今天看似赢得的战果送给他们。你构造了一个我无法解答的巨大谜团,赞不赞成又从何谈起呢?"

唐的脸上露出满意的神情。"你比任何人都了解我。尽管你没有西西里血统,但我把你培养成了一个西西里人。你说的都没错,但谜团终究有答案,你会在它完全编织好之前看明白的。你看得出每个人都必须接受我的话,而我会信守诺言。我要你们不折不扣地执行我的命令。可是,汤姆,现在最重要的就是尽快让迈克尔回家。把这个当成你脑子里和工作中的首要任务。打通所有的法律关节,我不在乎你花多少钱。他回家必须回得万无一失。咨询最好的刑事律师。我会给你几个法官的名字,他们会私下接见你。事成之前,我们必须严防一切背叛行为。"

黑根说:"我和你看法相同,不太担心确实存在的证据,更担心他们有可能炮制的伪证。警察的朋友还有可能在他被捕后杀死他。他们会在牢房里杀死他,让其他犯人顶罪。要我说,我们甚至不能让他被捕和受指控。"

唐·柯里昂叹息道:"我知道,我知道。这就是难点了,而且我们不能拖延太久。西西里也有麻烦。那边的年轻人不再服从长辈,老派的唐实在控制不住很多被美国驱逐回去的家伙。迈克尔有可能被卡在两者之间。我采取了一些预防措施,他目前隐蔽得还很好,但迟早有露馅的一天。这是我必须和谈的理由之一。巴齐尼在西西里有朋友,已经闻到了迈克尔的踪迹。你那个谜团有了一部分答案:我必须用和谈保证儿子的安全。没有别的办法。"

黑根没有费事问唐是怎么知道这些情报的,他甚至不吃惊。这确实解开了部分谜团。"我和塔塔利亚家族商谈细节的时候,要不要坚持他挑选没有案底的人担任贩毒中间商?法官恐怕不会愿意轻判有前科的人。"

唐·柯里昂耸耸肩。"他们应该有想到这一点的脑子。提一提,用不着坚持。我们尽我们所能,但他们被抓住的人要是有毒瘾,我们连一根指头都别动。就说实在无能为力。不过,你不说,巴齐尼自己也想得到。你注意到了吗?在这件事上,他怎么都不肯直接表态。光看表面,你有可能永远不知道他到底有没有卷入。这种人永远都不怕被输家连累。"

黑根大吃一惊:"你是说他从一开始就是索洛佐和塔塔利亚的后台?"

唐·柯里昂叹息道:"塔塔利亚是拉皮条的。他怎么可能斗得过桑蒂诺?这就是我不必搞清楚前因后果的理由。知道巴齐尼插手就足够了。"

黑根慢慢理解这句话。唐给了他一些线索,但还有很重要的内容没说。黑根知道那是什么,但他的地位不允许他多问。他道过晚安,起身离开。唐还有最后几句话要吩咐。

"记住,运用你的全部智慧,制订计划让迈克尔回家,"唐说,"还有一件事。和电话公司的人安排一下,每个月我都要拿到克莱门扎和忒西奥打进打出的所有通话清单。我并不怀疑他们。我发誓他们绝对不会背叛我。但在出事之前掌握所有微小的细节也不会有坏处。"

黑根点点头,走出门。他琢磨着唐有没有用什么手段监视他,随后又因为他的怀疑而羞愧。但此刻他放心了,确信教父那敏锐而复杂的头脑已经制订出了影响深远的行动计划,白天的谈判仅是一次战术撤退。这里潜藏着一个阴森的秘密,谁也没有提起,他本人不敢问,唐·柯里昂避而不谈。一切都指向未来算总账的那一天。

第二十一章

然而,近一年以后,唐·柯里昂才终于安排妥当,让儿子迈克尔偷渡返回美国。在这段时间里,整个家族绞尽脑汁,盘算切实可行的方案。甚至向已经和康妮一起住进林荫道的卡洛·里齐征求了看法(在这段时间里,他们又生了第二胎,一个儿子)。可是,所有方案都没有得到唐的批准。

最后还是布其奇奥家族的一场不幸解决了问题。布其奇奥家有个叫菲利克斯的小表弟,还不到二十五岁,在美国出生,比家族的任何成员都要有头脑。他拒绝进入家族的垃圾搬运业,娶了个英国血统的漂亮姑娘,进一步和家族划清界限。他晚上念书考律师,白天是邮局的一名文职人员。在这段时间里,他有了三个孩子,妻子很会持家,所以一家人靠他的薪水过日子,等他考取法学学位。

这位菲利克斯·布其奇奥和许多年轻人一样,以为努力完成学业,掌握职业技能,德行就将得到回报,让他过上体面的日子。事实证明并非如此。他依然自负,拒绝了家族的全部帮助。他有个年轻的律师朋友,神通广大,在一家大型法律事务所就职,前途无量,说服菲利克斯帮个小忙。这个小忙非常复杂,看似合法,牵涉到破产欺诈。被揭穿的几率顶多百万分之一。菲利克斯·布其奇奥想试试运气。这场骗局需要动用他在大学学到的法律技能,他觉得看起来犯法并不严重,说来好玩,甚至不触犯刑法。

傻瓜的故事我们长话短说,骗局被揭破了,律师朋友拒绝以任何手段帮助菲利克斯,连电话都不肯接。骗局的两名主犯都是精明的中年商人,由于计划出了纰漏而疯狂斥责菲利克斯·布其奇奥的法律手腕太笨拙,接着认罪并和州政府合作,指名道姓地说菲利克斯·布其奇奥是骗局主谋,说他用暴力威胁控制他们的公司,强迫他们与他合作,执行那些瞒天过海的方案。证词把菲利克斯和布其奇奥家族几个有暴力前科的叔伯兄弟联系了起来,证据确凿而致命。商人得到缓刑,逍遥法外。菲利克斯·布其奇奥入狱一到五年,服刑三年。家族没有向任何家族或唐·柯里昂请求援助,因为菲利克斯拒绝向他们求助,理当给个教训:只有家族才会向你施恩,家族比社会更加忠实,更加值得信赖。

总而言之,服刑三年后,菲利克斯·布其奇奥出狱回家,亲吻妻子和三个孩子,安安静静住了一年,随后用行动证明他毕竟还是布其奇奥家族的成员。他没有隐瞒罪行的打算,购买一把手枪,射杀了他那位律师朋友。接着,他找到那两名商人,在他们走出一家小餐馆的时候,冷静地开枪打穿两颗脑袋。他连看也没多看马路上的尸体一眼,走进小餐馆,点了一杯咖啡,坐等警察来逮捕他。

审讯迅速,判决无情。黑帮成员罪有应得坐牢,出狱后残忍杀害指认他的证人。这是公然嘲笑社会正义,民众、媒体和社会组织体系破天荒地意见一致,连耳朵软心肠软的人道主义者都要求送菲利克斯·布其奇奥上电椅。按照州长身边最亲密的政治助手的说法,动物收容所对疯狗有多同情,州长待他就有多慈悲。布其奇奥家族终于为他自豪了,只要能向更高一级法院上诉,花多少钱都愿意,但结论却无法改变。各种法律手续虽说能拖延一点时间,但菲利克斯·布其奇奥将死在电椅上。

布其奇奥家的一名成员希望能为这个年轻人做点什么,黑根应他的要求,请唐关注一下这个案件。唐·柯里昂断然拒绝。他又不是魔术师。布其奇奥家的请求完全不可能实现。但第二天,唐打电话叫黑根来他的办公室,吩咐他详详细细从头到尾讲一遍这个案子。等黑根说完,唐·柯里昂叫他请布其奇奥家族的首领来林荫道会面。

接下来的事情简单而绝妙。唐·柯里昂向布其奇奥家族的首领保证,菲利克斯·布其奇奥的妻子将得到一笔不菲的抚恤金,立刻交付给布其奇奥家族。作为回报,菲利克斯必须认罪,是他谋杀了索洛佐和麦克劳斯凯警长。

还有许多细节需要安排。菲利克斯·布其奇奥的坦白必须真实可信,因此他必须了解部分真实的细节。另外,他必须把警长牵涉进贩毒活动。要说服月亮餐馆的侍者,指认菲利克斯·布其奇奥是杀人犯。这需要一定的勇气,因为描述将有翻天覆地的变化:菲利克斯·布其奇奥比迈克尔·柯里昂矮得多也胖得多。不过这个问题交给唐·柯里昂解决。另外,由于被判死刑的年轻人笃信高等教育,也是大学毕业生,他会希望他的孩子也能念大学。因此,唐·柯里昂将一次性承担孩子的大学教育费用。他还要说服布其奇奥家族,原先的三条人命已经让菲利克斯·布其奇奥不可能得到豁免,多认罪只是给本已确定的命运贴上封条而已。

一切都安排妥当了,钱如数给到位,适当接触死刑犯,传达指示和建议。终于,计划实施,认罪登上所有报纸的头条。整件事获得巨大成功。可是,唐·柯里昂和以往一样谨慎,等到菲利克斯·布其奇奥处刑后又过了四个月,这才下令让迈克尔回家。

第二十二章

桑尼死后一年,露西·曼奇尼仍旧非常想念他,哀悼之情超过了任何浪漫故事里的情人。她不是像纯情少女或者忠贞妻子一样思念、渴求他。她也没有因失去"人生伴侣"而寂寞,或是想念他的健壮体魄。她怀恋的不是饱含感情的礼物、小女孩的英雄崇拜和他的笑容,也不是她说了什么惹人怜爱或者俏皮机智的话时他眼中好笑的亮光。

不。她想念他的理由更加重要:他曾是全世界唯一能让她的躯体完成爱情行为的男人。在她年轻而天真的脑袋里,仍旧相信只有他才有可能做到这件事。

如今一年过去了,她在内华达的芬芳微风中晒着日光浴。她的脚边坐着一个身材瘦削的金发年轻男人,他正在抚弄她的脚趾。两人在酒店的游泳池边消磨周日的下午时光,尽管周围有那么多人,男人的手还是顺着她赤裸的大腿滑了上来。

"喂,朱尔斯,停下,"露西说,"我还以为医生好歹不会像普通男人那么轻浮呢。"

朱尔斯咧嘴一笑:"我是拉斯维加斯的医生。"他轻挠她的大腿内侧,惊讶于一个小小动作就能惹得她那么兴奋。尽管她极力掩饰,但兴奋还是在脸上流露了出来。真是一个淳朴天真的姑娘。可是,他为什么就是无法让她就范呢?他必须搞清楚这一点,什么爱情失去就永远无法弥补之类的鬼话就算了吧。他的手底下是个活生生的器官,活生生的器官需要另外一个活生生的器官。朱尔斯·西格尔医生下定决心,今晚他要在房间里迈出这一大步。他原本打算不要花招就让她就范,但如果非得要花招的话,他可是行家——当然,都是出于对科学的兴趣,再说这可怜的孩子也想得要命。

"朱尔斯,停下,求你了,停下。"露西说,声音在颤抖。

朱尔斯立刻懊悔起来。"好的,宝贝儿。"他说。他把脑袋放在她的膝头,用柔软的大腿当枕头,打了个小盹。她的蠕动和她滚烫的下体让他觉得很有意思;她用手梳理他的头发,他开玩笑似的抓住她的手腕,像情人一样握在手里,实际上是在量她的脉搏——跳得很厉害,他今晚就能把她弄到手,解开这个谜团,看到到底是为什么。朱尔斯·西格尔医生满怀信心,沉沉入睡。

露西望着泳池边的人们。她怎么也不可能想到不足两年,生活就能变得这么厉害。她从没后悔过自己在康妮·柯里昂婚礼那天的"犯蠢"。那是她遇到过的最美好的事情,她在梦中一遍又一遍重温那一刻,就像她在婚礼之后的那几个月里一遍又一遍地重温一样。

桑尼每周找她一次,有时多些,从没少过。每次见他的前几天里,她的躯体经受着煎熬。他们对彼此的激情是最原始的那一种,没有掺杂诗意和任何形式的理性。那是最原始的天性,是肉欲之爱,是器官对器官的爱。

每次桑尼打电话说要来,她就确保公寓里备足晚餐和早餐所需的酒水和食物,因为他通常要到第二天上午才离开。他想饱尝她的滋味,正如她想饱尝他的滋味。他有公寓钥匙,每次一进门,她就会飞扑进他健壮的怀抱。两人都像野蛮人一样直接、原始,刚开始接吻就摸索着解对方的衣服,他把她举在半空中,她用双腿缠住他粗壮的大腿。他们站在门厅里做爱,就仿佛他们必须重演当初的第一幕,然后他就这么抱着她走进卧室。

他们会在床上做爱,会在公寓里一待就是十六个钟头,完全赤裸。她会给他做饭,丰盛的大餐。他有时候会接几个电话,显然是谈正经事,但她一个字也没听进去过。她会忙着玩弄他的躯体,爱抚它,亲吻它,用嘴巴吞没它。有时候他起身去拿饮料,从她身边走过,她忍不住要伸手触摸他赤裸的躯体,抓住他,和他做爱,就仿佛他身上那特殊的器官是一件玩具,一件构造特殊而精巧但纯粹的玩具,独立存在,能带来难以想象的销魂体验。刚开始她对自己的荒淫还有点羞愧,但很快发现这些行为也让情人开心,她彻底沦为他的胯下之臣使得他飘飘欲仙。他们的关系里有着动物般的单纯,彼此都很高兴。

桑尼的父亲在街上遇到刺杀,她立刻意识到情人也有危险。她独自待在公寓里,没有黯然垂泪,而是大声嚎哭——动物般的嚎哭。桑尼一连三个星期没来找她,她靠安眠药、酒精和愤懑过日子。她感觉到的痛楚是肉体上的痛楚,她的躯体疼痛难忍。后来他终于来了,她几乎每时每刻地抓着他不放。接下来他至少每周来一次,直到遇害。

她通过报纸得知他的死讯,那天晚上,她吞了大剂量的安眠药。不知为何,安眠药没有杀死她,而是让她非常难受,她跟跟跄跄地来到公寓的走廊上,晕倒在电梯门口,被人发现后送进医院。她和桑尼的关系很少有人知道,因此只在地摊小报上得到了几英寸的版面。

她在医院里的时候,是汤姆·黑根来医院探望和安慰她,也是汤姆·黑根给她在拉斯维加斯安排了一份工作,去桑尼的弟弟弗雷迪经营的酒店做事,还是汤姆·黑根说柯里昂家族将给她一笔年金,是桑尼给她准备的。黑根问她有没有怀孕,怀疑她就是为此吃安眠药的,她说没有。黑根问她桑尼在遇难的那天夜里有没有来见她,有没有打电话说要来见她,她说桑尼没有来见她,也没打过电话。说她每天下班后都在家里等桑尼。她对黑根说了实话。"他是我这辈子唯一爱过的男人,"她说,"我再也没法爱别人了。"她看见他露出一丝微笑,同时也有点诧异。"就那么难以置信吗?"她问,"他不是把小时候的你领回家了吗?"

"那时候的他是另外一个人,"黑根说,"长大后变成了另外一种男人。"

"对我来说不是,"露西说,"也许对别人来说都是的,但对我来说不是。"她还很虚弱,无法解释桑尼待她有多么温柔,从不对她发火,甚至都不烦躁和紧张。

黑根安排妥当,送她去了拉斯维加斯。有一套租来的公寓在等她,他亲自送露西去机场,请她答应,只要觉得孤单或者过得不顺心就打电话给他,他会尽可能地帮助她。

她登机之前,吞吞吐吐地问黑根:"桑尼的父亲知道你做的这些事情吗?"

黑根笑着说:"我不但代表自己,也代表他。他在这方面很老派,不会做不利于儿子的合法妻子的事情,但他觉得你还太年轻,桑尼应该更懂事才对。可你吃安眠药却吓住了大家。"他没有详细解释,在唐这样的人看来,一个人试图自杀是多么不可思议的事情。

在拉斯维加斯住了十八个月之后,她惊讶地发现自己过得还算开心。有些夜晚她会梦见桑尼,黎明前醒来后躺在那里,一边爱抚自己一边继续做梦,直到重新入眠。她一直没有新男人。拉斯维加斯的生活很合她胃口。每逢休息日,她就在酒店泳池游泳,泛舟米德湖上,驱车穿越沙漠。她瘦了下来,体形变得更好。她仍旧性感,但更接近美国,而不是古老的意大利风格。她在酒店的公关部门担任接待员,和弗雷迪没什么关系,不过弗雷迪每次见到她都要停下聊几句。她对弗雷迪的变化很吃惊。弗雷迪像个花花公子,衣着时髦,似乎对经营赌博饭店很有天赋。他控制的是客房部,赌场东家一般不插手这个行当。夏季漫长而炎热,加上也许过于活跃的性生活,弗雷迪也瘦了不少,好莱坞风格的服侍让他风度翩翩,潇洒得要命。

她到拉斯维加斯六个月后,汤姆·黑根来看她过得怎么样。除了工资,她每个月收到一张六百美元的支票。黑根解释说这笔钱必须做得像是另有来路,请她签署一份授权委托书,方便他调拨钱款。他还说她将从形式上拥有她工作的这家酒店的五"点"股份。她得办理内华达法律要求的所有法律手续,不过所有事情都由别人处理,她本人的不便将微乎其微。但是,没有他的同意,她不能和任何人讨论这方面的安排。她将在各方面得到法律的保护,每个月肯定能拿到那笔津贴。要是政府或执法机构有问题,她只要把所有的事情交给律师就不会有麻烦了。

露西同意了。她明白在发生什么,但并不介意被这么利用。似乎是个合情合理的小恩惠。可是,黑根又请她盯着点儿酒店里的事情,盯着点儿弗雷迪和弗雷迪的老板——他拥有和经营客房部,是大股东——露西说:"什么,汤姆,你不是要我监视弗雷迪吧?"

黑根笑着答道:"弗雷迪的父亲很担心他。他和莫·格林走得很近,我们只想确保他别招惹麻烦。"他没费神解释说唐之所以在拉斯维加斯这种荒漠里资助建设酒店,不单是为了给儿子提供避难所,也是想踏进更大规模商业活动的门槛。

这次会面过后不久,朱尔斯·西格尔来到酒店担任特聘医师。他非常瘦削英俊,魅力过人,当医生似乎有点过于年轻,至少在露西看来是这样。她因为手腕长了个肿块而认识了他。她担心了好几天,终于在一天上午走进医生在酒店的诊室。两个合唱队的歌舞女郎在候诊室里聊天,都是桃红肤色的金发美女,露西一直很羡慕这种美丽。她们貌若女神,但其中一个却在说:"我发誓,再得一次性病,我就不跳舞了。"

朱尔斯·西格尔医生打开诊室的门,示意一名歌舞女郎进去,露西真想转身就走,要是她的问题更加私密和严重,那就肯定走了。西格尔医生穿休闲裤,翻领衬衫。还好角质框眼镜帮了忙,气质显得沉静而稳重,不过总的来说让人觉得不太庄重。和很多骨子里的老派人一样,露西觉得和医学有关的事情不可能是随随便便的。

等她终于走进诊所,他的谈吐举止显得那么能安慰人,打消了她的全部顾虑。他很少开口,但并不唐突,而且不紧不慢。她问肿块是怎么回事,他耐心地解释说只是个很常见的纤维增生,不可能是恶性的,也不需要大惊小怪。他拿起一本厚厚的医学书,说:"伸出胳膊。"

露西犹犹豫豫地伸出胳膊。他第一次对她露出笑容:"我要让自己损失一笔外科手术费了,"他说,"我要用这本书砸平它。也许还会再冒出来,不过要是动外科手术摘除,你会破费一大笔,要缠绷带还有很多麻烦事,如何?"

她报以微笑。不知为何,露西完全信任他。"好的。"她说。接下来的一瞬间,沉重的医学书拍在她的手臂上,她惊叫一声。肿块几乎平了。

"有那么疼吗?"他问。

"没有,"她说。她看着他填写病历卡,"就这样?"

他点点头,没再多看她一眼。她起身离开。

一周后,他在咖啡馆遇到露西,到吧台前挨着她坐下。"胳膊怎么样?"他问。

她笑着答道:"很好。你真是不守常规,但确实有一手。"

他咧嘴一笑。"你还不知道我有多不守常规呢。我也不知道你有多有钱。《维加斯太阳报》刚发表了这家酒店的股东名单,露西·曼奇尼足足有十个点。我应该利用那个小肿块发一笔财啊。"

她没有吭声,忽然想起了黑根的提醒。他又咧嘴一笑。"别担心,我知道规矩,你只是傀儡而已,拉斯维加斯到处是这种人。今晚陪我看演出怎么样?我请你吃晚饭。还可以请你玩几把轮盘赌。"

她有点拿不准。他极力怂恿。最后,她说:"我去是想去,但你恐怕会对今晚的结果失望。我可不像拉斯维加斯的大部分女孩那么随便。"

"所以我才邀请你啊,"朱尔斯兴高采烈道,"我给自己开了休息一晚的处方。"

露西对他笑了笑,有点伤感地说:"就那么明显?"他摇摇头,她说:"好吧,那就吃个晚餐,不过轮盘赌的筹码我自己买。"

他们去吃晚餐看表演,朱尔斯逗得她很开心,用医学术语描述各种类型的赤裸大腿和胸部，但不是讥笑，而是善意的玩笑。吃过饭，他们在同一个轮盘下注，赢了一百多块。接下来，两人在月光下开车去顽石大坝，他试图和她做爱，但她在几次亲吻后开始抵抗，他知道她是真的不愿意，只得罢手。他欣然接受失败。"我说过不行了。"露西有点不好意思地责备道。

"要是我连试也不试，你会觉得受到了莫大的屈辱。"朱尔斯说。她不得不哈哈大笑，因为确实如此。

接下来的几个月里，他们成了好朋友。不是情侣，因为没有做爱，露西不允许。她看得出她的拒绝让他困惑，但没有像大多数男人那样受到伤害，这反而让她愈加信任他了。她发现在医生的职业外表下，他这个人狂放不羁，喜爱玩乐。每逢周末，他就开着一辆改装名爵轿车去加州赛车。有机会休假，他会深入墨西哥内陆，真正的蛮荒之地，他说陌生人在那儿会因为一双鞋丢掉性命，生活和一千年前一样原始。露西偶然得知他是个外科医生，曾经就职于纽约的一家著名医院。

她不禁对他为何接受酒店的工作感到更加困惑。她问起此事，朱尔斯答道："你告诉我你最隐秘的秘密，我就告诉你我的。"

她脸红了，没说下去。朱尔斯没有追问，两人的关系一如既往，她对这份温暖友情的依赖超出了自己的意料。

此刻，坐在泳池边，朱尔斯长着金发的脑袋搁在她的膝头，她对他产生了难以遏制的柔情。她的下体一阵胀痛，她的手指不由自主充满欲望地爱抚他的脖子。他似乎睡着了，没有注意到，单是感觉到他贴着自己，她就兴奋了起来。他忽然从她的膝头抬起脑袋，站起身，抓住她的手，领着她穿过草坪，走上水泥步道。她乖乖地跟着他，听凭他领着她走进他居住的一幢独立小屋。进了房间，他给两人调了两大杯酒。经过烈日暴晒和淫靡的念头，酒精径直冲进大脑，让她头晕目眩。朱尔斯搂住她，除了几小片浴衣之外赤裸裸的两具躯体彼此紧贴。露西喃喃道："不要。"但声音毫无说服力，朱尔斯也不加理睬。他很快脱掉她的胸罩，抚弄和亲吻她沉甸甸的双乳，接着剥掉她的短裤，一边亲吻她的躯体，她浑圆的肚脐和大腿内侧。他站起身，好不容易褪掉自己的短裤，搂紧她，两个人赤裸裸地彼此拥抱，倒在他的床上，她感觉到他进入了自己的身体——这就够了，光是那轻微的触感，就让她达到了高潮。高潮过后的那一瞬间，她从他的动作中读到了他的讶异。认识桑尼之前的那种耻辱感排山倒海而来，但朱尔斯把她的身体拉到床边，将她的双腿摆成一个特定的角度，她任由朱尔斯操纵她的四肢和躯体，他重新进入她的体内，亲吻着她，这次她感觉到了他，但更重要的是她看得出他也有了感觉，一路冲到高潮。

朱尔斯从露西的身上翻下来，她缩进床的一角，开始哭泣。她觉得太羞愧了。可就在这时,她惊讶地听见朱尔斯轻轻笑着说:"可怜又愚昧的意大利姑娘啊,这几个月你就是为这个在拒绝我?你个小笨蛋。"他把"你个小笨蛋"说得那么饱含善意和爱怜,她不禁转身面对他,他抱住她赤裸的躯体,说:"中世纪来的,你绝对是中世纪来的。"他的语气充满了安慰,因为她还在哭个不停。

朱尔斯点燃香烟,放进她的嘴里,她呛得直咳嗽,想哭也没法哭了。"你给我听好了,"他说,"你要是生在二十世纪的家庭文化里,按照像样的现代方式抚养长大,估计问题几年前就已经解决了。让我说说你的问题吧:这不是相貌丑陋、肤质糟糕和斜眼这种整容手术没法解决的问题,你的问题更像下巴上有个疣或痣,或者耳朵外廓不好看。别往性方面去想。别以为你有个男人没法爱的大筒子,因为不能给阴茎以必要的摩擦。你的问题是骨盆畸形,我们外科医生的叫法是骨盆底异位。通常出现在产后,但也有可能是天生结构不良。这个症状很常见,虽然一个小手术就能解决,但确实让很多女人一辈子活得凄惨。甚至有女人因此自杀。你的体型这么好,我都没往这方面想,我还以为是心理问题呢,因为我知道你的经历,你和桑尼什么的,你跟我说的已经够多了。来,我给你仔细检查一下,好确定到底要动多大的手术。你先去洗个澡。"

露西去浴室冲了个澡。朱尔斯很有耐心,不顾她的反对,命令她躺在床上,分开两腿。他的住处有备用的急诊包,此刻打开放在手边。床边的玻璃板小桌上放了些其他器具。他完全成了医生,检查她的身体,把手指探进体内摸来摸去。她觉得有点屈辱,他却亲亲她的肚脐,一脸漫不经心地说:"我这辈子第一次很享受这份工作。"他把露西翻过来,一根手指插进直肠摸来摸去,但另一只手充满爱意地抚摸她的脖颈。检查完,他把露西翻回正面,温柔地亲吻她的嘴唇,说:"宝贝儿,我要给你完全造个新的下面,然后我会亲自试用。第一次是以医学为目的,我要写论文拿到正式期刊上发表。"

朱尔斯从头到尾都带着善意和爱怜,显然非常关心她,露西克服了羞愧和尴尬。他甚至拿来书架上的医学课本,给她看一个类似的案例和纠正的手术过程。她非常感兴趣。

"况且也对健康有好处,"朱尔斯说,"要是不矫正,你的排泄系统以后会出大问题。要是不动手术,整个构造都会越来越脆弱。很多医生因为保守的观念问题无法诊断和矫正这种症状,很多女人因此遭受折磨,真是该死。"

"别说了,求你别再说了。"露西说。

他看得出她仍旧对自己的秘密有些羞愧,因为"丑陋的缺陷"而尴尬。尽管受过医学训练的头脑认为这蠢得可笑,但性格中敏感的一面也能让他理解她的心情,使得他下决心要让她感觉好受些。

"好了,既然我知道了你的秘密,现在轮到你听听我的了,"他说,"你一直问我来这儿干什么——这位东部最年轻最有才华的外科医生。"他嘲弄地复述报纸对他的描述,"真相是这样的:我是堕胎医生——本身并不那么坏,半个医疗行当嘛,可惜我被逮住了。我有个叫肯尼迪的医生朋友,我们一起实习过,这家伙正派得很,但答应拉我一把。我知道汤姆·黑根跟他说过,柯里昂家族欠他的人情债,所以需要帮忙尽管开口。他去找了黑根。指控很快撤销,但医学协会和东部的医院都把我列人了黑名单。于是柯里昂家族帮我安排了这份工作。挣钱不少,这份工作也需要我。歌舞女郎经常怀孕,要是直接来找我,堕胎实在再容易不过。我的刮宫手艺和你刮煎锅似的。弗雷迪·柯里昂简直让人忍无可忍。要是我没算错,从我来到现在,他已经搞大了十五个姑娘的肚子。我在认真考虑要不要跟他就性爱话题来一场父子般的恳谈。尤其是我已经给他治过三次淋病和一次梅毒了。弗雷迪这厮骑马不爱用马鞍。"

朱尔斯停了下来。他刚才是存心失言,这是破天荒第一次,是想让露西知道别人——包括她认识而且有点害怕的弗雷迪·柯里昂——也有不能见光的隐私。

"就当是你身体里的一根橡皮筋失去了弹性吧,"朱尔斯说,"切掉一截,会更紧、更有脆劲儿。"

"让我考虑一下。"露西说,但她知道自己肯定要做这个手术,因为她百分之百信任朱尔斯。她想到另一个问题:"需要多少钱?"

朱尔斯皱眉思考。"我没有做这种手术的设施,而且也不是这方面的专家。不过我在洛杉矶有个朋友,他是业内的最顶尖的高手,在最好的医院里有最优秀的设施。说起来,他给好多电影明星紧过皮,那些贵妇人发现光是拉脸拉胸部已经不足以让男人爱她们了。他欠我几个人情,所以一分钱都不必花。我帮他做堕胎手术。要不是会违反医生的伦理,否则我就告诉你都有哪些性感女神做过这个手术了。"

她立刻好奇起来。"哎呀,快说,告诉我吧,"她说,"求你了。"这可是最精彩的闲谈材料,朱尔斯有个好处,就是她可以随便展示女人的八卦天性,不必害怕被他取笑。

"答应和我共进晚餐,再一起过夜,我就告诉你,"朱尔斯答道,"我们要弥补因为你犯傻而错过的许多好时光。"

他的温情让露西爱他爱得无法自拔,甚至说出了这样的话:"你不必非得和我睡觉,你知道我现在是什么样子,不会有多少乐趣的。"

朱尔斯哈哈大笑:"你个小笨蛋,笨得难以置信。没听说过做爱还有其他方式吗?古老得多,也文明得多。你没那么天真吧?"

"哦那个。"她说。

"哦那个,"他模仿道,"好姑娘不那么做,男子汉不那么做。哪怕是一九四八年也不行。哎呀,亲爱的,我可以带你去拉斯维加斯一个小老太的家里去坐坐,她在西部狂野年代——记得是上世纪八十年代——是最热门的妓院里最年轻的老鸨。她喜欢回忆往事。知道她怎么说？那些枪手,那些阳刚男子汉,动不动就拔枪的牛仔,总央求女孩做'法国式',医学术语是口交,你的叫法是'哦那个'。难道没考虑过和你亲爱的桑尼做'哦那个'吗?"

她第一次让他真的吃了一惊。她转身面对他,表情只能以蒙娜丽莎的微笑来形容。医学头脑立刻开始胡思乱想:这莫非就是几个世纪的谜题的答案? 她静静地说:"我和桑尼什么都做过。"这是她第一次向任何人坦白这方面的事情。

两周以后,朱尔斯·西格尔站在洛杉矶那家医院的手术室里,望着朋友弗雷德里克·凯尔纳施展专业手法。露西进入麻醉状态之前,朱尔斯俯身悄声说:"我告诉他说你是我的心头肉,所以他会使劲儿往紧里箍。"不过前驱麻醉药已经让她昏昏欲睡,所以她没有笑,连嘴角都没动一动,但他的玩笑话确实带走了她对手术的恐惧。

凯尔纳医生以一杆进洞的信心划开切口。任何加固骨盆底的手术技法都要满足两个目标。一方面是缩短骨盆的肌肉吊索,收紧松弛部位。另一方面自然要打开阴道,将骨盆底的问题点向前拉到耻骨弓下方,减轻从正上方受到的压力。修复骨盆吊索的部分叫会阴缝补术。缝合阴道壁的部分叫阴道缝合术。

朱尔斯看见凯尔纳医生的动作谨慎了起来,切开的风险在于刀口过深,伤及直肠。这个病例颇为简单,朱尔斯研究过所有 X 光片和检验结果。应该不会出问题,但外科手术这东西总有出问题的可能性。

凯尔纳正在处理隔膜吊索,T 型钳夹住阴部皮瓣,露出括约肌和构成阴道的筋膜。凯尔纳缠着医用纱布的手指推开松软的结缔组织。朱尔斯盯着阴道壁,寻找静脉突出的迹象,那是直肠受损的危险信号。不过凯尔纳老伙计心里有数,他构造新阴部的轻松程度不亚于木匠钉起几块二乘四的木板。

凯尔纳缝合刀口,修掉多余的阴道壁,闭合"人口",去除赘肉,确保日后不会形成讨厌的凸起。凯尔纳并起三根手指,尝试伸进变窄了的阴道口,接着换成两根手指。两根手指勉强进去,他深入探查,抬头看了朱尔斯两眼,宝蓝色的眼睛在纱布口罩上方顽皮一闪,像是在问这下够窄了吧。他低头继续忙着缝合。

手术结束,他们把露西推进加护病房,朱尔斯向凯尔纳了解情况,凯尔纳很开心,这是一切顺利的信号。"完全没有并发症,好兄弟,"他对朱尔斯说,"里面什么也没长,非常简单的手术。她的身体弹性特别好,在这种病例里很罕见,现在她是一等一的寻欢作乐好伴侣了。我嫉妒你啊,好兄弟。当然了你们还得等一阵子,不过我保证你会喜欢我的手艺。"

朱尔斯哈哈笑道:"你是真正的皮格马利翁,医生,我说真的,你太了不起了。"

凯尔纳医生哼了一声:"都是小孩子的把戏,和你的堕胎差不多。社会要是更现实点儿,你我这种有真材实料的人,应该去做些更像样的事情,把这种破事丢给三流货好了。说起来,下个星期我要送个姑娘去你那儿,人很好,遇到麻烦的似乎总是这种人。今天的手术就算扯平了。"

朱尔斯摇头道:"谢谢,医生。你找个时间过来,我让你领略一下什么叫热情款待。"

凯尔纳歪了歪嘴:"我每天都在赌博,不需要你们的轮盘赌和掷骰子。我和命运头碰头的次数实在太多了。你在荒废生命,朱尔斯,再过几年,正经的外科手术你就全忘光了。到时候你还怎么混?"他转身离开。

朱尔斯明白凯尔纳的本意不是斥责而是提醒,但他还是顿时消沉了下去。露西至少要在加护病房住十二个钟头,他于是进城喝了个烂醉。喝醉有一部分原因是露西的问题解决得这么容易,他的心头大石落了地。

第二天早晨,他来医院探望露西,惊讶地发现床边已经有了两个男人,病房里到处都是鲜花。露西靠坐在几个枕头上,容光焕发。朱尔斯之所以惊讶,是因为露西早就和家里断了往来,特别叮嘱他只要不出问题就别通知家人。弗雷迪·柯里昂当然知道她要入院做个小手术,这是必要的,否则两人都没法请假;弗雷迪还告诉朱尔斯说酒店可以帮露西付账。

露西介绍他们认识,朱尔斯立刻认出了其中的一个男人。大名鼎鼎的约翰尼·方坦。另外一位是个健壮的大块头意大利人,模样有点傲慢,名叫尼诺·瓦伦蒂。他们和朱尔斯握手,然后就不再理睬他。两人和露西开玩笑,聊当年在纽约的旧邻居,聊朱尔斯不可能知道的人和事。他只好对露西说:"我等会儿再过来吧,我还得去见见凯尔纳医生呢。"

不过约翰尼·方坦已经开始向他发射魅力了。"哎,老兄,我们反正得走了,你陪着露西吧。好好照顾她,医生。"朱尔斯注意到约翰尼·方坦的声音有一种特别的嘶哑感,忽然想起他有一年多没公开演唱了,赢得奥斯卡奖也是因为表演。他难道这把年纪突然变声,而报纸为他保守秘密,所有人都为他保守秘密?朱尔斯喜欢内幕八卦,听着方坦的声音,尝试诊断他的问题。有可能只是发紧,或者是烟酒过度,甚至纵欲过度。声音里有种难听的粗粝感,他得丢掉甜美情歌王子的美名了。

"你听着像是得了感冒。"朱尔斯对约翰尼·方坦说。

方坦有礼貌地答道:"只是喉咙发紧,昨晚我试过唱歌。估计我得接受现实了,我的嗓子变了,上岁数了嘛,你明白的。"他对朱尔斯露出"去他妈的"笑容。

朱尔斯假装随便地说:"没请医生看看?也许很容易就能治好呢。"

方坦不再魅力四射。他冷冰冰地瞪着朱尔斯看了好一会儿。"我两年前做的第一件事情就是看医生。最好的专科大夫。我的私人医生,据说是加州最顶尖的一位。他们叫我多休息。没什么毛病,只是上岁数了。男人上了岁数,声音会跟着变化。"

说完,方坦不再搭理他,只关注露西,像是对所有女人那样对她发射魅力。朱尔斯继续听他说话。肯定是声带上长了东西。但专科医生怎么可能没有发现呢?难道是恶性的,还是不能动手术?要么还有别的原因?

他打断方坦的话:"上一次接受专科检查是什么时候?"

方坦显然被惹火了,但看在露西的面子上,尽量按捺住火气。"大概十八个月前。"他说。

"你的医生有没有给你定期检查?"朱尔斯问。

"还用你说?"约翰尼·方坦怒道,"他给我喷可待因,仔细检查。他说只是嗓子上了年纪,还有喝酒抽烟其他原因。难不成你比他还懂行?"

朱尔斯问:"哪个医生?"

方坦稍微有点自豪地说:"塔克,詹姆斯·塔克医生。对他有何高见?"

很耳熟,提起他就会想起电影明星、名媛和收费昂贵的疗养院。

"穿衣打扮很有一套。"朱尔斯笑呵呵地说。

方坦真的生气了。"你觉得你当医生比他强?"

朱尔斯哈哈笑道:"那得看你当歌手是不是比卡门·伦巴多强了。"他惊讶地看见尼诺·瓦伦蒂仰天狂笑,后脑勺撞在了椅背上。这个笑话似乎没那么好笑。他狂笑时吐出的气息有波旁威士忌的味道,瓦伦蒂先生——天晓得是何方神圣——大清早这个时辰就已经喝得半醉了。

方坦苦笑着对朋友说:"喂,他说笑话你笑成这样,我说笑话你怎么不笑?"露西伸手把朱尔斯拽到床边。

"他看着像个小混混,其实是个厉害的外科医生,"露西告诉两人,"如果他说他比塔克医生强,那他就肯定比塔克医生强。约翰尼,你就听他的吧。"

护士进来说他们得出去了,住院医生要给露西作检查,需要私密。朱尔斯开心地看见约翰尼·方坦和尼诺·瓦伦蒂上去亲吻露西的时候,露西转过头去,他们亲到的是面颊而不是嘴唇;不过他们似乎早有预料。她允许朱尔斯亲吻她的嘴唇,一边悄声说:"下午再过来,好吗?"他点点头。

回到走廊里,瓦伦蒂问他:"她做了什么手术?问题严重吗?"

朱尔斯摇摇头。"妇科的小毛病。完全是常规手术,相信我好了。我比你们更关心她,我希望能娶她。"

两人上上下下打量他,他只好问:"你们怎么知道她在这家医院?"

"弗雷迪打电话给我们,请我们过来看看,"方坦说,"我们是在同一个街区长大的。弗雷迪的妹妹出嫁的时候,露西是伴娘。"

"哦。"朱尔斯说。他不想流露出他全都清楚,也许因为他们都守口如瓶,尽量保护露西,守住她和桑尼那段情缘的秘密。

三个人顺着走廊向前走,朱尔斯对方坦说:"我在这儿有访问医生的待遇,愿不愿意让我看看你的喉咙?"

方坦摇头道:"我赶时间。"

尼诺·瓦伦蒂说:"他的嗓子价值百万,不能让无照医生随便看。"朱尔斯看见瓦伦蒂对他咧嘴一笑,显然站在他这一边。

朱尔斯喜滋滋地说:"我可不是无照医生。我是东海岸最厉害的年轻外科医生和诊断医师,直到被人指控非法堕胎。"

如他所料,这句话让他们认真对待他了。他承认自己的罪行,反而激发他们对他自封的头衔产生了信任。瓦伦蒂首先回过神来,"要是约翰尼不肯用你,我倒是有个女朋友想让你看看,不过要看的不是嗓子。"

方坦紧张地说:"需要多少时间?"

"十分钟。"朱尔斯说,这是骗人,但他相信骗人也有好处。除非在生死关头,真话和医疗实在合不来。

"好吧。"方坦说,声音变得更加低沉和嘶哑,透着恐惧。

朱尔斯请了个护士,要了一间诊疗室,这里没有他需要的所有设施,但也够用了。不到十分钟,他已经知道方坦的声带上有增生了——实在非常容易,塔克这个衣着入时的无能小人,混饭吃的好莱坞骗子,本应该一眼就看见的。天哪,那家伙说不定连行医执照都没有,就算有也应该被撤销。朱尔斯没有多看方坦和瓦伦蒂,他拿起电话,请医院的喉科专家下来。接着,他转过身,对尼诺·瓦伦蒂说:"看来你要多等一阵了,有事的话就先走吧。"

方坦瞪着他,一脸不敢相信的神色,"你这个混蛋,以为能把我留在这儿?你凭什么觉得我会让你动我的喉咙?"

朱尔斯自己都没法想象他能这么开心,他直勾勾地盯着方坦的眼睛。"你爱去哪儿就去哪儿,"他说,"但你的声带上有增生,在喉咙里。你要是愿意留下几个钟头,我们就能查明病因,搞清楚是恶性还是良性,决定是手术还是保守治疗。我可以给你解释清楚,我可以给你介绍全美国最顶尖的专科医生,你要是觉得有必要,大可以请他今晚就乘飞机来洛杉矶,反正你那么有钱。另外一方面,你也可以现在就出去,见你那个庸医朋友，或者提心吊胆，决心换个医生，或者再被介绍给另一个无能骗子。万一是恶性的，过段时间长得太大了，他们会切掉你的整个喉部，否则你就必死无疑。当然，你也可以一直提心吊胆过下去。留下，几个小时我们就能搞清病因。你难道还有什么更重要的事情？"

瓦伦蒂说："我们留下吧，约翰尼，管他的。我去楼下大厅打电话给电影公司。我保证不多嘴，只说有事耽搁住了。然后我再上来陪着你。"

这个下午过得很忙碌，但非常有价值。朱尔斯看过 X 光片和取样检验的结果，觉得医院喉科专家的诊断完全靠得住。检查到半中间，约翰尼·方坦满嘴碘酒，塞在嘴里的纱布卷害得他干呕不止，他企图打退堂鼓。尼诺·瓦伦蒂抓住他的肩膀，把他狠狠地按回椅子上。检查结束，朱尔斯对方坦得意地笑着说："肉赘。"

方坦没有反应过来。朱尔斯重复道："只是肉赘而已。很容易切除，和剥大红肠的皮差不多。过几个月你就一切正常了。"

瓦伦蒂欢呼一声，方坦却还是皱着眉头："然后呢，能唱歌吗？会影响我唱歌吗？"

朱尔斯耸耸肩："这我就没法保证了。不过你现在反正也没法唱歌，有什么区别吗？"

方坦厌恶地看着他。"小子，你不知道你在说什么，对吧？听上去是个好消息，其实，我有可能永远没法唱歌了，对不对？我有可能再也不能唱歌了？"

朱尔斯终于动气了。他一直在以真正的医生身份诊治方坦，乐在其中，他在帮这个王八蛋一个大忙，王八蛋却表现得像是被摆了一道。朱尔斯冷冰冰地说："听着，方坦先生，我是一名医学博士，你应该叫我医生，而不是小子。我说的确实是好消息。我本来以为你长的是恶性肿瘤，很可能需要切除整个发声器官，否则你会被它害死。我担心的是我也许不得不说你已经死定了。说'肉赘'这两个字的时候，我确实满心欢喜，因为你的歌声曾经带给我那么多快乐，在我还年轻、你还是一名响当当的艺人那会儿，帮我搞定了很多姑娘。可是你这个人实在是被宠坏了。怎么？你是约翰尼·方坦，所以就不可能得癌症，不会长无药可救的脑瘤，心脏不会衰竭？你以为你能永生不死？唉，人生又不完全是甜美的音乐，你要是愿意在医院里走一圈，就会看见什么是真正的苦难，就会给肉赘唱一首小情歌了。所以别说废话，该做什么就做什么。你那位衣冠楚楚的医生也许能帮你安排一个正经外科专家，但他自己要是企图窜进手术室，我建议你因为企图谋杀而逮捕他。"

朱尔斯转身走出房间，瓦伦蒂说："好样的，医生，就该这么教训他。"

朱尔斯又回过身。"你总是不到中午就喝得醉醺醺的？"

瓦伦蒂说："是啊。"使劲对朱尔斯微笑，开心得让朱尔斯不由压低了嗓门："你得想明白了，再这么喝下去，你这条命顶多还剩五年。"

瓦伦蒂跳着碎舞步蹒跚走向他，一把搂住朱尔斯，满嘴波旁威士忌的酒臭。他哄然笑道："五年？"仍旧笑个不停，"还要等那么久吗？"

手术后一个月，露西·曼奇尼坐在拉斯维加斯的酒店泳池旁，一只手端着一杯鸡尾酒，另一只手抚摸朱尔斯枕着她大腿的脑袋。

"用不着喝酒壮胆，"朱尔斯取笑道，"我在我们的套房里准备了香槟。"

"这么快，你确定没问题吗？"露西问。

"我是医生，"朱尔斯说，"今晚是我的大日子。说起来你有没有想到，我将是医学史上第一个试用自己手术结果的外科医生？空前绝后，知道吗？我打算兴高采烈地写报告寄给学术期刊。让我想一想，'术前的明显欣快感源于心理原因和外科专家兼指导者的高超手法，术后性交的高度快感则完全来自神经学'……"露西猛拽他的头发，他疼得大叫起来，只得住嘴。

她低头看着朱尔斯。"今晚你要是没有满足，那就只能怪自己了。"她说。

"我保证我的技术没问题。手术方案是我定的，只是让凯尔纳老兄做体力活罢了，"朱尔斯说，"我们养精蓄锐一下，今晚的研究会很耗时费力。"

他们上楼回到套房里——两人已经同居——露西不由惊喜：一顿丰盛的晚餐，香槟酒杯旁有个首饰盒，里面是一枚镶着偌大钻石的订婚戒指。

"看看，我对我的技术多有信心，"朱尔斯说，"现在就看你配不配合了。"

他待她非常体贴和温柔。刚开始她还有点害怕，被他一碰就想躲开，但很快就恢复了信心，感觉身体积蓄起了她未曾体验过的激情。第一次事毕，朱尔斯悄声说："我的技术不错吧？"她也悄声答道："哦，是的，不错，是的，不错。"两人相对大笑，开始了第二次。

第六部

第二十三章

流亡西西里五个月，迈克尔·柯里昂终于理解了父亲的个性和自己的命运。他理解了卢卡·布拉齐和冷酷的首领克莱门扎，理解了母亲为何听天由命，安然接受自己的角色。这是因为他在西西里看到了如果不和命运抗争，他们将落得什么结果。他理解了唐为什么总说"一个人只有一个命运"。他理解了人们为何蔑视权威和合法政府，为何触犯缄默规则的人都会遭到仇视。

迈克尔穿戴旧衣服和鸭舌帽，在巴勒莫的码头下船，辗转到西西里岛的内陆，黑手党控制的一个行省的心脏地带，当地的黑手党头目曾经得到过他父亲的帮助，因此欠他父亲很大一笔人情债。柯里昂镇就在这个行省，多年前唐迁居美国后拿镇名充当了姓氏。镇上已经没有唐的亲戚在世，女人年老逝世，男人不是死于仇杀就是也搬走了，有的去了美国或巴西，有的去了大陆的其他行省。他后来发现，这个贫穷小镇发生凶杀的频率在全世界也首屈一指。

迈克尔被安排以客人身份住进黑帮头目的单身叔叔家。这位叔叔年已七旬，是附近地区的医生。黑手党头目五十多岁，名叫唐·托马西诺，公开身份是管家，为西西里的一户望族管理一个大庄园。管家是豪门庄园的看管人，确保穷人不会强占无人开垦的土地，不会以任何方式暗自侵占，包括偷猎和未经许可的耕种。简而言之，管家就是富人以一定金额雇用的黑帮首领，保护富人的地产，防止穷人以合法或非法的手段对土地提出要求。假如有贫穷农户试图通过法律途径购买无人开垦的土地，管家就要用人身伤害或死亡威胁他。就这么简单。

唐·托马西诺还控制附近地区的用水权，拒绝罗马政府在当地建水坝。他的生财之道就是从他控制的自流井向居民卖水,这种水坝会摧毁他的生意,让水价变得过于便宜,摧毁几百年来辛苦建立起的整个水资源经济。不过,唐·托马西诺是个老派的黑手党首领,绝对不碰贩毒和卖淫。巴勒莫这种大城市涌现出的新一代黑手党首领与唐·托马西诺在这方面意见相左,受驱逐返回意大利的美国帮派分子影响了新一代首领,他们没有类似的顾虑。

这位黑手党首领格外肥壮,名副其实的"大肚汉",是个能在同伴中激起恐惧的角色。有他庇护,迈克尔什么也不用害怕,不过作为流亡者隐匿身份还是有必要的。因此,迈克尔的活动范围仅限于唐的叔叔、塔扎医生家的围墙之内。

塔扎医生身高近六英尺,在西西里人来说算是很高了,面颊红润,头发雪白,尽管年已七旬,每周还是要去巴勒莫光顾比他年轻得多的妓女,而且越年轻越好。塔扎医生的另一个癖好是读书。他什么书都读,喜欢找文盲镇民、农夫患者和庄园的牧羊人讨论他正在读的书,这让他在当地有了傻瓜的名声——书和他们能有什么关系呢?

每天傍晚,塔扎医生、唐·托马西诺和迈克尔坐在满是大理石雕像的大花园里,在西西里岛上,大理石雕像和黑红色的醉人葡萄一样,都像是变魔术似的从地里长出来的。塔扎医生喜欢讲述黑手党几百年来的丰功伟绩,迈克尔·柯里昂听得入迷。有时候连唐·托马西诺也会被芬芳的晚风、果香浓郁的醉人葡萄酒和花园里清雅宁静的氛围迷得忘乎所以,讲述起他的亲身经历。医生说的是传奇,唐是现实。

就在这个古老的花园里,迈克尔·柯里昂知道了长出父亲这颗果实的藤蔓之根。"黑手党"一词的原意是避难场所。一个突然出现的秘密组织后来以此为名,他们抵抗已经欺压了这个国家和人民几百年的统治者。西西里这片土地在历史上经受过绝无仅有的残酷蹂躏。宗教法庭不分贫富,对西西里人一律严酷拷问。罗马教廷册封的王爵占有土地,以绝对权力统治牧羊人和农夫。警察是权力的工具,和这些人难分彼此,因此西西里人嘴里的"警察"是骂人时最难听的脏话。

面对残暴的绝对权力,苦难中的人民害怕被击垮,学会了决不泄露怒火和恨意,决不空口威胁而让自己受到伤害,因为那就等于提醒对手,会迅速遭到报复。他们学会了社会就是敌人,于是在受到冤屈而寻找救济的时候,转而求助于叛逆的地下王国——黑手党。黑手党通过缄默规则巩固权力。在西西里乡村,陌生人连问怎么去最近的村镇都得不到礼遇和回答。黑手党成员能犯下的最大罪错莫过于告诉警察,他吃了谁的枪子或者被谁以任何方式伤害了。缄默规则成了人们的宗教。一个女人就算丈夫被杀、儿子被杀、女儿被强奸,也不能向警方透露罪犯的姓名。

政府无法实践正义,人们于是向罗宾汉般的黑手党求助。黑手党在某种程度上扮演了政府的角色。人们不管有什么急事,都会去找当地的黑手党头目。他是他们的社工,是随时能拿出一篮子食物和一份工作的地方长官,是他们的保护者。

可是,有一点塔扎医生没有说清楚,是迈克尔在接下来的几个月内自己了解到的:西西里的黑手党已经成了富人的非法武装,甚至是法律和政治体系的辅助警察,已经沦落成了堕落的资本主义体系,反共产主义,反自由主义,对任何形态的商业活动——无论规模有多小——都要强征一份税收。

迈克尔·柯里昂第一次明白了,他父亲这样的人为何选择当盗贼和杀人犯,而不是合法社会的普通成员。对于一个有灵魂的人来说,贫穷、恐惧和落魄实在可怕得难以承受。西西里人移民到了美国,只会想当然地认为政府也同样残忍。

塔扎医生周末照例去巴勒莫逛妓院,问迈克尔要不要同去,但迈克尔拒绝了。逃亡西西里使得他骨折的下巴无法得到像样的医治,左脸如今带上了麦克劳斯凯警长留给他的纪念品。骨头愈合得不太好,扯得侧脸有些歪斜,从左边看显得很邪恶。他对相貌一直颇为自负,破相比想象中更让他心烦意乱。疼痛来来去去,他倒是并不在意,塔扎医生给他开了些镇痛药。塔扎提出帮他治疗,迈克尔婉言谢绝。他来这儿已经够久,知道塔扎医生恐怕是西西里数一数二的差劲大夫。塔扎医生什么都读,唯有医学文献除外,他承认自己看不懂。他能通过医师考试,完全是有西西里最重要的黑手党首领从中斡旋,首领特地去了一趟巴勒莫,和塔扎的教授们讨论应该给他什么分数。这也说明了黑手党在意大利对社会是多么可怕的癌症。专长毫无价值,天赋毫无价值,努力毫无价值。黑手党教父把职业当礼物送给个人。

迈克尔有许多时间思前想后。白天,他在乡野散步,附庸于唐·托马西诺庄园的两名牧羊人不离左右。在西西里岛,黑手党时常招募牧羊人充当雇用杀手,牧羊人杀人也只是为了讨生活。迈克尔思考着父亲的组织。柯里昂帝国若是继续蓬勃发展,结果会和西西里岛的情况相同,像癌症一样毁掉整个国家。西西里已经成了鬼魂的岛屿,居民移民去了世界各国,只为了混口饭吃,或者是逃离因为追求政治和经济自由而遭到杀害的命运。

漫长的散步途中,最让迈克尔叹为观止的是壮丽秀美的风景。他走过乡间的柑橘园,枝叶搭成阴凉深邃的洞穴,古老沟渠穿插其中,公元前的巨蛇石像从毒牙间吐出活水。房屋样式模仿古罗马的别墅,有宽阔的大理石门廊和同样宽敞的拱顶房间,如今已经破败成废墟,只有离群的野羊居住。地平线上,嶙峋的山丘闪闪发亮,犹如漂白的骨骼垒在一起。花园和田地绿意盎然,仿佛透亮的绿宝石项链般点缀荒原。他有时候会一直走到柯里昂镇,一万八千居民的住所连绵不断,占据了近处山岭的侧面,从山上开采的黑色岩石搭起了一座座简陋小屋。过去一年间,柯里昂镇有超过六十起杀人案,死神的阴影笼罩着小镇。再向前走,费库萨森林打断了单调的平原风景。

他的两名牧羊人保镖总是扛着狼枪陪迈克尔散步。这种凶恶的西西里霰弹枪是黑手党最喜欢的武器。墨索里尼派高级警官去西西里清除黑手党,他做的第一件事就是下令拆墙,全西西里的石墙都不得高于三英尺,不让使用狼枪的凶手把石墙当作刺杀的埋伏地点。可惜用处不大,警官大人的解决办法是逮捕一切有黑手党嫌疑的男性,驱逐去苦役殖民岛。

盟军解放西西里岛之后,美军政府官员认为法西斯政权囚禁的必然是民主斗士,任命大量黑手党成员为村镇官员和军管政府的翻译。好运让黑手党重振旗鼓,反而比战前更加恐怖。

长途散步,晚上一瓶烈性葡萄酒和结结实实一大盘面条配肉食,迈克尔总是睡得很香。塔扎医生的图书室有很多意大利文的书籍,尽管迈克尔会说意大利方言,在大学里也选修过意大利语,读这些书仍旧劳神费力。口语逐渐没了口音,尽管他永远也没法假扮当地人,但冒充来自北方与瑞士和德国交界处的外省人已经没问题了。

变形的左脸让他更加像本地人。由于缺少医药,这种破相在西西里很常见。仅仅因为缺钱,小伤口就没法及时得到修补。很多孩童和成年人都有破相的伤疤,要是在美国,早就通过小手术或先进的医学手段修整得看不见了。

迈克尔时常想起凯,想起她的笑容和身体,每次想到自己连再见都没说就突然离开,良心就感到阵阵刺痛。奇怪的是,杀死那两个人却没有让他良心不安,索洛佐试图刺杀他的父亲,麦克劳斯凯警长打得他终生破相。

塔扎医生总是催他动手术,矫正偏向一侧的面部,特别是迈克尔经常问他要镇痛药——随着时间过去,疼痛越来越厉害,发作也越来越频繁。塔扎解释说眼睛下方有一根面部神经,向周围辐射出一整套复杂的神经丛。说起来,这正是黑手党拷问人最喜欢的位置,拷问人会用冰锥的锋利尖端在受害者脸上找到这个位置。迈克尔脸上的这根神经受到了伤害,也许有一小块碎骨扎进了那里。去巴勒莫的医院做个小手术就能一劳永逸地驱除痛楚。

迈克尔拒绝了。医生问为什么,迈克尔咧嘴笑道:"那是老家留给我的纪念。"

他其实并不在乎疼痛,这种疼痛更接近隐痛,是颅骨内搏动的轻微刺痛,仿佛马达在液体里旋转,清洗设备。

过了快七个月悠闲的乡村生活,迈克尔终于厌烦起来。也就在这个时候,唐·托马西诺变得非常忙碌,难得来他寄居的别墅做客。他和巴勒莫蓬勃发展的"新黑手党"有了冲突。那些年轻人靠战后兴旺的建筑业大发横财,借着这笔钱,开始侵蚀老派黑手党首领的乡村地盘,他们轻蔑地称老派首领为"胡子彼得"。唐·托马西诺忙着保护他的地盘。迈克尔没了老头子的陪伴,只能听塔扎医生的故事打发时间,而有些故事已经说了好几遍。

一天早晨,迈克尔决定远足去柯里昂镇另一头的山区。当然,那两位牧羊人保镖还是陪着他——并不是为了防范柯里昂家族的敌人,而是因为外乡人在这里独自乱逛实在过于危险。这个地区遍地土匪,黑手党的不同派别常年仇杀,危及所有人的生命。他还有可能被误认为农具屋小偷。

农具屋是田间地头用茅草搭建的小屋,存放农具,为下地劳动的人遮风挡雨,免得他们扛着农具长途跋涉往来村庄。西西里的农夫不住在他们耕种的土地上。那太危险了,任何一块可耕种的土地——假如归农夫所有——都异常珍贵。不,农夫住在村里,太阳一出来,他就出发去遥远的田地里耕耘,全凭步行。农夫来到他的农具屋,发现被人洗劫一空,那他可就倒霉了。他这是被人断了生计。事实证明法律毫无用处,黑手党于是接手,将农夫的利益置于羽翼之下,用典型的手段解决问题。黑手党追杀屠戮所有的农具屋窃贼。有无辜百姓受伤也是在所难免。要是迈克尔凑巧走过某个刚被洗劫一空的农具屋,如果没有人肯为他担保,很可能会被判定有罪。

就这样,在一个阳光灿烂的清晨,他开始步行穿过乡野,两名忠诚的牧羊人跟着他,其中一个生性淳朴,甚至有点痴傻,比死人还沉默,比印第安人还要面无表情。他有着西西里人中年发福之前的精瘦身材,名叫卡洛。

另一个牧羊人更外向,比较年轻,稍微见过些世面,尽管大部分是海洋,因为他是意大利海军的水手,只来得及文了个身,所在的舰艇就被击沉,他成为英国人的俘虏。不过,文身让他在村里挺有名气。西西里人通常不文身,一是缺少机会,二是没这个爱好(这位牧羊人叫法布雷奇奥,文身主要是想遮住腹部的一块红色胎记)。不过,黑手党成员的集市推车倒是都绘着华丽的风景画,精心绘制,笔法纯朴但画面美丽。总而言之,法布雷奇奥回到老家,胸膛上的文身并没有让他有多骄傲,不过文身图案的主题很贴近西西里的所谓"荣誉",在他毛茸茸的肚皮上一个丈夫刺死一对纠缠在一起的男女。法布雷奇奥和迈克尔说说笑笑,问他美国怎么样——他不可能向他们永远隐瞒他的真实国籍,但他们并不清楚他的身份,只知道他来这儿避难,他们不能乱说他的事情。法布雷奇奥有时会带给迈克尔一块还在渗奶珠的新鲜乳酪。

他们沿着尘土飞扬的乡间道路行走,经过一辆又一辆绘着艳丽图画的驴车。田地里满是粉色的花朵,橘树、杏树和橄榄树的花朵都在绽放。这曾让迈克尔倍感惊讶。迈克尔听别人说了那么多西西里人如何贫穷,还以为西西里是一片贫瘠的荒原,但见到的土地却遍地鲜花,散发着柠檬花香的气味。西西里的美丽让他不由感叹,人们怎能忍心离开。逃离伊甸园一样的家园,你就知道人类对同胞有多么残酷了。

他打算徒步走到海边的马扎拉村,晚上搭公共汽车回到柯里昂,耗尽全部精力,好好睡一觉。两个牧羊人的帆布背包里装满了路上吃的面包和乳酪。他们明目张胆地背着狼枪，像是要去打猎一整天。

这个早晨格外美丽。迈克尔的感觉就仿佛小时候夏天一早出门去打球。那时候的每一天都像刚冲洗过那么干净，刚画上去的那么鲜艳。今天也是这样。西西里遍地绚丽鲜花，橘和柠檬树的花香浓郁，尽管面部伤情严重压迫鼻窦，他也还是闻到了。

左脸的粉碎性骨折已经完全愈合，但骨头没有对齐，鼻窦受压导致左眼疼痛，还让他流涕不止，不但把一块又一块的手帕擦得黏糊糊的，还经常学着当地农夫的样子，冲着地面擤鼻子。而他从小就深恶痛绝这个习惯，有些年长的意大利人觉得手帕是英国佬的纨绔做派，就着马路边的阴沟擤鼻子，他见了就讨厌。

他觉得整张脸都"沉甸甸的"。塔扎医生说这都怪骨折愈合不良对鼻窦造成了压力。塔扎医生说他的症状叫颧骨蛋壳性碎裂，在开始愈合之前很容易处理，一个小手术就能解决，用类似调羹的器械把碎骨推回原位。但现在不行了，医生说，你只能去巴勒莫住院，做个叫"颌面修补术"的大手术，打碎骨头重新拼合。迈克尔听听就够了，他没有答应。比起疼痛和流鼻涕，更难以忍受的是脸上那种沉甸甸的感觉折磨着他。

那天他根本没有走到海边。走了十五英里，他和两名牧羊人就歇在凉爽湿润的橘树树荫下，吃着午餐喝葡萄酒。法布雷奇奥在唠叨什么他以后要去美国。吃喝完毕，他们懒洋洋地躺在树荫下，法布雷奇奥解开衬衫纽扣，伸缩腹部的肌肉，文身于是活了过来。胸口那对赤裸的男女开始蠕动，丈夫看得心急如焚，匕首在被刺穿的肉体里颤抖。三个人看得很开心。就在这时，西西里人所谓的"霹雳"击中了迈克尔。

橘树林子的另一头是几片狭长的绿色田地，属于某位男爵的庄园。顺着橘树林子向前，路边有一幢古罗马风格的别墅，模样像是刚从庞培城的废墟里挖出来的，宛如一座小型宫殿，有宽敞的大理石门廊和希腊式的廊柱，从廊柱中间出来了一群乡村姑娘，左右各有一名裹着黑衣的矮壮妇人。她们来自附近的村庄，显然刚向本地的男爵尽了传统义务，帮他打扫别墅或者是为他冬季暂住作准备，这会儿正要去田间采花装饰房间。她们采的是粉色的岩黄芪和紫色的紫藤花，还有橘树和柠檬树的花朵。姑娘们没有看见树荫下的三个男人，越走越近。

印着艳丽花朵的便宜衣服紧紧紧裹她们的身体。她们还不到二十岁，但阳光早早催熟了她们的肉体。三四个姑娘追着另一个姑娘跑向那丛橘树。被追赶的姑娘左手拿着一捧紫色大葡萄，用右手一颗一颗揪下葡萄，扔向追赶她的那些姑娘。她的满头卷发也是葡萄一样的黑紫色，身躯也和葡萄一样就要涨破皮肤。

就快跑到树丛，她忽然瞥见三个男人与周围颜色不同的衬衫，吓了一跳，猛地停下。她踮着脚尖站在那里，姿势像是准备逃跑的小鹿。她站得那么近，近得足以看清她的五官。

她的一切都是鸭蛋形的——鸭蛋形的眼睛、鸭蛋形的脸型、鸭蛋形的额头轮廓。她的皮肤是很精致的暗奶油色,眼睛很大,是黑紫红色或暗棕色,浓而长的睫毛都快遮住了这张可爱的脸庞。她嘴唇丰满但并不臃肿,甜蜜但并不软弱,被葡萄汁染成了深红色。她可爱得让人不敢相信眼睛,法布雷奇奥忍不住喃喃道:"耶稣基督啊,取了我的灵魂去吧,我要死了。"虽然是玩笑话,但嗓子有点沙哑。女孩像是听见了他的感叹,放下脚跟,转身逃向追赶她的伙伴。她的后腰在紧身衣裙下扭得像只小动物,既充满肉欲,又天真无邪。跑到伙伴身边,她又转过身,脸孔在炫目花朵的衬托下像个黑洞。她伸出一条胳膊,抓着葡萄的手指着树丛。女孩边跑边笑,矮壮的黑衣妇人连声责骂。

而迈克尔·柯里昂,他不由站起身,心脏扑腾扑腾跳个不停,觉得有点头晕。热血涌遍全身,流经四肢,冲击手指尖和脚趾尖。全西西里岛的香气都在风中涌动,橘子花、柠檬花、葡萄、各种野花。他的躯体像是抛弃灵魂,自己飘走了。他听见两个牧羊人放声大笑。

"你这是被霹雳打中了,嗯?"法布雷奇奥拍着他的肩膀说。连卡洛也变得友善,拍着他的胳膊说:"悠着点儿,朋友,悠着点儿。"语气含着情谊。那阵势就仿佛迈克尔被汽车撞了。法布雷奇奥递给他一瓶酒,迈克尔狠狠喝了一大口。他的头脑顿时清醒了。

"你们两个该死的恋羊崽子胡说什么啊?"他说。

两个人哈哈大笑。卡洛那张诚实的脸以最严肃的表情说:"你躲不过那道霹雳。被霹雳击中,有眼睛就看得见。哎呀,朋友,有什么不好意思的,有些男人还祈祷能天降霹雳呢。你很走运。"

迈克尔不怎么开心,因为别人这么容易就看穿了他的情绪。可是,这毕竟是他这辈子第一次撞见这种事情。和青春期的迷恋不一样,和他对凯的爱毫无相似之处,他对凯的爱的基础是凯的甜美和智慧,还有她明辨是非的眼光;而这次是排山倒海的占有欲望,女孩的面容在他的脑海里打下了不可磨灭的印记,他知道要是不能占有她,这张脸会在记忆里折磨他一辈子。他的生活顿时变得简单,集中在一个目标上,除此之外的一切都不值得分神哪怕一瞬间。在这段流放的时间里,他总是想着凯,但他猜想那段情缘再也不可能继续,甚至连友情都没法保持了。无论怎么说,他毕竟是个杀人犯,是个杀过人的黑手党成员。然而,此刻连凯都被完全驱逐出了脑海。

法布雷奇奥兴致勃勃地说:"我去村里看看,我们能问出她的身份。谁知道呢,说不定比我们想象的容易得手。霹雳只有一种解药,对吧,卡洛?"

　　另一个牧羊人严肃地点点头。迈克尔没有说话,跟着两个牧羊人顺着道路走向附近的村庄,那群姑娘刚才就消失在了这个村庄里。

　　村庄照例环绕带喷泉的中央广场而建。不过这个村庄在一条大路上,所以有几家商店、酒铺和一间小小的咖啡馆,小露台上摆着三张桌子。牧羊人找了张桌子坐下,迈克尔过去和他们作伴。前后左右找不到女孩的身影,毫无踪迹。村庄里似乎只有几个小男孩和一头游游荡荡的驴子。

　　咖啡馆的老板出来伺候客人。他身材魁梧,个子不高,再矮点儿就是侏儒了,他兴高采烈地和他们打招呼,把一盘鹰嘴豆摆在桌上。"生面孔呀,"他说,"听听我的建议如何? 试试我家的葡萄酒。葡萄是自己家农庄种的,酒是我的两个儿子亲手酿的。他们在葡萄里混了橙子和柠檬。保证是意大利最好的红酒。"

　　他们叫他拿一罐来,酒比他宣传的还要好,黑紫色,和白兰地一样有劲。法布雷奇奥对老板说:"我敢说你认识村里的每一个姑娘,对吧? 刚才在路上见到几个漂亮妞往这边走,其中有一个害我们朋友挨了一道霹雳。"他朝迈克尔打个手势。

　　咖啡店老板换个眼神,重新打量迈克尔。这张破相的脸和先前一样,还是平平常常,不值得看第二眼。不过一个挨了霹雳的男人就是另外一码事了。"你还是带几瓶酒回家吧,朋友,"他说,"否则今晚肯定睡不好。"

　　迈克尔问他:"知道一个满头卷发的姑娘吗? 奶油般的皮肤,眼睛特别大,特别黑。知道村里有这么个姑娘吗?"

　　老板只撂下一句"不,不知道这样的女孩",就转身从露台上回到了店里。

　　三个男人慢吞吞地喝着葡萄酒,喝完一罐,喊老板再来一罐。老板没有出现。法布雷奇奥走进店里,回来的时候做个鬼脸,对迈克尔说:"和我想的一样,我们说的正是他女儿,他在后面气得发狂,要让我们尝尝厉害。我们还是赶紧回柯里昂村吧。"

　　尽管已经在岛上住了几个月,但柯里昂还是不习惯西西里人在情爱方面的保守,而这次对西西里人来说也有点过头了。可是,两位牧羊人似乎觉得理所当然。他们在等他起身离开。法布雷奇奥说:"老杂种说他有两个儿子,身强力壮的好汉,他吹声口哨就能叫来。我们走吧。"

　　迈克尔冷冰冰地瞪着他。在此之前,他一直表现得像个温文尔雅的年轻人,一个典型的美国佬,只是藏身于西西里说明他肯定做了什么很有男子气的事情。这是牧羊人第一次见到柯里昂家族的眼神。唐·托马西诺知道迈克尔的真实身份和案底,待他向来很谨慎,拿他当同样"值得尊敬的人",但这两个没文化的羊倌对迈克尔有自己的看法,而且不怎么聪明。迈克尔冷冰冰的眼神,他刚硬发白的脸膛,浑身散发出的怒气,犹如冰块上流淌出的寒雾,止住了他们的笑声和热乎劲儿。

迈克尔看到他们恭敬得体的视线,说:"叫他出来见我。"

他们丝毫没有犹豫,扛起狼枪,走进昏暗凉爽的店堂。几秒钟后,两人夹着老板重新出现。矮胖的男人面无惧色,但怒气里有一丝警觉。

迈克尔靠在椅背上,打量了他几秒钟,然后非常平静地说:"我明白议论你女儿惹你生气了。请接受我的道歉,我在这里是陌生人,不太熟悉风俗。请允许我这么说:我对你和她都毫无不尊敬的意思。"

牧羊人保镖深受触动。和他们说话的时候,迈克尔从没用过这个语气。尽管是在道歉,但声音里透着命令和权威的感觉。老板耸耸肩,更加警觉了,知道不是在和普通农夫打交道。"你是谁,你对我女儿有什么想法?"

迈克尔毫不迟疑地说:"我是美国人,来西西里躲藏,逃避美国警察的追捕。我叫迈克尔。你可以向警察告密,挣一大笔钱,可你女儿不但会失去自己的父亲,还会失去一个丈夫。我无论如何都想认识你的女儿,在你的允许和你家族的监管下认识一下,以我全部的礼数和全部的尊重认识一下她。我想认识她,和她说话,要是彼此都觉得合适,我想娶她。要是不合适,你就再也不会见到我了。她也许会觉得我很讨厌,这就不是人力能挽救的了。可是,要是时机恰当,我会把岳父应该了解的事情全部告诉你。"

三个男人惊愕地瞪着他,法布雷奇奥敬畏地悄声说:"真是好一道霹雳。"老板终于没那么趾高气扬、满脸不屑了,连怒气都没那么笃定了。最后,他说:"你是朋友们的朋友吗?"

普通西西里人绝对不会大声说出"黑手党"这个词,所以店老板这等于是在问迈克尔是不是黑手党的成员。这是问一个人属不属于黑手党的通常问法,但一般不会直接向当事人提出。

"不,"迈克尔说,"我在这里是陌生人。"

老板重新审视他,看他破相的左脸,看西西里少有的两条长腿。他打量着明目张胆扛枪的两个牧羊人,想起他们怎么走进咖啡馆,说他们的东家要和他聊聊。老板吼叫着要那个王八蛋从他家露台滚蛋,一名牧羊人却说:"听我一句,你最好亲自出去和他聊聊。"他不由自主走了出来。此刻他意识到最好对这个陌生人以礼相待,于是勉强道:"星期天下午来吧。我叫维泰利,我住在村外山坡上的高处。你先来咖啡馆,我带你上去。"

法布雷奇奥想说什么,迈克尔用一个眼神制止了他,牧羊人的舌头冻在了嘴里。维泰利也注意到了这一点。迈克尔起身伸出一只手,老板紧紧握住,满脸笑容。他要打听一下,要是答案不如意,反正可以让两个儿子带着霰弹枪迎接迈克尔。老板在

"朋友们的朋友"圈里也有不少关系。不过,直觉告诉他这就是西西里人信奉的不期而遇的好运气,女儿的美貌将让她不愁吃穿,家族兴旺。其实倒也不错。村里有些年轻人已经开始围着女儿打转,这张破相的脸足以完成吓跑他们的必要任务。为了表达善意,维泰利送了他们一瓶最好最冰的葡萄酒。他注意到付钱的是一名牧羊人。这让他的心里更加有数了,迈克尔说了算,另外两个只是他的手下。

迈克尔失去了远足的兴致。他们找到一家车行,雇用汽车和司机送他们回柯里昂镇。还没到吃晚饭的时候,塔扎医生多半就从牧羊人嘴里听说了前后经过。晚上,坐在花园里,塔扎医生对唐·托马西诺说:"我们的朋友今天吃了一道霹雳。"

唐·托马西诺似乎并不吃惊,他咕哝道:"真希望巴勒莫的那帮年轻人也能吃一记霹雳,好让我喘口气。"他说的是巴勒莫那些大城市里涌现的新派黑手党首领,正在挑战他这种旧体系的中坚力量。

迈克尔对托马西诺说:"我想请你吩咐两个羊倌一声,星期天别跟着我。我要去女孩的家里吃饭,不希望他们在旁边转来转去。"

唐·托马西诺摇摇头:"你是你父亲托付给我的,所以别对我提这种要求。另外呢,我怎么听你已经在说结婚了?在我派人和你父亲通气之前,这种事绝对不可能发生。"

迈克尔·柯里昂说得很小心,这毕竟是一位值得尊敬的长者。"唐·托马西诺,你了解我的父亲。要是有人拒绝他,他的耳朵马上会什么也听不见,直到答应了才会恢复听觉。唉,他已经被我拒绝了好几次。保镖的事情我理解,我不想招惹麻烦,他们星期天陪我去好了,但结不结婚我说了算。既然我不允许父亲干涉我的私生活,那么要是允许你这么做,岂不是在侮辱他吗?"

黑手党头目叹息道:"唉,好吧,看来这个婚是非结不可了。我知道你是被霹雳打中了。她是个正派人家的好姑娘。你要是侮辱了她家门楣,她父亲肯定会追杀你,你肯定会流血。另外,我和这家人很熟,我不会允许这种事发生。"

迈克尔说:"她也许会受不了我的长相,另外她年纪很小,会觉得我太老,"他见到两个男人在对他笑,"我需要钱买礼物,最好还能有辆车。"

唐点点头。"都交给法布雷奇奥安排吧,他很机灵,在海军学过机修。我明天早上给你些钱,顺便通知一下你父亲——这是我的义务。"

迈克尔对塔扎医生说:"有什么办法能止住这该死的鼻涕吗?我不想让姑娘看见我总在擦鼻子。"

塔扎医生说:"可以在你出发前给你敷药,会让你感觉有点发麻,但别担心,你一时半会儿还不能亲她。"医生和唐都被这句俏皮话逗乐了。

　　星期天之前,迈克尔拿到一辆阿尔法罗密欧,有点破旧,但还能开。他搭巴士去了一趟巴勒莫,为姑娘及其家人置办礼物。他得知姑娘叫阿波罗妮亚,每晚总挂念她可爱的面容和好听的名字,不使劲喝酒就睡不着,医生家的几位老女仆得到命令,每晚要在他床边放一瓶冰好的葡萄酒。他每晚都喝个精光。

　　星期天,随着响彻西西里全境的教堂钟声,他开着阿尔法罗密欧去了那个村子,在咖啡馆门口停车。卡洛和法布雷奇奥带着狼枪坐在后排,迈克尔叫他们在店里等,别跟着他去老板家。咖啡馆今天歇业,露台上空无一人,维泰利靠在栏杆上等他们。

　　几个人互相握手,迈克尔带着三个装礼物的小包,跟着维泰利爬上山坡。维泰利的住处比普通村合宽敞得多,他家显然不穷。

　　室内的陈设很熟悉,有几尊罩着玻璃罩的圣母像,圣母像脚下闪烁着祈祷蜡烛的红光。两个儿子在等他们,同样身穿星期天穿的黑衣。两个年轻人顶多二十出头,身强力壮,经常下地干活,模样比较成熟。母亲身材健壮,和丈夫一样矮胖身材。没有那姑娘的身影。

　　先是一轮彼此介绍,迈克尔连听也没听,众人在一个房间里落座,这里多半是客厅,但也有可能是正式的用餐室。房间里塞满了各色家具,不怎么宽敞,但就西西里的标准而言,已经是中产阶级方能享受的浮华生活了。

　　迈克尔向维泰利先生和维泰利夫人奉上礼物。给父亲的礼物是个金质雪茄剪,给母亲是在巴勒莫能买到的一匹最好的布料。还有一件礼物是给那姑娘的。维泰利夫妇收下礼物,但感激中有所保留。礼物给得有点早,通常要到第二次登门拜访才送礼。

　　父亲用乡下男人对男人的语气对迈克尔说:"别以为我们家就那么低贱,会随便欢迎陌生人进门。但唐·托马西诺以个人名义为你作保,整个行省没有一个人会怀疑这位好人的信誉,所以我们才愿意欢迎你。可是,有句话我要说清楚,如果你对我女儿是认真的,那么我们就必须先知道一下你和你家族的情况。你应该能理解,你们家也是这个国家出去的。"

　　迈克尔点点头,有礼貌地说:"只要你想知道,我随时愿意都有问必答。"

　　维塔利阁下举起一只手。"我这人不喜欢打听是非。先看有没有必要好了。现在你是以唐·托马西诺的朋友身份进我家门的。"

　　尽管鼻腔内部敷了药,但迈克尔竟然闻到那姑娘出现在了房间里。他转过身,姑娘就站在通往里屋的拱门门口。那是鲜花和柠檬花的香味,可她乌黑的卷发上没有簪花,纯黑色的裙装上——显然是她最好的主日礼服——也没有装饰。她瞥了迈克尔一眼,微微一笑,端庄地垂下眼睛,在母亲身边坐下。

　　迈克尔又有了那种气短的感觉,洪水般涌遍全身的与其说是情欲,不如说是疯狂的占有欲。他第一次理解了意大利男人那闻名遐迩的嫉妒。此时此刻，要是有谁敢碰一下这女孩，妄图宣称拥有她，从他手里夺走她，他就会毫不犹豫杀死对方。他想占有她，就像吝啬鬼想占有金币那样痴狂，就像小佃农想拥有一片土地那样饥渴，想把她锁在房间里，囚禁她，只有他一个人能碰。他甚至不想让别人看见她。她扭头对一个哥哥微笑，迈克尔想也没想就向他投去杀人的眼神。全家人都看见了，认为是挨了"霹雳"的典型症状，顿时放下心来。结婚之前，这位年轻人将是女儿手里的面团。结婚以后情况当然会有变化，但那也无所谓了。

迈克尔在巴勒莫也给自己买了些新衣服，此刻不再是衣着简陋的乡下人，全家人看得出他肯定是个唐。和他想象中的不一样，脸伤并没有让他显得邪恶；另一边侧脸英俊非凡，弥补了破相的一边。这点伤在西西里再怎么说也称不上破相，因为要和他比较的是许多身体上遭遇了极度不幸的人。

迈克尔直勾勾地望着姑娘，她可爱的鸭蛋脸。他见到她的嘴唇近乎于紫蓝色，颜色和嘴唇里流淌的鲜血一样深。他不敢直呼她的名字，只好说："我那天在橘树丛见到了你，你转身逃跑，希望我没有吓坏你。"

女人抬起眼睛，看了他仅仅一瞬间。她摇摇头，但那双眼睛可爱得让迈克尔不得不转开视线。母亲凶巴巴地说："阿波罗妮亚，和可怜的小伙子说两句吧，他赶了许多里路来见你。"但女孩长且黑的睫毛一动不动，翅膀般遮住双眼。迈克尔把用金纸裹着的礼物递给她，她接过去放在膝头。父亲说："打开吧，女儿。"但她的手没有动。这双棕色的小手像是属于顽童。母亲探身拿起包裹，不耐烦地打开，但下手很有分寸，不想扯破昂贵的包装纸。见到红色天鹅绒的首饰盒，她犹豫片刻，她这双手还没拿过这种东西，不知道怎么打开暗扣。不过她还是凭借本能打开了，取出礼物。

礼物是一条沉重的金链，可以当项链佩戴，全家人倍感敬畏，不但因为显然很值钱，更因为在这个社会里，金子质地的礼物就等于最认真的表白，不亚于求婚，至少也是有求婚的意图。他们不再怀疑陌生人的诚恳，也不再怀疑他的家世。

阿波罗妮亚仍旧没有去拿礼物。母亲举到她眼前让她看，她抬起长长的睫毛，只看了一眼，就转而直视迈克尔，小鹿般的棕色眼睛很严肃，用意大利语说："谢谢。"这是迈克尔第一次听见她说话。

声音仿佛天鹅绒，充满了少女的柔嫩和羞怯，听得迈克尔的耳朵嗡嗡作响。他不敢看她，只和她父母说话，因为看她会让他失魂落魄。不过他还是注意到了，尽管她的衣服很保守，宽宽大大的，但她的肉体仍旧散发着纯粹的肉欲，如亮光般射穿布料。他还注意到她涨红了脸，热血涌到脸上，暗奶油色的肤色变得更深了。

最后，迈克尔起身准备离开，全家人跟着站了起来。他们郑重其事地道别，握手的时候,女孩终于站在了他面前,肌肤相贴让迈克尔像是触了电,她的手温暖而粗糙——乡民的皮肤。父亲送他下山上车,请他下周来吃星期天的正餐。迈克尔点点头,但知道自己不可能忍耐一星期之久。

他没有苦苦等待。第二天,他没带那两个牧羊人,开车来村里,坐在咖啡馆的花园露台上,同女孩的父亲聊天。维泰利先生动了恻隐之心,叫老婆和女儿下山来咖啡馆和他们一起坐坐。这次就没那么尴尬了。阿波罗妮亚不再那么羞怯,话也稍微多了些。她身穿日常的印花衣服,更加适合她的肤色。

第三天,还是照旧。只是这次阿波罗妮亚戴着他送的金链。迈克尔对她微笑,知道这是在给他打暗号。他送阿波罗妮亚上山,她母亲紧随其后,但这也阻止不了两个年轻人的身体挨挨蹭蹭,阿波罗妮亚绊了一下,撞在他身上,他只得伸手扶住她,她的身体是那么温暖,那么充满活力,在迈克尔的血液里掀起阵阵波澜。他们看不见维泰利夫人在背后忍不住笑了,因为她的女儿是一头小山羊,还裹着尿布的时候就在这条路上上下下了,怎么可能绊跤?她笑是因为在婚礼之前,这位年轻人只能用这个办法摸摸她的女儿了。

如此,两周一晃而过。迈克尔每次来都要送她礼物,她的羞怯越来越少。不过,他们见面的时候总有女方家里的长辈盯着。她只是个农村姑娘,没多少文化,对这个世界一无所知,但她对生活有着鲜活的渴望,再加上语言的障碍,她显得格外有趣。一切都按照迈克尔的愿望顺利进行。姑娘不但迷上了他,还知道他肯定很有钱,婚礼定于两周后的星期天举行。

唐·托马西诺终于插手。他收到从美国传来的话:迈克尔做事可以不受约束,但必要的预防措施还是一样也不能少。因此,唐·托马西诺自命为新郎的长辈,他的保镖到场也就顺理成章了。卡洛、法布雷奇奥和塔扎医生都算是柯里昂家族出席婚礼的代表。新郎和新娘将住进塔扎医生那幢有石墙包围的别墅。

婚礼是普通的乡村婚礼。新郎新娘和来宾组成队伍,步行从新娘家走向教堂,村民站在街道上,朝他们撒鲜花。婚礼队伍把糖衣杏仁——传统的结婚糖果——扔给邻居,剩下的糖果在新娘的婚床上堆成白色糖山,不过这里的婚床只是个象征,因为他们将在柯里昂镇外的别墅度过初夜。婚宴要持续到午夜,但新郎新娘会早早乘那辆阿尔法罗密欧离开。到了要离开的时候,迈克尔惊讶地发现新娘请母亲陪他们一起去柯里昂镇。父亲解释说姑娘年纪还小,是处女,有点害怕,新婚之夜过后的早晨需要有人陪她说说话;万一出什么岔子,还能把她拨回正轨——情况有时候会变得很棘手,对吧?迈克尔发现阿波罗妮亚看着他,小鹿般的棕色大眼里含着疑虑。迈克尔对她笑了笑,点头答应。

就这样，他们开车载着岳母回到柯里昂镇外的别墅。不过年长的妇人见到塔扎医生的女仆就咬起了耳朵，抱了抱女儿，留下一个吻就走了。迈克尔和新娘总算可以单独走进宽敞的卧室。

阿波罗妮亚在斗篷底下还穿着婚纱。嫁妆箱和行李从车里送进了房间。小桌上有一瓶葡萄酒和一盘小婚礼蛋糕。两人的眼睛总往华盖大床瞅，姑娘站在房间正中央，等待迈克尔先采取行动。

此刻他单独和她在一起了，合法地拥有她了，不再有障碍阻挡他享用每晚都要梦到的这具躯体和这张面容了，但迈克尔却无法走近她。他望着她摘下新娘的头纱，搭在椅背上，把新娘的花冠放在小梳妆台上。梳妆台上有一排迈克尔派人从巴勒莫买来的香水和面霜。姑娘用视线清点了一遍。

迈克尔关掉灯，心想姑娘在等待黑暗遮蔽身体，好脱下身上的衣服。可是，西西里的月光却从敞开的窗户里洒了进来，金光亮如白昼，迈克尔过去关百叶窗，但留了一条缝，免得房间里太闷热。

姑娘还站在小桌边，迈克尔只好走出房间，到走廊另一头的卫生间去了。他同塔扎医生和唐·托马西诺在花园里喝了杯葡萄酒，妇人们正忙着铺床。他以为回去的时候会见到阿波罗妮亚身穿睡衣，已经躺在了床上。他惊讶地发现母亲还没向女儿传授过这一点。也许阿波罗妮亚本来希望他能帮她脱衣服。不过，迈克尔相信她还太腼腆，太纯真，做不出这么主动的事情。

回到卧室里，他发现房间一片漆黑，有人完全关上了百叶窗。他摸索着走到床边，辨认出阿波罗妮亚裹着被单的身影，她背对着他，蜷成一团。迈克尔脱掉衣服，赤裸裸地钻到被单里。他伸出一只手，摸到的是丝绸般的赤裸皮肤。她没有穿睡衣，这份大胆激励了迈克尔。他小心翼翼地慢慢按住她的肩膀，轻轻用力，让她转过来面对他。她缓缓转身，他的手摸到了她的乳房，那么柔软，那么丰满，她飞快地钻进他的怀抱，两具肉体紧紧贴在一起，激起一道微弱的电流，他终于搂住了她，深深亲吻她温暖的嘴唇，把她的肉体和乳房按在自己身上，一翻身骑上了她的身体。

她的肉体和毛发如绸缎般紧绷，她的欲望也起来了，初生的情欲促使她贴紧迈克尔。他进入她的身体，她轻轻惊叫一声，身体静止了一秒钟，紧接着使劲一挺下体，两条光滑的大腿缠住迈克尔的臀部。来到高潮，两具身体死死纠缠，拼命互相擦蹭，彼此分开就仿佛临终前的颤抖。

那天晚上和接下来的几周，迈克尔·柯里昂终于理解了淳朴百姓为何如此珍视处女。这是一段他从未体验过的肉欲时光，让他体会到了雄性的力量。头几天，阿波罗妮亚简直成了他的奴隶。精力旺盛的姑娘得到信赖和怜爱，刚刚摆脱处女身份，被唤起了性意识,甘美得仿佛熟透的水果一般。

她一个人就点亮了别墅里颇为阴郁的男性气氛。新婚之夜后的第二天,她把母亲送回家,以活泼的少女魅力主持餐桌。唐·托马西诺每天和他们共进晚餐,随后坐进满是戴着血红花环的雕像的花园,边喝葡萄酒边听塔扎医生讲那些老故事,因此晚上总是过得很愉快。夜里回到卧室,新婚的两人接连几个小时狂热做爱。迈克尔怎么也尝不够阿波罗妮亚那雕像般的美丽肉体,怎么也看不够她蜜色的皮肤和闪着情欲光芒的棕色大眼。她散发着美妙的清新气味,性欲激发的肉体气息,近乎于甜香,是可怕的催情剂。她的处女激情和他的勃发情欲相得益彰,两人往往到黎明时才筋疲力尽地睡着。有时候,尽管已经疲惫但还不想睡觉,迈克尔就坐在窗台上望着沉睡的阿波罗妮亚的赤裸身躯。她的面容在睡梦中也那么可爱,迈克尔以前只在意大利圣母绘本里见过,艺术家的笔法再怎么夸张,你也看得出那肯定是处女。

婚后第一周,他们时常开着阿尔法罗密欧外出野餐和游玩。唐·托马西诺私下告诉迈克尔,结婚让西西里人都知道了他的出现和身份,因此必须采取预防措施,应付柯里昂家族的敌人——他们的长臂也伸进了岛上的避难地。唐·托马西诺在别墅周围安排了武装警卫,牧羊人卡洛和法布雷奇奥在石墙内值勤。迈克尔和妻子只能在别墅地界内活动。迈克尔教阿波罗妮亚读写英语和绕着石墙内沿开车,借此消磨时光。在这段时间里,唐·托马西诺忙得不可开交,很少陪他们。塔扎医生说他还在和巴勒莫城的新黑手党闹不和。

一天夜里在花园,一位在别墅做事的老年村妇端来一碟新鲜橄榄,然后转身问迈克尔:"大家都说你是纽约教父唐·柯里昂的儿子,真的吗?"

迈克尔见到唐·托马西诺气得直摇头,他们的秘密如今已经众所周知。可是,这个干瘪老太的眼神却那么热切,知不知道实情对她来说似乎很重要,迈克尔于是点点头。"你认识我父亲?"他问。

老妇人名叫菲洛蒙娜,皱皱巴巴的棕色面容像个核桃,皮壳裂开,露出褐色的牙齿。迈克尔来别墅这么久,她还是第一次对他微笑。"教父救过我的命,"她说,"还有我的脑子。"她朝脑袋打个手势。

她显然还想说什么,迈克尔用微笑鼓励她。她畏畏缩缩问:"卢卡·布拉齐死了,真的吗?"

迈克尔又点点头,惊讶地看见老妇人露出如释重负的表情。菲洛蒙娜在胸前画个十字,说:"上帝宽恕我,但我希望他的灵魂在地狱里受煎熬,直到永恒。"

迈克尔回想起他从前对布拉齐的好奇,直觉突然告诉他,老妇人知道黑根和桑尼一直不肯告诉他的某些事情。他给老妇人斟了一杯酒,请她坐下。"给我说说我的父亲和卢卡·布拉齐,"他温和地说,"我知道部分情况,但他们是怎么成为朋友的? 布拉齐对我父亲为何那么忠诚? 别害怕,请告诉我。"

菲洛蒙娜那张皱巴巴的脸和葡萄干似的黑眼睛转向唐·托马西诺,唐·托马西诺用某种方式表达了同意。于是菲洛蒙娜讲起她的故事,陪他们度过这个夜晚。

三十年前,菲洛蒙娜是纽约的接生婆,在第十大道为意大利移民服务。意大利女人总是怀孕,她的生意颇为兴隆。医生遇到难产都要向她请教。她的丈夫开了个杂货店,生意也很不错——但他已经死了,愿他可怜的灵魂安息——可是,他喜欢打牌和玩女人,没想过为艰难时日存钱。总而言之,三十年前那个该诅咒的晚上,正经人早就上床休息了,忽然有人来敲菲洛蒙娜的门。她并不害怕,因为谨慎的孩子总是挑这个时辰降临罪恶尘世,她穿上衣服打开门。门口站着的是卢卡·布拉齐,当时就已经声名狼藉了。另外,大家都知道他是单身汉。菲洛蒙娜马上慌了神。她以为布拉齐是来收拾她丈夫的,她丈夫说不定一时犯傻,拒绝帮布拉齐什么小忙。

可是,布拉齐这次倒是肩负着最普通的任务,说有个女人快要临盆,住处离这附近有段距离,她必须跟他走。菲洛蒙娜立刻觉得有什么地方不对劲。那天晚上,布拉齐凶恶的脸就像个疯子,显然被什么魔鬼摄了心神。她不想去,说她只给她了解情况的女人接生,但他捞出一大把绿票子塞进她手里,粗声大气地命令她别磨蹭。她害怕,不敢拒绝。

街上停着一辆福特,司机和卢卡·布拉齐是一路货色。开了不到三十分钟,他们过桥来到长岛市的一幢板房小屋。屋子能住两户人家,现在显然只有布拉齐和他的同党,因为厨房里还有几个混混在打牌喝酒。布拉齐拉着菲洛蒙娜上楼进卧室。床上是个漂亮姑娘,像是爱尔兰血统,脸化着浓妆,一头红发,肚子胀得像母猪。可怜的姑娘怕得要死,见到布拉齐,她惊恐得转过头去——对,就是惊恐——布拉齐那张邪恶面孔上的憎恨表情,她这辈子也没见过更可怕的东西(菲洛蒙娜又在胸前画个十字)。

长话短说,布拉齐走出房间。他的两个手下协助接生婆,孩子生下来了,母亲筋疲力尽,陷入沉睡。布拉齐被叫过来,菲洛蒙娜用多余的毯子裹起婴儿,把小包裹递给他,"这个女儿是你的吧,接着。我的任务完成了。"

布拉齐凶恶地瞪着她,癫狂占据了他的整张脸。"对,是我的,"他说,"但我不要这个种的东西活下去。给我拿到地下室,扔进锅炉。"

菲洛蒙娜有一瞬间以为她听错了什么。"种"这个字用得她大惑不解。他难道想说这姑娘不是意大利人? 还是说这姑娘是最低贱的品种,简而言之就是妓女? 还是在说从他下体出来的东西就不配活下去? 她确信布拉齐开了个粗鲁的玩笑,随口说:"反正是你的孩子,你爱怎么处理都随你。"她再次试图把包裹递给他。

筋疲力尽的母亲醒来了,转身面对他们,刚好看见布拉齐使劲一推小包裹,婴儿砸在菲洛蒙娜的胸口。她用微弱的声音喊道:"卢卡,卢卡,我真抱歉。"布拉齐转身面对她。

太可怕了,此刻的菲洛蒙娜说,真是可怕。他们就像两头疯狂的野兽,根本不是人类,对彼此的憎恨弥漫在整个房间里。这一瞬间,什么都不存在了,连这个新生儿都不存在了。但其中又有一种怪异的激情:那种魔鬼般的嗜血欲望,实在有悖于自然,你知道这两个人将在地狱里永受煎熬。卢卡·布拉齐转过身,对菲洛蒙娜严厉地说:"照我说的做。我让你发财。"

菲洛蒙娜吓得不敢说话。她摇摇头,好不容易才挤出声音:"你自己动手,你是父亲,你喜欢怎么做就怎么做。"但布拉齐没有应声,而是从衬衫里掏出匕首。"我会割了你的喉咙。"他说。

她肯定陷入了休克状态,因为下一段记忆就是他们都来到了地下室,站在四四方方的铸铁锅炉前。菲洛蒙娜还抱着毯子里的婴儿,婴儿毫无声息(如果她大哭,如果我当时够机灵,使劲掐她一下,菲洛蒙娜说,那个魔鬼也许会发发善心)。

大概是哪个男人打开了炉门,她看见了火光。再一转眼,她和布拉齐单独站在地下室里,周围的水管在渗水,泛着一股耗子的臭味。布拉齐又抽出了匕首。毫无疑问,要是不从命,他就会杀死她。火光,布拉齐的眼睛。他那张脸,就是魔鬼的雕像,不是人类,没有理智。他把菲洛蒙娜推向敞开的炉门。

说到这里,菲洛蒙娜沉默下去。她并拢双手,放在膝头,直直地望着迈克尔。他知道她要什么,知道她想告诉他,但不想用自己的声音。他轻声问:"你做了吗?"她点点头。

她又喝了一杯葡萄酒,在胸前画个十字,祈祷几句,这才继续说下去。她收到一沓钞票,被车送回家。她明白要是敢走漏一个字,就得搭上自己的一条命。两天后,布拉齐杀死了婴儿的母亲,那个爱尔兰姑娘,警方随即逮捕了他。菲洛蒙娜吓得失魂落魄,跑去找教父,说了这件事情。教父命令她保守秘密,他会处理好一切的。布拉齐当时还没有为唐·柯里昂做事。

唐·柯里昂还没来得及摆平事情,卢卡·布拉齐在牢房里企图自杀,用一块玻璃划破喉咙。他被送进监狱的医院,在他养伤的时候,唐·柯里昂前前后后全都安排妥当了。警察知道卢卡·布拉齐犯案,却无法向法庭证明,只好释放了他。

尽管唐·柯里昂向菲洛蒙娜保证说她既不需要害怕卢卡·布拉齐,也不用担心警方,但她还是活得提心吊胆。她的精神几近崩溃,做不了老本行。最后,她说服丈夫卖掉杂货店,两人一起返回意大利。丈夫是个好人,菲洛蒙娜把一切都告诉了他,他完全理解。可是,他这人意志不够坚定,在意大利挥霍掉了两人在美国做苦力挣来的钱。他去世之后,菲洛蒙娜成了佣人。故事说到这里结束。她又喝了一杯葡萄酒,对迈克尔说:"我祝福你父亲的大名。我每次只要开口,他就会送钱给我,他从布拉齐手上救了我。转告他,我每晚都为他的灵魂祈祷,他不需要畏惧死亡。"

她离开后,迈克尔问唐·托马西诺:"她说的是真事吗?"黑手党头目点点头。迈克尔心想,难怪谁也不肯跟他说实话。非同一般的故事。非同一般的卢卡。

第二天早晨,迈克尔想和唐·托马西诺讨论一下所有事情,却得知一名信使传来紧急消息,老头子赶到巴勒莫去了。晚上,唐·托马西诺回来,把迈克尔叫到一旁。他说,美国来了消息。他悲痛得说不出口的消息。桑蒂诺·柯里昂被杀了。

第二十四章

清晨,西西里柠檬色的阳光洒满迈克尔的卧室。他睁眼醒来,感觉到阿波罗妮亚光滑的身体贴着他睡得热烘烘的皮肤,于是怀着爱意叫醒她。两人做爱完毕,尽管已经完全占有了她好几个月,但他仍旧惊叹于她的美丽和激情。

她走出卧室,去走廊另一头的卫生间盥洗更衣。迈克尔没有穿衣服,早晨的阳光让身体充满活力,他点燃香烟,懒洋洋地躺在床上。今天是他们在这幢别墅的最后一天。唐·托马西诺安排他去西西里南岸的另一个小镇。阿波罗妮亚怀孕刚第一个月,打算回家先住几个星期,随后再去迈克尔的新藏身处。

昨天晚上,阿波罗妮亚上床以后,唐·托马西诺和迈克尔在花园里坐下。唐既烦躁又疲惫,承认他很担心迈克尔的安全。"结婚让你暴露了,"他对迈克尔说,"真奇怪,你父亲怎么不安排你换个地方躲躲。我正在和巴勒莫的年轻土佬闹纠纷。我提出的安排很公平,允许他们湿湿嘴,比他们应得的还要多,可那群人渣什么都想要。我无法理解他们的心态。他们试着搞了些小花样,但我没那么容易死。他们必须明白,我这么强大,他们不可能轻易打败。但和年轻人打交道就是有这个坏处,能干归能干,但说不通道理,总想霸占一口井里的所有水。"

唐·托马西诺告诉迈克尔,牧羊人法布雷奇奥和卡洛将继续担任保镖,和他一起乘阿尔法罗密欧离开。唐·托马西诺今晚就要和他告别,因为明早天一亮他就要去巴勒莫处理事情。另外,迈克尔不能把这步棋告诉塔扎医生,因为医生打算去巴勒莫过夜,保不准会说漏嘴。

迈克尔知道唐·托马西诺处境不妙。武装保镖绕着别墅石墙彻夜巡逻,几个信得过的牧羊人背着狼枪总在屋里转悠。唐·托马西诺本人也全副武装,一名私人保镖亦步亦趋。

　　早晨的阳光越来越强烈。迈克尔揿熄烟头,按照大多数西西里男人的打扮,穿上工装裤、工装衬衫和鸭舌帽。他光着脚探出卧室窗户,见到法布雷奇奥坐在一把花园椅上。法布雷奇奥正在懒洋洋地梳理浓密的黑发,狼枪漫不经心地扔在花园桌上。迈克尔吹声口哨,法布雷奇奥抬头望向窗户。

　　"备车,"迈克尔低头喊道,"我五分钟后出发。卡洛呢?"

　　法布雷奇奥站起身,衬衫没有系纽扣,胸口文身的红蓝线条露在外面。"卡洛在厨房喝咖啡,"法布雷奇奥说,"你夫人也去吗?"

　　迈克尔眯起眼睛望着他。他忽然想到,法布雷奇奥最近这几周似乎总盯着阿波罗妮亚看。当然,他还没胆大包天得敢对唐的朋友的妻子下手,在西西里,没有比这更存心找死的事情了。迈克尔冷冷地说:"不,她要先回自己家,过几天再和我们会合。"他目送法布雷奇奥急匆匆地走向石屋,那里是存放阿尔法罗密欧的车库。

　　迈克尔去走廊的另一头洗漱。阿波罗妮亚已经走了,多半在厨房亲手为他准备早餐,洗掉心里的内疚,因为她想在去西西里的另一头之前,再回家多看两眼。唐·托马西诺会派人送她去迈克尔躲藏的地方。

　　下楼走进厨房,老妇人菲洛蒙娜端上咖啡,不好意思地对他说再见。"我会向父亲转达你的问候。"迈克尔说,她使劲点头。

　　卡洛走进厨房,对迈克尔说:"车开出来了,要我帮你拎行李吗?"

　　"不用了,我自己拎,"迈克尔说,"阿波拉呢?"

　　卡洛露出好笑的表情:"她坐在驾驶座上,想踩油门想得要命。她不用去美国就会变成美国人啦。"在西西里有农妇尝试驾驶汽车,这可是闻所未闻的稀奇事。迈克尔偶尔允许阿波罗妮亚开着阿尔法罗密欧绕着石墙内侧兜圈,但总坐在她身旁,因为她有时候想踩刹车,却一脚踏在油门上。

　　迈克尔对卡洛说:"叫上法布雷奇奥,到车上等我。"他走出厨房,跑上楼回卧室。他已经收拾好了行李。拎起皮箱前,他朝窗外张望了一眼,见到车停在门廊前,而不是厨房门口。阿波罗妮亚坐在车里,双手抓着方向盘,像是小孩子在玩耍。卡洛把午餐提篮放在后座上。这时,迈克尔见到法布雷奇奥走出了别墅大门,似乎要去外面办什么事,不禁有点烦心。这家伙在干什么? 他见到法布雷奇奥扭头张望,神情不知怎的有点鬼祟。他得好好教训一下这个牧羊人了。迈克尔走下楼梯,决定去厨房找菲洛蒙娜再打个招呼,和她郑重道别。他问老妇人:"塔扎医生还在睡觉吗?"

　　菲洛蒙娜皱巴巴的老脸淘气地笑了笑。"老公鸡等不到日出。医生昨晚就去巴勒莫了。"

迈克尔哈哈大笑。他从厨房走出别墅,柠檬花的香味沁透了他堵塞的鼻窦。他见到十步外的车道上,阿波罗妮亚在车里对他挥手,明白她是要他站在原处,等她把车开过来。卡洛笑嘻嘻地站在车旁,一只手抓着狼枪。法布雷奇奥仍旧不见踪影。就在这个时刻,没有经过任何推理,一切线索忽然在脑海里汇聚,迈克尔对姑娘喊道:"不!不!"可是,随着阿波罗妮亚发动引擎,剧烈的爆炸淹没了他的叫声。厨房门应声而碎,迈克尔被甩出去足足十英尺,狠狠摔在别墅的墙上。从屋顶震落的石块砸在肩膀上,他躺倒在地,又一块石头砸在他头上。在他失去意识之前,他只来得及看见阿尔法罗密欧只剩下了四个轮子和连接车轮的钢梁。

再次恢复知觉,他所在的房间似乎非常暗,他听见有人说话,但嗓子压得很低,听不清字词,只是些许声音。出于动物的本能,他试着假装还在昏迷,但说话声随即停止,有人在床边的椅子上俯身凑近他,声音也变得清晰,说:"哎呀,他总算醒来了。"一盏灯点亮,白热烈火般的光线炙烤眼球,迈克尔扭过头去。脑袋特别沉重,非常麻木。这时,他认出浮在上空的那张脸属于塔扎医生。

"让我稍微看看你,然后就关灯。"塔扎医生轻声说。他忙着用小手电照迈克尔的眼睛,"你会好起来的。"塔扎医生扭头对房间里的另一个人说:"你可以和他说话了。"

坐在床边椅子上的是唐·托马西诺,迈克尔这会儿看清了他的面容。唐·托马西诺在说:"迈克尔,迈克尔,能和我说话吗?还是想休息?"

抬起一只手打手势比说话容易,迈克尔这么做了,唐·托马西诺说:"是法布雷奇奥把车从车库里开出来的吗?"

迈克尔微微一笑——他不知道自己在笑,这个笑容表示同意,不同寻常,令人胆战心惊。唐·托马西诺说:"法布雷奇奥失踪了。听我说,迈克尔,你昏迷了近一周。明白吗?大家都以为你死了,所以现在你很安全,他们已经不再追杀你了。我送信通知了你父亲,他说用不了多久,你就可以返回美国。这段时间里,你就在这儿静养。你在山上,这儿是我的一个特别农庄,很安全。按理说你已经死了,巴勒莫的那些人与我讲和,他们的目标本来是你。他们想杀死你,但希望做得像是其实在追杀我。这一点你要记在心里,其他事情都交给我处理吧。你休养身体,悄悄待着。"

迈克尔记起了前后经过,知道妻子死了,卡洛也死了。他想到厨房里的老妇人,不记得她是不是跟着他走出了别墅。他哑着嗓子说:"菲洛蒙娜?"唐·托马西诺静静地说:"除了爆炸害她流鼻血,没受什么伤。别担心。"

迈克尔说:"法布雷奇奥。告诉你的牧羊人,谁交出法布雷奇奥,会获得全西西里最好的牧场。"

塔扎医生和唐·托马西诺都松了一口气。唐·托马西诺从手边的桌子上端起玻璃杯,仰起头,喝着琥珀色的烈酒。塔扎医生坐在床沿上,有点心不在焉地说:"知道吗? 你是鳏夫了。这在西西里很少见。"像是这点区别能安慰他似的。

迈克尔示意唐·托马西诺靠近。唐在床沿上坐下,俯下头。"告诉我父亲,把我弄回去,"迈克尔说,"告诉我父亲,我希望当他的儿子。"

迈克尔等了一个月,从重伤中恢复过来,又等了两个月,各种必要的手续和安排才完全就绪。他从巴勒莫飞到罗马,从罗马飞到纽约。在这段时间里,法布雷奇奥始终下落不明。

第七部

第二十五章

凯·亚当斯拿到大学学位,接受了新罕布什尔家乡一所小学的教职。迈克尔消失后的头六个月,她每周打电话向迈克尔的母亲询问情况。柯里昂夫人很友善,最后却总是说:"你是个好姑娘。忘了米基吧,找个好丈夫。"这份直率并没有冒犯凯,她明白迈克尔的母亲这么说是出于关心,她的处境不可能有出路。

第一个学期结束,她决定去纽约买些好衣服,见见大学里的女同学。她还想在纽约找个更有意思的工作。她过了两年老处女的生活,读书教书,拒绝约会,拒绝一切活动,哪怕不再打电话到长滩以后也是这样。她知道她不能再这么过下去,自己正一天天变得暴躁和阴沉。可是,她却始终相信迈克尔会写信给她,或者想办法捎信给她。他不这么做就等于羞辱她,他居然这么不信任她,实在惹人伤心。

她搭早班火车出发,下午三四点住进酒店。当初的女同学都有工作,她不想打扰她们,打算晚上再打电话到她们家里。坐火车很疲劳,她没有外出购物的心情。她孤零零地坐在旅馆房间里,回想起迈克尔和她在旅馆里做爱的往事,不禁心情低落。是这种凄凉的心情,使得她拿起电话,打给长滩找迈克尔的母亲。

一个粗鲁的男人接听电话,她觉得纽约口音很重。凯请他找一下柯里昂夫人。等了几分钟,凯听见那个口音浓重的声音问她是谁。

凯有点尴尬。"我是凯·亚当斯,柯里昂夫人,"她说,"不记得我了?"

"怎么会?记得,当然记得,"柯里昂夫人说,"你怎么后来不打电话啦?结婚了吗?"

"唉,还没有,"凯说,"忙着工作。"迈克尔的母亲显然因为她不再打电话而有些生气,凯不由吃了一惊。"有迈克尔的消息吗?他没事吧?"

电话另一头沉默良久,最后传来了柯里昂夫人有力的声音:"米基回家了。他没打给你,没去见你?"

凯觉得胃里一阵发虚,委屈得想哭。她好不容易开口,有点语不成声:"他回家多久了?"

柯里昂夫人说:"六个月。"

"哦,我明白了。"凯答道。她确实明白了。迈克尔的母亲知道他待她实在过于轻贱,这让她觉得热辣辣的羞耻一波波袭来。紧接着,愤怒涌起。对迈克尔的愤怒,对他母亲的愤怒,对所有外国佬的愤怒,这些不通礼数的意大利人,就算做不了情人,也可以保持体面的友谊啊!就算迈克尔不想要她这个床伴,不再想娶她,也该明白她有多关心他啊!他难道以为她是那种愚昧的意大利姑娘,会因为奉献了贞操而又被抛弃就会自杀或者大吵大闹?她尽量冷静地说:"我明白了,非常感谢,"她说,"很高兴迈克尔回家了,一切安好。我只是想知道一下而已。我不会再打电话来了。"

柯里昂夫人的声音很不耐烦,像是没听见凯在说什么。"要见米基,就来这儿。给他一个大大的惊喜。你叫辆车,我吩咐看门的替你付车钱。你告诉出租车司机,车钱给他双份,否则他就不肯来长滩。不过你别付钱。门口我丈夫的手下会付钱。"

"我不能去,柯里昂夫人,"凯冷冰冰地说,"迈克尔要是想见我,早就打电话到我家里了。他很明显不想继续我们的关系。"

柯里昂夫人轻快地说:"你是个好姑娘,两条腿很漂亮,但没什么脑子,"她咯咯笑道,"你来看我,不是米基。我想和你聊聊。你马上来。别付车钱。我等你。"电话咔嗒一声断了。柯里昂夫人挂断了电话。

凯可以再打过去,说她来不了,但她知道她必须见迈克尔一面,和他说说话,哪怕只是礼貌闲谈也行。假如他已经回家,没有隐瞒行踪,就说明他已经从麻烦中脱身,可以过正常人的生活了。她跳下床,开始为见他作准备。她精心梳妆打扮。要出门的时候,她望着镜子里的自己。她比迈克尔失踪前更漂亮了吗?还是他会觉得我老了、没吸引力了?她的体型更有女人味了,臀部更加浑圆,胸部更加丰满。按理说意大利人就喜欢这样,可迈克尔却总说他就喜欢她瘦巴巴的。唉,有什么关系呢?迈克尔显然并不想再和我有什么瓜葛,否则六个月前一回到家就应该打电话给我了。

她拦下一辆出租车,司机拒绝送她去长滩,直到她对司机甜甜一笑,说按里程双倍付钱。车程近一小时,自从上次拜访,长滩的林荫道变了很多。林荫道四周筑起了铁栏杆,路口有一道大铁门。一个穿休闲裤、白上衣和红衬衫的男人过来开门,把脑袋探进车窗,看了看计价器,掏出一把钞票塞给司机。凯看见司机没有反对,对到手的数额颇为满意,于是下车走过林荫道,走向最中央的那幢屋子。

开门的是柯里昂太太本人,她用温暖的拥抱欢迎凯,凯不由吃了一惊。柯里昂太太又用赞赏的视线上下打量凯。"多漂亮的姑娘啊,"她说得毋庸置疑,"唉,我的儿子怎么那么傻。"她拉着凯进门,走进厨房,大浅盘已经盛满食物,炉子上煮着咖啡。"迈克尔马上就到家,"她说,"给他个惊喜吧。"

两人坐下,老妇人逼着凯多吃点,一边怀着极大的好奇心问东问西。得知凯是老师,来纽约是为了探访以前的女同学,今年只有二十四岁,她喜形于色。她频频点头,就仿佛这些事实印证了心里的猜测。凯紧张极了,只懂得问一句答一句,别的什么都没说。

她首先隔着厨房的窗户瞥见了他。一辆车在屋前停下,另外两个男人钻出车门,随后是迈克尔。他站直身,和另外两个男人里的一个说话。他的左脸暴露在她的视线之内。这半边脸受过伤,凹下去了,就像洋娃娃的脸被顽皮孩童踢了一脚。奇怪的是,破相在她眼中并没有损害他的英俊,却引得她淌出了眼泪。他转身准备进屋,她见到他取出一块雪白的手帕,捂住嘴巴和鼻子,压了几秒钟。

她听见门打开了,他的脚步声从门厅转向厨房,他出现在厨房里,见到了凯和他的母亲。他似乎不为所动,只是微微一笑,破相的左脸使得他没法咧嘴。凯本想用最冰冷的语气说一声"你好吗",却从座位上跳起来,扑进他的怀抱,把脸蛋埋在他的肩膀上。他亲吻她湿漉漉的面颊,抱紧她,等她哭完,然后领着她出门上车,挥手赶开保镖,带着凯驱车离开。她用手帕擦掉残余的化妆,就算是补妆了。

"我可不想哭成这样的,"凯说,"但谁也没有告诉我,他们把你伤成了这个样子。"

迈克尔笑着摸了摸受伤的半边脸。"你说这个?没什么。只是让我鼻窦不舒服。现在回来了,我有时间就去治一治。我不能给你写信或者用别的方式联系你,"迈克尔说,"你首先必须理解这一点。"

"好吧。"她说。

"我在市里有个地方,"迈克尔说,"我们现在就过去,还是先找家餐馆吃顿饭、喝两杯?"

"我不饿。"凯说。

他们向纽约开去,两人都沉默了一阵子。"你拿到学位了吗?"迈克尔问。

"拿到了,"凯说,"我现在是小学老师。他们找到了杀死警察的真凶吗?所以你才可以回家?"

迈克尔有好一会儿没有回答。"是啊,找到了,"他说,"纽约的报纸全登了。你没读到?"

凯笑了起来，他否认自己是杀人犯，她不由松了一口气。"我们镇上只有《纽约时报》，"她说，"这条新闻估计塞在最后面的八十九页上。我要是读到了，肯定会早些打电话给你母亲。"她停了停，又说，"真有意思，听你母亲说话的语气，我都快相信事情真是你做的了。你回来之前，我们喝咖啡的时候，她还在说认罪的那个疯子如何如何。"

迈克尔说："说不定我母亲刚开始也相信了。"

"你的亲生母亲？"凯问。

迈克尔咧嘴一笑。"母亲和警察一样，总把事情往坏里想。"

迈克尔把车停进桑树街的一家修车铺，老板似乎认得他。他领着凯拐弯走向一幢相当老旧的褐石大屋，屋子颇为符合这个破败的街区。迈克尔用钥匙打开前门，走进室内，凯发现装饰昂贵而舒适，堪比百万富翁的市区联排别墅。迈克尔领着凯上楼，楼上的套房包括宽敞的客厅、大厨房和一扇通往卧室的门。客厅的一角是吧台，迈克尔给两人调酒。他们坐进沙发，迈克尔静静地说："我们不如去卧室吧。"凯喝了一大口酒，对他微笑。"好的。"她说。

凯觉得做爱和以前同样美妙，只是迈克尔变得更粗鲁直接了，不像以前那么温柔。就好像他对她也有所防范，但她不打算抱怨。隔阂是会逐渐消失的。说来有趣，她心想，男人遇到这种情况往往更加敏感。她发觉时隔两年，和迈克尔做爱仍旧是天底下最自然而然的事情，就仿佛他从没离开过一天。

"你应该给我写信，应该信任我的，"她贴在迈克尔的身上说，"我会遵守新英格兰的缄默规则。扬基佬的嘴巴也可以很紧，你知道的。"

迈克尔在黑暗中轻声笑着说："我没想到你会等我。发生了那些事情，我真的没想到你还会等我。"

凯很快回答："我一直不相信是你杀了那两个人。听你母亲似乎相信了的时候也许除外。但我心里从来就不相信。我太了解你了。"

她听见迈克尔喟然叹息。"我有没有杀人并不重要，"他说，"你必须理解这一点。"

他冷酷的声音让凯不明所以。她说："你就直说吧，到底是不是你？"

迈克尔在枕头上坐起来，黑暗中火光一闪，他点燃香烟。"如果我向你求婚，你在回答之前是不是非要我先回答这个问题？"

凯说："我不在乎，我爱你，真的不在乎。如果你也爱我，就不该害怕告诉我实话。不该害怕我会去报告警察。就这么简单，对不对？你其实真是黑帮，对吧？可我并不在乎。我在意的只是你显然不爱我。你回家这么久，连个电话都不打给我。"

迈克尔抽着香烟，烟灰掉在凯赤裸的脊背上。她轻轻一抖，开玩笑地说："别折磨我了，我是不会说的。"

迈克尔没有笑，语气有点茫然。"知道吗？回到美国，见到家里人，父亲、母亲、妹妹康妮、汤姆，我并不那么开心。好归好，但我根本不在乎。可今晚回到家里，见到你在厨房里，我开心极了。要你说，这算不算是爱？"

"要我说，已经足够接近了。"凯答道。

他们又做了一回爱。这次迈克尔温柔多了。他出去给两人斟酒，回来时坐进面对床的扶手椅。"我说正经的，"他说，"愿不愿意嫁给我？"凯对他微笑，示意他上床。迈克尔报以微笑。"说正经的，"他说，"我不能事无巨细全告诉你。我现在为父亲工作了。他在培养我接管家族的橄榄油生意。但你知道我的家族有敌人，我的父亲有敌人。你说不定年纪轻轻就要当寡妇，这个可能性虽说微乎其微，但毕竟存在。我不能把办公室每天发生了什么一五一十全告诉你。我不能把生意场上的事情全告诉你。你会成为我的妻子，但没法成为我的人生伴侣——大家是这么说的，对吧？不是彼此对等的伴侣。这个不可能。"

凯在床上坐起来，打开床头柜上的大台灯，点燃香烟，靠在枕头上，平静地说："你想说你确实是黑帮，对不对？你想说你要为杀人和各种与杀人有关的罪行负责。想说我不能过问你的那部分生活，甚至连想都不能想。这算什么？简直是恐怖电影里怪物在求美丽的姑娘嫁给他。"迈克尔咧嘴一笑，破相的半边脸转过来对着凯，凯后悔道："天哪，迈克，我根本没注意到那块该死的地方，我发誓，真的没有。"

"我知道，"迈克尔笑着说，"我现在还挺喜欢的，只是害得我经常流鼻涕。"

"你说要认真的，"凯继续道，"我们要是结婚，我会过上什么样的生活？就像你母亲？意大利家庭主妇，养几个孩子，收拾收拾屋子？要是出事怎么办？我怀疑你迟早要坐牢。"

"不，绝对不可能，"迈克尔说，"被杀？有可能。坐牢？不可能。"

他的信心让凯笑出了声，这个笑声很有意思，混合了骄傲和因骄傲而起的喜悦。"你凭什么这么说？"她说，"说真的，告诉我。"

迈克尔叹息道："有许许多多事情我不能告诉你，也不想告诉你。"

凯沉默许久。"既然你回来了好几个月都不肯打电话给我，为什么又想要我嫁给你？我在床上有那么好？"

迈克尔郑重其事地点点头。"对，"他说，"不过我不费吹灰之力就能享受到，为什么要为了这个求你嫁给我呢？听着，你现在不需要回答我。我们继续见面。你回去和父母商量一下。听说你父亲也很强硬。听听他的建议吧。"

"你还没有回答我的问题呢,你为什么要我嫁给你?"凯说。

迈克尔从床头柜的抽屉里取出一块白手帕,捂住鼻子擤了一下,擦掉鼻涕。"这是不嫁给我的最好的理由,"他说,"有个家伙总在身边擤鼻子,怎么受得住?"

凯不耐烦地说:"快说,说正经的,我在问你问题呢。"

迈克尔抓着那块手帕。"好吧,"他说,"只此一次。天底下我只对你有爱恋和关心的感觉。我没有打电话给你,是因为没想到发生了那些事情之后,你仍旧对我感兴趣。是啊,我可以追求你,哄骗你,但我不想那么做。我信任你,所以愿意告诉你一件事,但你别说给别人听,哪怕是我父亲。如果一切顺利,柯里昂家族将在五年内完全合法化。要实现这个想法,就必须处理好一些非常棘手的事情——所以我说你也许会成为很有钱的寡妇。说到我为什么想娶你,好吧,因为就是想要你,想要成家。我想要孩子,是时候了。我不希望孩子受到我的影响,就像我受到我父亲的影响那样。倒不是说我父亲存心影响了我。他没有这么做过,他甚至根本不希望我参与家族生意,他更希望我去当教授或医生。可惜事与愿违,我不得不为家族战斗。因为我爱我父亲,敬重我父亲。我不知道还有谁比他更值得尊敬。他是好丈夫和好父亲,对活得不那么幸运的人来说是好朋友。他还有另外一面,但对我,对他的儿子来说并不重要。总而言之,我不希望我们的孩子遇到这种事情。我希望他们能受到你的影响,希望他们像真正的美国孩子那样长大,成为真正的美国人,里里外外都是。他们或者他们的儿孙也许能进入政界,"迈克尔笑了笑,"说不定还能出个美国总统呢。没什么是不可能的。在达特茅斯上历史课的时候,我们研究过历届总统的背景,有些人的父亲和祖父没被绞死就算是走运了。不过我的孩子当医生、音乐家和老师也不错。他们绝对不能参与家族生意。等他们到那个年纪,我早就退休了。你和我会加入什么乡村俱乐部,过着富裕美国人简单而美好的生活。你觉得我的求婚词听起来怎么样?"

"非同凡响,"凯说,"不过当寡妇那部分似乎没有细说。"

"可能性微乎其微,我提起只是为了让你全面了解情况。"迈克尔用手帕擦了擦鼻子。

"我没法相信,没法相信你是这样的人,你从骨子里就不是,"凯说,露出大惑不解的神情,"我从头到尾都不理解,事情怎么会变成这样。"

"嗯,我不会继续解释下去了,"迈克尔柔声说,"说真的,你不需要思考这方面的事情,如果我们结婚,这些和你、和我们的生活都没有任何关系。"

凯摇摇头。"你凭什么想娶我,凭什么转弯抹角说你爱我,你对我没说过这个字,却说你爱你的父亲,但你从没说过爱我,你怎么可以不信任我,连生活里最重要的事情都不告诉我? 你怎么能娶一个你无法信任的女人? 你父亲信任你母亲,这点我很清楚。"

"那是当然,"迈克尔说,"但不等于他会把所有事情都告诉她。另外,你要知道,他有理由信任她。不但因为他们结了婚,她是他的妻子,而且她在生孩子还不那么安全的时候为他生了四个孩子,而是她在别人对他开枪以后护理他、保卫他。我母亲信任我父亲。四十年来,我母亲最忠诚守护的就是我父亲。等你做到这些,我会告诉你一些你其实并不想知道的事情。"

"我们必须住在林荫道吗?"凯问。

迈克尔点点头。"我们会有自己的一幢屋子,情况没你想象的那么坏。我父母不会打扰我们。我们可以过我们自己的生活。可是,在解决所有问题之前,我只能住在林荫道。"

"因为住在外面对你很危险。"凯说。

认识迈克尔这么久,这是凯第一次见他动怒。令人胆寒的森冷怒火并没有通过姿态或语调的变化表现出来,而是一股如死亡般从他身上散发出的寒意,凯知道要是她最终决定不嫁给迈克尔,促使她下定决心的就会是这股寒意。

"问题出在电影和报纸宣传的那些狗屎东西,"迈克尔说,"你对我父亲和柯里昂家族有了错误的看法。我最后再解释一次,以后不会再说了。我父亲是个生意人,想供养老婆孩子,帮助日后也许会遇到麻烦的朋友。他不接受我们所在社会的规矩,因为这些规矩会束缚他,迫使一个拥有极大魄力和非凡性格的人去过并不适合他的生活。你必须理解一点:他认为他和总统、首相、最高法院的法官和州长这些大人物是对等的。他拒绝遵守别人制定的规矩,拒绝忍气吞声过日子。但是,他最终的目标是带着一定的权势进入这个社会,因为社会并不保护不具备权势的个体。另外一方面,他的行为也遵守他的一套伦理道德,他认为这套伦理道德优于社会的法理结构。"

凯向他投去难以置信的眼神。"太荒唐了,"她说,"要是每个人都这么想怎么办?社会还怎么运转? 我们岂不是要回到穴居时代? 迈克尔,说归说,但你不相信,对吧?"

迈克尔对她笑了笑:"我只是在复述我父亲的信念。我只是希望你能了解,不管他是什么人,总之他不缺乏责任感,至少他创造的社会里是这样。他不是你心中端着机关枪扫射的暴徒。他是个负责任的男人,只是方式与众不同。"

"那么,你的信念是什么?"凯平静地问。

迈克尔耸耸肩。"我的信念是家庭,"他说,"是你和我们也许会组成的家庭。我不相信社会能保护我们,不愿意把命运交给别人处置,那些家伙唯一的本事就是哄骗大众投票给他们。但这只是暂时的。我父亲的时代已经结束。他过去能做的事情,今天要做就必须冒极大的风险。无论喜不喜欢，柯里昂家族都必须融入社会。但就算要融入，我也希望我们能带着自己的巨大权势融入，简而言之就是金钱和其他价值的所有权。我希望我的后代能活得尽可能地安稳，然后再融入大众的命运。"

"可是，你曾经志愿参军保卫国家，曾经是战争英雄，"凯说，"是什么让你改变了看法？"

迈克尔答道："这样谈是没有什么结果的。也许我只是一个传统的保守派，就像你老家长大的那些人。我自己照顾自己的利益。政府并没有为人民做多少事情，事情就是这样，但并不是真的这样。我只能这么说：我必须帮助我的父亲，我必须站在他身旁，而你必须作出决定，要不要站在我身边。"他对凯笑着说，"看来结婚真不是个好主意。"

凯拍拍床铺。"结婚我还拿不准主意，不过我有两年没亲近过男人了，不会轻易放过你。你给我过来。"

他们又躺在了床上，台灯熄灭。她在迈克尔耳边说："相信我说的吗？你离开后我没碰过别的男人。"

"相信。"迈克尔说。

"你呢？"她换上更温柔的声音。

"有过，"迈克尔说。他感觉到她有点绷紧了身体，"但过去这六个月没有。"这是实话。自从阿波罗妮亚死后，凯是第一个和他做爱的女人。

第二十六章

布置华丽的套房俯瞰酒店后面的人工仙境；缠在树上的橙色装饰灯照亮了移植而来的棕榈树，沙漠的星光下，两个巨大的游泳池闪着深蓝色的微光。地平线上的砂石山峦环绕着霓虹闪烁的拉斯维加斯。约翰尼·方坦放下厚实的灰色花边窗帘，转身回到房间里。

房间里有特别安排的一组四个人：一个赌区经理，一个荷官，一个替补人手，还有穿着暴露制服的鸡尾酒女招待，他们正在为私人赌局作准备。尼诺·瓦伦蒂躺在会客区的沙发上，手里的玻璃杯里灌满了威士忌。他望着赌场人员布置二十一点牌桌，又在马蹄形赌桌前放上六把舒适的软椅。"好极了，好极了，"他用半醉不醉的含糊声音说，"约翰尼，来陪我和这帮混蛋赌几把。我运气不错，我们要赢他们一个片甲不留。"

约翰尼在沙发前的脚凳上坐下。"你知道我不能赌博的，"他说，"尼诺，感觉怎么样?"

尼诺·瓦伦蒂咧嘴笑道:"好得很。半夜总有妹子上来陪我,吃点东西,再回到牌桌前。你知道我赢了赌场差不多五万块吗?他们磨磨叽叽跟我折腾了快一个星期。"

"知道,"约翰尼·方坦说,"你要是死了,希望把钱留给谁?"

尼诺一口喝光杯里的烈酒。"约翰尼,你这个浪荡鬼的名声到底是怎么来的?约翰尼啊,你死气沉沉的。老天,这儿游客的乐趣都比你多。"

约翰尼说:"是啊,要我扶你上牌桌吗?"

尼诺挣扎着从沙发上起身,牢牢地在地毯上站稳脚跟。"我自己就行。"他说,松手任由酒杯落地,走向刚刚搭好的牌桌,步履还算坚定。发牌手已经准备好了。看台子的站在发牌手背后,替补发牌手坐在远离牌桌的椅子上。鸡尾酒女招待坐在另一把椅子上,正对尼诺·瓦伦蒂,他打什么手势她都看得见。

尼诺用指节敲敲绿色台呢。"筹码。"他说。

看台子的掏出衣袋里的记事簿,填了张欠条,连同墨水笔放在尼诺面前。"给您,瓦伦蒂先生,"他说,"按常规,五千块起板。"尼诺在欠条最底下随手签名,看台子的把欠条收进衣袋,朝发牌手点点头。

发牌手的手指灵活得不可思议,从牌桌的暗格里拈出几摞黑黄相间的百元筹码。不到五秒钟,尼诺面前就多了五摞高度相同的百元筹码,一摞十枚。

绿色台呢上刻出了六个比纸牌稍大的白色方框,每个方框对应一名玩家的座位。尼诺把赌注放在其中三个方框里,一个方框一枚筹码,代表他收三把牌,每把一百块。三把他都没再要牌,因为庄家的明牌是六点,很容易爆掉——也确实爆掉了。尼诺收起筹码,扭头对约翰尼·方坦说:"今晚兆头不错,你说呢,约翰尼?"

约翰尼笑了笑。请尼诺这种赌棍在赌博前签借条很少见,对豪客而言,通常说句话就顶用了。赌场大概害怕尼诺会因为喝酒忘记他的欠账,他们可不知道尼诺有个好记性。

尼诺赢个不停,第三盘结束,他朝鸡尾酒女招待勾勾手指。她走到房间另一头的吧台前,端来满满一玻璃杯他喜欢的黑麦威士忌。尼诺拿起酒杯,换到另一只手里,伸手搂住女招待。"陪我坐坐,宝贝儿,玩两把,送点运气给我。"

鸡尾酒女招待长得很漂亮,但约翰尼看得出她全是虚情假意,再怎么装也装不出半分真心。她对尼诺绽放灿烂的笑容,但真正垂涎的是黑黄相间的筹码。妈的,约翰尼心想,她想要就给她呗。他懊悔的只是尼诺没有用钱买来更好的货色。

尼诺让女招待替他玩了几盘,赏她一枚筹码,拍拍她的屁股,叫她起身滚蛋。约翰尼示意她端杯酒来。酒端来了,可她的动作像是在出演有史以来最做作的电影里最做作的一个镜头。她把所有魅力射向了不起的约翰尼·方坦,眼里放出悉听尊便的光芒,步态卖弄十二万分的性感,嘴巴微微张开,像是怀着一肚子欲火,打算见什么吞什么。她怎么看都像发情的雌兽,可惜只是表演而已。约翰尼·方坦心想,唉,天哪,又是这种人。想拉他上床的女人最喜欢这么接近他,但只在他烂醉的时候才管用,而他此刻毫无醉意。他对姑娘露出著名的笑容,说:"谢谢你,宝贝儿。"姑娘看着他,分开嘴唇,露出"谢谢你才对"的笑容,眼神变得迷离,网眼丝袜裹着的长腿带着绷紧的身躯微微后仰,肉体里像是在积蓄巨大的张力,乳房愈加丰满鼓胀,就快撑破薄得可怜的上衣了。紧接着,她全身轻轻一颤,几乎释放出一股性欲的震荡波。简直就像约翰尼·方坦只用一个微笑和一句"谢谢你,宝贝儿"就让她高潮了。演得漂亮,约翰尼第一次见到演得这么漂亮的。可惜如今的他已经知道这是演戏。睡这种女人一般得不到什么乐趣。

他望着女招待坐回椅子上,自己慢悠悠地喝着酒。他不想再看一次刚才的小把戏了,今晚他没这个情绪。

过了一个小时,尼诺·瓦伦蒂撑不住了。他先是向前一歪,又晃晃悠悠地向后倒,接着直挺挺地从椅子上摔向地面。还好看台子的和替补发牌手见到他开始摇晃就冲了上来,在他着地前抓住了他。他们扶起他,架着他穿过分开的帘幕,走进套房的卧室。

约翰尼望着这一幕,鸡尾酒女招待帮两个男人脱掉尼诺的衣服,给他盖上罩单。看台子的数了数尼诺的筹码,掏出那一小本借款单,记下数字,守在桌边,盯着庄家的筹码。约翰尼问他:"他这样有多久了?"

看台子的耸耸肩。"他今晚昏得比较早。第一次发作的时候,我们叫来了酒店的医生,他用什么药救醒瓦伦蒂先生,教训了他一顿。可尼诺说再见到他昏过去就不必叫医生了,把他放到床上,第二天早晨自己会好的。我们照他吩咐的做。他运气不错,今晚又赢了一大笔,快三千块。"

约翰尼·方坦说:"唉,今晚还是叫酒店的医生来一趟吧。要是有必要就去赌场那头广播一声。"

差不多过了十五分钟,朱尔斯·西格尔才走进套房。约翰尼见到他就生气,这家伙从来就没个医生的样子。今晚他上身是件松松垮垮的蓝色白边针织马球衫,赤脚穿着一双白色山羊皮便鞋,却拎着个传统的黑色出诊包,模样实在可笑。

约翰尼说:"你得想想办法,找个半截的高尔夫球袋装你那些吃饭家伙。"

朱尔斯心领神会地笑着说:"是啊,医学院的拎包就是太累赘了。大家见了就害怕。至少该换个颜色。"

他走向尼诺躺着的那张床，打开诊疗包，对约翰尼说："多谢你那张顾问费的支票。你太大方了。我做的事情不值那么多。"

"不值个屁，"约翰尼说，"陈年往事就别提了。尼诺这是怎么了？"

朱尔斯飞快地检查心跳、脉搏和血压，从包里取出注射器，漫不经心地扎进尼诺的胳膊，推了一管药水。尼诺睡梦中的面容没了蜡像一般的惨白色，血色回到面颊上，像是血脉恢复了畅通似的。

"诊断起来很简单，"朱尔斯欣然答道，"他第一次在这儿昏倒的时候，我抓住机会给他检查了身体，做了几项化验，在他恢复知觉前把他送进医院。他有糖尿病，轻度成年二型，只要好好吃药，节制饮食，其实不是什么大毛病。但他置之不理，打定主意要喝死自己。他的肝功能正在衰退，大脑也会受到影响。现在他处于糖尿病导致的轻度昏迷之中。我的建议是把他关起来。"

约翰尼顿时放了心。事情还不严重，尼诺只需要照顾好自己就行。"你是说弄进那种戒酒瘾的地方？"约翰尼问。

朱尔斯走向房间另一头的吧台，给自己倒了杯酒。"不，"他说，"我说的是真的关起来。也就是疯人院。"

"别逗了。"约翰尼说。

"我没开玩笑，"朱尔斯说，"精神病学的那些东西我并不完全懂，但我知道不少，职业需要嘛。你的朋友尼诺可以恢复得相当不错，前提是肝损伤不能太严重，但这个就只有到尸检的时候才能知道了。他真正的问题在脑袋里。简而言之，他根本不在乎死不死，说不定就是想自杀。在解决这方面的问题之前，他是没指望的，所以我才说要把他关起来，接受必要的精神病学治疗。"

有人敲门，约翰尼过去开门。来的是露西·曼奇尼，她扑进约翰尼的怀抱，亲吻他。"天哪，约翰尼，见到你太好了，"她说。

"好久不见啊。"约翰尼·方坦说。他注意到露西变了。她苗条了不少，衣服比从前好得多，穿在她身上显得尤其美丽。她把头发剪得有几分男孩子气，非常适合脸型。他从没见过她这么年轻漂亮的样子，脑子里闪过在拉斯维加斯找她作伴的念头。和这么一个漂亮妞四处逛逛倒是乐事一桩。不过，还没等他点燃魅力，就想起她是医生的人。唉，算了吧。他换上朋友对朋友的笑容，说："大半夜的，你跑到尼诺的房间里来干什么？"

她一拳打在他肩膀上。"我听说尼诺病了，朱尔斯上来看他。我只是想看看能不能帮忙。尼诺没事吧？"

"没事，"约翰尼说，"他会好起来的。"

朱尔斯·西格尔瘫倒在沙发上。"好个屁,"朱尔斯说,"我建议我们坐在这儿等尼诺醒过来,然后说服他自己人院治疗。露西,他喜欢你,你也许能帮上忙。约翰尼,你如果是他真正的朋友,那就应该配合我。否则尼诺老兄的肝脏很快就是某个大学实验室的展品 A 了。"

医生的轻浮态度让约翰尼很不高兴。他以为他是老几?他正想说什么,却听见床那边传来了尼诺的声音:"喂,老朋友,给我倒杯酒好吗?"

尼诺坐在床上,他朝露西笑着说:"嘿,小宝贝,到老尼诺这儿来。"他张开怀抱,露西在床沿坐下,抱了抱尼诺。奇怪的是,尼诺的脸色现在并不难看,几乎算是正常了。

尼诺打个响指。"来吧,约翰尼,给我倒一杯。时间还早。牌桌他妈的上哪儿去了?"

朱尔斯喝了一大口酒,对尼诺说:"你不能喝酒,你的医生禁止你喝酒。"

尼诺恶狠狠地说:"我的医生?去他妈的。"话刚出口,演戏似的后悔表情就浮现在他脸上。"嘿,朱尔斯,是你啊。你不就是我的医生吗?哥们,我说的不是你。约翰尼,给我倒一杯,否则我下床自己倒。"

约翰尼耸耸肩,走向吧台。朱尔斯冷漠地说:"我说过了,他不能喝酒。"

约翰尼知道朱尔斯为什么惹他生气。这位医生说话总那么冷静,无论内容多么紧迫,说起来也从不拿腔拿调,声音始终低沉而克制。就算他在警告什么,那么警告也只存在于字词之中,声音本身永远四平八稳,仿佛事不关己。光是这一点就足以让约翰尼动怒,端了一杯威士忌给尼诺。他先对朱尔斯说:"一杯酒杀不死他,对吧?"然后把酒递给尼诺。

"对,杀不死他。"朱尔斯说得很平静。露西紧张地看看他,想说什么,一转念又停下了。尼诺接过威士忌,一仰脖灌了下去。

约翰尼低头对尼诺微笑,他们在表演给混蛋医生看。突然,尼诺使劲喘息起来,脸色涨得发紫,他透不过气,哼哼唧唧地使劲吸气,身体像鱼似的向上跃起,整张脸挣得血红,眼珠突出。朱尔斯出现在床的另一边,面对约翰尼和露西。他抓住尼诺的脖子,按住尼诺,把注射器的针头插进肩膀和脖子相接的地方。尼诺软瘫下去,挣扎得没那么用力了,没多久,他倒在枕头上,眼睛紧闭,陷入沉睡。

约翰尼、露西和朱尔斯回到套房的会客区,围着宽大结实的咖啡桌坐下。露西拿起海蓝色的听筒,叫了咖啡和食物送上楼。约翰尼在吧台前给自己调酒。

"你知道他喝了威士忌会有那个反应?"约翰尼问。

朱尔斯耸耸肩。"对,相当确定。"

约翰尼生气地说:"那你为什么不警告我?"

"我警告你了。"朱尔斯说。

"警告的方式不对，"约翰尼冷冰冰地怒吼道，"你算是什么狗屁医生？你压根儿就不关心。说什么要把尼诺送进疯人院，你就不能说疗养院？你就喜欢跟人对着干，对吧？"

露西低头盯着膝盖。朱尔斯只是对方坦笑道："谁也拦不住你把那杯酒递给尼诺。你就非得显示一下你不接受我的警告、我的命令？还记得嗓子那档事过后，你请我当你的私人医生吗？我拒绝你是因为我知道我跟你合不来。医生认为他是神明，是现代社会的高等祭司，这是他的奖赏之一，但你不可能用这种态度对我。神明归神明，但我非得拍你的马屁。你们这些人的好莱坞医生都是一个德性。那些家伙倒是从哪儿找出来的啊？妈的，他们是不懂还是根本不在乎？他们肯定知道尼诺出了什么问题，但只给他吃各种各样的药物，让他有一口气就行。他们身穿丝绸正装，舔你的屁眼，只因为你是手握大权的电影人，而你反过来认为他们是了不起的医生。演艺圈啊，医生们哪，总得有点心肝吧？对吧？可是，他们根本不在乎你的死活。唉，我有个小小的爱好，虽然听起来难以置信，却正是治病救人。我没有拦住你把那杯酒给尼诺，就是想让你看看他喝了会有什么结果。"朱尔斯倾向约翰尼·方坦，声音仍旧沉静，不含感情，"你的朋友已经离死不远。明白不明白？要是不接受治疗和严格的护理，他就死定了。高血压、糖尿病和坏习惯让他随时有脑溢血的危险。他的大脑会砰地炸开。这么说够形象的吧？没错，我说的就是疯人院。我要你明白他需要什么。否则你就什么都不会做。跟你实话实说好了。把他关进去，你还能救你这位好哥们儿一命，否则就亲亲他，和他说再见吧。"

露西嗳嚅道："朱尔斯，亲爱的，朱尔斯，别这么凶。有话好好说。"

朱尔斯站起身。约翰尼·方坦不无满足地注意到，他平时的冷静不翼而飞，说话时也没了那种缺乏重音的沉稳语气。

"你以为这是我第一次在这种情况下劝说你这种人吗？"朱尔斯说，"这是我的日常工作。露西叫我别那么凶，那是因为她真的不懂。知道吗？我经常这么和别人说，'肉别吃那么多，否则你会死；烟别抽那么多，否则你会死；工作别那么卖力，否则你会死；酒别喝那么凶，否则你会死。'谁也不听我的。知道为什么吗？因为我说的不是'明天你就会死'。但今天我可以告诉你，尼诺说不定明天就会死。"

朱尔斯走到吧台前，给自己又调了一杯酒。"怎么说，约翰尼？同意把尼诺关进去吗？"

约翰尼说："我也不知道。"

朱尔斯在吧台前几口喝完一杯酒，又斟满酒杯。"知道吗？说来有趣，你可以抽烟抽死,喝酒喝死,工作累死,甚至吃死。这些都是做得到的。从医学角度来说,唯一做不到的是性交把自己搞死,但人们却在这方面设置了各种障碍。"他顿了顿,喝完酒,"即便如此,麻烦也还是会有,至少对女人来说是这样。我诊治过绝对不能再怀孕的女人。'非常危险',我这样嘱咐她们。'你会死的',我实话实说。一个月后,她们又冒出来,红着脸说'医生,我好像有了',当然,她们想堕胎。'但这非常危险',我还是这么说。那时候我说话还动感情呢。她们会笑着对我说,'可是,我丈夫和我都是严守教规的天主教徒啊。'原话。"

有人敲门,两名侍者推着装满食物和银咖啡壶的餐车进来,从餐车底下取出活动小桌支起来。约翰尼打发他们离开。

他们在桌边坐下,喝着咖啡,吃着露西点的三明治。约翰尼往后一靠,点燃香烟。"这么说,你确实救过不少人的命,怎么会变成堕胎医生的?"

露西第一次开口:"他想帮助有麻烦的姑娘,有些姑娘说不定会自杀,或者为了取掉孩子做些危险的事情。"

朱尔斯对她微笑,叹息道:"事情没那么简单。当时我好不容易当上外科医生。按照棒球运动员的说法,我有一双好手。可是,我实在太出色了,把自己吓得屁滚尿流。打开某个倒霉蛋的肚皮,我看一眼就知道他死定了。手术还是要做,但我知道癌症或肿瘤还会复发,却满脸堆笑说些屁话送他们回家。有个可怜的姑娘来看病,我切掉她一个乳房。一年后她又来了,我切掉另一个乳房。又过了一年,我从她肚子里像掏瓜瓤似的摘除东西。再然后? 她就死了。丈夫呢? 只会打电话来问,'化验结果怎么说? 化验结果怎么说?'

"于是我另外雇了个秘书接这种电话。只在病人做好检查、化验和手术的准备以后才见她们。我尽量少和患者接触,因为我太忙。最后,我只允许丈夫和我谈两分钟。'晚期。'我就这么说。他们就好像没听见似的。他们理解意思,但就是听不见。刚开始我还以为自己不知不觉地压低了声音,于是存心扯着嗓门说。可他们还是听不见。有个家伙居然问我,'初期? 到底是什么意思?'"朱尔斯哈哈大笑,"初期,晚期,去他妈的。我开始接堕胎的活儿。轻松简单,大家高兴,就好像洗碗清理水槽。这就是我的行当呀。我喜欢极了,我喜欢当堕胎医生。我不认为两个月的胚胎是人类,所以一点问题也没有。我帮助遇到麻烦的年轻女孩和已婚女性,钱挣得很不错。我离开了第一线。警察逮我的时候,我感觉像是逃兵被抓了回来。不过我运气挺好,朋友四处打点,把我弄了出来,但大医院不允许我再拿刀。于是我就在这儿了。一遍又一遍劝人活命,但是和从前一样,大家都就当没听见。"

"我没有,"约翰尼·方坦说,"我正在考虑呢。"

露西改变话题。"约翰尼,你来拉斯维加斯干什么?好莱坞栋梁忙累了来松松骨头,还是为了工作?"

约翰尼摇摇头。"迈克尔·柯里昂要见我,和我谈谈。他今晚和汤姆·黑根一起飞过来。露西,汤姆说他们也要见你。知道是怎么一回事吗?"

露西摇摇头。"明晚所有人要一起共进晚餐。弗雷迪也去。我估计事情和酒店有关系。赌场最近一直在亏钱,不应该的。唐大概派迈克来查账。"

"听说迈克总算把他的脸修整好了。"约翰尼说。

露西笑道:"大概是凯说服了他。他们结婚的时候他都不肯。真是想不通。样子那么吓人,还害得他不停流鼻涕。他早就该修整好才对。"露西顿了顿,"柯里昂家族把朱尔斯叫去参加手术,让他当顾问和观察员。"

约翰尼点点头,干巴巴地说:"是我推荐的。"

"哦,"露西说,"总而言之,迈克说他想为朱尔斯做些事情,所以明晚邀请我们一起吃饭。"

朱尔斯边想边说:"他谁也不信任。他提醒我注意每个人的一举一动。手术本身很简单,常规手术而已。有执业资格的人都能开这个刀。"

套房的卧室传来响动,他们望向帘幕。尼诺又醒来了。约翰尼过去坐在床沿上。朱尔斯和露西走到床脚停下。尼诺对他们挤出惨淡的笑容:"好吧,我就不自作聪明了。我觉得糟糕透了。约翰尼,记得一年前我们在棕榈泉和那两个女人吗?我向你发誓,我一点也不嫉妒。我很高兴。约翰尼,相信我吗?"

约翰尼安慰道:"当然,尼诺,当然相信你。"

露西和朱尔斯对视一眼。就他们对约翰尼·方坦的了解,很难相信他会从尼诺这种老朋友手里横刀夺爱。为什么时隔一年尼诺还要说他不嫉妒呢?同一个想法掠过两人的脑海:尼诺打算像浪漫小说似的喝死自己,是因为某个姑娘抛弃了他,投入了约翰尼·方坦的怀抱。

朱尔斯又检查了一下尼诺的情况。"我叫个护士到房间里陪你一晚,"朱尔斯说,"你必须卧床休息几天。不开玩笑。"

尼诺微笑着说:"好的,医生,但护士千万别太漂亮了。"

朱尔斯打电话叫护士,然后和露西离开。约翰尼坐进床边的椅子,等待护士。尼诺重新沉沉睡去,一脸筋疲力尽的神色。约翰尼想起尼诺说对一年前的事不嫉妒的话。约翰尼从来没有想到过尼诺会嫉妒。

一年前,约翰尼·方坦执掌的电影公司,他坐在自己豪华的办公室里,心情前所未有地低落。这可真是奇怪,因为他制作的第一部电影——他本人担纲,尼诺领衔——

挣了个盆满钵满。一切都很顺利，大家各司其职，费用没有超过预算。参与者全都大发其财，杰克·沃尔茨少说也要夭寿十年。另外两部电影正在制作之中，一部由他本人担纲，另一部由尼诺担纲。尼诺实在太适合扮演那种魅力四射的愣头青小情人了，女人恨不得把他搂进乳沟里。他简直就是点石成金，钞票滚滚而来。教父透过银行得到分红，这尤其让约翰尼开心。他证明了教父对他的信心。可是，这些对他今天的心情毫无帮助。

如今他已经是成功的独立制作人了，手里的权力和他当歌手时同样大，甚至更大。漂亮女人和从前一样扑进他怀里，不过目的更加现实。他有了私人飞机，过得比以前更奢侈，享受商人能享受而歌手不能享受的特别减税待遇。那么，他到底是为了什么不开心呢？

他很清楚理由。他脑门疼，鼻腔疼，喉咙瘙痒。挠痒止痒的办法只有一个，就是唱歌，但他害怕得不敢尝试。他为此打过电话给朱尔斯·西格尔，问他什么时候开嗓子才安全，朱尔斯说只要他愿意，随时都可以。于是，他尝试了一次，声音嘶哑而难听，他黯然放弃。第二天，喉咙疼得厉害，和切除肉赘前的疼法截然不同——甚至更疼，火烧火燎。他不敢继续尝试，害怕他会永远失声，或者毁了嗓子。

要是不能唱歌，其他的一切又有什么意义呢？其他的一切都狗屁不如。他真正了解的东西只有唱歌。也许全世界没有人比他更加了解唱歌和他的音乐。他现在明白了，自己就有这么出色。唱了这么多年，他已经成了真正的专家。别人没法告诉他什么对什么错，他不需要向任何人请教。他打心底里了解。多么浪费，多么他妈的浪费啊。

今天是星期五，他决定与维吉尼亚和两个女儿度周末。他和往常一样，先打电话说他要来。其实是给她一个拒绝的机会。她从不拒绝。离婚这么多年了，一次也没有拒绝过。因为她绝对不会阻拦女儿见到父亲。多好的女人啊，约翰尼心想。碰到维吉尼亚算他走运。尽管他知道他对维吉尼亚的关心胜过了他对其他女人的关心，但他们还是不可能回到床上去。也许等六十五岁他退休以后，两人可以一起隐居，从此不问世事。

现实却击碎了他的梦想，来到维吉尼亚家，他发现维吉尼亚不太高兴，两个女儿也不怎么乐意见到他，因为母亲本来答应让她们和几个女伴去加州的一个牧场度周末，可以骑骑马什么的。

他对维吉尼亚说尽管让她们去牧场，然后乐呵呵地吻别女儿。他很理解她们的心情。有哪个孩子宁可陪着闷闷不乐的父亲——况且还是个擅离职守的父亲——而不是去牧场骑马玩乐呢？他对维吉尼亚说："我喝几杯就走。"

"好的。"她说。今天她心情低落——少见,但看得出来。她过的这种生活也确实不容易。

她看见他拿了个特别大的杯子斟酒。"你倒是为什么要给自己打气?"维吉尼亚问,"你过得那么万事如意。我做梦都没想到过你当商人会这么出色。"

约翰尼对她笑了笑。"其实并不难。"他说,心里想:原来问题出在这儿。他了解女人,明白维吉尼亚之所以心情低落,是因为她认为约翰尼过得称心如意。女人最不喜欢见到男人过得太遂心,见了就生气,让她们难以用情感、性爱和婚姻纽带拴住男人。约翰尼只好说:"我要是不能唱歌,有没有这些又有什么区别呢?"更多是为了哄她开心,而不是发自己的牢骚。

维吉尼亚气恼道:"天哪,约翰尼,你已经不是毛头小子了。你都三十五多了。为什么还要傻乎乎地操心唱不唱歌呢?你当制片人反正挣得更多。"

约翰尼好奇地打量着她。"因为我是歌手,我喜欢唱歌。老不老和这个又有什么关系呢?"

维吉尼亚不耐烦道:"我反正从来不喜欢你唱的歌。现在既然你显露出了制作电影的本事,那么你不能唱歌反而让我高兴。"

约翰尼怒道:"你他妈放什么屁。"两人都被这话吓了一跳。他气得发抖。维吉尼亚怎么可以这么想,她怎么可以这么恨他?

维吉尼亚见他受到伤害,却露出微笑,那句话实在伤人,他当然有理由动怒。她说:"那些女人因为你唱歌那德性追着你跑的时候,你觉得我是什么感觉?我要是光屁股上街引得男人追着我跑,你会有什么感觉?你唱歌就是这个德性,我巴不得你嗓子坏掉,再也没法唱歌。不过,那都是离婚前的事情了。"

约翰尼喝完酒。"你什么都不明白。一点也不明白。"他走进厨房,打电话给尼诺。他三言两语安排好,两人一起去棕榈泉度周末,又给了尼诺一个女孩的号码,这个女孩是新人,他早就想搞到手。"她会给你带个朋友,"约翰尼说,"我一小时后到你家。"

他出门的时候,维吉尼亚冷冰冰地和他道别。他根本不在乎,他对维吉尼亚生气的次数屈指可数,这是其中一次。去他妈的,他打算肆意放松一个周末,排出体内所有的毒水。

果不其然,到了棕榈泉一切顺心如意。约翰尼在棕榈泉有自己的屋子,每年的这个季节总有人打扫照看。两个姑娘年纪很轻,会玩得很开心,不至于贪婪地索求帮助。几个闲人到泳池旁陪他们,到晚餐时间才离开。尼诺带着他那个姑娘回屋,为晚餐换衣服,趁着晒了太阳的身子还暖和,见缝插针打一炮。约翰尼没这个心情,于是让他的姑娘——蒂娜,是个娇小玲珑的金发美人——上楼去自己冲澡。和维吉尼亚吵完架之后,他总是提不起兴致跟别的女人上床。

他走进玻璃墙围起的天台客厅,这儿有一架钢琴。和乐队巡演的时候,他会为了逗观众开心偶尔摆弄几下钢琴,所以他也能勉强弹点假模假式的月光小夜曲。他坐在琴凳上,边弹边随意哼唱,声音很轻,断断续续一两个单词,不算真在唱歌。不知不觉间,蒂娜走进客厅,给他倒了一杯酒,挨着他在钢琴前坐下。他弹了几首曲子,她跟着他哼唱。他把蒂娜留在钢琴前,自己上楼去冲澡。在浴室里,他唱了几小段——更接近念白。他穿上衣服,回到楼下。客厅里还是只有蒂娜一个人;尼诺大概和女人干得正欢,要么是又在拼命喝酒。

蒂娜走到室外,望着游泳池,约翰尼重新在钢琴前坐下,开始唱他的一首老歌。喉咙里没了烧灼感。音调还有点喑哑,但韵味十足。他望向天台,蒂娜还在外面,玻璃门关着,她听不见。不知为何,他不希望别人听见他的歌声。他换上一首自己最喜欢的老情歌,唱得全情投入,就仿佛他在对观众演唱,放开嗓门,等待熟悉的灼痛感涌上喉头——却迟迟没有等来。他听着自己的歌声,声音起了变化,但他还是很喜欢。现在的歌声更沉稳,属于成熟的男人,而不是毛头小子:浑厚,他心想,沉稳而浑厚。他轻松自如地唱完那首歌,坐在钢琴前思考着。

尼诺在他背后说:"不坏啊,老伙计,真的不坏。"

约翰尼猛地转身。尼诺一个人站在门口,没有带他的女孩。约翰尼松了一口气。他不在乎让尼诺听见。

"是啊,"约翰尼说,"把那两个女孩赶走Ⅱ巴,打发她们回家。"

尼诺说:"要打发你自己打发。她们都是好姑娘,我不想害得她们伤心。再说我刚和我的姑娘打了两炮。我要是连饭都不请她就打发她回家,她会觉得我是什么人啊?"

去他妈的,约翰尼心想。就让那两个姑娘随便听吧,声音难听又怎样呢?他在棕榈泉认识一位乐队领班,他拨通号码,要一把曼陀林琴给尼诺。乐队领班反对道:"妈的,加州哪儿有人弹曼陀林!"约翰尼吼道:"叫你送你就送!"

屋里塞满了录音器材,约翰尼支使两个姑娘开关设备和调音量。吃完晚餐,约翰尼开始工作。尼诺弹曼陀林伴奏,他唱了一遍他所有的老歌。他一口气从头唱到尾,完全不需要顾忌嗓子。他的嗓子好得很,他觉得他能永远唱下去。不能唱歌的几个月里,他经常琢磨怎么唱歌,思考该怎么把词句唱得和年轻时不一样。他在脑海里尝试各种微妙的重音变化。此刻他在现实中唱了出来。实际唱的时候常常出错,在脑海里感觉明明很对头,大声唱出来反而不怎么好听。大声唱出来,他心想。他不再听自己的歌声,而是把注意力都放在演绎上。他的节拍偶尔不那么准确,但问题不大,只是有点生疏罢了。他的脑袋里有个节拍器,一向可靠,只需要稍加练习就能恢复。

最后,他终于停下。蒂娜走过来,眼睛闪闪发亮,吻了他很久。"我总算知道我母亲为什么不肯漏掉你的任何一部电影了。"她说。换了别的时候,这句话恐怕都不太得体,但此刻约翰尼和尼诺一起哈哈大笑。

他们回放录音,约翰尼听清了自己的声音。嗓子变了,天上地下的区别,但毫无疑问,仍旧是约翰尼·方坦在唱歌。正如他早先注意到的,声音变得更浑厚和沉稳,但同时也更像男人而非男孩子的歌声了。声音里有了更多的情感和个性。技巧更是远远超过从前,说是炉火纯青也不为过。现在他这么生疏还能如此动听,等恢复了最佳状态,他要厉害成什么样子啊?约翰尼对尼诺笑着说:"真的有我想象中那么好吗?"

尼诺若有所思地看着他喜气洋洋的脸。"太他妈好了,"他说,"不过先看看你明天还能不能唱歌再说。"

尼诺居然这么悲观,约翰尼有点受伤。"狗娘养的,你知道你不可能唱得这么好。别担心明天了。我感觉好极了。"那天晚上他没有再唱歌。他和尼诺带着两个姑娘去参加一场派对,蒂娜在他床上过夜,可惜他的表现不尽如人意。姑娘有点失望。可是,去他妈的,不可能一天事事遂心吧,约翰尼心想。

第二天早晨,他醒来时满心担忧,隐约害怕嗓子恢复是他夜里梦见的。等他确定不是梦见的,又害怕嗓子会再次失灵。他走到窗口,轻轻哼唱,然后穿着睡衣去了客厅。他在钢琴上弹起一首歌,过了几个小节,开始尝试跟唱。刚开始他没有放开喉咙,但嗓子既不痛也不嘶哑,于是他放声歌唱。声音准确而浑厚,他根本不需要用劲。轻松,太轻松了,犹如行云流水。约翰尼意识到坏日子已经到头,他已经完全恢复。现在就算电影拍砸他也不在乎,昨晚他和蒂娜没搞成他也不在乎,维吉尼亚会因为他又能唱歌而恨他,他还是不在乎。这时候他只有一点小小的遗憾。假如嗓子是在他给女儿唱歌时恢复的,那该有多好啊。那样的话就太好了。

酒店的护士推着装药品的小车走进房间。约翰尼起身,低头望着尼诺,尼诺正在沉睡,也许正在一点一点死去。他知道尼诺并不嫉妒他的嗓子恢复。他明白尼诺嫉妒的只是嗓子恢复让他那么高兴,他依旧那么在乎唱歌。因为现在尼诺·瓦伦蒂显然对任何让他愿意活下去的事情都丧失了兴趣。

第二十七章

那天夜里，迈克尔·柯里昂很晚才赶到拉斯维加斯，遵照他的命令，没有人在机场接他。只有两个人陪着他，一个是汤姆·黑根，另一个是新保镖艾尔伯特·奈利。

酒店留出最豪华的套房给迈克尔及随行人员。需要迈克尔会见的人已经等在了套房里。

弗雷迪用热情的拥抱欢迎弟弟。弗雷迪壮实了很多，模样变得更和善，喜气洋洋的，而且比从前时髦多了。他身穿做工考究的灰色丝绸正装，配饰一件不少，精心修剪的发型堪比电影明星，脸刮得很干净，容光焕发，指甲也经过仔细打理。和四年前被仓皇送出纽约的那个人相比，他起了翻天覆地的变化。

他仰起上半身，怀着情谊打量迈克尔。"脸修整好了，你漂亮了不知道多少倍。你妻子总算说服你了，对吧？凯怎么样？她什么时候过来看看我们？"

迈克尔对哥哥微笑道："你看起来也好得很。凯本来想来，但她又怀上了，而且有一个孩子要照看。再说这次我来是为了公事，弗雷迪，明天晚上或者后天上午就得飞回去。"

"先吃点东西吧，"弗雷迪说，"酒店的大厨可厉害了，你会尝到这辈子最好吃的饭菜。你快去冲个澡，换身衣服，出来这儿就都准备好了。我已经让你要见的人都排好队了，他们就在外面等着，你准备好了我叫一声就行。"

迈克尔轻快地说："把莫·格林留到最后，请约翰尼·方坦和尼诺上来和我们吃饭，还有露西和她的医生朋友。我们边吃边聊。"他转身对黑根说，"汤姆，还要加上什么人吗？"

黑根摇摇头。弗雷迪欢迎他就远不如对迈克尔那么热情了，不过黑根也能理解。弗雷迪上了父亲的黑名单，弗雷迪当然要责怪顾问没有帮他摆平。黑根倒是愿意帮他这个忙，但他并不清楚弗雷迪为何会引起父亲的恶感。唐并没有具体说原因，只是表达了不悦的情绪。

迈克尔的套房里支起餐桌，众人落座时已经过了十二点。露西亲吻迈克尔，没有说他的脸比手术前好看了许多。朱尔斯·西格尔倒是毫无顾忌，他打量着修复后的颧骨，对迈克尔说："手术很成功，接缝没有问题。鼻窦还好吧？"

"很好，"迈克尔说，"谢谢你帮忙。"

吃饭的时候，大家的注意力放在迈克尔身上。他们都注意到他的言行举止酷似唐。说来奇怪,他也在众人心里激起了同样的尊重和敬畏,他本人却安之若素,还尽量让大家不要拘束。黑根和平时一样,宁可不引人瞩目。他们不认识的新保镖艾尔伯特·奈利也很安静和低调。他说他不饿,坐进靠近房门的扶手椅,读起一份本地的报纸。

喝完几杯酒,吃过东西,他们打发走侍者。迈克尔对约翰尼说:"听说你的声音和以前一样好,以前的歌迷全回来了。我要恭喜你。"

"谢谢。"约翰尼说。他很好奇:迈克尔为什么想见他,要请他帮什么忙?

迈克尔对众人说:"柯里昂家族正在考虑集体迁居拉斯维加斯。卖掉我们在橄榄油生意里的全部份额,定居拉斯维加斯。唐、黑根和我已经讨论过了,我们认为这里就是家族的未来。不是说现在或者明年。前后安排需要两年、三年,甚至四年。不过整体计划就是这样。我们的几个朋友是这家酒店和赌场的大股东,所以这里将是我们的根据地。莫·格林将把股份卖给我们,这里将完全由家族的朋友掌握。"

弗雷迪的圆脸顿时紧张起来。"迈克,你确定莫·格林肯卖?他没和我提过,而且他热爱这个行当。我不觉得他会卖。"

迈克尔静静地说:"我会出一个他无法拒绝的提议。"

他说话的语气平平常常,效果却让人胆寒,也许因为这正是唐最喜欢的说法之一。迈克尔对约翰尼·方坦说:"唐指望你能帮我们起步。按照我们的理解,娱乐业是吸引赌客的重要因素。我们希望你能签个合同,一年举办五次表演,每次为期一周。希望你在电影业的朋友也能这么做。你已经帮了他们很多忙,现在可以让他们还人情债了。"

"没问题,"约翰尼说,"我愿意为教父做任何事情,迈克,你知道的。"可是,他的声音里却有一丝犹疑。

迈克尔笑着说:"你和你的朋友都不会因此亏钱的。你会得到酒店的股份,你认为足够重要的朋友也可以得到股份。你不相信我也无妨,我跟你实话实说,这是唐的原话。"

约翰尼连忙说:"我相信你,迈克。但长街有十几家酒店和赌场正在兴建。等你们进来,市场有可能已经饱和,竞争者早已站稳脚跟,你们也许会来得太迟。"

汤姆·黑根开口道:"其中三家酒店是柯里昂家族的朋友资助建设的。"约翰尼立刻明白了,柯里昂家族拥有其中三家酒店及其赌场,也就是说有很多股份可供支配。

"我这就去办。"约翰尼说。

迈克尔转向露西和朱尔斯·西格尔。"我欠你的人情,"他对朱尔斯说,"听说你想回去继续开膛破肚,很多医院因为你从前给人堕胎,不肯让你用他们的设施。我想听你亲口说,你真有这个愿望吗?"

朱尔斯笑着说："应该是吧,但你不了解医学界。你拥有的权势对他们来说毫无意义。你恐怕帮不了我的忙。"

迈克尔漫不经心地点点头。"你当然说得对。不过,我有几个朋友——都是很有声望的人——打算在拉斯维加斯开办一家大型医院。按照这个城市的发展势头和规划,很快就会需要这么一家医院。要是安排得好,他们也许会允许你进入手术室。妈的,他们能弄几个你这么出色的外科医生来这荒郊野外哪?或者有你一半出色的?我们这是帮医院一个大忙,所以你再坚持一下吧。听说你和露西要结婚了?"

朱尔斯耸耸肩。"等我看见自己的前程再说。"

露西淘气地说:"迈克,你要是不开那家医院,我死了都是老处女。"

众人哄堂大笑,只有朱尔斯除外,他对迈克尔说:"如果我接受这份工作,那可不能有什么附加条件。"

迈克尔冷冰冰地说:"没有附加条件。我欠你一个人情,只是想还你这个人情。"

露西细声细气地说:"迈克,你别生气。"

迈克尔对她笑笑。"我没生气,"他转向朱尔斯,"你那么说可真是不动脑子。柯里昂家族为你做了不少安排。我会蠢到逼你做你不愿意的事情吗?就算我真的逼你了,你又能怎样?你遇到麻烦的时候,有别人抬起哪怕一根手指帮你吗?听说你想回去当真正的外科医生,我花了很多时间看我能不能帮忙。结果是我能。我不是在逼你做任何事情。可是你至少应该把我当朋友,为朋友做点你愿意做的事。这就是我的条件。当然,你也可以拒绝。"

汤姆·黑根低下头,忍不住笑了。唐本人恐怕也没法说得更好了。

朱尔斯涨红了脸。"迈克尔,我不是那个意思。我万分感谢你和你的父亲。忘了我刚才的话吧。"

迈克尔点点头。"好的。在医院建成开业之前,你将是四家酒店的医学主管。给自己组织一个队伍吧。你的薪水相应提高,等会儿你和汤姆慢慢商量。另外,露西,有件更重要的事情我要交给你。基本上是协调以后将在酒店游乐中心开设的所有商铺。财务方面的协调。也许还有招聘在赌场为我们工作的女孩,诸如此类的。要是朱尔斯不肯娶你,你至少会是个有钱的老处女。"

弗雷迪一直在怒气冲冲地抽雪茄。迈克尔扭头面对他,和气地说:"弗雷迪,我只是替唐跑腿的。他要你做什么,当然会亲口告诉你,不过我保证肯定是件大事,足以让你高兴。大家都说你在这儿做得非常出色。"

"那他为什么生我的气?"弗雷迪郁闷地说,"就因为赌场在亏钱?那部分又不是我负责的,那是莫·格林的地盘。我到底要怎么做,老头子才满意啊?"

"别担心。"迈克尔说。他转向约翰尼·方坦，"尼诺去哪儿了？我还以为能见到他呢。"

约翰尼耸耸肩。"尼诺病得厉害。护士在房间里照顾他。这位医生说应该把他关进去，说他这是想自杀。可这是尼诺啊！"

迈克尔真的吃了一惊，若有所思道："尼诺为人一直很好，我没听说他做过任何不像话的事，说过让人不舒服的话。他什么都不太在乎，除了喝酒。"

"是啊，"约翰尼说，"钞票滚滚而来，他有很多工作可以接，唱歌、拍电影都行。他如今拍一部电影能拿五万块，他却不屑一顾。他根本不在乎成不成名。我和他是多年的好朋友，从没见过他做什么让人讨厌的事情。可这个混蛋现在却要把自己喝死。"

朱尔斯正要说话，忽然有人敲了敲套房的门。坐在扶手椅上的男人离门最近，却没有过去开门，而是继续埋头读报，这让他有些吃惊。黑根起身去开门。莫·格林把他往旁边一推，大踏步走进房间，身后跟着两名保镖。

莫·格林是个英俊潇洒的匪徒，当年在布鲁克林以"谋杀有限公司"的行刑人出道，后来插手赌博业，向西发展，寻找生财之道；他第一个看到了拉斯维加斯的光明前途，建起长街上的第一家酒店赌场。他一怒之下就要杀人的暴脾气还在，酒店里没有人不害怕他，弗雷迪、露西和朱尔斯·西格尔也不例外。他们总是尽量避开他。

他板着那张英俊的脸，对迈克尔·柯里昂说："我一直在等着和你谈话，迈克，我明天还有很多事情要做，所以我觉得还是今晚就碰个头吧。你说呢？"

迈克尔·柯里昂望着他，表情友好而诧异。"没问题，"他说着朝黑根打了个手势，"汤姆，给格林先生倒杯酒。"

朱尔斯注意到叫艾尔伯特·奈利的男人正在仔细观察莫·格林，看也不看靠在门上的两名保镖。他知道只要在拉斯维加斯，就绝对不可能爆发暴力冲突。拉斯维加斯在规划中将是美国赌徒的合法天堂，暴力会给这套计划带来致命打击，因此各方严禁使用暴力。

莫·格林对保镖说："拿些筹码给这些朋友下去玩两手，酒店请客。"他指的显然是朱尔斯、露西、约翰尼·方坦和迈克尔的保镖艾尔伯特·奈利。

迈克尔·柯里昂点点头，赞同道："好主意。"听到他发话，奈利起身准备和别人一起出去。

互道珍重之后，房间里只留下了弗雷迪、汤姆·黑根、莫·格林和迈克尔·柯里昂。

格林把酒杯放在桌上，勉强控制住怒气说："我听说柯里昂家族要买断我的股份？只有我让你们出局，你们休想买断我。"

迈克尔通情达理地说:"你的赌场一直在亏钱,这很不合理,你的经营方式有问题,我们也许能比你做得好。"

格林粗声粗气地大笑道:"狗杂种,我帮助你们,在你们倒霉的时候收留了弗雷迪,现在却要赶我走了?真是好算计啊。谁也不能赶我走,我有很多朋友愿意给我撑腰。"

迈克尔仍旧很平静,说起话来通情达理:"你收留弗雷迪是因为柯里昂家族支援了你一大笔钱,让你完成酒店的装修,充实赌场的本金。还因为西海岸的莫雷纳里家族肯担保他的安全,你收留他,他们帮了你几个忙。柯里昂家族和你互不相欠。我不知道你为什么生气。你随便说个价码,只要合情合理,柯里昂都愿意掏腰包,这有什么不对的呢?有什么不公平呢?你的赌场在亏钱,我们这是在帮你。"

格林摇着头说:"柯里昂家族已经没有当初的力量了。教父身体不行了。其他家族正在把你们赶出纽约,你们以为这儿遍地软蛋。听我一句劝,迈克,你连试也别试。"

迈克尔轻声细气地说:"所以你就可以在大庭广众之下扇弗雷迪的耳光喽?"

汤姆·黑根大吃一惊,扭头望向弗雷迪。弗雷迪·柯里昂涨红了脸。"迈克,小事一桩。莫没有恶意。他有时候会失去控制,但我和他还是好朋友。对吧,莫?"

格林警觉起来。"对,当然。有时候为了经营,我也只能动手打人。我对弗雷迪生气,是因为他睡了每一个鸡尾酒女招待,放任她们上班摸鱼。我和他争执起来,只能教训教训他。"

迈克尔不动声色,对哥哥说:"你被教训了,弗雷迪?"

弗雷迪愠怒地盯着弟弟,没有回答。格林哈哈笑道:"他一次带两个上床,玩三明治。弗雷迪,我不得不承认,你对女人确实有一手。被你搞过以后,谁都满足不了她们了。"

黑根发现这句话打了迈克尔一个措手不及。他和迈克尔对视一眼。这大概就是唐对弗雷迪不悦的真正原因了。唐在性这方面很老脑筋。他觉得弗雷迪一次和两个女人寻欢作乐,完全是伤风败俗。莫·格林这种人动手教训他更是有损柯里昂家族的尊严,这是他上了父亲黑名单的另一个原因。

迈克尔站起身,下了逐客令:"我明天就回纽约,所以你考虑一下价码吧。"

格林气急败坏地说:"狗娘养的,你以为能随便打发我?老子能打飞机前杀的人就已经比你多了。我要飞到纽约去和唐本人谈。我要让他开个价码。"

弗雷迪紧张地对汤姆·黑根说:"汤姆,你是顾问,你可以和唐谈一谈,提点建议。"

听到这里,迈克尔冷酷的一面终于爆发在两个人身上。"唐已经半退隐了,"他说,"现在家族生意由我负责。我已经撤掉了汤姆的顾问位置。他以后在拉斯维加斯将完全担任我的律师。他过几个月就带着家人搬到拉斯维加斯来,开始办理所有法律手续。因此,你们要是有话要说,那就对我说好了。"

没有人回答。迈克尔正色道:"弗雷迪,你是我的哥哥,我尊重你。但以后请不要支持与家族作对的人。我连提也不会向唐提起。"他扭头对莫·格林说:"不要侮辱正在尽量帮助你的人。你最好把力气用在查清楚赌场为何亏钱上。柯里昂家族投入了大笔资金,却没有得到相应的回报,但我这次来仍旧不是为了指责你,而是对你伸出援手。唉,你要是宁可朝我的援手吐口水,那就是你的事情了。我不会多说什么。"

他自始至终没有提高声音,但这番话却让格林和弗雷迪清醒了过来。迈克尔盯着他们,从桌边走开,意思是说他们可以离开了。黑根过去开门,两人连晚安都没说就出去了。

第二天早晨,迈克尔·柯里昂收到莫·格林的口信:无论什么价码,他都不肯出售股份。送信的是弗雷迪。迈克尔耸耸肩,对哥哥说:"回纽约之前,我想先见见尼诺。"

来到尼诺的套房,他们发现约翰尼·方坦在沙发上吃早饭。朱尔斯拉起了卧室的帘幕,在里面检查尼诺的情况。等了好一阵,帘幕终于拉开。

尼诺的模样吓了迈克尔一跳。他整个人都垮了,两眼无神,嘴巴微张,脸上所有的肌肉都耷拉着。迈克尔坐在床沿上,说:"尼诺,能和你叙叙旧可真好。唐经常问起你的近况。"

尼诺咧嘴一笑——还是以前那个笑容,"告诉他,我快死了。告诉他,演艺圈比橄榄油生意还要危险。"

"你会好起来的,"迈克尔说,"你有什么烦心事,只要家族帮得上忙的,尽管告诉我。"

尼诺摇摇头。"没有,"他说,"真的没有。"

迈克尔和他又聊了一会儿,起身离开。弗雷迪送他和他的手下去机场,迈克尔坚持叫他离开,不用等飞机起飞。迈克尔与汤姆·黑根和艾尔伯特·奈利登上飞机,迈克尔扭头问奈利:"记住他的长相了?"

奈利拍拍脑门。"拍了大头照,编号存在这儿了。"

第二十八章

回纽约的航班上,迈克尔·柯里昂放松心情,想打个瞌睡,可惜未能如愿。人生中最艰难的时光正在接近,说不定甚至会要了他这条命。不可能继续推迟了。一切都已准备就绪,他们采取了所有的预防措施,足足耗费两年时间。无法继续拖延下去了。上周,唐正式向首领和柯里昂家族的其他成员宣布退隐,迈克尔知道这是父亲在用他的方式说时机已经成熟。

他回美国就快三年,和凯结婚已经超过两年。他的这三年花在了学习家族生意上。他长时间和汤姆·黑根探讨,长时间和唐谈话。他惊讶地发现柯里昂家族的财富和权势竟然如此可观。家族在纽约中城拥有大量昂贵地产,都是整幢的办公楼。家族暗中与华尔街两家证券经纪公司合作,是时装中心几家公司的合伙人,拥有长岛几家银行的股份;而这些都还没算非法的赌博生意。

回顾柯里昂家族过去的活动时,迈克尔觉得有件事情特别有意思:家族向一群唱片盗版商收过保护费。盗版商复制和出售著名歌手的唱片,一切都仿造得天衣无缝,因此从没被逮住过。他们批发卖给零售店,歌手和唱片公司当然拿不到一分钱。迈克尔注意到盗版使得约翰尼·方坦损失惨重,因为那段时间恰好在他失声之前,他的唱片在全国最为畅销。

他向汤姆·黑根问起这事,唐为什么允许盗版商损害他教子的利益?黑根耸耸肩。生意就是生意。再说了,当时约翰尼刚和青梅竹马的老婆离婚,娶了玛格特·艾什顿,唐对他非常不满,他因此上了唐的黑名单。

"那些人后来为什么罢手?"迈克尔问,"被警察逮住了?"

黑根摇摇头。"康妮的婚礼过后不久,唐就收回了保护。"

正符合他经常见到的模式:唐帮助不幸的人,而这些人的不幸又有一部分要归咎于他。不一定出于狡诈或计划,很可能只是因为他在各方面都有利益,也许这就是宇宙的固有性质:善与恶内在联系,宇宙本身就是这样。

迈克尔在新英格兰与凯成婚,没有大张旗鼓,只有她的父母和她的少数几个朋友参加。他们随后搬进长滩林荫道的一幢屋子。迈克尔惊讶地发现凯与他父母还有住在林荫道的其他人相处得很好。她很快就有了,真是个传统的意大利好老婆,这一点帮了她很大的忙。两年后的今天,她刚刚怀上了第二个孩子。

凯会在机场接他,她总喜欢到机场接他,每次他外出归来,她总是分外开心。他见了也很开心。但今天是个例外。这次旅程结束,意味着他终于要启动酝酿已有三年的大行动了。唐正在等他,首领也在等他,而他,迈克尔·柯里昂将发布命令,作出即将左右他和家族命运的决定。

每天早晨,凯·亚当斯·柯里昂起床喂婴儿吃早饭的时候,总会看见保镖开车送柯里昂妈妈离开林荫道,一小时后返回。凯很快得知婆婆每天清晨都要去教堂。老太太经常在回来的路上顺便拜访她,喝杯咖啡,看看新得的孙子。

柯里昂妈妈的开场白永远是问凯为什么不考虑皈依天主教,罔顾凯的孩子已经受洗成为新教徒。凯不禁觉得有必要问一问老太太,她为什么每天清晨都要去教堂,天主教徒非得如此吗?

老太太像是以为这会阻止凯皈依天主教,连声说:"噢,不,不是的,有些天主教徒只在复活节和圣诞节去教堂。你愿意去几次就去几次。"

凯笑着说:"那你为什么每天都要去呢?"

柯里昂妈妈用最自然不过的语气说:"我去是为了我丈夫,"她指着脚下说,"免得以后去那儿。"她顿了顿,又说,"我每天为他的灵魂祈祷,这样他就可以去那儿了。"她指了指天上。她说话时满脸顽皮笑容,像是在偷偷摸摸忤逆丈夫的意志,又像在说这个目标注定失败。她说话的语气也像是在开玩笑,是个意大利老太婆的黑色笑话。和平时一样,只要丈夫不在身边,她对伟大的唐就有点不太尊重。

"爸爸最近心情如何?"凯有礼貌地问。

柯里昂妈妈耸了耸肩。"自从吃了那几枪,他就像换了个人,把事情全交给迈克,自己成天侍弄菜园——他的辣椒,他的番茄。就仿佛他仍旧是个农夫。唉,男人,都是一个样。"

上午晚些时候,康妮·柯里昂会领着两个孩子穿过林荫道找凯聊天。凯喜欢康妮,喜欢她的活泼性格,喜欢她对哥哥迈克尔显而易见的偏爱。康妮教凯怎么做意大利菜,偶尔也带她上更专业的菜肴来供迈克尔品尝。

今天上午康妮和往常一样来了,问凯怎么看她的丈夫卡洛,问迈克尔是不是表里如一地喜欢卡洛。卡洛和家族一直不怎么合得来,但这两年似乎走上了正道。他在工会干得不错,但必须干得非常卖力,每天很晚才回家。康妮常说卡洛是真心喜欢迈克尔。可话也说回来,每个人都喜欢迈克尔,就像每个人都喜欢她父亲。迈克尔是唐的翻版。由迈克尔来经营家族的橄榄油事业真是再好不过了。

凯早就看出来了,康妮每次说到她丈夫和家族的关系,总是紧张兮兮地期待着对卡洛的嘉许之词。康妮对迈克尔喜不喜欢卡洛简直到了提心吊胆的地步,只有傻瓜才看不出这一点。一天晚上,她向迈克尔说起这件事,又说起谁也不谈论桑尼·柯里昂,甚至提都不提他的名字,至少在她面前是这样。有一次,凯尝试向唐和唐的妻子表达哀悼之情,得到的却是近乎于无礼的沉默和不加理睬。她也试过让康妮谈谈她的大哥,同样未能成功。

桑尼的妻子珊德拉带着孩子搬去佛罗里达和父母团聚。家族作了必要的财务安排,保证她和孩子过上舒适的生活,因为桑尼并没有留下任何资产。

迈克尔不情愿地解释了桑尼遇害那晚的经过:卡洛打老婆,康妮打电话回林荫道,接电话的是桑尼,气疯了冲出家门。因此,康妮和卡洛当然总是提心吊胆,害怕家族的其他成员会怪罪她间接导致了桑尼遇害,或者责怪她丈夫卡洛。实情并非如此。证据摆在眼前:家族给了康妮和卡洛一幢林荫道的屋子,提拔卡洛进工会担任重要职务。卡洛也改邪归正,戒酒戒嫖,不再自作聪明。家族对他这两年的表现和态度很满意。没有人因为过去的事情责怪他。

"我们为什么不找个晚上请他们来家里,你来安慰一下自己的妹妹呢?"凯说,"她多可怜,总是提心吊胆,生怕你对她丈夫有看法。你亲口告诉她,叫她别再胡思乱想。"

"这我做不到,"迈克尔说,"我们家里从来不讨论这种事情。"

"我可以把你的这些话告诉她吗?"凯说。

这个建议明显合乎情理,迈克尔却花了很长时间思考,凯不禁困惑起来。最后,迈克尔说:"我觉得不应该,凯,我觉得这么做没有半点好处。她还是会担心。任何人都无能为力。"

凯愣住了。她觉察到尽管康妮很爱迈克尔,迈克尔对妹妹却比他对其他人总是冷淡一点。"你不会因为桑尼的事情责怪康妮吧?"她问。

迈克尔叹了口气。"当然不会,"他说,"她是我的妹妹,我一直很喜欢她。我为她感到遗憾。卡洛改邪归正了,但骨子里他不是个好丈夫。这种事谁都无能为力,我们就别再提了吧。"

唠叨不符合凯的天性,因此她没再多嘴。另外,她早就知道逼问迈克尔毫无益处,他会变得冷酷而乖戾。她知道全世界只有她能压迈克尔一头,但也知道经常这么做只会毁掉这种能力。还有,和迈克尔在一起两年,她更加爱他了。

她爱迈克尔是因为他总是非常公正,非常罕见。但他确实对周围的每一个人都那么公正,哪怕在最小的细节上也决不武断。她看得到迈克尔现在手握大权,经常有人登门向他请教和求助,对迈克尔顺服而恭敬,但真正让她分外喜爱迈克尔的却是另外一件事情。

迈克尔带着破相的脸从西西里回来以后,每一名家族成员都尝试过劝说他接受整容手术。迈克尔的母亲每天追着他跑。一个星期天,柯里昂全家在林荫道聚餐,她对迈克尔吼道:"你这模样简直是电影里的匪徒,老天在上,就算为了你可怜的老婆,去修整一下你那张脸吧。也免得你成天流鼻涕,活像爱尔兰醉汉。"

坐在桌首的唐看在眼里,他问凯:"他的模样让你难受吗?"

凯摇摇头。唐对妻子说:"他已经不归你管了,事情也和你没关系了。"老妇人立刻安静下来。倒不是说她有多害怕丈夫,而是当众和他争论会显得不尊重他。

可就在这时候,康妮——唐的掌上明珠正在厨房烹制周日大餐,炉火把她的脸蛋烘得红扑扑的——从厨房走进房间,说:"我觉得他应该把脸修整好。他受伤前是家里最英俊的。来吧,迈克,就答应了吧。"

迈克尔望向她,一脸的心不在焉,仿佛根本没听见大家都在说什么。他没有回答。

康妮走到父亲身旁站住。"你给他下命令。"她对唐说,双手亲热地放在唐的肩膀上,轻轻按摩父亲的脖颈。全家只有她能这么亲近唐,她对父亲的爱令人感动,是小女孩的那种无条件的信赖。唐拍拍她的一只手,说:"我们都要饿死啦,先把面条端上来再聊天。"

康妮转向丈夫,说:"卡洛,你劝劝迈克,让他修整一下他的脸,说不定他会听你的。"她的语气暗示迈克尔和卡洛·里齐是朋友,关系比卡洛与家里其他人都要好。

卡洛晒得黝黑,金发剪得考究,梳得整齐,喝着家酿葡萄酒说:"谁也不能左右迈克的想法。"自从搬进林荫道,卡洛就变了个人。他知道他在家族里的位置,从不越轨。

在这整件事里存在一些凯搞不懂的东西,一些说不清道不明的东西。同为女人,她看得出康妮是在有意蛊惑父亲,尽管做得很漂亮,甚至发自内心,但并不自然。卡洛的回答就像个大男人磕头如捣。迈克尔却对一切视而不见。

凯并不在意丈夫的破相,但很担心破相引起的鼻窦毛病。手术不但能修复面容,也能治好鼻窦,因此她希望迈克尔能住院接受必要的治疗。可是,尽管奇怪,但她能理解丈夫对破相的留恋之情。她知道唐也理解。

凯生完第一个孩子以后,迈克尔问她:"你希不希望我去修整我的脸?"

凯吃了一惊,点点头。"你知道孩子是什么样的,等儿子长大,意识到你的面容不正常,他心里会不舒服的。我不想让我们的孩子见到。我根本不在乎,迈克尔,我说真的。"

"明白了,"他对凯微笑着说,"我去做。"

他等凯出院回家,作了全部必要的安排,然后入院治疗。手术很成功。面颊上的凹痕已经几不可查。

家族里人人高兴,康妮则是最高兴的一个。她每天拖着卡洛去医院探望迈克尔。迈克尔回家那天,她使劲拥抱迈克尔,亲吻他,赞赏道:"现在你又是我最英俊的哥哥了。"

只有唐不为所动,耸耸肩,评论道:"有什么区别呢?"

凯满心感激。她知道接受手术违反了迈克尔本人的意愿。他之所以接受,是因为凯求了他,因为全世界只有她能迫使迈克尔做违背自己心意的事情。

迈克尔从拉斯维加斯返回的那天下午,洛可·兰坡开着豪华轿车去林荫道接凯,送她去机场迎接丈夫。丈夫每次出城回来,她都要去机场接他,主要是因为住在宛如堡垒的林荫道上,没有他,她觉得非常孤单。

她看着迈克尔与汤姆·黑根和新来的艾尔伯特·奈利走下飞机。凯不太喜欢奈利,奈利那种不动声色的暴戾让她想起卢卡·布拉齐。她注意到奈利走在迈克尔的侧后方,锐利的视线扫过附近每一个人。奈利首先瞅见了凯,拍拍迈克尔的肩膀,要他往凯的方向看。

凯扑进丈夫的怀抱,迈克尔轻轻亲了她一下,放开手。他、汤姆·黑根和凯坐进豪华轿车,艾尔伯特·奈利却不见了。凯没有注意到奈利和另外两个男人钻进了另一辆车,护送豪华轿车回到长滩。

凯从来不问生意谈得好不好。两人心照不宣,连这种礼节性的问题说出口都会很尴尬,倒不是说他不会给个同样礼节性的回答,而是这么一问一答,就会提醒两人想到这场婚姻还有一片禁区永远无法被纳入疆域。凯已经不在乎了。可是,听迈克尔说他今晚要向父亲汇报拉斯维加斯之行的结果,她还是忍不住失望地皱了皱眉。

"抱歉,"迈克尔说,"明晚我们去纽约看戏吃饭,好吗?"他拍拍凯的腹部,她怀孕已近七个月了。"等孩子出生,你又要忙得不可开交。唉,你真像是意大利人。两年两个孩子。"

凯反唇相讥:"你呢? 你真像扬基佬。回家第一个晚上就花在生意事上。"不过,她是面带微笑对丈夫说这句话的,"不会很晚回来吧?"

"十二点以前,"迈克尔说,"你要是累了就别等我。"

"我等你。"凯说。

那天晚上的会议在唐·柯里昂家的拐角书房举行,与会者有唐、迈克尔、汤姆·黑根、卡洛·里齐和克莱门扎与忒西奥两位首领。

这次会议的气氛不像平时那么融洽。自从唐·柯里昂宣布半退隐和迈克尔接管家族生意以来,众人的关系就有些紧张。家族这种巨型组织的控制权一向不是父子相传的。换了其他家族,克莱门扎和忒西奥这种有权势的首领也有资格接替唐的位置。

至少也能得到允许,分裂成立自己的家族。

另外,唐·柯里昂和五大家族和谈之后,柯里昂家族的实力就走上了下坡路。巴齐尼家族如今无疑是纽约地区最有权势的家族,与塔塔利亚家族结盟后,占据了柯里昂家族原有的地位。他们同时在暗地里蚕食柯里昂家族的势力,靠武力挤进赌博领域,测试柯里昂家族的反应,发现反击乏力,于是建立起自己的簿记点。

听到唐的退隐消息,巴齐尼家族和塔塔利亚家族欢欣鼓舞。迈克尔也许能证明他也是个人物,狡诈程度和影响力在十年内却不可能追上唐。柯里昂家族明显是在走下坡路。

家族确实遭遇了严重的挫折。事实证明弗雷迪只适合管小客栈,是妈妈的宝贝——无法更加准确的言传,总是像个贪婪的婴儿,总是叼着母亲的奶头不放——简而言之就是没有男子气概。桑尼遇害也是一场灾难。桑尼在世时令人恐惧,不可轻视。他当然也犯过错误,派自己的弟弟迈克尔去杀土佬和警长。尽管从战术角度说是必要的一步棋,但从长期战略的角度看,事实却证明他犯了个严重错误,最终迫使唐从病床上爬起来,害得迈克尔失去了宝贵的两年经验和训练,没能在父亲的监护下学习。还有,任命一名爱尔兰人当顾问是唐这辈子唯一一次犯傻。论狡诈,爱尔兰人无论如何也比不上西西里人。各大家族观点一致,他们自然更尊敬巴齐尼—塔塔利亚联盟,而非柯里昂家族。他们对迈克尔的看法是他不如桑尼那么有魄力,虽说比较有智慧,但仍旧比不上他的父亲。这个继承人资质平庸,不值得过于畏惧。

另外,尽管唐息事宁人的政治家风度受人们的敬佩,但他不为桑尼复仇却严重损害了家族的威信。大家认为他的政客手腕缘于软弱。

在座众人都清楚这些问题,有几个人甚至深信不疑。卡洛·里齐喜欢迈克尔,但不像害怕桑尼那样害怕他。克莱门扎也是,尽管赞赏迈克尔做掉土佬和警长的精彩表演,却忍不住觉得迈克尔过于软弱,当不了唐。克莱门扎希望能得到允许,组建自己的家族,分离出柯里昂家族,建立自己的帝国。可是,唐已经表示过不行了,克莱门扎非常尊重唐,不可能违抗他——除非局势失控。

忒西奥看好迈克尔。他感觉到这个年轻人没这么简单,巧妙地隐藏起了某种力量,他戒心很重,生怕把真正的实力暴露在公众视线之下,遵循唐的教诲:让朋友低估你的优点,敌人高估你的缺陷。

唐本人和汤姆·黑根当然最了解迈克尔。要是唐对儿子有能力取回家族的地位缺乏百分之百的信心,他肯定不会退隐。黑根在过去两年间担任迈克尔的老师,惊讶地发现迈克尔迅速掌握了错综复杂的家族生意。他不愧是教父的儿子。

克莱门扎和忒西奥之所以不喜欢迈克尔,是因为他不但削弱了两人组织的实力,而且毫无重建桑尼手下的想法。柯里昂家族如今只有两个作战单位,人数也大不如前。克莱门扎和忒西奥认为这是自寻死路,特别是巴齐尼和塔塔利亚还正在蚕食他们的帝国。因此,今天他们希望这些错误能在唐召开的特殊会议上得到纠正。

迈克尔首先汇报拉斯维加斯之行,指出莫·格林拒绝出售股份。"不过,我们会给他一个他无法拒绝的出价,"迈克尔说,"你们都知道柯里昂家族打算把活动中心移向西部。我们将拥有长街的四家酒店赌场。但事情不可能一天就办成,我们需要时间打好基础。"他直接对克莱门扎说:"彼得,你和忒西奥,我希望你们毫无疑问、不加保留地再跟我干一年。一年结束,你们都可以从柯里昂家族分裂出去,自立门户,组建自己的家族。当然,不用说,我们的友谊仍旧一如既往,我根本不会动别的念头,因为那样是侮辱你们和你们对我父亲的尊敬。但是,在此之前,我希望你们能听从我的领导,不要有什么顾虑。各方正在谈判,你们认为难以解决的问题终究会得到解决。因此,还请二位耐心一些。"

忒西奥发言道:"莫·格林想和你父亲谈谈,为什么不让他谈呢?唐有本事说服任何人,谁都抵挡不了他的说理。"

唐回答了他的问题:"我已经退隐了,要是插手,会损害迈克尔的威信。另外,我恐怕不怎么愿意和那家伙谈。"

忒西奥记起他听说过莫·格林曾在拉斯维加斯的酒店扇弗雷迪·柯里昂耳光。事情恐怕不会这么简单,他往后一靠。莫·格林死定了,他心想。柯里昂家族没兴趣说服他。

卡洛·里齐发言道:"柯里昂家族打算完全停止纽约的生意?"

迈克尔点点头。"我们正在出售橄榄油生意,能交出去的东西都会转给忒西奥和克莱门扎。卡洛,你不用担心你的工作。你是土生土长的内华达人,熟悉这个州,认识当地人。等我们去了拉斯维加斯,我指望你能担任我的右手。"

卡洛往后一靠,满意得满脸通红。他的机会来了,他将进入权力核心。

迈克尔继续道:"汤姆·黑根不再担任顾问,他将是我们在拉斯维加斯的律师。两个月后,他会带着家人定居拉斯维加斯,只担任律师。从现在这一分钟开始,任何人都不能找他谈其他的事情。他是律师,只是律师。不得怀疑汤姆,这是我的意愿。再说了,如果需要建议,还有比我父亲更好的顾问吗?"众人哈哈大笑,但对笑话之外的信息心领神会。汤姆·黑根已经出局,不再拥有任何权力。每个人都瞥了一眼黑根的反应,但他面无表情。

克莱门扎带着胖子的气音呼哧呼哧地说:"那么,一年之后,我和忒西奥就全靠自己了?"

"也许不到一年，"迈克尔亲切地说，"当然了，你也可以留在家族之内，你说了算。不过，我们的大部分实力将向西迁移，所以你最好组织起自己的力量。"

忒西奥平静地说："这样的话，我希望你能允许我们招募新人，充实部下。巴齐尼家族的王八蛋不断吞噬我的领土。我觉得应该给他们上一堂礼貌课了。"

迈克尔摇头道："不，没有好处。不要轻举妄动。这些事情都将通过谈判解决，我们在离开前会厘清所有的头绪。"

忒西奥不那么容易低头。他冒着招致迈克尔反感的风险，直接对唐说："请原谅，教父，看在我们多年友谊的分上，请原谅我。但是，我认为你和你儿子在内华达的事情上是大错特错了。没有纽约的实力做后盾，你怎么可能在那里成功？两边的命运相互关联。你们离开以后，巴齐尼和塔塔利亚对我们来说过于强大，我和彼得会陷入麻烦，迟早向他们臣服，虽说巴齐尼不合我的口味。我想说的是，柯里昂家族应该在强盛中转移，而不是在虚弱时。我们应该巩固组织，至少要收复斯坦顿岛的失地。"

唐摇摇头："我已经讲和了，请记住，我不能食言。"

忒西奥拒绝认输："大家都知道自从和谈以后，巴齐尼一直在挑衅。再说，如果迈克尔是柯里昂家族的新首领，他为什么不能采取他认为合适的行动呢？你的话不能束缚他的手脚。"

迈克尔突然插嘴，完全以首领的口吻对忒西奥说："各方正在谈判的一些事情能解答你的疑问，打消你的疑虑。要是我的话对你来说还不够，那就问问你的唐好了。"

忒西奥意识到他已经越界。要是胆敢问唐，迈克尔将成为敌人。他只好耸耸肩，说："我说这些不是为了自己，而是为了家族。我能照顾好自己。"

迈克尔对他友善地笑了笑："忒西奥，我从来没有怀疑过你。永远也不会。请你信任我。我在这些方面比不上你和彼得，但我毕竟有我的父亲当领路人，表现不会太差，我们都会见到好结果的。"

会议到此结束。重要消息是克莱门扎和忒西奥将得到允许，带着各自的人手组建家族。忒西奥掌管布鲁克林的赌博和码头工会，克莱门扎掌管曼哈顿的赌博和家族在长岛的赛马内线。

两位首领出门时不怎么满意，还有点不安。卡洛·里齐迟迟不肯离开，希望终于等来了家族正式接纳他的日子，但很快发现迈克尔并没有这个意思。他把唐、汤姆·黑根和迈克尔单独留在拐角书房里。艾尔伯特·奈利送他出大门，卡洛注意到奈利站在门洞里，目送他穿过水银灯照耀下的林荫道。

书房里，三个男人放松下来，只有在同一幢屋子里住了许多年的一家人才能这么轻松。迈克尔给唐倒了杯茴香酒，给汤姆·黑根倒了杯苏格兰威士忌。他给自己也斟了一杯烈酒,这是很少见的事情。

汤姆·黑根首先开口:"迈克,你为什么把我排除出去?"

迈克尔面露讶色。"你是我在拉斯维加斯的一号部下。我们要尽量合法,你将负责法务。还有比这个更重要的职位吗?"

黑根笑得有点哀伤。"我说的不是这个。我说的是洛可·兰坡在背着我秘密组建人手,说的是你直接指挥奈利,而不是通过我和某位首领。当然,除非你也不知道兰坡在干什么。"

迈克尔轻声说:"你是怎么发现兰坡的人?"

黑根耸耸肩。"别担心,风声没有走漏,其他人都不知道。但是,我这个位置看得见所有动静。你允许兰坡拥有自己的生计,给了他很大的自由,所以他的小帝国需要人手。然而,他每招募一个人都必须向我报告。我注意到他放在工资单上的人对所承担的职务来说都有点过于优秀,就所履行的职责而言拿的薪水又有点过于丰厚。顺便说一句,你选兰坡算是选对了人。他干得好极了。"

迈克尔做个鬼脸。"要是被你注意到了,显然还不够好。再说兰坡也是唐选的。"

"好吧,"汤姆说,"那么,我为什么被排除出去了?"

迈克尔面对他,也不避讳,而是直截了当说道:"汤姆,你不适合在开战时当顾问。这次转移局势将变得很险恶,我们可能要被迫应战。另外,我也想把你撤下火线,以防万一。"

黑根涨红了脸。要是唐这么说,他或许愿意低头接受。可是,迈克有什么资格作出如此突然的决定呢?

"好吧,"他说,"但说起来,我赞同忒西奥的看法。我认为这步棋你完全走错了。你的迁移是出于虚弱,而非强盛。这么做从来不会有好下场。巴齐尼就像一条狼,他会一条胳膊一条腿地撕烂你,其他家族恐怕不会冲出来帮助柯里昂家族。"

唐终于开口:"汤姆,这不单是迈克尔的主意。我在这些方面向他提供建议。有些事情非做不可,但我实在承担不起这么大的责任了。这是我的愿望,不是迈克尔的。我从来不认为你是个不称职的顾问,但我认为桑蒂诺是个不称职的唐——愿他的灵魂安息。他确实很勇猛,但不适合在我遭遇小小不幸的时候领导家族。谁又能想到弗雷迪会追着女人的屁股跑呢?所以,你别难过。我完全信任迈克尔,正如我完全信任你。出于某些不能告诉你的原因,你绝对不能参与接下来的事情。另外,我跟迈克尔说过,兰坡的秘密人手逃不过你的眼睛。你看,我对你多么有信心。"

迈克尔笑着说:"实话实说,汤姆,我没想到真会被你看出来。"

黑根知道他们是在宽慰他。"也许我还能帮忙。"他说。

迈克尔摇摇头，斩钉截铁道："你出局了，汤姆。"

汤姆喝完酒，在离开前温和地责备了迈克尔一句。"你和你父亲差不多同样出色，"他告诉迈克尔，"但有件事你还得学着点。"

"什么？"迈克尔有礼貌地问。

"怎么对别人说不。"黑根答道。

迈克尔郑重其事地点点头。"你说得对，"他答道，"我会记住的。"

黑根离开后，迈克尔开玩笑地对父亲说："其他的你都教过了，现在请告诉我，怎么用别人喜欢的方式对他们说不。"

唐走到大书桌前坐下。"你不能对你爱的人说不，至少不能经常说。这就是秘诀。要是非说不可，也得听起来像是肯定。或者想办法让他们自己说。你得耐心，不怕麻烦。可话也说回来，我毕竟是个守旧的人，你是摩登的新一代，用不着都听我的。"

迈克尔笑道："对。不过，你也同意让汤姆出局，对吧？"

唐点点头。"他不能卷入这些事。"

迈克尔静静地说："我想现在可以告诉你了，我打算采取的行动不仅是为了给阿波罗妮亚和桑尼报仇，从方向上说也是正确的。忒西奥和汤姆对巴齐尼的判断很正确。"

唐·柯里昂点点头。"复仇这盘菜，凉了最好吃，"他说，"我并不想和谈，但我知道不和谈你就不可能活着回来。我吃惊的是巴齐尼居然最后还试了一次。也许在和谈之前就安排好了，他想取消也取消不了。你确定那次的目标不是唐·托马西诺？"

迈克尔说："他们就希望弄得看起来是这样。计划本来很完美，连你都不会起疑心。只可惜我侥幸活了下来。我看见法布雷奇奥走出大门，逃之夭夭。我回来以后当然全调查清楚了。"

"他们找到了那个牧羊人吗？"唐问。

"找到了，"迈克尔说，"一年前找到的。他在水牛城开了家小比萨店。改名换姓，用假护照和假证件。牧羊人法布雷奇奥活得相当不赖。"

唐点点头。"所以，没必要继续等下去了。你打算什么时候发动？"

迈克尔说："我想等凯生完孩子。以防事情出差错。我让汤姆去拉斯维加斯定居，这样大家就不会觉得他和事情有关系了。我觉得一年以后的今天就很适合。"

"你全都准备好了？"唐问，他说话时没有看迈克尔。

迈克尔柔声说："你没有参与，不需要负责，我承担全部责任。我拒绝你哪怕只是行使否决权。你现在要是尝试行使否决权，我就脱离家族，走我自己的路。你仍旧不需要负责。"

唐沉默半晌,最后长叹一声。他说:"那就这样吧。也许这就是我退隐的原因,也许这就是我把所有事情交给你的原因。我已经做完了我这辈子的苦工,已经硬不起这个心肠。有些职责,连最优秀的人也无法永远承担。这就是其中之一。"

在这一年里,凯·亚当斯·柯里昂生下第二个孩子,仍旧是男孩。她生得很顺利,没有遇到任何麻烦,回到林荫道时受到了皇家贵妇的欢迎。康妮·柯里昂送了婴儿一套意大利手工制作的丝绸用品,非常贵重,非常漂亮。她告诉凯:"这是卡洛发现的,我找不到特别喜欢的东西,他跑遍纽约,就想弄点特别的好礼物。"凯微笑道谢,明白她应该把这桩好事告诉迈克尔。她越来越像西西里人了。

同样在这一年里,尼诺·瓦伦蒂死于脑溢血。他的辞世登上小报头版,因为由约翰尼·方坦制作、尼诺·瓦伦蒂担纲的电影几周前开画,票房火爆,尼诺成了大明星。小报说约翰尼·方坦亲自安排葬礼,仪式将不对外开放,只有家人和亲友可以参加。一则煽情报道甚至说,在一次访谈中,约翰尼·方坦将朋友之死归咎于他本人,说他应该强迫朋友接受治疗,记者把约翰尼·方坦写成敏感但无辜的旁观者,面对悲剧像平常人一样自我谴责。约翰尼·方坦将儿时伙伴尼诺·瓦伦蒂打造成了电影明星,朋友做到这个份上已经足够了。

柯里昂家族只有弗雷迪参加了这场在加州举办的葬礼。露西和朱尔斯·西格尔参加了。唐想去,但他刚刚遭遇了一次轻微的心脏病发作,害得他卧床一月不起。他只好送了个大花篮。艾尔伯特·奈利以家族正式代表的身份赶赴西海岸。

尼诺葬礼后两天的好莱坞,莫·格林在电影明星情妇家中遭到枪杀;艾尔伯特·奈利直到近一个月后才重新在纽约露面。他从加勒比度假归来,简直晒成了黑人。迈克尔·柯里昂用微笑和几句嘉许之词欢迎他,其中提到奈利将额外得到一笔"生计"——东区一个公认特别挣钱的簿记点的收入。奈利颇为满意,因为他生活的这个世界令人满意,履行职责的人能获得恰当的奖赏。

第八部

第二十九章

迈克尔·柯里昂对一切意外都采取了预防措施。他的计划无懈可击,防备坚不可摧。他很耐心,希望用一整年时间做足准备。然而,他并没能得到这必需的一年时间,因为命运站在了他的反面,而且来势汹汹,他猝不及防:因为辜负了迈克尔·柯里昂的正是教父,了不起的唐本人。

一个阳光灿烂的星期天早晨,女人都去了教堂,唐·维托·柯里昂换上园艺服:松垮垮的灰色长裤,褪色的蓝衬衫,土黄色的旧呢帽,配一条脏兮兮的灰色丝绸帽带。唐这几年长了不少体重,声称伺候番茄藤纯粹是为了健康——但他骗不了任何人。

实际情况是他喜欢照料花园,他喜欢大清早花园的景色,让他回想起六十年前在西西里的童年时光,但又没有恐惧,没有父亲之死带来的悲恸。你看,一行行豆苗开出了小小的白花,苗壮的大葱茎秆筑起篱笆。花园的另一头有个带喷嘴的大桶,装满了稀释的牛粪,那是上佳的花园肥料。脚边是他亲手搭建的四方木架,粗白绳捆扎起彼此交错的木条。番茄藤已经爬满木架。

唐忙着给花园浇水。水必须在日出前浇完,否则日头会把水变成棱镜,聚热灼伤生菜的叶子。阳光比水重要,水当然也很重要,但阳光和水若是调配不当,就会酿成大祸。

唐在花园里走来走去搜寻蚂蚁。要是有蚂蚁,就说明菜地里有蚜虫,因为蚂蚁总是跟着蚜虫跑,那他就得喷杀虫药了。

他准时浇完水。阳光越来越热,唐心想,"小心,要小心。"不过,还有几株豆苗需要用木杆支起来,他再次弯下腰。伺候完最后这行豆苗,他就回屋歇息。

突然,太阳好像降到了头顶。舞动的金色斑点充满了天空。唐跪倒在地,迈克尔的大儿子穿过花园跑向他,炫目的黄色光芒包裹着那孩子。唐当然不会被骗住,他太老练了:死神就躲在那团黄色光球背后,正准备扑向他,唐挥手赶开孩子——刚好来得及——胸膛里像是挨了几记重锤,他喘不上气,一头栽倒在地。

孩子跑去找父亲。迈克尔·柯里昂和林荫道门口的几个男人冲进花园,发现唐趴在地上,双手攥着两把泥土。他们抬起唐,把他放在石板天井的阴凉处。迈克尔在父亲身边跪下,抓着父亲的手,另外几个人去叫救护车和医生。

唐费了最大的力气,睁开眼睛,最后看了儿子一眼。心脏病严重发作把红脸膛变成了铁青色。他已在弥留之际。他闻着花园的香味,黄色的光球刺得眼睛生疼,他悄声说:"生活如此美丽。"

他没有看到女人的眼泪,死在她们从教堂回来之前,死在救护车和医生赶到之前。他死在男人之间,握着他最爱的儿子的手。

葬礼极其隆重。五大家族的唐和首领悉数出席,忒西奥和克莱门扎家族也一样。约翰尼·方坦不顾迈克尔的劝告,坚持参加葬礼,登上小报头条。方坦向报纸发表声明,说维托·柯里昂是他的教父,是他这辈子认识的最像样的男人,能得到家族允许,向他表示最后的敬意,他只感到非常荣幸,才不怕你们知道。

守灵仪式按照传统习俗在林荫道他的故居举行。亚美利哥·邦纳塞拉的手艺从没这么出色过,他还清了所有的人情债,为他的老朋友、他的教父精心化妆,简直像是母亲在打扮要出嫁的女儿。人人都说连死神都无法取走唐脸上的高贵与尊严,说得亚美利哥·邦纳塞拉心里充满了不言而喻的自豪和奇异的力量感。只有他知道突如其来的死亡从多大程度上改变了唐的面容。

老朋友和旧部下都来了。纳佐里尼带着妻子、女儿、女婿和孙子孙女来了;露西·曼奇尼和弗雷迪从拉斯维加斯来了;黑根及其妻子和儿女来了,旧金山、洛杉矶、波士顿和克利夫兰的几位唐都来了。抬棺人是洛可·兰坡和艾尔伯特·奈利、克莱门扎和忒西奥,当然还有唐的两个儿子。林荫道和两边的所有屋子都摆满了花篮。

报社记者和照相师守在林荫道的大门口,还有一辆大家都知道属于联邦调查局的小货车,探员带着电影摄影机在车里拍摄这个史诗般的场面。有几个记者试图混进去,发现大门和围栏有保安把守,拿不出证件和请帖就进不去。他们得到了良好的招待,还不时有饮料和点心送出来,但就是不许他们进去。他们试着和出来的人攀谈,却只收获了冷冰冰的视线和沉默。

迈克尔·柯里昂与凯、汤姆·黑根和弗雷迪在拐角图书室度过了这一天的大部分时间。人们被引荐到他面前,向他表达哀悼之情。迈克尔对所有人都以礼相待,但有几个人称他"教父"或"唐"的时候,只有凯注意到他因为不悦而抿紧了嘴唇。

克莱门扎和忒西奥也来加入了核心团体,迈克尔亲自为他们斟酒。他们聊了些生意上的事情。迈克尔说林荫道连同所有的住宅将出售给一家房产开发与建筑公司,获利极为丰厚,再次证明了唐的商业天赋。

他们都明白这说明整个帝国都将搬往西部,说明柯里昂家族正在变现他们在纽约的势力。这个动作等的是唐的完全退隐或辞世。

有人说这幢屋子有近十年没这么济济一堂了,上次人声鼎沸还是康丝坦齐娅·柯里昂和卡洛·里齐的婚礼。迈克尔走到窗口,望着花园。也就是这么多年前,他和凯坐在花园里,做梦也没想到他的命运竟会如此离奇。父亲死前的最后一句话是"生活如此美丽"。迈克尔不记得父亲对死亡发表过任何看法,仿佛唐太尊敬死神,不愿妄加评论。

现在该去墓地了,该埋葬伟大的唐。迈克尔挽起凯的手臂,出门去花园加入送葬的人群。他背后是两名首领和他们的兵卒,接下来是教父在世时赐福过的卑微凡人。面包师纳佐里尼、寡妇科伦坡和她的几个儿子,他严厉但公正地统治过的王国的众多臣民。甚至有一些往日的敌手也来送他最后一程。

迈克尔把这一切都看在眼里,绷着脸露出礼貌的笑容。他不为所动,但他心想,要是我离世时也能说一句"生活如此美丽",那么其他的也就不再重要。要是我能这么相信自己,那么其他的还有什么关系呢?他将追随父亲的脚步。他将照顾他的孩子、他的家庭和他的王国。不过,他的孩子将在另一个世界里长大,将成为医生、艺术家、科学家、州长、总统。任何人。他将帮助他们融入人类的大家庭,但他这个强大而谨慎的父亲,必须警惕地注意那个大家庭的一举一动。

葬礼后的第二天早晨,柯里昂家族所有最重要的高级成员在林荫道聚首。快到正午时分,他们被召进唐生前居住的屋子。迎接他们的是迈克尔·柯里昂。

拐角的图书室几乎挤满了人。有两位首领,克莱门扎和忒西奥;有洛可·兰坡,一脸通情达理的精明相;有卡洛·里齐,非常安静,他很清楚自己的位置;有汤姆·黑根,不顾他彻底洗白的身份,在危急时刻留了下来;艾尔伯特·奈利,尽量贴近迈克尔,给新唐点烟调酒,在柯里昂家族遭此大难的时候,显示出坚定不移的忠贞。

唐的辞世对家族是个巨大的不幸。没了他,家族的实力似乎损失了一半,几乎失去了与巴齐尼—塔塔利亚联盟谈判的全部筹码。房间里每个人都明白这一点,正在等着听迈克尔怎么说。在他们眼中,迈克尔还不是新唐,还没有赢得这个地位和头衔。要是教父还活着,他也许能保证儿子顺利继位,但现在就说不准了。

迈克尔等奈利倒完酒,然后平静地说:"我只想告诉在座诸位,我明白大家的感受。我明白你们都尊敬我父亲,但现在不得不为自己和家人担忧。有些人在思考这件事将如何影响我们已经制订的计划和我已经作出的承诺。嗯,答案是这样的:不会有任何影响。一切照常进行。"

克莱门扎摇了摇他那颗水牛般的大头,他铁灰色的头发蓬乱,五官嵌在层层堆叠的肥肉中间,表情很不愉快。"巴齐尼和塔塔利亚家族将下重手攻击我们,迈克,你只能要么应战,要么坐视。"众人注意到克莱门扎不但没有用唐的头衔称呼他,甚至只用了昵称"迈克"。

"我们等着看,"迈克尔说,"让他们首先破坏和平。"

忒西奥用他柔和的声音说:"他们已经破坏了,迈克。他们今天早晨在布鲁克林开设了两个簿记点。分局负责制订保护名单的警长给了我这个消息。一个月后,我在布鲁克林连个挂帽子的地方都不会有了。"

迈克尔若有所思地盯着他。"你没有对此采取行动吧?"

忒西奥摇着他雪貂似的小脑袋说:"没有,我不想给你找麻烦。"

"很好,"迈克尔说,"按兵不动。我想对你们说的暂时只有这一句。按兵不动。怎么挑衅都不要反击。给我几周时间厘清头绪,看看风会往哪个方向吹。到时候我会为在座各位谈成条件最好的交易。到时候我们再开最后一次会,做出最后的决定。"

他没有搭理他们的惊讶,艾尔伯特·奈利开始送他们出去。迈克尔突然说:"汤姆,你留下几分钟。"

黑根走到面对林荫道的窗口,目送奈利将两位首领、卡洛·里齐和洛可·兰坡送出戒备森严的大门,这才转身对迈克尔说:"所有的政治关系都接过来了吗?"

迈克尔懊丧地摇摇头。"不是全部的。本来还需要三个月时间,唐和我就在忙这个。不过法官已经全在我手上了,这是首先交接的,还有国会里几个最重要的角色。纽约的党魁当然不是问题。柯里昂家族比别人想象的要强大得多,但我希望做得更加万无一失。"他对黑根笑着说,"我猜你已经完全想通了。"

黑根点点头。"其实并不难。除了你要我退出行动的原因。不过我换上西西里人的脑袋,最后连这点也想明白了。"

迈克尔笑道:"老头子说你肯定能想通,但我现在不能再让你过舒服日子了。我这儿需要你。至少接下来几周需要你。你最好给拉斯维加斯打个电话,和你妻子交待一下。就说你要多逗留几周。"

黑根沉思道:"你认为他们会对你下手?"

迈克尔叹了口气:"唐指点了我。他们会通过我身边的人下手。巴齐尼会安排某个和我很亲近、我肯定不会怀疑的人对我下手。"

黑根对他笑着说："就像我这样的人。"

迈克尔笑着答道："你是爱尔兰人，他们不会信任你。"

"我是德美混血儿。"黑根说。

"对他们来说还是爱尔兰人，"迈克尔说，"他们不会来找你，也不会找奈利，因为奈利是警察。再说你们和我过于亲近。他们不能冒险。洛可·兰坡还不够亲近。不，只能是克莱门扎、忒西奥或卡洛·里齐。"

黑根轻声说："我压卡洛。"

"等着瞧，"迈克尔说，"不需要等太久。"

实际上只等到了第二天上午，黑根和迈克尔正在吃早饭，迈克尔去图书室接了个电话，回到厨房对黑根说："安排好了。一周后我将和巴齐尼会面。唐逝世后必须缔结新的和约。"迈克尔笑了起来。

黑根问："打电话给你的是谁？接洽的是谁？"两人都知道，柯里昂家族里谁去接洽，谁就是叛徒。

迈克尔露出哀伤而懊悔的笑容，答道："忒西奥。"

早餐剩下的时间里，两人默不作声。黑根边喝咖啡边摇头道："我昨天都敢发誓不是卡洛就是克莱门扎，没想到会是忒西奥。他是这群人里最优秀的。"

"也是最有智慧的，"迈克尔说，"他做了他眼中最聪明的事情。他出卖我，让巴齐尼做掉我，由他继承柯里昂家族。他觉得继续站在我这边，他迟早会颗粒无收。他估计我不可能获胜。"

黑根犹豫了一下，逼着自己问道："他的估计有多准确？"

迈克尔耸耸肩。"情况看起来很糟糕，但只有我父亲才明白，政治关系和政治力量比得上十个组织。我认为我已经掌握了父亲的大部分政治力量，但知道这一点的只有我。"他对黑根露出鼓励的笑容，"我会让他们叫我唐的，但对于忒西奥，我觉得很难过。"

黑根说，"你答应和巴齐尼会面了吗？"

"答应了，"迈克尔说，"一周后的今晚。布鲁克林，忒西奥的地盘——我在那儿会很安全。"他又放声大笑。

黑根说："在此之前，请多加小心。"

迈克尔第一次对黑根冷淡起来。"我不需要顾问给我这种建议。"他说。

柯里昂与巴齐尼两个家族和平谈判前的这一周里，迈克尔向黑根展示了他能有多么小心。他一步也不踏出林荫道，见人也总是带着奈利。麻烦事只有一桩：康妮和卡洛的大儿子要去天主教堂受坚信礼，凯请求迈克尔当孩子的教父。迈克尔一口回绝。

"我很少求你，"凯说，"看在我的面上，这次就答应了吧。康妮想得都要发疯了。卡洛也是。对他们来说非常重要。迈克尔，求你了。"

她看得出她这么坚持让迈克尔很生气，以为他仍旧会拒绝，但他却点点头，说："好吧，但我不能离开林荫道。叫他们安排神父来这儿给孩子举行仪式。花多少钱我都肯付。教会要是找麻烦，我就让黑根去谈。"

就这样，与巴齐尼家族会面前的一天，迈克尔·柯里昂成为了卡洛·里齐和康妮·里齐的大儿子的教父。他的礼物是一块极其昂贵的手表和金表链。卡洛在家里举办了一场小型酒会，他邀请了两位首领、黑根、兰坡和林荫道的全部住户，其中当然也包括唐的遗孀。康妮激动得忘乎所以，整个晚上没完没了地拥抱和亲吻哥哥和凯。连卡洛·里齐都变得感情外露，瞅到机会就握着迈克尔的手，叫他教父——这是意大利的旧风俗。迈克尔也从没这么容易亲近和谈笑风生。康妮咬着凯的耳朵说："我想卡洛和迈克这下算是真正的朋友了。这种纽带总能把两个人联系起来。"

凯捏了捏她的手臂。"我也很高兴。"

第三十章

艾尔伯特·奈利坐在布朗克斯的公寓里，小心翼翼刷着以前当警察时的蓝色制服。他解下警徽，放在桌上准备抛光。制式枪套和手枪挂在椅背上。这套熟悉的琐碎规程莫名其妙地让他高兴，妻子离开他快两年了，他很少会这么高兴。

他娶丽塔的时候，她还在念高中，他也刚当上警察。她是个黑发的腼腆姑娘，来自一个古板的意大利家庭，晚上十点以前必须回家。奈利全心全意爱上了她，爱她的纯真，爱她的品行，也爱她黝黑的肤色和美貌。

刚开始，丽塔·奈利狂热地迷恋着丈夫。他力大无穷，她看得出人们害怕他，既因为他的力量，也因为他黑白分明、决不动摇的是非观。他很少拐弯抹角。要是不赞同某个团体或个人的看法，他要么避而不谈，要么直截了当地说出他的不满。他从不礼节性地随意附和。他拥有地道的西西里脾气，发起火来实在恐怖。当然，他从不对妻子动怒。

区区五年，奈利成了纽约警队最令人畏惧同时也是最诚实的警察，但他有他自己的一套执法标准。他讨厌地痞流氓，见到一群流氓半夜三更在路口寻衅滋事，就会断然采取行动。他的身体强壮得出奇，这一点连他自己都没有完全意识到。

一天晚上，他在中央公园西路跳下巡逻车，叫住六个身穿黑色丝绸外套的小流氓。

他的搭档很了解奈利，留在驾驶座上，不想掺和进去。六个小伙子都不到二十岁，在街上拦人讨烟抽，用的是年轻人的那种威胁手法，并没有真的伤害什么人。他们还调戏路过的女孩，色迷迷的德性更像法国佬，而不是美国人。

奈利命令他们贴着隔开中央公园和第八大道的石墙站好。虽是黄昏时分，但奈利带着他最喜欢的武器：一支特大号的手电筒。他从不拔枪，因为没这个必要。他动怒的时候脸色十分吓人，加上制服，平常的小流氓见了就腿软，毫无例外。

奈利问第一个身穿黑色丝绸外套的小伙子："你叫什么？"小伙子答了个爱尔兰名字。奈利说："滚远点儿，今晚再让我见到就钉死你。"他用手电筒比划了一下，小伙子快步溜走。奈利按同样套路打发走了接下来的两个小伙子。可是，第四个小伙子报上的是个意大利名字，笑嘻嘻地看着奈利，像是在说我们有血缘关系。奈利明显是意大利血统的长相，他盯着小伙子看了几秒钟，毫无必要地问了一句："意大利人？"小伙子信心十足地咧嘴一笑。

奈利却抡起手电筒冲他脑门来了一下。小伙子跪倒在地，前额皮开肉绽，血流如注，但只是皮肉伤。奈利粗声粗气地对他说："狗娘养的，你让意大利人丢脸了。你败坏了我们的名声。给我站起来。"他一脚踢在小伙子的侧腹部，不轻但也不重，"回家去，别在街上鬼混。再让我逮住你穿这种衣服，我就送你进医院。现在给我回家。算你走运，我不是你老子。"

奈利懒得再问剩下的两个小流氓，只是赏了他们屁股几脚，告诉他们今晚别被他看见第二次。

这种遭遇战总是打得非常迅速，不等人群聚集起来，旁观者抗议他的暴行，事情就已经结束。奈利会钻进巡逻车，搭档开车就走。当然了，偶尔也会碰到一两个想打架的硬骨头，甚至会拔出匕首。这些人算是倒了大霉。奈利动起手来迅速又残忍，打得他们鲜血横流，然后抓起来扔进巡逻车。他们将被捕，受控袭警。不过，案子通常要等他们出院才能开始审理。

最后，上头调奈利去联合国大厦地区巡逻，主要原因是他不够尊重分局领导。联合国那些有外交豁免权的家伙把豪华轿车随便停在马路上，根本不在乎警方的规定。奈利向分局抱怨，上司叫他别生事，就当没看见好了。一天晚上，乱停的车辆堵得一条小马路彻底瘫痪。时间已经过了午夜，奈利从巡逻车里取出特大号手电筒，把一辆辆车的挡风玻璃砸得稀烂。就算是高级外交官，想在几天之内修好挡风玻璃也不怎么容易。抗议信雪片般涌入分局，要求惩处这种破坏行径。砸碎挡风玻璃后一周，真实情况传到某个人耳中，艾尔伯特·奈利被调往哈莱姆。

不久后的一个星期天，奈利带着妻子去布鲁克林，探望他孀居的姐姐。和所有西西里人一样,艾尔伯特·奈利对姐姐有着激烈的爱护之情,每几个月总要探望一次,看她是不是一切都好。姐姐比奈利大很多,儿子已经二十岁,叫托马斯,缺乏父亲的指引,活得不怎么规矩。他卷入过几起小型争斗,最近变得越来越野。奈利曾经动用过警队里的关系,让偷了东西的小伙子免于起诉。那次他尽量按捺住脾气,警告外甥说:"汤米,你害得我姐姐掉眼泪,我得让你走走正道了。"这是舅舅对外甥的友善忠告,而不是威胁。汤米虽然是布鲁克林这个最凶悍的街区上最凶悍的孩子,仍旧害怕他的艾尔舅舅。

　　这次看望姐姐的时候,汤米星期六很晚才回家,一直在房间里睡觉。母亲进去叫醒他,叫他穿上衣服,和舅舅舅妈一起吃星期日的正餐。汤米粗鲁的声音从门缝里传了出来:"我他妈才不在乎,让我睡觉。"他母亲只好回到厨房里,抱歉地笑了笑。

　　于是他们没有管他,自己吃饭。奈利问姐姐,汤米有没有惹来真正的麻烦,她摇摇头。

　　奈利和妻子正准备出门,汤米总算起床了。他含含糊糊打了个招呼,走进厨房,居然对母亲叫道:"喂,妈妈,给我做点东西吃行吗?"但这不是请求,而是娇生惯养的孩子在任意支使母亲。

　　母亲尖声说:"吃饭的时候起床就有饭吃,现在我才不给你做饭呢。"

　　这种难堪的场面其实不算什么,但刚睡醒的汤米还有点起床气,犯了错误。"唉,去你妈的,少他妈唠叨了,我自己出去吃。"话刚出口,他就后悔了。

　　艾尔舅舅像猫扑耗子似的跳到他身上。不但因为他姐姐今天受了侮辱,还因为他私下里显然经常和母亲这么说话。汤米从不敢在舅舅面前说这种话。今天他实在是疏忽了——算他倒霉。

　　就在两个惊恐的女人眼前,艾尔伯特·奈利不慌不忙、冷酷无情地揍了外甥一顿。刚开始这小子还企图自卫,但很快就放弃了,拼命求饶。奈利几个耳光扇得他嘴唇肿胀流血。他抓着这小子的脑袋一下一下地撞墙,一拳一拳打在肚子上,又把他按倒在地,拿他的面门擦地毯。他叫两个女人等一等,拖着汤米下楼坐进车里。他在车里吓得汤米屁滚尿流。"要是我姐姐再告诉我,你用这种语气和她说话,今天这顿打相比之下就会像是小姑娘亲了你一口,"他说,"我要你改邪归正。你上去吧,告诉我妻子,我在车里等她。"

　　两个月后,艾尔伯特·奈利值夜班回家,发现妻子离开了他。她收拾了所有衣服,逃回娘家。她父亲说丽塔害怕他,说因为他的脾气,她害怕和他一起生活。艾尔听得愣住了,不敢相信。他从没打过妻子,甚至没有威胁过她,对她只有爱。她的离开让他大惑不解,决定过几天去她家里找她谈一谈。

　　不幸的是,第二天夜里,他值班时惹出了大麻烦。他接警出车去哈莱姆处理一起人身攻击案件。和平时一样,车还没停稳,他就跳出车门。时间已经过了十二点,他带着超大号手电筒。出事地点一眼就能看见。一幢公寓楼门前聚集了一群人。一个黑人女人对奈利说:"有个男人拿刀划一个小女孩。"

　　奈利冲进门洞。走廊尽头有一扇门开着,里面灯火通明,他听见有人呻吟。他一边摆弄手电筒,一边顺着走廊过去,进了那扇敞开的门。

　　地上躺着两个人,险些绊倒他。一个是二十五岁左右的黑人妇女,另一个是个黑人小女孩,顶多十二岁。两人身上脸上都被剃刀划得血淋淋的。奈利看见肇事者就在客厅里。他认识那家伙。

　　凶手叫瓦克斯·贝恩斯,臭名昭著的皮条客、毒贩子和暴力犯罪者。此刻他吸了毒,两眼暴突,血淋淋的剃刀在手里微微发颤。两周前贝恩斯当街严重伤害一名妓女,奈利逮捕了他。当时贝恩斯对他说:"喂,哥们,别多管闲事。"奈利的搭档也说什么黑鬼喜欢自相残杀就由他们去吧,但奈利还是把贝恩斯抓回分局。贝恩斯第二天就被保释出去了。

　　奈利向来不怎么喜欢黑人,在哈莱姆做事更是让他越来越讨厌他们。黑人吸毒酗酒,让老婆工作或者卖屁股挣钱。他看不管这些混蛋。贝恩斯明目张胆犯法激怒了他,见到小女孩被剃刀划得浑身是血让他恶心。他冷静地在心里作了决定:他不会抓贝恩斯回警局。

　　可是,目击证人已经从背后涌进公寓:楼里的几个住户和巡逻车上的搭档。

　　奈利命令贝恩斯:"放下刀子,你被捕了。"

　　贝恩斯哈哈大笑。"哥们,你不开枪就别想逮捕我,"他举起剃刀,"还是说你想尝尝这个?"

　　奈利动作飞快,搭档来不及拔枪。黑人一刀刺来,奈利超乎凡人的反应神经让他用左手掌挡开攻击,他用右手抡圆了手电筒砸过去,一下子打在贝恩斯的脑袋侧面,打得贝恩斯醉汉似的两腿打结。剃刀从手里掉下来,他毫无还手之力,因此奈利的第二下完全是多余的,警局听证会和刑事审判后来在目击者和搭档的证词下证明了这一点。奈利用手电筒从上向下砸在贝恩斯的头顶上,这一下力量大得可怕,敲碎了手电筒的玻璃,珐琅护垫和灯泡崩出来,飞到了房间的另一头。手电筒沉重的铝合金外壁也弯了,多亏里面的电池,才没有折成两截。住在公寓楼里的一位黑人看得目瞪口呆,后来为检方作证说:"哥们,那黑鬼的脑壳够硬的。"

　　可是,贝恩斯的脑壳终究还是不够硬。这一击砸塌了他的头盖骨。两小时后他在哈莱姆医院咽气。

艾尔伯特·奈利因为滥用暴力在警局内部受到指控，只有他一个人倍感意外。他遭到停职处理，检察官又提出刑事指控。他被控过失杀人，判决有罪，入狱一到十年。这时候他对社会的愤怒和憎恨达到了顶点，根本不在乎坐牢。他们居然说我是罪犯！居然因为我杀了黑鬼皮条客那么一个禽兽就送我进监狱！女人和小女孩被划得惨不忍睹，终生破相，人还躺在医院里，他们居然不管不顾！

他并不害怕监狱，既因为他是警察，也因为他的罪名情有可原，肯定会得到照顾。他的几个伙伴已经向他保证，他们会找朋友打招呼。只有他岳父，一位精明的老派意大利人，布朗克斯一家鱼市场的老板，明白艾尔伯特·奈利这种人在监狱里恐怕活不过一年。要么是他被同牢房的囚犯杀死，要么是他杀死同牢房的囚犯。女儿因为那些只有女人才明白的愚蠢理由抛弃了这么一个好丈夫，他为此一直有些愧疚，于是动用他在柯里昂家族的关系人（他向柯里昂家族的一名代表交保护费，还把最好的鱼当礼物送给柯里昂家族），请求家族出手援助。

柯里昂家族知道艾尔伯特·奈利。这位守法而彪悍的警察算是个传奇人物，名声在外，不可等闲视之，哪怕去掉制服和佩枪，仍旧值得敬畏。柯里昂家族对这种人向来感兴趣。他的警察身份倒是并不重要。很多年轻人在拥抱真正的命运之前都走错过路。时间和运气会改正错误。

提醒汤姆·黑根注意的是彼得·克莱门扎，他对优秀人才的嗅觉很敏锐。黑根看着警方案卷的复本，听克莱门扎讲完，最后说："看来我们又多了一个卢卡·布拉齐。"

克莱门扎使劲点头。胖归胖，他那张脸却没有平常胖子的慈祥感。"我也是这么想的。应该交给迈克自己处理。"

就这样，还没等艾尔伯特·奈利从临时拘留所转入州北他的埋骨之地，就得到通知说法官看了新材料和高级警官的书面陈述，重新审议后决定判他缓刑，就此释放。

艾尔伯特·奈利不是傻瓜，他的岳父也不喜欢闷声做好事。奈利查清前因后果，答应和丽塔离婚，以此偿还岳父的人情债。接着，他前往长滩酬谢恩人。当然，事先已经做好了安排。迈克尔在图书室接见他。

奈利一本正经地表达感谢，见到迈克尔热情地接受了他的谢意，他不禁既惊又喜。

"妈的，我怎么能让他们这么对待西西里的同胞？"迈克尔说，"应该发你一个大奖章才对，但那些该死的政客除了游说团体，什么都不关心。听着，我要是没有仔细调查一番，看到你遭受的待遇有多么不公正，本来也不会挺身而出。我的手下和你姐姐谈过，她说你一向照顾她和她的儿子，说你怎么让那小子改邪归正，没有让他走错路。你的岳父说你是全世界最好的小伙子。这可真是少见。"迈克尔很得体地没有提起奈利的妻子离开了他。

两人聊了一阵。奈利向来话少,遇到迈克尔·柯里昂却聊得很投机。迈克尔只比他大五岁,但奈利感觉像是在和比他大得多的人说话,和一位足以当他父亲的长者说话。

最后,迈克尔说:"既然已经把你弄出了监狱,我不能看着你走投无路。我帮你安排点事情做吧。我在拉斯维加斯有产业,你凭借经验可以当酒店的保安。还是说你想做什么小本生意?我可以和银行说句话,帮你贷款当资本。"

奈利感激得尴尬起来,但出于自尊,他还是拒绝了,最后说:"缓刑期间,我必须留在法院的管辖范围之内。"

迈克尔兴致勃勃地说:"这些都不值一提。我搞得定。别惦记什么监管了,我想办法抽掉你那张黄纸,免得银行找麻烦。"

黄纸指的是警方的刑事犯罪记录,通常在法官酌情定罪时呈交给法官。奈利在警队的时间已经足够长,知道许多暴徒之所以能得到法官的轻判,就是因为警方的记录科受贿,呈交了一份干干净净的黄纸。听见迈克尔·柯里昂说他办得到这种事,他并不吃惊;他吃惊的是他们竟然肯为他费这么多的力气。

"如果需要帮助,我一定会联系你的。"奈利说。

"好的,很好。"迈克尔说,他看看手表,奈利以为这是逐客令,起身准备离开,但他又吃了一惊。

"吃午饭了,"迈克尔说,"来和我们家一起吃个饭吧。我父亲说他很想见见你。我们去他家。我母亲大概做了煎辣椒、炒蛋和香肠。真正的西西里风味。"

艾尔伯特·奈利,从他还小的时候算起,从他十五岁父母过世算起,这无疑是他过得最愉快的一个下午。唐·柯里昂和蔼可亲,得知奈利父母出生的小村庄离他老家只有几分钟车程,他真是高兴极了。大家聊得开心,食物美味,红艳艳的葡萄酒味道醇厚。奈利不禁觉得他终于碰到了人生知己,他明白他不过是个普通客人,但也知道他能在这么一个世界里找到永久的安身之地,获得幸福。

迈克尔和唐送他出门上车。唐握着他的手说:"你是个好小伙子。我的儿子迈克尔,我一直在教导他经营橄榄油生意,我年纪大了,很想退休。他来找我,说希望插手你那桩小事。我说你好好学习橄榄油生意吧,但他就是不肯安生。他说有个好小伙子,西西里人,别人正在使坏收拾他。我今天告诉你这些,是想说他做得对。见过你以后,我很高兴我们费了那些周折。哪,要是我们还能为你做点什么,尽管吩咐一声就是了。明白吗?我们乐意为你效劳。"(回想起唐的仁慈,奈利希望伟大的老头子还活着,能见到他今天将如何帮助家族。)

奈利花了不到三天就下定决心。他明白柯里昂家族在拉拢他,但也明白其他的道理。他被社会谴责和惩罚的行为,正是柯里昂家族欣赏他的地方。他知道在柯里昂家族,他会过得比在外面这个世界里更加高兴。他还知道柯里昂家族的限制比较少,因此更加强大。

他再次拜访迈克尔,向迈克尔摊牌。他不想去拉斯维加斯,愿意接受家族在纽约的职位。他清楚表示愿意效忠。迈克尔受到触动,奈利看得分明。工作安排好了,迈克尔坚持要奈利先去迈阿密度个假,住在家族的酒店里,家族承担费用,预付一个月薪水,让他有足够的现金好好享受人生。

这次度假是奈利第一次品尝到奢侈的味道。酒店的人特别照顾他,总说:"唉,你可是迈克尔·柯里昂的朋友。"风声传开,他得到最豪华的套房,而不是打发一般普通关系户的小房间。酒店夜总会的经营者介绍了几个漂亮姑娘给他。返回纽约的时候,奈利的人生观有了细微的变化。

他被分配进克莱门扎手下,人才大师仔细考验他。必要的预防措施终归不能放下。他毕竟曾经是警察。不过,尽管奈利曾经身处围墙的另一边,但他的暴虐天性打消了人们的顾虑。不到一年,他就杀了第一个人,再也不能回头。

克莱门扎对他赞不绝口。奈利是奇迹,是卢卡·布拉齐再世。克莱门扎甚至夸口说他会超过卢卡。毕竟奈利是他发现的嘛。就身体条件而言,奈利确实出类拔萃,反射神经和协调能力比得上乔·迪马乔。克莱门扎也明白他这种人驾驭不了奈利。经过安排,奈利直接为迈克尔·柯里昂效力,中间只有汤姆·黑根一层必不可少的缓冲。他是"特殊人物",薪水很高,但没有自己的营生,比方说簿记点或雇用打手。他明显对迈克尔·柯里昂尊敬得五体投地,黑根忍不住开玩笑对迈克尔说,"现在你有了你的卢卡。"

迈克尔点点头。他确实做到了。艾尔伯特·奈利到死都会是他的人。诀窍当然来自唐本人的传授。学习生意经的时候,接受父亲教导的那些漫长日子里,迈克尔曾经问父亲:"你怎么会用卢卡·布拉齐这种人,禽兽不如的一个人?"

唐开始教导他。"世界上有些人呢?"他说,"嚣张跋扈找死的人。你肯定见到过这种人。赌桌上吵得不可开交,只是因为挡泥板被刮了一下就怒气冲冲跳下车,不清楚对方的底细就肆意羞辱和威胁别人。我见过一个家伙,傻得出奇,存心撩拨一群危险角色,他自己却没有半点能耐。这种人到处乱逛,嘴里喊着'杀了我,杀了我'。迟早会碰见愿意成全他们的人。我们每天读报都能见到这种人。他们当然会给别人带来巨大的损害。

"卢卡·布拉齐就是这种人,但他很有本事,因为长期以来谁也奈何不了他。绝大多数这种人和我们毫无关系,但布拉齐是一件可以利用的凶险武器。既然他不怕死,存心找死,那么诀窍就在于,让他唯独不想死在你的手里。他害怕的事情只有一件——不是死亡,而是他或许会死在你手里。到那个时候,他就完全属于你了。"

这是唐死前最有价值的训导之一,迈克尔用这套办法让奈利成为了他的卢卡·布拉齐。

此时此刻,艾尔伯特·奈利独自坐在布朗克斯的公寓里,准备再次换上警察制服。他仔细刷干净制服,接下来打算擦亮枪套。还有警帽,帽舌得好好清理,厚底黑皮鞋要擦得闪闪发亮。奈利干得很起劲。他已经找到了他在世界上的位置,迈克尔·柯里昂绝对信任他,今天他不会辜负这份信任。

第三十一章

同一天,两辆豪华轿车停在长滩林荫道上。一辆等着送康妮、她母亲、丈夫和两个孩子去机场。卡洛·里齐一家要去拉斯维加斯度假,为迁居做些准备工作。迈克尔不顾康妮的抗议,向卡洛下了命令,没有花时间解释说他要在柯里昂和巴齐尼两个家族会谈前撤空林荫道。事实上,会谈本身就是高度机密,只有家族的几名首领知道内情。

另外一辆豪华轿车等着送凯和孩子去新罕布尔探望父母。迈克尔还得留在林荫道,有些紧急事务需要他处理。

昨天夜里,迈克尔送信给卡洛·里齐说需要他在林荫道多留几天,本周晚些时候再去和妻儿会合。康妮大发雷霆,打电话找迈克尔,但迈克尔已经进城了。这会儿,她用视线在林荫道搜寻哥哥的踪迹,但他和汤姆·黑根在闭门密谈,禁止打扰。卡洛送康妮上车,康妮吻别卡洛。"等你两天,你要是不来,我就回来抓你。"她威胁道。

卡洛还她一个好丈夫的笑容,充满性暗示。"我会去的。"他说。

她探身出车窗。"你估计迈克尔为什么要你留下?"她问,担忧地皱起眉头,模样老气,毫无吸引力可言。

卡洛耸耸肩。"他答应过要给我找个好差事,也许就是想谈谈这个,至少听起来有这意思。"卡洛不知道柯里昂与巴齐尼两大家族定于当晚会谈。

康妮急切地说:"真的吗?"

卡洛点点头,叫她放心。豪华轿车驶出林荫道大门而去。

第一辆豪华轿车离开,迈克尔出来送别凯和两个儿子。卡洛也过来祝凯一路平安,度假愉快。第二辆豪华轿车也徐徐开动,驶出大门。

迈克尔说:"很抱歉,卡洛,我必须要你留下。一两天就行。"

卡洛马上说："没关系,完全没关系。"

"很好,"迈克尔说,"你守在电话旁,我准备好了就打给你。我还有别的事情要办。好吗?"

"当然,迈克,那当然。"卡洛说。他走进自己家,打电话给他在韦斯特伯里偷偷养的情妇,答应晚上溜出来见她。他打开一瓶黑麦威士忌,坐下等待。他等了很久很久。中午过后不久,车辆开始陆续进门。他看见克莱门扎走下一辆车,没几分钟过后,忒西奥走下另一辆。一名保安把两人领进迈克尔的住处。几小时后,克莱门扎离开了,但忒西奥没再露面。

卡洛在林荫道走了一圈,呼吸新鲜空气,顶多十分钟。他熟悉在林荫道值勤的所有保镖,甚至和其中几个关系不错。他有心找他们闲聊打发时间,却惊讶地发现今天的保镖都是生面孔,他一个也不认识。更让他惊讶的是负责把守大门的居然是洛可·兰坡,卡洛知道洛可在家族里地位很高,除非发生了什么异乎寻常的事情,否则不可能前来执行这种琐碎任务。

洛可友好地对他笑了笑,打声招呼。卡洛有点紧张。洛可说:"咦,还以为你和唐在一起快活呢。"

卡洛耸耸肩。"迈克要我等他一两天,有什么事情要交给我。"

"是啊,"洛可·兰坡说,"我也是。结果他打电话叫我守门。唉,管他的,他说了算。"语气像是在说迈克尔比不上他的父亲——有点不太恭敬。

卡洛假装没听见他的语气。"迈克知道他在干什么。"他说。洛可默然接受他的谴责。卡洛说再见,转身走向住所。有事情发生了,但洛可不知道内情。

迈克尔站在客厅的窗口,望着卡洛在林荫道走来走去。黑根端来一杯烈性白兰地。迈克尔欣然接受,喝了一口。黑根在身后轻声说:"迈克,你必须开始行动,是时候了。"

迈克尔叹了口气:"真希望不是这么快,真希望老头子能多活一段时间。"

"不会出错的,"黑根说,"我都没有完全看穿,别人就不用说了。你安排得非常妥当。"

迈克尔从窗口转过身。"很大一部分是老头子策划的,我以前真的不知道他到底有多精明,不过我猜你应该知道。"

"谁比得上他呢?"黑根说,"不过计划非常优美,无懈可击,所以你的水平也不差。"

"看到结果再说吧,"迈克尔说,"忒西奥和克莱门扎在林荫道吗?"

黑根点点头。迈克尔一口喝掉剩下的白兰地。"叫克莱门扎来见我。我要亲自向他下达指示。我连一眼都不想见到忒西奥。告诉他,我准备半小时后和他一起去和巴齐尼会谈。接下来,克莱门扎的人会关照他的。"

黑根用平淡的语气问:"不可能放忒西奥一马?"

"不可能。"迈克尔说。

州北,水牛城,一条小街上的一家小比萨店,生意兴隆。随着午餐时间过去,顾客越来越少,店员从窗口端起盛着剩下几块比萨的铁皮托盘,放在砖砌烤炉的架子上。他看了看炉膛里还在烤的一片比萨。奶酪还没有开始鼓泡。等他转身面向柜台,招待街上的客人,赫然见到一个满脸凶相的年轻人站在那儿。年轻人说:"给我一块。"

店员拿起木铲,把一块凉比萨放回炉膛里加热。客人没有等在外面,而是推门进了店堂。店里这会儿没有客人。店员打开炉门,取出烘热的比萨,放在纸碟上端给客人。客人却没有付钱,而是目光灼灼地盯着店员。

"听说你胸口有个漂亮文身,"客人说,"能从你衬衫领口看到最顶上一点,能让我看个完整吗?"

店员愣住了,无法动弹。

"解开衬衫。"客人说。

店员摇摇头。"我没有文身,"他的英语口音很重,"有文身的是值夜班那位。"

客人哈哈大笑。笑声刺耳而勉强,听了让人难受。"别逗了,解开衬衫让我看看。"

店员开始后退,想绕到炉子的另一头去。客人的手抬过柜台,手里握着枪。他开火了。子弹击中店员的胸口,掀得他撞在炉子上。客人朝他的身体开了第二枪,店员跌倒在地。客人绕过货架,弯下腰,扯开衬衫的纽扣。胸口满是鲜血,但文身清晰可辨,彼此纠缠的男女和刺穿身体的匕首。店员无力地抬起一条胳膊,像是要保护自己。枪手说:"法布雷奇奥,迈克尔·柯里昂向你问候。"他举起枪,枪口离店员的颅骨仅有几英寸,他扣动扳机,然后走出店堂。路边有辆车敞着门在等他,他跳上车,汽车迅速开远。

大门口铸铁廊柱上的电话响了,洛可·兰坡拿起听筒。对方说:"你的包裹准备好了。"然后咔嗒一声挂断。洛可钻进车里,驶出林荫道。他走琼斯海滩堤道——也就是桑尼·柯里昂遇害的那条路——来到旺托的火车站停下。另外一辆车正在等他,车里有两个人。他们沿着日出公路开了十分钟,拐进一家汽车旅馆的前院。洛可·兰坡把两个人留在车上,自己走向一幢山间木屋风格的小别墅。洛可一脚踢得门和铰链分了家,蹿进房间。

七十岁的菲利普·塔塔利亚赤裸得像个婴儿,站在躺着一个年轻女人的床上。菲利普·塔塔利亚满头浓密的黑发，阴毛却是铁灰色。他的身体柔软而丰润，仿佛雏鸟。洛可一口气把四颗子弹打进他的腹部，转身跑回车上。两个男人在旺托火车站放他下车，他开自己的车一路回到林荫道。他进屋和迈克尔·柯里昂谈了几句，又出来继续守门。

艾尔伯特·奈利一个人在公寓里，整理好了他的制服。他慢慢穿上，裤子、衬衫、领带、上衣、枪套、武装腰带。停职时他交回了佩枪，但行政手续上的疏忽大意让警队忘了收回徽章。克莱门扎找了一把无法追查的点三八警用手枪给他。奈利拆开枪，上油，检查击铁，重新装配，咔嗒咔嗒扣了几次扳机。他把子弹装进弹膛，准备出发。

他把警帽放进厚纸袋，穿上普通人的大衣，盖住警服。他看看手表。离车到楼下来接他还有十五分钟。他把十五分钟用在了对镜打量自己上。没有问题，怎么看都是真正的警察。

等他的车里有两个洛可·兰坡的手下坐在前排。奈利坐在后座上。车驶向闹市区，离开公寓所在的区域之后，他脱掉普通人的大衣，放在脚边。他扯开纸袋，戴上警帽。

车到五十五街和第五大道路口在道旁停车，奈利钻出车门。他顺着大道向前走。重新穿上警服，走在他巡逻过无数次的街道上，他的感觉很奇怪。人群熙熙攘攘。他走向商业区，到洛克菲勒中心停下，马路对面是圣派屈克大教堂。他在第五大道靠近他的这一侧瞥见了要找的那辆豪华轿车。车孤零零地停在一串"禁止停车"和"禁止临时停车"的红色标记之间。奈利放慢步伐。他来早了。他停下来，掏出告票簿涂涂写写，然后继续前进。他走到豪华轿车侧面，用警棍敲敲挡泥板。司机诧异地抬起头。奈利用警棍指了指"禁止停车"标记，示意司机开走。司机扭过头去。

奈利走到马路上，到驾驶座敞开的车窗前停下。司机是个满脸凶相的流氓，正是他喜欢收拾的那种类型。奈利用存心侮辱人的语气说："我说，有点眼色行不行，是要我把告票塞进你的屁眼呢，还是乖乖给我滚蛋？"

司机不为所动。"你最好先去分局问一问。要是发我一张票能让你开心，你就尽管开给我好了。"

"他妈的滚远点儿，"奈利说，"否则我把你拖下车，揍得你屁滚尿流。"

司机不知从哪儿掏出一张十块钞票，只用一只手就叠成个小方块，抬起胳膊想塞进奈利的口袋。奈利回到人行道上，朝司机勾勾手指。司机从车上下来。

"请出示驾驶执照和车辆登记证。"奈利说。他本想把司机弄到路口的另一边去，但现在做不到了。奈利从眼角瞥见三个矮胖男人走下中心大厦的台阶，朝马路而来。那是巴齐尼和两名保镖，正要去见迈克尔·柯里昂。他刚看见他们，一名保镖就抢先跑上来,看巴齐尼的座驾出了什么事情。

保镖问司机:"什么事?"

司机没好气地说:"我收了张告票,没大事。这家伙肯定是新来的。"

这时,巴齐尼和另一名保镖也走近了,巴齐尼吼道:"他妈的搞什么?"

奈利在告票簿上写完,把驾驶执照和车辆登记证还给司机。他把告票簿放回臀部口袋,手收回来的时候顺势拔出了点三八警枪。

他把三颗子弹打进巴齐尼酒桶般的胸膛,另外三个人这才醒过神来,纷纷蹲下躲闪,而此刻奈利已经冲进人群,转过拐角,跳上正在等他的轿车。车飞速驶上第九大道,转向下城区。来到切尔西公园附近,奈利已经扔掉了警帽,换掉衣服,穿上普通人的大衣,他钻进另一辆正在等他的轿车。他把枪和警服留在前一辆车上,自然会有人处理。一小时后,他安然回到长滩林荫道,向迈克尔·柯里昂汇报。

忒西奥在老唐住处的厨房等待,正在喝咖啡的时候,汤姆·黑根进来了。"迈克准备好了,"黑根说,"你给巴齐尼打个电话,通知他出发。"

忒西奥起身走向墙上的电话,拨通巴齐尼在纽约的办公室,劈头就说:"我们出发去布鲁克林了。"他挂断电话,对黑根微笑,"希望迈克今晚能给大家谈个好交易。"

黑根肃然道:"相信他一定会。"他陪忒西奥走出厨房,来到林荫道上,走向迈克尔的住处。来到门口,一名保镖拦住他们,"老板说他坐另一辆车,叫你们先出发。"

忒西奥皱起眉头,扭头对黑根说:"该死,他不能这么做,会打乱我的所有安排。"

这时,又有三名保镖在他们周围冒了出来。黑根轻声说:"我也不能跟你去了,忒西奥。"

雪貂脸首领一瞬间就全明白了,也默然接受。他有半秒钟浑身发软,随即恢复正常。他对黑根说:"告诉迈克,纯粹为了生意,我一向喜欢他。"

黑根点点头。"他理解。"

忒西奥犹豫片刻,柔声说:"汤姆,不能放我一马?看在过去的份上?"

黑根摇摇头,"我不能。"他说。

他目送四名保镖围拢忒西奥,押他登上一辆等待的车。他有点难过。忒西奥曾经是柯里昂家族最优秀的部下。除了卢卡·布拉齐,老唐最倚重的应该就是他。这么精明的一个人,活到这么大的年纪,却犯下致命的判断错误,实在太不幸了。

卡洛·里齐还在等待迈克尔接见他,许多人来来去去,看得他惶恐不安。显然出了什么大事,但看起来他被排除在外了。他等得不耐烦了,打电话给迈克尔。接电话的是一名室内保镖,他去叫迈克尔,回来说迈克尔叫他少安毋躁,很快就来找他。

卡洛又打给情妇,保证请她吃夜宵,在她家过夜。迈克尔说很快就来找他,不管要谈什么,一两个钟头肯定够了。开车去韦斯特伯里还要四十分钟左右。时间来得及。他答应他一定赶到,甜言蜜语哄她,免得她生气。挂断电话,他决定先换衣服,节省会面后的时间。刚穿上干净衬衫,他就听见有人敲门。他马上醒悟过来,迈克尔打电话找他,却总是忙音,于是派手下来叫他了。卡洛过去开门,巨大的恐惧淹没了他,感觉整个身体都要瘫软下去了。站在门口的是迈克尔·柯里昂,面容正是卡洛·里齐时常在噩梦中见到的死神。

站在迈克尔·柯里昂背后的是黑根和洛可·兰坡。他们面容肃穆,像是虽说十二万分的不情愿,但还是不得不向朋友报告坏消息。三个人走进屋子,卡洛·里齐领着他们进了客厅。他从起初的震惊中恢复过来,以为刚才是神经过敏大发作了。可是,迈克尔一开口,他才真的魂飞魄散,险些呕吐。

"桑蒂诺的事,你要给我一个交代。"迈克尔说。

卡洛没有吭声,假装听不懂。黑根和兰坡分开,各自占领一面墙壁。他和迈克尔面对面站着。

"你把桑尼卖给了巴齐尼,"迈克尔的声音很平稳,"你和我妹妹演了一套小闹剧,是不是巴齐尼哄你说,这么做能骗柯里昂家的人上当?"

卡洛·里齐吓得胆战心惊,说起话来不顾体面,没有丝毫自尊。"我发誓我是清白的,我以我孩子的命发誓,我是清白的。迈克,别这么对我,求你了,迈克,别这么对我。"

迈克尔静静地说:"巴齐尼死了,菲利普·塔塔利亚也死了。今晚我要清算家族的老账。你少跟我说你是清白的,老实承认对你有好处。"

黑根和兰坡诧异地望着迈克尔。他们心想,迈克尔毕竟还比不上他的父亲。有必要逼着叛徒承认有罪吗?他的罪行已经铁证如山,这种事情能证明到这个程度已经到头了。答案显而易见,但迈克尔对他是否正确还不够有信心,还害怕自己不够公正,还有一丝一毫的难以确定,只有卡洛·里齐本人坦白才能打消他的疑虑。

迈克尔没有等来回答,他近乎和蔼地说:"别那么害怕。难道我会让我的妹妹当寡妇、让我的外甥失去父亲吗?再怎么说,我都是你的一个孩子的教父呀。唉,对你的惩罚就是把你赶出家族的生意。我会送你上飞机去拉斯维加斯和妻儿团聚,你就留在那儿好了。我会给康妮一份津贴。就是这样。但请不要总说什么我是清白的,不要侮辱我的智力,惹我生气。是谁接触你的,塔塔利亚还是巴齐尼?"

知道自己不会被杀,甘美的欣慰感觉犹如泉涌,怀着一肚子挣扎求生的希望,卡洛·里齐喃喃答道:"巴齐尼。"

"好的,很好,"迈克尔柔声说,他挥了挥右手,"你可以走了。等在外面的车会送你去机场。"

卡洛首先出门,另外三个人紧随其后。天已经黑了,但林荫道和平时一样灯火通明。一辆车驶近停下,卡洛认出是自己那辆。司机是个生面孔,后座远离他这边的地方还坐着个人。兰坡打开前门,示意卡洛上车。迈克尔说:"我会打电话通知你妻子说你已经上路。"卡洛坐进车里,冷汗浸透了丝绸衬衫。

车徐徐启动,轻快地驶向大门。卡洛扭头想看他认不认识后座上的人。就在这时,克莱门扎一挥手,用绳索勒住卡洛·里齐的脖子,动作伶俐而优雅,就像小女孩把缎带套上小猫的头颈。克莱门扎猛地一拽,光滑的细绳嵌进卡洛·里齐的皮肤,身体弹上半空,仿佛鱼儿上钩。克莱门扎死死卡住他,收紧绳子,直到他的身体软瘫下去。车里突然臭气熏天,死亡临近使得括约肌松弛,卡洛失禁了。保险起见,克莱门扎又等了几分钟才松手,把绳子收起来放回衣袋里。他躺回后座靠背上,卡洛的尸体软绵绵地靠在车门上。几秒钟过后,克莱门扎摇下车窗,放掉臭气。

柯里昂家族取得了彻底的胜利。就在这二十四小时内,克莱门扎和兰坡允许各自的手下大开杀戒,惩罚擅自闯入柯里昂家族的外来者。奈利接管了忒西奥的人。巴齐尼家族的簿记点就此歇业,巴齐尼手下两个最高等级的执法人在桑树街的意大利餐馆吃完晚饭,正优哉游哉地剔着牙,却被枪击身亡。一个声名狼藉的赛马掮客在场上大胜一晚,回家路上同样被杀。滨水区两个盘子最大的放债人失踪,几个月后才在新泽西的沼泽地现身。

这次凶残的攻击使得迈克尔·柯里昂确立了名声,柯里昂取回他们在纽约各大家族中的卓然地位。他之所以受人尊敬,不但因为可敬的战术天赋,还因为巴齐尼和塔塔利亚两个家族的大部分首领立刻投靠了他。

要是没有妹妹康妮的歇斯底里大发作,迈克尔·柯里昂的胜利简直称得上完美无瑕。

康妮把孩子留在拉斯维加斯,和母亲飞回家。她按捺住丧夫的痛苦,等豪华轿车开进林荫道才爆发。母亲还没来得及拦住她,她就跑过卵石马路,冲进迈克尔·柯里昂的住处,在客厅找到迈克尔和凯。凯起身走向她,想安慰她,姐妹似的拥抱她,但愣在了那里,因为康妮对她的哥哥大吼大叫,又是咒骂又是斥责。"卑鄙的狗杂种,"她尖叫道,"你杀了我丈夫。你等我们的父亲去世才动手,这样谁也拦不住你了,你杀了他。你因为桑尼怪罪他,一直怪罪他,所有人都怪罪他。可你就不为我想一想。你从来不在乎我。我现在该怎么办,该怎么办?"她号啕大哭。迈克尔的两名保镖站在她背后,等待迈克尔的指示。迈克尔却面无表情地站在那儿,等待妹妹发泄完怒火。

凯用惊恐的声音说:"康妮,你昏头了,别说这种话。"

康妮从歇斯底里中恢复过来,声音饱含怨毒,"你以为他为什么总对我那么冷淡?你以为他为什么把卡洛留在林荫道?他从头到尾都知道他要杀了我丈夫,但我父亲还活着的时候他不敢。我父亲会阻止他。他知道,所以他只是静静等待,还答应当我们孩子的教父,不就是为了麻痹我们吗?铁石心肠的杂种。你以为你了解你丈夫?你知道他把多少人和我家卡洛一起杀了吗?读读报纸就知道。巴齐尼、塔塔利亚,还有好多。我哥哥杀了他们。"

她说着说着又歇斯底里发作起来,想朝迈克尔的脸膛吐口水,但嘴里没有唾液。

"送她回家,给她找个医生。"迈克尔说。两名保镖立刻抓住康妮的胳膊,把她拖出屋子。

凯惊魂未定,问丈夫:"她为什么要说那些话?迈克尔,她怎么会那么想?"

迈克尔耸耸肩。"她歇斯底里发作了。"

凯望着丈夫的眼睛。"迈克尔,不是真的吧,求求你,告诉我,不是真的。"

迈克尔疲惫地摇摇头。"当然不是。请你相信我,这次我允许你过问我的事务,我也愿意给你一个答案。不是真的。"他的语气从未如此令人信服。他直视凯的眼睛。他动用了两人在婚姻中建立起的全部互相信任,希望她能相信他。她不能继续怀疑下去了。她后悔地笑了笑,扑进他的怀里,亲吻丈夫。

"我们都需要喝一杯了,"她说,走进厨房去取冰,在厨房里听见前门开了,走出来,她看见保镖带着克莱门扎、奈利和洛可·兰坡进门。迈克尔背对着她,她走了两步,好看清丈夫的侧脸。这时,克莱门扎向她丈夫打招呼,用的是最正式的称呼。

"唐·迈克尔。"克莱门扎说。

凯看见迈克尔如何站在那里,接受他们的臣服。他让凯想起罗马的雕像,那些罗马古代帝王的雕像,他们凭借神授的君权,掌握臣民的生死大权。他一只手撑着腰,侧脸流露出冷酷而尊贵的威权,身体站得随便而傲慢,重心落在略微后撤的一条腿上。首领站在他面前。就在这一刻,凯知道了,康妮指责迈克尔的话全都是真的。她回到厨房,默默哭泣。

第九部

第三十二章

经过一年微妙的政治运作,柯里昂家族的血腥胜利终告完整,迈克尔·柯里昂成为全美国最强盛的黑帮家族的首领。过去这十二个月,迈克尔的时间平均分配,一半在长滩林荫道的指挥总部,另一半在拉斯维加斯的新家。一年过去,他决定停止在纽约的所有活动,卖掉全部住宅和林荫道的地产。为此,他带全家回东海岸最后再看看。他们住了一个月,结束生意,凯打包托运家里的物品。有无数琐碎小事需要办理。

柯里昂家族的地位已经毫无争议,克莱门扎组建了自己的家族。洛可·兰坡接任柯里昂家族的首领。内华达,艾尔伯特·奈利负责家族控制的所有酒店的保安工作。黑根也属于迈克尔的西部家族组织。

时间医治了旧伤。康妮·柯里昂和哥哥迈克尔言归于好。事实上,那次癫狂指责后不到一周,她就因为说的那些话向迈克尔道歉,向凯保证说那些都不是真的,只是突然丧夫后的歇斯底里疯话罢了。

康妮·柯里昂轻而易举地找到了新丈夫,服丧不到一年,就把一个来柯里昂家族当秘书的好小伙子弄上了床。这个年轻人来自一个可靠的意大利家庭,毕业于美国最顶尖的商校。迎娶唐的妹妹自然让他前程无忧。

凯·亚当斯·柯里昂听取天主教的教诲,最终皈依,柯里昂家大为高兴。两个儿子按照要求也被领入教会。迈克尔本人对这个动向却不怎么满意。他更愿意让孩子当新教徒,新教更符合美国的主流。

凯惊讶地发现自己爱上了内华达的生活。她喜欢这里的景致,山丘和峡谷里华美的红色岩石,灼热的沙漠,不经意出现、令人心旷神怡的湖泊,甚至包括炎热的天气。

两个儿子骑着矮种马四处溜达。她有了真正的仆人,而不是保镖。迈克尔的生活也正常多了。他拥有一家建筑公司,参加商人俱乐部和市民委员会,颇为关心当地政治,但又不公开插手。这样的生活确实不错。清空纽约的住处,拉斯维加斯将成为永久的家园,这让凯很高兴。她不喜欢回纽约,所以最后这次回来之后,她以最高的效率和速度打包托运,今天是最后一天了,她急于离开纽约的心情就像长期住院的病患终于能够出院。

最后这天,凯·亚当斯·柯里昂在黎明醒来。她听见林荫道外传来卡车的轰鸣声。卡车将搬空这些住宅的全部家具。柯里昂家族下午乘飞机回拉斯维加斯,柯里昂妈妈也要走。

凯走出浴室,迈克尔靠在枕头上抽烟。"你到底为什么每天一大早都要去教堂?"他说,"星期天我倒是不在乎,但平时为什么也要去? 你和我妈真是一个毛病。"他摸黑打开了床头灯。

凯坐在床沿上,开始穿丝袜。"你知道刚皈依的天主教徒是什么样,"她说,"比其他人更加热心呗。"

迈克尔伸手去摸她的大腿,摸到了尼龙长筒袜以上热乎乎的皮肤。"别摸了,"她说,"今天早晨我要领圣餐。"

她从床上起身,迈克尔没有试图挽留。他微笑着说:"既然你这个教徒这么严守教规,为什么经常允许孩子不去教堂呢?"

她有点不安,心生警觉。他打量着她,用那种她暗暗称之为"唐的眼神"的目光。"他们有的是机会,"她说,"回到家里,我会逼着他们多去的。"

她吻别迈克尔,走出屋门,外面已经暖和起来了。夏天的艳阳红彤彤地升起。凯走向林荫道的大门口,她的车停在那里。柯里昂妈妈身穿寡妇的黑衣服,已经坐在车里等她。这已经成了例行的套路:早弥撒,每天清晨,同去同回。

凯亲吻老妇人皱纹交错的面颊,坐到驾驶座上。柯里昂妈妈怀疑地问:"你吃早饭了?"

"没有。"凯说。

老妇人赞许地点点头。凯有一次忘了领圣餐前从午夜开始不得进食的规定,那是很久以前了,但柯里昂妈妈从此就不再信任她,每次都要问清楚。"感觉还好吧?"老妇人问。

"挺好。"凯答道。

清晨的阳光下,小教堂显得冷冷清清。彩色玻璃挡住炽热的阳光,里面很凉快,适合安歇。凯搀扶婆婆爬上白色石阶,让她走在前面。老妇人喜欢坐前排,靠近圣坛。

凯在台阶上又等了几分钟。她在最后这一刻总是不太情愿,总是有点害怕。

最后,她还是走进凉爽而黑暗的教堂,指尖蘸了圣水画十字,用湿指尖飞快地碰了碰干燥的嘴唇。圣坛前的蜡烛红光闪烁,基督钉在十字架上。凯先跪拜,然后走进她的那排座位,跪在硬木条上,等待招呼她领圣餐。她低着头,像是在祈祷,其实心里并没有做好准备。

只有置身于昏暗的拱顶教堂之中,她才允许自己思索丈夫的另一面,思索一年前那个可怕的夜晚,他如何存心利用两人间的信任和爱,哄骗她相信他的谎言,相信他没有杀害他的妹夫。

她曾经离开过他,不是为了这件事,而是为了这个谎言。第二天早晨,她带着孩子去了新罕布什尔的父母家。她没有留下任何话,甚至不清楚自己打算怎么办。迈克尔马上就明白了。第一天他给凯打了个电话,随后再也没有打扰她。一周后,一辆纽约牌照的豪华轿车来到她家门前,车里坐着汤姆·黑根。

她和汤姆·黑根度过了一个漫长而难熬的下午,她一生中最难熬的一个下午。两人去小镇外的树林里散步,黑根并没有好言相劝。

凯犯了个错误,她试着说些冷酷无礼的话,可惜并不适合这个角色。"迈克派你来威胁我?"她问,"还以为会是几个'弟兄'钻出车门,端着冲锋枪逼我回去。"

自从认识黑根以来,凯这还是第一次见他动怒。他恶声恶气地说:"我就没听过这么孩子气的屁话。没想到你这样的女人会说出这种话。别逗了,凯。"

"好吧。"她说。

两人走在绿意盎然的乡间小路上。黑根轻声问:"你为什么逃跑?"

凯说:"因为迈克尔对我撒谎,因为他当了康妮儿子的教父,愚弄了我。他背叛了我。我不能爱这么一个男人。我忍受不了。我不能允许他当我的孩子的父亲。"

"真不知道你在说什么。"黑根说。

她转向黑根,怒气有了正当的理由。"我是说他杀了自己的妹夫。明白吗?"她顿了顿,"还有,他对我撒谎。"

两人默默地走了好一会儿,最后,黑根说:"你不能确定这些都是事实。为了讨论起见,姑且假设是真的——请记住,我没有说就是真的——但假如我能证明他有正当理由呢?或者说,有可能性很大的正当理由?"

凯看着他,嘲笑道:"这还是我第一次见到你律师的一面,汤姆,可不是你最好的那一面。"

黑根咧嘴笑笑。"好吧,你听我说完。假如是卡洛把桑尼诱人圈套,出卖了桑尼呢?假如卡洛那次是存心殴打康妮,就为了引出桑尼,而敌人知道他会走琼斯海滩堤道呢？假如卡洛曾经花钱至桑尼于死地呢？那你怎么想？"

凯没有回答。黑根继续道："假如唐，这位可敬的男人，下不了狠心做他应该做的事情，杀死女儿的丈夫为儿子复仇呢？假如最终他不堪忍受，指定迈克尔继承事业，知道迈克尔会肩负起他的重担，承受那份罪责呢？"

"那都是历史了，"凯说，泪如泉涌，"大家现在都很高兴，为什么不能原谅卡洛呢？为什么不能好好活下去，忘了这件事呢？"

她领着黑根走过草场，来到树荫下的小溪旁。黑根坐在草地上，叹了口气。他环顾四周，又叹口气，说："换了这个世界，也许真的可以。"

凯说："他已经不是娶我的那个男人了。"

黑根轻笑一声。"如果还是，那他已经死了，而你是寡妇。也就没什么难题了。"

凯怒道："你这话是什么意思？来，汤姆，一辈子总得说一次实话。我知道迈克尔做不到，但你不是西西里人，你可以把实话告诉一个女人，可以把女人看作平等的同类。"

黑根又沉默良久，最后摇头道："你错怪了迈克。你生气是因为他对你撒谎。唉，他提醒过你，永远不要过问生意上的事情。你生气是因为他当了卡洛儿子的教父，但那是你逼他接受的。实话实说，这确实是一步好棋，方便对卡洛采取行动。赢得对方的信任，这是经典的战术手段。"黑根苦笑道，"这么说够坦诚了吧？"但凯已经低下了头。

黑根继续道："我再多跟你说些实话吧。唐去世后，有人设计要杀迈克。知道是谁吗？忒西奥。因此忒西奥必须被处决。卡洛必须被处决。因为背叛是不能宽恕的罪行。迈克尔可以宽恕他们，但他们永远无法宽恕自己，因此反而更危险。迈克尔真的很喜欢忒西奥，更爱自己的妹妹。可是，如果放过忒西奥和卡洛，那就是对你和孩子、对他的整个家庭、对我和我的家人的失职。他们会对我们所有人、所有人的生命构成危险。"

凯听着这番话，泪水滚滚而下。"是迈克尔派你来说服我的吗？"

黑根望着她，真的吃了一惊。"不是，"他说，"他叫我告诉你，你要什么都可以，愿意干什么就干什么，但一定要照顾好孩子，"黑根笑了笑，"他叫我告诉你，你是他的唐——当然，只是开玩笑。"

凯伸手按住黑根的胳膊。"他没有命令你把另外这些事告诉我？"

黑根犹豫片刻，像是在考虑要不要说实话。"你还是不明白，"他说，"如果你把我今天的话告诉迈克尔，那我就死定了。"他顿了顿，"全世界只有你和你的孩子是他无法伤害的。"

过了漫长的五分钟,凯从草地上起身,开始返回住处。就快到家的时候,凯对黑根说:"吃完晚饭,你能用车送我和孩子回纽约吗?"

"我来就是为了这个。"黑根说。

回到迈克尔身边一周后,她去找神父,请神父指引她皈依天主教。

教堂的最深处响起钟声,召唤罪人悔改。凯按照教规,握拳轻捶胸口以示悔罪。钟声再次敲响,随着沙沙的脚步声,来领圣餐的人离开座位,走向圣坛前的栏杆。凯起身加入队伍。她在圣坛前跪下,教堂深处又传来钟声,她攥紧拳头,再次捶打心口。神父来到她的面前。她仰起头,张开嘴,接受薄如纸片的面饼。这是最可怕的一刻。她必须等待面饼融化,吞下去,才能做她来这里要做的事情。

她洗清罪孽,这个哀求者蒙受神恩,垂下头,交叠双手,放在圣坛栏杆上。她挪动重心,减轻身体对膝盖的压迫。

她排空所有思绪,忘记自己,忘记孩子,忘记所有的愤怒、所有的反抗和所有的疑问,然后,她怀着发自肺腑的恳切愿望——渴望相信,渴望上帝能听到她的心声——为迈克尔·柯里昂的灵魂念诵必不可少的祷词,卡洛·里齐被杀后的每一天都是这样。